The SAGE Dictionary of
CRIMINOLOGY

EUGENE MCLAUGHLIN and JOHN MUNCIE
3RD EDITION

Los Angeles | London | New Delhi
Singapore | Washington DC

Los Angeles | London | New Delhi
Singapore | Washington DC

SAGE Publications Ltd
1 Oliver's Yard
55 City Road
London EC1Y 1SP

SAGE Publications Inc.
2455 Teller Road
Thousand Oaks, California 91320

SAGE Publications India Pvt Ltd
B 1/I 1 Mohan Cooperative Industrial Area
Mathura Road
New Delhi 110 044

SAGE Publications Asia-Pacific Pte Ltd
3 Church Street
#10-04 Samsung Hub
Singapore 049483

Editor: Natalie Aguilera
Editorial assistant: James Piper
Production editor: Rachel Eley
Marketing manager: Sally Ransom
Cover design: Joni Strudwick
Typeset by: C&M Digitals (P) Ltd, Chennai, India
Printed in India at Replika Press Pvt Ltd

First edition published 2001
Reprinted 2001 and 2003
Second edition published 2006
Reprinted 2007, 2008, 2009, 2010 (twice) and 2011

This third edition published 2013

Library of Congress Control Number: 2011943769

British Library Cataloguing in Publication data

A catalogue record for this book is available from
the British Library

ISBN 978-1-44620-082-7
ISBN 978-1-44620-083-4 (pbk)

Praise for the Second Edition

If the first edition was an invaluable guide for students, the second is well nigh indispensable. I can think of no better starting point for those wanting a 'quick fix' on any given criminological topic.
Professor Tony Jefferson, Keele University

Since its initial publication in 2001, I've steadfastly kept *The SAGE Dictionary of Criminology* within easy reach of my desk, referring to it countless times in writing articles, books, and lectures. I've found it to be a remarkable book – a comprehensive dictionary, certainly, but as much so a significant achievement in intellectual inquiry. It may seem odd to say of a dictionary, but it really is one of my favourite books; the only book that can replace it on my deskside bookshelf is this second edition, whose new entries confirm the editors' grasp of contemporary criminology in all its excitement and complexity.
Professor Jeff Ferrell, Texas Christian University

The welcome inclusion of entries on contemporary theoretical and policy concerns ranging from Anti-social Behaviour, Eco-crime and Emotions through Forensic Anthropology, Globalisation, Governance and Mentoring to Sex Crime, Virtual Criminology and What Works?, adds to the well established strengths of the first edition. The entries, all written by established scholars, provide a clear, concise and critical introduction to criminological concepts and constitute an invaluable resource for all criminology students and academics.
Professor Hazel Croall, Glasgow Caledonian University

It is unusual for a dictionary to be interesting, but this one manages to be both compelling and useful for faculty and students across a range of disciplines and orientations who are commonly interested in criminology. *The SAGE Dictionary of Criminology* is also distinctive in providing a literally encyclopaedic compendium of information that has been carefully placed in social, cultural and political contexts.
Professor Lynn Chancer, Hunter College, City University of New York

The list of new entries is quite impressive. Once you've read them, you start to wonder how come that the first edition of *The SAGE Dictionary of Criminology* already felt so complete.
Dr René van Swaaningen, Erasmus University, Rotterdam

Thoughtful evaluations of the key concepts criminologists must think about by quality contributors who include many of the world's leading criminologists.
Professor John Braithwaite, Australian National University

The compilers have done criminology a tremendous service. This dictionary is an invaluable resource for students and teachers and I'm certain will be a key reference work for years to come.
Professor Tim Newburn, London School of Economics

Great dictionaries inform, intrigue and investigate. McLaughlin and Muncie's perceptive collection does all three. *The SAGE Dictionary of Criminology* is wide and accessible enough to interest anyone concerned with crime, the law and the panoply of issues and explanations that surround them. This admirable volume will inform, guide and contribute to debates in the years ahead.
Ellis Cashmore, Professor of Culture, Media and Sport, Staffordshire University, author of *Dictionary of Race and Ethnic Relations* and co-editor of *Dictionary of Cultural Theorists*

McLaughlin and Muncie have assembled an impressive list of international contributors and have succeeded in putting together a wonderfully entertaining book ... the dictionary belongs on every criminologist's bookshelf.
Professor George Mair, Liverpool John Moores University (*Criminal Justice: An International Journal* 2:2)

The main strength of the project ... lies in its attempts at integration of a wide range of themes and theoretical perspectives under one set of covers.
Professor John Raine, University of Birmingham (*Youth Justice* 2:1)

There is a genuine international feel to the compilation as a whole ... Nowadays, such has criminology grown, it is barely possible to keep up even in a narrowly defined sub-field, and a new dictionary is essential. Anyway, we will all have to read it because our students will. What a relief that it is such a pleasure to do so.
Jason Ditton, University of Sheffield (*British Journal of Criminology* 43:2)

Contents

About the Editors

Eugene McLaughlin is Professor of Criminology at the University of Southampton, UK. His first academic post was at the University of Hong Kong and he was at The Open University before moving to City University London. Professor McLaughlin has written extensively on policing and police reform, police–community relations, criminal justice policy reforms and criminological theory. His most recent books are *The Sage Handbook of Criminological Theory* (with Tim Newburn, Sage, 2010) and *The New Policing* (Sage, 2007). His current research concentrates on: the policing of multi-pluralist societies; the mediatization of crime and criminal justice policy; the politics of law and order; and new developments in critical criminological theory. He is an Associate Editor of *Crime, Media and Culture* and is a former Co-Editor of *Theoretical Criminology*.

John Muncie is Emeritus Professor of Criminology at The Open University, UK. He is the author of *Youth and Crime* (Sage, 3rd edition, 2009) and has published widely on issues in comparative youth justice and children's rights including the co-edited companion volumes *Youth Crime and Justice* and *Comparative Youth Justice* (Sage, 2006). He has produced numerous Open University texts and readers including *Crime: Local and Global* (Willan, 2010), *Criminal Justice: Local and Global* (Willan, 2010), *Criminological Perspectives: Essential Readings* (Sage, 2nd edition, 2003), *The Problem of Crime* (Sage, 2nd edition, 2001), *Crime Prevention and Community Safety* (Sage, 2001) and *Imprisonment: European Perspectives* (Harvester, 1991). He has also contributed nine volumes to *The Sage Library of Criminology* (Sage, 2007–2009). He is Co-Editor of the Sage journal *Youth Justice: An International Journal*.

List of Contributors

Editors

Eugene McLaughlin, University of Southampton, UK
John Muncie, The Open University, Milton Keynes, UK

Administrative Support

Sarah-Jane Boyd, Sage Publications, UK (3rd edition)
Pauline Hetherington, The Open University, UK (1st and 2nd editions)
Sue Lacey, The Open University, UK (1st edition)

International Advisory Board

Pat Carlen, University of Kent, UK
Stuart Henry, San Diego State University, USA
Tony Jefferson, University of Keele, UK
Victor Jupp, formerly University of Northumbria, UK
Pat O'Malley, University of Sydney, Australia
Joe Sim, Liverpool John Moores University, UK
Elizabeth Stanko, Metropolitan Police, London, UK
René van Swaaningen, Erasmus University Rotterdam, The Netherlands

Authors (current position/position held at time of entry authorship)

Katja Franko Aas, Oslo University, Norway
Robert Agnew, Emory University, Atlanta, USA
Peter B. Ainsworth, formerly University of Manchester, UK
Bruce Arrigo, School of Professional Psychology, Fresno, California, USA
Gregg Barak, Eastern Michigan University, USA
Piers Beirne, University of Southern Maine, USA
Ben Bowling, University of London, UK
Trevor Bradley, Victoria University, Wellington, New Zealand
Sheila Brown, University of Sheffield, UK
Eamonn Carrabine, Essex University, UK
Stephen Case, University of Swansea, Wales, UK
Geertrui Cazaux, University of Southern Maine, USA
Kathryn Chadwick, Manchester Metropolitan University, UK
John Clarke, The Open University, UK
Roy Coleman, Liverpool University, UK

LIST OF CONTRIBUTORS

Iain Crow, University of Sheffield, UK
Chris Cunneen, University of New South Wales, Australia
Kathleen Daly, Griffith University, Brisbane, Australia
Julia Davidson, Kingston University, UK
Deborah H. Drake, The Open University, UK
Anna Duncan, Victoria University, Wellington, New Zealand
Adam Edwards, Cardiff University, Wales, UK
Paul Ekblom, University of the Arts, London, UK
Martin Evison, Sheffield University, UK
Clive Emsley, The Open University, UK
Jeff Ferrell, Texas Christian University, USA
Matthew Follett, formerly Leicester University, UK
Alan France, University of Auckland, New Zealand
Loraine Gelsthorpe, University of Cambridge, UK
Peter Gill, Liverpool John Moores University, UK
Barry Goldson, Liverpool University, UK
David Greenberg, New York University, USA
Chris Greer, City University London, UK
Nic Groombridge, St Mary's College, London, UK
Ben Gunn, HMP Erlestoke, UK
Willem de Haan, University of Groningen, The Netherlands
Kevin Haines, University of Swansea, Wales, UK
Simon Hallsworth, London Metropolitan University, UK
Lynn Hancock, Liverpool University, UK
Keith Hayward, University of Kent, UK
Frances Heidensohn, London School of Economics, London, UK
Stuart Henry, San Diego State University, USA
Paddy Hillyard, Queen's University Belfast, Northern Ireland, UK
Clive Hollin, University of Leicester, UK
Ross Homel, Griffith University, Brisbane, Australia
Tim Hope, Salford University, UK
Barbara Hudson, University of Central Lancashire, UK
Gordon Hughes, Cardiff University, Wales, UK
Mark Israel, University of Western Australia, Australia
Ruth Jamieson, Queen's University, Belfast, Northern Ireland, UK
Tony Jefferson, Keele University, UK
Yvonne Jewkes, Leicester University, UK
Victor Jupp, University of Northumbria, UK
Roger Kern, Eastern Michigan University, USA
John Kerr, City University, London, UK
Gloria Laycock, University College London, UK
Maggy Lee, University of Hong Kong, China
Ronnie Lippens, Keele University, UK
Shadd Maruna, Queen's University, Belfast, Northern Ireland, UK
Roger Matthews, University of Kent, UK
Eugene McLaughlin, University of Southampton, UK
Dragan Milovanovic, Northeastern Illinois University, USA
Gerry Mooney, The Open University, UK
Wayne Morrison, Queen Mary and Westfield College, London, UK
John Muncie, The Open University, UK

Karim Murji, The Open University, UK
David Nelken, University of Macerata, Italy
Pat O'Malley, University of Sydney, Australia
Emma J. Palmer, University of Leicester, UK
Ken Pease, University of Huddersfield, UK
Hal Pepinsky, Indiana University, USA
Graham Pike, The Open University, UK
Mike Presdee, University of Kent, UK
Jill Radford, University of Teesside, UK
Joseph Rankin, Eastern Michigan University, USA
Roger Sapsford, University of Teesside, UK
Esther Saraga, The Open University, UK
Phil Scraton, Queen's University, Belfast, Northern Ireland, UK
James Sheptycki, York University, Canada
Michael Shiner, London School of Economics, UK
Joe Sim, Liverpool John Moores University, UK
Richard Sparks, University of Edinburgh, Scotland, UK
Peter Squires, University of Brighton, UK
Elizabeth Stanko, Metropolitan Police, UK
Colin Sumner, freelance author, UK
Maggie Sumner, Westminster University, London, UK
René van Swaaningen, Erasmus University Rotterdam, The Netherlands
Charles R. Tittle, North Carolina State University, USA
Steve Tombs, Liverpool John Moores University, UK
Kyle Treiber, University of Cambridge, UK
Tonia Tzannetakis, University of Athens, Greece
Claire Valier, University of London, UK
Barry Vaughan, Institute of Public Administration, Ireland
Sirpa Virta, Tampere University, Finland
Alison Wakefield, Portsmouth University, UK
Sandra Walklate, University of Liverpool, UK
Reece Walters, Queensland University of Technology, Australia
Louise Westmarland, The Open University, UK
Nicole Westmarland, Durham University, UK
Rob White, University of Tasmania, Australia
Dick Whitfield, Probation Office, Kent, UK
Dave Whyte, University of Liverpool, UK
Chris A. Williams, The Open University, UK
David Wilson, University of Central England, Birmingham, UK
Anne Worrall, Keele University, UK
Jock Young, John Jay College of Criminal Justice, New York, USA

List of Entries

LIST OF ENTRIES

Preface to the First Edition

The compilation of the dictionary has been a truly collective endeavour and could not have been developed without the generous help, support and suggestions of many different people. From the outset the editors have been supported by an international advisory board with representatives from the USA, Australia and the Netherlands as well as the UK. They provided invaluable advice in drawing up an initial list of key terms which had international and universal significance and furnished the editors with the names of specialist academics worldwide. As a result the dictionary has been immeasurably enhanced by contributions from criminological researchers and authors, of whom many are the leading scholars in their field. With more than 250 entries written by 69 academics and practitioners from Europe, USA, Australia and New Zealand, never before has the work of so many criminologists – often with widely differing perspectives – been brought together in a single endeavour. We are indebted to them all.

A work of this nature has also been a necessarily lengthy and complex exercise in collaboration, collation, formatting, timetabling and processing. Without the formidable administrative and secretarial skills of Sue Lacey and Pauline Hetherington of the Social Policy Department at the Open University it would not have been possible at all. Last but not least we express sincere thanks to Gillian Stern and Miranda Nunhofer and the team at Sage for their invaluable support, assistance and care for this project.

Preface to the Second Edition

The compilation of this second edition of *The SAGE Dictionary of Criminology* has once again been a truly collective endeavour and could not have been developed without the generous help, support and suggestions of many different people. When compiling the first edition in 2000 the editors were supported by an international advisory board with representatives from the USA, Canada and the Netherlands as well as the UK. They provided invaluable advice in drawing up an initial list of key terms which had international and universal significance and furnished the editors with the names of specialist academics world-wide. As a result the dictionary has been immeasurably enhanced by contributions from criminological researchers and authors, of whom many are the leading scholars in their field. For this second edition we have been greatly assisted by welcome feedback from numerous advisors and reviewers who have revealed to us the dictionary's major strengths and weaknesses. We hope that this constructive dialogue with our criminology colleagues will continue. This edition retains all of the pre-existing entries in their original form but is now considerably enhanced with the addition of some forty new entries covering such diverse (and previously omitted) topics as offender profiling, terrorism, globalisation, mentoring and psychopathy as well as a discussion of emergent concepts and perspectives such as eco-crime, virtual criminology, crime science and forensic anthropology. With now more than 290 entries written by 94 academics and practitioners from Europe, USA, Canada, Australia and New Zealand, we have once more attempted to reflect the divergent interests of all those who lay claim to the subject matter of criminology. We remain indebted to them all.

A work of this nature has also been a necessarily lengthy and complex exercise in collaboration, collation, formatting, timetabling and processing. A special, and immense debt of gratitude is owed to Sue Lacey and Pauline Hetherington of the Social Policy Department at the Open University for their formidable administrative and secretarial skills that made the first edition possible. For the second edition this administrative burden has been carried solely by Pauline Hetherington. Needless to say without this level of professional support the dictionary would not have come to fruition at all. Last but not least we again express sincere thanks to Gillian Stern for championing the dictionary in the first place and to Miranda Nunhofer, Caroline Porter and the team at Sage for their unfailing support and assistance and care for this ongoing project.

Preface to the Third Edition

The compilation of this third edition of *The SAGE Dictionary of Criminology* has once again been a truly collective endeavour and could not have been developed without the generous help, support and suggestions of many different people. When compiling the first edition in 2000 the editors were supported by an international advisory board with representatives from the USA, Canada and the Netherlands, as well as the UK. They provided invaluable advice in drawing up an initial list of key terms which had international and universal significance, and furnished the editors with the names of specialist academics world-wide. As a result the dictionary has been immeasurably enhanced by contributions from criminological researchers and authors, of whom many are the leading scholars in their field. For this third edition we have been greatly assisted by welcome feedback from numerous advisors and reviewers who have revealed to us the dictionary's major strengths and weaknesses. We hope that this invaluable advice from our criminology colleagues will continue. This edition retains all of the pre-existing entries in their original form but is now considerably enhanced with the addition of new entries covering such diverse (and previously omitted) topics as art crime, defiance, gangs, life course theory and risk factor research, as well as a discussion of emergent concepts and perspectives such as public criminology, green criminology and global criminology. With now more than 300 entries written by over 100 academics and practitioners from across Europe, the USA, Canada, Australia, New Zealand and China, we have once more attempted to reflect the divergent interests of all those who lay claim to the subject matter of criminology. We remain indebted to them all and look forward to their involvement in a re-formatted fourth edition.

A work of this nature has also been a necessarily lengthy and complex exercise in collaboration, collation, formatting, timetabling and processing. A special, and immense, debt of gratitude is owed to Sue Lacey and Pauline Hetherington of the Social Policy and Criminology Department at the Open University for their formidable administrative and secretarial skills that made the first and second editions possible. This administrative responsibility was ably taken on by Sarah-Jane Boyd at Sage Publications for the third edition. Sarah-Jane had the extra responsibility of tracking down our original contributors. Needless to say, without this level of professional support the dictionary would not have come to fruition at all. Last but not least we again express our sincere thanks to Gillian Stern for championing the dictionary in the first place and to Miranda Nunhofer, Caroline Porter and Natalie Aguilera at Sage for their unfailing support, assistance and care over the past twelve years for this ongoing project. Without the enthusiastic support of Sage this academic endeavour would not be possible.

EM/JM
January 2012

Editors' Introduction

The SAGE Dictionary of Criminology explores the categories of thought, methods and practices that are central to contemporary criminological study. Unlike many other dictionaries or encyclopaedias in this area, its starting point is not to elucidate particular legal powers or criminal justice procedures but to unravel issues of theoretical and conceptual complexity.

The dictionary was constructed on the principle that criminology is a contested, contradictory and interdisciplinary discourse marked by constant incursion, interactions, translations, deviations and transgressions. Competing theoretical perspectives meet and sometimes they are able to speak to, listen to and understand each other, while at other times they appear not to share any common discourse. There is, therefore, no one definition of 'criminology' to be found in this dictionary, rather a multitude of noisy, argumentative criminological perspectives which in themselves often depend and draw upon knowledges and concerns generated from elsewhere. As a result the dictionary deliberately includes pieces that depart from traditional agendas, transgress conventional boundaries and suggest new points of formation and avenues for cross-discipline development. Many of the entries will be of vital importance in understanding criminology in terms of what it is intellectually struggling to become. A canonical closure or discursive unification of criminology, or indeed a move beyond criminology, is no more possible in the twenty-first century than it was at the beginning of the twentieth century. New modes of information exchange and the unprecedented mobility of ideas rule out both disciplinary parochialism and the assertion of authoritative positions. This is what will give criminology its intellectual strength and ensure that the field of criminological studies remains dynamic and relevant for future generations of students.

The rationale of the dictionary can best be explained by way of a detailing of its scope and structure. In compiling this dictionary every effort has been made to ensure that it is broadly representative and inclusive in tone, reflecting the international field of criminology in its eclectic, diverse and expansive dimensions. Though these appear in alphabetical order the choice of entries has been guided by four organizing principles. Each entry is:

- a major theoretical position;
- a key theoretical concept;
- a central criminological method; *or*
- a core criminal justice philosophy or practice.

Each entry is also central to the field, standing either as an intellectual benchmark or as an emergent thematic in the shifting and expanding field of criminological studies. As a result the dictionary provides a comprehensive introduction to criminological theory, its diverse frames of reference and its expansive modes of analysis.

In addition it aims throughout to be fully international and deliberately avoids legal terms and cases which are specific to particular criminal justice jurisdictions. For the same reason it also deliberately avoids legally defined acts of crime – such as theft, burglary, murder and so on – but does include those 'crimes' which are either emergent – such as cybercrime and animal abuse – or those with a wider theoretical resonance – such as corporate crime, serial killing, hate crime and so on.

In selecting these entries we have been particularly concerned to help students to think through and utilize key concepts, methods and practices and to complement as well as supplement the teaching materials already used in university- and college-based criminology and related courses. It is designed as an interactive learning resource for students in the fields of criminology, criminal justice studies, the sociology of crime and deviance, socio-legal studies, jurisprudence, criminal law studies, social policy, youth studies and social work.

To ensure maximum accessibility each entry starts with a short statement or *definition* which sets out the basic parameters of the concept itself. From that point onward any comparability with an orthodox dictionary ends. The section that follows – *distinctive features* – is more encyclopaedic in style and allows for some detailed comment on the concept's origins, development and general significance. Throughout we have encouraged authors to reflect critically and freely on criminology's historical knowledge base and on potential future developments. A final section – *evaluation* – has also been included for all of those concepts considered to have the greatest theoretical weight and lasting legacy. This allows for an initial considered and critical assessment of how particular theoretical positions have been or can be debated, challenged and reworked. As a guide we have encouraged entries of up to 1500 words each.

Each entry is then also cross-referenced with other *associated concepts* in the dictionary in order to facilitate a broader and in-depth study. Finally each entry concludes with a list of selected *key readings* to reinforce the aim of the dictionary as a learning resource to be built upon by the reader. We are also aware that for many students an initial entry into criminological study is as much through the names of particular authors as it is through a particular key concept. To this end the dictionary concludes with both a *subject* and a *name index* to further enhance its accessibility. All of these features are designed to facilitate the dictionary's use as a *study guide* for introductory courses in the field, as a *source of reference* for advanced study, as a *supplement* to established textbooks and as a *reference guide* to the specialized language of theoretical and conceptual criminology. Patient reading will uncover the full range of connections to be made across the entries and their associated concepts.

The idea for this dictionary originated during a series of conversations between ourselves and Gillian Stern, then Commissioning Editor for Criminology at Sage, in London and Milton Keynes in the late 1990s. The overwhelmingly positive response to the first and second editions inspired us to continue with our project of mapping the expansive and diverse concerns of criminology and to make these concerns accessible to as wide a range of different audiences as possible. We continue to view this dictionary as part of our ongoing dialogue with/in criminology and fully intend to produce further editions which will allow us to further expand upon the range of theoretical perspectives, concepts, methodologies and emergent issues and also give all existing authors the opportunity to revise and update their original contributions. We will persist with our efforts to be as inclusive and internationalist as possible and continue to emphasize the importance of both a theory-led and globally-oriented criminology. To this end we continue to welcome feedback as well as any possible future contributions to what must be, by necessity, a project that will always remain 'unfinished'.

Eugene McLaughlin
John Muncie
January 2012

ABOLITION

Definition

In criminology and criminal justice, the term 'abolition' currently refers to the attempt to do away with punitive responses to criminalized problems. It is the first step in the abolitionist strategy, followed by a plea for dispute settlement, redress and social justice. In more general terms it refers to the abolition of state (supported) institutions which are no longer felt to be legitimate. Historically, the term has been used in the fight against slavery, torture, prostitution, capital punishment and prison.

Distinctive Features

Though the literal meaning of the verb 'to abolish' suggests differently, penal abolition should not be interpreted in absolute terms. Abolitionists do not argue that the police or courts should be abolished. The point is that crime is not to be set apart from other, non-criminalized, social problems and that the social exclusion of 'culprits' seldom solves problems. Instead, crime problems should be treated in the specific context in which they emerge and reactions should be oriented towards reintegration rather than exclusion. Neither do abolitionists argue against social control in general terms. It is indeed hard to imagine social coexistence without any form of social control. The problem is the top-down, repressive, punitive and inflexible character of formal social control systems. It is these specific characteristics of penal control

which are to be abolished (Bianchi and van Swaaningen, 1986).

Abolitionists question the ethical calibre of a state that intentionally and systematically inflicts pain upon other people. They point out that, because generally accepted goals of general and special prevention cannot be supported with empirical data, the credibility of the whole penal rationale is at stake. Depenalization (pushing back the punitive character of social reactions) and decriminalization (against the labelling of social problems as crimes) are the central strategies of abolition. Stan Cohen (1988) has identified five other 'destructuring moves' which are part of the politics of abolition: decarceration (away from prison), diversion (away from the institution), decategorization (away from offender typologies), delegalization (away from the state) and deprofessionalization (away from the expert). In a next, positive or reconstructive phase, a distinction is made between abolitionism as a way of thinking (an alternative way of understanding the problem of crime and punishment) and as a way of acting (a radical approach to penal reform).

In their attempts at depenalization, abolitionists first pointed their arrows at the prison system. This struggle has its roots in prisoners' movements or a religiously inspired penal lobby (Mathiesen, 1974; van Swaaningen, 1997). During the early 1980s, the attention shifted to the pros and cons of non-custodial measures as alternatives to prison. Warnings against the net-widening effects were contrasted with their potential value in the attrition of the penal system. The recognition that sanctioning-modalities at the end of the penal chain do not change its punitive, excluding character focused attention on the diversion of cases in preliminary phases, with the aim of preventing the stigmatizing effects of both trial and punishment. This phase was followed by the advocacy of a whole alternative procedural rationale, in which non-punitive responses to social problems were promoted, including forms of social crime prevention designed to address the structural contexts of crime (de Haan, 1990).

Notably, Nils Christie's and Louk Hulsman's abolitionist perspectives contain many implicit references to Habermas's idea of the 'colonization of the lifeworld'. The 'decolonization' of criminal justice's 'system rationality' is another object of abolition. Though the tension Habermas observes between systems and lifeworlds does not lead him directly to a rejection of the criminal justice system, he does argue against the degeneration of criminal justice into a state-instrument of crime control in which the critical dimension of power is ignored. Thus, penal instrumentalism is another object of abolition which can be derived from Habermas.

A further aim of abolition is related to the constitution of moral discourse. In Western, neo-liberal societies, values like care and empathy are delegated to the private sphere and are thereby excluded from public, or political, ethics. These latter ethics are dominated by abstract, so-called 'masculine' notions such as rights, duties and respect, which outrule more subjective, contextually determined 'feminine' notions such as care and empathy. The dominance of abstract approaches of rights results in a morality that is oriented towards a generalized other, whereas a feminist approach is oriented towards a concrete other. Thus, abolitionism also implies the abolition of the 'masculine', individualistic, neo-liberal values upon which our penal systems are built (van Swaaningen, 1989).

René van Swaaningen

Associated Concepts: abolitionism, community justice, critical criminology, deconstruction, redress, the state

Key Readings

Bianchi, H. and van Swaaningen, R. (eds) (1986) *Abolitionism: Towards a Non-Repressive Approach to Crime.* Amsterdam: Free University Press.

Cohen, S. (1988) *Against Criminology.* New Brunswick, NJ: Transaction.

de Haan, W. (1990) *The Politics of Redress: Crime, Punishment and Penal Abolition.* London: Unwin Hyman.

Mathiesen, T. (1974) *The Politics of Abolition.* London: Martin Robertson.

van Swaaningen, R. (1989) 'Feminism and abolitionism as critiques of criminology', *International Journal for the Sociology of Law,* 17 (3): 287–306.

Van Swaaningen, R. (1997) *Critical Criminology – Visions From Europe.* London: Sage.

ABOLITIONISM

Definition

A sociological and political perspective that analyses criminal justice and penal systems as social problems that intensify rather than diminish crime and its impact. On this basis prisons (the initial focus of study) reinforce dominant ideological constructions of crime, reproduce social divisions and distract attention from crimes committed by the powerful. Abolitionists advocate the radical transformation of the prison and punishment systems and their replacement with a reflexive and integrative strategy for dealing with these complex social phenomena.

Distinctive Features

Liberal approaches to the study of the prison are built on a number of often competing and contradictory goals: rehabilitation, general prevention, incapacitation, punishment and individual and collective deterrence. Abolitionism, which emerged out of the social movements of the late 1960s, challenges these liberal perspectives by arguing that in practice the criminal justice system and prisons contribute little to the protection of the individual and the control of crime. In the words of the Dutch abolitionist Willem de Haan, the prison 'is counter productive, difficult to control and [is] itself a major social problem'. Crime is understood as a complex, socially constructed phenomenon which 'serves to maintain political power relations and lends legitimacy to the crime control apparatus and the intensification of surveillance and control' (de Haan, 1991: 206–7). At the same time abolitionists are critical of liberals' unquestioning acceptance of prison reform. For abolitionists like Thomas Mathiesen liberal reform can never have a positive effect because it reinforces and bolsters the system, thus perpetuating processes of brutalization for the confined. Alternatively, 'negative reforms' are supported for their potential to challenge and undermine the system leading eventually to the demise of prisons. Abolitionists advocate a system that deals with crime as a socially constructed phenomenon. Crime should be responded to not by the negativity of a system built on punitive exclusion but by a reflexive and participatory system of inclusion built on redress, social policy, mutuality and solidarity: 'The aim is compensation rather than retaliation; reconciliation rather than blame allocation. To this end, the criminal justice system needs to be decentralized and neighbourhood courts established as a complement or substitute' (de Haan, 1991: 211–12). Abolitionism therefore 'implies a negative critique of the fundamental shortcomings of the criminal law to realize social justice', while simultaneously offering both an alternative way of thinking about crime and a 'radical approach to penal reform' (van Swaaningen, 1997: 117).

It is also important to note that abolitionism is not an homogeneous theoretical and political movement but one that varies across cultures. Not only has it been principally a European phenomenon (Davies, 1998), but within Europe there have also been different strands to the movement with some pointing to the distinct differences between European and British movements. In Europe early abolitionists such as Mathiesen, Christie, Bianchi and Hulsman advocated an alternative vision for criminal justice politics. Second generation abolitionists – neo-abolitionists – accept many of the abolitionist principles, including the rejection of both the concept of crime and 'penality as the ultimate metaphor of justice' (van Swaaningen, 1997: 116, 202). However, British neo-abolitionists such as Box-Grainger, Ryan, Ward, Hudson and Sim also advocated engaging in more interventionist work to develop a 'criminology from below', which

> in utilizing a complex set of competing, contradictory and oppositional discourses, and providing support on the ground for the confined and their families, has challenged the hegemony around prison that has united state servants, traditional reform groups and many academics on the same pragmatic and ideological terrain. In a number of areas ... such as deaths in custody, prison conditions, medical power, visiting, censorship and sentencing these groups have conceded key points to the abolitionist argument and have moved onto a more radical terrain where they too have contested the construction of state-defined truth around penal policy. (Sim, 1994: 275–6)

Evaluation

In light of the huge increase in prison populations around the globe and the continuing rise in both reported crimes and crimes audited in victimization and self-report studies, abolitionism offers an important series of insights into the role of the prison and its failures at the beginning of the twenty-first century. The perspective continues to pose the key question: is prison the answer to the problem of crime, even allowing for an expanded definition to include crimes committed by the powerful?

There have been a number of issues raised and criticisms made of the abolitionist position. Most have come from those who, like abolitionists, would see themselves as part of a theoretical and political tradition that was on the critical wing of politics and social science. Left realists would criticize abolitionists for their idealism and for their 'anarcho communist position' which is 'preoccupied with abolishing or minimizing state intervention rather than attempting to make it more effective, responsive and accountable' (Matthews, 1990, cited in Sim, 1994: 265).

Abolitionists would reject the charge of idealism and as noted above would point to the influence that they have had on a number of political debates and social policies in terms of making the state more accountable. For example, the issue of deaths in custody which became a major political debate in the UK in the 1980s and 1990s not only involved individuals who were part of the abolitionist movement; it also had a significant hegemonic impact on liberal reform groups by pulling them onto a more radical and critical terrain in terms of demanding political action to deal with the devastating impact of these deaths on the families and friends of the deceased (Sim, 1994). Abolitionists would also say that the problem with criminology is that it suffers from too little utopian and idealistic thought rather than too much.

Feminist writers have also drawn attention to the problem of violent men and what should be done to protect women from the predations of, for example, men who rape. This raises the broader question of dangerousness and the nature of the response that is needed to deal with dangerous individuals. What, for example, do we do with those who engage in serial killing and who are overwhelmingly men? Abolitionists would agree that violence against women is a major issue across societies which should be taken and responded to seriously, but would also maintain that simply confining violent men inside can often only mean detaining them in institutions where the pervasive culture of masculinity is likely to reinforce misogynist views around male power and women (Sim, 1994). Therefore they would say that the nature of the institutions and the broader culture which objectifies women and equates heterosexuality with domination and power need to be addressed.

In addition they would argue further that dangerousness is a social construction in that there is a range of behaviours that can have immense implications for individual and group safety but which are rarely, if ever, labelled dangerous. The non-implementation of health and safety laws would be an example of this. Finally, abolitionists would suggest that the distinction between normal and abnormal, which lies at the heart of positivist thought, and which dominates debates about violence and dangerousness, is also problematic. They would point to the killings carried out by, and the non-prosecution of, the 'normal' men who murdered hundreds of innocent men, women and children in Vietnam in 1968 as an example of the social construction of dangerousness. This crime took place 15 months before the infamous Manson murders in the USA. This latter case has become deeply embedded in popular and political consciousness while the former case has largely been forgotten.

At another level, Angela Davies (1998: 102–3) has argued that while the European abolitionist tradition has offered many important insights into the nature of the prison, 'there is no sustained analysis of the part anti-racism might play in the theory and practice of abolitionism'. This is particularly important when it is recognized that prison populations around the world contain a disproportionate number of people who are drawn from ethnic minority backgrounds.

For the future, abolitionists have increasingly connected with the emerging discourses and debates around human rights and social justice which they see as mechanisms for developing negative reforms, thereby promoting a response to social harm that is very different from the destructive prison and punishment systems that currently exist.

Joe Sim

Associated Concepts: abolition, critical criminology, hegemony, left idealism, redress, social constructionism, social justice, the state

Key Readings

Bianchi, H. and van Swaaningen, R. (eds) (1986) *Abolitionism: Towards a Non-Repressive Approach to Crime.* Amsterdam: Free University Press.

Davies, A. (1998) 'Racialized punishment and prison abolition', in J. James (ed.), *The Angela Y. Davies Reader.* Oxford: Blackwell.

de Haan, W. (1991) 'Abolitionism and crime control: a contradiction in terms', in K. Stenson and D. Cowell (eds), *The Politics of Crime Control.* London: Sage.

Mathiesen, T. (1990) *Prison on Trial.* London: Sage.

Sim, J. (1994) 'The abolitionist approach: a British perspective', in A. Duff, S. Marshall, R.E. Dobash and R.P. Dobash (eds), *Penal Theory and Practice: Tradition and Innovation in Criminal Justice.* Manchester: Manchester University Press.

van Swaaningen, R. (1997) *Critical Criminology: Visions From Europe.* London: Sage.

ACTION RESEARCH

Definition

A form of research, often evaluative in nature, which has the intention of influencing the future direction of practice and policy.

Distinctive Features

The origins of action research are generally traced to the work of Kurt Lewin (1943), who envisaged that social research should seek to address certain goals. In many forms of enquiry the researcher seeks to distance him- or herself from the topic being researched and from the parties to social action. The action researcher, in contrast, enters into a dialogue with the parties to social action, transmitting results at certain points during the investigation so that the parties involved can make changes to the ways in which they are proceeding and sometimes to the aims they are seeking to achieve. The consequences of these changes are then studied in turn and further feedback and change may take place in an iterative process.

Such a process can also have consequences for the research design and methods originally adopted by the researcher(s), which may have to change in order to accommodate new developments in social action. Action research is therefore a dynamic model of research which requires time for reflection and review.

Action research has been used in community-based initiatives, such as community development projects and crime prevention programmes, in order to inform the future progress of social intervention. An example of action research in practice can be found in an evaluation of a domestic violence project where 'regular feedback was given to the project in order that this could inform subsequent developments'. Here the difficulties of achieving 'longer term reflections and change' when beset by shorter term 'operational' issues were noted (Kelly, 1999).

Evaluation

Action research has also been employed where participants and researchers share a commitment to achieving a particular end, such as anti-racist action, feminist approaches to working and the pursuit of human rights (see for example Mies, 1993). Action research raises questions about the extent to which the researcher can remain aloof and detached from social action; the researcher may be regarded more as an actor with a particular set of skills and experience. Action research can also have the aim of empowering participants in social action. This may be achieved by enabling participants to have more control over their lives and communities, or by increasing the research skills of participants so that they have a greater ability to monitor, evaluate and reflect on their activities themselves, or both of the foregoing. One such development has been the attempt to empower user interests in public service evaluations. 'User' research has a 'commitment to changing the balance of power between those who provide and those who receive services', with the interests of service users being enhanced through the research process (Barnes, 1993).

Iain Crow

5

Associated Concepts: evaluation research, praxis, reflexivity

Key Readings

Barnes, M. (1993) 'Introducing new stake-holders: user and researcher interests in evaluative research – a discussion of methods used to evaluate the Birmingham Community Care Special Action Project', *Policy and Politics*, 21 (1): 47–58.

Everitt, A. and Hardiker, P. (1996) *Evaluating for Good Practice.* Basingstoke: Macmillan.

Greenwood, D.J. and Levin, M. (1998) *Introduction to Action Research: Social Research for Social Change.* London: Sage.

Kelly, L. (1999) *Domestic Violence Matters: An Evaluation of a Development Project.* Home Office Research Study No. 193, Research, Development and Statistics Directorate. London: HMSO.

Lewin, K. (1943) 'Forces behind food habits and methods of change', *Bulletin of the National Research Council,* 108: 35–65.

Mies, M. (1993) 'Towards a methodology for feminist research', in M. Hammersley (ed.), *Social Research: Philosophy, Politics and Practice.* London: Sage.

ACTUARIALISM

Definition

Refers to the suite of risk calculation techniques that underpin correctional policies.

Distinctive Features

Actuarialism is most closely associated with the 'new penology' writings of Malcolm M. Feeley and Jonathan Simon. The term 'new penology' had been floating around American criminal justice circles for several years before Feeley and Simon finally pulled the various components together. They argue that in response to the need for more accountability and rationality a radical shift took place in correctional policy in the USA during the 1980s. The old transformative rationales for the correctional system were replaced by the actuarial language of probabilistic calculations and statistical distributions that were applicable to populations. Rather than concentrating on individuals, the system shifted towards targeting and managing specific categories and sub-populations. Management was to be realized through the application of increasingly sophisticated risk assessment technologies and practices. This shift also enabled the system to construct its own measures of success and failure and to predict its own needs. In many respects Feeley and Simon viewed actuarialism as both the logical consequence of the original utilitarian penal reform project and a radical departure in that the system had moved beyond any interest in reform or rehabilitation. The correctional system under actuarialism becomes a hyper-rational processing system that fulfils the mandate it has been given. For them actuarialism logically connected with neo-liberal socio-economic policies which produced surplus populations that had to be contained and controlled. In the UK actuarialism is most closely associated with the work of the probation service, whose professional task is risk assessments of the likelihood of re-offending and the threat posed to communities.

Eugene McLaughlin

Associated Concepts: managerialism, prediction studies, rational choice theory, risk, risk factor research, situational crime prevention

Key Readings

DiLulio, J. (1987) *Governing Prisons: A Comparative Study of Correctional Management.* New York: The Free Press.

Feeley, M. and Simon, J. (1992) 'The new penology: notes on the emerging strategy of corrections and its implications', *Criminology*, 30 (4): 452–74.

Simon, J. (1988) 'The ideological effect of actuarial practices', *Law and Society Review*, 22: 771–800.

Simon, J. and Feeley, M. (1995) 'True crime: the new penology and public discourse on crime', in T. Blomberg and S. Cohen (eds), *Punishment and Social Control.* New York: Aldine de Gruyter.

ADMINISTRATIVE CRIMINOLOGY

Definition

A term coined by Jock Young in the 1980s to refer to the reconstitution of establishment criminology in the UK and USA in the aftermath of the demise of positivist-inspired correctionalist theory and practice and the emergence of radical criminology. Administrative criminology concentrates on the nature of the criminal event and the setting in which it occurs and assumes that offenders are rational actors who will attempt to weigh up the potential costs and benefits of their actions. The goal of administrative criminology is to make crime less attractive to offenders.

Distinctive Features

The term 'administrative criminology' encompasses a large number of writers from a variety of academic backgrounds involved in a wide range of research sites. They are united by their acceptance of dominant definitions of what constitutes the problem of crime; their lack of interest in the social causes of crime; their further acceptance of the need for their research to be applied to aid policy development and decision making; their support for rational choice or 'opportunity' approaches to specific offenders and specific offences; their advocacy of 'what we know' and 'what works' criminal justice policies; their proposing modesty and realism in making claims about what can be achieved; and their being either employed within the criminal justice system or acting as paid advisers to criminal justice officials.

For Jock Young, the work of James Q. Wilson (in the USA) and Ronald V. Clarke (in the UK) has been vital to the emergence of a fully fledged administrative criminology. Administrative criminology's starting point is that despite the massive investment in welfare in the 1960s and a sustained period of prosperity, crime rates escalated to unprecedented levels in many Western societies. Wilson took this startling fact as proof that social democratic theorizing on the causes of and solutions to crime was seriously flawed. He argued that it was time to go back to basics on criminal justice policy. Criminologists should concentrate their efforts on producing policies that addressed what the public was afraid of, namely 'predatory' street crimes such as muggings, assaults, robberies, burglaries and so on, that were carried out by strangers. Crime reduction rather than social engineering should be the focus of criminal justice policies. The benefit of engaging in focused research and evaluated pilot studies was to produce rigorous knowledge and avoid costly mistakes. Scepticism about the role of the criminal justice system in crime control also meant that policy makers needed to think about how to integrate practical crime control into other aspects of public policy.

In the UK Clarke, a senior researcher at the Home Office, reached similar conclusions to Wilson and began to formulate an approach to 'commonplace crime' that was not hindered by what he viewed as the limitations of mainstream criminological theorizing, particularly its failure to develop realistic and practical policy recommendations. From Clarke's perspective, criminal justice policy makers cannot do much about the desire of some young men to become involved in delinquency and criminal activity. However, most offenders are involved in a rational choice structuring process that consists of evaluating the perceived risks in the commission of a particular offence, the rewards that are likely to be realized, and the skills and resources required to execute a criminal act successfully. As a consequence, criminal justice policy makers should concentrate their efforts on reducing the physical opportunities for offending and increasing the chances of offenders being caught and punished. This focus on how a criminal's decision making in a given situation is influenced by her/his perception of risk, effort and reward led to the development of a suite of opportunity reduction techniques to increase the effort associated with committing a crime; multiply the risks of crime; reduce the rewards of crime; and remove the excuses for crime. The techniques and strategies chosen must be appropriate to the specifics of the crime committed and their setting.

Evaluation

Such situational crime prevention policy initiatives lend themselves to evaluation for effectiveness and this has enabled administrative criminologists to develop evidence-based, problem-solving approaches to crime reduction. Administrative criminology's other concern is to reorganize the state's crime control efforts in order to make these as efficient, effective and focused as possible. It has no particular sentimental attachment to the criminal justice system and is willing to advocate managerialization, actuarialization and privatization.

By the end of the 1990s administrative criminologists had become increasingly sophisticated in formulating and defending their perspective, going so far as to present 'opportunity' as a 'root cause' of crime.

Eugene McLaughlin

Associated Concepts: actuarialism, crime science, experimental criminology, managerialism, opportunity theory, public criminology, rational choice theory, routine activity theory, situational crime prevention

Key Readings

Clarke, R.V. (ed.) (1997) *Situational Crime Prevention: Successful Case Studies,* 2nd edn. New York: Harrow and Heston.

Cornish, D. and Clarke, R.V. (eds) (1996) *The Reasoning Criminal: Rational Choice Perspectives on Offending.* New York: Springer-Verlag.

Felson, M. and Clarke, R.V. (1998) *Opportunity Makes the Thief: Practical Theory for Crime Prevention* (Police Research Group Paper 98). London: The Home Office.

Newman, G., Clarke, R.V. and Shoham, S. (eds) (1997) *Rational Choice and Situational Crime Prevention.* Aldershot: Ashgate.

Sherman, L., Gottfredson, D., MacKenzie, D., Eck, J., Reuter, P. and Bushway, S. (1997) *Preventing Crime: What Works, What Doesn't, What's Promising: A Report to The United States Congress.* Available at http://www.ncjrs.org/works/index.htm

Wilson, J.Q. (1983) *Thinking about Crime.* New York: Basic Books.

AETIOLOGY

See: Causation

ANARCHIST CRIMINOLOGY

Definition

Anarchism is one of the most difficult political ideologies to conceptualize and define, primarily because there is no single anarchist ideology and because of the degree of misrepresentation by its political opponents. It is a meeting place for a bewildering number of philosophies, belief systems and practices and originated as a reaction to the emergence of the nation state and capitalism in the nineteenth century. Anarchists are united, first and foremost, by a belief that the state is coercive, punitive, exploitative, corrupting and destructive. Alternative forms of mutual aid and voluntary organization that are non-authoritarian, non-coercive, non-hierarchical, functionally specific and decentralized are advocated.

Distinctive Features

A number of specifically anarchist principles have been developed from the work of Max Stirner (1806–56), Pierre Joseph Proudhon (1809–65), Mikhail Bakunin (1814–76), Peter Kropotkin (1842–1921) and Emma Goldman (1869–1940). In general these principles do not conceive of a disorderly or chaotic society, rather a more expansive form of social order without the state. This social order will maximize individual freedoms and encourage voluntary association and self-regulation. A broad spectrum of anarchist thought also wishes to replace monopoly forms of capitalism and private property with collectivist forms of ownership. According to sympathetic criminologists such as Jeff Ferrell, there cannot be a fully fledged anarchist criminology because this would be a contradiction in terms. However, Peter Kropotkin's writings on law and state authority still stand as a key reference point for any emergent anarchist criminology.

Kropotkin argues that law is useless and harmful, sustaining mass criminality and generating social pathologies. Laws protecting private property and the interests of the state are responsible for generating between two-thirds and three-quarters of all crime. The body of criminal law that is geared towards the punishment and prevention of 'crime' does not prevent crime and degrades society because it fosters the worst human instincts and obedience to the status quo and bolsters state domination.

Kropotkin insists that the majority of crime will disappear the day private property ceases to exist and human need and cooperation rather than profits and competition become the organizing principle of social life. Alternative forms of social solidarity and inclusive notions of social justice, rather than state-run systems of criminal justice and the fictional 'rule of law', can contain anti-social behaviour. Here, there are obvious links to the core principles underpinning abolitionism, left idealism and peacemaking criminologies.

Anarchists would deny that their vision relies on disorder, violence and lawlessness. However, the belief that anarchism originates in everyday struggle rather than abstract theorizing leads to the advocacy of direct or creative action and 'propaganda by deed'. The resultant protest and resistance tactics and set-piece confrontations which are vital to the renewal of theory and practice bring anarchist groups into confrontation with the forces of law and order and they thus risk potential criminalization. It is in this moment that the stereotypical representation of the nihilistic anarchist is conjured up in the news media.

Evaluation

Anarchist theory provides criminologists with:

- an uncompromising critique of law, power and the state;
- the promise of un-coercive social relationships;
- the possibility of alternative forms of dispute settlement and harm reduction;
- a form of political intervention that may be appropriate to an increasingly complex and fragmented world where conventional forms of politics are becoming increasingly redundant;

- the basis to develop both libertarian and communitarian criminologies.

Jeff Ferrell (1995: 106) sums up the possibilities of anarchist criminology: 'At its best, anarchism and the process of justice that flows from it constitute a sort of dance that we make up as we go along, an emerging swirl of ambiguity, uncertainty, and pleasure. Once you dive into the dance, there are no guarantees – only the complex rhythms of human interaction and the steps that you and others invent in response. So, if you want certainty or authority, you might want to sit this one out. As for the rest of us: start the music.'

Eugene McLaughlin

Associated Concepts: abolitionism, left idealism, peacemaking criminology, the state

Key Readings

Ferrell, J. (1995) 'Anarchy against the discipline', *Journal of Criminal Justice and Popular Culture*, 3 (4): 86–106.
Ferrell, J. (1999) 'Anarchist criminology and social justice', in B.A. Arrigo (ed.), *Social Justice/Criminal Justice*. Belmont, CA: Wadsworth.
Kropotkin, P. (1996) 'Law and authority', in J. Muncie, E. McLaughlin and M. Langan (eds), *Criminological Perspectives: A Reader*. London: Sage.
Tifft, L.L. (1979) 'The coming re-definitions of crime: an anarchist perspective', *Social Problems*, 26: 392–402.

ANIMAL ABUSE

Definition

Any act that contributes to the pain, suffering or unnatural death of an animal or otherwise threatens its welfare. Animal abuse may be physical, psychological or emotional; may involve active maltreatment or passive neglect or omission; and may be direct or indirect, intentional or unintentional.

Distinctive Features

Species-specific indicators indicate the impact on the psychological and physical welfare of animals. Specific health, physiological, ethological and production indicators (when the animals are incorporated in production processes, e.g. animal husbandry) can be determined, from which a violation of animals' welfare can be assessed. Reduced life expectancy, impaired growth, impaired reproduction, body damage, disease, immuno-suppression, adrenal activity, behaviour anomalies and self-narcotization are indicators of poor welfare. Welfare thus depends not solely on an animal's subjective experiences. Although poor welfare and suffering often occur together, suffering is no prerequisite for poor welfare. When an act or omission entails negative effects on an animal's welfare – to be assessed using these species-specific indicators – it can be classified as animal abuse. But scientific uncertainty about many aspects of animals' mental state or emotional life requires the use of a precautionary principle: an act should be regarded as animal abuse if we are unsure if it has a detrimental effect on the welfare of an animal. Following the descriptions of 'battered child syndrome' and 'battered woman syndrome', attempts should also be made to identify the clinical signs and pathology of physical abuse of companion animals, as specified in 'battered pet syndrome'.

Evaluation

The apparent importance of animal abuse has recently been highlighted through its complex relationship with child abuse and domestic violence (Lockwood and Ascione, 1998). One line of research has examined the supposed links between animal abuse and other expressions of family violence, for example, child abuse and woman abuse. It has been found that several forms of violence often co-exist with different categories of victim. The presence of animal abuse might indicate that other family members are also potential victims; acknowledging this connection can help in the prevention of human interpersonal violence. Other research has examined the correlation between animal abuse committed by children and the development of aggressive or violent behaviour at later stages in life. Here, it has been found that children abusing animals are more likely subsequently to exhibit aggressive and violent tendencies towards humans. Animal abuse in childhood is thus seen to signify a need for interventions by a variety of social and human service agencies.

The importance of detecting and preventing animal abuse has tended to become a justifiable and legitimate field of research, action and intervention, precisely because of its connection with expressions of human interpersonal violence. However, this is an anthropocentric or speciesist approach to animal abuse. Several philosophers have established the moral significance of animals in their own right. Because animals are sentient living beings, with interests and desires, and are 'subjects-of-a-life', they are taken into the circle of moral consideration (Regan and Singer, 1989). Speciesism thus stands for a prejudice or biased attitude favouring the interests of the members of one's own species against those of members of other species. As with other systems of discrimination like racism and sexism, speciesism rests on the domination and subordination of others, here solely based on the fact that animals are not human (Adams and Donovan, 1995). A non-speciesist and more sensitive definition of animal abuse focuses on the interests of animals and the consequences of animal abuse for their welfare (Beirne, 1995; Cazaux, 1999). It rests not on an exhaustive enumeration of possibly abusive acts or omissions (e.g., burning, poisoning, assault, neglect, etc.) but on the effects of practices on animals' physical and psychological welfare.

Henceforth, this definition of animal abuse invalidates the distinction between animal cruelty and animal abuse. The effects of abuse on animals' welfare are independent of offenders' sadistic, malicious or benign propensities. Nor should the definition of animal abuse include the anthropocentric phraseology 'unnecessary suffering' – often inscribed in animal welfare laws – since this lends legitimacy to animal suffering that is deemed necessary for economic, political or scientific reasons. For example, from a non-speciesist viewpoint, bestiality is not an offence of decadence or sexual indecency but, because of its similarity to the sexual assault of women and children, it should be called 'an interspecies sexual assault' (Beirne, 1997).

Animal abuse refers not only to individual cases of socially unacceptable practices, such as the abuse of companion animals, but also to several institutionalized systems founded on the exploitation and subordination of animals which are by many viewed as socially acceptable. These include the abuse of animals in agriculture, hunting, fishing, trapping, entertainment and sports, and in experimental research.

What is classified as animal abuse is thus independent of human intention or ignorance, socially sanctioned or socially rejected norms, and labels of necessary or unnecessary suffering. It is also independent of whether the animal victim is categorized as a companion animal, a wild animal, livestock, or an experimental animal, and covers both single and repeated or institutionalized incidents of animal abuse.

Geertrui Cazaux and Piers Beirne

Associated Concepts: family crime, green criminology, hidden crime, violence

Key Readings

Adams, C.J. and Donovan, J. (eds) (1995) *Animals and Women.* London: Duke University Press.

Beirne, P. (1995) 'The use and abuse of animals in criminology: a brief history and current review', *Social Justice,* 22 (1): 5–31.

Beirne, P. (1997) 'Rethinking bestiality: towards a concept of interspecies sexual assault', *Theoretical Criminology,* 1 (3): 317–40.

Cazaux, G. (1999) 'Beauty and the Beast: animal abuse from a non-speciesist criminological perspective', *Crime, Law & Social Change,* 31 (2): 105–25.

Lockwood, R. and Ascione, F.R. (eds) (1998) *Cruelty to Animals and Interpersonal Violence.* West Lafayette, IN: Purdue University Press.

Regan, T. and Singer, P. (eds) (1989) *Animal Rights and Human Obligations.* London: Prentice-Hall.

ANOMIE

Definition

A state of ethical normlessness or deregulation, pertaining to either an individual or a society. This lack of normative regulation leaves individuals without adequate ethical guidance as to their conduct and undercuts social integration.

Distinctive Features

Anomie is one of the foundational concepts of modern criminological thought. Its prominence in American theorizing (where it forms the basis of 'strain' theory) is largely due to the interpretation given to anomie in the work of Robert Merton. His 1938 article 'Social Structure and Anomie' has proven to be one of the most influential articles in the history of sociology. Whilst Merton's theory is now seen as reductionist and somewhat mechanistic in the view it offers of human agency, fertile ground can still be found in Durkheim's original late nineteenth-century formulation of anomie. This is largely due to the scope of his questioning. Along with some fellow Europeans (i.e., Marx, Nietzsche and Weber), Durkheim was concerned with grappling with the new problems of modernity and sought to identify the key features underlying social change. With modernity human desires and passions seemed freer and the pace of change was dramatic: how then was 'social solidarity' or social cohesion possible? Durkheim did not pose the question so much in terms of 'What are the forces driving us apart?', rather he asked: 'What is it that keeps us together? How is society itself possible? What are the roles and "functions" of humans and social institutions? And how are we to learn about it in order that we may adapt to change?'

Durkheim locates the driving force of modernity in the twin factors of the division of labour and the freeing of desire. Society is to be conceived as a 'moral milieu' which positions and constitutes the individual. Individuals experience social reality through their differential positioning in the social division of labour. Humans are motivated by the pursuit of pleasure and the satisfaction of desire and they attain happiness when their possibilities for satisfying desire are not at odds with the social realities of the division of labour. But what happens when the cultural regulation of desire breaks down and desire is released as a mobile, infinite capacity transcending the limitations on satisfaction inherent in any division of labour?

In his doctoral thesis, first published in 1893, Durkheim argued that the consequences of anomie, or the failure of moral regulation, were clear in

> the continually recurring conflicts and disorders of every kind, of which the economic world offers so sorry a spectacle. For, since nothing restrains the forces present from reacting together, or prescribes limits to them that they are obliged to respect, they tend to grow beyond all bounds, each clashing with the other, each warding off and weakening the other ... Men's passions are stayed only by a moral presence they respect. If all authority of this kind is lacking, it is the law of the strongest that rules, and a state of warfare, either latent or acute, is necessarily endemic. (Durkheim, 1984: xxxii–xxxiii)

Durkheim thus explicitly reverses Hobbes's picture of 'the war of all against all' inherent in the state of nature. Whereas for Hobbes this was the purely natural or pre-social state, which humans overcome by creating a powerful sovereign to lay down definitions of meaning (laws) and enforce obedience, Durkheim places this state of social war and crime as a product of society, a result of the breakdown of moral regulation. Modernity is characterized by increasing individualism, by an autonomy of thought and action, but this autonomy is dependent upon greater interdependency in the division of labour and increased complexity within the collective consciousness: 'liberty itself is the product of regulation'. The task for 'advanced societies' was to achieve a balance between the functions of the division of labour, law and culture, 'the conditions that dominate social evolution'. With the old certainties disappearing, the individual finds him- or herself without a secure footing in reality, and anomie threatens. In times of economic crisis, either dramatic increases in prosperity or disasters, anomie may become the normal state of being: 'greed is aroused without knowing where to find its ultimate foothold. Nothing can calm it, since its goal is far beyond all it can attain. Reality seems valueless by comparison with the dreams of fevered imaginations; reality is therefore abandoned, but so too is possibility when it in turn becomes reality: A thirst for novelties, unfamiliar pleasures, nameless sensations, all of which lose their savour once known' (Durkheim, 1984: 254).

So what was the solution to this state of anomie? While Durkheim personally argued that the solution to the normative deregulation causing anomie could not be the imposition of normative restructuring through violence and the manipulation of cultural symbols – the solution that both fascism and state Stalinism were later to offer – he bequeathed few theoretical tools for integrating studies of culture, class and perceptions of social 'reality'. The understanding of anomie which was to be developed within criminology was constrained by its centrality to the middle range theorizing of Robert Merton (1938).

Writing shortly after the social democratic compromise of the 'new deal', Merton identified the key cultural message of modernist American culture as the 'success' goal, in particular 'money-success'. A 'strain to anomie' resulted from a disjuncture between cultural goals and legitimate means of achievement. Specifically, the new technologies of advertising put forward a cultural goal of economic affluence and social ascent, but individuals, differentially positioned in the social structure, understood that the institutionally available means may or may not enable personal success. Whilst the majority of Americans may 'conform' others might 'innovate' – by accepting the cultural goal but rejecting the institutionally available means. Particularly for those located in the lower reaches of the social structure, crime could therefore be a reaching for the American dream, albeit sought through illegitimate channels. Merton's theory was further developed with the 'differential opportunity' theorizing of Cloward and Ohlin (1960), and anomie has proved a fertile, if somewhat elusive, concept to build upon, recently informing Agnew's (1992) 'positive' strain theory.

Evaluation

Merton's theory struck a deep chord with many. It seemed to offer a way of constraining crime by improving the legitimate life chances of those who otherwise may make the choice to innovate deviantly. However, the positivist tendencies of American sociology meant that any concept that was difficult to operationalize into survey questions or mathematically inscribable data remained elusive rather than accepted and always open to the charge of weak sociology.

Anomie is thus a highly suggestive concept, but one that is difficult to operationalize. What are we to make of this? Perhaps the intellectual history of anomie reflects the impossibility of achieving a 'transparent' sociology, capturing the true 'experience' of the subject. Durkheimian sociology had a normative element; it was for modern society to arrive at a state of scientific self-consciousness. This would aid the creation of moral individualism in that mankind would attain an objective knowledge of how things stood, of the functional interdependency of all upon all. But this dream of happiness as attunement to our shared knowledge of the state of reality has been undercut by the relentless division of labour, by 'reality' in 'late-modern' 'Western' societies being characterized by oscillation, plurality and perspectivism, rather than stability. The technological intensification of cultural reproduction – via the advent of generalized communication, the mass media, the Internet – gives us a sea of information, rendering 'our' experience communicable to a translocal set of 'fellow-feelers' while appearing inconsistent and superficial to our 'others'. Few would see the function of modern 'art' as to offer representations of the 'absolute' or gateways into the eternal truths of the human condition; rather it is designed to 'shock' or draw the observer into the experience of ambiguity and ambivalence. Within criminology, understanding anomie offered the hope that criminological theorists could demonstrate particular policy recommendations, namely that crime could be averted by reconciling the means available to agents through the goals offered by culture. If agents could be assured that they could achieve the cultural goals through legitimate or 'normal' means (education, employment, etc.), then the strain to deviance would lessen. But in the globalized capitalism of the late-modern condition, at least within Western societies, multiple goals and fractured and overlapping identities appear the norm. The very concept of deviance loses its grip. Moreover, the range of candidates available as cultural goals, not just consumerism but the enhancement of power or the creation of personal identity as a life choice, renders the technological fix of adjusting 'means to ends' a mirage. The concept of anomie may take on the role of an existential prop – never quite fitting within any criminological theory, but always hinting at something of fundamental importance in the human condition.

Wayne Morrison

Associated Concepts: differential association, functionalism, relative deprivation, social control theory, strain theory, subculture

Key Readings

Agnew, R. (1992) 'Foundation for a general strain theory of crime and delinquency', *Criminology*, 30 (1): 47–87.

Cloward, R. and Ohlin, L. (1960) *Delinquency and Opportunity.* New York: The Free Press.

Downes, D. and Rock, P. (1998) 'Anomie', in *Understanding Deviance: A Guide to the Sociology of Crime and Rule Breaking*, 3rd edn. Oxford: Oxford University Press.

Durkheim, E. (1970) *Suicide* (trans. S.A. Solovay and J.H. Mueller, ed. G.E.G. Catlin). New York: The Free Press.

Durkheim, E. (1984) *The Division of Labour in Society* (trans. W.D. Halls). Basingstoke: Macmillan.

Merton, R.K. (1938) 'Social structure and anomie', *American Sociological Review*, 3: 672–82.

ANTI-SOCIAL BEHAVIOUR

Definition

The concept of anti-social behaviour (ASB) is usually invoked to refer to such issues as youths hanging about causing trouble, noise, vandalism, abandoned vehicles, litter, graffiti and drunkenness. But definitions of ASB are highly contested and, in the eyes of many, legally quite imprecise. Its definition in Britain has been intentionally left very wide, involving, according to the Home Office, 'acting in a manner that caused or was likely to cause harassment, alarm or distress to one or more persons not of the same household (as the defendant)'.

Distinctive Features

The concept of ASB has seen a rapid rise to prominence since the 1990s, particularly in Britain. It is even said to be the 'number one concern' of the British people and tackling it was given a central place in the 2004–08 Home Office Strategic Plan. Some commentators (Tonry, 2004) argue that New Labour virtually 'invented' the concept and as a result ASB is seen as being inextricably bound up with New Labour's politics of crime and disorder and the strategies of governance emerging therefrom. However, while it is true that few people were talking about ASB before the mid-1990s, the concept also has an important historical pedigree that we should not overlook.

Its recent history can be traced back to Wilson and Kelling's highly influential (1982) 'broken windows' article, where the concept of 'incivilities' was originally employed to describe a range of offensive and disorderly behaviours and conflicting relationships in fractured and deprived communities in the USA. Often implicit in this analysis was an association between such degraded behaviours and an 'underclass' way of life. Wilson and Kelling's thesis was also the stated basis for the NYPD's high profile 'zero tolerance' crackdown on 'quality of life' offences.

These understandings of the problem in 'high crime/sink estate' areas corresponded closely to the developing urban management and community crime prevention agendas in the UK. The residualization of social housing typically made problems even more acute. Crime and harassment compounded difficulties with housing management. Conservative proposals for 'probationary' or introductory tenancies culminated in new enforcement powers in the 1996 Housing Act (Flint, 2002) whilst a 1995 Labour policy document, *A Quiet Life: Tough Action on Criminal Neighbours*, expanded the notion of ASB, placing it firmly at the centre of the Party's approach to community-oriented crime and disorder management. This housing management focus has remained a key aspect of ASB – media horror stories about 'neighbours from hell' are not uncommon.

More often than not, however, ASB is seen as related to the activities of young people. Youth, therefore, represents a second, and increasingly prominent, strand in the contemporary discourse of ASB (Squires and Stephen, 2005). This was especially well reflected in *Misspent Youth*, the 1996 Report of the Audit Commission, itself promptly followed by New Labour's White Paper *No More Excuses*, which declared its intention to 'break the links between anti-social behaviour and crime'. Anti-social behaviour, therefore, understood as a kind of pre-delinquent nuisance, was central to the ensuing new youth justice strategy which prioritized early interventions that were designed to 'nip crime in the bud'.

Evaluation

Viewing ASB as a form of pre-delinquency connects us to its much older conception which has now been largely sidelined in favour of the enforcement-based approach of the present day. This perspective, developed in the USA in the late 1940s, focused upon the identification of behavioural and personality disorders in childhood, centred around a broadly conceived 'anti-social personality disorder' that was used to predict future delinquency. This conception of a psychosocial pathology requiring welfare and treatment interventions no longer commands mainstream attention today even though there is strong evidence of the prevalence of behavioural and personality disorders amongst young offender groups. Treatment-based approaches for delinquency fell foul of complaints about 'net-widening' although precisely the same complaint could be made of anti-social behaviour enforcement actions today. Rather than severing them, early interventions make connections between ASB and later criminality. Intervening early to 'nip crime in the bud' intensifies the processes of scrutiny and surveillance to which young people are subjected. To use a fishing analogy, wider nets with thinner mesh mean catching more. Newer proposals envisage allowing a wider range of persons (including parish councils and community panels) to initiate (or nominate young people for) ASBO (Anti-Social Behaviour Order) proceedings. Therefore, to develop the analogy, there will also be more people fishing.

That this was precisely the intention behind the government's ASB strategy in England and Wales may be gleaned from comments in a Home Office report on ASBOs. The early 1990s witnessed a rising tide of complaints about the policing of youth-related crime and disorder. Official strategies favouring diversion were increasingly discredited as a misguided liberal tolerance that was preventing the police from responding forcefully and effectively. The view then developed that an 'enforcement deficit' had emerged, with young people apparently able to flout the law with impunity and engage in acts of anti-social behaviour 'in the full knowledge that there were few criminal sanctions that could touch them'. This situation often caused great frustration: 'anti-social behaviour is often used as a synonym for problems with young people' (Campbell, 2002). In the first 30 months following the 1998 Crime and Disorder Act, three-quarters of the ASBOs in England and Wales were issued for people under 21 years of age.

Although it was originally envisaged that each year up to 5000 ASBOs would be handed out, even after five years the overall total had not reached 2500. Nevertheless the government appeared to be convinced of the merits of this 'quicker and easier' approach to ASB enforcement. In 2003 it published a White Paper, *Respect and Responsibility: Taking a stand against ASB,* reiterating its contractual model of inclusion and social responsibility. This was followed, later in the year, by the Anti-Social Behaviour Act which established a new, Home Office-led *Together* campaign to develop a national ASB action plan. The use of Acceptable Behaviour Contracts and ASBOs was to be promoted while new powers, such as Closure Notices (for premises used in drug-dealing) and Curfews and Dispersal Orders (to disperse congregations of young people causing fear and alarm in residential areas), were also introduced. As in the case of ASBOs, the promise of quicker and easier enforcement undoubtedly has some appeal to police and complainants alike but misgivings have been voiced about the increasingly discretionary enforcement that may result. For example, the police have always 'moved on' young people causing a nuisance and Dispersal Orders may chiefly represent the formalization and realignment of the law around existing police practices. The government, by contrast, concerned that some Crime and Disorder Reduction Partnerships were not taking the threat of ASB seriously enough, also announced that it would be looking for improvements in performance by despatching 'ASBO ambassadors' from areas considered to be working well to those judged to be underperforming.

Yet ASB has another history, one that is often overlooked in the ever-decreasing circles of contemporary problem analysis, opinion polling and impact evaluation that have become so central a feature of modern governance. At the end of World War II, Hermann Mannheim (1946) discussed ASB, seeing it as a series of harms perpetrated against the community and contrary to the spirit and purposes of social reconstruction. He specifically referred to 'profiteering' and the non-payment of taxes, not simply the breach of criminal laws. In due course, mainstream criminology rather declined this more radical and expansive agenda but now seems more willing to pick up the issue. Compared with today's conception of ASB, however, Mannheim's perspective raises two key issues. First, during times of rapid social change (post-war Britain and today's late modernity) it may be necessary to assert the values of community and social inclusion more forcefully. However, second, anti-social behaviour is not solely the preserve of the poorest or the young.

Peter Squires

Associated Concepts: 'broken windows', communitarianism, community policing, community safety, deviance, juvenile justice, net widening, social capital, zero tolerance

Key Readings

Campbell, S. (2002) *A Review of Anti-Social Behaviour Orders,* Home Office Research Study 236. London: Home Office.
Flint, J. (2002) 'Social housing agencies and the governance of anti-social behaviour', *Housing Studies,* 17 (4): 619–37.
Mannheim, H. (1946) *Criminal Justice and Social Reconstruction.* London: Routledge & Kegan Paul.
Squires, P. and Stephen, D. (2005) *Rougher Justice: Young People and Anti-Social Behaviour.* Cullompton: Willan.
Tonry, M. (2004) *Punishment and Politics: Evidence and Emulation in the Making of English Crime Control Policy.* Cullompton: Willan.
Wilson, J. and Kelling, F. (1982) 'Broken windows – the police and neighbourhood safety', *Atlantic Monthly,* 249 (3): 29–38.

APPRECIATIVE CRIMINOLOGY

Definition

An approach that seeks to understand and appreciate the social world from the point of view of the individual, or category of individual, with particular reference to crime and deviance.

Distinctive Features

The designation 'appreciative criminology' owes much to use of the term 'appreciative studies' by Matza (1969) to refer to specific studies of deviant subcultures such as those of the hobo, the juvenile gang, the drug-taker. Such studies are characterized by observing, sometimes by participation, the social world of deviants with a view to producing an appreciative account of the deviant's own story in his or her own terms. Theoretically, appreciative criminology is influenced by the interactionist perspective which developed in social psychology and sociology in the 1930s and which received further impetus in the 1960s and 1970s, for example in connection with new deviancy theory. Interactionism offers an alternative to positivist ways of thinking about crime and criminality. Amongst other things, positivism started from assumptions such as: there are categories of individuals who are criminal and who have characteristics which clearly distinguish them from non-criminals; the explanations for criminality lie in individual pathologies; such pathologies are the causes and determinants of criminality. Instead, interactionism offers a framework which emphasizes human choice and free will rather than determinism; a view of crime and deviance as something which is generated in interactions rather than as a characteristic of individual backgrounds; and an assumption that social action and the social world are flexible, changing and dynamic rather than fixed, objective and external. Above all, appreciative studies took from interactionism the notion that there can be variability of meanings in social contexts and in society in general, rather than consensus. The aim of appreciative studies was, and is, to describe, understand and appreciate the social meanings and interpretations which categories of individuals attribute to events, contexts and others' actions. Such studies are epitomized in the title of Howard Parker's (1974) book *View from the Boys,* a study of male juvenile gangs in Liverpool based on the perspectives of the gang members themselves.

Methodologically, appreciative studies have been influenced by the ethnographic tradition in social research. Ethnography, which liberally means description ('graphy') of cultures ('ethno'), has its roots in social anthropology and the study of pre-industrial societies. Subsequently it has been adapted to the examination of subcultures in complex society. Ethnography has a number of methodological commitments which make it especially appropriate to appreciative studies of deviant subcultures using an interactionist framework. First, there is a commitment to studying the social world from the point of view of the individuals being studied. Second, it is assumed that there can be a multiplicity of perspectives rather than just one, and also that each is equally valid for the people who hold them. Third, social perspectives (and the social meanings, definitions, labels and stereotypes which comprise them) cannot be separated from social interactions. Therefore, particular attention should be paid to the ways in which people interact in specific social contexts. Fourth, there is a belief that such observation should be naturalistic; that is, individuals should be studied behaving as they would normally and naturally do so. It is for this reason that ethnographers often rely on participant observation although that is not the only form of data collection used.

The Chicago School of Sociology of the 1920s and 1930s was a source of classic appreciative studies. Researchers adapted some of the techniques of social anthropologists to study the subcultures of crime within their city (in addition to using a statistical analysis of crime rates to map zones of the city). They produced books with titles such as *The Jack Roller* (Shaw, 1930), *The Hobo* (Anderson, 1923) and *The Gang* (Thrasher, 1927). There was particular emphasis on the transitional zone of the city with indicators of social disorganization such as a high turnover of population, poor housing and a high incidence of crime.

Appreciative studies captured the culture of crime in this zone and also the mechanisms by which this culture was transmitted. In doing so, the Chicago sociologists emphasized the distinctiveness of the deviant subcultures and their separation from mainstream society. In the 1960s and 1970s there was a resurgence of ethnographic studies, linked to an interactionist framework, but with a particular slant towards the process of labelling. For example, Howard Becker's (1963) study of marijuana smokers was influential in generating a greater concern with the ways deviant and non-deviant worlds meet and interact rather than with their separation. This was part of the emergence of labelling theory as a radical response to the predominance of positivist conventional criminology. Becker was not interested in asking questions about the causes of smoking marijuana; instead he focused on the question of how and why marijuana users come to be defined and labelled as deviant. This involved looking at interactions between the would-be deviant and the agencies of social control.

Evaluation

The critiques that can be levelled at appreciative criminology are those which, in terms of theory, can be levelled at interactionism, and which, in terms of methodology, can be directed at ethnography. For example, explanations of crime and deviance that are grounded in interactions in small-scale contexts run the risk of neglecting wider social structural dimensions of power, inequality and oppression (although for some a synthesis based on theorizing at different levels is feasible). Methodologically, ethnographic studies endure the criticisms that they lack generalizability to wider contexts and – being reliant on the deviants themselves for data – are not scientific or objective. There is also the possibility that taking an appreciative stance is synonymous with glorifying the criminal. This does not find sympathy with those who emphasize the need to face up to the reality of crime and the consequences of it for victims.

Such criticisms apart, appreciative studies have provided a rich vein within criminology and have also described and explained criminal and deviant subcultures which would not otherwise have been made visible by other theoretical and methodological approaches.

Victor Jupp

Associated Concepts: Chicago School of Sociology, cultural criminology, ethnography, interactionism, labelling, new deviancy theory, participant observation, subculture

Key Readings

Andersen, N. (1923) *The Hobo: The Sociology of the Homeless Man.* Chicago: University of Chicago Press.

Becker, H. (1963) *Outsiders: Studies in the Sociology of Deviance.* New York: The Free Press.

Matza, D. (1969) *Becoming Deviant.* Englewood Cliffs, NJ: Prentice–Hall.

Parker, H. (1974) *View from the Boys.* Newton Abbot: David and Charles.

Shaw, C.R. (1930) *The Jack Roller.* Chicago: University of Chicago Press.

Thrasher, P.M. (1927) *The Gang.* Chicago: University of Chicago Press.

ART CRIME

Definition

As with the art world, art crime is difficult to define. Comprising numerous illicit activities and grey areas of the law, it involves criminal acts that range from theft (including looting), damage (iconoclasm), deception (fakes, forgeries, fraud, and ransom) and trafficking, to graffiti.

Distinctive Features

Lacking regulation, the art world is fluid and its organizational basis creates the flows that help amplify it into one of immense value. Globally, the cultural economy and heritage are characterized by huge worldwide sales and very large visitor numbers for art displays. In London alone, eight museums now have more than a million visitors annually.

A lack of evidence means that the often-regurgitated figure that globally art crime is worth billions of pounds should be treated with caution as it is very difficult to substantiate (www.interpol.com). For example, in the UK, it is extremely hard to verify the actual extent of art theft because it is recorded under the wider categorization of property crime. Large figures serve to highlight the crime, but they also confuse our understanding as they bring together numbers from disparate types of art crime. However, in spite of contentious figures and a lack of empirical evidence, it is clear that day-to-day criminal acts are endemic and involve huge sums. Various types of people participate in art crime, such as insiders, conmen, art connoisseurs, the psychologically challenged, the politically motivated, opportunists, organized criminals, governments, the military and artists. Though the disparate types of art crime pose very different challenges, the threat usually centres on money. The transnational nature of the crime is highlighted by the fact that much stolen art passes through the hands of criminal gangs in countries other than from where the art was stolen. This is significant because criminals are using art and antiques to fund crime internationally.

Encapsulating the challenges faced by modern securitization and policing networks, art crime requires specialization, expertise and resources. These frequently violent crimes are often met by a lack of public police attention. With a few exceptions (such as that of Italy which has a large, well-manned unit or France and Germany which have services managing national databases), in most countries it is a marginalized area of public policing. For example, in the UK, the Metropolitan Police Service's Art and Antiques Unit, in spite of a history of success, lacks staff and only has jurisdiction over London.

The prevention and detection of art crime have a complex matrix of security providers. As with many spaces in modern society, within the locations where art is displayed or stored, it is often private security technical staff that 'do' this security inside 'security bubbles'. In some large cities (particularly capitals), this security can be 'public' owing to the large amount of state run locations that own and display art. Overall, a range of people will be involved in the securitization and policing of art, including onsite security personnel (and other staff), art installers, transportation companies, the owners, government agencies (including ministries of culture and customs), the public police, private detectives, private security companies and consultancies, lawyers, the insurance industry, surveyors and loss adjusters working for insurance companies, databases and Interpol.

Evaluation

While researching art crime in 1994, Conklin found very little social scientific research and relied largely on media sources. A decade later, Mackenzie (2005) found the situation had hardly changed. There is now more available literature, both factual and fictional; however, while there is criminological research this often centres on specific areas. For instance, academics such as Mackenzie, Polk, Bowman, and Lane et al. have focused much of their research on the area of looting and the entrance of stolen objects into the art/antiquity market. Research from the legal perspective provides a valuable source of information, particularly as different legal systems (e.g., in the UK and USA compared to France and Italy) affect policing and security measures owing to differing ownership laws concerning good-faith purchases.

Criminologists have a crucial role both in broadening our general understanding of different art crimes and in undertaking specific policy-based research. But how art crime is understood poses difficult questions. For example, the ownership or provenance of a work of art can be contentious. An artwork might also have an elaborate history that is linked either directly or indirectly with crime; from being originally looted or stolen from another location, involved as a fake or forgery, or the victim of damage, turning up in a drug deal, to being part of a 'reward' that is uncomfortably close to a ransom. The grey area of the art world is exemplified by some looted art and antiquities now being viewed as licit, and also by the ways that pieces are 'authenticated' by the art world (Bowman, 2008). Furthermore, an artwork, such as a graffiti mural, can start life as a crime but then be

protected or sold to general acclaim. To achieve a proper understanding of art crimes, the different types must not be amalgamated together as they pose very different challenges.

The large emphasis on risk management and the prevention of crime by security and policing nodes, particularly insurance companies, shows the preventative measures to be more important than either recovery or the criminal involved. Among these are situational crime prevention (especially the use of technology), environmental design, the use of databases, documenting the objects, and buyers being self-responsible. This highlights the cross-disciplinary nature of research into these crimes, with criminology, law, architecture and geography all being involved. However, in spite of the preventative measures, many locations are still vulnerable to crimes involving fakes, forgeries and criminal damage, and also to different types of theft (such as looting where the technological advances coupled with the economic hardships of some people in the source countries make the crime attractive, even if those committing the original crime are ultimately being exploited: see Bowman 2008).

With the transnationality of many art crimes and securitization and policing having to involve a range of agencies both nationally and internationally, the crucial question is less about who is best suited to undertake the security, and more about how different people (with their range of motivations and interests) can work together to produce the most effective preventative security (as well as investigations and recoveries), and, crucially in neo-liberal terms, one by which they all benefit. The insurance companies are central to the security terrain. Fluidity in the art world creates profits and, in line with Ewald's (1991: 208) view that 'insurance allows enterprise', insurance is the driving force behind institutions taking 'risks' such as putting on blockbuster exhibitions with loans of artworks moving around the world (even after previous thefts during loans) and handling the security of this art. The ownership of huge amounts of art by states also means that governments can be very involved as well. In the UK, while not purchasing insurance, the state follows a similar model both for creating flows of art (with the consequent 'risk') and for securing its art and that which is deemed to be shown in the public interest.

Different criminological theories have been used to try and understand art crime. For example, Conklin (1994), Mackenzie (2005), Polk (1999) and Lane et al. (2008) have used Routine Activity theory in their work. The basic features of this theory exist in many art crimes. This reflects a crime science focus; however, it is important not to ignore the criminality aspects, particularly those concerning the people who perpetrate the different stages of the crimes. Other theories include flag effect (Conklin, 1994; Mackenzie 2005), target hardening (Polk, 1999), and cognitive mapping theory (Mackenzie, 2005).

Art is one of the few remaining unregulated fields and is also a world that has problems dealing with thieves within it. The contemporary relevance of different art crimes to criminology is clear. Its fluid threat, exemplified by the theft of sculptures when prices for certain metals rise, encapsulates the challenges posed by profit-driven criminals and transnational crime to the locations in which art is kept and, also, to the many varied public sector and private agencies and stakeholders involved in the securitization and policing of art around the world.

John Kerr

Associated Concepts: corporate crime, globalization, hidden crime, opportunity theory, organized crime, routine activity theory

Key Readings

Bowman, B.A. (2008) 'Transnational crimes against culture: looting at archaeological sites and "grey" market in antiquities', *Journal of Contemporary Criminal Justice*, 24 (3): 225–242.

Conklin, J. (1994) *Art Crime*. Westport, CT: Praeger.

Ewald, F. (1991) 'Insurance and risk', in G. Burchell, C. Gordon and P. Miller (eds), *The Foucault Effect: Studies in Governmentality*. Chicago: University of Chicago Press.

Lane, D., Bromley, D., Hicks, R. and Mahoney, J. (2008) 'Time crime: the transnational organisation of art and antiquities theft', *Journal of Contemporary Criminal Justice*, 24 (3): 243–262.

Mackenzie, S. (2005) *Criminal and Victim Profiles in Art Theft: Motive, Opportunity and Repeat Victimisation*. Available at http://ssrn.com/abstract = 1003988

Polk, K. (1999) 'Who wins and who loses when art is stolen or forged?' Paper presented at the Art Crime: Protecting Art, Protecting Artists and Protecting Consumers Conference, convened by the Australian Institute of Criminology, Sydney, 2–3 December.

AUTHORITARIAN POPULISM

Definition

Conceptualized as an essential aspect of how social democratic states and their institutions respond to crises within advanced capitalist political economies, authoritarian populism explains how increasingly repressive punitive laws and sanctions gain popular legitimacy. This mobilization of state power aims to manage consent, organize regulation and secure hegemony through an increasingly authoritarian political agenda derived from political disaffection and discontent. It reaffirms reactive and reactionary discourses established around the 'collapse' of democracy, the 'breakdown' in law and order, the 'militancy' of the unions, the 'decline' in moral values and so on. These discourses are exploited through political and media 'campaigns', thus generating 'moral panics' within popular discourse and social reaction.

Distinctive Features

Basing his analysis on the proposition that 'state-monopolized physical violence permanently underlies the techniques of power and mechanisms of consent' within Western capitalist democracies, Poulantzas (1978: 81) claimed that during the 1970s a new *form* of state had emerged: 'authoritarian statism ... intensified state control over every sphere of socio-economic life *combined with* radical decline of the institutions of political democracy and with draconian and multiform curtailment of so-called "formal" liberties' (1978: 203–4). Repressive measures depended on the actual exercise of state-sanctioned violence and, significantly, on its internationalization through ideological acceptance or, for those who opposed the rise of authoritarianism, through *mechanisms of fear*.

For Stuart Hall, Poulantzas had made a defining contribution to the critical analysis of the 'exceptional shifts' towards authoritarianism within Western social democracies. Yet he also felt that Poulantzas had misread the strategy of anti-statism prevalent within the radical right – a strategy representing itself as anti-statist to win popular support while disguising the reality of honing state centralism. More importantly, Poulantzas had neglected the purposeful and orchestrated construction and manipulation of popular consent. Herein lay the essence of Hall's claim for authoritarian populism: 'harness[ing] ... support [of] some popular discontents, neutraliz[ing] opposing forces, disaggregat[ing] the opposition and incorporat[ing] *some* strategic elements of popular opinion into its own hegemonic project' (Hall, 1985: 118).

Hall's response to, and development of, Poulantzas's thesis emerged from his work with colleagues at the Centre for Contemporary Cultural Studies, Birmingham, UK, during the 1970s. In their exhaustive analysis of the 'crisis' in the UK political economy, Hall et al. (1978: 303) identified 'deep structural shifts' which had resulted in 'the extension of the law and the courts at the level of political management of conflict and the class struggle'. As the state had become more directly interventionist within the economy, establishing the foundation for capitalist reconstruction through the libertarianism of the 'free-market', it became both necessary and 'legitimate' for 'public opinion to be actively recruited in an open and explicit fashion in favour of the "strong state" ... [characterized as] the ebb and flow of authoritarian populism in defence of social discipline' (1978: 304–5).

For Hall et al. (1978: 317–20) the 'crisis' that was 'policed' through the gradual development of *legitimate coercion* comprised four distinct elements: a crisis of and for British capitalism; a crisis of the 'relations of social forces' derived in the economic crisis; a crisis of the state in mobilizing popular consent for potentially unpopular socio-economic strategies; a crisis in political legitimacy, in social authority, in hegemony; and the imposition of 'social authority' and societal discipline. The authors identified the collapse of postwar social-democratic consensus and the consolidation of New Right ideology as a fundamental shift in the balance of social forces – from consent to coercion – inherent within social democracies; a shift they characterized as the emergence of an exceptional form of the capitalist state.

Further expanding the thesis, Hall (1979: 19) proposed that the 'language of law and order is sustained by moralisms ... where the great syntax of "good" versus "evil", of civilized and uncivilized standards, of the choice between anarchy and order constantly divides the world up and classifies it into its appointed stations'. By appealing to 'inherent' social values and evoking an overarching moral imperative, law and order rhetoric appealed to a collective common sense, 'welding people to that "need for authority" ... so significant for the Right in the construction of consent to its authoritarian programme'. Populism, however, was not simply a 'rhetorical device': it operated on 'genuine contradictions' and reflected a 'rational and material core' (1979: 20).

Hall (1980: 3) considered the 'drive' towards a 'more disciplinary, authoritarian kind of society' to be 'no short-term affair'. It embodied a 'regression to a stone-age morality' promoted by politicians, together with, in popular discourse, 'a blind spasm of control: the feeling that the *only* remedy for a society which is declared to be "ungovernable" is the imposition of order, through a disciplinary use of law by the state'. Thus, the 'shift "from above" [was] pioneered by, harnessed to and, to some extent, legitimated by a popular groundswell below', a populism exemplified by 'a sequence of "moral panic"' (Hall, 1985: 116).

Evaluation

The most strident critique of authoritarian populism came from Jessop et al. (1988). Concentrating on its application to the rise and consolidation of Thatcherism in the UK they argued it over-emphasized the significance of ideology and downplayed structural relations of political economy. It was too concerned with the 'relative autonomy' of language and discourse, neglected the political economy of the New Right (preferring instead to focus on its 'hegemonic project') and 'generate[d] an excessive concern with the mass media and ideological production at the expense of political and economic organization ...' (1988: 73). They rejected the idea that Thatcherism had secured hegemony and achieved a new expression of collective 'common-sense'; the New Right had neither a broad consensus nor political legitimacy for its objectives. Further, Hall was criticized for idealizing the gains of postwar social democracy and for failing to address the political economic determinants of global economic restructuring.

The ensuing debate was severe. Hall denied that authoritarian populism had been conceived as a *comprehensive* analysis of Thatcherism. It was 'preposterous' to claim that he had suggested that Thatcherism had secured hegemony. Rather, it constituted a politics, shared by Western capitalist states and hegemonic in 'conception and project', whose 'dominance' had become 'self-evident' by the mid-1980s (Hall, 1985: 119). Returning to Gramsci, he concluded it was 'impossible to conceptualize or achieve' hegemony without accepting the economy as the 'decisive nucleus' around which civil society consolidated (1985: 120).

As academic hostilities cooled it became clear that the significance of authoritarian populism conceptually lay in its contribution to theorizing the political and ideological dimensions of the authoritarian shift and its populist appeal for stronger laws, imposed order and tighter discipline. What remained unexplored was the foundation of popular authoritarianism within the wider society, given – as Hall and others recognized – that people are not mere 'dupes'. Historically, an authoritarian streak can be detected within the collective psyche which appears to transcend cultural and regional differences. Further, authoritarian responses to orchestrated moral panics, not derived in economic crises or which occur during periods of relative economic expansionism, require consideration.

Yet Hall's analysis – combining Gramsci, Laclau and Poulantzas – demonstrated that advanced capitalism is served, serviced, but rarely confronted by state institutions whose decision makers share its ends, if not always its means, via a coincidence of interests expressed in a common and dominant ideology. In functioning, the state – exemplified by the rule of law, its derivation and administration – tutors and guides the broad membership of society. State institutions are sites for the regeneration and reconstruction of ideas as well as policies. This process, sensitive to and informing of popular discourses, serves to defend the structural contradictions and inequalities of advanced capitalism whether in recession (crisis) or in growth (reconstruction). In this climate, authoritarian populism serves as a poignant reminder that if consensus cannot be forged, it will be forced.

Phil Scraton and Kathryn Chadwick

Associated Concepts: criminalization, critical criminology, hegemony, moral panic, punitiveness, the state

Key Readings

Hall, S. (1979) 'The Great Moving Right Show', *Marxism Today,* January: 14–20.
Hall, S. (1980) *Drifting into a Law and Order Society.* London: The Cobden Trust.
Hall, S. (1985) 'Authoritarian populism: a reply to Jessop et al.', *New Left Review,* 151: 115–24.
Hall, S., Critcher, C., Jefferson, T., Clarke, J. and Roberts, B. (1978) *Policing the Crisis: Mugging, the State and Law and Order.* London: Macmillan.
Jessop, B., Bennett, K., Bromley, S. and Ling, T. (1988) *Thatcherism.* Cambridge: Polity Press.
Poulantzas, N. (1978) *State, Power, Socialism.* London: Verso.

BEHAVIOUR MODIFICATION

Definition

Early theories of learning gave rise to a range of strategies, termed behaviour modification, aimed at changing behaviour. These practical techniques were widely used with a range of groups, including offenders. As theories of learning became more sophisticated and their research base grew, so their application, in the associated methods of behaviour change, developed accordingly.

Distinctive Features

The early learning theorists maintained that behaviour is functionally related both to its setting (i.e., the antecedent conditions) and to its consequences (via reinforcement and punishment). It follows from this position that a given behaviour can be changed by modifying both the setting events and the outcomes for the behaviour.

The strategy of bringing about behavioural change through modification of the environment is called *stimulus control* and is a standard technique in behaviour modification (Martin and Pear, 1992). This strategy is evident in situational crime prevention where the aim is to reduce offending by, say, reducing opportunity or increasing the chances of detection. Similarly, behaviour change can be attempted by modifying the consequences that follow a given behaviour. There is a range of established methods that focus on control of reinforcement and punishment contingencies to bring about behavioural change. Token economy programmes are one such method, in which optimal behaviours are strengthened by rewarding tokens or points which can later be exchanged for tangible rewards. Token economies were used in the American prison system for a period of time but were discontinued for ethical reasons.

As well as bringing about behavioural change through a modification of antecedents and consequences, the focus can be on the behaviour itself. The rationale underpinning this particular strategy is that changing behaviour will elicit different outcomes from the environment. In turn, these new outcomes will then reinforce and strengthen the new behaviour, thereby bringing about behavioural change. Strategies that focus explicitly on overt behaviour are often termed *behaviour therapy,* although the basic theory is the same as that informing behaviour modification. In the 1970s the notion of skills training in health services was developed and quickly became widespread in the form of assertion, life and social skills training. Skills training with offenders became popular and was used with a range of types of offender, including sex offenders and violent offenders (Hollin, 1990a).

As behavioural theory developed to produce social learning theory, behaviour modification and behaviour therapy evolved into cognitive-behavioural therapy. A number of particular techniques have become associated with cognitive-behavioural practice: these techniques include self-instructional training, thought stopping, emotional control training and problem-solving training (Sheldon, 1995). The method of change underpinning this approach is that by bringing about a change in internal (psychological and/or physiological) states and process, this covert change will, in turn, mediate change at an overt behavioural level. Changes in overt behaviour will then elicit new patterns of reinforcement from the environment and so maintain the behaviour change. Cognitive-behavioural methods have been widely used with offender groups and particularly with young offenders (Hollin, 1990b).

In practice, behaviour change techniques are seldom used in isolation: it is more common to see amalgams of techniques in the form of *multi-modal programmes*. Such programmes might include elements such as problem-solving skills training, social skills training and emotional control training. Given the complexity of many of the problems for which cognitive-behavioural therapy has been used, including offending, it is appropriate that change is sought by attending to a range of aspects of an individual's functioning. If the cognitive-behavioural model has several interrelated constituents, then attempts at change will be well served by attending to a range of those aspects rather than one in isolation. There are several multi-modal programmes designed for offender groups, including Reasoning and Rehabilitation (Ross et al., 1988) and Aggression Replacement Training (Goldstein et al., 1998).

One of the main concerns lies in the abuse of behavioural methods. First, when these powerful methods are used inappropriately by untrained personnel; second, when they are used with people, such as prisoners, who are not in a position to give free consent.

Clive Hollin

Associated Concepts: cognitive behaviourism, conditioning, differential reinforcement, situational crime prevention, social learning theory, 'what works'

Key Readings

Goldstein, A.P., Glick, B. and Gibbs, J.C. (1998) *Aggression Replacement Training: A Comprehensive Intervention for Aggressive Youth,* 2nd edn. Champaign, IL: Research Press.

Hollin, C.R. (1990a) 'Social skills training with delinquents: a look at the evidence and some recommendations for practice', *British Journal of Social Work,* 20: 483–93.

Hollin, C.R. (1990b) *Cognitive-Behavioural Interventions with Young Offenders.* Elmsford, NY: Pergamon Press.

Martin, G. and Pear, J. (1992) *Behaviour Modification: What It Is and How To Do It,* 4th edn. Englewood Cliffs, NJ: Prentice-Hall.

Ross, R.R., Fabiano, E.A. and Ewles, C.D. (1988) 'Reasoning and rehabilitation', *International Journal of Offender Therapy and Comparative Criminology,* 32: 29–35.

Sheldon, B. (1995) *Cognitive-Behavioural Therapy: Research, Practice and Philosophy.* London: Routledge.

BEHAVIOURISM

See: Conditioning

BIFURCATION

Definition

A concept – built on the 'just deserts' premise – which seeks to reserve incarceration solely for those offenders who pose a risk to the community, whilst also finding community-based penalties for less serious offenders.

Distinctive Features

Bifurcation is a reaction to at least two different forces within transnational criminal systems. First it is a reaction to the expansion of the penal estates of several Western democracies, which has seen the prison populations of, for example, the USA quadruple since the early 1980s, with a corresponding growth in expenditure on maintaining the penal estate. This expansion is in turn partly a reaction to the neo-conservativism of Republicans in the USA and the Conservatives in England and Wales, the latter coming to power in 1979 and the former with the election of Ronald Reagan in 1980.

With increasing numbers of people being incarcerated, politicians came under increasing pressure to reduce the amount of money being spent on maintaining the infrastructure of the penal estate. One way of doing this was to reserve imprisonment only for those people who posed a risk to the public and to find alternative punishments for largely nonviolent offenders. By adopting this policy a government could appear to be 'tough and soft simultaneously' (Pitts, 1988: 29). This has been described as 'penal pragmatism' (Cavadino and Dignan, 1992) and further interpreted as a reaction to the 'penal crisis'.

In England and Wales bifurcation is most commonly associated with the Criminal Justice Act of 1991. In the words of the White Paper which preceded the Act – *Crime, Justice and Protecting the Public* – for most offenders imprisonment has to be justified in terms of public protection, denunciation and retribution otherwise it can be an expensive way of making bad people worse. The prospects of reforming offenders are usually much better if they stay in the community, provided the public are properly protected (Home Office, 1990).

The passage of the 1991 Act did reduce the prison population significantly; it fell from 45,835 in October 1992 to 41,561 in January 1993. This downward trend continued until expansionist policies reappeared in the wake of the murder of 2-year-old James Bulger by two 10-year-olds in 1993, and the 'prison works' speech of the then Home Secretary, Michael Howard, in the same year (Wilson and Ashton, 1998).

The second force at the heart of bifurcation is the theoretical concept of just deserts. Put simply, this is a return to elements of classical criminology which suggest that 'the punishment should fit the crime'. As such prisons should not be filled with minor property offenders – who in fact fill most prisons in Western democracies – but with offenders who pose a risk to the public, and who would be dangerous if not incarcerated. Just deserts is therefore also a recognition that prisons do not rehabilitate offenders and instead often stigmatize them, thus making it more difficult for them to reintegrate into society.

Evaluation

Bifurcation showed limited success in England and Wales in that the passage of the 1991 Criminal Justice Act did reduce the prison population significantly. However, it is noteworthy that this was a concept that was unable to withstand the popular 'commonsense' clamour to increase prison numbers, largely as a reaction to a tragic but atypical murder and when political expediency determined a different course of action. In short, when it was in the British government's interest to appear 'tough' on criminals as well as crime, bifurcation became politically irrelevant.

David Wilson

Associated Concepts: classicism, just deserts, neo-conservative criminology

Key Readings

Bottomley, A.K. (1980) 'The "Justice Model" in America and Britain: development and analysis,' in A. Bottoms and R. Preston (eds), *The Coming Penal Crisis: A Criminological and Theological Exploration*. Edinburgh: Scottish Academic Press. pp. 25–52.

Cavadino, M. and Dignan, J. (1992) *The Penal System: An Introduction*. London: Sage.

Home Office (1990) *Crime, Justice and Protecting the Public* (cm 965). London: HMSO.

Pitts, J. (1988) *The Politics of Juvenile Crime*. London: Sage.

Wilson, D. and Ashton, J. (1998) *What Everyone in Britain Should Know About Crime and Punishment*. London: Blackstone's.

BIOLOGICAL CRIMINOLOGY

Definition

The basic premise of biological criminology is that certain people are born to be criminal through the inheritance of a genetic or physiological predisposition to crime. Environmental conditions are not ignored but viewed as potential triggers of the biological force. As behaviour is viewed as reflecting a prewritten, often inherited, code, criminality lies beyond individual control. Accordingly biological criminology is overwhelmingly positivist in nature.

Distinctive Features

Early positivists such as Lombroso, Ferri and Garafalo identified the criminal in terms of physical stigmata. Physical anomalies with hereditary origins (such as large cheekbones, a flat nose and thick eyebrows) were thought to mark out a criminal propensity. The notion of the criminal as defective reworks Darwin's theory of evolution. As humans develop they learn how to adapt to their environment. Those who do not are viewed as an atavistic throwback to an earlier stage of evolution and thus as pre-social and more criminally inclined. In his later work Lombroso placed less emphasis on the atavistic nature of all criminality. By 1897 he claimed that the 'born criminal' applied to only a third of all criminals. To this he added the categories of the epileptic, the insane and the 'occasional criminal'. The latter exhibited no inbred anomalies, but turned to crime as a result of a variety of environmental conditions. His later work also attempted to measure the effect of climate, rainfall, the price of grain, banking practices, a poor education and the structure of government, Church and religion on occasional criminality. However, he never totally abandoned the notion that criminals were abnormal and nor did he ever allow for the possibility that criminality could be 'normal'.

Several attempts have subsequently been made to test biological and genetic theories. A study of 3,000 prisoners in London in the 1910s discovered a high correlation between the criminality of spouses, as well as between parents and their children and between brothers. Poverty, education and broken homes were poor correlates. It was argued that criminality was passed down through inherited genes. Accordingly, in order to reduce crime, it was increasingly recommended that people with such inherited characteristics should not be allowed to reproduce. This logic was fertile ground for the growth of *eugenics,* a doctrine concerned with 'improving' the genetic selection of the human race. Evidence from the Cambridge Study in Delinquent Development established in the 1960s also continued to suggest that crime did indeed run in families. From a base of 397 families, half of all convictions were concentrated in just 23 of these. Convictions for one family member were strongly related to the convictions for each of the other family members. Three-quarters of convicted mothers and convicted fathers also had a convicted child.

Further, more sophisticated research directed at isolating 'a genetic factor' has been carried out with twins and adoptees. This has attempted to test two key propositions:

1 that identical (monozygotic or MZ) twins have more similar behaviour patterns than fraternal (dizygotic or DZ) twins;
2 that children's behaviour is more similar to that of their biological parents than to that of their adoptive parents.

In a review of research carried out between 1929 and 1961, Mednick and Volavka (1980) noted that, overall, 60 per cent of MZ twins shared criminal behaviour patterns compared to 30 per cent of DZ twins. More recent work has also found a lower, but still significant, level of association. Christiansen's (1977) study of 3,586 pairs of twins in Denmark uncovered a 52 per cent concordance for MZ groups and a 22 per cent concordance for the DZ groups. The evidence for the genetic transmission of some behaviour patterns thus appears to be quite strong. However, telling criticisms have also been made of this line of research. For example, a tendency to treat identical twins more alike than fraternal twins may account for greater concordance. Thus the connection between criminality and genetics may be made through environmental conditions, derived from the behaviour of parents or from twins' influence on each other's behaviour.

As a result, Mednick et al. (1987) proposed that studying adoptions would be a better test of relative genetic effect, particularly if it could be shown that the criminality of biological parents and children was similar even when a child had grown up in a completely different environment. Using data from over 14,000 cases of adoption in Denmark from 1924 to 1947, Mednick et al. concluded that some factor is indeed transmitted by convicted parents which increases the likelihood that their children – even after adoption – will be convicted for criminal offences. As a result, this type of research continues to attract research funding and publicity. In 1994 the Centre for Social, Genetic and Development Psychiatry was established at the Maudsley Hospital in South London to examine the role genetic structures play in determining patterns of behaviour (including crime). In 1995 a major international conference was also held behind closed doors to discuss the possibility of isolating a criminal gene – the basis of which rested on the study of twins and adoptees (Ciba Foundation, 1996). In one of the best-selling social science books of the decade, *The Bell Curve* (New York, Basic Books, 1994), Herrnstein and Murray claimed that American blacks and Latinos are disproportionately poor not because of discrimination, but because they are less intelligent. Further, they suggested that IQ is mainly determined by inherited genes and that people with a low IQ are more likely to commit crime because they lack foresight and are unable to distinguish right from wrong. Such theory indeed remains politically and popularly attractive because it seems to provide *scientific* evidence which clearly differentiates 'us' from 'them'. If certain people are inherently 'bad' then society is absolved of all responsibility. Such reasoning is, of course, most characteristic of totalitarian regimes,

whether those in Nazi Germany or the former USSR or in programmes of forced therapy practised in the USA.

Further research has examined the effect of a wide range of biochemical factors. These have included: hormone imbalances; testosterone, vitamin, adrenalin and blood sugar levels; allergies; slow brain-wave activity; lead pollution; epilepsy; and the operation of the autonomic nervous system. None of the research has, as yet, been able to establish any direct causal relationships. While some interesting associations have been discovered – for example between male testosterone levels and verbal aggression, between vitamin B deficiency and hyperactivity, and between stimulation of the central portion of the brain (the limbic) and impulsive violence – it remains disputed that such biological conditions will automatically generate anti-social activities, which in turn will be translated into criminality.

Evaluation

Most critical commentaries on this work, notwithstanding the question of its ethical position, have argued that each fails to recognize the potential effect of a wide range of environmental factors. The high correlation in the criminality of family members could be explained by reference to poor schooling, an inadequate diet, unemployment, common residence or the cultural transmission of criminal values. In other words, criminality may not necessarily be an inherited trait, but instead learned from or generated by a plethora of environmental factors. The usual comparative controls of criminal and non-criminal are doubly misleading here. Offenders in custody are not representative of criminals in general, but constitute a highly selected sub-set of those who have been apprehended, charged and convicted. Control groups of the non-criminal are almost certain to include some individuals who have committed crimes but whose actions have remained undetected. Indeed most current research in this tradition would not claim that biological make-up *alone* can be used as a sufficient explanation of crime. The question of exactly *what* is inherited remains unanswered.

Rather, some biological factors may generate criminality but only when they interact with certain other psychological or social factors. Whilst correlational analysis may suggest that criminality is transmitted in certain families, it is now acknowledged that this does not allow us to distinguish the relative importance of genetic and environmental factors. Characteristics that are linked to offending (e.g., intelligence, impulsivity, aggressiveness) could be genetically transmitted, but not criminality *per se*.

It is now more common to find biology considered as but one element within *multiple factor* explanations. For example, Wilson and Herrnstein (1985) argue that individuals have the free will to choose criminal actions when they believe that the rewards will outweigh any negative consequences. Such a decision (freely made) is, however, influenced by inherited constitutional factors. A low IQ, an abnormal body type and an impulsive personality, it is argued, will predispose a person to make criminal decisions, but criminality is not a matter of nature versus nurture, but of nature *and* nurture. This approach is a defining characteristic of *socio-biology*, developed in the 1970s and heralded by its advocates as a way forward in unifying the social and natural sciences. Generally, it is argued that some people carry with them the potential to be violent or anti-social and that environmental conditions can sometimes trigger anti-social responses. Socio-biologists view biology, environment and learning as mutually interdependent factors. Sociopathy may not be inherited, but a biochemical preparedness for such behaviours is present in the brain, which, if given a certain type of environment, will produce anti-social behaviour (Jeffery, 1978).

Nevertheless, the search for biological, physiological or genetic correlates of criminality is continually hampered because it is practically impossible to control for environmental and social influences and thus to be able to measure precisely the exact influence of a genetic effect.

John Muncie

Associated Concepts: determinism, dispositional theories, genetics, individual positivism, somatotyping

Key Readings

Christiansen, K.O. (1977) 'A review of studies of criminality among twins', in S. Mednick and K.O. Christiansen (eds), *Biosocial Bases of Criminal Behaviour*. New York: Gardner.

Ciba Foundation Symposium 194 (1996) *Genetics of Criminal and Antisocial Behaviour*. Chichester: Wiley.

Jeffery, C.R. (1978) 'Criminology as an inter-disciplinary behavioural science', *Criminology*, 16 (2): 149–69.

Mednick, S. and Volavka, J. (1980) 'Biology and crime', in N. Morris and M. Tonry (eds), *Crime and Justice*, vol. 2. Chicago: University of Chicago Press.

Mednick, S.A., Gabrielli, W. and Hutchings, B. (1987) 'Genetic factors in the etiology of criminal behaviour', in S. Mednick, T. Moffit and S. Stack (eds), *The Causes of Crime: New Biological Approaches*. Cambridge: Cambridge University Press.

Wilson, J.Q. and Herrnstein, R.J. (1985) *Crime and Human Nature*. New York: Simon and Schuster.

BIRMINGHAM 'SCHOOL'

Definition

Refers to work emerging from the Centre for Contemporary Cultural Studies at the University of Birmingham (CCCS). Some of this work was particularly influential in media studies, criminology and youth studies. Whether the output described in this manner was ever coherent and systematic enough to be called a 'School' remains an open question.

Distinctive Features

The Centre for Contemporary Cultural Studies was a postgraduate research unit established at the University of Birmingham by Professor

Richard Hoggart in 1964 and one which continued (in various guises) until it was closed by the University in 2002, despite a local, national and international outcry. Exploring the significance of popular cultural forms and practices, the Centre played a leading role in the creation of the new field of Cultural Studies. Its work was intellectually innovative, drawing on a range of resources including literary theory, anthropology, sociology and social history. Its practice was also innovative, as much of its research and writing was undertaken collectively in groups working on specific themes and issues. The Centre also published its work in a variety of forms: a famous series of Stencilled Papers (written by members of the subgroups) and an in-house journal (*Working Papers in Cultural Studies*) that subsequently became a series of publications with an external publisher (Hutchinson).

Identifying culture as a field for social analysis, the CCCS found itself challenging existing orientations to culture as high culture (the conventionally recognized and valorized cultural products consumed by social elites); to culture as folk or popular culture (the tradition values, practices and forms being uprooted or cast aside in processes of industrialization and urbanization); and to culture as mass culture (the pessimistic reading of commodified or mass mediated culture dominant in the United States). Instead, the CCCS treated culture as a field of politically contested meaning in which struggles over social domination and subordination were conducted through how meanings were made, distributed and used. Cultural Studies took shape around such questions and these led to a variety of theoretical and political orientations. Across its four decades, the Centre drew on theories from European Marxism, post-structuralism, feminism, post-colonialism and psychoanalysis to explore how they would contribute to the analysis of the political significance of cultural forms, formations and practices.

Although the work of the CCCS ranged over many fields, perhaps the most salient here involved questions of youth, deviance and the mass media. Paul Willis had undertaken an ethnography of 'bikers' in Birmingham before he produced his study of working-class

boys' transition from school to work that was to become one of the most famous CCCS texts. In *Learning to Labour* (1977), Willis explored the paradox by which the group that was most resistant to the formal world of schooling ('the lads') acquired in the process the cultural skills, practices and orientations that enabled their transition into waged work. The 'subcultures group' was one of the Centre's working groups during the 1970s and explored stylistically defined subcultures (Teddy Boys, Mods, Skinheads and so on), developing accounts that resisted unifying conceptions of generation or psychodynamic views of adolescence.

Instead, processes of class and generational formation were fore-grounded and the Birmingham approach gave much attention to the symbolic work or signifying practices through which particular groups of young working-class men defined both themselves and their place. This influential work was published in a number of forms, most obviously as *Resistance through Rituals* (Hall and Jefferson, 1976; originally *Working Papers in Cultural Studies*, 7/8, in 1974). The collection – and its orientation towards class cultures and youth subcultures – shaped much subsequent work in youth studies. Perhaps the most strongly semiotic version of the work on style was developed by Dick Hebdige, whose book *Subculture: The Meaning of Style* (1979) explored subcultures as the site of symbolic exchanges between black and white youth.

Indeed, the original subcultures work and its predominant focus on white male working-class youth was both challenged and drawn into new directions by others working at the Centre. Gender formations were examined by Angela McRobbie (who, with Jenny Garber, had contributed the only article to identify gender dynamics and the cultural practices of young women in *Resistance through Rituals*). A number of her essays were collected together in *Feminism and Youth Culture* (1991). A second line of development followed questions of race, racial formation and the racialization of British society. Paul Gilroy's work, individually and as a member of the collective group that produced a CCCS volume called *The Empire Strikes Back*, was central to the process of thinking British culture as a profoundly racialized formation. His book, *There*

Ain't No Black in the Union Jack (1987), inaugurated a powerful and persistent engagement with the diasporic culture of the Black Atlantic and a critical enquiry into the problems of a post-imperial British culture. As with the other studies mentioned here, Gilroy's work was influential in shaping the trajectory of Cultural Studies – both in the UK and in North America – and had an impact well beyond the field.

Finally, many of the key features of the Birmingham School's work in the 1970s came together in *Policing the Crisis* (Hall et al., 1978). This collective study focused on the claim that street crime – in the specific guise of 'mugging' – marked a social crisis, a breakdown in social order, that could only be resolved by the tougher policing and sentencing of the young men who were its perpetrators. The book moves outwards from one specific case (in Birmingham in 1973) to examine the different contexts that came together to promote the move to a 'Law and Order Society'. These included the mass media (drawing on Stanley Cohen's work on 'folk devils and moral panics'); the role of political and juridical agents in constructing 'the mugger' as a national danger; the role of the imagery of street crime imported from the USA; and Britain's multiplying crises – economic, social, political – as it moved into a crisis of consent. Hall and his co-authors treated this as a crisis of hegemony (developing an idea by the Italian Marxist Antonio Gramsci) and stressed the ways in which the imagery of the British social order (and its descent into disorder) was profoundly racialized.

The book's analysis of the move towards a Law and Order Society anticipates much of the authoritarian turn in the New Right, or Thatcherite, governments of the 1980s. Stuart Hall (at that time the Director of the CCCS, and later a Professor of Sociology at The Open University) developed an analysis of Thatcherism that described it as a politics of 'authoritarian populism'. Some commentators have suggested that the UK has not yet stopped policing the crisis. The book has since been influential in criminology, sociology and politics, as well as standing as one of the exemplary texts of Cultural Studies for the way that it developed a *conjunctural analysis* of the crisis.

Evaluation

Cultural Studies in Birmingham has been subjected to a variety of critical evaluations. Some have been what might be called 'disciplinary' disputes, in which people in established fields (sociology, literature, history) bemoaned the lack of discipline in the approaches taken in Cultural Studies. Others have been worried by the growth and geographical dispersal of Cultural Studies as an academic field, including a concern that the British – and later American – varieties of the subject have been too dominant, producing exciting growth in counter-hegemonic regionalized approaches to the subject.

More specifically, the approaches to youth subcultures and social disorder discussed above have provoked critical responses, ranging from challenges to an over-focus on stylistic versions of youth, to a critique of the excessive focus on class as well as the view that the idea of 'resistance' displaced attention from politics, thereby celebrating forms of socially regressive or consumption-centred behaviour. The Birmingham 'School' has been criticized both for its attachment to Marxism and for its 'Marxism-lite' – the view that it lacked a properly materialist political economy.

Despite these many critical evaluations, the work of the Birmingham Centre has proved profoundly influential both in shaping the field of Cultural Studies and in its impact on other disciplines and fields of study, the sociology of youth, media studies, (cultural and critical) criminology and social policy. Whether its members ever did agree sufficiently about the theory and practice of Cultural Studies to be called a 'School' seems doubtful.

John Clarke

Associated Concepts: authoritarian populism, critical criminology, cultural criminology, feminist criminologies, Marxist criminologies, racialization, social constructionism, subculture

Key Readings

Gilroy, P. (1987) *There Ain't No Black in the Union Jack: The Cultural Politics of Race and Nation.* London: Hutchinson.

Hall, S. and Jefferson, T. (eds) (1976) *Resistance Through Rituals: Youth Subcultures in Post-war Britain*. London: Hutchinson (originally published in 1974 as *Working Papers in Cultural Studies*, 7/8).

Hall, S., Critcher, C., Jefferson, T., Clarke, J. and Roberts, B. (1978) *Policing the Crisis: Mugging, The State and Law'n'Order*. London: Macmillan.

Hebdige, D. (1979) *Subculture: The Meaning of Style*. London: Routledge.

McRobbie, A. (1991) *Feminism and Youth Culture: From Jackie to Just 17*. Basingstoke: Macmillan.

Willis, P. (1977) *Learning to Labour: How Working Class Kids get Working Class Jobs*. Farnham: Ashgate.

'BROKEN WINDOWS'

Definition

'Broken Windows' is arguably one of the most influential and widely cited articles in North American criminology. It was published originally by James Q. Wilson and George Kelling in 1982 and updated by Kelling and Coles (1996). Using a mixture of research findings on policing and self-proclaimed 'common sense', Wilson and Kelling produced a working theory about the role of the police in promoting neighbourhood safety through reducing the fear of crime.

Distinctive Features

The image of 'broken windows' is used to explain how neighbourhoods descend into incivility, disorder and criminality if attention is not paid to their maintenance. An unrepaired broken window signals to law-abiding and criminals alike that no one cares. Gradually other windows in the building will be smashed and this will reinforce the sense that the local community and the authorities have relinquished ownership and that disorder is tolerated. For them, petty disorderly acts, which are not necessarily breaches of the criminal law, trigger a chain reaction that undermines community safety and paves the way for serious criminality. If a neighbourhood or a street is perceived to be increasingly disorderly and unsafe, people will modify their behaviour accordingly. Fearful of being harassed, they will avoid or withdraw from these areas or move through them as quickly as possible: meanwhile respectable residents, aware that things will deteriorate, will move out or fortify their homes. Because only the weak and vulnerable are left behind this leaves the neighbourhood open to colonization by drug dealers, pimps and prostitutes and other 'street criminals'. It is they who will then lay claim to ownership of the streets and will set the appropriate norms of behaviour. The human equivalents of these 'broken windows' are down-and-outs, rowdy teenagers and importuning beggars: 'The unchecked panhandler is, in effect, the first broken window'. Thus, policy makers should pay attention to the policing of these disorderly and disreputable individuals because it is they who will create the conditions within which more serious forms of criminality can flourish.

According to Wilson and Kelling, shifts in policing styles also leave certain neighbourhoods and streets exposed to such a chain reaction. The authors step back to ask why the public are so supportive of foot patrols even though this particular policing style has been discredited as a method of effective crime control. For them it is because foot patrolling heightens the sense of public safety and the impression of social order. Experienced foot patrol officers, with a sense of duty and an aura of authority, intuitively recognize that their primary role is 'order maintenance' and 'community safety' rather than crime fighting or law enforcement. This form of police work enables these officers to become intimately acquainted with the law-abiding and respectable as well as criminals and the disreputable. They can also notice indicators of routine normality and that which is out of the ordinary. Their task is to order social relations and activities on the streets and use their discretionary powers to regulate disorderly tendencies through a reinforcement of communal norms and informal social controls. As a consequence, the police enjoy the confidence and support of the community because they are effective in responding to and dealing with the 'quality of life' matters that exasperate people on a daily basis. In a neighbour-hood where policing is defined as a collaborative effort between patrol officers and the community, there is considerably less likelihood of disorder and incivilities going unchecked and fewer oppor-tunities to break windows with impunity.

However, from the 1970s onwards the nature of police–community relations changed as a result of: the police claiming that the fight against high profile, serious crime was their priority; deploying officers in patrol cars; con-centrating resources in high-crime areas; the bureaucratization and professionalization of police work; the emergence of a strident civil rights culture; and the decriminalization of vic-timless crimes. As a result police officers became more distant from local communities and less able and willing to intervene in petty 'non-police' matters. In neighbourhoods at risk of tipping over into disorder, 'de-policing' had a disastrous effect because it meant that respectable residents had no support from the authorities.

Wilson and Kelling (1982: 36) thus argued for a *return* to old-fashioned, community-oriented 'order maintenance' police work and to employ-ing such methods in neighbourhoods where these would make a qualitative difference. The primary police task should be to protect areas and support communities where 'the public order is deteriorating but not unreclaimable, where the streets are used frequently but by apprehensive people, where a window is likely to be broken at any time, and must quickly be fixed if all are not to be shattered'. It is a waste of police resources to concentrate on crime-ravaged neighbourhoods that are beyond redemption.

Evaluation

The compelling analysis underpinning 'Broken Windows' fed into policy discussions about the need for new approaches to urban policing. What is significant is that it lends itself to both benign and authoritarian policy responses and mission statements. It could be argued that 'problem oriented policing' strategies are premised on a similar type of understanding of the role of the police in stabilizing urban communities and how police legitimacy can be secured through responding to 'quality of life issues' and prioritizing

crime prevention. It has also played an important role in the development of the 'signal crime' perspective (see Innes, 2004). However, its core argument has also been adapted to justify aggres-sive street policing tactics such as those practised in New York in the 1990s. The NYPD's 'zero tolerance' crime-fighting strategy returned offic-ers to street patrolling and mandated them to target the broad spectrum of low level miscon-duct and widespread anti-social behaviours which made the city feel unsafe and disorderly. There is considerable disagreement over how much of the remarkable improvement in the New York crime rate could be attributed to the 'broken windows' strategy. However, what is beyond dispute is that Wilson and Kelling reop-ened a debate on what the core role of the police should be and how policing should be organized.

Eugene McLaughlin

Associated Concepts: anti-social behaviour, com-munitarianism, community policing, COMP-STAT, defensible space, problem oriented policing, right realism, social capital, zero tolerance

Key Readings

Bratton, W.J. (1997) 'Crime is down in New York: blame the police', in N. Dennis (ed.), *Zero-Tolerance Policing: Policing a Free Society.* London: Institute of Economic Affairs.

Goldstein, H. (1990) *Problem-Oriented Policing.* New York: McGraw-Hill.

Innes, M. (2004). 'Signal crimes and signal dis-orders: notes on deviance as communicative action'. *British Journal of Sociology*, 55: 335–355.

Kelling, G.L. and Coles, C.M. (1996) *Fixing Broken Windows: Restoring Order and Reducing Crime in Our Communities.* New York: Touchstone Books.

Skogan, W. (1990) *Disorder and Decline: Crime and the Spiral of Urban Decline in American Neighborhoods.* New York: The Free Press.

Wilson, J.Q. and Kelling, G. (1982) 'Broken windows', *Atlantic Monthly,* 249 (3): 29–38.

Young, J. (1997) 'Zero tolerance: back to the future', in A. Marlow and J. Pitts (eds), *Planning Safer Communities.* London: Russell House Publishing.

C

CAPITAL PUNISHMENT

Definition

Punishment by execution – either by hanging, electrocution, firing squad, gas chamber, lethal injection or beheading. Capital punishment can be imposed for a range of offences, but in Western countries, except in exceptional circumstances, it is usually reserved for murder.

Distinctive Features

Capital punishment by hanging was used in England and Wales between 1016 and 1964, and between 1900 and 1949 there were 751 people hanged, of whom 87 were women. The purpose of capital punishment seems to have been both retributive and to act as a deterrent. Until 1868 hangings were public affairs. The last public execution was that of the Irish nationalist Michael Barrett in May 1868, with some 2,000 people attending (Potter, 1993: 94). These public events were usually drunken affairs, with spectators often using the occasion as an opportunity to commit further crimes, thus turning what was intended as a solemn state ritual – which was supposed to reflect the power of the law – into a shambles (Ignatieff, 1978: 21–4). After May 1868 executions took place behind the prison's walls with an increasing standardization of the process of death, with the result that a uniform scaffold apparatus was adopted as well as a standard length and thickness of rope, and tables of 'drops' were published in order that executioners – a profession which also became increasingly specialized – could judge the execution in relation to the condemned's height and weight. Although executions were private, selected members of the public were allowed to attend. For example, in August 1868 at the hanging of Thomas Wells in Maidstone Gaol (the first person to be executed in prison) 16 reporters were present so as to be able to describe the final moments of the demise of the condemned man for the morning papers (Potter, 1993: 95). The 1965 Murder (Abolition of the Death Penalty) Act ended capital punishment except in exceptional circumstances – such as treason, arson in HM Dockyards and piracy – for a trial period of five years. Its actual abolition occurred in England and Wales in December 1969.

This trend towards the abolition of public executions, and thereafter capital punishment itself, has been a process most obviously observed in Western Europe. There has been a tendency to treat capital punishment as a somewhat closed policy issue, especially as those former Warsaw Pact countries which have applied to join the Council of Europe have signalled their intention to move to abolition. Indeed Russia has also reduced the number of offences for which the death penalty can be imposed. However, the abolitionist cause has not had much impact on several regions of the world. So, for example, as Hood (1996) advises, most of the Middle East and North African states have expressed strong support for the continued use of capital punishment, which reflects their Islamic beliefs and law. China also continues to use capital punishment enthusiastically and only one Caribbean country has abolished the death penalty since 1965.

By far the most vocal and visible retentionist advocate of capital punishment has been the United States of America. In 1999, for example, there were some 3,000 people on 'death row' awaiting execution in the 37 states that have retained the death penalty. Of note, concern has been expressed that blatant racial discrimination operates in the application of capital punishment in the USA. So, for example, the killers of white people were 11 times more likely to be condemned to death than the murderers of African Americans. Discrimination in the application of the death penalty can be seen most obviously by focusing on the murder victim's race. In Georgia, for example, prosecutors sought the death penalty in 70 per cent of the cases where the murderer was African American and the victim was white, but when there was a white murderer and the victim was African American the same prosecutors sought the death penalty in only 15 per cent of cases (Donziger, 1996). Others have drawn attention to how politicians use the issue of capital punishment symbolically for electoral advantage. So, for example, it has been suggested that Bill Clinton scheduled the execution in Arkansas of a brain-damaged black man – Rickey Ray Rector – during his Presidential campaign bid in 1992 so as to demonstrate his toughness on crime and punishment. On the eve of his execution Mr Rector is reported to have been barking like a dog, laughing inappropriately, and on being offered his last meal, asking to save his dessert 'until later'.

The most consistently debated question about capital punishment is whether or not it has a deterrent effect, and this remains the most common justification for the death penalty by retentionist countries. However, comparative studies of neighbouring abolitionist and retentionist states in the USA have suggested that abolition is not associated with higher murder rates in general, or with higher murder rates of police or prison officers in particular (Hood, 1996: 166). Even where a deterrent effect has been detected, critics would still debate whether the decision to murder is a matter of rational choice, and whether data on executions and murder are reliable. In his comprehensive study, undertaken on behalf of the United Nations Committee on Crime Prevention and Control, Hood (1996: 167) concluded that 'research has failed to provide scientific proof that executions have a greater deterrent effect than life imprisonment. Such proof is unlikely to be forthcoming. The evidence as a whole still gives no positive support to the deterrent hypothesis.'

David Wilson

Associated Concepts: deterrence, punitiveness, retribution, right realism, the state, state crime

Key Readings

Bedau, A.H. (1998) *The Death Penalty in America: Current Controversies.* New York: Oxford University Press.
Donziger, S. (ed.) (1996) *The Real War on Crime: The Report of the National Criminal Justice Commission.* New York: Harper Collins.
Garrell, U.A.C. (1994) *The Hanging Tree: Execution and the English People 1770–1868.* Oxford: Clarendon Press.
Hood, R. (1996) *The Death Penalty: A World-Wide Perspective.* Oxford: Clarendon Press.
Ignatieff, M. (1978) *A Just Measure of Pain: The Penitentiary in the Industrial Revolution, 1750–1850.* Harmondsworth: Penguin Books.
Potter, H. (1993) *Hanging in Judgement: Religion and the Death Penalty in England.* London: SCM Press.
Sarat, A. (ed.) (1998) *The Killing State.* New York: Oxford University Press.

CARCERAL SOCIETY

Definition

The concept of the emergence and existence of a carceral society was first suggested by Michel Foucault in his (1977) book *Discipline and Punish: The Birth of the Modern Prison.* In this book not only does Foucault attack the idea that prisons have somehow become more enlightened and humanitarian – that they have progressed – but he also tries to unmask the disciplinary nature of modern society, of which prison is but one manifestation.

Distinctive Features

Discipline and Punish opens with a description of the gruesome torture of the regicide Damiens in 1757, and is almost immediately counterbalanced in the text by the detailed plans for a young offender institution some seventy years later. However, the reader is not meant to infer from these descriptions that somehow punishment has become more humane or enlightened – the book stands as a full-frontal attack on modernism – but rather how prisons punish in other ways, which might be less public and individualized, but which are equally gruesome. Moreover, punishment is no longer intended to alter individual behaviour, but rather becomes the basis on which physical and social structures are created within society and not just within prisons, and which thus alters the behaviour of everyone. For Foucault the key words are inspection, surveillance and power, which in relation to prison were symbolized by Bentham's Panopticon.

What is of interest is that Foucault saw these 'carceral impulses' swarming outside of the Panopticon and other penal institutions: 'their mechanisms have a certain tendency to become de-institutionalized, to emerge from the closed fortresses in which they once functioned and to circulate in a "free" state' and thus 'infecting' schools, hospitals and factories. Their purpose was to observe, inspect and ultimately control the general population, a disciplinary impulse that he saw at work in a variety of locations and within a variety of organizations – from religious and charity groups, to the development of a centralized police force in France.

Evaluation

The concept can be applied within a variety of Western societies that have sought to control the behaviour of their inhabitants, not on the basis of controlling the behaviour of individual members of that society but rather of the population as a whole. So many more areas of social life are being subjected to categorization, surveillance, prevention, organized forms of control and 'compliance systems' of both a formal and informal nature. Inevitably this has also meant that the number of people who come to be managed by the criminal justice system has increased, and the massive growth of, for example, the prison populations of the USA and England and Wales is testimony to this expansion. Hand in glove we have also seen, for example, the increased use of CCTV, airport security checks and random urine checks at work. At another level there is greater awareness of 'lifestyle controls' in the form of no-smoking zones, or evidence that some businesses may not hire people who are overweight.

Foucault's work is filled with rich historical insight and has re-emerged as a powerful tool with which to analyse more contemporary concepts such as risk management, actuarialism and population control which are often incorrectly presented as 'theory neutral'.

David Wilson

Associated Concepts: actuarialism, governance, governmentality, net widening, panopticism, penality, situational crime prevention, social control, target hardening

Key Readings

Bogard, W. (1996) *The Simulation of Surveillance: Hypercontrol in Telematic Societies.* Cambridge: Cambridge University Press.

Driver, F. (1984) 'Power, space and the body: a critical reassessment of Foucault's *Discipline and Punish*', *Society and Space*, 3: 425–46.

Foucault, M. (1977) *Discipline and Punish: The Birth of the Modern Prison.* London: Allen Lane.

Gandy, O. (1993) *The Panoptic Sort.* Boulder, CO: Westview Press.

CARNIVAL (OF CRIME)

Definition

A description and analysis of popular festive behaviour as a necessary act of irrational excess and excitement in opposition to the dominant accepted values of the restraint, sobriety and rationality of modern industrial life. Transgression and crime are understood as an integral part of the performance of carnival, no longer restricted to festivals but as an enjoyable part of popular everyday life and a site of resistance to rationality.

Distinctive Features

The most important analysis of the nature of carnival is that of the work of Mikhail Bakhtin (1984), who stressed that the structure and imagery of carnival seek to legitimate its participants' behaviour thus making it a period of licensed misrule. A characteristic of carnivalesque transgression is the open defiance of dominant authority structures and values, thereby putting the transgressor in a position of power as their behaviour turns the social world 'upside down'. Such social behaviour is full of irrational, senseless, offensive acts performed in a time of disorder, transgression and doing wrong in an otherwise ordered world where such acts would be considered criminal.

Contemporary theorists of popular culture (e.g., Docker, 1996) have analysed the place of carnival in popular pleasure including media entertainment, whilst cultural criminologists have looked at the pleasure of doing wrong (Katz, 1988; Presdee, 2000). The latter highlight the notion that carnival functions as a playful and pleasurable resistance to authority where those normally excluded from the discourse of power celebrate their anger at their exclusion. Cultural criminologists maintain that, through the dual processes of the scientific rationality and containment of contemporary everyday life, carnival has shattered and its fragments and debris are now to be found not in the pleasure and excitement of organized carnival but in acts of transgression and crime (Presdee, 2000). Without a partly licensed and organized carnival

'form', the carnivalesque emerges more unrehearsed and unannounced and often in a more violent and criminal way. Lyng (1990) has described such performance as 'edgework' – intense and often ritualised moments of pleasure and excitement which accompany the risk, danger and skill of transgression and which come to play a key part in the construction of shared subcultural meaning.

Many pleasurable activities, such as rave culture, drug taking, body modification, the use of the internet, joy riding and SM activities, contain elements both of the carnivalesque and of crime, whilst the political demonstration 'The Carnival against Capitalism' that erupted at the 30 November 1999 meeting of the World Trade Organization in Seattle, USA, evidenced a global carnival of crime and pleasure, partially organized through the Internet, which showed that practical politics (such as the demonstrations by 'Reclaim the Streets' and 'Tree Dwellers' in the UK) can cause widespread disruption – and can be criminal yet immensely pleasurable to participants.

The carnival as analysed by Bakhtin resulted in a return to law and order and led to reintegration into the existing structures of social life. Today, as carnival explodes into everyday life, there is no longer an inevitable return to law and order. The expectation has grown that crime as carnival will be continually performed without shame and without social reintegration.

Mike Presdee

Associated Concepts: anarchist criminology, cultural criminology, cybercrime, hedonism

Key Readings

Bakhtin, M. (1984) *Rabelais and His World.* Bloomington: Indiana University Press.
Docker, J. (1996) *Postmodernism and Popular Culture: A Cultural History.* Cambridge: Cambridge University Press.
Ferrell, J. and Sanders, C.R. (1995) *Cultural Criminology.* Boston, MA: Northeastern University Press.

Katz, J. (1988) *Seductions of Crime: Moral and Sensual Attractions in Doing Evil*. New York: Basic Books.

Lyng, S. (1990) 'Edgework: a social psychological analysis of voluntary risk taking', *American Journal of Sociology*, 95: 851–86.

Presdee, M. (2000) *Cultural Criminology and the Carnival of Crime*. London: Routledge.

CAUSATION

Definition

The key proposition of causal analysis is that certain antecedent individual and social factors will invariably and unconditionally have a certain effect.

Distinctive Features

To establish that one factor is the cause of another, we have at least to show that the supposed cause precedes the supposed effect in time and, ideally, that the effect occurs always and only when the cause occurs. (Social causation is generally complex, however, and it may take a combination of causes to produce an effect. We may also find that a cause does not determine an effect absolutely, but only probabilistically: the cause may make the effect more likely but not always and inevitably produce it.) We should note that an association between the supposed cause and the effect is a *necessary* condition for causation but not a *sufficient* one. To demonstrate causation beyond argument it is necessary to establish the mechanism by which the cause brings about the effect.

In social and criminological research we seldom speak absolutely of 'causes', but rather of 'antecedents' or 'influences' or 'predisposing factors'. Rarely is it possible, even in theory, to argue that an antecedent factor leads deterministically to its effect; we are more likely to want to say that it renders a behaviour more likely or influences the way in which events and actions are interpreted. The exception is when treatments or ways of handling offenders or crimes are being evaluated. Here we shall want to show that the treatment or form of handling *does* have the desired effect and is the only reasonable explanation for the effect's occurrence.

The essence of causal analysis, in criminological as in all other research, is control of alternative explanations. In an *experiment* this control is delivered as part of the design of the study: a treatment or manipulation is shown to lead to the effect and the study is designed so that all other explanations for the effect can be ruled out. Where experiments are not possible or ethical (i.e., in most criminological research) then statistical control is used to rule out alternative explanations.

Roger Sapsford

Associated Concepts: correlational analysis, determinism, experiments, multivariate analysis, positivism, prediction studies

Key Readings

Belson, W.A. (1975) *Juvenile Theft: The Causal Factors*. London: Harper & Row.

Glueck, S. and Glueck, E. (1950) *Unravelling Juvenile Delinquency*. Cambridge, MA: Harvard University Press.

Sapsford, R. and Jupp, V. (eds) (1996) *Data Collection and Analysis*. London: Sage.

CHAOS THEORY

Definition

Sometimes referred to as complexity theory, and one of the emerging perspectives in postmodern criminology, this is the study of orderly disorder. Chaos theory is the study of dynamic systems that exhibit both 'determinism' and 'free will'. Modernist thought has constructed determinism and free will as dualities; chaos theory argues both can be at work in complex, dynamic systems.

Distinctive Features

Chaos theory had already been anticipated by Nietzsche (cited in Babich, 1996: 109): 'the total character of the world ... is in all eternity chaos'. Order appears only as an imposition or as 'aesthetic anthropomorphisms', as 'semiotic fictions' according to Nietzsche. In the early 1990s a number of theorists in America (Bruce Arrigo, Dragan Milovanovic, Hal Pepinsky, Robert Schehr, T.R. Young) began applying chaos theory to criminology, law and sociology (Milovanovic, 1997). Chaos theory includes several key conceptualizations.

Attractors Four types of attractors have been identified: point, cyclic/periodic/limit, torus and strange. Each lives in 'phase space', a map portraying dynamic systems in movement in their various phases. Attractors are regions in phase space toward which dynamic systems move. The point attractor reflects movement toward a point in phase space. A swinging pendulum (the dynamic systems) eventually comes to rest at a point. This 'point' attracts trajectories to it. The periodic, cyclic or limit attractor is seen as a circle with each point on the circle depicting at least two dimensions simultaneously. A swinging pendulum, with no frictional forces, will move back and forth traversing space and changing momentum. This could be depicted in phase space as a circle with the two axes marked position and momentum. Hence, any point on this circle represents simultaneously its location and momentum. For both the point and periodic attractor, modernist thought would have no problem with the determinacy involved.

The next two attractors become increasingly 'fuzzy'; one sees both order and disorder existing. Modernist thought is hard pressed to explain them. A torus attractor looks very much like an inflated inner tube. If our pendulum was connected with a worn hinge it would wobble as it moved in its trajectory. Hence this introduces the third degree of freedom. To depict this we would include movement in the form of a line winding itself around the outside of the torus. In other words, the torus depicts two coupled cyclic attractors. Where the two coupled systems repeat frequencies in a ratio way we have a periodic torus; where they don't, we have a quasiperiodic torus. The shape of the torus itself does indicate there is overall order in the system (read 'determinism' or stability); however, within the torus, or at any moment, an accurate prediction escapes us (thus a degree of

instability, or if you will 'free will'). The strange attractor combines order and disorder (orderly disorder), and is the most indeterminate of the four attractors. The most celebrated strange attractor is the butterfly attractor, which looks very much like a pair of butterfly wings. Each wing represents an 'outcome basin', or a region toward which trajectories move. These attractors can both exhibit a form (i.e., the shape of a butterfly wing) or order, stability, or can even be interpreted as having a degree of determinism, and also disorder (i.e., within the wings, indeterminacy prevails). Thus within each wing are trajectories portraying the dynamic system in movement in its various phases, but no accurate prediction can exist: hence we have instability, disorder, indeterminacy or 'free will'.

Bifurcation diagram (logistic mapping) This phase map was developed in early studies of gypsy moth populations. It was found that rather than linear development, non-linear movement appears in the form of 'period doubling'. Here, with increasing input of some major variable, results do not follow neat predictable outcomes. Rather, initially periodic attractors develop as solutions to the question of what size population, but, with additional proportional input, bifurcations or splitting exist, where first 2 solutions (periodic attractors) then 4, then 8, 16, 32 and so on emerge. In other words, proportional inputs did not produce proportional results and various attractors appear: first, point, then periodic, then torus, and then strange attractors. After that, deep chaos is experienced where prediction escapes us. However, within these latter regions, called far-from-equilibrium conditions, order spontaneously arises out of disorder. These pockets of order are called 'dissipative structures'.

Far-from-equilibrium conditions Modernist thought privileges order, stability, homeostasis, equilibrium, structural functionalism. Chaos theory argues for inherent instabilities. Thus disorder, instability and far-from-equilibrium conditions are privileged. Within these regions both order and disorder live side by side, not as dualisms. Within these regions 'structures' are extremely sensitive to perturbations. Even very small inputs can produce disproportionate effects. Thus contrary to the privileging of bureaucratic structures as is assumed in homeostatic systems, 'dissipative structures' appear which are only temporary structures of stability.

Dissipative structures These 'structures' are characterized as always in process; they are both 'structures' and also dissipating – that is, in constant reconfiguring modes of being. They offer only temporary stability points. They exist in far-from-equilibrium conditions. Unger's (1987) blueprint for a 'super-liberal' society entails the emergence of these dissipative structures (without his naming them as such).

Iteration This is a process by which one begins with a simple algorithm, plugs in an initial value, solves this, takes the result, plugs this back into the algorithm, solves this, plugs the solution into the initial algorithm, and so on. It is feedback. What one finds is that even a very slight variance can, with a number of subsequent iterations, produce large, disproportional effects. In empirical criminology rounding and dismissing 'minor' variables in calculating 'variance explained' may overlook important factors once iterated. One of the classic forms produced by a simple algorithm and iteration is the Mandelbrot set.

Sensitivity to initial conditions Chaos theory shows that especially in far-from-equilibrium conditions, even with small perturbations, or even with some small change in initial starting values in iterations, large, unintended and disproportional results occur: 'a butterfly flapping its wings in Southeast Asia produces a hurricane in Florida'. A school-crossing guard taking interest in a child in the ghetto may, upon iteration, produce a person transcending his/her adverse environment.

Non-linearity Modernist thought privileges linear developments, perhaps best expressed in syllogistic reasoning and deductive logic in legal reasoning. Chaos theory indicates that complex systems often exhibit 'jumps', singularities and unintended consequences. Even beginning with a deterministic mathematical formula can produce unexpected, non-linear changes.

Fractals and fractal geometry Modernist thought privileges Euclidean geometry with its whole integer dimensions (0, 1, 2, 3, etc.). Chaos theory indicates that within these integer dimensions an infinite number of others exist. The classic question of how long is the coast of England is answered by: it's infinite; it depends on the measuring device; use a yardstick and you will get one result, use a foot-stick, you will get another result, use an 'inch stick' and there is yet another result. With each measurement the distances will increase. Fractals are useful for getting away from Boolean logic, as in yes–no answers privileged in legal logic. The truth is always somewhere in between. Fractal geometry opens up 'space' in which alternative visions may appear.

Evaluation

Chaos theory has been applied in criminology (see for example Milovanovic, 1997) to explain rural crime, banditry, property crime, gender and racial violence, organized crime, corporate crime, white collar crime; in modelling Richard Quinney's critical theory in criminology; in developing a 'chaos of violence'; and in juvenile delinquency research. In law, several applications have been developed: it has been integrated with semiotic analysis; it has been applied to explain the role of the American legal system; it has been shown to be relevant in forensic psychology to explain the insane defendant; it has also been shown how the law imposes coordinates on the body and language by which reality gets constructed in restricted ways; it has been demonstrated that the law operates much like an 'autopoietic' system (e.g., a dissipative structure); and it has been applied in decision making in law. In social justice it has been used to explain models of a more just society (Henry and Milovanovic, 1996); the spontaneous development of new forms of organization in single room occupancy areas; the development of new models of society that are more sensitive to being human; as the basis of a new approach in social movement theory. It has also been applied to a critique of existing mediation programmes (Schehr and Milovanovic, 1999).

The methodological thrust of doing chaos theory involves:

1 locating the attractors hidden in complex data sets;
2 determining how many attractors exist in that data set;
3 finding the change point(s) at which new attractors are produced (for purposes of social control);
4 identifying the key parameters which drive the system into ever more uncertainty (for purposes of developing humanistic social policy);
5 determining which setting of those key parameters is acceptable to the whole society.

Chaos theory is one of the perspectives within postmodern criminology. It continues to find wide application areas in criminology and law. Several theorists have integrated chaos theory with other perspectives within postmodern analysis to develop a model that draws from the innovative conceptual tools offered. Perhaps the greatest influence has been on those who are eager to develop novel ways of approaching old problems.

Dragan Milovanovic

Associated Concepts: constitutive criminology, postmodernism, post-structuralism

Key Readings

Babich, B. (1996) 'The order of the real: Nietzsche and Lacan', in D. Pettigrew and F. Raffaoul (eds), *Disseminating Lacan*. Albany, NY: State University of New York Press.
Henry, S. and Milovanovic, D. (1996) *Constitutive Criminology*. London: Sage.
Milovanovic, D. (1996) 'Postmodern criminology', *Justice Quarterly*, 13 (4): 567–609.
Milovanovic, D. (ed.) (1997) *Chaos, Criminology, and Social Justice: The New Orderly (Dis)Order*. Westport, CT: Praeger.
Schehr, R. and Milovanovic, D. (1999) 'Conflict mediation and the postmodern: chaos, catastrophe, and psychoanalytic semiotics', *Social Justice*, 26 (1): 208–32.
Unger, R. (1987) *False Necessity*. New York: Cambridge University Press.

CHICAGO SCHOOL OF SOCIOLOGY

Definition

A school of sociological enquiry renowned for establishing links between environmental factors and crime.

Distinctive Features

To understand the Chicago School it helps to know something of Chicago itself. In little over a century – largely as a result of its significant geographical location – Chicago grew from an obscure frontier trading-post to become one of the world's greatest cities with a population that, by 1930, had exceeded 3 million. One of the striking features of this phenomenal expansion was the extent to which it had become home to a panoply of ethnic groups: not only was the city a point of gravitation for migrating African Americans keen to escape the poverty and repression of the rural South, it was also a destination point for large numbers of European immigrants. Consequently, by 1900 Chicago was an amalgam of disparate social worlds and conflicting identities. Against this socially turbulent background, a new school of sociological enquiry emerged.

The starting point for the Chicago School was Robert Park's 'theory of human ecology'. Derived from his observations of early plant ecologists, Park postulated that human communities were closely akin to any natural environment in that their spatial organization and expansion were not the products of chance, but instead were patterned and could be understood in terms analogous to the basic natural processes that occur within any biotic organism. Thus Park maintained that the city could be thought of as a super-organism: an amalgamation of a series of subpopulations differentiated either by race, ethnicity, income group or spatial factors. Accordingly, each of these groups acted 'naturally' in that they were underpinned by a collective or organic unity. Furthermore, not only did each of these 'natural areas' have an integral role to play in the city as a whole, but in addition each community or business area was inter-related via a series of 'symbiotic relation-ships'. Close observation of these relationships enabled Park to conclude that just as in any natural ecology, the sequence of 'invasion-dominance-succession' was also in operation within the modern city.

Park's thoughts on the social ecology of the city were developed by his colleague Ernest Burgess (Park et al., 1925), whose *concentric zone theory* contended that modern cities expanded radially from their inner-city core in a series of concentric circles. Burgess identi-fied five main zones within Chicago, each two miles wide. At the centre was the business district, an area of low population and high property values. This in turn was encircled by the 'zone in transition', a place characterized by run-down housing, high-speed immigra-tion, and high rates of poverty and disease. Surrounding that zone, in turn, were zones of working-class and middle-class housing, and ultimately the affluent suburbs. Of greatest importance to the Chicagoans, however, was the zone in transition. This was the oldest residential section of the city and was com-prised primarily of dilapidated, ghetto hous-ing that was unlikely to be renovated because of its proximity to the busy commercial core. The affordability of accommodation in these neighbourhoods ensured that the zone served as a temporary home for thousands of immi-grants who were too poor to afford lodgings elsewhere in Chicago. A pattern quickly emerged whereby immigrant families only remained in the zone for as long as it took them to become sufficiently economically established to move out and 'invade' an area further away from the business district. Consequently, this was an area of great flux and restlessness – a place in which communal ties were lost, traditional shared folkways were undermined, and impersonal relations prevailed. Such neighbourhoods were some-times described as 'socially disorganized', and it was within these un-integrated urban spaces that the members of the Chicago School sought to unearth the substantive causes of crime and deviance.

These Chicagoans set about assiduously researching the city's many social problems. Taking their lead from Park, they proceeded from the premise that the best way to identify the causes of social problems such as crime was by close observation of the social proc-esses intrinsic to urban existence. To facilitate this task the School developed innovative new research methods such as *participant observa-tion* and *the focused interview*. Such techniques enabled them to 'enter the world of the devi-ant' and compile ethnographic data on hobos and taxi-dancers, racketeers and street-gang members. The result was a series of stunning qualitative and appreciative studies (see for example Anderson, 1923; Shaw, 1930) that not only provided great insight into many diverse urban subcultures, but also went a long way to establishing a theorized method-ology for studying social action.

Arguably, it is the findings that emerged from the School's empirical work that remain its most enduring legacy. Clifford Shaw and Henry McKay (1942) set about statistically testing the assumption that crime was greater in disorganized areas than elsewhere in the city by plotting juvenile delinquency court statistics onto Burgess's concentric circle model. Their findings had immense impli-cations for criminology. Simply stated, they found that delinquency rates were at their highest in run-down inner-city zones and pro-gressively declined the further one moved out into the more prosperous suburbs. Of critical importance, they also identified that this spa-tial patterning of juvenile crime remained remarkably stable (often over very long peri-ods of time) irrespective of the neighbour-hood's racial or national demographic composition. These findings allowed Shaw and McKay to conclude that delinquency was a product of sociological factors within the zone of transition rather than individual pathology or any inherent ethnic characteris-tics. This was a momentous breakthrough that did much to dispel earlier criminological theories that located the root cause of crime within the individual. Having established this important position, Shaw and McKay went on to claim that socially disorganized neighbourhoods perpetuated a situation in which delinquent behaviour patterns were *culturally transmitted*. In contrast to orderly neighbourhoods where community integration was strong and 'conventional values' were deeply ingrained, in disorganized environments – because of the paucity of supervision and the collapse of community provisions – the prevailing value-system was likely to be both conducive to, and supportive of, delinquent behaviour. In other words, criminal conventions and delinquent traditions were 'transmitted down through successive generations of boys, in much the same way that language and other social forms are transmitted' (1942: 166). This observation, along with Edwin Sutherland's (1939) related theory of *differential association*, was an important strand in subsequent criminological theories that attempted to account for crime by reference to deviant subcultures.

Evaluation

The work of the Chicago School had a considerable influence on the development of criminological theory. In particular, it helped crystallize thinking and give structure to the nascent and very disparate movements within the then fledgling discipline of sociology.

By developing innovative research methodologies, the School laid the foundations for a new type of 'appreciative', reflexive, qualitative analysis. More importantly, by identifying the important relationship between environmental factors and crime, the School greatly compromised the (then still popular) belief that criminality was a product of innate biological or pathological factors. Vitally, it established the importance of a detailed appreciation of the social lifeworlds of individuals for understanding the meaningfulness of their behaviour. Despite its many achievements, however, the School has not been without its critics.

A common criticism, challenging the usefulness of the ecological model, is that the theory of human ecology contained certain fallacious assumptions – not least that the work of the Chicagoans (in particular that of Shaw and McKay) implied that *individual* action can be explained *solely* by the larger environment in which that individual resided. This later famously became known as the 'ecological fallacy'. Similarly, the key concept of 'social disorganization' has been questioned on the grounds that it was held by the Chicagoans to be both the cause of delinquency *and* the proof that it existed. This tautological 'like-causes-like' fallacy is recognized today as being fundamentally flawed.

Major reservations have also been expressed about the wisdom of basing empirical research into juvenile delinquency upon official statistics. Aside from the obvious criticism that Shaw and McKay consistently failed to acknowledge that crime rates are always the product of *social construction*, the 'delinquency areas' scrutinized in their research were often locations in which delinquents *resided* and thus not necessarily the same neighbourhoods in which they committed their crimes.

A further criticism concerns the failure of the Chicagoans to place the everyday world of crime and deviance within the wider economic or political context. So concerned were Park and his followers with the day-to-day processes of urban life and the ways in which these concerns impinged upon and contributed to crime in the city, that they neglected to consider fully the underlying forces of capitalist development that also played a major role in shaping social life and determining patterns of urban segregation in Chicago.

Keith Hayward

Associated Concepts: appreciative criminology, community crime prevention, geographies of crime, participant observation, social ecology

Key Readings

Anderson, N. (1923) *The Hobo: The Sociology of the Homeless Man*. Chicago: University of Chicago Press.

Faris, R.E.L. (1967) *Chicago Sociology, 1920–1932*. Chicago: University of Chicago Press.

Park, R.E., Burgess, E.W. and McKenzie, R.D. (eds) (1925) *The City.* Chicago: University of Chicago Press.

Shaw, C.R. (1930) *The Jack-Roller: A Delinquent Boy's Own Story.* Chicago: University of Chicago Press.

Shaw, C.R. and McKay, H.D. (1942) *Juvenile Delinquency and Urban Areas.* Chicago: University of Chicago Press.

Sutherland, E. (1939) *Principles of Criminology,* 3rd edn. Philadelphia: J.B. Lippincott.

CHILD ABUSE

See: Family crime; Violence

CLASSICISM

Definition

An approach to the study of crime and criminality which is underpinned by the notion of rational action and free will. It was developed in the late eighteenth and early nineteenth centuries by reformers who aimed to create a clear and legitimate criminal justice system based upon equality. At its core is the idea that punishment should be proportionate to the criminal act and viewed as a deterrent. Further assumptions include the notion of individual choice within a consensual society based upon a social contract and the common interest.

Distinctive Features

One of the central features of the classical perspective within criminology is the emphasis upon voluntarism and hedonism. Individualism and self-interest are placed at the forefront of explanations about why some people commit crime and how they should be punished. One of the first proponents of this approach was the Italian philosopher Cesare Beccaria, with his work on the right to punish and methods to prevent crime, first published in 1764. He argued that society should create laws that may infringe upon the personal liberty of a few, but result in the greater happiness of the majority. His approach to the prevention of crime was that the pain of punishment should be greater than the potential pleasure resulting from the act. Hence, the punishment should be proportionate to the harm it causes society.

Another early advocate of this utilitarian approach was the philosopher and penal reformer Jeremy Bentham, who argued that punishment should be calculated to inflict pain in proportion to the damage to the public interest. As this philosophy was developed into criminological and legal definitions of crime, formal equality before the law and the similarity of criminals and non-criminals was emphasized in penal policy. In contrast to positivist approaches, which were developed in the late nineteenth century by Lombroso and Ferrero (1895) and Ferri (1901), for example, classicists maintained that the reasoning individual had simply made an error of judgement in committing a criminal act – a violation of the social contract. To prevent this recurring the individual must be sure of swift, sharp and certain punishment, so that, according to Beccaria, crime and punishment would be associated in the human mind.

Evaluation

As an alternative to the apparently cruel, harsh system based on terror, absolute control and paternal benevolence which had preceded Beccaria and Bentham's ideas, leading to reforms to the legal system, classicism appears to offer a reasonably fair and more transparent philosophy of punishment. It provides a benchmark by which other theories can be compared and an important philosophical underpinning for anti-positivistic paradigms that emphasize free will. What it fails to take into account, however, are the reasons or causes of societal inequality or conditions within which individuals are said to be propelled to commit certain acts that may violate legal codes. Classical criminologies assume that there is an agreed collective set of values or goals, ignoring the possibility of conflicting groups or aims. Although Beccaria conceded that there are pre-rational individuals (children) and sub-rational people (the mentally insane), he failed to acknowledge that social conditions may affect 'rational' judgement. Furthermore, unlike later neoclassicists, Beccaria did not view crime as a rational response to certain social conditions such as poverty, although he did concede that the poor may have to be deterred more forcefully than other members of society.

Critiques offered by positivist criminologists also suggest that social and individual forces, such as biology, physiology and the environment, create situations which may lead individuals to commit certain acts. Early theorists, mentioned above, proposed that some particular bodily difference, such as skull size, could identify and predict a propensity towards crime (see for example Lombroso and Ferrero, 1895). Later on, psychologists working within positivist frameworks argued that there could be an individual explanation in terms of personality characteristics which might predispose some people to commit crime. By contrast, classicism maintains that although hedonistic, pleasure-seeking principles may lead some people to make errors of judgement, they are essentially similar to those who do not commit such acts. Furthermore, in terms of gender this perspective fails to take into account the disparity between rates of offending between men and women. One of the questions this type of critique raises is the inability to explain these differences in terms of offending as an irrational act or individual error.

Another difficulty with the classical school is that it assumes a rational, legal and 'just' system, ignoring functionalist arguments regarding the necessary and beneficial aspects of crime. It seems unable to account for white collar and corporate crime or the 'dark' figure of crime because, if self-report studies are to be believed, 'crime' is a regular and common occurrence. This questions the extent to which the majority of individuals in society can be argued to be acting in an 'irrational' manner, if this is indeed the case.

Louise Westmarland

Associated Concepts: free will, functionalism, neo-conservative criminology, positivism, rational choice theory

Key Readings

Beccaria, C. (1764) *On Crimes and Punishments* (reprinted 1963). New York: Bobbs-Merrill.

Beirne, P. (1993) *Inventing Criminology: Essays on the Rise of Homo Criminalis.* Albany, NY: SUNY Press.

Bentham, J. (1791) *Collected Works of Jeremy Bentham* (reprinted 1843). London: J. Bowring.

Ferri, E. (1901) 'Causes of criminal behavior', reprinted 1968 in S.E. Grupp (ed.), *The Positive School of Criminology: Three Lectures by Enrico Ferri.* Pittsburgh: University of Pittsburgh Press.

Lombroso, C. and Ferrero, W. (1895) *The Female Offender.* London: Fisher Unwin.

Roshier, B. (1989) *Controlling Crime: The Classical Perspective in Criminology.* Milton Keynes: Open University Press.

COGNITIVE-BEHAVIOURAL THERAPY

See: Behaviour modification; Social learning theory

COGNITIVE-BEHAVIOURISM

Definition

'Cognitive-behaviourism' emerged from the combination of two theoretical traditions in psychological research and psychotherapy. These were behaviourism, which provided a stimulus-response analysis of behaviour based on classical conditioning theory (Watson, 1924), and cognitive-based theories, such as social learning theory (Bandura, 1977, 1986), which emphasized the role of internal cognitive factors in learning.

Distinctive Features

The initial formulation of behavioural theory focused on the relationship between environmental stimuli and humans' observable behaviour through the process of learning. The process through which learning was proposed to occur was conditioning, whereby the consequences of actions would determine whether these were reinforced or extinguished (Skinner, 1938). The first shift away from strict behavioural interpretations of behaviour through the environmental rewards and punishments of an individual's actions was known as social learning theory (Bandura, 1977, 1986). This approach proposed that as well as learning from external reinforcers in the environment, people could also learn behaviours through vicarious reinforcement (that is, through observing the consequences of other people's actions) and self-reinforcement (when their behaviours would result in feelings of pride about their own actions). Research into learned helplessness also began to show that in some circumstances animals and people were not able to generate avoidant responses despite being given opportunities to learn these. This was supported by other work suggesting a mediating effect of self-efficacy and self-regulation through the use of inner-language on behaviour. As these findings began to be incorporated into behavioural therapies, the term 'cognitive-behavioural' came into use in the mid-1970s. As such, cognitive-behaviourism represents the relationship between the environment, cognition, feelings and behaviour (Meichenbaum, 1995).

This increasing interest in cognition and cognitive processes to explain behaviour was paralleled by research into information processing, which when applied to behaviour gave rise to the social information processing approach. This emphasizes the specific cognitive processes which deal with the verbal and non-verbal information that we use in our interactions with other people. These processes include encoding information and making a mental representation of the situation, identifying one's goals or outcomes, accessing or constructing responses, and deciding upon a response. Biases or cognitive distortions at any of these stages can lead to inappropriate behaviours, with a large body of research linking them to aggressive and anti-social behaviour (see Crick and Dodge, 1994).

As an approach, cognitive-behaviourism has been applied to explain and change a range of human behaviour, including criminal behaviour. Furthermore, although cognitive-behaviourism is psychological in origin it shares some similarities with certain criminological theories, such as differential learning theory and differential association theory, in that it involves relationships between learning, cognition and behaviour.

When applied to intervening with offenders, cognitive-behavioural approaches reflect the fact that it is an amalgam of two previously separate theories (behaviourism and cognitivism). Therefore, a range of methods or techniques can be labelled cognitive-behavioural, which will place a greater or lesser focus on behaviour and/or cognition. Behaviour modification and behaviour therapy draw heavily upon pure behaviourist theory, in that they view dysfunctional behaviour as learned through conditioning. Therefore, they use methods based upon conditioning theory in order to try to reduce unwanted behaviours and replace these with more appropriate ones. Social skills training is made up of a group of techniques and has often been adopted for use with offenders following evidence that many persistent offenders have deficits in their social skills. Interventions of this type typically involve modelling, role-play, instruction, coaching and feedback by trainers.

Another set of common cognitive-behavioural techniques used with offenders is social problem-solving training, in which problematic thinking skills that lead to criminal behaviour are addressed in order to replace these with more appropriate skills that will be more likely to promote pro-social behaviour. These techniques are based upon empirical research showing that offenders tend to have poor social cognitive skills (Ross and Fabiano, 1985). Thus, interventions aim to improve their problem awareness and recognition, ability to generate alternative solutions, means–end thinking skills, consequential thinking, empathy and social perspective taking, moral reasoning and abstract thinking skills. In this way the emphasis is on how people think and the process of thinking, rather than the content of their thoughts. This is typically done through interactive sessions using role-play, repetition and feedback, with an emphasis on modelling and reinforcement techniques. The importance of using concrete examples from offenders' lives in doing this is also recognized, in order to make the new skills relevant and improve the likelihood that they will be generalized beyond the intervention setting.

Other cognitive-behavioural interventions focus on challenging offenders' distorted cognitions, such as their schema and attitudes. For example, work with sexual offenders may attempt to challenge beliefs about committing sexual acts with young children. A final and important set of techniques in the cognitive-behavioural area concerns relapse prevention, with techniques to address this being built into interventions that can be used for a number of behaviours.

Evaluation

One criticism of cognitive-behaviourism is that it does not consist of one true theory, and so there is no single cognitive-behavioural method for intervention. Instead it consists more of a group of ideas and techniques that are based on a shared general theoretical framework relating to the conceptualization of the link between environment, cognition, feeling and behaviour. In addition, it has also been argued that many current cognitive-behavioural approaches to behaviour neglect the wider sociological factors. The theoretical framework of cognitive-behaviourism certainly has the scope to allow this to happen and it is to be hoped that it will be achieved at some point in the future.

Emma J. Palmer

Associated Concepts: conditioning, differential association, sex crime, social learning theory, 'what works'

Key Readings

Bandura, A. (1977) *Social Learning Theory.* Englewood Cliffs, NJ: Prentice-Hall.
Bandura, A. (1986) *Social Foundations of Thought and Action: A Social Cognitive Theory.* Englewood Cliffs, NJ: Prentice-Hall.
Crick, N.R. and Dodge, K.A. (1994) 'A review and reformulation of social information-processing mechanisms in children's social adjustment', *Psychological Bulletin,* 115: 74–101.
Meichenbaum, D.H. (1995) 'Cognitive-behavioural therapy in historical perspective', in B. Bongar and L.E. Beutler (eds), *Comprehensive Textbook of Psychotherapy: Theory and Practice.* New York: Oxford University Press.
Ross, R.R. and Fabiano, E.A. (1985) *Time to Think: A Cognitive Model of Offender Rehabilitation.* Johnson City, TN: Institute of Science and Arts.
Skinner, B.F. (1938) *The Behaviour of Organisms.* New York: Appleton-Century-Crofts.
Watson, J.B. (1924) *Behaviorism.* Chicago: The People's Institute.

COHORT STUDIES

Definition

Cohort studies involve the collection of data from the same group of respondents over a period of time. Research employing the cohort approach can be either qualitative or quantitative. Researchers adopting a qualitative approach might seek to conduct in-depth interviews with a group of respondents on a longitudinal basis, whilst researchers employing a more quantitative approach might survey the same sample of respondents over a period of time. Cohort studies are a form of longitudinal study.

Distinctive Features

Cohort studies are employed where there is a desire to explore patterns of behaviour over time, or where there is an interest in following life events, and increasingly these are being used in evaluation research where there is a desire to observe the impact of rehabilitative programmes upon recipients. The aims of cohort-based research are to identify what motivates groups of people to behave as they do, to describe life events, and sometimes to explore the impact of programmes or policies.

The form that cohort research takes will be dependent upon the methodological techniques employed within a particular study. Typically a sample of respondents will be selected at the outset of a study on the basis of some defining characteristic. The respondents may, for example, share the same birthday or the same interest or might perhaps have been convicted of a particular offence at a given time. This group of respondents or participants will be asked to participate in the research over a specified time period and then contacted at regular intervals in order to participate in interviews or complete questionnaires.

Some cohort studies are based upon the analysis of secondary data. In the case of criminological research such data may have been collected by criminal justice agencies in the course of their work. As the data already exist the researcher may select a cohort of individuals and attempt to trace their criminal histories. One such study was conducted by Peter Marshall (1998), in which he aimed to estimate the number of men in England and Wales who had received convictions for a variety of sexual offences. The work was based upon data from the Home Office Offender Index, a database which stores information on all convictions from 1963 to the present. Marshall calculated estimates on the basis of five cohort samples of men born between 1953 and 1973. The men's criminal histories were compiled by 'sampling one in thirteen records from each year – based upon all birthdays in four weeks of each year' (1998: 2). Marshall was able to estimate the number of men convicted of sexual offences in England and Wales, and found that at least 260,000 men aged 20 or over had been convicted of a sexual offence in the 1993 population, 110,000 of whom had committed a sexual offence against a child. Of his cohort of men born in 1953, approximately one in 60 had a conviction by age 40 for some type of sexual offence (this included less serious forms of sexual offending).

Evaluation

The value of quantitative cohort research lies in its ability to provide a great deal of data regarding respondents' lives and motivations over a long period of time. As the work is not conducted in a retrospective fashion, problems associated with respondents recalling past events are also diminished. The advantages are similar in qualitative work, except that in addition rich detailed data may be collected on an ongoing basis, thereby providing a fuller picture of respondents' lives rather than a snapshot.

Relatively few cohort studies have been conducted by social researchers given the resources associated with the design and management of such projects. Another key problem arises in attempting to retain the original sample over time. Some respondents may be inaccessible as the study progresses or might wish to withdraw from the research altogether. A great deal of effort is involved in retaining the cooperation of respondents. A further problem arises in that the production of findings will be slow, given the long-term nature of cohort research.

Julia Davidson

Associated Concepts: developmental criminology, longitudinal study, risk factor research, social survey, time series design

Key Readings

Marshall, P. (1998) *The Prevalence of Convictions for Sexual Offending* (Home Office Research Findings Briefing, No. 55). London: HMSO.
Sapsford, R. and Jupp, V.R. (eds) (1996) *Data Collection and Analysis.* London: Sage.

COMMUNITARIANISM

Definition

The broad philosophical and sociological tradition in which there is an emphasis on the centrality of informal, communal bonds and networks for the maintenance of social order. It is critical of individualistic, liberal theories of social behaviour and 'society', invoking notions of 'social beings' and 'community' rather than 'atomized individuals'. It has both conservative and radical variants.

Distinctive Features

The intellectual pedigree of this body of ideas/perspective is one displaying a decidedly mixed 'parentage'. Apart from the important connections back to Aristotelian notions of civic republicanism and Judaeo-Christian ideas of communion, the expression of communitarian aspirations is also associated with socialist and anarchist thinking. Furthermore, communitarian philosophy may also be linked to a conservative sociological tradition in which a critique of Enlightenment's project may be discerned. As a result of this heterodox pedigree, communitarianism may be said to 'break' with traditional ideas of right and left. Thus, for example, within much communitarian thought, both the market and the (welfare) state are viewed as dangers to the vibrant, organic community.

Liberalism's emphasis on individual rights and freedoms and abstract notions of 'enlightened self-interest' is subject to a critique for its neglect of the inherently social nature of humans. In contrast, communitarians point to the collective character of human existence in which obligation and mutual dependency are to the fore. Questions about solidarity and belonging are central to communitarianism in all its versions. Social compliance in turn derives primarily from informal cultural controls built into everyday relations. Much of its appeal then is to real people in specific, morally bounded communities rather than through abstract notions of liberty and individual rights. Herein lies its strong conservative appeal.

The sociologist and populist 'guru' Amitai Etzioni (1994) is the most prominent contemporary proponent of the conservative communitarian project to undertake a 're-moralization' of society. In Etzioni's words, 'Communitarians call to restore civic virtues, for people to live up to their responsibilities and not to merely focus on their entitlements, and to shore up the moral foundations of society.' At times Etzioni is quite explicit in harking back to a vision of a more stable, orderly and lawful past based on an idealized image of small-town America. Accepting that there was discrimination against women and ethnic minorities in the past, Etzioni nevertheless expresses concern that the assumed, previous bedrock of moral consensus has not been replaced by anything of substance other than 'a strong sense of entitlement and a weak sense of obligation'. The contemporary weakness of community is identified as both the cause of most of our ills (including crime and disorder) and also its potential saviour, when 're-moralized'.

Quite specific suggestions are put forward by conservative communitarians on law and order which further reinforce the dominant motifs of obligation and the shoring up of our moral foundations. Apart from support for vigilant 'self-policing' in the community, this communitarian agenda appears to encourage a Draconian and public version of 'shaming' offenders. The bottom line for authors like Etzioni, however, in their diagnosis of the problem and solution of crime and disorder, always appears to be the existence of a tight and homogeneous community.

There is also a radical variant of communitarianism in which the principles of spontaneous solidarity, rules of reciprocity and small-scale communities with participatory democracy are centre stage. Bill Jordan captures the working definition of 'community' adopted in this body of work as follows: it is 'the voluntary exchanges within systems of mutual obligation that include members through reciprocity, sharing and redistribution' (Jordan, 1996: 186). In contrast to moral authoritarian communitarianism, radical communitarians are keen to emphasize that individual moral autonomy needs to be assured and realized through specific projects and commitments. The good society is defiantly pluralistic and mutual tolerance is a crucial feature of it.

According to radical communitarians, in recent years neo-liberal societies have witnessed a deterioration in social relations due to a denial of access for the poor to majority goods and thus their experience of majority power as unjust. As a consequence, both the autonomy of poor people as citizens and quality of life in the community have been jeopardized. Such processes of social exclusion and polarization do not necessarily destroy communities in any simple sense but radical communitarian commentators recognize that new forms of particularistic communities do emerge in the absence of any notion of a shared, common good. It is argued that marginalization, inequality and exclusion lie at the root of much crime and anti-social activities. As a consequence, the radical communitarian agenda on crime prevention gives ethical priority to decisions over *redistribution and reintegration* which in turn allows all members to participate both in the decisions themselves and, crucially, in the shared life of their communities. Unless such developments take place, it is suggested, the decay in consent and in allegiance to democracy and civil order will continue and with it the growth of more coercive and authoritarian methods of government and social control. The politics of enforcement will gather greater force.

A major contribution to the radical communitarian debate on crime, disorder and the decline of communities in the USA is found in the work of Elliot Currie (1997). Currie contends that the most serious problem facing contemporary USA is that its most disadvantaged communities are sinking into a permanent state of terror and disintegration. Radical communitarian commentators like Currie argue that behind the growth of crime is a *cultural* as well as a *structural* transformation of poor communities. In this regard, there are some common themes to both the conservative and radical communitarians. The connecting points are around the concern with cultural deprivation and morality.

However, there are also important breaks between the two variants of communitarianism, as exemplified in the radical version's concern with structural inequalities, promotion of diversity and the key and positive role of the state in addressing social 'wounds'.

Evaluation

Moral authoritarian or conservative communitarianism has been widely criticized for the following reasons:

- a normative emphasis on one moral community at the expense of a sociological recognition of the plurality and diversity of actually existing communities;
- a desire to return to a traditional and nostalgic past;
- a neglect of power structures in human societies or at least a naturalization of hierarchical relations;
- a critique of personal rights and a call for duties but a failure to critique property rights;
- a glorification of past solidaristic communities together with a failure to conceptualize the crucial importance of struggles versus oppression in the creation of collectivist communities;
- finally, a naive and exclusivist call for a return to the 'traditional' family as the means to prevent social ills, including crime.

Within the popular conservative variant of communitarianism, there is a vision of a unitary, homogeneous community sustained by strongly held moral certainties, celebrating in turn mono-culturalism and setting, and, albeit at times implicitly, a morally prescriptive agenda for the social exclusion of marginalized and 'deviant' categories of people.

The extent to which the aspirations for a radical communitarian agenda are realizable in the face of both the authoritarian penal populism and the fragmentation of communities in neo-liberal societies remains open to further debate. There also remains a lack of empirical substantiation for its participatory democratic visions of civil society and vibrant, expansive and tolerant communities. Furthermore, the key question remains as to what might create the more redistributive economic strategies upon which these radical communitarian visions of crime prevention and social reconstruction are dependent.

Community remains a deeply problematic word which is often derided by social scientists and yet is hard to live without. It may be a necessary fiction, evoking as it does the fundamentally collective, shared and interdependent quality of our existence and the pull of the local on most of our lives (and especially those of the poor and disadvantaged).

Gordon Hughes

Associated Concepts: abolitionism, anti-social behaviour, community crime prevention, community safety, left realism, restorative justice, shaming

Key Readings

Currie, E. (1997) 'Market, crime and community', *Theoretical Criminology*, 1 (2): 147–72.
Etzioni, A. (1994) *The Spirit of Community: The Reinvention of American Society.* New York: Touchstone.
Hughes, G. (2000) 'Communitarianism and law and order', in T. Hope (ed.), *Perspectives on Crime Reduction.* Dartmouth: Ashgate.
Jordan, B. (1996) *A Theory of Poverty and Social Exclusion.* Cambridge: Polity Press.

COMMUNITY CORRECTIONS

Definition

A catch-all term for the range of correctional strategies and programmes for dealing with the punishment, treatment or supervision of offenders without recourse to penal custody.

Distinctive Features

Community corrections are generally viewed as being synonymous with 'alternatives to custody' and may range from the use of supervisory probation orders, community service orders, rehabilitation programmes, half-way houses, electronic tagging and home curfews, to the adoption of even more Draconian, shaming corrections in the community. There is a marked diversity of programmatic activities which have a 'community-based' label. Across the world, such strategies and programmes still generally exist on the 'borderlands' of criminal justice and social welfare, in which a mix of the principles of punishment, care and treatment is evident. They are particularly associated with the work of the probation or correction services in most Western jurisdictions (Hamai et al., 1995). Community corrections have been popularly perceived as 'soft options' when compared with custodial sentences, and widespread debate continues to rage over their 'effectiveness', however this is defined. They have also been popularly viewed as marginal to the 'real work' of criminal justice, namely custody, despite the use of community penalties outnumbering those sentenced to custody in most countries. In the USA, for example, there were 1.5 million adults sentenced to penal custody as against 3 million on parole in 1994.

The changing nature of community corrections and sentences has been driven by a heady mix of populist political motives, pragmatic managerial and economic concerns as well as philosophical and moral principles. As Tim May (1994: 860) notes, 'attempts therefore to improve an evolutionary theoretical scheme on the spread of community-based sentences must be treated with caution.'

A recent shift in the wake of dominant New Right thinking across many neo-liberal societies has seen the move from 'welfare' to 'punishment' models of community corrections and the populist punitive political call for such community sentences to be 'tough'. Indeed, in the USA use of the term 'corrections' rather than 'treatment' is itself indicative of the sullied reputation of treatment models of rehabilitation (National Advisory Commission on Criminal Justice Standards and Goals, in Carter and Wilkins, 1976). More generally, since the 1980s the 'professional-therapeutic' rationale has been replaced by a 'punishment-administrative' rationale of community sentences (May, 1994). Apart from the shift to make community sanctions 'tougher', the other key, related shift is that of concentrating on the administrative and managerial technicalities of such corrections, with particular emphasis placed on cost and effectiveness.

Evaluation

The contemporary picture of community penalties and treatment programmes across many societies is confusing and messy. Many of these programmes are currently overlaid with contradictory objectives and concerns, including such issues as managerialist effectiveness, value for money, public protection, victim satisfaction, and responsibility of the offender, as well as some vestiges of rehabilitation and restoration. And this situation is not helped by 'community' being such a slippery and promiscuous word. According to critics of the appeal to community in criminal justice practices, the rise of community-based, non-incarcerative sanctions is particularly dangerous due to their potential for widening the net of social control from inside the prison and out into the community (Cohen, 1985). However, such sweeping, if seductive, generalizations are open to question from existing trends (Bottoms, 1983). There is also the danger that criticisms of community-based programmes may serve to vacate the political space for those forces who want to increase the profile of retributive and incarcerative penalties yet further.

Like probation, community corrections are always practised in 'the shadow of prison'. We seem incapable of conceptualizing other penalties except in terms of their relationship to imprisonment. This is perhaps why nonincarcerative sanctions and programmes attract such popular suspicion. Across the world, it would seem that non-incarcerative measures are increasingly concerned with the 'punitive' restriction of liberty, surveillance and monitoring rather than treatment and welfare. An alternative vision is put forward by Ann Worrall to this depressing scenario in her argument that such measures should be viewed as constituting a sphere of social control which is quite separate from that of the prison, based on self-government and normalizing instruction. This would result in a widening of the net of inclusion (Worrall, 1997: 151).

Gordon Hughes

Associated Concepts: bifurcation, managerialism, neo-conservative criminology, net widening, probation, rehabilitation, social control

Key Readings

Bottoms, A. (1983) 'Neglected features of contemporary penal systems', in D. Garland and P. Young (eds), *The Power to Punish*. London: Heinemann.
Carter, R. and Wilkins, L. (1976) *Probation, Parole and Community Corrections*. New York: John Wiley.
Cohen, S. (1985) *Visions of Social Control*. Cambridge: Polity Press.
Hamai, F., Ville, R., Harris, R., Hough, M. and Zvedic, U. (eds) (1995) *Probation Around the World*. London: Routledge.
May, T. (1994) 'Probation and community sanctions', in M. Maguire, R. Morgan and R. Reiner (eds), *Oxford Handbook of Criminology*. Oxford: The Clarendon Press.
Worrall, A. (1997) *Punishment in the Community*. London: Longman.

COMMUNITY CRIME PREVENTION

Definition

The strategy which prioritizes the participation of members of the community in the active prevention of crime and related incivilities. It is also associated with explanations which look for the causes of crime and disorder in the fabric of the community and the wider social environment.

Distinctive Features

The strategy was most famously pioneered by the Chicago School of Sociology in the early twentieth century, which focused on the communal 'pathology' behind high rates of crime and delinquency in urban environments. Its enduring legacy is the rationale of community development. Key individuals of the Chicago School, such as Shaw and McKay (1969), were at pains to develop practical ways of modifying those aspects of socially disorganized community life which fostered delinquency and criminal careers among its members. The strategy which emerged, and is now often termed 'community crime prevention', was one which targeted specific problem neighbourhoods and sought to compensate poor communities for their lack of a 'normal' institutional infrastructure by initiating programmes of community development. The success of the Chicago School's own programmes has been widely questioned but it has nevertheless influenced subsequent community interventions across the globe (Hope, 1995).

Appeals to community in crime prevention initiatives remain popular among both practitioners and politicians. This is in no small part due to the seductive rhetoric of 'community' in a world where traditional, tightly knit and cohesive communities appear to be the exception rather than the rule. It is also linked to the perceived growing problem of policing the most deprived and marginalized urban communities and a recognition that the solution to problems may require the participation of the involved communities themselves. In practice, many researchers have noted that the active role of the community is often limited to rhetoric rather than practice. Contemporary strategies of community crime prevention – increasingly termed 'community safety' – are generally multi-agency in character and involve both situational techniques (such as CCTV) and some limited social initiatives, such as the 'self-help policing' of Neighbourhood Watch schemes. Overall, such strategies are generally 'top-down' in character with limited 'bottom-up' participation.

Evaluation

Despite the lack of tangible, measurable successes, by the 1990s multi-agency community crime prevention appeared to be a phenomenon whose 'time had come' on the global stage. However, for some critics, the appeal to community sits more comfortably at the level of rhetoric than practice. According to other critical commentators, the idea that the solution to neighbourhood crime problems can be achieved primarily through the self-help efforts of residents is fundamentally flawed. Tim Hope (1995: 78), for example, argues that instead of communitarian self-help, disintegrating urban communities may need significant investment in their institutional infrastructure to offset powerful tendencies towards the destabilization of poor communities within the urban free-market economy.

There are some important conceptual and political questions with regard to the popular appeal to 'community' in crime control discourses. For example, the nature of the community to which such appeals in dominant political discourses on law and order are made is itself often a highly selective rhetorical device. Crawford (1997) notes that it is (wrongly) assumed in the dominant discourse that the lack of community necessarily leads to decline and thus crime, whereas 'more' community equals less crime. Furthermore, community is assumed to be a defence against 'outsiders' and will also be characterized by homogeneity rather than diversity. In accord with a long tradition of sociological scepticism on the use of this slippery word, Crawford alerts us to the exclusionary and bounded 'majoritarian' mode of legitimation which is likely to result from the particular effects of the dominant discourse on multi-agency 'community' crime prevention and community safety, not least leading to the demonization of the labelled 'other' and 'outsider'.

Most contemporary sociologists and criminologists are deeply sceptical about the use of appeals to community in crime control 'talk' and practice. According to Garland (1996), appeals to, and the use of, community as a new means of 'governing' crime may again be best understood as part of a wider adaptation to the realization of high crime rates as a normal 'social fact' in late modernity. More than this, they are part of a 'responsibilization strategy' by means of which the state devolves the responsibilities for crime prevention onto agencies, organizations, groups and individuals outside of the state and persuades them to act appropriately. According to this logic, the sources of crime and also the means for its control and prevention are viewed as positioned in the behaviour and attitudes of individual citizens and their local communities.

However, this grand theoretical critique may be guilty of neglecting countervailing forces that are at work on the wider social fabric and of underplaying the possibility of 'unsettlements' of the state's dominant agenda on crime control.

We may, for example, ask what of mobilization around community as symbolic of new resistances and solidarities in opposition to the central state's programme of popular penalism and 'privatized prudentialism'?

Despite the criticisms noted above, the idea that communities *do* have a key role to play in crime prevention remains influential in criminological circles. The argument that community 'breakdown' is a key contributing factor in patterns of rising crime and delinquency, and claims that some communities are being excluded from 'mainstream' social life in a period of increased social polarization and greater social inequality, remain powerful. Again, it is wise to be wary about the novelty of such ideas. The Chicago School in the USA in the 1920s and 1930s claimed to have identified a crucial link between the disorganized and disadvantaged community and the growth and sustenance of criminality. Thus similar claims and arguments about community tend to re-occur within different historical contexts, highlighting the continuing potency of community ideas.

Gordon Hughes

Associated Concepts: Chicago School of Sociology, communitarianism, community justice, community safety, crime prevention, governance, left realism, self-policing, social exclusion

Key Readings

Crawford, A. (1997) *The Local Governance of Crime.* Oxford: The Clarendon Press.
Garland, D. (1996) 'The limits of the sovereign state: strategies of crime control in contemporary society', *British Journal of Criminology,* 33 (4): 445–71.
Hope, T. (1995) 'Community crime prevention', in M. Tonry and D. Farrington (eds), *Building a Safer Society: Strategic Approaches to Crime.* Chicago: University of Chicago Press.
Shaw, C. and McKay, H. (1969) *Juvenile Delinquency and Urban Areas.* Chicago: University of Chicago Press.

COMMUNITY JUSTICE

Definition

The term is deployed generally to describe a range of conflict resolution strategies, usually associated with informal, popular or restorative forms of justice.

Distinctive Features

The term 'community justice' has begun to enter the vocabulary of those who work with offenders and victims, although few are sure what it means (Nellis, 2000). That said, the word has a long tradition in criminological thought, having been deployed in analyses of popular and informal justice. It is also particularly associated with abolitionist and communitarian perspectives/traditions in criminology (see Christie, 1977). The current, growing popularity of the term among practitioners and policy makers is in part linked to the recognition that state-administered systems of justice are expensive, unduly bureaucratic and slow, individualized in their response to offenders and neglectful of the needs of victims and the wider community. Abolitionists have long shared these misgivings but the main impulse of the abolitionist critique of traditional formal criminal justice is based on the criminalizing consequences of disintegrative shaming and retributive punishment and the failures of contemporary criminal justice policy owing to its overbearing reliance on imprisonment. Communitarians of different varieties share the abolitionist bias towards informal, reintegrative and educational solutions. However, they also openly accept that punishment is the inevitable concomitant of law enforcement with censure as a mostly legitimate response to wrong-doing, and with denunciation in the name of the victim and the common good as morally appropriate (Nellis, 2000).

The claims of community justice are also evident in populist law and order interpretations of the limitations of the formal and legalistic system of criminal justice. Vigilantism and public shaming are common expressions of this variant of the movement for community justice.

However, the contemporary appeal to community justice in criminal justice systems and for policy-makers and practitioners is based on less extreme criticisms of, and organizational departures from, formal, adversarial justice than that associated with either abolitionism or populist punitiveness. In effect, the practice of community justice is for the most part aimed at an organizational reform of parts of the justice system which are viewed as failing due to high costs, poor coordination and a lack of participation and involvement on the part of lay actors in the process. There are clear parallels with the emergence of the strategy of multi-agency community safety and crime reduction. The actual claims for returning justice to the community (however defined) appear to have more to do with rhetoric and legitimation than actual practice. Instead, community justice as realized in specific criminal justice and social welfare systems tends to be a not-so-new or radical strategy based on multi-agency work with relatively low tariff

offenders in which the active involvement of the victim, offender and other relevant members of the community is encouraged. Among the most influential examples of such institutional practices in contemporary societies are the 'reintegrative shaming' initiatives such as Family Group Conferences and sentencing circles and the widely used penalties such as community service orders for 'shallow end' offenders. Is it then mostly a 'rebranding' of the status quo? According to proponents of community justice, it offers to open up further possibilities in ways that other terms and ideas do not. In particular, there is hope that over time new practices might develop which will tilt the centre of gravity away from imprisonment and mass social exclusion and towards the creation of inclusive communities which would also be freer from crime (Nellis, 2000). Prime among these new possibilities are initiatives in restorative justice, such as reparation and compensation schemes and victim–offender mediation initiatives.

Evaluation

There are some important reservations to be made about the contemporary appeal to community and communal participation in criminal justice. Community justice initiatives have tended to define community loosely if at all, and critics have noted the wide variety of forms that these initiatives often take. In particular, the dangers of populist appeals to a 'participatory' politics of enforcement in crime control are evident. The 'off-loading' by central government of crime control practices onto communities, however 'represented', does have its dangers for the central state, not least in the creation of volatile new spaces such as vigilantism. The rise of vigilantism is evident in the examples of 'communities' taking the law into their own hands against 'paedophiles' and 'persistent' offenders. We need to be wary of opening up criminal justice issues to democratic participation at precisely the moment when relations of trust between groups of citizens and between citizens and government have been at their weakest. In order to counteract the dangers of a reactionary and exclusivist moral majoritarian backlash against the criminalized, Jordan and Arnold (1995: 180) argue that 'balanced democratic governance may require the public power to repair social conflicts through actions in other spheres before attempting to open up criminal justice policy for public participation'. In other words, there may be a key role to be played by the state in healing the wounds in the social fabric by measures of social justice before 'the community' can be allowed to participate in an inclusive politics of crime control and social justice.

Gordon Hughes

Associated Concepts: abolitionism, communitarianism, community crime prevention, community safety, governance, governmentality, redress, restorative justice, shaming

Key Readings

Christie, N. (1977) 'Conflicts as property', *British Journal of Criminology,* 17 (1): 1–19.
Galaway, B. and Hudson, J. (1996) *Restorative Justice: International Perspectives.* Monsey, NY: Criminal Justice Press.
Jordan, B. and Arnold, J. (1995) 'Democracy and criminal justice', *Critical Social Policy,* 44/45: 171–80.
Nellis, M. (2000) 'Creating community justice', in K. Pease, S. Ballintyne and V. McLaren (eds), *Key Issues in Crime Prevention, Crime Reduction and Community Safety.* London: IPPR.

COMMUNITY POLICING

Definition

A philosophy of policing that promotes community-based problem-solving strategies to address the underlying causes of crime and disorder and fear of crime and which provides reassurance. It is a process by which crime control is shared, or co-produced, with the public, and a means of developing communication with the public, thus enhancing quality of life for local communities and building police legitimacy.

Distinctive Features

Community policing is one of the most popular contemporary approaches to policing. It emerged in response to evidence which indicated that the police could not fight crime by themselves. It was also seen as a mechanism for improving police–public relationships and in particular aimed to gain the trust and confidence of minorities. Community-oriented policing (COP) stresses community engagement, partnerships and participation. Problem oriented policing (POP) is a more analytical and intelligence-led strategy but in practice they overlap.

For Eck and Rosenbaum (1994) 'community policing' is a 'plastic' concept because the range and complexity of the programmes encompassed by it are large and evolving. Not surprisingly, many definitions of community policing consist of a list of its numerous features and possible dimensions. A good illustration of this approach is 'The Nine Ps of Community Policing' by Trojanowicz: philosophy, personalized, policing, patrols, permanent, place, proactive, partnership and problem solving. In practice then, there is no general consensus as to what community policing actually entails and it can take various forms, for example 'policing by consent', 'neighbourhood policing', 'proximity policing', 'problem oriented policing'. The common denominator is that these initiatives and processes broadly follow the same principles. Central to community policing initiatives are local police/community partnerships and problem oriented approaches.

- Local policing requires a process of organizational decentralization. Officers need to be assigned to the same beat so that they can establish the trust and confidence of local people and secure an intimate day-to-day knowledge of local conditions. Officers also need to be given more operational freedom and uncommitted patrol time to tailor their work to local demands and optimize contact with the community.

- Forging meaningful partnerships with the community requires a degree of deprofessionalization on the part of the police. Active community involvement in deliberations about policing priorities obliges the police to be open about issues such as strategies and resourcing.
- Problem oriented policing identifies the underlying causes of crime and disorder that the community feels most strongly about and constructs tailor-made strategies that have the support of local people. It also enables police officers and communities to alter the conditions and circumstances that encourage criminal and disorderly behaviour.

Community policing holds out the promise of reduced levels of crime and disorder, improved quality of life for the community, enhanced relationships between the police and the community, a supportive environment for police operations and greater job satisfaction for police officers. There is no single recipe for successful community policing. However, for it to work it requires the entire police force to adopt a broader concept of policing and a transformation of the mindset of all police officers.

Evaluation

Community policing philosophy is strongly linked to the concepts of democracy and policing by consent, based on a respect for fundamental human rights. Community policing is thus a guarantee for police legitimacy, continuously justifying and renewing the police mandate. Public policing, as a common good, can be sustained through community policing. The production of genuine community policing is not possible unless it is constructed within a framework of democratic accountability that prioritizes public service. A critical criminological approach to community policing stresses its contextual and ethnocentric character and questions its transferability.

Community policing processes vary considerably. In some countries it has become the dominant philosophy, in others it has assumed orthodoxy, and elsewhere cultural resistance, organizational and legal factors, together with political and economic exigencies, have prevented any notable developments (Brogden, 1999). By taking account of local power relations, Lyons (1999) examines the degree to which community policing reflects and enhances the power of those already in privileged positions. Community policing can, from this perspective, be seen as a form of social engineering or political control.

Contemporary variants of community policing, for instance 'reassurance policing', have been built upon its philosophical basis. Community-led policing initiatives are now seen by governments in various jurisdictions as a necessary support for investment and regeneration strategies as well as crucial to the building of social capital in disadvantaged communities. In this context, intelligence-led policing should be seen as a complementary and not a competitive approach, supporting community safety partnerships and community policing. Community policing may also be viewed as a radical police reform, a response to police–community problems or crime-fighting failures, or more broadly as a governmental means to enhance quality of life for local communities. In all these forms it serves as the dominant contemporary legitimation of policing and as justification for a publicly-funded police service.

Sirpa Virta

Associated Concepts: 'broken windows', policing, problem oriented policing, responsibilization, social capital, zero tolerance

Key Readings

Brogden, M. (1999) 'Community policing as cherry pie', in R.I. Mawby (ed.), *Policing Across the World*. London: UCL Press.
Eck, J.E. and Rosenbaum, D.P. (1994) 'The new police order: effectiveness, equity

and efficiency in community policing', in D.P. Rosenbaum (ed.), *The Challenge of Community Policing: Testing the Promises.* London: Sage.

Fielding, N.G. (1995) *Community Policing.* Oxford: Clarendon Press.

Lyons, W. (1999) *The Politics of Community Policing.* Ann Arbor: University of Michigan Press.

Skogan, W.G. (ed.) (2004) *Community Policing: Can it Work?* Belmont, CA: Wadsworth.

Skogan, W.G. and Hartnett, S.M. (1997) *Community Policing, Chicago Style.* New York: Oxford University Press.

Trojanowicz, R.C. (1998) *Community Policing: A Contemporary Perspective.* New York: Anderson.

COMMUNITY SAFETY

Definition

The strategy which seeks to move beyond a police-driven crime prevention agenda to involve other agencies and generate greater participation from all sections of the 'community'. It has been particularly associated with local 'partnership' strategies of crime and disorder reduction from local authorities. However, it is a capacious phrase which may also refer to strategies aimed at improving community safety from harms from all sources, not just those acts classifiable as 'crimes'.

Distinctive Features

By the 1990s community safety could be viewed as the 'rising star' of crime prevention. The use of this referent, rather than crime prevention, may reflect a diminished confidence in formal criminal justice agencies which, when compared to the networks of civil society, have a limited impact on patterns of crime. It also involves an expanded role that must be played by an array of voluntary and commercial organizations and responsible ('responsibilized') individuals in 'partnership'

with statutory agencies, all of which now represent a key feature of the politics of social defence in increasingly fearful and divided societies. The subtext of community safety then is that of a holistic, managerialist approach allied to the promotion of community activism and of a logic of responsibilization – with the consequence that blame is placed on fellow citizens rather than on the wider social arrangements that generate harms. Multi-agency strategies of community safety are most pronounced in the UK, where they have become a statutory feature of local crime and disorder reduction policies. As legislated in the UK, it is merely a style of crime reduction/prevention – 'a synonym of crime prevention with fluffy overtones added' (Pease and Wiles, 2000).

More generally across the world, community safety also often appears to be a means by which many powerful sectional interests within civil society are able to 'lock', 'light' and 'zone' themselves out of harm's way, whilst areas blighted by de-industrialization and acute levels of victimization are least likely to have the material resources, political connections and civic associations that meaningful community safety presupposes (Hope, 1995).

Viewed more broadly, community safety refers to the absence of likely or serious harms, whether caused by human agency or otherwise (Pease and Wiles, 2000). This pan-hazard paradigm offers a challenge to dominant, compartmentalized thinking about harms in which each agency seeks to reduce the harms that are traditionally central to its compartmental function. It is concerned with dangers from whatever source, not just crime but also, for example, traffic and transport, housing and working conditions. This approach to harm reduction and the promotion of public safety is not as yet common, necessarily involving what is often termed 'joined-up thinking'. It also necessitates sustained, multi-agency coordinated attention being paid to access to, and the delivery of, welfare and health services, and educational and employment opportunities, as well as confronting institutionalized discrimination and vested power interests. But there are potential advantages to rethinking community safety as strategies aimed at minimizing the number and seriousness of harms rather than focusing on crime prevention alone: not least in order that serious harms caused by non-human agency may take their rightful place among reasons to be fearful (Pease and Wiles, 2000).

Evaluation

The debate on whether community safety and crime prevention amount to the same thing or whether they carry different connotative baggage is still nascent and unfinished. As Pease and Wiles note, community safety is a phrase to be preferred (over crime prevention and crime and disorder reduction) only if safety refers to the likely absence of harms (and particularly serious harms) from all sources and not just from human acts that are classifiable as crimes. In particular this requires a shift in focus away from harming a person and towards the harming circumstance. If used narrowly we are likely to see the emergence of double standards here – whereby some of us are protected from attacks by others while others of us choke on polluted air or are victimized as a result of inadequate protective building design.

Many academic commentators have sought to debunk the idea of community on various counts (for being nebulous, nostalgic, intrinsically oppressive and so forth). According to many academic commentators, 'community safety' is at best a 'feel good' word marked by extreme vagueness. It is generally seen to exist more happily at the level of rhetoric rather than practice, where it is limited by some serious structural constraints (Gilling, 1997). Critics of community safety have also alerted us to the dangers of appeals to community in the politics of criminal justice and crime prevention, not least for their tendency to produce intolerance towards those viewed as 'outsiders'. But the idea of community also has a long association with the solidarity struggles of the weak and the poor. If it did not exist then it would need to be invented.

Community safety remains a 'wicked issue', not just for the challenges it raises for not easily compartmentalized practices and policies about harm reduction, but also for the theoretical, moral and political challenges associated with its nascent and contested agenda in the new governance of crimes and harms (Hughes, 2000).

Gordon Hughes

Associated Concepts: communitarianism, community crime prevention, community justice, governance, left realism, multi-agency crime prevention, self-policing, social crime prevention, social harm

Key Readings

Crawford, A. (1997) *Local Governance of Crime.* Oxford: The Clarendon Press.

Gilling, D. (1997) *Crime Prevention: Theory, Policy and Practice.* London: UCL Press.

Hope, T. (1995) 'Community crime prevention', in M. Tonry and D. Farrington (eds), *Building a Safer Society.* Chicago: University of Chicago Press.

Hughes, G. (2000) 'In the shadow of crime and disorder: the contested politics of community safety', *Crime Prevention and Community Safety,* 2 (4): 47–60.

Pease, K. and Wiles, P. (2000) 'Crime prevention and community safety: Tweedledum and Tweedledee?', in K. Pease, S. Ballintyne and V. McLaren (eds), *Key Issues in Crime Prevention, Crime Reduction and Community Safety.* London: IPPR.

COMMUNITY SENTENCES

Definition

Penalties, imposed on offenders by criminal courts, that do not involve imprisonment. These include various forms of reprimand, financial penalties, supervision and unpaid work, and are sometimes referred to as 'non-custodial' sentences or 'alternatives to prison'.

Distinctive Features

Although community sentences vary around the world, it is possible to classify them in three ways: self-regulatory, financial and supervisory (Worrall, 1997). Self-regulatory penalties involve some form of public admonition or reprimand which is assumed to be sufficiently shaming of itself to deter the offender from further law-breaking. Financial penalties are of two kinds: fines are both retributive and deterrent in purpose and are generally paid to the central administration of a criminal justice system; compensation is paid (through the courts) to the victim of a crime and is intended to provide reparation. Supervisory sentences are imposed when courts believe that the offender is unable to stop committing crimes without support or surveillance and they may contain one or more of three elements: rehabilitation (through education, therapeutic programmes, counselling and welfare advice), reparation (through unpaid work for the community) and incapacitation (through curfews and electronic monitoring).

Some community sentences have long histories, while others have been introduced more recently. For example, in many countries the origins of probation (the main form of supervision) can be traced back to the late nineteenth century, whereas community service (unpaid work) was introduced in the 1960s and 1970s and electronic monitoring in the 1980s.

Expansion in the use of supervisory sentences since the 1970s has been due to a desire by many governments to be seen to be finding less expensive, but equally demanding, alternatives to imprisonment. This has been termed the 'decarceration' debate and resulted from a loss of confidence in the 1950s and 1960s in the 'rehabilitative ideal' (based on the discredited therapeutic possibilities of institutions). In reality, such expansion has been an accompaniment, rather than an alternative, to a rising prison population.

Evaluation

Community sentences have many advantages over imprisonment. They allow offenders to retain family, work and social ties while, at the same time, giving them the opportunity to repair the damage they have done to the community and resolve the personal and social problems which may have led to their offending in the first place. They enable an offender to avoid the stigma of imprisonment and the risk of becoming embedded in a criminal culture as the result of a constant association with other criminals in prison. Community sentences are also far less costly to administer than imprisonment.

Despite these advantages, community sentences have an 'image' problem. Although many more offenders receive some form of community sentence than are imprisoned, penal debates and policies focus overwhelmingly on prisons and neglect other forms of punishment. Attempts to raise the profile of community sentences have encountered a number of obstacles.

First, and of most significance, is the public and media perception that community sentences are but a poor substitute for the 'real punishment' of prison. Viewed as 'soft options', such sentences are often represented in policy documents as weak and undemanding 'let offs', which do not command public confidence. There is, therefore, a constant search undertaken by advocates of community sentences to include more and more demanding conditions which will distinguish 'intermediate sentences' (as they are sometimes called) from traditional welfare-oriented supervision (Byrne et al., 1992; Petersilia, 1998). Second is the obstacle of unfair and inconsistent sentencing. Despite increasingly sophisticated guidelines on the use of community sentences, there remain concerns that certain groups of offenders are overrepresented in prison for reasons that may have little to do with the seriousness of their offences. Community sentences tend to be available only to the relatively advantaged socially – those with sufficient money to pay a fine, those who are employed, and those who are perceived to be able to 'benefit' from supervision. Third is the obstacle of 'net-widening' – a term which entered the criminal justice vocabulary in the 1960s in the wake of labelling theory. With the proliferation of alternatives to custody comes the danger that instead of keeping people out of prison, community sentences will simply draw more and more people into the 'net' of the criminal justice system and thereby increase the likelihood that they will eventually end up in prison. With 'net-widening' comes the concept of the 'dispersal of discipline' (Cohen, 1985) which proposes that community sentences will extend the restrictions of liberty experienced in prison to the community outside the prison walls. The electronic monitoring of offenders in their own homes is a concrete example of this concept. The fourth obstacle is that of enforcement. Ensuring compliance with community sentences is notoriously difficult and courts have the right to send to prison any offender who fails to pay a fine or who breaches the conditions of a supervisory order. In this way, community sentences always function 'in the shadow' of imprisonment.

Anne Worrall

Associated Concepts: community justice, decarceration, electronic monitoring, incapacitation, net widening, probation, rehabilitation, reparation, restorative justice, shaming

Key Readings

Brownlee, I. (1998) *Community Punishment: A Critical Introduction.* Harlow: Addison Wesley Longman.

Byrne, J.M., Lurigio, A.J. and Petersilia, J. (1992) *Smart Sentencing: The Emergence of Intermediate Sanctions.* London: Sage.

Cohen, S. (1985) *Visions of Social Control.* Cambridge: Polity Press.

Mair, G. (1997) 'Community penalties and the probation service', in M. Maguire, R. Morgan and R. Reiner (eds), *The Oxford Handbook of Criminology,* 2nd edn. Oxford: Oxford University Press.

Petersilia, J. (ed.) (1998) *Community Corrections.* Oxford: Oxford University Press.

Worrall, A. (1997) *Punishment in the Community: The Future of Criminal Justice.* Harlow: Addison Wesley Longman.

COMPARATIVE CRIMINOLOGY AND CRIMINAL JUSTICE

Definition

Comparative studies of criminal justice seek to describe, explain, interpret and evaluate differences in the way offensive conduct is defined and sanctioned (Nelken, 2010).

Distinctive Features

Comparative studies may be interested in differences in what is and is not forbidden, in the justifications of punishment or regulation, in measures used to deal with conduct that is sanctioned, with who is involved (e.g., lay people or private business), or how crime and criminal justice is reported by the media

Studying what others do may just be a matter of curiosity – variously motivated, and even morbid on occasion. Whatever misgivings they may have about how their own system works, most people are even more suspicious of what goes on when their fellow citizens end up being tried abroad. But we may also have a more open-minded interest in apparently strange ideas and practices, including our own practices seen in the light of what others do and think. Comparative criminal justice, like criminology and criminal justice in general, is also an area of enquiry pursued because of its potential for policy application.

Those who undertake studies of this kind will seek to borrow some institution, practice, technique, idea or slogan so as to better realize their own values – or (sometimes) to change them. They may aim to learn from those places with high incarceration rates what *not* to do, or else try to become more like places with low prison rates such as Scandinavia or Japan. Alternatively they may want to help others change their systems, for example by exporting new police systems to South Africa or restoring the jury system in Russia. Or they may be moved to cooperate and collaborate in the face of 'common threats'. In order to achieve such aims they may also have to explain and understand how others go about making comparisons for their own practical purposes.

Many of those seeking to understand how things are done elsewhere will want to improve their own criminal justice systems by taking other places as a foil. Both Cavadino and Dignan (2006) and Lacey (2008), for example, offer explanations of the differences in prison rates in Europe so as to prove that a growing punitiveness is not the only game in town and not the sole path that can be taken. Lacey's recommendations are intended to show politicians in England and Wales that they can – if they wish – get themselves out of the hole they themselves have helped dig, where each party finds itself obliged to outbid the other on being 'tough on crime'. Taken too far, however, this line of argument becomes self-defeating. The reasons for why we make comparisons cannot provide the only criterion for a successful comparison. If we have failed to understand another system properly we can hardly make use of 'it' to throw light on our own arrangements. It remains true, however, that any cross-cultural comparison emerges from a given cultural context and has to be able to make sense to the audience(s) for whom it is intended.

Reference to cross-national and cross-cultural research may often be the best way to show criminology's claims to be more than local truths. But comparative criminal justice offers a number of other potential benefits (and challenges) that go beyond simply adding to the pool of potential variables that can be used in building criminological explanations. Trying to understand one place in light of another allows us to move closer to a holistic picture of how crime and its control are connected. Another (under-emphasized) benefit of the comparative approach is that it permits or even requires the sort of dialogue about who is entitled to define crime and criminal justice that is too often truncated in domestic criminology because of the hierarchy of credibility between those who write about crime and the usually low status offenders and deviants they write about.

By contrast, when comparative criminologists seek to describe or explain what goes on in other places they frequently find that there are locally-based criminologists (or others with high credibility) able and willing to take issue with them, whether they come to criticize or to praise. For many criminologists, the main interest of comparative criminal justice lies in the formulating and testing of explanatory hypotheses – for example regarding which countries use prison more. Others may be interested in evaluating a system, what goes on in the various 'stages' of criminal justice, or what is achieved by any of its constituent organizations or networks.

Evaluation

In learning about and evaluating other systems of criminal justice we need to navigate between two opposing (or at least contrasting) dangers. On the one hand there is the risk of being ethnocentric – of 'confusing the familiar with the necessary'. Here we will fall into the trap of assuming that the links between social factors, crime and criminal justice that we find persuasive are also ones that apply generally, and that what *we* do, our way of thinking about and responding to crime, is universally shared, or, at least, that it would be right for everyone else. Alternatively there is the temptation of relativism (which again can be either cognitive or normative). Here the claim is that we will never ever really grasp what others are doing, or that there can be no trans-cultural basis for evaluating whether what they or we do is right.

For some leading post-war authors the point of comparative work was precisely so as to 'uncover etiologic universals operative as causal agents irrespective of cultural differences between different countries'. The protocols of this kind of positivist 'scientific' approach to explanation guide cross-national literatures on matters such as the effects on crime of different penalties. Other comparative enquiries attempt to establish cross-national similarities in agency practices, for example in the ranking police give to the relative seriousness of various types of police misconduct (Klockars et al., 2004). There is currently renewed interest in establishing and spreading 'evidence-based', trans-cultural knowledge of 'what works' in responding to crime. By contrast, there are authors who contest this search for universals and suggest the point of comparative research is rather to undermine the pretensions of positivistic criminology. For them, a careful examination of foreign criminal justice practices suggests that it is above all the certainties buried in universalizing approaches to explanation – such as the claim that all systems will find ways of relieving case-load pressures (for example through plea-bargaining or its 'functional equivalents'), or that criminal law must always serve the interests of the powerful – that will turn out to be cultural rather than scientific truisms.

David Nelken

Associated Concepts: global criminology, globalization, policy transfer

Key Readings

Cavadino, M. and Dignan, J. (2006) *Penal Systems: A Comparative Approach.* London: Sage.
Klockars, C.B., Ivkovich, S.K. and Haberfeld, M.R. (eds) (2004) *The Contours of Police Integrity.* London: Sage.
Lacey, N. (2008) *The Prisoners' Dilemma: Political Economy and Punishment in Contemporary Democracies.* Cambridge: Cambridge University Press.
Larsen, N. and Smandych, R. (eds) (2008) *Global Criminology and Criminal Justice: Current Issues and Perspectives.* Buffalo, NY: Broadview.
Nelken, D. (2010) *Comparative Criminal Justice: Making Sense of Difference.* London: Sage.
Nelken, D. (ed.) (2011) *Comparative Criminal Justice and Globalisation.* Aldershot: Ashgate.

COMPARATIVE METHOD

Definition

The selection and analysis of cases which are similar in known ways and which differ in other ways, with a view to formulating or testing hypotheses.

Distinctive Features

The types of cases which are the basis for comparison can vary and include individuals, groups, institutions, situations, cultures, geographical areas and time periods. Where different societies or cultures are compared it is common to refer to cross-cultural comparison. Comparison can be used both to develop and to test hypotheses.

One way of developing hypotheses is by using the process of theoretical sampling, which is closely associated with qualitative, ethnographic research. This process involves the selection of cases for analysis (such as settings, groups or individuals) with a view to forming generalizations about how and why such cases differ. For example, this could involve the observation of beat police officers and criminal investigation officers in order to form generalizations about the differing ways in which they take decisions and the factors that influence this decision taking. Often comparison takes place by maximizing and minimizing differences, for example by ensuring that all officers are of the same age, sex, social class and ethnic background whilst they differ in terms of the nature of their police role and police training. The process can be continuous as the researcher seeks out new cases and maximizes and minimizes other differences in order to modify and extend hypotheses. For example, this could involve comparing decision making by beat and criminal investigation officers in both urban and rural areas. When no extra insight can be gained by further comparisons the stage of theoretical saturation has been reached. Another way of developing research questions or hypotheses is by the examination of 'deviant' or 'critical' cases in comparison with cases that are close to the norm. For example, this could involve comparing a geographical area that has an extremely high level of crime with areas that are close to the average in order to formulate generalizations about factors that could account for these differences of extreme.

Using comparison for hypothesis testing can be illustrated by forms of statistical analysis (although qualitative research also tests hypotheses, by using a process known as analytic induction). Assume that a researcher wishes to test a hypothesis that the level of crime in geographic areas is associated with levels of unemployment. This can be done by grouping areas according to their level of unemployment (high, medium, low). Each of the three categories of area will be measured in terms of their average level of crime, and statistical tests can be applied in order to provide evidence as to whether differences between the areas are so substantial and significant that levels of crime must be associated with levels of unemployment (or vice versa).

The comparative method is reflected in different research styles. For example, the use of quasi-experimental or evaluative designs to assess policy initiatives involves a comparison of the two groups or areas, one of which receives the policy initiative whilst the other does not. The two groups are compared before and after the introduction of the initiative with regard to the feature at which the policy is aimed. This two-way comparison (of two groups on a before–after basis) facilitates some evaluation of the effectiveness of the policy initiative. The comparative method in social surveys is illustrated by the way in which categories of people in a sample (for example, men and women; old and young) are compared in terms of their having or not having an attribute (for example, a scale that measures 'fear of crime'). Qualitative, ethnographic work emphasizes the development of generalizations and of 'grounded theory' by systematic comparisons of cases in terms of their similarities and differences. The cases that are compared will include interactions, social meanings, contexts, social actions and cultural groups. Because this is a continuous rather than a once and for all activity, it is sometimes referred to as the constant comparative method. Other methods that use comparison include content analysis (the comparison of documents), historical research (the comparison of historical periods) and analysis of official statistics (the comparison of areas, groups or time periods in terms of social indicators).

Comparison permeates different stages of research. For example, in research design it is illustrated by the ways in which samples are selected for study so as to compare subsets on some variables while holding others constant.

At the analysis stage different areas or social groups can be compared on a variable at the same point in time (cross-sectional analysis), or the same areas or groups can be compared on a variable at different points in time (longitudinal analysis). Sometimes the comparison will take place after the publication of results from several researchers working independently, for example, in examining the conclusions of projects from different parts of the world to consider how different societies deal with domestic disputes. In other cases researchers from different countries will collaborate to produce inter-societal comparisons (see for example Van Dijk et al., 1990; Mawby and Kirchoff, 1996).

Evaluation

Comparison is an essential part of research methodology. It involves deliberately seeking or anticipating comparisons between sets of observations. Without comparison with a baseline or against a control group it is not possible to reach plausible and credible conclusions. However, this requires the clear establishment of a baseline and the ability to control for factors the researcher does not wish to vary.

Victor Jupp

Associated Concepts: content analysis, ethnography, evaluation research, social survey

Key Readings

Mawby, R. and Kirchoff, G. (1996) 'Coping with crime: a comparison of victims' experiences in England and Germany', in P. Davies, P. Francis and V. Jupp (eds), *Understanding Victimization.* Newcastle: University of Northumbria Press.

May, T. (1997) *Social Research: Issues, Methods and Process.* Buckingham: Open University Press.

Van Dijk, J.J.M., Mayhew, P. and Killias, M. (1990) *Experiences From Across The World: Key Findings of the 1989 International Crime Survey.* Deventer, The Netherlands: Kluwer.

COMPSTAT

Definition

An abbreviation of either 'computer statistics' or 'comparative statistics'. It refers to the interactive managerial template that the New York Police Department (NYPD) constructed to drive up police performance in the high profile war against crime and disorder it launched in the mid-1990s.

Distinctive Features

By the early 1990s an assumed consensus emerged that criminality and lawlessness were such problems in New York that they were impacting not just on residents' quality of life but also on the very economic viability of the metropolis. In 1993, Rudolph W. Giuliani ran a successful mayoral campaign promising to implement tough measures to reverse the city's law and order crisis. William Bratton, Giuliani's new police commissioner, committed himself to reforming the NYPD to enable it to launch an unprecedented crackdown on crime across the city. Bratton, an enthusiastic supporter of Wilson and Kelling's 'broken windows' thesis, had previously restructured the New York Transit police to reclaim the subway system from petty criminals, drug addicts, beggars, youth gangs, graffiti artists and the homeless. The resultant crime-busting campaign in New York generated international headlines for Bratton's philosophy of 'zero-tolerance', 'quality-of-life', 'order maintenance' policing and also COMPSTAT, the managerial tool used to drive the anti-crime agenda.

According to Bratton, he had inherited a police department that was highly centralized, over-specialized and preoccupied with power and divisive in-house politics. A generation of senior NYPD officers had been socialized into a bunker mentality of avoiding public scandal and controversy. They had also been ideologically handcuffed by the findings of criminologists and police scholars who insisted that changes in policing strategy or extra resourcing would have little or no meaningful impact on the city's crime rate. The rank and file were thoroughly demoralized having been reduced to 'drive-on-by' tactics and community 'de-policing' in an effort to keep the crime statistics politically manageable. Bratton's deputy Jack Maple concluded that the NYPD had effectively surrendered the nation's premier city to the criminals and anti-social elements.

Bratton insisted that crime, disorder and fear could be dramatically reduced if the NYPD was re-formed as a proactive, crime-fighting organization with a 'work the streets to get results' mentality. He also realized from experience that if the radical multi-faceted reform process was rolled out on anything other than a departmental-wide basis, the new policies would be ignored, resisted or adhered to in a half-hearted, perfunctory manner. Bratton and his team integrated as many officers as possible into the proposed reform process, providing middle managers and front-line supervisors with the opportunity to identify what needed to be done to turn around the dysfunctional NYPD. Power and resources were subsequently decentralized to commanders, giving them the authority to run their precincts as mini-police departments and to take overall responsibility for driving down gun crime, drug crime, domestic violence, youth crime, auto crime, quality-of-life misdemeanours and police malpractice. The degree of control commanders exercised over personnel and resources was also expanded.

Popular accounts of Bratton's years in charge of the NYPD tend to focus on his operationalization of the 'broken windows' thesis. However, the NYPD was also reoriented managerially towards the idea of evidence-based policing interventions. The quality of the spatial and chronological crime data that the department was working with was enhanced. This necessitated overhauling the recording and reporting practices to produce accurate and timely intelligence on crime patterns and trends and introducing a relentless follow-up and assessment of the impact of police tactics. On a weekly basis, each police unit was required to compile a statistical summary of the week's crime as well as a briefing on significant cases, crime patterns and police activity. This was forwarded to what became known as the COMPSTAT unit where it was then collated and analysed to produce a weekly report which was both contemporaneous and comparative in nature.

At legendary COMPSTAT performance review meetings in the high-tech 'command centre' at NYPD headquarters, Precinct Commanders and those in charge of specialist units and teams were cross-questioned in a highly confrontational manner about what was being done to tackle crime 'hotspots', emerging crime trends and significant cases in their areas. These early morning meetings were attended by senior NYPD officers as well as representatives from other municipal departments and criminal justice agencies. As the presentations became more sophisticated, computerized, colour-coded maps and graphs of 'real time' crime and enforcement data were projected onto video projection screens to offer a much more detailed, multi-levelled analysis of how police tactics were impacting on crime and disorder across different neighbourhoods. COMPSTAT was also expanded to cross-reference data on 'quality-of-life' offences as well as data on neighbourhood demographics and dynamics gleaned from other municipal agencies and departments.

The COMPSTAT team was also able to generate Commander Profile Reports which were used to analyse: how well commanders were motivating and managing personnel; their effectiveness in addressing departmental priorities; their degree of understanding of the neighbourhood dynamics encompassed by the precinct. COMPSTAT therefore enabled the department to reach down into the organization in order to comprehend the quality of the human resources it had at its disposal. The underlying message disseminated through the COMPSTAT meetings was that as far as the NYPD was concerned, crime reduction was a business enterprise like any other. As a result of the 'rough and tumble' intensity of early COMPSTAT meetings, a significant number of Precinct Commanders opted for early retirement or were replaced. The full

COMPSTAT meetings were subsequently supplemented by precinct- and borough-level preparation and debriefing meetings.

Evaluation

According to Bratton and Maple, COMPSTAT – 'the Swiss Army knife of police management':

- mandated the NYPD to re-police the streets;
- installed an aggressive results-oriented accountability culture;
- re-established the principle of police custodianship of the city;
- identified and rewarded high-performing senior officers;
- encouraged a problem-solving, evidence-based mentality;
- tracked the impact of different forms of police activity and deployment levels;
- motivated officers to think outside of the existing bureaucratic box;
- broke down departmental insularity and a fiefdom mentality;
- spread a 'best practice' culture across the department;
- matched resources and personnel against priorities;
- pushed accountability relentlessly downwards, with each supervisory level of the organization interrogating the one below about performance matters.

Versions of COMPSTAT were adopted by other police departments for the following reasons. First, it coincided with an emerging consensus that the police had a vital if unfulfilled role to play in crime control. Second, it coincided with advances in the development of off-the-shelf GIS software that had relevance to policing problems. Third, COMPSTAT had legitimacy because it emerged from inside the police rather than being imposed by politicians. Fourth, it was very clear in its requirements and had no major resource implications. Fifth, COMPSTAT was part of a post-community policing strategy to empower police officers to get back to their core business of law enforcement and take pride in taking as many criminals off the streets as possible and restoring and maintaining order on behalf of the law-abiding citizen. Finally, it was directly associated with the first real success story in policing for decades. Even before COMPSTAT the crime rate had been falling in New York. However, it plunged in 1994 with a 12 per cent reduction in reported crime. This was followed by even more dramatic reductions in the next three years. The New York figures accounted for one-third of the decrease in crime in the USA in this period. By the late 1990s the NYPD had acquired the reputation of being the leader in big city policing. New York's COMPSTAT-driven crime figures seemed to prove that serious crime problems could be tackled by launching an aggressive attack on petty crime, anti-social behaviour and the most visible signs of neighbourhood disorder. Key personnel involved in the New York 'crime miracle' were recruited to command other US police departments and to advise police forces world-wide on how to 'fix windows', restore order and improve the quality of neighbourhood life.

Bratton's critics highlighted the negative consequences of COMPSTAT's macho 'blood on the carpet' version of crime reduction, noting how it was endorsing an aggressive street policing style that had little respect for civil liberties and was focused on a politically powerless underclass. Instances of police brutality, the unjustifiable use of force, and the paramilitarization of police attitudes were inevitable and would trigger anti-police sentiments in certain New York neighbourhoods. It was also pointed out that (a) crime had fallen in US cities that had opted for community policing rather than the NYPD model and (b) the crime crash in New York was due to a set of complicated, interconnected structural transformations rather than to COMPSTAT and 'broken windows'. Other critics argued that Bratton needed to acknowledge that many of the departmental changes which he took credit for had been initiated by a previous generation of police reformers in the NYPD.

Eugene McLaughlin

Associated Concepts: anti-social behaviour, 'broken windows', community policing, governance, managerialism, problem oriented policing, zero tolerance

Key Readings

Bratton, W. (1998) *Turnaround: How America's Top Cop Reversed the Crime Epidemic.* New York: Random House.
Giuliani, R.W. (2002) *Leadership.* New York: Talk Mirimax Books.
Green, J. (1999) 'Zero tolerance: a case study of police policies and practices in New York City', *Crime and Delinquency,* 45 (2): 171–87.
Karmen, A. (2000) *New York Murder Mystery: The True Story Behind the Crime Crash of the 1990s.* New York: New York University Press.
Kelling, G. and Coles, C. (1997) *Fixing Broken Windows.* New York: Free Press.
Maple, J. (1999) *The Crime Fighter: How You Can Make Your Community Crime Free.* New York: Broadway Books.

CONDITIONING

Definition

The processes by which an organism's behaviour is related to, or conditioned by, the environment; often used to mean *learning*.

Distinctive Features

In the history of psychology, the term conditioning is most closely associated with the Russian Nobel prizewinner Ivan Pavlov (1849–1936). Pavlov was a physiologist whose work was concerned with the canine digestive system: it was in the course of this experimental work that he observed an unusual pattern of salivation in dogs. Dogs naturally salivate at the sight of food (a reflex or *unconditioned response*), but Pavlov also observed that his dogs salivated at cues such as the sound of food pails in the laboratory.

Clearly dogs are not born with the capacity to salivate at the sound of clanking metal, so there must be another explanation for their behaviour. In a series of famous experimental studies Pavlov established that it was the close temporal pairing of sound and the appearance of food that elicited the wayward salivation. In other words, the sound became associated with the food so that the sound elicited the animal's behaviour. Thus, the salivation had become conditional to the sound and so could be thought of as a *conditioned response*. This process of learning by association is called *classical conditioning*.

The concept of classical conditioning is fundamentally important in advancing the position that the origins of behaviour lie not within the organism but are located in the environment. Thus, the way in which a person behaves can be understood by reference to that person's environment rather than their inner world.

The discovery of the phenomenon of learning by association surfaced alongside the emergent discipline of psychology in American universities in the early 1900s. At that time psychology in Europe was dominated by Freudian theory, so perhaps it is not surprising that the emerging New World departments of psychology searched for a fresh theoretical paradigm. The key figure in the struggle for this new paradigm was the academic researcher John B. Watson (1878–1958). Watson rejected the non-scientific theories prevalent in Europe and looked to formulate a new basis for psychology. In his vision the task would be to understand behaviour, not by drawing on the ghost in the machine of psychodynamic forces and the niceties of philosophical debate, but by producing empirical evidence that was firmly based within a scientific tradition. Such an experimental approach to psychology would be informed by evolutionary biology, neuroscience and the principles of conditioning. The focus of this endeavour would be behaviour, and the work of Pavlov and his contemporaries would be the starting point. Watson's position, expounded in a classic paper published in 1913, 'Psychology as the Behaviorist Views It', finally gave behaviourism to the academic world.

Can behaviour really be viewed as a string of classically conditioned responses? B.F. Skinner (1904–90) took Watson's vision and developed behaviourism into a dominant force in psychological method and thought. Acknowledging the role of learning by association, Skinner's significant contribution was to cultivate the notion of learning through the consequences of behaviour, and hence to the unfolding of *radical behaviourism*. In simple terms, Skinner's experimental work demonstrated that as behaviour acts upon the environment the resultant environmental consequences of that behaviour then act to increase or decrease the probability of future instances of such behaviour. A behaviour which produces consequences that the individual finds rewarding and then increases the rate of behaviour is said to be *reinforced*; a behaviour which produces consequences that the individual finds aversive and decreases the rate of behaviour is said to be *punished*. (In the technical sense used here, punishment simply means that a behaviour decreases in frequency.) Further, the organism learns that the environmental conditions, or setting events, will signal the likelihood that a certain behaviour will produce certain consequences. The relationship between a setting event, the behaviour and its consequences is called *a three-term contingency*. The process of learning through consequences is referred to as *operant* (or *instrumental*) *conditioning*.

In operant conditioning, behaviour is understood in terms of an interaction between the person and the environment. The environment influences the person and the person influences the environment. The range of environmental influences on our behaviour is vast: the list would encompass political, economic, educational and legal systems, images in the popular media, and the words and actions of friends, peers and parents. All of these environmental forces, to a greater or lesser extent, shape our behaviour; our behaviour, to a greater or lesser extent, moulds the world in which we live.

Evaluation

The notion of conditioning received a bad press in novels such as *Brave New World* and *Clockwork Orange*, which to some extent influenced popular views of the motives of advocates of theories of conditioning. Indeed, several academic and professional commentators have dismissed theories of learning by impugning the characters of their proponents.

It is noticeable that since Skinner's death several texts have attempted to give a more rounded picture of behaviourism (Nye, 1992; O'Donohue and Kitchener, 1999).

There are two critical lines to consider in the evaluation of conditioning. First, the rejection of mentalism as an explanatory concept, with the associated forsaking of free will as a vehicle for accounting for human actions. Second, the gap in understanding, at a psychological and physiological level, of the way in which conditioning takes place.

Clive Hollin

Associated Concepts: behaviour modification, cognitive-behaviourism, differential association, free will, opportunity theory, personality theory, rational choice theory, social learning theory

Key Readings

Bjork, D.W. (1993) *B.F. Skinner: A Life.* New York: Basic Books.
Davey, G. (ed.) (1981) *Applications of Conditioning Theory.* London: Methuen.
Lee, V.L. (1988) *Beyond Behaviorism.* Hillsdale, NJ: Lawrence Erlbaum.
Nye, R.D. (1992) *The Legacy of B.F. Skinner: Concepts and Perspectives, Controversies and Misunderstandings.* Belmont, CA: Wadsworth.
O'Donohue, W. and Kitchener, R. (eds) (1999) *Handbook of Behaviorism.* San Diego, CA: Academic Press.
Watson, J.B. (1913) 'Psychology as the behaviorist views it', *Psychological Review,* 20: 158–77.

CONFLICT THEORY

Definition

Conflict theory is usually contrasted with positivism or those theories that assume a basic consensus exists in society. It has taken three major forms. *Culture conflict* theory focuses on clashes between conduct norms. *Group conflict* theory relates such clashes directly to the position of elites and the wielding of political power. *Class conflict* theory views power differentials in the context of the systematic generation of structured inequalities in capitalist societies. All stress that to understand crime we must also understand the interests served by criminal law and the way in which those in authority use their power.

Distinctive Features

According to consensus theory, society is held together by a common acceptance of such basic values as right and wrong. Because of this common agreement social order is largely harmonious and predictable. On the other hand, conflict theory argues that there is little agreement on basic values. Society is composed of many competing groups, each of which promotes different interests. Conflict, rather than stability, is the fundamental characteristic of social order. Power and authority are reflections of social, economic and political inequality. Law is a means that the powerful use to enforce their own interests at the expense of others.

Thorsten Sellin (1938) was the first to argue that conflict causes crime. He noted that modern societies were characterized by social anonymity, poorly defined personal relationships and the existence of a wide variety of competing groups, which meant that however certain groups behaved they would always violate the norms of some other group. Crime occurs when the law of one group is extended to cover the domain of another (as in cultural migration) and when differentiation occurs within one group (as in disputes over law enforcement). The conduct which the state denotes as criminal is related directly to the decisions of those who wield political power and control the legislative and judicial manifestations of authority. George Vold (1958) extended this analysis through the concepts of 'group conflict' and 'political organization'. He argued that groups conflict with each other when the goals of one can be achieved only at the expense of others. Each of the many interest groups will attempt to secure its own interests by lobbying the legislature to enact laws in their favour. Groups that are able to do so will curb the behaviour of competing groups. As a result the process of law-making, law-breaking and law enforcement is a direct reflection of fundamental conflicts between interest groups and the relative power that they hold. Patterns of criminalization reflect the different degrees of political power wielded by various social groups. Criminality becomes a normal and natural response for groups struggling to maintain their own way of life.

During the 1960s several criminologists, also influenced by labelling, further refined criminological conflict theory. In the USA Austin Turk (1969) developed the thesis by accounting for specific processes of criminalization in societies based on relationships of conflict, domination and subordination between authorities and subjects. Richard Quinney's (1970) work set out a number of propositions to establish the social reality of crime. Crime was defined as human conduct created by authorized agents in a politically organized society. Criminal definitions describe behaviours that conflict with the interests of those who possess the power to shape public policy. The social reality of crime is constructed by the formulation and application of criminal definitions by 'certain social segments', their diffusion within the rest of society, the development of behaviour patterns related to criminal definitions and the construction of criminal conceptions. As such, the defining quality of crime lies not in criminal behaviour but in the power to criminalize. The greater the social conflict, the more likely it is that the powerful will criminalize the behaviour of those who would challenge their interests.

Chambliss (1975) and Quinney in his (1974) work subsequently developed conflict theory by relating such pluralist notions as 'social segments' to specific class divisions and specific modes of economic production. Class conflict theory, derived from Marxism, included the premises that:

- acts are defined as criminal because it is in the interest of the ruling class to define them as such;

- the ruling class will violate laws with impunity while members of the subject classes will be punished;
- criminal behaviour is a consequence of the repression and brutalization of capitalism;
- criminal law is an instrument of the state used to maintain the existing social order;
- crime diverts the working class's attention from the exploitation they experience; it contains their resistance;
- crime will persist in capitalist societies because of the fundamental tendency of such societies to promote inequality and class conflict.

In these ways, conflict theory has produced a series of complex analyses of why certain behaviours are criminalized by the state while others are not, and how a capitalist economic system is itself capable of generating certain patterns of crime.

Evaluation

Conflict theory has taken many forms within the rubric that conflict is natural to society. Initial formulations adopted an interactionist or pluralist view of conflicting interest groups; later formulations, influenced by Marxism or political anarchism, have emphasized the centrality of structured class inequalities and ruling class power. The heyday of conflict theory came with the political turmoil of 1960s and 1970s America. By the mid-1970s it had been largely superseded by the New Criminology and critical criminology that had developed in the UK. Its key propositions that law always arises from conflict and that criminalization always serves the interests of the ruling class have been severely tested. Such *a priori* generalizations have either been outrightly rejected by neo-conservative criminology or critiqued by critical criminology as one-dimensional and deterministic. Conflict theory tends to view the relationship between power and consciousness as relatively simple. It suggests that crime only exists when it is recognized by the powerful or when one is in a position of disadvantage in an unequal society. It fails to grasp adequately the fluidity and negotiation of class relations, whilst more or less ignoring those of 'race' and gender. But whatever its limitations its lasting legacy is to have started the process of politicizing criminology, turning attention to the fact that the study of crime cannot adequately proceed in isolation from the study of criminal law.

John Muncie

Associated Concepts: criminalization, critical criminology, interactionism, labelling, Marxist criminologies, new criminology, radical criminologies, the state

Key Readings

Chambliss, W. (1975) 'Toward a political economy of crime', *Theory and Society*, 2: 149–70.
Quinney, R. (1970) *The Social Reality of Crime.* Boston, MA: Little, Brown.
Quinney, R. (1974) *Critique of the Legal Order.* Boston, MA: Little, Brown.
Sellin, T. (1938) *Culture, Conflict and Crime.* New York: Social Science Research Council.
Turk, A. (1969) *Criminality and Legal Order.* Chicago, IL: Rand McNally.
Vold, G. (1958) *Theoretical Criminology.* New York: Oxford University Press.

CONFORMITY

See: Social control theory

CONSTITUTIVE CRIMINOLOGY

Definition

A postmodernist theoretical perspective that draws on several critical social theories, most notably symbolic interactionism, phenomenology, social constructionism, structural Marxism, structuration theory, semiotics, chaos theory and affirmative postmodernism. The core of the constitutive argument is that crime and its control cannot be separated from the totality of the structural and cultural contexts in which it is produced, nor can it lose sight of human agents' contribution to those contexts (Henry and Milovanovic, 1994, 1996).

Distinctive Features

Constitutive theory rejects the argument of traditional modernist criminology that crime and offenders can be separated from social processes of societal production and analysed and corrected in isolation from the whole. Nor is crime understandable as a determined product of cultures and structures. Instead of setting out to identify factors that 'cause' offending, constitutive criminology seeks to examine the relations that co-produce crime.

Constitutive criminology is founded on the proposition that humans are responsible for actively creating their world with others. They do this by transforming their surroundings through interaction with others, not least via discourse. Through language and symbolic representation humans identify differences, construct categories, and share a belief in the reality of that which is constructed that orders otherwise chaotic states. It is towards these social constructions of reality that humans act.

In the process of investing energy in their socially constructed, discursively organized categories of order and reality, human subjects not only shape their social world; they are also shaped by it. They are co-producers and co-productions of their own and others' agency. Constitutive criminology is about how some of this socially constructed order, as well as some of the human subjects constituted within it, can be harmed, impaired and destroyed both by the process and by what is built during that process: ultimately, by each other as fellow subjects.

Constitutive theorists argue that the co-production of harmful relations occurs through society's structure and culture, as these are energized by active human subjects – not only as offenders, but also as social categories such as victims, criminal justice practitioners, academics, commentators, media reporters and producers of film and TV crime shows, and most generally, as investors, producers and consumers in the crime business. They look at what it is about the psycho-socio-cultural matrix (the cloth of crime) that provides the discursive medium through which human agents construct 'meaningful' harms to others. The approach taken, therefore, shifts the criminological focus away from narrow dichotomized issues focusing either on the individual offender or on the social environment. Instead, constitutive criminology takes a holistic conception of the relationship between the 'individual' and 'society' which prioritizes neither one nor the other, but examines their mutuality and interrelationship.

According to constitutive criminologists, a major source of harmful relations emanates from structures of power. Unequal power relations, built on the constructions of difference, provide the conditions that define crime as harm. Constitutive criminology defines crime as the harm resulting from humans investing energy in harm-producing relations of power. Humans suffering such 'crimes' are in relations of inequality. Crimes are nothing less than people being disrespected. People are disrespected in numerous ways but all of these have to do with denying or preventing us becoming fully social beings. What is human is to make a difference to the world, to act on it, to interact with others, and together to transform the environment and ourselves. If this process is prevented we become less than human; we are harmed. Thus constitutive criminologists define crime as 'the power to deny others their ability to make a difference' (Henry and Milovanovic, 1996: 116).

Constitutive criminology also has a different definition of criminals and victims from that of modernist criminological theories. The offender is viewed as an 'excessive investor' in the power to dominate others. Such 'investors' put energy into creating and magnifying the differences between themselves and others. This investment of energy disadvantages, disables and destroys others' human potentialities. The victim is viewed as a 'recovering subject', still with untapped human potential but also a damaged faith in humanity. Victims are more entrenched, more disabled, and suffer loss. Victims 'suffer the pain of being denied their own humanity, the power to make a difference. The victim of crime is thus rendered a nonperson, a non-human, or less complete being' (Henry and Milovanovic, 1996: 116).

This reconception of crime, offender and victim thus locates criminality not in the person, nor in the structure or culture, but in the ongoing creation of social identities through discourse, and leads to a different notion of crime causation. To the constitutive theorist crime is not so much *caused* as *discursively constructed* through human processes of which it is but one. Consciously striving to reconstruct the discourse of the excessive investor at both a societal and a systemic level, crime feeds off itself, expanding and consuming the energies intended to control it. Put simply, crime is the co-produced outcome not only of humans and their environment but also of human agents and the wider society, through its excessive investment – to the point of obsession – in crime, through crime shows, crime dramas, crime documentaries, crime news, crime books, crime films, crime precautions, criminal justice agencies, criminal lawyers and criminologists. All are parasitic of the crime problem, but as constitutive criminology suggests, they also contribute to its ongoing social and cultural production and its ongoing reproduction.

Evaluation

The implications of constitutive theory are first, that crime must be deconstructed as a recurrent discursive process, and second, that conscious attempts must be made at reconstruction with a view to preventing recurrence. Given this interrelated nature of social structures and human agents and their social and cultural productions in the co-production of crime, constitutive criminology calls for a justice policy of reconstruction. This is achieved through *replacement discourse* that 'is directed toward the dual process of deconstructing prevailing structures of meaning and displacing them with new conceptions, distinctions, words and phrases, which convey alternative meanings ... Replacement discourse, then, is not simply critical and oppositional, but provides both a critique and an alternative vision' (Henry and Milovanovic, 1996: 204–5). The new replacement constructions are designed to displace crime as moments in the exercise of power and as control. They offer an alternative medium by which social constructions of reality can take place. This is not a unitary medium but, as Smart (1990: 82) has argued, refers instead to 'subjugated knowledges, which tell different stories and have different specificities' and which aim at 'the deconstruction of truth' and the power effects of claims to truth. Instead of replacing one truth with another, replacement discourse invokes a 'multiplicity of resistances' to the ubiquity of power (1990: 82). Beyond resistances, the concept of replacement discourse offers a celebration of unofficial, informal, discounted and ignored knowledges through its discursive diversity. In terms of diminishing the harm experienced from all types of crime (street, corporate, state, hate, etc.), constitutive criminology talks of 'liberating' replacement discourses that seek a transformation of both the prevailing political economies and the associated practices of crime and social control. Constitutive criminology thus simultaneously argues for an ideological as well as a materialistic change; one without the other renders change that is only in partial. In short, constitutive criminology argues for a transpraxis which is deconstructive, reconstructive and sensitive to the dialectics of struggle.

Stuart Henry and Dragan Milovanovic

Associated Concepts: chaos theory, crime, deconstruction, Marxist criminologies, newsmaking criminology, postmodernism, praxis, social harm

Key Readings

Barak, G. (1994) *Media Process and the Social Construction of Crime: Studies in Newsmaking Criminology.* New York: Garland.

Henry, S. and Milovanovic, D. (1994) 'The constitution of constitutive criminology', in D. Nelken (ed.), *The Futures of Criminology.* London: Sage.

Henry, S. and Milovanovic, D. (1996) *Constitutive Criminology: Beyond Postmodernism.* London: Sage.

Henry, S. and Milovanovic, D. (eds) (1999) *Constitutive Criminology at Work: Applications to Crime and Punishment.* New York: State University of New York Press.

Smart, C. (1990) 'Feminist approaches to criminology, or postmodern woman meets atavistic man', in L. Gelsthorpe and A. Morris (eds), *Feminist Perspectives in Criminology.* Milton Keynes: Open University Press. pp. 70–84.

CONTAINMENT THEORY

Definition

Developed by Walter Reckless in the 1950s, this social-psychological approach to understanding the causes of crime and conformity falls under the more general heading of social control theories. The main assumption is that strong inner controls (especially a positive self-concept) and outer controls (particularly the family) act to insulate or buffer adolescents from delinquency.

Distinctive Features

Containment theory is one of a number of related social control explanations that depict how social-psychological factors as well as social institutions restrain individuals from violating societal norms. Reckless (1967) is credited with developing this theoretical approach during the 1950s and 1960s. As one of the earlier social control theorists, he was curious as to why some boys in high crime neighbourhoods did not break the law. He speculated that a positive self-concept or attitude (inner containment) was the key variable that could explain why some did not turn to crime even in the face of outside or external pressures, especially delinquent peers.

Reckless divided explanatory factors into two general categories: those that are either 'inner' or 'outer' to the individual psyche, and those variables that act as either criminogenic or controlling behavioural influences. Inner containment and pushes are internal social-psychological influences, whereas outer containments, pressures and pulls are external to the individual. Inner and outer containments act as defences against deviation, thus insulating or buffering a young person from the criminogenic influences of society's pushes and pulls.

Inner pushes are social-psychological states and include such factors as a need for immediate gratification, hostility, restlessness, discontent, alienation and frustration. *External pressures and pulls* include deviant companions, membership of criminal subcultures, poverty, unemployment, limited occupational opportunities, a minority status and other inequalities.

Outer containments are external to the individual psyche or personality and act as buffers or insulators, encouraging conformity to the community and legal norms. External controls include effective parental supervision and discipline, conforming or positive peer influences, membership of organizations interested in the activities of their members, etc. *Inner containments* are self-controls that develop during socialization and include such components as a good self-concept, goal directedness, a well-developed superego, and a high frustration tolerance. Inner containment is also generally seen as a product of favourable external socializing agencies such as teachers and peers and especially parents.

Although both inner and outer containments comprise defences against deviance, inner containments (especially a positive self-concept) received the most theoretical and empirical attention from Reckless and his associate Dinitz (1967). Together they spent over a decade investigating the effects of inner containment, concluding that a precondition of conforming behaviour is a positive self-concept which acts as an insulator against delinquency. Indeed, they argued that young people growing up even in the most criminogenic areas can insulate themselves against deviance through the maintenance of what they considered to be the strongest defence against delinquency – a positive self-concept.

If a young person's outer containments are weak, the internal and external pressures and pulls must be controlled by the inner control system. On the other hand, if the outer buffers are strong and effective, the inner containment system does not have to play such a significant role. Thus, Reckless believed that strong inner containments could compensate for weak outer containments, and vice versa. His 'Prediction Model' specified that deviance would be greatest when both inner and outer controls are weak and lowest when both control systems are strong. In those instances in which one is weak and the other strong, he believed that weak inner containment would have a higher probability of criminality than weak outer containment.

Evaluation

Despite claims by Reckless that containment theory could explain most forms of delinquency – that it is both social and psychological in nature, and that unlike most other (macro) theories it can be used to explain individual case histories – the theory has been harshly criticized. Many consider its concepts too vague and the theory too broad to produce testable hypotheses. No conceptual information is offered concerning the interrelations among delinquency and the various combinations of inner and outer containment and environmental pressures, pushes and pulls. Accordingly, no interactions are hypothesized among inner and outer containments, pushes and pulls. Jensen (1970) points out that, other than his rather vaguely stated 'prediction model', Reckless's theory appears to be little more than an inadequate classification scheme, since apparently there is no rationale for classifying its variables as pushes, pulls or inner and outer containments other than in terms of the behaviours to be explained.

Although differential involvement in delinquency is explained somewhat differently by the various social control theories, there is much conceptual overlap between Reckless and subsequent theorists such as Hirschi (1969). For example, 'delinquent companions' (environmental pulls or attachments), 'conventional activities' (outer containment or involvement), 'educational expectations' (inner containment or commitment), and 'attitudes toward the law' (inner containment or belief) are variables and concepts that are integral to both theories (Rankin, 1977).

Nevertheless, Reckless's theory has been criticized as conceptually vague, with little empirical evidence that a positive self-concept or self-esteem is negatively related to crime and delinquency. In addition he did not explain *why a* negative self-concept makes adolescents vulnerable to delinquency, nor could he account for those adolescents with bad self-concepts who were not delinquent. A number of research studies found little association between self-esteem and delinquency – a finding that was contrary to the key containment hypothesis. Thus, the main flaw of containment theory is this lack of empirical evidence linking the concept to crime and delinquency. This has led to containment theory being superseded by subsequent social control theories, especially Hirschi's (1969) theory of the social bond.

Joseph Rankin and Roger Kern

Associated Concepts: neutralization (techniques of), social control theory

Key Readings

Hirschi, T. (1969) *Causes of Delinquency.* Berkeley, CA: University of California Press.
Jensen, G. (1970) 'Containment and delinquency: analysis of a theory', *University of Washington Journal of Sociology*, 2: 1–14.
Rankin, J. (1977) 'Investigating the interrelations among social control variables and conformity', *Journal of Criminal Law and Criminology*, 67: 470–80.
Reckless, W. (1967) *The Crime Problem.* New York: Appleton-Century-Crofts.
Reckless, W. and Dinitz, S. (1967) 'Pioneering with self-concept as a vulnerability factor in delinquency', *Journal of Criminal Law, Criminology and Police Science*, 58: 515–23.

CONTENT ANALYSIS

Definition

A strategy of research which stresses an objective, systematic and quantitative approach to the analysis of documents. Typically, it is concerned with the manifest content and surface meaning of a document rather than with deeper layers of meanings or with differing interpretations which can be placed on the same content.

Distinctive Features

In its widest sense, content analysis can refer to analysis of the content of all types of document by whatever means. The range of documents examined by criminologists can include diaries, letters, newspapers, magazines, stories, essays, official documents, memoranda and research reports. Here, content analysis is used in a specific sense to refer to the positivist approach to documentary analysis which, according to Holsti (1969), has the following features. First, the procedures should be objective in that each step in the research process should be carried out on the basis of explicitly formulated rules so that different researchers following the same procedures will get the same results. Second, procedures must be systematic, that is, rules must be applied with consistency. Third, content analysis should have generality, by which is meant that findings must have theoretical relevance. Fourth, content analysis should be quantitative and include counting the frequency with which certain words or themes appear in documents. Finally, content analysis should be concerned with the manifest content and surface meaning of a text rather than with deeper layers of meaning.

Typically, research designs will cluster around one or more of the following questions: What are the characteristics of the content? What inferences can be made about the causes and generation of content? What inferences can be made about the effects of content on readers or viewers? For example, in characterizing films watched by adolescents the researcher may categorize these as 'high', 'medium' or 'low' in terms of violence by counting the number of actions in each film which s/he defines as 'violent'. Or research on the images of youth portrayed by popular newspapers may categorize and count the number of articles which portray a 'positive', 'negative' or 'neutral' image. In such cases, the definition of the relevant categories comes from the researcher. Once the categories are delineated, the analysis of content is often a technical process and may be carried out using the appropriate computer software.

Evaluation

The positivist approach to content analysis emphasizes the manifest contents of documents which are subsequently categorized according to definitions provided by the researcher. The latent meanings of the content and the possibility of differing interpretations by 'producers' and 'receivers' are not treated as problematic nor as a prime focus of interest. By way of contrast, an interpretative (or interactionist) approach places social meanings at the centre of any analysis, that is, meanings attributed to the contents of documents by producers and by the variety of audiences. In doing so, the interpretative tradition is at odds with the positivist assumptions of a correspondence between intent, content and effect on different audiences and also at odds with the belief that there is a common universe of meanings uniting all relevant parties. What the interpretative tradition brings to the research agenda is a focus on the ways in which meanings are assigned both by authors and audiences and the subsequent consequences. It would, for example, be interested in the ways in which the same documents placed before a court of law

can be interpreted differently by defendants, prosecutors, jurors and the judge. The interpretative approach to documents is very close to the ethnographic tradition in social research.

Whilst accepting the possibility of a multiplicity of meanings and interpretations, the critical tradition adds further dimensions, for example by examining the ways in which the contents of documents come to be treated as 'knowledge' and also the role of such knowledge in the exercise of power. This could be at a societal level, by analysing the ways in which official reports define certain forms of action as illegitimate and thereby justify the exercise of state power against certain sections of society; or it can be at a micro level, by analysing the ways in which police and probation records result in the ways in which an individual is dealt with in the criminal justice system.

Victor Jupp

Associated Concepts: documentary analysis, ethnography, interactionism, positivism

Key Readings

Holsti, O.R. (1969) *Content Analysis for the Social Sciences and Humanities*. Reading, MA: Addison-Wesley.

Jupp, V.R. and Norris, C. (1993) 'Traditions in documentary analysis', in M. Hammersley (ed.), *Social Research: Philosophy, Politics and Practice*. London: Sage.

Scott, J. (1990) *A Matter of Record*. Cambridge: Polity Press.

CONTROL BALANCE THEORY

Definition

A general, integrated theory to explain deviant behaviour by individuals or organizations, although it explains conformity and submission as well. Deviant behaviour consists of acts disapproved of by the majority of a group or that typically bring about negative social reactions. Since criminal behaviour is usually deviant, the theory also explains most crime.

Distinctive Features

Theoretically, the likelihood of deviance in some form is predictable from a *control imbalance* and a motivation-producing provocation. A *control imbalance* exists when the control a social entity (individual or organization) can exercise over things, circumstances or individuals is greater or less than the control to which the social entity is subject. Relative amounts of total control are registered as control ratios, which can show balance, deficits or surpluses.

With a given control imbalance and a motivating provocation, specific deviance is chosen from acts within a restricted range of *control balance desirability* (CBD). Since the degree of CBD varies among acts, all misbehaviours can be arrayed over a continuum of CBD. The range of the CBD continuum from which an act is chosen is related to a person's control ratio, opportunity, possible counter-control the act will likely attract, and the person's self-control. Choosing a particular deviant act is called control balancing – weighing the perceived gain in *control* from possible deviant behaviour against the counter-control that it may produce.

Being rooted in social statuses, personal characteristics and organizational affiliations, control ratios are global and situational. All people are assumed to want to gain more control, regardless of how much or how little they already have, and actors are assumed to rely principally on deviant behaviour in trying to overcome *control imbalances*. However, a pre-existing desire to extend control does not produce deviance unless it is brought into awareness by situational circumstances, and other conditions also exist. Actors become motivated toward deviance when sharply reminded of their control imbalances, especially if these reminders involve denigration or humiliation and they perceive that deviance can help. Motivation may lead to deviance

if the behaviour is possible in the situation (opportunity) and the potential counter-controls do not outweigh (or are not perceived as outweighing) the potential gain in control to be realized from misbehaviour. Because opportunities for deviance of some kind are omnipresent and the chances of controlling reactions are highly variable, some kinds of deviance will always provide favourable balances. As a result, the strength of motivation predicts the chances of deviance in some form. If researchers measure the chances of subjects committing each of a large number of deviant acts, along with their control ratios and motivation, they should find those with control imbalances who are motivated to be much more likely to commit one or more of the acts than are those with balanced controls. The control ratio and motivation, however, are not sufficient to predict the exact act to be committed.

Because serious deviant acts have the greatest potential for increasing one's control, a motivated person will first contemplate committing one or more of them. But serious acts also imply great potential counter-control. Therefore, only those with small control deficits or any degree of control surplus can realistically resort to serious misbehaviour. As a result, deviantly motivated people will cognitively slide along a continuum of CBD to find an 'appropriate' deviant act. Those with balanced control ratios are more conformist because they are less likely to become motivated toward deviance and they face greater potential counter-control. By contrast, overwhelming control deficits will reduce the ability to imagine alternatives, leading to submission.

Those with control deficiencies are frequently motivated by reminders of their relative helplessness while those with surpluses are often motivated by not receiving the deference they expect. The specific act of deviance resulting from a converge of a control imbalance, provocation and motivation, opportunity, and control balancing reflects its CBD, which is composed of two elements: (1) the act's likely long-range effectiveness in altering a control imbalance; and (2) the extent to which the act requires the direct and personal involvement of the perpetrator with a victim or an object affected by the deviance. When the theory's theoretical causal variables converge for a given individual, that person will choose from among various deviant acts with *similar scores* on the CBD continuum.

An actor with a control ratio between the second and third quartiles of a continuum from maximum deficit to maximum surplus (excluding the balanced zone) is liable for acts somewhere between the second and third quartiles of CBD, provided that: the actor has sufficient self-control to avoid 'unrealistic' action; there is opportunity to do them; and the risk of counter-control does not outweigh the gain from the deviant act. The choice of deviant act is also influenced by such things as moral commitments, intelligence, habits and personality.

Thus, an unbalanced control ratio, in combination with deviant motivation, will lead to the choice of a specific deviant act within a restricted range on the CBD continuum. The zone from which the deviant act is chosen narrows with the increasing inclusion of theoretical variables. Taking all the theoretical variables into account allows the range of likely deviant acts to be quite narrow, though it may still contain a large number of different acts with similar CBD. Thus, the theory cannot predict the choice of a specific deviant act, such as stealing an object or assaulting a spouse.

Evaluation

The validity of the theory currently rests mainly on argument. The original statement (Tittle, 1995) was quickly recognized as worthy of attention, but only limited tests were conducted. The research that was conducted, though challenging some aspects of the theory, nevertheless suggests that control imbalances are important predictors of deviance. Those empirical challenges and logical critiques led to a major revision (Tittle, 2004a). That refined version has not yet been tested, so whether the theory fulfils its theoretical promise remains to be seen.

Charles R. Tittle

Associated Concepts: opportunity theory, prediction studies, rational choice theory, social control theory

Key Readings

Tittle, C.R. (1995) *Control Balance: Toward a General Theory of Deviance.* Boulder, CO: Westview.
Tittle, C.R. (2001) 'Control balance', in R. Paternoster and R. Bachman (eds), *Contemporary Theories.* Los Angeles, CA: Roxbury. pp. 315–34.
Tittle, C.R. (2004a) 'Refining control balance theory', *Theoretical Criminology*, 8: 167–184.
Tittle, C.R. (2004b) 'Control balance theory and violence', in M.A. Zahn, H. Brownstein and S.L. Jackson (eds), *Violence: From Theory to Research.* Cincinnati, OH: Anderson.

CONTROL THEORY

See: Containment theory; Control balance theory; Social control theory

CONVERSATIONAL ANALYSIS

Definition

A research methodology in the social sciences which analyses naturally occurring conversation systematically, using tape recordings and transcripts. It aims to 'describe people's methods for producing orderly social interaction' (Silverman, 1993: 120).

Distinctive Features

Conversational analysis is a research technique particularly associated with the broader research perspective of ethnomethodology, which emerged in the 1960s as a reaction against the 'grand theorizing' and 'abstracted empiricism' of earlier sociologists such as Talcott Parsons (Heritage, 1984). Ethnomethodology emphasizes the importance of studying the ways in which people routinely ascribe meaning to daily events in specific, local, social contexts. Consequently, the ways in which people talk to each other become worthy of study in their own right. This emphasis on naturally occurring speech counteracted previous preferences for researcher-dominated methods such as structured interviews, observation or the experimental manipulation of behaviour. All these approaches, it was argued, produced only 'glossed' or idealized interpretations of how research subjects presented themselves within a pre-conceived theoretical framework and denied the researcher access to the genuine 'raw' data of mundane social interaction.

The underlying assumptions of conversational analysis are that spoken interaction is organized in identifiable, stable structural patterns and that its meaning is dependent on the context. Therefore, it is not possible to engage in *a priori* theoretical construction or interpretation of motives or meaning, in the absence of a detailed examination of actual conversation. It is also important that no aspect of the conversation (for example, pauses or overlapping speech) should be dismissed as irrelevant. For this reason, conversations must be tape recorded and later transcripts will need to include every detail of the process, rather than being 'tidied-up' versions of interviews. Analysis of transcripts involves paying close attention to the sequencing of timed intervals and the characteristics of speech production such as volume, emphasis and intonation. These features are indicated by the use of written symbols which constitute the agreed conventions of conversational analysis (Ten Have, 1999).

The core tool of conversational analysis is the concept of the 'adjacency pair', a term used by Harvey Sacks (Heritage, 1984) to describe a sequence of two utterances which are adjacent, produced by different speakers, ordered as a first and second part and in such a way as the first part requires a particular second part. Examples of common adjacent pairs are 'question–answer', 'greeting–greeting', 'offer–acceptance/refusal'. The concept of the 'adjacency pair' is a template not only for describing conversational action but also for interpreting it. It can be used to demonstrate how the first speaker uses his or her action as the basis for interpreting the second speaker's response – and how the second speaker then continues the process. This sequencing leads on to the other key aspect of conversational analysis which concerns an obligation on the part of participants to listen, understand and turn-take. Turn-taking is viewed as the mechanism by which actors will display to each other that they are engaged in social interaction. A violation of this turn-taking (for example, by interrupting, 'talking over' someone, or failing to respond to an invitation to speak) indicates a failure of social competence. Conversational analysis is also interested in 'lexical choice' – the words and descriptive terms which speakers select in differing contexts – and in 'interactional asymmetries'. Heritage (1997) identifies four potential sources of asymmetry which may exist between participants in institutional talk – inequalities of status, 'knowhow' (that is, an understanding of the institution), knowledge and rights to knowledge. All these factors would shape, and would also be detectable in, any conversation between, for example, a magistrate, a solicitor and a defendant in court.

Evaluation

Although conversational analysis is a useful tool for studying ordinary interactions in a variety of criminologically relevant situations, it may be of particular value in the study of 'institutional talk'. Here, an understanding of the basic structures and sequences of conversation can be extended to an understanding of how criminal justice institutions, such as courts and prisons, function (Atkinson and Drew, 1979). Of particular interest are the ways in which professionals routinely legitimate or account for their actions. However, conversational analysis is a highly technical methodology which is not readily accessible to novice researchers. Of more practical use may be the similar, but broader and less technical approach of discourse analysis.

Anne Worrall

Associated Concepts: discourse analysis, ethnography

Key Readings

Atkinson, J.M. (1982) 'Understanding formality: the categorization and production of "formal" interaction', *British Journal of Sociology*, 33: 86–117.
Atkinson, J.M. and Drew, P. (1979) *Order in Court: The Organization of Verbal Interaction in Judicial Settings.* London: Macmillan.
Heritage, J. (1984) *Garfinkel and Ethnomethodology.* Cambridge: Polity Press.
Heritage, J. (1997) 'Conversation analysis and institutional talk', in D. Silverman (ed.), *Qualitative Research: Theory, Methods and Practice.* London: Sage.
Silverman, D. (1993) *Interpreting Qualitative Data: Methods for Analysing Talk, Text and Interaction.* London: Sage.
Ten Have, P. (1999) *Doing Conversation Analysis: A Practical Guide.* London: Sage.

CONVICT CRIMINOLOGY

Definition

Convict criminology is a branch of critical criminology started by convict and ex-convict academics who were dissatisfied with mainstream criminological considerations of crime, crime control and justice. It is fundamentally concerned with challenging existing definitions of crime, the over-reliance on prison, and the shortcomings and injustices of the criminal justice system. Convict criminology emerged, in part, out of dissatisfaction amongst ex-convict and convict students and academics with the research, theory and academic work on prisons and prisoners. In addition, however, it was a response to the continued failure of mainstream criminologists, the general public and criminal justice practitioners to fully appreciate the convict perspective. This failure, according to convict criminology, is evidenced in the persistent representation of convicts as 'inferior' or 'deviant' and the continued tolerance of criminal justice processes that are inhumane and counterproductive (Ross and Richards, 2003).

Distinctive Features

Convict criminology first emerged in the United States where imprisonment rates are – by far – the highest in the world. Its development as a distinctive area of criminology was facilitated by the organization of a special session of 'convict criminologists' at the 1997 American Society of Criminology (ASC) annual meeting. Amongst those in attendance were Charles Terry, Alan Mobely, Richard S. Jones, Stephen C. Richards and Edward Tromanhauser, and the 'original felonious sociologist', John Irwin (Irwin, 1970; now sadly deceased). Jeffrey Ian Ross and Stephen Richards (2003: 2–5) argued that six factors contributed to the formation of, and the idea for, a branch of criminology informed primarily by the perspectives of convicts and ex-convicts. First, despite the formidable gains made in theoretical criminology by critical and radical perspectives that had begun to highlight the structural inequalities, injustices and failures of criminal justice, much of even critical criminological scholarship remained the work of privileged intellectuals. There persisted, therefore, a lack of scholarly work that fully appreciated the perspectives and experiences of those caught up in criminal justice processes. Second, developments within victimology and the emergence of constitutive criminology created a space and method for the voices of marginalized groups and their experiences to be expressed and for these to form 'replacement discourses' (Ross and Richards, 2003: 3; see also Henry and Milovanovic, 1996). This broader movement within criminology created the opportunity for convict voices to contribute to wider criminological and penological debates. Third, and perhaps most obviously, the continued failure of prisons, and the persistent lack of acknowledgement in society, political discourse and mainstream (particularly administrative) criminology of the completeness of this failure, demanded illumination from a convict perspective. Fourth, the growing strength of prisoners' rights movements in the United States in particular assisted in raising the consciousness of convicts and ex-convicts regarding the legal and political injustices that they were being subjected to. Fifth, despite the fact that writings on prison life from an insider perspective have been with us as long as prison itself, it cannot be said that the majority of these formed a coherent body of work. Many prison texts were not written with the intention of grounding them in academic theory or method. The notion of forming a 'school' of convict criminology, therefore, emerged in part as a movement seeking to encourage and facilitate more autoethnographic and other research accounts of prisons and crime by academics-turned-convicts or convicts-turned-academics. Finally, and related to the previous point, the emergence of convict criminology might also be seen as an inevitable result of existing convict criminologists applying ethnographic methods to describe and analyse their research area. The centrality of ethnography in the work of convict criminologists has added considerable depth to the foregoing body of penological work that has used quasi-ethnographic methods to understand prison life. The formation of the school of convict criminology highlights a crucial point, namely that the ethnographic accounts of convict criminologists are, of course, true ethnographies, which other non-convict criminologists are unable to undertake. As such, convict criminology has been able to establish a firm ground from which to challenge ethnographic or other types of prison research, conducted by non-convict researchers, that fail to adequately capture the perceptions and experiences of prisoners.

Convict criminology was formed, and continues to be led by, ex-convicts who are now academic faculty. It is explicitly not, however, an elitist branch of criminology and is principled about not being so. Those who count themselves amongst the convict criminological community possess varying levels of academic achievement and skill. The 'school' aims for inclusivity and collaboration on the common project of building first-hand expertise into the subject matter of criminology and its methods (Ross and Richards, 2003: 6). Further, the growing number of convict criminologists who carry academic credentials strongly positions them to challenge the way crime is constructed, to argue against the persistence of viewing it as the result of 'individual pathology', and to debate the power structures associated with defining 'what crime is' and who the targets of criminal 'justice' are.

The academic project of convict criminology is to challenge mainstream (particularly administrative) criminology and criminal justice and penal practice. The social justice movement within convict criminology is, first, to transform the way prison research is conducted, and second, to work toward policy forms that centralize the humanity of those who become caught up in the criminal justice system in order to make its processes significantly more humane (Ross and Richards, 2003: 10).

Evaluation

Convict criminology is still a small school within critical criminology, but growing. It has members from around the world, though its strongest base still remains within the United States. It offers an important contribution to criminological knowledge from the first-hand perspectives and expertise of those who have been victimized by the processes of the criminal justice system. Importantly, convict criminology as a strand of critical criminology unites the voices of ever increasing numbers of men and women whose research draws on first-hand experiences of the harms associated with prison and the way crime is constructed and controlled. This activist component of convict criminology is of crucial importance as prisoner numbers have begun to increase in many countries world-wide. It is well positioned to offer alternative discourses that challenge the persistent construction of crime as 'individual pathology'. As more prisoners or ex-prisoners become academics (and vice versa), the so-called 'inferiority' or 'pathology' of those who find themselves in prison is fundamentally challenged. However, the extent to which this strand of criminology will be able to continue to grow remains questionable. Increasing prisoner numbers and commensurate reductions in the provision of higher education within prisons may ensure that convict criminology remains a small collective. Such trends also mean that the activist role of critical criminology assumes even greater importance, which may well benefit from a more coordinated engagement with politicized prisoner movements.

In sum and most crucially, the emergence of convict criminology and the collection of voices it includes under its banner has presented significant challenges to the hegemony of the prison as an effective crime control tool by illuminating with stark and chilling clarity the many social and personal harms associated with its use.

Deborah H. Drake and Ben Gunn

Associated Concepts: abolition, abolitionism, constitutive criminology, critical criminology, ethnography, labelling, social constructionism

Key Readings

Henry, S. and Milovanovic, D. (1996) *Constitutive Criminology: Beyond Postmodernism.* London: Sage.
Irwin, J. (1970) *The Felon.* Englewood Cliffs, NJ: Prentice-Hall.
Newbold, G. (2000) *Crime in New Zealand.* Palmerston North, New Zealand: Dunmore.
Palombo, J.E. (2009) *Criminal to Critic: Reflections Amid the American Experiment.* Plymouth, UK: Lexington Books.
Ross, J.I. and Richards, S.C. (eds) (2003) *Convict Criminology.* Belmont, CA: Thomson-Wadsworth.
Ross, J.I. and Richards, S.C. (eds) (2009) *Beyond Bars: Rejoining Society after Prison.* New York: Alpha Books.
Terry, C.M. (2002) *Overcoming Prison and Addiction.* Belmont, CA: Thomson-Wadsworth.

CORPORATE CRIME

Definition

Illegal acts or omissions, punishable by the state under administrative, civil or criminal law, which are the result of deliberate decision making or culpable negligence within a legitimate formal organization. These acts or omissions are based in legitimate, formal, business organizations; made in accordance with the normative goals, standard operating procedures and/or cultural norms of the organization; and are intended to benefit the corporation itself.

Distinctive Features

Attention to corporate crime has a long tradition that can be traced back to the work of Bonger in Western Europe and Ross in the USA in the early 1900s. With Sutherland's groundbreaking work in the 1940s, the phenomenon of corporate crime received greater prominence, but also came to be conflated with the concept of white collar crime, a conflation which remains problematic (Nelken, 1994). A recent, significant stage in conceptual clarification was the distinction between 'occupational' and 'organizational' crimes (Slapper and Tombs, 1999: 15–18).

Much research into corporate crime has sought to overcome the absence of utilizable official statistics in almost all national jurisdictions by documenting the scale of such offending. Further, quantitative corporate crime research using large data sets, typically focusing upon the largest corporations such as the *Fortune 500* in the USA (Sutherland, 1983; Clinard and Yeager, 1980), has sought to isolate empirical correlates of offending, such as industry, size, profitability and so on. Findings from such empirical efforts remain contentious, save for the overwhelming conclusion that offending is widespread and pervasive. Various strands of qualitative work have also been undertaken around corporate crime. One focus has been case studies of a particular event, very often with a view to determining via social science that a particular corporate activity constitutes illegality in the absence of any successful legal action. Much academic work has also been devoted to specific types or categories of crime, most notably around financial crimes, crimes committed directly against consumers, crimes arising directly out of the employment relationship, and crimes against the environment. Finally, there have been several industry-specific case studies, notably in the car, chemicals, financial services, oil and pharmaceuticals sectors. Taken together, these bodies of work demonstrate the scale and pervasiveness of corporate crimes across societies and also support the now almost universally accepted claim that the economic (not to mention physical and social) costs of corporate offending far outweigh those associated with 'conventional' or 'street' offending.

Much of this work has proceeded either at the margins of, or beyond, criminology. This is partially explained by the fact that criminology remains wedded to state-defined crime and criminal law, each of which are largely understood in individualistic and interpersonal terms; it is little surprise that much of the work around corporate crime has hailed from critical criminologies, which are based upon a commitment to a critique of dominant definitions of crime and criminal law, while at the same time examining processes of criminalization (and, by implication, non-criminalization). Corporate crime research also faces enormous methodological difficulties and may be relatively unattractive to the funders of research, as well as being unlikely to produce immediately utilizable policy proposals – all of which may further explain its relative omission from dominant criminological agendas.

Evaluation

Conceptual disputes as to what constitutes corporate crime still persist, with many pursuing classic arguments regarding the 'proper' domain of criminology. One consequence of the relative marginality of corporate crime research to criminology is the amount of theoretical underdevelopment that surrounds this concept. Moreover, the field of corporate crime has constantly suffered from problems of legitimacy, not least because of its extensions to the term 'crime' to cover those acts or omissions punishable beyond the criminal law but also as a result of its desire to include as 'crimes' acts or omissions that have never been defined as such under any criminal justice process. These shifts beyond both the criminal law and formal legal processes have frequently left corporate crime researchers open to charges of moralizing.

Other conceptual disputes can be understood as necessary responses to changing social phenomena, such as the seemingly increasingly complex relationships between legitimate and illegitimate organizations.

There are good reasons why corporate crime research – leading to both empirical and theoretical development – should, and may well, proliferate. These include: the spread of the corporate form, as privatization has been championed across nation-states; diversification in the nature of corporate structures and organization; the apparent internationalization of much corporate activity; associated claims regarding the growing power of corporations vis-à-vis national governments and populations, and the resistance associated with these trends; the dogged persistence of so-called 'quality of life' issues such as environmental protection, which came to prominence in the Western capitalist states from the 1960s onwards; and the increasing exposure of the active role of corporations in human rights atrocities. Against these trends, and militating against corporate crime research, should be noted the power of corporations to secure, via their political allies, a decriminalization of their activities through the introduction of various forms of self-regulation or through simple deregulation, each of which represents a significant trend in contemporary capitalist nation-states (Snider, 2000).

Corporate crime research remains crucial to critical agendas within and around criminology – because a focus upon corporate crime entails continual scrutiny of the coverage and omissions of legal categories; the presences and absences within legal discourses;

the social constructions of these categories and discourses; their underpinning of, treatment within and development through criminal justice systems; and the ways in which particular laws are enforced (or not enforced), interpreted, challenged and so on.

Steve Tombs and Dave Whyte

Associated Concepts: art crime, criminalization, critical criminology, critical research, deviance, globalization, hidden crime, human rights, Marxist criminologies, organized crime, radical criminologies, the state, state crime, transnational organized crime, white collar crime

Key Readings

Clinard, M. and Yeager, P. (1980) *Corporate Crime.* New York: The Free Press.

Minkes, J. and Minkes, L. (2008) *Corporate and White Collar Crime.* Los Angeles: Sage.

Nelken, D. (1994) 'White-collar crime', in D. Nelken (ed.), *White-Collar Crime.* Aldershot: Dartmouth.

Slapper, G. and Tombs, S. (1999) *Corporate Crime.* London: Longman.

Snider, L. (2000) 'The sociology of corporate crime: an obituary. (Or, Whose knowledge claims have legs?)', *Theoretical Criminology,* 4 (2): 169–206.

Sutherland, E. (1983) *White-Collar Crime: The Uncut Version.* New Haven, CT: Yale University Press.

CORRELATIONAL ANALYSIS

Definition

Correlation is the association of two variables – the predictability of the values of one from the values of another. We speak of a *positive* correlation, when high values on one variable predict high values on the other, and a *negative* correlation, when high values on one variable predict low values on another. Examples here would be height and weight (a positive correlation) and fitness and exhaustion after exercise (a negative correlation).

Distinctive Features

The degree of correlation is generally expressed as a *correlation coefficient* – with Pearson's product-moment coefficient being the most commonly used – which varies between +1 (a perfect positive correlation) and −1 (a perfect negative correlation). A value of zero would mean no correlation whatsoever, with the value on one variable offering no help at all in predicting the value on another. The correlation coefficient expresses the extent to which the values on the two variables can be fitted to a joint prediction line, with a high value of the coefficient indicating a very good fit and a low value a very poor one (see Figure 1). Correlational analysis usually deals with linear relationships – ones that can be fitted by a straight line – while other related methods are needed for predicting non-linear relationships. Figure 2 illustrates linear and non-linear relationships.

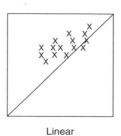
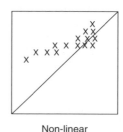

A relatively high correlation   A relatively low correlation

Figure 1 *Good and poor correlation*

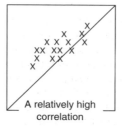
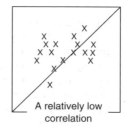

Linear   Non-linear

Figure 2 *Linear and non-linear relationships*

More than one variable can be combined via multiple regression into a *multiple correlation coefficient* (see Figure 3), estimating how well a dependent variable can be predicted from an array of possible causal influences. The analysis will also generally permit the researcher to determine which variables are necessary for

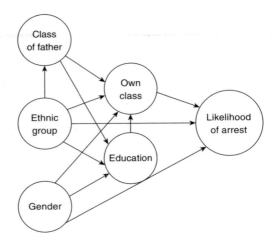

Figure 4   *Path analysis*

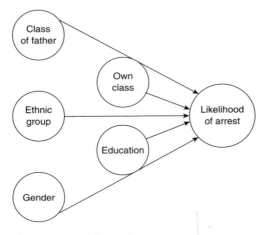

Figure 3   *Multiple correlation*

the prediction and which can be discarded as they are not adding anything further. An elaboration of this method, *path analysis*, permits the testing of hypotheses about chains of influence by taking into account relationships between the possible causes as well as relationships with the dependent variable. Paths on the diagram which turn out not to be statistically significant are deleted to leave a clear indication of the direct and indirect influences on the dependent variable suggested by the data (see Figure 4).

The technique of *partial correlation* is one of the ways in which we may control for alternative explanations by statistical means. A partial correlation coefficient expresses the relationship between a dependent and an independent variable with the effect of a third variable removed. For example, in an analysis of the effects of age on offending behaviour we might control for extent of previous criminal behaviour by partialling out (removing) the effects of previous convictions.

Evaluation

Correlational analysis is used to assess the degree of influence of one variable on another – for example, the extent to which social circumstances, childhood experiences and personality characteristics may provide explanations for subsequent criminal behaviour. The old maxim, however, is that 'correlation does not prove causation'. Correlation is a necessary condition for establishing causal influence – if one variable influences another, it must be correlated with it – but it is not a sufficient one. It is always possible that a third variable, which is not present in the analysis, may be an explanation both for the effect and for the apparent cause.

Roger Sapsford

Associated Concepts: causation, multivariate analysis

Key Readings

Hood, R. (1992) *Race and Sentencing*. Oxford: The Clarendon Press.
Sapsford, R.J. (1999) *Survey Analysis*. London: Sage.

CRIME

Definition

Crime is not a self-evident and unitary concept. Its constitution is diverse, historically relative and continually contested. As a result an answer to the question 'what is crime?' depends upon which of its multiple constitutive elements is emphasized. This in turn depends upon the theoretical position taken by those defining crime.

Distinctive Features

Key elements in determining crime are: (1) harm; (2) social agreement or consensus; and (3) the official societal response. 'Harm' includes the nature, severity and extent of the harm or injury caused and the kind of victim harmed. 'Consensus' refers to the extent of the social agreement about whether victims have been harmed. 'Official societal response' refers to the existence of criminal laws specifying under what conditions (such as intent and knowledge of the consequences) an act resulting in harm can be called crime, and the enforcement of such laws against those committing acts that harm. These dimensions have emerged from, and been differently emphasized by, six basic theoretical traditions – legal, moral consensus, sociological positivism, rule-relativism, political conflict and power-harm.

In early formulations, a simple relationship was assumed between each of the three key dimensions, such that if an action caused harm, people would be outraged and would then enact laws that the state would enforce in order to penalize the perpetrator. Thus emerged what became known as the moral or consensus position on crime which states that crimes are acts which shock the common or collective morality, thereby producing intense moral outrage among people. In founding this view Durkheim stated that 'an act is criminal when it offends the strong, well-defined states of the collective consciousness' (1984 [1893]: 39). Specifically, crime was a term used 'to designate any act, which, regardless

of degree, provokes against the perpetrator the characteristic reaction known as punishment' (1984 [1893]: 31). As a result, the basic definition of crime became behaviour defined and sanctioned by criminal law. Thus there is no crime without law, and law is based on the 'injury' or 'harm done'. In a seminal statement reflecting the Durkheimian consensus view, Michael and Adler (1933: 5) asserted that 'criminal law gives behaviour its quality of criminality' and that 'the character of the behaviour content of criminal law will be determined by the capacity of behaviour to arouse our indignation' (1933: 23).

Evaluation

Several flaws in the legal consensus view of crime led to various critical challenges that stemmed from those holding different theoretical positions. The first problematic is the issue of what harm has been caused and what counts as harm. Even classical thinkers in the eighteenth century disagreed about this. The concept of 'harm', according to Cesare Beccaria, refers to restrictions on the freedom of individuals to accumulate wealth. Beccaria identified three categories of crimes based upon the seriousness of their harm *to society*. The most grave of these were those perpetrated against the state, followed by crimes that injured the security and property of individuals; last in importance, were crimes that proved disruptive to the public peace. But for Jeremy Bentham, harms were behaviours that caused 'pain' rather than restrictions of the freedom to accumulate wealth. Bentham discussed 12 categories of pain whose measurement was necessary in order to give legislators a basis on which to decide whether to prohibit an act. He believed that no act ought to be an offence *unless* it was detrimental to the community. An act would be detrimental if it harmed one or more members of the community. Bentham elaborated on a list of offence categories that he considered to occupy five classes: public offences, semi-public offences, self-regarding offences (offences that were only detrimental to the offender), offences against the state, and multiform or anomalous offences. Each would carry a punishment determined by the circumstances. Bentham declared that only harms to others should be criminal offences; cases of public morality and transactional crimes where 'consent has been given' need not be subject to the criminal law. In considering crime as defined in law therefore, the concern is not with those who commit crime, only with those acts that harm others.

A related issue is who should determine whether a consensus of outrage exists on whether harm has been committed. Those who have been termed 'sociological positivists' argued that the measure of such consensus or outrage was the purview of social scientists. Thorsten Sellin (1938), for example, advocated a science of criminal behaviour that would be free from the politics of criminal law, legislators and lawyers. Scientists would instead employ their own value-neutral techniques to measure independently whether harm had been caused and to establish whether outrage existed and through these means they would then establish scientific definitions of crime (1938: 20–1). Sellin proposed to do this by basing it on a study of naturally existing 'conduct norms' rather than using legally constructed laws. This 'would involve the isolation and classification of norms into universal categories, transcending political and other boundaries, a necessity imposed by the logic of science' (1938: 30). The problem here is the assumption that science, and the scientific process itself, are any more free of influence than law (Schwendinger and Schwendinger, 1970).

Rule-relativists further argued that the meaning of what is defined in law or in moral consensus is not fixed but varies. They argued that what is defined as crime in law is historically, temporally and culturally relative. Their insight highlights the role of changing rather than absolute values about crime. Their challenge to the strict legal view of crime has been developed further by social constructionist arguments which show how what is regarded as harm will depend on the social context and situational meaning, which will be shaped by the interaction between interest groups, such as offender, victim, community organizations and police agencies in the local setting. The emergence of an act as an 'offence' depends on how these groups negotiate and honour the claims that harm has been created.

The legal consensus position is also criticized because it ignores the politics of lawmaking. Radical conflict theorists claim that what ends up being defined as crime will depend on having the power to define and the power to resist criminalizing definitions. Indeed, if interests influence the law creation process, then not all acts causing indignation or outrage will be legislated against. Only those harms that powerful interests deem worthy will be subject to criminalization. As Edwin Sutherland (1940) first stated, this would mean that many harms, particularly those perpetrated by powerful corporations, remain outside the criminal law, even though they may be subject to civil regulation. For Sutherland, an adequate definition of crime would need to be based on an expanded definition of harm that included 'social injury'. Similarly, Quinney (1977) wanted to expand the definition of crime to include not only the legal harms resulting from economic domination in a capitalist society, but also the crimes of governments and their agencies of social control. However, legalists such as Paul Tappan (1947) vigorously disagreed with expanding the legal definition, arguing that without adhering strictly to the law the concept of crime was open-ended and meaningless.

But for those taking a critical conflict perspective, an adequate definition of crime must be based on a definition of harm that is tied neither to the law nor consensus but to an independent notion of 'human rights'. Without such independent anchoring of the definition of crime those who are victimized are subject to the tyranny of moral majorities or the bias of powerful interests who determine the law. Because of this the harms that result from racism, sexism, ageism, or from 'insidious injuries' perpetrated by corporations through harmful work conditions or products, were for years not acknowledged either in society or in the law (Schwendinger and Schwendinger, 1970).

Postmodernist criminologists have also developed the idea that harm must be related to a concept of humanity and therefore they would argue for a dynamic conception of the different ways that humanity can be harmed. The postmodernist constitutive approach to defining crime goes beyond powerful groups and classes to include the total context of powerful relations in situational and global contexts. For example, Henry and Milovanovic (1996: 104) state that 'crimes are nothing less than moments in the expression of power such that those who are subjected to these expressions are denied their own contribution to the encounter and often to future encounters.' They argue that crime 'is the power to deny others ... in which those subject to the power of another, suffer the pain of being denied their own humanity, the power to make a difference'; they also distinguish between 'harms of reduction' and 'harms of repression' (1996: 103). Harms of reduction occur when an offended party experiences the loss of some quality relative to their present standing that results from another's action. Harms of repression (or oppression) result from the actions of another that limit or restrict a person from achieving a future desired position or standing, though one achieved without harming others. Harms of repression have also been described as crimes against human dignity: 'acts and conditions that obstruct the spontaneous unfolding of human potential' (Tifft, 1995: 9).

The idea of criminalizing the use of power to reduce or suppress another is particularly important in order to expose the previously hidden crimes of gender oppression, sexual harassment, hate crime and racism that critical theorists have long complained are neglected in the legal and consensus definitions. It is also central to the unveiling of white collar, corporate and state crimes. Indeed, the analysis of power relations in the creation of crime highlights the intersecting forces of class, race and gender relations which coalesce in law and social institutions to legitimize harm and thereby render legalized relations, relations of harm. It follows, therefore, that the law itself can create crime, not merely by definition but by its use of power over others and its concealment of the harms of others within the protection of law (Tifft, 1995).

Finally, there has been increased recognition of the need to integrate each of the different dimensions of crime. This began explicitly with John Hagan's (1985) notion of the pyramid of crime which was further developed by Henry and Lanier (1998) in their notion of the 'prism of crime'. The aim of these approaches is to capture the multiple dimensions of crime simultaneously, rather than emphasizing any one element as predominant. Henry and Lanier's prism, for example, affords a way of incorporating individual and social harm; crimes of the powerful and those of the powerless; crimes that are invisible as well as those that are highly visible; and crimes that are selectively enforced as well as those more consistently enforced. In this way they aim for a more comprehensive definition that transcends the politics of the law-making process.

Stuart Henry

Associated Concepts: art crime, conflict theory, constitutive criminology, corporate crime, crimes against humanity, family crime, hate crime, hidden crime, integrative criminology, labelling, organized crime, political crime, sex crime, social harm, state crime, transnational organized crime, war crimes

Key Readings

Durkheim, E. (1984) [1893] *The Division of Labor in Society.* New York: The Free Press.

Hagan, J. (1985) *Modern Criminology.* New York: McGraw–Hill.

Henry, S. and Lanier, M. (1998) 'The prism of crime: arguments for an integrated definition of crime', *Justice Quarterly,* 15 (4): 609–27.

Henry, S. and Milovanovic, D. (1996) *Constitutive Criminology: Beyond Postmodernism.* London: Sage.

Michael, J. and Adler, M.J. (1933) *Crime, Law and Social Science.* New York: Harcourt Brace and Jovanovich.

Quinney, R. (1977) *Class, State, and Crime.*
New York: David McKay.
Schwendinger, H. and Schwendinger, J. (1970)
'Defenders of order or guardians of human
rights?', *Issues in Criminology,* 5: 123–57.
Sellin, T. (1938) *Culture, Conflict and Crime.*
New York: Social Science Research Council.
Sutherland, E.H. (1940) 'White-collar criminal-
ity', *American Sociological Review,* 5: 1–12.
Tappan, P.R. (1947) 'Who is the criminal?',
American Sociological Review, 12: 96–102.
Tifft, L.L. (1995) 'Social harm definitions of
crime', *The Critical Criminologist,* 7: 9–13.

CRIME CONTROL MODEL

Definition

A crime control perspective or model which
stresses that the primary function of the
criminal courts is to punish offenders and, by
so doing, to control crime.

Distinctive Features

The 'crime control' model involves a system of
criminal justice which has as its primary aim the
need to repress criminal conduct. The courts are
thus more guardians of law and order than
upholders of impartial justice. The failure of law
enforcement to bring criminal conduct under
tight control is viewed as leading to the breakdown of public order and thence to the disappearance of an important condition of human
freedom. That is, whilst crime and disorder
remain inadequately checked then the law-
abiding citizen may become the victim of all
sorts of unjustifiable invasions of his or her
interests. The security of person and property is
diminished and therefore the liberty to function
as a member of society. The inherent claim is
that the criminal justice process is a positive
guarantor of social freedom. In order to achieve
this high purpose, the crime control model
requires that primary attention is given to the
efficiency with which the criminal process operates to screen suspects, determine guilt, and
secure appropriate punishment (Packer, 1964).

While 'due process' values prioritize civil
liberties in order to ensure that the innocent
are acquitted (even at the risk of acquitting
some who are guilty), 'crime control' values
stress the goal of convicting the guilty (even
at the risk of convicting some who are innocent, or of infringing some civil liberties). In
a 'crime control' model, formal rules of procedure are often seen as obstacles standing
in the way of securing a defendant's conviction. As the ultimate aim is to punish offenders and to deter future crime, the criminal
justice system cannot afford a high acquittal
rate; the system must work efficiently and
speedily to apprehend and convict offenders. Packer (1964) likens the crime control
model to an assembly line or a conveyor belt
which, beginning with a presumption of
guilt, moves the offender to workers at fixed
stations who perform on each case to bring
it one step closer to being a finished product
or a closed file.

It is argued that the main tool of the pre-
modern model of crime control was the
spectacular, public, bloody punishment of
the offender who had offended sovereign
power. The 'Bloody Code' of crime control,
as criminal justice was popularly referred to
in eighteenth-century England, was however
supplemented by more traditional, communitarian mechanisms of social control (custom and informal means) which had survived
from the feudal era. Following criticisms
from classical reformers there was new
interest in rationality, formalism and legality. The lasting philosophical influence of
classicist views on crime and its prevention
is perhaps to be found in utilitarianism and
what has been called social contract theory
(Hughes, 1998). According to this perspective, punishment of the offender is only justifiable in terms of its contribution to the
prevention of future infringements on the
well-being and happiness of others. Social
contract theory derives from the idea that
the power and authority of governments to
control crime (through punishment amongst
other means) stems from an unwritten, but
none the less binding, contract entered into
by members of society whereby they agree

to certain measures in order to secure their freedom against the invasive actions of others. Following this, Garland (1996) refers to 'sovereign crime control', meaning that the state is there to provide security, law and order, and crime control within its territorial boundaries.

A key meaning of the 'crime control model', therefore, relates to the wide range of mechanisms employed by the state – from the introduction of police forces to control disruptive behaviour, to developing institutions for criminal justice and corrections, and from situational crime prevention to multi-agency crime prevention work and other sophisticated modes of community control – in order to achieve crime control ends.

Evaluation

There are strong criticisms that the adoption of a 'crime control model' leads to harsh penalties and unnecessarily intrusive measures (Hudson, 1996). It is clearly associated with 'get tough', 'prisons work' and 'zero tolerance' policies. Yet such movements in criminal justice do not reflect unalloyed scientific endeavour; rather, they reflect political concerns (Stenson and Cowell, 1991).

Some radicals view the crime control measures of the criminal justice system as largely ineffective and even criminogenic. Many concerned with justice for juveniles, for instance, have argued that there should be as little intervention in young offenders' lives as possible on the basis that criminal justice interventions might well exacerbate their offending. Others would suggest that the most effective forms of crime control are those that relate to deep social and economic structures, which seemingly contribute to the onset of crime in the first place.

In a deeply pessimistic but important review of crime control, Nils Christie (1993) has argued that this has now become an industry – one with an unlimited potential for growth that also presents a very real danger regarding the value of human life.

Loraine Gelsthorpe

Associated Concepts: crime prevention, criminal justice, deterrence, due process model, governmentality, social control, zero tolerance

Key Readings

Christie, N. (1993) *Crime Control As Industry*. London: Routledge.

Garland, D. (1996) 'The limits of the sovereign state: strategies of crime control in contemporary society', *British Journal of Criminology*, 36 (4): 445–71.

Hudson, B. (1996) *Understanding Justice*. Buckingham: Open University Press.

Hughes, G. (1998) *Understanding Crime Prevention*. Buckingham: Open University Press.

Packer, H. (1964) Two models of the criminal process', *University of Pennsylvania Law Review*, 113: 1–68.

Stenson, K. and Cowell, D. (eds) (1991) *The Politics of Crime Control*. London: Sage.

CRIME MAPPING

See: COMPSTAT; Crime science; Geographies of crime

CRIME NEWS

Definition

News stories about crime, deviance and punishment are ubiquitous in modern society. Quite simply, crime is newsworthy. But crime news follows markedly different patterns to both the 'reality' of crime and its representation in official statistics, and is frequently said to be 'manufactured' along ideological lines.

Distinctive Features

In the simplest of terms, crime news is event-orientated, and focuses on specific – usually atypical – criminal incidents rather than on crime trends or on wider debates around causes, prevention or policy. Research carried out in the UK and the USA indicates that crime reporting is more prevalent than ever before, and that interpersonal crimes, particularly those of a violent or sexual nature, are both over-reported in relation to their statistical occurrence, and frequently described in a manner which graphically sensationalizes them. This tendency has led to accusations that the media skew public perceptions of crime and fuel fears among those least likely to be victims. Some studies have also found that the police reinforce journalistically-produced concerns about 'crime waves' and that audiences over-estimate the proportion of crimes solved (cf. Wykes, 2001).

The question of how 'deliberate' these mis-representations are is a subject of enduring debate, with opinions broadly falling into either a radical or liberal pluralist perspective (Greer, 2003). Underpinned by Marxist theory, the radical argument claims the function of the news media is to manufacture consent around elite ideas in the name of public or national interests. Culturally dominant groups and opinion leaders are able to advance a 'primary definition' of crime-related issues, which frames the terms for any ensuing debate. Meanwhile, alternative definitions may not get aired simply because there is no longer the spread of sources there once was. By contrast, liberal pluralists argue that recent processes of deregulation and privatization (especially, though by no means exclusively, in North America and Western Europe) have succeeded in removing the media from state regulation and censorship and encouraged open competition between media institutions, leading to a previously unimaginable extension of public choice and the possibility of 'counter-definitions'. Thus, according to this perspective, while we can still identify a dominant economic class in a conceptual sense, it does not constitute a coherent political force. Traditional ideological inequalities formed along lines of class, gender and race no longer inhabit the static positions they once may have, and – thanks to mass education, social mobility and the rise of a media-driven 'celebrity culture' – the contemporary 'ruling class' is more culturally diverse than ever before.

Given its favourable characterization of the media industries, it is unsurprising that, while the radical 'dominant ideology' perspective has been influential within the academy, pluralism has been championed by practitioners and policy makers (Greer, 2003). But these differences aside, what all commentators agree on is that, given that the time and space available for news in most mediums are finite, crime news is selected, shaped and presented according to certain 'news values' – professional benchmarks which alert us to the fact that crime news normalizes particular interests and values.

This normalization occurs as a result of two interconnected factors in the production–consumption process. The first relates to the structural determinants of news production: the over-reporting of crimes that have been 'solved'; the deployment of reporters at institutional settings such as courts where they are likely to come across interesting stories; the need to create stories which fit production schedules; a concentration on specific crimes at the expense of causal explanations; considerations of personal safety resulting in camera operators covering incidents of public disorder from behind police lines; an over-reliance on 'official', accredited sources for information; and so on. The second factor which shapes news values concerns the assumptions that media professionals make about their consumers. Potential news items are sifted and selected, words are edited, and visual images are chosen with a particular market in mind, while those stories which are of no perceived interest or relevance to the target audience are discarded (Wykes, 2001).

The first scholars to identify a set of news values were Galtung and Ruge (1965/1973). Their concern was with news reporting generally, but their view that events were more likely to be reported if they were unexpected, unambiguous, of a significant threshold in terms of dramatic impact, and negative in essence clearly made them relevant to crime news. Following their analysis, another influential work was published by Chibnall in 1977. Specifically concerned with British crime news between 1945 and 1975, Chibnall outlined eight professional imperatives, including dramatization, simplification, novelty, high-status persons and immediacy. A more recent attempt to develop these classic studies and identify a set of news values specifically tailored towards crime and media analysis in the twenty-first century is that of Jewkes (2004). While remaining faithful to certain fundamentals, this account nonetheless recognizes that as society changes so too do the cultural and psychological triggers which condition responses within media consumers and, correspondingly, influence the construction of crime narratives. Britain is a very different place now to what it was half a century ago and contemporary news reports contain references to crimes that were unknown then – road rage, joy-riding, carjacking, ecstasy dealing, illegal immigration, cyberstalking and identity theft, among others. Meanwhile, non-violent crimes such as property offences which, in the postwar period, constituted nearly a quarter of stories in *The Times* (Reiner, 2001) are now so commonplace that they are rarely mentioned in the national media unless the victim is well known. Moreover, the media landscape has changed almost beyond recognition and audiences are both more sophisticated and more sceptical than at any time previously – certainly they possess sufficient media-savvy to know when they are on the receiving end of political 'spin'. In our media-saturated times, then, Jewkes (2004) highlights the values of risk, individualization, violence, children, sex, celebrity, and a right-wing, conservative consensus as key determinants of crime newsworthiness.

Evaluation

News values help to explain the broad profile of media representations of crime and control. Liberal pluralists argue that the reasons for the media's preoccupation with certain types of crime are largely pragmatic and economic. They are, after all, in the business of selling newspapers and gaining audience ratings, and it is serious crimes – especially those involving women and children – which are least common and therefore most 'newsworthy'. In addition, it must be remembered that most

consumers of crime news are seeking to engage with stories on an emotional level, and journalists and editors are well-attuned to the fact that 'giving the public what they want' frequently involves stirring passions and provoking moral outrage. However, the desire to accommodate public tastes has prompted radical critics to accuse the media of catering to what the first Director General of the BBC, Lord Reith, called the 'lowest common denominator' of an audience. Since the British media were deregulated in the early 1990s, the criticism has intensified and broadcast and print media have been accused of 'dumbing down' their news coverage and measuring newsworthiness by the degree of amusement, shock or revulsion a story provokes. The identification of key news values seems to support this view. They illustrate that the news media do not systemically cover all forms and expressions of crime and victimization, and that they pander to the most voyeuristic desires of the audience by exaggerating and dramatizing relatively unusual crimes, while also ignoring or downplaying the crimes that are most likely to happen to the 'average' person. At the same time, they will sympathize with some victims while blaming others (Jewkes, 2004).

The purpose, value and 'effects' of crime news remain contested. The expansion of the media may be regarded as a cultural expression of democracy giving voice to new forms of political engagement – a trend that can only intensify as more people access global news organizations via the Internet. While the interests of contemporary audiences may be regarded as populist and trivial, the fact is that more people consume news today than have at any time previously. Furthermore, there is a valuable investigative tradition in journalism which continues to play an important role in the spheres of crime prevention and control, and in uncovering police corruption and miscarriages of justice. However, there is also a strong argument to suggest that the news media's concentration on crimes of sex and violence, especially against vulnerable individuals, heightens anxieties and results in a greater public mandate for increasingly punitive forms of punishment to combat what is perceived as a continually spiralling crime rate and a criminal justice system that is ineffective and 'soft on crime'.

Yvonne Jewkes

Associated Concepts: fear of crime, moral panic, newsmaking criminology, public opinion, social constructionism, social reaction, stereotyping

Key Readings

Chibnall, S. (1977) *Law and Order News.* London: Tavistock.

Galtung, J. and Ruge, M. (1965/1973) 'Structuring and selecting the news', in S. Cohen and J. Young (eds), *The Manufacture of News: Deviance, Social Problems and the Mass Media.* London: Constable.

Greer, C. (2003) *Sex Crime and the Media: Sex Offending and the Press in a Divided Society.* Cullompton: Willan.

Jewkes, Y. (2004) *Media and Crime.* London: Sage.

Reiner, R. (2001) 'The rise of virtual vigilantism: crime reporting since World War II', *Criminal Justice Matters,* 43: 4–5.

Wykes, M. (2001) *News, Crime and Culture.* London: Pluto.

CRIME PREVENTION

Definition

Any action taken or technique employed by private individuals or public agencies aimed at the reduction of damage caused by acts defined as criminal by the state. Given that crimes are events proscribed only by legal statute, it is not surprising that there is a huge plethora of activities and initiatives associated with the term 'crime prevention'.

Distinctive Features

Crime prevention in its broadest sense has a long history, stretching back to the first use of locks and bolts to protect persons and property. However, it was only during the last three decades of the twentieth century that it emerged as a key institutional feature of criminal justice systems and related sites of social control across most contemporary societies. It is also during this recent period that we have seen a massive output of criminological writing aimed at classifying different types of crime prevention. Crime prevention is a chameleon concept which cannot be neatly or unproblematically defined. There continue to be many different meanings to crime prevention and in turn divergent policies and practices associated with the notion.

There is no consensus among criminologists with regard to how best to define the phenomenon of crime prevention. Instead, there are competing models and typologies, often of a limited theoretical nature, and seemingly driven by rather narrow technical concerns about the measurement and evaluation of 'success' or 'failure'. One of the leading experts on the evaluation of crime prevention initiatives, Ken Pease, has recommended exercising caution towards any attempt to look for universality in the techniques of prevention since, when we consider the prevention of crime, we are in fact looking at a set of events that are joined together only by their proscription by statute (Pease, 1997: 659).

A popular means of defining crime prevention in criminology in the late twentieth century has been in terms of the distinction between situational and social strategies of prevention (to complicate matters further, the social strategies are often termed 'community' crime prevention). Situational crime prevention chiefly concerns opportunity reduction, such as the installation of surveillance technology in public spaces to reduce the opportunities for the theft of vehicles or crimes against victims. Social crime prevention is focused chiefly on changing social environments and offenders' motivations. Social crime prevention measures thus often tend to focus on the development of schemes to deter potential or actual offenders from future offending. Both situational and social crime prevention approaches tend to be what is termed 'multi-agency' in orientation, rather than being driven by one agency alone, such as the police. Common to both elements of this distinction is the claim to be less damaging than traditional (retributive) justice approaches. Also common to both situational and social prevention is a narrow focus on 'street crime' and specific categories of offender (young, working-class males) rather than other social harms and offenders.

Another approach to classifying types of crime prevention is that there are three major models of crime prevention, borrowed from theorizing in medical epidemiology (Weiss, 1987). First, there is 'primary' crime prevention involving the reduction of criminal opportunities without reference to criminals. In primary crime prevention attention is paid to the crime event rather than the motivated offender. In the second type of crime prevention, termed 'secondary', the focus is on changing people before they do something criminal. Here then attention rests on the prevention of criminality. Finally, 'tertiary' crime prevention focuses on the truncation of the criminal career, or a reduction in the seriousness of offending, for example through the treatment of known offenders.

Another attempt to provide a comprehensive typology of crime prevention strategies is found in Tonry and Farrington (1995). These authors distinguish four major strategies of crime prevention (law enforcement, developmental, communal and situational). According to law enforcement strategy, criminal laws exist and are enacted so that fewer of the proscribed acts take place and general prevention in turn is the primary justification for maintaining a system of criminal punishment. This traditional law enforcement approach to both crime prevention and punishment operates chiefly through deterrence, incapacitation and rehabilitation. Developmental preventive interventions are designed to prevent the development of criminal potential in individuals, especially targeting the risk and protective factors discovered in studies of human development. Community prevention is designed to change the social conditions that influence offending in residential communities. And situational prevention involves interventions that are designed to prevent the occurrence of crimes, especially by reducing opportunities and increasing risks.

Evaluation

Despite the plethora of activities and definitional distinctions noted above, there remains the continuing dominance of a narrow focus in administrative criminology on 'what works' as crime prevention techniques (most associated with situational crime prevention 'fixes'). Viewed critically, this technicist focus is limiting and runs the risk of missing the broader sociological and political context in terms of which trends in crime prevention need to be understood. It may be noted that the concern with evaluating policies and initiatives for reducing or managing crimes may mean that crime prevention experts lose sight of the wider levers of crime, disorder and harms in contemporary societies.

According to critical authors, the 'growth industry' around crime prevention, crime reduction and community safety – which includes the academic criminological community – reflects important wider social transformations in contemporary societies (Crawford, 1997; Hughes, 1998; O'Malley, 1992). This insight is crucial to the recognition that developments in crime prevention are not just well-intentioned technical solutions or responses to specific new crime events, but also reflect broad trends in social control and the governance of diverse and often fragmented populations. In particular, the increasing emphasis on (at best) crime reduction and (more pragmatically) risk management associated with an 'actuarialist' model of justice may reflect the decline of the nation state's claims to sovereignty over crime control and may further accentuate trends towards social exclusion along with 'safety' increasingly becoming the 'club'-like privilege of the privileged and affluent.

Gordon Hughes

Associated Concepts: administrative criminology, community safety, crime control model, fear of crime, governance, governmentality, multi-agency crime prevention, realist criminologies, situational crime prevention, social crime prevention, surveillance, 'what works'

Key Readings

Crawford, A. (1997) *The Local Governance of Crime.* Oxford: The Clarendon Press.

Hughes, G. (1998) *Understanding Crime Prevention: Social Control, Risk and Late Modernity.* Buckingham: Open University Press.

O'Malley, P. (1992) 'Power, risk and crime prevention', *Economy and Society,* 21 (3): 251–68.

Pease, K. (1997) 'Crime prevention', in M. Maguire, R. Morgan and R. Reiner (eds), *The Oxford Handbook of Criminology,* 2nd edn. Oxford: The Clarendon Press.

Tonry, M. and Farrington, D. (1995) *Building a Safer Society: Strategic Approaches to Crime.* Chicago: University of Chicago Press.

Weiss, R. (1987) 'Community and crime prevention', in E. Johnson (ed.), *Handbook on Crime and Delinquency.* New York: Greenwood Press

CRIME REDUCTION

Definition

Crime reduction is formally defined as any activity that seeks to lower the numerically measured instances of actions legally proscribed as criminal. However, it is often used interchangeably with crime prevention to refer to activity that has as its primary aim the reduction of problems associated with behaviour defined as criminal. It is also defined as a criminological approach that gives primacy to numerical measurement and a scientific evaluation of effectiveness, whilst simultaneously not engaging in discussions on political context and ideology.

Distinctive Features

The term 'crime reduction' has a relatively short official history in the UK. Although the terms 'crime reduction' and 'crime prevention' tended to be used interchangeably during the 1980s and 1990s, Home Office publications changed the terminology with the introduction of the Crime Reduction Programme in 1999. The 'crime reduction' approach as defined here also exists in the USA, although the governmental terminology has remained that of crime prevention (Sherman et al., 1997).

'Community safety' can also be distinguished from both crime prevention and crime reduction because it encompasses a wider brief (Home Office, 1991), although the three terms are often used interchangeably. Separating crime reduction from crime prevention and community safety provides a rationale, therefore, for defining it as a policy-orientated criminological approach that is based upon quantity and therefore is about reducing the number of actions defined as criminal. The primary focus is one of diminishing the volume and consequences of crime. Regardless of the locale of policy implementation, the key concern is to utilize existing resources as efficiently as possible so that a reduction in the observable number of actual events can be recorded (Ekblom, 2000).

The current aspiration of the Crime Reduction Programme is to gather evidence of 'what works' based on 'evidence' and cost (Tilley, 2001: 82). This emphasis reflects the broader project of New Public Management (NPM) processes that are a hallmark of neo-liberal government. This is an approach to governing across the public policy field that prioritizes performance monitoring for efficiency and effectiveness, with an emphasis on measuring outputs to show value for money.

Evaluation

There are two crucial assumptions underpinning 'crime reduction'. First, there is an acceptance that crime cannot be prevented but merely reduced. Crime is seen as an inevitable part of everyday life. Second, there is the assumption that cost effectiveness is pivotal. There is an inherent political consequence to accepting both of these assumptions. The former does not see criminal activity as something that can be prevented at the source of causation, for example through socio-economic change, while the latter accepts as legitimate present levels of resources. This is a form of political pragmatism which implies that politically controversial or expensive crime reduction strategies cannot be considered.

A further aspect of quantitatively measured crime reduction is a lack of recognition of the importance of *process* in determining such reductions. One could point to the suggestion that the quickest way to reduce recorded crime is not to arrest anyone; however, that would only be superficially successful on purely numeric grounds. The issue therefore is whether such an approach provides success that is constructed and/or driven by ideology, pragmatic politics or sheer convenience. Evidence-led policy risks being dominated solely by that which is readily amenable to measurement (Tilley, 2001: 83). This then raises questions about viewing crime reduction as being value/ideologically neutral; whether it is based on evidence that is produced without political influence, and then applied in a similarly value-free way. These issues of 'neutrality' are also problematic when applied, as much crime reduction activity is, to notions of the 'community'. The latter is also not something that can easily be 'neutrally' defined and measured.

The role of political context is one of the most debated issues in the criminological discourse around crime reduction. Use of the term 'crime reduction' can be seen as being more politically convenient than 'prevention', with the latter being a more speculative enterprise, in that one cannot necessarily quantitatively show that something has been prevented. If something stopped it occurring, one cannot necessarily measure that nonoccurrence. Crime reduction is also an approach that fails to recognize, or seeks to ignore, the political context in which acts defined as crimes occur (see the debate in the *British Journal of Criminology* between Morgan and Hughes and Edwards (2004, 44 (4): 619–21). Prevention can also be less politically convenient because it is more difficult to establish that an act did not occur because of a specific intervention being used, for example CCTV. Also some prevention activities are founded upon assumptions about the role that political and economic structural factors (such as employment prospects or the lack of them) play in producing offending behaviour, and are thus more demanding in terms of structural and economic change.

In theory, 'crime reduction' approaches have scientifically measurable and cost effective outcomes. In practice, at the local level, practitioners operate within a complex of political, cultural, geographical, economic and historical contexts, and so any approach to crime control has value-laden motivations and political outcomes (Stenson and Edwards, 2001). However, the 'crime reduction' approach still remains extremely influential at all levels of policy making. Its criminological strength, according to its critics, is that it carries both illuminating comment on how 'new products and technologies create modern "desires" and "needs" which may take criminal forms' and also a capacity to place crime science at the centre of modern crime control (Hughes et al., 2002: 331–2).

Matthew Follett

Associated Concepts: community crime prevention, community safety, crime prevention, crime science, governance, managerialism, 'what works'

Key Readings

Ekblom, P. (2000) 'The conjunction of criminal opportunity', in S. Ballintyne, K. Pease and V. McLaren, (eds), *Secure Foundations*. London: IPPR.

Home Office (1991) *Safer Communities: The Local Delivery of Crime Prevention through the Partnership Approach* (Morgan Report). London: Home Office.

Hughes, G., McLaughlin E. and Muncie, J. (2002) 'Teetering on the edge: the futures of crime control and community safety', in G. Hughes, E. McLaughlin and J. Muncie (eds), *Crime Prevention and Community Safety: Future Directions*. London: Sage.

Sherman, L., Gottfredson, D., MacKenzie, D., Eck, J., Reuter, P. and Bushway, S. (1997) *Preventing Crime: What Works, What Doesn't, What's Promising: A Report to the United States Congress*. Available at http://www.ncjrs.org

Stenson, K. and Edwards, A. (2001) 'Crime control and liberal government: the "third way" and the return to the local', in K. Stenson and R. Sullivan (eds), *Crime, Risk and Justice*. Cullompton: Willan.

Tilley, N. (2001) 'Evaluation and evidence-led crime reduction policy and practice', in R. Matthews and J. Pitts (eds), *Crime, Disorder and Community Safety*. London: Routledge.

CRIME SCIENCE

Definition

Crime science was launched in April 2001 as a new discipline directed at the prevention and detection of crime and the reduction of disorder in ethically acceptable ways. It involves the application of scientific principles – including the formulation of explanatory theory, the application of logic, the use of rational argument, and the empirical testing of hypotheses through the collection and analysis of data – to the problems of crime and disorder. The precise contours of crime science, however, are still evolving (Laycock, 2005).

Distinctive Features

The first Institute of Crime Science was established in the School of Public Policy at University College London in 2001. Crime science offers an umbrella under which an entire range of separate scientific disciplines can be encouraged to contribute to the crime reduction agenda. Centrally relevant current disciplines include criminology, particularly environmental criminology, and forensic science, but geography, economics, chemistry, psychology, engineering, computer science and many other primary areas of study are also relevant to the control of crime and disorder. Their application has often been neglected due to the emphasis on the criminal justice system as the principal means of crime control. One of the challenges of crime science is how better to join together these various base disciplines in a coherent approach to crime and disorder.

Science is seen to contribute to the control of crime and disorder in at least three ways – by better understanding its nature within a social context; by contributing to the design of places, goods, services, policies and management practices so as to minimize crime; and by improving the detection of crime through the application of forensic and other scientific approaches. As a discipline, crime science can also increase the capacity of detectives, and other agents with a detection remit, to think in a more evidentially robust and scientific manner.

In some respects crime science challenges the way in which contemporary western democracies typically characterize crime and disorder and attempt to deal with it. Rather than concentrating on detection, arrest and sentencing, crime scientists would typically focus on the offence itself, and an analysis of the characteristics of common classes of offending, with the aim of developing effective preventive methods as a first step. In this respect, the approach can be compared to the response to an air crash or other accident where the primary concern is to ensure that the event is not repeated.

Crime science also emphasizes the evolutionary nature of crime methods and the extent to which crime preventers and offenders are locked into an arms race, with new technologies being used both to prevent crimes and to assist in their perpetration (Ekblom, 1997).

In contributing to our understanding of crime and its prevention, crime science draws on the theories of environmental criminology, including crime pattern theory (Brantingham and Brantingham, 1993), routine activity theory (Felson, 2002), rational choice theory (Cornish and Clarke, 2003) and situational crime prevention (Clarke, 1997). These theories help to explain where, why and how crimes happen and thus to indicate potential methods of prevention. When specific preventive measures are being developed other sciences might become relevant, such as electronic engineering when designing secure mobile telephony systems, computer science when securing aspects of the Internet, or electrical engineering when considering the design of deadlocks and immobilizers on motor vehicles.

When prevention fails, science – and the technologies derived from it – can be used to assist in the detection of offenders. Although many techniques used by forensic scientists are now well established, recent developments in DNA technology have opened up new possibilities. If these and other future developments are to be effectively exploited in delivering improvements in detection rates, there needs to be a greater understanding of the ways in which this might be done. Crime scientists would advocate a more holistic approach to the transfer of these technologies to the workplace and would also be interested in ensuring that there was appropriate training and a comprehensive understanding of the principles underlying the new approaches. To take DNA technology as an example, although it may not be necessary for a working detective to understand the underlying science, it is probably advisable for senior officers to appreciate the statistics that may or may not support the conclusions they wish to draw from DNA evidence.

Crime science, like the natural sciences, emphasizes the need for experimentation and hypothesis testing in the development of crime policies. In doing so it is concerned with controlling for chance and bias in the process. There is an emphasis throughout any experimental or evaluation exercise on determining the mechanism through which any particular initiative might work in the context of its application (Pawson and Tilley, 1997). In addressing the efficacy of crime control measures there is, therefore, an interest not only in what works but also in how and where.

With such an emphasis on experimentation, crime science has an obvious interest in the integrity, accuracy, validity and reliability of data on crime and disorder. Improving the skills and knowledge base of police and associated professionals, whose work involves the collection and analysis of such data, is a current area of activity for crime scientists and is likely to remain so for some time.

Evaluation

It is too soon to say what value, if any, crime science adds to society's approach to crime control. There is a considerable research literature which is critical of the view that science has anything significant to offer to the control of socially defined behaviours such as those classed as criminal or disorderly, and to that extent crime science may have an uphill battle. Nevertheless, criminal behaviour is still behaviour and the discipline of psychology, in common with other empirically-oriented sciences, is founded on the belief that all behaviour is amenable to scientific study and that it can be modified without recourse, necessarily, to oppressive measures.

Gloria Laycock

Associated Concepts: administrative criminology, crime prevention, experimental criminology, opportunity theory, public criminology, rational choice theory, routine activity theory, situational crime prevention

Key Readings

Brantingham, P.L. and Brantingham, P.J. (1993) 'Environment, routine and situation: toward a pattern theory of crime', in R.V. Clarke and M. Felson (eds), *Routine Activity and Rational Choice Advances in Criminological Theory*, vol. 5. New Brunswick, NJ: Transaction Press.
Clarke, R.V. (1997) 'Introduction', in Ronald V. Clarke (ed.), *Situational Crime Prevention: Successful Case Studies*, 2nd edn. New York: Harrow and Heston.
Cornish, D. and Clarke, R.V. (2003) 'Opportunities, precipitators and criminal decisions: a reply to Wortley's critique of situational crime prevention', in M. Smith and D.B. Cornish (eds), *Theory for*

Situational Crime Prevention, Crime Prevention Studies, vol. 16. Monsey, NY: Criminal Justice Press.

Ekblom, P. (1997) 'Gearing up against crime: a dynamic framework to help designers keep up with the adaptive criminal in a changing world', *International Journal of Risk, Security and Crime Prevention*, October, 2/4: 249–65.

Felson, M. (2002) *Crime and Everyday Life*, 3rd edn. Thousand Oaks, CA: Sage.

Laycock, G. (2005) 'Defining Crime Science', in M. Smith and N. Tilley (eds), *Crime Science: New Approaches to Preventing and Detecting Crime*. Cullompton: Willan.

Pawson, R. and Tilley, N. (1997) *Realistic Evaluation*. London: Sage.

Associated Concepts: genocide, hate crime, human rights, human trafficking, state crime, torture, war crimes

Key Readings

Bassiouni, M.C. (1999) *Crimes Against Humanity in International Law*. The Hague: Kluwer Law.

Gutman, R. and Rieff, D. (eds) (1999) *Crimes of War: What the Public Should Know*. New York: Norton.

Ratner, S.R. and Abrams, J.S. (1997) *Accountability for Human Rights*. Oxford: The Clarendon Press.

Robertson, G. (2000) *Crimes Against Humanity*. Harmondsworth: Penguin.

CRIMES AGAINST HUMANITY

Definition

The International Military Tribunal at Nuremberg impressed the concept of crimes against humanity into international law. These crimes were defined as the 'murder, extermination, enslavement or deportation, and other inhumane acts committed against any civilian population, before or during the war, or persecutions on political, racial or religious grounds in the execution of or in connection with any crime within the jurisdiction of the Tribunal, whether or not in violation of the domestic law of the country in question.' The international criminal tribunals for the former Yugoslavia and Rwanda added the crimes of rape and torture to the inventory of crimes against humanity. Crimes against humanity are different from genocide because they do not require the intention to eradicate, or attempt to eradicate, a national, ethnic, racial or religious group by mass murder. They are distinguishable from war crimes in that they apply in times of peace as well as war.

Eugene McLaughlin

CRIMINAL CAREERS

Definition

Ordered sequences of criminal law violations. An important difference between occupational and criminal careers is that the positions in occupational careers are usually legitimate, are often established by formal organizations, and frequently follow a standard pattern. Criminal law violations are less widely approved and usually do not involve organizationally defined positions. The concept is distinct from the linguistically similar phrase, 'career criminals'.

Distinctive Features

A criminal career has a beginning and an end; its trajectory is characterized by age of onset, age of desistance, frequency of violations of each type of crime, and the probabilities of switching between offence categories. Individuals, organizations and places may have criminal careers. Most research and theorizing has concerned the criminal careers of individuals.

Criminal career research confronts a number of methodological issues. Some of the most important are:

- The validity of different types of data (official records, self-reports, the reports of others). Often the trajectories derived from different sources are similar, but in some cases, those constructed from official records will differ from those based on non-official sources. Arrest statistics show aggregate levels of violence rising to a peak in late adolescence and early adulthood, and then declining. Observations of children, however, suggest that aggressive behaviour may be highest at ages 1 or 2, and then declines gradually with age. Because small children are weak, do little damage, and are not considered fully responsible for their actions, their aggression is handled informally, and thus is often neglected in studies of criminal careers.

- Aggregate data or individual-level data? A good deal of theorizing has been based on aggregate-level data. For a number of different offences, at different times and in different places, rates of aggregate involvement in crime rise with age and then decline. Quite different patterns of individual starts, stops and frequencies can yield the same aggregate pattern. To distinguish among these different patterns, data on individual careers are required.
- Cross-sectional or longitudinal analyses? In a one-shot, cross-sectional study, information about crime is collected from individuals of different ages at a single time. This design cannot distinguish age effects from cohort effects. Longitudinal research following one or more cohorts over time cannot distinguish the effects of age from period. No design can disentangle the linear effects of age, period and cohort. Researchers have typically dealt with this issue by assuming that one or more of these effects is zero.

Research on aggregate patterns has established that the age distribution of involvement in crime has changed dramatically over the past 200 years, that it differs from country to country, and is offence-specific. Studies of individual careers show trajectory shapes to be person-specific. There is a substantial degree of continuity in individual criminal involvement:

those with high levels of involvement at one time tend to have high levels at later times. Yet change does occur, with many careers ending in adolescence or early adulthood.

Research has identified numerous antecedents of the early onset of criminality in early childhood traits and family characteristics. Subsequent trajectories are influenced by marriage, employment, changing patterns of peer association, imprisonment, and participation in treatment programmes. Studies differ on whether offences tend to become more serious as careers progress.

Most offenders are not specialists. Superimposed on a pattern of random switching between crimes is a modest degree of specialization. Specialization is somewhat greater for white collar criminals and sex offenders.

Evaluation

The strength of the criminal career perspective is that it directs attention towards changes in patterns of criminal behaviour over the life course and also towards the dependence of age, or stage of career, on factors that influence criminal behaviour.

Thus far, research on criminal careers has tended to be individualistic: little attention has been paid to the possible mutual dependence of co-offenders' career trajectories. Statistical analyses have tended to lump offences of different kinds together, possibly obscuring differences among offences. Studies of crime switching have tended not to examine the temporal shape of trajectories.

Career research has concentrated on the 'common' crimes of interpersonal violence, theft, vandalism, illegal drug use, status offences and public order offences. Little research has been done on careers in consumer fraud, stock market fraud, insurance fraud, price-fixing, insider trading, tax evasion, offering and soliciting bribes, embezzlement, espionage, money laundering, arms trafficking, child molesting, perjury, making and distributing pornography, war crimes, police and prison guard violence, and genocide. Some of these offences can be carried out only by those who meet advanced educational standards and who hold office in legitimate organizations. For these offenders, onset is expected to be late and involvement to occur at older ages. Predictors of common criminality (for example, an impulsive personality, childhood aggressiveness, inadequate parental supervision in childhood, school difficulties and a low socio-economic status) may not predict involvement for these offences. Marriage and employment may not promote desistance, as they do for routine violence and property offences. Late initiators of careers in 'common' crimes have also been little studied.

David Greenberg

Associated Concepts: cohort studies, cross-sectional design, desistance, deterrence, developmental criminology, deviance, deviancy amplification, labelling, life course theories of crime, longitudinal study, recidivism, risk factor research

Key Readings

Blumstein, A., Cohen, J., Roth, J.A. and Visher, C.A. (eds) (1986) *Criminal Careers and 'Career Criminals',* 2 vols. Washington, DC: National Academy Press.

Farrington, D.P. (1997) 'Human development and criminal behaviour', in M. Maguire, R. Morgan and R. Reiner (eds), *The Oxford Handbook of Criminology,* 2nd edn. Oxford: The Clarendon Press.

Greenberg, D.F. (ed.) (1996) *Criminal Careers,* 2 vols. Aldershot, and Brookfield, VT: Dartmouth.

Le Blanc, M. and Frechette, M. (1989) *Male Criminal Activity from Childhood through Youth: Multilevel and Developmental Perspective.* New York: Springer-Verlag.

Thornberry, T. (ed.) (1997) *Developmental Theories of Crime and Delinquency.* New Brunswick, NJ: Transaction.

Tonry, M., Ohlin, L. and Farrington, D.P. (eds) (1991) *Human Development and Criminal Behavior.* New York: Springer-Verlag.

CRIMINAL JUSTICE

Definition

The process through which the state responds to behaviour that it deems unacceptable. Criminal justice is delivered through a series of stages: charge, prosecution, trial, sentence, appeal, punishment. These processes and the agencies which carry them out are referred to collectively as *the criminal justice system*.

Distinctive Features

The framework of criminal justice is laid down by legislation specifying the penalties available in consequence of various crimes, and the powers, rules and procedures for each process and agency. In the UK, legislation has generally prescribed maximum penalties, leaving considerable discretion to courts in deciding the actual penalty in individual cases. The life sentence for murder has traditionally been the only mandatory sentence. Other countries have more prescriptive penal codes, with less discretion available to courts. In recent years, the UK has followed other jurisdictions, especially the USA, in introducing more mandatory sentences. Discretion has been reduced at all points in the system. Under the slogan 'truth in sentencing', politicians have decreed that offenders should serve the sentence pronounced by the court, or at least a fixed percentage of it, rather than have the length of sentence actually served determined by prison governors or probation officers through decisions about early release or the early termination of community orders.

Life imprisonment is the most severe punishment in most Western countries. The important exception here is the USA, where use of the death penalty had increased during the 1990s; several states which did not have it have introduced or re-introduced the death penalty. In most years, Texas carries out the highest number of executions. By contrast, Eastern European countries seeking membership of the European Union have abolished the death penalty, as part of moves to bring their criminal justice systems into line with the European Convention on Human Rights.

In the 1980s, several high-profile cases in England and Wales were shown to have resulted in wrongful convictions. Concern with these miscarriages of justice led to a Royal Commission on Criminal Justice in 1993. Some changes in procedures resulted, among the most important of which was the requirement upon prosecutors to disclose evidence more fully to the defence before trial. Gradually, however, these concerns have faded, and by the mid-1990s a widespread perception that too many guilty people were being acquitted had led to further changes which swung the balance of advantage back towards the prosecution.

Theoretical analysis of criminal justice has focused on the tension between the objective of crime control and the values of due process. Although crime control, or crime reduction, is obviously the overall aim of criminal justice, it is limited by the rights accorded to defendants. Crime control and due process were represented as alternative models of criminal justice by Herbert Packer (Sanders and Young, 1994). If crime control is the dominant consideration, severe penalties may be imposed: penalties designed to ensure the protection of the public through the removal or incapacitation of the offender, so there is no chance of a further offence. Establishing guilt 'beyond reasonable doubt' may seem less important than demonstrating the consequences of crimes. Due process values emphasize fairness and equality in criminal justice, and respect the rights of offenders, in order that there should be proper safeguards through representation, rules of evidence, and the prosecution having to establish guilt according to rigorous standards of proof. Due process models also expect the punishment to be proportionate to the seriousness of the offence, and not to be degrading or inhumane. The 1980s are said to have been characterized by the dominance of due process values, while there was a marked swing towards crime control in the 1990s.

Criminologists have been interested in the possibility and extent of discrimination in criminal justice. Unemployment, race and gender have been shown to influence criminal justice decision making. High unemployment rates correlate with high imprisonment rates; black offenders have been found to be more likely than their white counterparts to be imprisoned; being female is associated with receiving probation where male offenders might receive a fine or other non-interventive sentence. There is some disagreement among criminologists about whether women's criminal justice treatment is more or less severe than that for males, but also a general agreement that this is different. Conversely, any consensus about the extent of different treatment due to race has been harder to establish; however, a general agreement exists that if there is any difference, it is evidenced by the greater severity that is directed towards black offenders.

Barbara Hudson

Associated Concepts: crime control model, discretion, discrimination, disparity, disproportionality, due process model, penality, probation, social justice

Key Readings

Ashworth, A. (1994) *The Criminal Process.* Oxford: Oxford University Press.

Ashworth, A. and Wasik, M. (eds) (1998) *Fundamentals of Sentencing Theory.* Oxford: The Clarendon Press.

Davies, M., Croall, H. and Tyrer, J. (1995) *Criminal Justice: An Introduction to the Criminal Justice System in England and Wales.* Harlow: Longman.

Hood, R. (1992) *Race and Sentencing: A Study in the Crown Court.* Oxford: The Clarendon Press.

Lacey, N. (1994) *Criminal Justice.* Oxford: Oxford University Press.

Sanders, A. and Young, R. (1994) *Criminal Justice.* Oxford: Butterworths.

CRIMINALIZATION

Definition

Crime is a status conferred on and ascribed to certain non-approved acts legislated against and, by due process of the law, punished. Derived in social reaction theory, criminalization is the institutionalized process through which certain acts and behaviours are labelled as 'crimes' and 'outlawed'. It reflects the state's decision to regulate, control and punish selectively. Critical theorists have developed this analysis further, arguing that criminalization does not occur in a vacuum. It is influenced by contemporary politics, economic conditions and dominant ideologies, and contextualized by the determining contexts of social class, gender, sexuality, 'race' and age.

Distinctive Features

While it is clear that certain acts and behaviours receive widespread disapproval and condemnation transcending time, place and culture, much that is declared 'unlawful' and defined as 'crime' is derived from a social and societal reaction. Not all harmful acts are defined as crimes and not all crimes are necessarily harmful. Criminalization represents the technical process through which acts are defined as crimes, legislated against, regulated through law enforcement and, via the courts, punished. Further, however, it is a political, economic and ideological process through which individuals and identifiable groups are selectively policed and disciplined.

Reflecting on a postwar USA, Spitzer (1975) argued that criminalization specifically targeted those whose 'behaviour, personal qualities, and/or position threaten the social relations of production', challenging the established economic order, the 'process of socialization for productive and non-productive roles', and the 'ideology which supports the functioning of capitalist society'. The deviant status ascribed to such 'problem populations' is the product of a process of social categorization. For Spitzer, critical analysis 'must examine where these images and definitions came from' and 'what they reflect about the structure of and priorities in specific class societies ...'.

Although criticized for economic reductionism, Spitzer placed class and marginalization firmly on the labelling and social reaction agenda. In other words, crime and criminalization were inextricably, although not always, linked to subordination and oppression within advanced capitalist societies. This discussion reasserted the importance of Marx's analysis of the relative surplus population within developing capitalism and its threat to the social order and economic conditions. The political management of the relative surplus population, of the marginalized, relies on the rule of law and its selective enforcement to discipline oppositional forces embodying strategies of surveillance, regulation and control.

Within the UK, Box (1983) demonstrated how contemporary economic crises impacted on the criminalization of subordinate groups. Ideological constructions derived from nineteenth-century social conditions were mobilized in the 1980s, best illustrated by continua that dichotomized the rough and the respectable, the undeserving and deserving poor, the subversive and the conforming. The rough, undeserving and dangerous 'underclass' – the 'enemy within' – necessitated hardline policing, tougher sentencing and secure containment. The implication was that imprisonment had to be used to control and regulate problem populations, particularly during economic recessions.

Critical analysis, however, contests the simplistic claim that rising unemployment and increased poverty will inevitably lead to crime and thus a swelling prison population. Box and Hale (1982: 22) recorded a more complex picture in which imprisonment was 'not a direct response to any rise in crime, but is an ideologically motivated response to the perceived threat posed by the swelling population of economically marginalized persons'. They contended that increases in street crime, for example, managed by the rhetoric and practices of authoritarian 'law and order' responses, was a myth that was constructed with the political objective of strengthening criminal justice control agencies.

In the USA, Currie (1998: 185) reflected that in 1967 the Kerner Commission on Urban Disorders brought the country to a law and order crossroads. He noted a common agreement that 'we could never imprison our way out of America's violent crime problem', that tackling violent crime meant 'attacking social exclusion' and 'making a real rather than rhetorical commitment' to defeating the material realities of crime and exclusion. The USA took another road, and at the end of the century 'bursting prisons, devastated cities and [a] violent crime rate unmatched in the "developed" world' were the result. According to Parenti (1999), a right-wing cultural backlash provided the basis for an ideological reaffirmation of the 'underclass' as marginals by choice rather than circumstance.

Marginalization and criminalization together protect, reinforce and reproduce established order interests whether these are political, economic, or both. Coercive intervention, however, requires not only authority but also legitimacy: 'The power to criminalize is not derived necessarily in consensus politics but is implicitly a political act. Criminalization [reflects] ideologies associated with marginalization and it is within these portrayals that certain actions are named, contained and regulated ... a powerful process because it mobilizes popular approval and legitimacy in support of powerful interests within the state' (Scraton and Chadwick, 1991: 172–3). Thus popular support has to be won for state policies and law reforms that are essentially authoritarian, including the normalization of 'special powers'. It is the political management of negative reputations and violent identities – developed, consolidated, transmitted and reproduced through ideologies of the 'other' – which underwrites a hardening process of criminalization.

Evaluation

The radical critique at the heart of critical analysis within criminology in the USA, UK and Europe in the 1970s was criticized for its economic reductionism and false universalism. It was accused of over-simplification regarding its proposed close association of class, marginalization and criminalization. The critique noted that crime, deviance and social conflict were complex and could not be reduced to material causation (unemployment, poverty, poor housing and so on).

Neo-classical, conservative criminologists considered concepts such as criminalization to be little more than justifications for crimes committed by individuals who had made informed choices and should be held responsible for their acts. As conservative analysis reasserted its position through the consolidation of 'underclass theory'; it was matched by the emergence of 'ethical socialists' who also emphasized 'dismembered families', 'lone mothers', a lack of civic responsibility and lifestyle choice as the primary causes of poverty and violent crime. Taken together, these critiques reaffirmed individual and social pathologies as the underlying conditions in which much crime was rooted.

From their roots within radicalism, self-styled 'left realists' in the UK argued that the critical analysis had been flawed by economic reductionism, leading to 'left idealism' and a failure to 'take crime seriously'. This created a heated debate in which critical criminologists argued that the associated structural processes of marginalization and criminalization could not be confined to the relations of production and distribution. They emphasized the significance of patriarchy, heterosexuality, 'race' and age as institutionalized and oppressive constructs, subordinating and marginalizing people at the political-ideological as well as the political-economic level.

Conceptually, criminalization explains the structural conditions in which certain acts are defined as crimes and subsequently policed and punished. It explores the creation and political management of identities in the determining contexts of societal power relations. And it also provides an understanding of the criminal justice clampdown, the rise in punitive legislation, and the authoritarian shift within social democratic states. This clampdown has been exemplified in the UK by the mantra 'tough on crime, tough on the causes of crime' which underpins a multi-agency or matrix approach to social discipline: zero tolerance and 'quality of life' policing, as well as increased surveillance, targeting and hardline interventions. With the criminal justice 'net' widening to include 'anti-social' behaviour, and to regulate children at a very early age, the criminalizing context has been further extended.

Kathryn Chadwick and Phil Scraton

Associated Concepts: authoritarian populism, crime, critical criminology, emergency legislation, labelling, left realism, net widening, racialization, radical feminism, risk, social harm, social reaction, surveillance, the state, underclass

Key Readings

Box, S. (1983) *Power, Crime and Mystification.* London: Tavistock.

Box, S. and Hale, C. (1982) 'Economic crisis and the rising prisoner population in England and Wales', *Crime and Social Justice,* 17: 20–35.

Currie, E. (1998) *Crime and Punishment in America.* New York: Metropolitan Books.

Parenti, C. (1999) *Lockdown America: Police and Prisons in the Age of Crisis.* London: Verso.

Scraton, P. and Chadwick, K. (1991) 'Challenging the new orthodoxies: the theoretical imperatives and political priorities of critical criminology', in K. Stenson and D. Cowell (eds), *The Politics of Crime Control.* London: Sage.

Spitzer, S. (1975) 'Towards a Marxian theory of deviance', *Social Problems,* 22: 368–401.

CRITICAL CRIMINOLOGY

Definition

Critical criminology applies critical analysis to the 'discipline' of criminology, the study of crime and the administration of criminal justice. It emphasizes the contextualizing relationship of structure and agency, locating the 'everyday', routine world within structural

and institutional relations. It locates 'crime', 'deviance' and 'social conflict' within their *determining contexts* rather than being obsessed with *causation*. It endeavours to broaden the scope of analysis to include a consideration of *harm* rather than crime, *social justice* rather than criminal justice, *treatment* rather than punishment, and discourses of *human rights* rather than discipline and control. The structural relations of production and distribution, reproduction and patriarchy, and neo-colonialism are identified as the primary determining contexts within which the interrelationships and mutual dependencies of structural forms of oppression can be understood.

Distinctive Features

Breaking with traditional, academic criminology which prioritized liberalism, pluralism and reformism, radical criminology emerged in the early 1970s. In Britain, the National Deviancy Conference (NDC) was formed, uniting academics, practitioners and campaigners in the pursuit of a radical alternative to mainstream criminology. From the NDC developed the 'New Criminology' which set the radical agenda via the proposal for a 'fully social theory' of deviance. This involved establishing theoretical connections between the law, the state, legal and political relations and the functions of crime. Its objective was to evolve a Marxist perspective prioritizing a political-economic focus on class and class relations. Implicit in this analysis was the connection between class, crime and the state, with 'crime control' providing the coercive means through which threats to the established social and economic order would be identified and regulated. It was the state, through its legislation, that would establish official means of crime control – hence the state's role to guarantee *continuity*, to manage *conflict*, and to *reproduce* the dominant social and economic order.

In responding to this 'radical' direction in criminology, critics targeted its implied economic reductionism. They suggested that within critical analysis the rule of law and its relations were reduced to functional subsidiaries of the political economy. In European societies, notably Scandinavia, Holland and West Germany, the development of radical criminology was more inclined towards abolitionism: 'the product of the same counter-cultural politics of the 1960s which gave rise to the cultural radicalism of the "new" or "critical" criminology' (Cohen, 1996: 3).

Throughout the 1980s profound differences emerged within critical criminology that were experienced most acutely in Britain. Key proponents of 'New Criminology' redefined themselves as 'left realists'. The primary proposition was that 'crime' needed to be 'taken seriously' and 'confronted' by politicians, policy makers and academics. Emphasizing crime, crime prevention and civil disorder, the left realist solution to the problem of crime proposed a democratic, multi-agency approach geared to a more equal distribution of resources and a reformed system of legal justice. Central to the work of left realism has been the labelling and rejection of 'idealism' in radical criminology, exposing the political and theoretical weaknesses of 'left idealism' as economically reductionist and deterministic. Critical criminology, however, cannot be so lightly dismissed.

According to Scraton and Chadwick (1991) a 'second phase' in the development of critical criminology can be identified. Established theoretical principles have not been rejected but refined, redeveloped and extended. The initial call from new criminology to locate the world of everyday life within broader structural relations remains a defining principle, setting the agenda for the consolidation of critical analysis within criminological theory. Significant here is the relationship between 'structure' and 'agency'. Agency refers to the experiential, everyday world of diverse social relations and interaction. Structure encompasses the world of institutions and structural relations – and their histories – which set the boundaries for social interaction and personal opportunity within society, containing and regulating social relations.

Moreover, while critical analysis remains committed to an economic analysis focusing on the relations of production and distribution – emphasizing class relations and the dynamics and consequences of advanced capitalism and globalization – other interrelated centres of power and their institutional relations are also prioritized. These include the structural relations of reproduction and dependency, emphasizing the global domination of women and the complexities, yet universality, of contrasting patriarchies. Also significant are the structural relations of neo-colonialism, emphasizing the pervasiveness of institutional racism and its imperialist legacy, and connecting slavery, colonization, immigration and migration. Scraton (1991: 93) identifies these structural relations as the 'determining contexts' of social action and human potential. These are relations embodying exploitation, oppression and subordination. They are relations of power, both economic and political, underpinned by deep ideological traditions and their contemporary manifestation.

A further important dimension of critical criminology is the relationship between power and knowledge. For Foucault (1980), power is not unidimensional but dispersed throughout society, not resting with one dominant state, sovereign or class. Power and knowledge imply each other. Crucially, the power–knowledge axis permeates and sustains official discourses. For critical theorists, official discourses are developed and reproduced through the primary determining contexts of class, 'race' and gender. Discrimination resulting from these determining contexts is experienced daily, interpersonally, at the level of agency. Yet they also have a structural significance in that classism, racism, sexism and heterosexism are institutionalized and oppressive constructs. They inform legislation, policy and practice throughout institutions, organizations and professions. It is through the process of institutionalization that the relations of domination and subordination gain their legitimacy and achieve structural significance.

The processes of marginalization and criminalization are central in explaining and analysing the relationship between the law, crime, punishment and the state. Critical theorists argue that there is a direct relationship between economic crises and the political responses of state and judiciary, leading to the marginalization and criminalization of certain groups. While economic changes bring political responses, through state action, when such action is coercive or involves the use of force and violence, it has to be legitimated. This is the dichotomy between coercion and consent. Critical criminology demonstrates that the process of criminalization protects, reinforces and reproduces the political, economic and social interests of an established order. The process requires institutional legitimacy and also the winning of popular consent for state policies and legal shifts that are essentially authoritarian. Negative reputations, stereotyped images and collective, violent identities – the stuff of 'folk devils' – are transmitted through ideologies. The state institutional response relies heavily on winning 'hearts and minds' in pursuing this ideological appeal through popular discourse. Political, economic and ideological forces, then, are intricately connected in the creation, maintenance and portrayal of the process of criminalization.

Evaluation

Critical criminology contests and rejects the knowledge base, theoretical traditions and imperatives of administrative criminology. It also challenges the emphases of left realist analyses, arguing that this approach remains locked into – and constrained by – definitions, policies and practices shaped and administered within the criminal justice priorities of social democratic states. While taking 'crime' seriously, it also retains a commitment to the location of 'crime', 'deviance' and 'conflict' within the determining contexts of power and their institutionalized relations.

Critical criminology also incorporates a human rights discourse and agenda. This development reaffirms that 'advanced' democracies, whatever their claims for upholding the principles of equality and liberty, embody and reproduce the structural inequalities of global capitalism, patriarchy and neo-colonialism. These inequalities are woven

into the fabric of the state and civil society – hegemonic rather than ideological. They are supported and reproduced through what Foucault calls 'regimes of truth'. Critical analysis has focused on the structure, procedures and appropriateness of the criminal justice process (from the derivation of laws to the administration of punishments) in identifying their specific and cumulative deficit in revealing 'truth' and delivering 'justice'. A human rights discourse, agenda and process provide a processual and procedural alternative to the administration of the law and criminal justice (Cohen, 1993, 1996). It is also a priority for critical criminology in challenging the context and consequences of state-sanctioned regimes of truth.

Kathryn Chadwick and Phil Scraton

Associated Concepts: abolitionism, authoritarian populism, Birmingham 'school', convict criminology, criminalization, critical research, human rights, left idealism, Marxist criminologies, new criminology, post-colonial criminology, public criminology, radical criminologies, radical feminism, the state

Key Readings

Cohen, S. (1993) 'Human rights and crimes of the state: the culture of denial', *Australian and New Zealand Journal of Criminology*, 26 (2): 97–115.

Cohen, S. (1996) 'Crime and politics: spot the difference', *British Journal of Sociology*, 47 (1): 1–21.

Foucault, M. (1980) *Power/Knowledge: Selected Interviews and Other Writings, 1972–1977* (ed. C. Gordon). Brighton: Harvester Wheatsheaf.

Scraton, P. (1991) 'Recent developments in criminology: a critical overview', in M. Haralambos (ed.), *Developments in Sociology: An Annual Review* (No. 7). Ormskirk: Causeway Press.

Scraton, P. and Chadwick, K. (1991) 'Challenging the new orthodoxies: the theoretical imperatives and political priorities of critical criminology', in

K. Stenson and D. Cowell (eds), *The Politics of Crime Control.* London: Sage.

Sim, J., Scraton, P. and Gordon, P. (1987) 'Crime, the state and critical analysis', in P. Scraton (ed.), *Law, Order and the Authoritarian State: Readings in Critical Criminology.* Milton Keynes: Open University Press.

CRITICAL RESEARCH

Definition

Critical social research begins with the premise that 'knowledge', including the formalized 'domain assumptions' and boundaries of academic disciplines, is neither value-free nor value-neutral. Rather, knowledge is derived and reproduced, historically and contemporaneously, in the structural relations of inequality and oppression that underpin established social orders. Challenging the quantitative foundations of positivism and the interpretive foundations of phenomenology, critical research endeavours to locate the experiential realities of individuals and communities (agency) within their historical, structural and reproductive contexts (structure).

Distinctive Features

Writing in the late 1950s, and demonstrating a growing scepticism for mainstream social science and its application within the USA, Wright Mills (1959: 20) criticized the 'bureaucratic techniques which inhibit sociological inquiry by "methodological" pretensions', its 'obscurantist conceptions' and its trivializing of 'publicly relevant issues' by an overstated 'concern with minor problems'. Such 'inhibitions, obscurities and trivialities' had created a crisis for a form of state-supported social research which decontextualized people's lives, experiences and opportunities. For Wright Mills, researching and teaching at the height of McCarthyism, sociology had 'lost its reforming push', and its 'tendencies towards fragmentary problems and scattered causation' had been 'conservatively turned to the use of the corporation, army and the state'.

Throughout the 1960s in the USA and Western Europe the radical critique of social sciences consolidated. It proposed that commissioned research was conceptualized and designed to further the material interests of the powerful, in political and economic institutions, at the expense of the powerless. Of particular concern was how social research was used to serve and service the military–industrial complex and its international, expansionist objectives. The radical critique claimed that crime and other social problems which were the consequence of structural inequality, economic deprivation and cultural discrimination were reconstructed through mainstream social research as the inevitable outcomes of individual or community pathologies.

Central to the critique was the assertion that social science, far from being constituted by 'value-free', 'objective' or 'scientific' disciplines independent of each other and distinct from societal relations, was directly implicated in the maintenance and reproduction of social order. In its applications and interventions social science was a part of, rather than apart from, the political, economic and social developments geared to regulating conflict and managing change. Thus its emphases and methodologies reflected its purpose and utility.

Within criminology the radical critique emphasized the significance of social conditions and structural inequalities in the creation of 'crime', 'deviance', disorder and conflict. Challenging the traditions of criminality, causation, pathologization and correction, critical research switched the emphasis to socio-legal definitions, social and societal reactions, and the structural contexts of daily interaction within communities. As Wright Mills had proposed: the 'most fruitful distinction with which the sociological imagination works' operates 'between the *personal troubles* of the milieu and the *public issues* of social structure' (1959: 8; emphases added).

Thus, critical social research 'is underpinned by a critical-dialectical perspective' committed to 'dig[ging] beneath the surface of historically specific, oppressive social structures' (Harvey, 1990: 1). Initially critical research was concerned with class-based oppression but the emergence of second-wave feminist analyses and anti-racist research extended critical methodologies to all structural forms of oppression and their integration. Critical research 'delv[es] beneath ostensive and dominant conceptual frames in order to reveal the underlying practices, their historical specificity and structural manifestations' (1990: 4). In this context, critical research is not only historically grounded, it is also concerned with the political-ideological context as well as the political-economic determinants which shape and legitimate the social conditions of structural inequality. This includes the institutional arrangements through which official discourse and academic knowledge are produced, and confers legitimacy on existing social arrangements.

As Hudson (2000: 177) notes, 'of all the applied social sciences, criminology has the most dangerous relationship to power: the categories and classifications, the labels and diagnoses and the images of the criminal produced by criminologists are stigmatizing and pejorative.' Such conceptions and their application inform 'strategies of control and punishment' and impact individually and collectively on 'rights and liberties'. Thus it is through critical social research that the power–knowledge axis, at the heart of Foucault's discussion of the material reality of societal 'regimes of truth', is exposed and deconstructed.

The search for knowledge and truth – epistemology – has been central to research traditions. Critical social research challenges the academic knowledge base which serves to reproduce dominant power relations and their structural inequalities. Of particular significance is official discourse, reflecting and reinforcing the 'view from above', conferring legitimacy on political and economic institutions and their operation. As regimes of truth are constructed they become the institutionalized and professionalized manifestations of knowledge. Thus 'knowledge' becomes 'institutionally appropriate', exercised and delivered through the interventions of professional 'experts'. By mobilizing the politics of reputation and representation, those 'knowledges' considered inappropriate,

non-legitimate or oppositional are marginalized and disqualified. Critical social research challenges official discourses as well as the power, authority and legitimacy of state institutions. Within criminology the 'object of investigation is the cluster of theories, policies, legislation, media treatments, roles and institutions that are concerned with crime, and with the control and punishment of crime' (Hudson, 2000: 177).

Connected to the *object* and *substance* of critical research is *reflexivity*, through which 'myths' and 'hidden truths' are revealed and people are helped 'to change the world for themselves' (Neuman, 1994: 67). The objective of reflective, qualitative action research in revealing 'the underlying mechanisms that account for social relations' is to 'encourage dramatic social change from grass-roots level' (1994: 67). As Stanley (1990: 15) comments in her discussion of feminist praxis, 'succinctly the point is to change the world, not only to study it'. Unpopular with governments and state institutions, criticized for reductionism and over-simplification and deprived of significant funding, critical research has been a highly successful antidote to the functional, self-serving apologism of administrative criminology and the decontextualized relativism – particularly regarding power – of postmodernist discourses on crime and punishment.

Phil Scraton and Kathryn Chadwick

Associated Concepts: action research, criminalization, critical criminology, discourse analysis, feminist research, reflexivity

Key Readings

Harvey, L. (1990) *Critical Social Research*. London: Sage.

Hudson, B. (2000) 'Critical reflection as research methodology', in V. Jupp, P. Davies and P. Francis (eds), *Doing Criminological Research*. London: Sage.

Neuman, W. (1994) *Social Research Methods: Qualitative and Quantitative Approaches*. Boston, MA: Allyn and Bacon.

Scraton, P. (ed.) (1987) *Law, Order and the Authoritarian State: Readings in Critical Criminology.* Milton Keynes: Open University Press.

Stanley, L. (ed.) (1990) *Feminist Praxis.* London: Routledge.

Wright Mills, C. (1959) *The Sociological Imagination.* New York: Oxford.

CROSS-SECTIONAL DESIGN

Definition

A design in which a cross-section of the population is selected for study, and data are collected from or about each selected case at one particular point in time.

Distinctive Features

The term 'cross-sectional design' often refers to a type of social survey in which subsets of a population are selected to be part of a sample. Where the subsets are represented in direct proportion to their existence in the population it is common to refer to 'proportionate cross-sectional designs'. Where subsets are not selected in proportion to their presence in the population – perhaps to give greater weight to the views of minority groups – the term 'disproportionate cross-sectional design' is used. Because data are collected from sample members at one single point in time, cross-sectional surveys are sometimes also known as 'one-shot designs'.

One-shot cross-sectional surveys are appropriate to obtaining representative 'snapshots' of the population in terms of basic attributes (such as class, age, ethnicity) and also in terms of subjective variables (such as opinions and attitudes). In the United Kingdom, police forces are required by legislation to carry out crime audits of their area, including a survey of the general public's views on the ways in which the community is policed. One-shot cross-sectional surveys are well suited to this purpose. Sometimes cross-sectional surveys are also used to collect retrospective data, for example observations about what sample members did in the past or had done to them. At the analysis stage an attempt is made to correlate past actions, behaviours or events with contemporary attributes, attitudes or other subjective feelings. For example, crime surveys will seek to connect respondents' previous victimization of crime with current fears about the possibility of further victimization.

The term 'cross-sectional design' also relates to the use of official statistics and other social indicators to describe geographical areas at any given point in time. For example, the Chicago School of urban sociology used delinquency rates (amongst others) to 'map' the city of Chicago in the 1930s. This was the basis for a concentric circle theory of urban development, and the mapping of the city in terms of such rates resembled a cross-section from an onion. Such statistical analysis was used alongside detailed ethnographic accounts of the 'underside' of life within different concentric circles.

Evaluation

Cross-sectional designs provide a relatively cheap and quick means for describing populations along a number of variables at any point in time. They also facilitate the search for patterns of relationships between variables, for example various indicators of social exclusion (such as unemployment, poor housing standards, low educational standards) and levels of criminal and disorderly actions.

As indicated earlier, cross-sectional surveys sometimes collect retrospective data – about past experiences, perhaps – with a view to correlating past experiences with present actions or attitudes. Such correlations subsequently form the basis for causal inferences suggesting, say, that previous experience of victimization engenders present fears of crime. There are, however, difficulties with this. For example, there are doubts about the reliability of respondents' memories of past experiences. More crucially, correlations indicating potential relationships between past experiences and current attitudes and feelings do not by themselves provide sufficient evidence of causality. What is also needed is direct evidence of time-ordering and of causal forces. Sometimes this can be provided by longitudinal surveys, in which a sample of individuals is studied over a long period of time (indeed sometimes a life-time).

A further problem with cross-sectional studies is related to one of their strengths, namely that they provide snapshots at a particular point in time. However, this means that such studies are not useful vehicles for examining social change in society or for mapping social trends over time. One way of overcoming this is to take equivalent samples at different points in time and collect data on the same variables with a view to examining changes or trends. This is known as a 'trend' or a 'time series' design, an example of which is the British Crime Survey, which seeks to examine changes and trends in victimization.

Victor Jupp

Associated Concepts: Chicago School of Sociology, longitudinal study, official criminal statistics, sampling, social survey, time series design, victim surveys

Key Readings

Jupp, V.R. (1996) *Methods of Criminological Research*. London: Routledge.
Mayhew, P. (1996) 'Researching crime and victimization: the BCS', in P. Davies, P. Francis and V. Jupp (eds), *Understanding Victimization*. Newcastle, University of Northumbria: Social Sciences Press.

CULTURAL CRIMINOLOGY

Definition

An emergent theoretical orientation that investigates the convergence and contestation of cultural, criminal and crime control processes. Cultural criminology emphasizes the role of image, style, representation and meaning, both within illicit subcultures and in the mediated construction of crime and crime control.

Distinctive Features

As developed by Ferrell (1999), Ferrell and Sanders (1995) and other theorists, cultural criminology incorporates a number of orientations regarding the cultural construction of crime and crime control. At its most basic, cultural criminology seeks to import the insights of cultural studies into criminology, building especially from the pioneering work of the Birmingham Centre for Contemporary Cultural Studies in the 1970s on subcultural symbolism and mediated social control. Similarly, cultural criminology operates from the postmodern propositions that style is substance, that meaning resides in representation, and that crime and crime control can therefore only be understood as an ongoing spiral of intertextual, image-driven 'media loops' (Manning, 1998). Undergirding the use of these contemporary perspectives in cultural criminology are somewhat more traditional projects: the expansion of existing interactionist understandings and the sharpening of critical analysis in criminology. Cultural criminologists attempt to develop the 'symbolic' in 'symbolic interaction' by exploring the stylized dynamics of illicit subcultures and the representational universes of the mass media. Similarly, they seek to unravel the complex circuitry through which the meaning of crime and crime control is constructed, enforced and resisted.

These theoretical orientations inform the methodologies favoured by cultural criminologists. As employed within cultural criminology, ethnographic research draws on sociological, anthropological and cultural-studies traditions to investigate nuances of meaning developed within particular cultural milieux and to explore the situated dynamics of illicit subcultures. At its extreme, such research is designed to develop a form of criminological *verstehen* whereby the researcher approaches an empathic, appreciative understanding of the meanings and emotions associated with crime and crime control. Alternatively, other cultural criminologists utilize methods of media and textual analysis to develop critical, scholarly readings of mediated crime and crime control accounts. Such scholarship investigates both historical and contemporary texts, ranging from newspapers, film and television to popular music, comic books and cyberspace. Recently, cultural criminologists have also begun to integrate these two methodological frameworks in exploring the ongoing confluence of illicit subcultures, media constructions and public meanings.

Framed by these theoretical and methodological orientations, cultural criminological analysis has developed in a number of areas. First, cultural criminology conceptualizes crime as a subcultural phenomenon organized around symbolic communication, shared aesthetics and collective identity. Given this, cultural criminologists focus especially on the dynamics of subcultural style as defining both the internal characteristics of illicit subcultures and external, mediated constructions of them (Hebdige, 1979). In addition, cultural criminologists highlight the intensities of collective experience and emotion within illicit subcultures, as embodied in moments of edgework and adrenalin, and as given meaning within shared vocabularies of motive.

If cultural criminologists in this sense conceptualize crime as culture, they also explore the ways in which culture comes to be reconstructed as crime. Focusing on 'culture wars' fought around issues of art and obscenity, alternative musical forms like punk and rap, and the allegedly criminogenic effects of television and film, researchers reveal the looping, reflexive process by which such media-generated popular culture forms are in turn criminalized by campaigns of moral enterprise which are themselves fought in the mediated realm of sound bites, press conferences and newspaper headlines. In this sense, 'cultural criminalization' occurs – that is, the mediated representation of popular culture forms as criminal or criminogenic, with or without attendant legal proceedings. Significantly, this process also embodies contemporary political dynamics, as moral entrepreneurs and cultural reactionaries utilize mediated channels to delegitimate alternative or illicit subcultures.

Cultural criminologists likewise explore the broader mediated construction of crime and crime control. Research in this area focuses not only on everyday media texts, but also on the complex, reciprocal interconnections between the criminal justice system and the mass media that shape such texts. Much of this work builds from, and in some cases reconceptualizes, Cohen's (1972) classic model regarding the invention of folk devils and the generation of moral panic around issues of crime and deviance. In this sense, this work examines the cultural dynamics by which certain activities come to be constructed as crime and threat, while others are left 'unconstructed'. It further emphasizes the ironies inherent in the marketing of crime as both threat and entertainment.

Threaded through all these areas of enquiry is a concern with relations of power, control and resistance. Cultural criminologists emphasize the new and often insidious forms of coercion and control that emerge within mediated 'wars' on crime and within the everyday consumption of crime as drama and entertainment. At the same time, they highlight the forms of resistance that emerge as audiences remake and reverse mediated meanings and as illicit subcultures embody their insubordination in stylized identities and collectively meaningful experience. Moreover, cultural criminology itself is designed to operate as a form of intellectual resistance, as a counter-discourse on contemporary crime issues that through 'newsmaking criminology' (Barak, 1994) and other public practices can generate alternative images of crime and crime control.

Evaluation

Despite a common focus on representation and meaning in the investigation of crime and crime control, much of the work in cultural criminology has remained divided between the study of illicit subcultures on the one hand and mass media texts on the other. Yet such a sharp disjunction misses a number of key dynamics regarding crime and culture, including the reconstruction of mass media texts by various subcultures and audiences; the production of localized, situated media by illicit subcultures and crime control agencies alike; and the subsequent appropriation of these situated images and symbols by the mass media. As noted previously, some recent work in cultural criminology has in fact begun to address this problem, by linking subcultural dynamics, organizational imperatives and situated media to broader, mass media constructions of crime and crime control, and by highlighting the reflexive process by which each party to public crime controversies remakes and recontextualizes the meanings of the other. Less promising is the ability of cultural criminologists to address issues of audience and audience meanings; as is the case with much media analysis and criticism, the epistemic activities of audiences remain more imagined than investigated.

Cultural criminologists are also just beginning to explore a number of key domains in which culture, crime and crime control converge. Contemporary policing is coming to be conceptualized as a set of semiotic practices entangled with 'reality' television programmes, everyday public surveillance, and the symbolism and aesthetics of police subcultures themselves. Public controversies regarding homeless populations, street gangs, graffiti crews and other marginalized groups are beginning to be investigated as conflicts over the construction of meaning and identity in public domains, and thus over ownership of 'cultural space'. Numerous investigations of embodied emotions – of pleasure, fear and excitement as the affective forces driving both crime and crime control – continue to emerge. Perhaps most importantly, cultural criminology is beginning to move beyond its British and US roots to explore the contested convergence of cultural and criminal dynamics in a variety of world settings, and to investigate the migration of illicit meanings across real and imagined borders.

Finally, as a nascent theoretical perspective, cultural criminology perhaps constitutes to this point less a completed, definitive paradigm and more an eclectic constellation of critiques linked by sensitivities to image and representation in the study of crime and crime control. Oriented as they are towards the multiplicity of meanings and indeterminacy of images continually developing around crime and crime control, though, cultural criminologists themselves would likely embrace cultural criminology as an always unfinished project, open to emerging configurations of culture, crime and crime control, and to emerging critiques of them.

Jeff Ferrell

Associated Concepts: appreciative criminology, Birmingham 'school', carnival (of crime), constitutive criminology, critical criminology, discourse analysis, ethnography, interactionism, newsmaking criminology, postmodernism, public criminology, social constructionism, subculture

Key Readings

Barak, G. (ed.) (1994) *Media, Process, and the Social Construction of Crime: Studies in Newsmaking Criminology.* New York: Garland.
Cohen, S. (1972) *Folk Devils and Moral Panics.* London: MacGibbon and Kee. (New edition, Oxford, Martin Robertson, 1980.)
Ferrell, J. (1999) 'Cultural criminology', *Annual Review of Sociology,* 25: 395–418.
Ferrell, J. and Sanders, C.R. (eds) (1995) *Cultural Criminology.* Boston, MA: Northeastern University Press.
Ferrell, J., Hayward, K., Morrison, W. and Presdee, M. (2004) *Cultural Criminology Unleashed.* London: Glass House Press.
Hebdige, D. (1979) *Subculture: The Meaning of Style.* London: Routledge.
Manning, P.K. (1998) 'Media loops', in F. Bailey and D. Hale (eds), *Popular Culture, Crime, and Justice.* Belmont, CA: West/Wadsworth.

CYBERCRIME

Definition

Cybercrimes are illegal acts committed with the assistance of, or by means of, computers, computer networks, the Internet, and web-based information and communications technologies (ICTs).

Distinctive Features

Broadly speaking, cybercrimes can be classified into two categories: crimes that cannot be committed in any other way or against any other type of victim (in other words, where the computer or online service is the target of the offence; for example, unauthorized access to systems, tampering with programs and data, and planting viruses); and familiar or conventional crimes that are facilitated by ICTs ('cyber' versions of identity theft, stalking, paedophile activities, hate crime, trading counterfeit goods, and so on). In some cases, criminal activities may encompass both categories, involving qualitatively new offences enabled by technologies and, at the same time, exploiting technology within more traditional activities such as planning, intelligence, logistics and finance. Finally, there are a number of behaviours that are not strictly cybercrimes, insofar as they are not illegal, but they may still constitute what most people would consider harmful to some users (such as some forms of pornography, gambling, unsolicited e-mail, unregulated sales of medicines and prescription drugs, etc.). Newman and Clarke (2003) have identified 26 crimes that have been made possible by ICTs, together with estimates of their extent or cost. They summarize the criminogenic attributes of cybercrimes in the acronym SCAREM: Stealth (cyberspace makes carrying out furtive crimes much easier), Challenge (an intellectual climate among hackers that is usually summed up as a desire to 'beat' the system), Anonymity (an aspect of cyberspace that is obviously conducive to committing crime and not getting caught), Reconnaissance (the Net provides a context in which informed criminals can plan their operation, survey all possible targets, and then act accordingly), Escape (in an environment where the identity and location of the offender are unknown and frequently unknowable, the opportunities for escape without leaving a trail of evidence are extremely high), and Multiplicity (cyberspace offers the opportunity to commit multiple crimes and create millions of victims simultaneously).

Evaluation

When it comes to assessments of crime and crime control in cyberspace there are essentially two diametrically opposed viewpoints. One is an upbeat – some would say, idealistic – outlook that new technologies are democratizing and the fact that control over content rests not with one powerful interest group, but potentially with each and every user, makes the cyber-environment a great social leveller where we can all 'police' each other. The other assessment of cybercrime is a negative response which ranges from gloomy resignation to shrill warnings about an apocalyptic meltdown. In popular discourse, including media discussions of cybercrime, it is the latter which dominates. Inevitably, our reliance on ICTs in nearly every aspect of our public and private lives raises important concerns about security, trust and control. In part, feelings of vulnerability may arise from the speed with which the personal computer (PC) became ubiquitous in everyday life in the 1980s and 1990s, and the rate at which 'new generation' technologies – variously called 'pervasive computing', 'ubiquitous computing' or 'ambient intelligence' – continue to be developed with unpredictable outcomes. Furthermore, the fear that hackers and virus writers are becoming less concerned with technical mastery for its own sake, and are also becoming explicitly criminal in intent, may be a consequence of the more general anxiety concerning terrorist threats post-9/11. Meanwhile, the childhood experience has undergone a major reorganization in advanced societies over the last half-century, with children subjected to a greater degree of protective control and regulation than ever before. As young people's horizons of play become increasingly restricted to the immediate environs of the home and home computer, fears have multiplied about their potential exposure to pornographic material and to paedophiles posing as fellow children in order to 'groom' their victims. The combination of these factors has resulted in high levels of global anxiety and numerous media-fuelled scares concerning the problem of cybercrime – which combine technological determinism with more generalized fears about the nature and prevalence of risk in the late-modern world.

The widespread notion that cyberspace is a playground for criminals is reinforced by pessimistic assessments of the effectiveness of law and order agents to control and combat it. The sheer size and scope of the Internet, the volume of electronic traffic it facilitates, the varying moral and legal responses to cybercrime in different countries, and other inter-jurisdictional difficulties such as a lack of co-operation or compatibility between police forces, combine to ensure that the police feel they remain in a perpetual game of 'catch-up' with the criminally-minded individuals who lurk in the shadowy corners of cyberspace. For example, organized criminals have been quick to exploit legal loopholes exposed within countries that have relatively relaxed attitudes to cybercrime. At the turn of the new millennium, Russia became a major source of child pornography because it had no specific laws governing the production or circulation of such material. Thus, while numerous criminal groups from other countries used Russian Internet sites to broadcast child pornography around the world, it was estimated that less than 1 per cent of the content was actually produced in Russia. Online casinos have also proliferated on the Internet – unsurprisingly since gambling is illegal in many jurisdictions. Other factors thought to have resulted in a widening gap between the activities of online offenders and those who monitor and police them, are the under-reporting of cybercrimes by victims (who, in many cases may not be aware that they have been victimized), a police culture which tends to be conservative and technology-averse, and limited resources. Given that cybercrime is potentially as limitless as cyberspace itself, any funding strategy quickly begins to resemble a bottomless money pit (Jewkes, 2003b).

Cyberspace has been identified as one of the fastest growing sites for crime and transgression (Thomas and Loader, 2000) and the next generation of ICTs – which will integrate online digital technology ever more closely into everyday life – will raise important questions of ownership, governance, security, surveillance, privacy, trust and vulnerability, among others. So complex is the global computing and communications environment that it is difficult to formulate a coherent response, to cybercrime or to predict future threats. In an environment where speed of transmission vastly outpaces the speed of response, and in which the computer power available at a constant price is doubled every 18 months (a principle known as Moore's law), many users will be willing to adopt technologies before they fully understand the issues they raise (Foresight, 2004). It is somewhat surprising, therefore, that – with a few exceptions – academic criminologists have been slow to address the criminogenic attributes of cyberspace.

Yvonne Jewkes

Associated Concepts: crime prevention, cultural criminology, globalization, hidden crime, risk, transnational organized crime

Key Readings

Foresight (2004) *Cyber Trust and Crime Prevention Project Executive Summary*. London: Department of Trade and Industry (www.foresight.gov.uk).

Jewkes, Y. (ed.) (2003a) *Dot.cons: Crime, Deviance and Identity on the Internet*. Cullompton, Devon: Willan.

Jewkes, Y. (2003b) 'Policing cybercrime', in T. Newburn (ed.), *Handbook of Policing*. Cullompton, Devon: Willan.

Newman, G.R. and Clarke, R.V. (2003) *Superhighway Robbery: Preventing E-Commerce Crime*. Cullompton, Devon: Willan.

Thomas, D. and Loader, B.D. (2000) *Cybercrime: Law Enforcement, Security and Surveillance in the Information Age*. London: Routledge.

Wall, D.S. (ed.) (2001) *Crime and the Internet*. London: Routledge.

D

DECARCERATION

Definition

The process that refers to a deliberate move away from the use of imprisonment as the central and predominant penal sanction, usually towards the use of alternative sanctions in the community.

Distinctive Features

Although criticisms against the form and level of prison use and the search for alternatives can be traced back at least to the nineteenth century, decarceration as a distinct process is a contemporary phenomenon. As part of what Cohen (1985) has termed the destructuring impulse in the 1960s, the decarceration movement grew in popularity at a time when the very idea of an institutional response to deviance was subject to a sustained critique. The prison system and total institutions in general were condemned as degrading, ineffective in terms of their stated goals (they could neither deter nor rehabilitate), counterproductive (they cemented deviant careers), and as part of the crime problem rather than its solution. Many proponents of decarceration have since argued for displacing the use of specific parts of the prison system (for example, juvenile detention), while others have concentrated on advocating alternative sanctions. Community-based corrections and treatments are regarded as more humane, less stigmatizing and more effective than institutional measures in the control of criminals and other problem populations. Intervention should be aimed at reintegration rather than segregation.

From a Marxist perspective, the prison system represents the symbol *par excellence* of a class society and of class justice. By inflicting coerced discipline and incarcerating predominantly young people, the unemployed and ethnic minorities, it reproduces hegemonic power relations in society. Critical studies on the association between imprisonment and unemployment, the repression of political dissent, human rights violations by the prison system, and overcrowding and inhumane prison conditions which have led to deaths and revolts, have served to highlight the role of the prison system as a repressive and ideological state apparatus. In this sense, decarceration is to be fought for as part of the class struggle.

Decarceration has also been closely associated with the abolitionist social movements and the radical penal lobby in Western Europe, Scandinavia and North America. Thomas Mathiesen (1986) advocated the principle of the 'unfinished' character of alternatives to prison and campaigned for 'negative' reforms that would ultimately lead to prison abolition. As academic involvement increased and the focus widened from solely the prison system to include the penal system, abolitionism developed as a new paradigm in criminology and as an alternative approach to crime and crime control.

Evaluation

Most Western criminal justice systems have witnessed some form of reduction in the use of custody at various times, but decarceration has not had a profound effect in decentring the prison system both in terms of actual prison population and its position in penal thinking. Critics have also pointed to the unintended and perverse consequences of decarceration. Scull (1984) has argued that treatment in the community often amounted to benign neglect, leaving people to fend for themselves without the care and supervision that they required. In his seminal work on the transformations in social control strategies, Cohen (1979, 1985) suggested that the extension of community corrections seemed to fit Foucault's model of 'dispersed discipline'. In the case of the decarceration of delinquents and criminals, old institutions remain while new community sanctions and supervisory punishments intended as 'alternatives' to custody are used as supplements to custody, thereby widening the net for social control. Greater rather than fewer numbers of deviants are drawn into the correctional continuum. The network of control agencies expands both physically and territorially. And the boundaries between liberty and confinement become blurred through the development of home curfews, tracking and tagging.

Whilst the decarceration critique continues to be influential, it does not necessarily reflect the current diverging control trends. In the case of the mentally ill, for example, the state-sponsored closing down of hospitals and asylums has continued to take place but mainly as a response to the retrenchment of welfare policies and fiscal pressures. Vass (1990) has also warned that an uncritical acceptance of the decarceration critique can lead to an impasse as well as a paralysis of inventive thought and praxis.

Maggy Lee

Associated Concepts: abolition, abolitionism, community sentences, diversion, penality, penology, radical non-intervention, social control, transcarceration

Key Readings

Cohen, S. (1979) 'The punitive city: notes on the dispersal of social control', *Contemporary Crises*, 3: 83–93.
Cohen, S. (1985) *Visions of Social Control: Crime, Punishment, and Classification.* Cambridge: Polity Press.
Mathiesen, T. (1986) 'The politics of abolition', *Contemporary Crises*, 10: 81–94.
Scull, A. (1984) *Decarceration: Community Treatment and the Deviant – A Radical*

View, rev. edn. Englewood Cliffs, NJ: Prentice-Hall.
Vass, A. (1990) *Alternatives to Prison – Punishment, Custody and the Community.* London: Sage.

DECONSTRUCTION

Definition

A literary and social scientific method of analysis most closely linked to postmodernism. Deconstructionists identify communication, whether spoken or written, as the construction of a 'text' that can be endlessly interpreted and re-interpreted, where meaning is always a departure from, rather than an arrival at, ultimate truths. Deconstructionists recognize that texts convey multiple, contradictory and hidden meanings that can only be provisionally examined and decoded. Thus, as a method of enquiry, it reveals some of the hidden assumptions and embedded values (i.e., ideology) conveyed, either knowingly or not, through the construction of a given text.

Distinctive Features

Deconstruction has been popularized chiefly by Jacques Derrida. In part, as a response to the objectivistic, absolutistic and positivistic sciences, Derrida's critique of Western epistemology and intellectual thought (i.e., 'logocentrism') reveals the hidden contradictions in which truth claims are asserted. Termed 'the metaphysics of presence', he examines how any value can be placed in relation to its corresponding binary term (e.g., white *vs.* black, straight *vs.* gay, objective *vs.* subjective, male *vs.* female). The value of the first term stems, in part, from the value of the second term; however, the value of the second term stems, in part, from the value of the first term. What this mutual interdependence demonstrates is that neither value can be privileged, despite the fact that we do this all the time in our constructed texts. Indeed, the first term becomes dominant, and the second repressed.

The metaphysics of presence shows us how, through communication, the first value is identified as a presence, active, privileged, while the second value is rendered an absence, passive, dismissed. The task of deconstruction is to show how these 'hierarchies' are basic to all phenomena and to demonstrate the way in which the texts that constitute these hierarchies can be decoded. Thus, the aim of deconstruction is to transform that which is absent into that which is felt and made present.

The deconstructionist strategy to decode existing power relations conveyed through a text is termed the 'reversal of hierarchies'. By turning the terms in binary opposition 'on their heads', so to speak, the implied and unspoken tension is revealed and their interdependence is made manifest. Further, deconstructionists like Derrida explain this mutual interdependence through the concept of *différance* (with an 'a'). *Différance* implies three meanings: (1) that the two terms in binary opposition 'differ' from one another to maintain their meaning; (2) that the two terms in binary opposition 'defer' to one another in the sense of implying the other term; and (3) that the two terms in binary opposition 'defer' to one another to maintain their interdependence.

Relatedly, deconstruction advocates the 'free play of the text'. Once a text (e.g., a legal narrative) is constructed, it is liberated, to some significant degree, from its author. That is to say, the narrative has a meaning beyond what was intended by the author – even if the author could exhaust his/her own intended meaning. For example, our understanding of homosexuality, the death penalty, mental illness, homelessness, abortion, drug addiction, politics, art, the presidency, and so on, is today considerably different from what it would have been twenty-five years ago. Deconstructionists tell us that this is because the meaning of each of these texts is historically situated; that is, different contexts create different meanings, and these various meanings are never exhaustible. This logic gives rise to the deconstructionist claim of 'foundationless' knowledge (i.e., truths that are absent from original, structured, anchored realities). Nihilist deconstructionists conclude that if all is relative, why bother to effect any change? Affirmative deconstructionists conclude that there are positional, provisional, relational truths (i.e., contingent universalities) that warrant attention when the voices and ways of knowing for those most silenced (i.e., the metaphysics of presence) necessitate wholesale support and recognition.

Evaluation

Modernity's quest for exactness, precision and ultimate truths finds considerable critique in the face of deconstructionism. As a method for uncovering hidden assumptions and values, deconstruction reveals how all texts (e.g., legal, criminological) are informed by ideology. The Critical Legal Studies Movement has relied heavily on deconstructionism to advance this position in relation to legal doctrines, the Constitution and statutory law. Criminology, although more slow in applying the tools of deconstruction, has raised similar questions in relation to criminological theory, criminal law and criminal behaviour. Postmodern critical criminology has been the leading exponent of this deconstructionist agenda.

Bruce Arrigo

Associated Concepts: critical criminology, discourse analysis, postmodernism, post-structuralism, virtual criminology

Key Readings

Caputo, J. (ed.) (1997) *Deconstruction in a Nutshell: A Conversation with Jacques Derrida.* New York: Fordham University Press.

Cornell, D., Rosenfeld, M. and Carlson, D. (eds) (1992) *Deconstruction and the Possibility of Justice.* New York: Routledge.

Derrida, J. (1973) *Speech and Other Phenomena.* Evanston, IL: Northwestern University Press.

Derrida, J. (1976) *Of Grammatology.* Baltimore, MD: Johns Hopkins University Press.

Derrida, J. (1978) *Writing and Différance.* Chicago: University of Chicago Press.

Derrida, J. (1981) *Positions.* Chicago: University of Chicago Press.

DECRIMINALIZATION

Definition

A process that refers to a removal of the labelling of social problems or deviant behaviours as crimes.

Distinctive Features

Decriminalization grew out of the abolitionist critique of penal responses to criminalized problems. It is based on a rejection of the penal reconstruction of reality (with its associated concepts such as crime, guilt and punishment) and its paralysing effect on attempts to address underlying social problems and circumstances. Abolitionists pointed to the top-down, repressive, punitive and inflexible character of penal control, the appropriation of conflicts from their owners, and the fundamental shortcomings of criminal law to realize social justice, and argued that criminal law sanction should be replaced by dispute settlement and redress. In policy terms, decriminalization means that social policy instead of crime policy is needed when dealing with the social problems and conflicts that are currently singled out as the problem of crime. Hulsman (1986) and de Haan (1990) have even argued for abandoning the very notion of 'crime' in criminology and for criminologists to talk and think about problematic events, troubles, harms, conflicts or mistakes instead.

Decriminalization has also been closely associated with a labelling approach to crime and deviance. If, as labelling theorists suggested, social reaction does not reduce offending but instead confirms deviant careers, then the reach of reaction should be reduced. In the narrowest sense, decriminalization involves taking certain offences (such as minor drug use and offences against public morality) out of the realm of criminal law. For example, proponents of the decriminalization of drugs generally point to the costly, counterproductive and unsuccessful efforts of law enforcement as a response to drug use. Next to a full, *de jure* decriminalization,

many proponents would also advocate a *de facto* decriminalization. This means that certain acts will not be prosecuted even though they will formally remain illegal. Opponents, however, will often argue that decriminalization would increase use, thereby increasing the serious cost to society.

Evaluation

Decriminalization has been used as a measure in penal reform in most Western criminal justice systems, with varying degrees of success in halting the trend of criminalization and challenging the crime control and punishment nexus. Wider developments of managerialism in criminal justice have meant that decriminalization is sometimes used as an attractive label for the state to clean up the criminal justice system's caseload and to transfer petty offences to alternative modes of control that offer the involved person less protection against arbitrary measures than a criminal law suit would. Critics have also argued that a *de facto* decriminalization of certain offences often involves an expansion of the policy discretions of the prosecution and the police (as in the use of police cautioning for minor drug-related offences). Mass settlements of offences by administrative or financial means are presented as forms of decriminalization, while their punitive character is retained.

Maggy Lee

Associated Concepts: abolition, abolitionism, criminalization, decarceration, diversion, labelling, social harm, redress

Key Readings

de Haan, W. (1990) *The Politics of Redress: Crime, Punishment and Penal Abolition.* London: Unwin Hyman.

Hulsman, L. (1986) 'Critical criminology and the concept of crime', in H. Bianchi and R. van Swaaningen (eds), *Abolitionism: Towards a Non-Repressive Approach to Crime.* Amsterdam: Free University Press. pp. 25–41.

DEFENSIBLE SPACE

Definition

The use of a range of architectural and environmental measures that are designed to reduce crime by encouraging communities to protect their public and private spaces from external intrusion.

Distinctive Features

During the 1920s researchers at the University of Chicago began to record how rates of crime persisted in certain areas of cities even when the composition of their populations had changed. Such observations led to the conclusion that it was not the nature of individuals, but the nature of particular neighbourhoods, that determined levels of disorder. By the 1960s a school of architectural determinism had emerged (Jacobs, 1961) in which features of the built environment were viewed as intrinsically criminogenic. The control of crime and disorder, it was argued, would best be achieved by restructuring residential environments so that they were controlled by local communities that had been empowered to mark out and defend their own territories. The most famous exponent of such work was the American architect Oscar Newman (1972). He defined defensible space as a range of mechanisms, real and symbolic barriers, strongly defined areas of influence, and improved opportunities for surveillance that when combined together would bring an environment under the control of its residents.

Newman argued that poorly designed buildings, such as the high-rise tower block, housing large low-income families, produced crime rates that were as much as three times higher than adjacent lower-rise buildings with socially identical residents and a similar population density. For Newman a combination of indifferent architects, land speculators, corporate financiers and city planning departments had contrived to build the maximum amount of housing space at the lowest cost without any consideration of the social

consequences of doing so. The high-rise double-loaded corridor apartment tower has no 'defensible space' other than the interior of the apartment itself. Everything else – the lobby, stairs, elevators and corridors – is a 'nether world of fear and crime'. Newman's solution to creating secure environments was fourfold:

- *Enhance territoriality* – by sub-dividing places into zones of influence that would discourage outsiders and encourage residents to defend their areas.
- *Increase surveillance* – by positioning windows so that residents could survey the exterior and interior public areas of their environment.
- *Improve image* – by redesigning buildings to avoid the stigma of low-cost or public housing.
- *Enhance safety* – by placing public housing projects within urban areas that were perceived to be safe.

Whilst Newman's approach has been critiqued as over-general and neglectful of social factors, it has still proved influential in a number of ways. Certain design features, such as improving external lighting, reducing anonymous open spaces, increasing pedestrian access and resetting windows to allow for greater surveillance, have been implemented in numerous housing projects worldwide. For example, in the late 1970s new models of spatial segregation appeared in the USA with the emergence of 'common interest communities'. Affluent Americans were opting to lock themselves away in carefully screened co-operative housing schemes and defended residential enclaves.

The most obvious way of reducing opportunities for crime lies in the use of physical barriers. This target hardening, involving locks, bolts, gates, guard dogs, security screens and so on, appears to be highly effective. Improving access and windows security on public housing estates is known to reduce the incidence of burglaries. Controlling access – historically evident in the moats and portcullises of medieval castles – has found its contemporary form in entry phones, electronic personal identification measures, fencing around apartment blocks and street closures. The key paradox which surrounds the effectiveness of 'defensible space' and other situational crime prevention measures is generally referred to as the problem of displacement. The possible displacement effects are:

- *temporal* – the movement of crime/disorder to a different time;
- *tactical* – the continual committal of crime, but by more sophisticated means;
- *target* – the movement of crime to different targets;
- *spatial* – the movement of criminal activity to different places.

Early empirical work appeared to support the premise of spatial displacement in particular. Increasing the police presence in one area of New York brought about a reduction in street crime, but also seemed to increase the level of crime in surrounding precincts. However, Clarke (1991) has argued that even when such displacement occurs it is unlikely ever to be complete. If the displacement is to crimes of lesser seriousness or to areas where the burden of victimization is more evenly spread, then it may be considered 'benign' rather than 'malign' (Barr and Pease, 1990). As a result, the issue of displacement remains unresolved. Nevertheless, the concept of defensible space has also come to be linked with two other unwelcome developments. First, continual surveillance suggests the emergence of a fortress society in which fear of crime and distrust stimulate a ever-expanding network of barricades. Second, the current growth in the capacity and penetration of electronic surveillance (such as CCTV) conjures up images of a totalitarian 'Big Brother' state.

John Muncie

Associated Concepts: Chicago School of Sociology, geographies of crime, panopticism, situational crime prevention, social control, surveillance

Key Readings

Barr, R. and Pease, K. (1990) 'Crime placement, displacement and deflection', in N. Morris and M. Tonry (eds), *Crime and Justice: A Review of Research*, vol. 12. Chicago: University of Chicago Press.

Blakely, E.J. and Snyder, M. (1997) *Fortress America*. Washington, DC: Brookings Institution.

Clarke, R.V. (1991) *Situational Crime Prevention: Successful Case Studies*. New York: Harrow and Heston.

Davis, M. (1994) *Beyond Blade Runner: Urban Control and the Ecology of Fear*. Westfield, NJ: Open Magazine Pamphlet Series.

Jacobs, J. (1961) *The Death and Life of Great American Cities*. Harmondsworth: Penguin.

Newman, O. (1972) *Defensible Space: People and Design in the Violent City*. London: Architectural Press.

DEFIANCE THEORY

Definition

Within the realm of criminality, defiance is a discernible increase in the (a) prevalence, (b) frequency, or (c) seriousness of offending caused by a 'proud, shameless reaction' to the application of the criminal sanction (Sherman, 1993). Angry defiance can be specific, individual, general or collective in nature. Direct defiance is an offence committed against a sanctioning authority whereas indirect defiance is an offence committed against a target representing the sanctioning authority responsible for triggering the anger.

Distinctive Features

Researching compliant and defiant behaviour is at the core of the criminological enterprise. There is a significant psychological literature on 'Oppositional Defiant Disorder' as an important manifestation of Attention-Deficit-Hyperactivity Disorder and Anti-Social Behaviour Disorder. The 'defiant child' is blamed for having unrealistic expectations which when not realized will spark their frustration, antipathy, rage and retaliation. Symptoms include an abrupt loss of temper; being argumentative; refusing to comply with adults' requests or rules; deliberately annoying behaviour; blaming others for their own mistakes or misbehaviour; being easily annoyed by others; becoming angry and resentful, and spiteful or vindictive. It is this range of behaviours that brings them into direct conflict with adult authority figures. A core part of this literature concentrates on how to communicate with and manage the 'defiant child'. According to Sherman (1993), researching the emotional reaction to an application of the criminal sanction is critical when attempting to formulate an effective control for crime and deviance. Deterrence theory claims that prompt, guaranteed and proportionally severe punishments will deter or reduce future offending. Labelling theory insists that criminal sanctions are criminogenic in that they produce secondary deviance, deviancy amplification and an increase in future offending. For Sherman there has been remarkably little thought given to 'angry defiance' – an act that encompasses an *open* rejection of and resistance to authority as well as revenge.

The backdrop to defiance theory is a foregrounding of the significance of differential reactions to criminal sanctions in deterring or intensifying criminal behaviour. Sherman attempted to combine Braithwaite's (1989) work on re-integrative and dis-integrative shaming practices; Tyler's (1990) work on fairness, justice and legitimacy; and Scheff and Retzingers' (1991) work on the emotional response to sanctions. For Sherman the reaction to the criminal sanctioning experience is determined by: the *legitimacy* of the sanctioning process; the strengths of the *social bonds* between the offender and the sanctioning authority and the community in whose name the sanctioning authority was acting; the *nature of the shame* shown by the offender; and the *sources of 'pride'* (positive or negative) the offender feels in the aftermath of the criminal sanctioning. Defiance of the criminal sanction or enforcement authority occurs when the offender: perceives the criminal

sanction to be unfair; is poorly bonded to or alienated from the enforcement authority or the community the authority represents; defines the action as stigmatizing and rejecting; and denies or refuses to acknowledge the shame the criminal sanction has actually caused them to suffer. Criminal sanctions are defined as unfair when the sanction is perceived to be unjust and/or where the sanctioning authority disrespects the offender or the group to which that offender belongs

Sherman predicts three reactions to criminal sanctions defined as 'unfair' – irrelevance, deterrence or the 'angry defiance' of poorly bonded offenders who experience the sanction as unjust punishment. They deny the shame they feel and react with indignant rage. The unacknowledged shame in turn generates an emotion of 'angry pride' at defying the punishment. This pride lowers the willingness to self-regulate and inclines the defiant offender to repeat the offence whilst transferring responsibility for that offending onto the punishment or enforcement authority. In the process, the victims or targets of the offending become vicarious surrogates for the enforcement authority or the community. Sherman (1993) advocated a 'science of sanction' with randomized experiments being used to research how offenders would perceive and interpret the criminal sanction. In addition, qualitative methods needed be used in order to observe the criminal sanctioning processes and the experience of criminal sanctioning. The research agenda laid out by defiance theory would include perceptions of the fairness or unfairness of: the law being enforced; the sanction for a given offence; and treatment by criminal justice agencies. For Sherman one of the most important questions to research is how offenders choose to accept or deny shame. Bouffard and Piquero (2010) have connected defiance theory with life course explanations of persistent offending. They have concluded that accepting or denying the shame of the criminal sanction may not be the key feature which determines whether defiance occurs. Rather, defining the criminal sanction as unfair and being poorly bonded are more critical determining factors of persistence.

Evaluation

It remains uncertain as to whether we should define 'defiance' as a theory or a concept. What focusing on defiance does allow us to do is to foreground the importance of understanding and researching differential reactions to being sanctioned by the criminal law in the deterrence or intensification of criminal behaviour. The most recent policy research effort has been expended on trying to establish why and when desistance happens. And desistance is the outcome for the majority of minor offenders. A critical task therefore has been to understand how desistance occurs amongst serious adolescent offenders or which factors have a significant influence on this process. This could be complete desistance or slowing down the rate of offending if 'ex-offenders' remain criminally active. Researching the emotional registers of offenders, through the lens of self-esteem and self-respect, is one significant result. 'Growing out of crime' and adopting 'law abiding behaviour' necessarily involves complicated behavioural, cognitive and emotional processes and pathways. However, socio-cultural changes are creating the conditions for a significant number of young offenders to refuse to desist from offending. At the same point as new technologies of social control premised upon conformity, obedience and compliance are being introduced, defiance, disobedience, non-cooperation and non-compliance are being culturally valued and to a degree becoming the normalized default response in a variety of situations. Being caught rather than the application of the criminal sanction is the source of embarrassment, shame and anger.

Eugene McLaughlin

Associated Concepts: desistance, deterrence, labelling, life course theories of crime, shaming

Key Readings

Bouffard, L.A. and Piquero, N.C. (2010) 'Defiance theory and life course explanations of persistent offending', *Crime & Delinquency*, 56 (2): 227–252.

Braithwaite, J. (1989) *Crime, Shame and Reintegration*. Cambridge: Cambridge University Press.
Scheff, T.J. and Retzinger, S.M. (1991) *Emotions and Violence: Shame and Rage in Destructive Conflicts*. Lexington, MA: Lexington Books.
Sherman, L.W. (1993) 'Defiance, deterrence and irrelevance: a theory of criminal sanction', *Journal of Research in Crime and Delinquency*, 30 (4): 445–473.
Sherman, L.W. (2010) 'Defiance, compliance and consiliance', in E. McLaughlin and T. Newburn (eds), *The Sage Handbook of Criminological Theory*. London: Sage.
Tyler, T. (1990) *Why People Obey the Law*. New Haven, CA: Yale University Press.

DELINQUENCY

Definition

A term, loosely used, to refer to any kind of youthful misbehaviour.

Distinctive Features

Criminologists frequently use the concepts of 'crime' and 'delinquency' interchangeably, especially when their object for study is young people. However, there are crucial differences. Whilst a legal definition of crime refers to behaviour prohibited by criminal law, delinquency is also applied to all manner of behaviours that are deemed to be undesirable. It is capable of capturing not only the legally proscribed, but also waywardness, misbehaviour, incorrigibility, the 'anti-social', and that which is believed to constitute the 'pre-criminal'. Much of this ambiguity derives from the establishment of separate systems of juvenile justice that have been designed not only to punish and treat offenders but also to protect the vulnerable and neglected. All Western jurisdictions stipulate that under a certain age young people cannot be held fully responsible for their actions. It is widely assumed that juveniles are *doli incapax* (incapable of evil), but how certain age groups – child, juvenile, young person, adult – are perceived and constituted in law is not universally agreed upon. Taking Europe as an example, the age of criminal responsibility in England and Wales is 10, in France 13, in Germany 14, in Spain 16, and in Belgium 18. Each is a socially and historically specific concept and as such is liable to review and change. For example, in England and Wales in the late 1990s the presumption that had been enshrined in law since the fourteenth century that those under 14 were incapable of criminal intent was abolished.

In the USA under the statutes of various states delinquency is in part specifically defined, but also retains a series of vague and imprecise standards that rest on the need to intervene early to prevent future offending or tackle assumed family or psychological problems. Determinations of what might constitute reprehensible behaviour extend a court's jurisdiction to establish conduct rather than purely legal norms. These are often referred to as status offences – that is, the violation of formal or informal rules which are applied only to certain sections of society. The focus is less on the offence itself and more on who commits it. In the USA such status offences as being incorrigible, a truant or sexually precocious apply solely to children.

Most historians would agree that delinquency was first identified as a major social problem in the early nineteenth century. Social surveys and empirical investigations permitted a problem to be identified but they presupposed existing conceptions of how young people should behave, what relation should exist between different age groups, and what should be the appropriate role of the family. In the early nineteenth century, with the rapid growth of industrial capitalism, factory production and high density urban populations, the condition of the labouring classes became the focus for considerable middle-class concern – whether this was because of a fear of their revolutionary potential, disgust at their morality or alarm at their impoverishment and criminal tendencies. In England, these fears were galvanized around dramatic images of gangs of 'naked, filthy, roaming, lawless and deserted children'. Accurate estimations of the extent of 'delinquency' were impossible, not least because of its ill-defined nature. Susan Magarey (1978) contends that there may have been some justification for these growing fears, particularly in the newly recorded prison statistics of the 1830s. The number of under-17s imprisoned increased from some 9,500 in 1838 to some 14,000 in 1848. However she finds that this rise is explicable, less with reference to 'increased lawlessness' and more with changes to the position of children in relation to the criminal law and the subsequent criminalization of behaviour for which previously there may have been no official action. In particular, the Vagrancy Act 1824 and the Malicious Trespass Act 1827 considerably broadened legal conceptions of 'criminality' to include, for example, the suspicion of being a thief, gambling on the street and scrumping apples from orchards and gardens. Previous nuisances were transformed into criminal offences. Moreover, the remit given to the Metropolitan Police in 1829 included the apprehension of 'all loose, idle and disorderly persons not giving good account of themselves'. This alone made many more street children liable to arrest. In these ways juvenile delinquency was 'legislated into existence'.

John Muncie

Associated Concepts: anti-social behaviour, crime, deviance, juvenile justice, subculture

Key Readings

Magarey, S. (1978) 'The invention of juvenile delinquency in early nineteenth century England', *Labour History* (Sydney), 34: 11–25.

May, M. (1973) 'Innocence and experience: the evolution of the concept of juvenile delinquency in the mid-nineteenth century', *Victorian Studies*, 17 (1): 7–29.

Tappan, P. (1949) *Juvenile Delinquency*. New York: McGraw-Hill.

West, D. and Farrington, D. (1973) *Who Becomes Delinquent?* London: Heinemann.

West, D. and Farrington, D. (1977) *The Delinquent Way of Life*. London: Heinemann.

DEMONIZATION

Definition

The act of condemning or denouncing evil that is attributed to demonic influence or powers.

Distinctive Features

Demonology refers to possession by evil spirits, as well as to the construction of a catalogue of enemies. In both cases the object of demonization is an 'other', an out-group to which the blame for misfortune is attributed, and its purpose is to erect and reaffirm certain moral and social boundaries. In terms of attribution theory, the argument would be that bad events require an explanation or causes and that demonization is a method for assigning blame or guilt. Denunciation fosters a dichotomization of 'us' and 'them' that serves to shore up the moral barricades of society. Historically, witchcraft has been a key source for demonology. Witches were connected to wicked acts prompted by the devil. The strongly sexualized and gendered dimension in this should not be ignored, such as the 'insatiable' sexual appetite attributed to women. The nature and scale of reaction in such events have been seen as a defensive reaction by religious groups seeking to maintain moral boundaries, particularly at times of rapid social change. For Erikson (1966) deviance manifests itself in the form that is most feared, suggesting that demons are defined by psychic needs.

In modern times the objects of demonization have been ideological and political deviants whose 'wickedness' is attributed to some shadowy and ambiguous force that enables them to perform feats beyond ordinary human capabilities – sometimes this is connected with a conspiracy theory. Thus, the subversion myth is a narrative that explains why things have gone wrong by attributing blame or demonizing certain groups or individuals by holding them responsible for bad events or occurrences (Goode and Ben-Yehuda, 1994). The cast list of demonized groups is extensive, including Jews under the Third Reich, and those who were subject to the Soviet show trials and the McCarthy era in the USA. These state crimes are instances of the mass production – or fabrication – of deviance that signify the need for society to take exceptional measures to protect itself, connecting the concept of demonization to scapegoating and moral panics. Homosexuals, abortionists, drug users, migrants and asylum seekers, as well as counter-cultural movements, have all been objects of scapegoating and demonization. Furthermore, countries have also been demonized, for instance the reputation of some 'terrorist' Islamic states has been linked to Islamophobia and Eurocentrism.

In more mundane terms the identification of folk devils such as particular youth cultures has been the basis for labelling outsiders who are then treated as legitimate targets of self-righteous anger and deserving of punishment. A folk devil is treated as the embodiment of evil and, as such, is stripped of all positive characteristics and ascribed negative ones. This occurs through a symbolization process in which 'images are made much sharper than reality' (Cohen, 1972: 43). New folk devils are placed into, and connected with, a gallery of contemporary folk devils that may underlie a moral panic. The identification of groups and their characteristics is listed in a stereotypical manner by the media and reaffirms their negative characteristics; this may also set in process deviancy amplification. Goode and Ben-Yehuda (1994) have emphasized the need to pay careful attention to the specific social context of demonization – in particular its timing, content and targets.

Evaluation

Like scapegoating, the term 'demonization' is loosely used in a generalized way that makes it difficult to assess its usefulness, unless there is some attention given to the details of the discursive process of attribution. Historical work on witchcraft has connected demonization to a cosmology that invokes and attributes evil to some people or groups. Modern instances of demonization seem to focus on conservative moral rhetorics reacting to the erosion of a 'way of life', thereby linking demonization to moral enterprise and symbolic crusades to bolster moral barricades.

Karim Murji

Associated Concepts: deviancy amplification, folk devil, moral panic, racialization, scapegoating, social censure, stereotyping

Key Readings

Cohen, S. (1972) *Folk Devils and Moral Panics.* London: MacGibbon and Kee (new edition, Oxford, Martin Robertson, 1980).

Erikson, K. (1966) *Wayward Puritans.* New York: Wiley.

Goode, E. and Ben-Yehuda, N. (1994) *Moral Panics: The Social Construction of Deviance.* Oxford: Blackwell.

Pfohl, S. (1985) *Images of Deviance and Social Control: A Sociological History.* New York: McGraw-Hill.

DENIAL

Definition

The various processes by which individual actors, social groups or states either 'block, shut out, repress or cover up certain forms of disturbing information [about wrong doing] or else evade, avoid or neutralize' its consequences (Cohen, 1995: 19).

Distinctive Features

Classic accounts of the denial of responsibility would include Sykes and Matza's (1957) seminal work on 'techniques of neutralization', which identified five major techniques for denying or deflecting the blame for wrongdoing away from the perpetrator. These were: a denial of responsibility for the act; a denial of the injury caused; a denial of the victim; a condemnation of the condemners; and an appeal to higher loyalties. Somewhat later, Scott and

Lyman (1968) made the crucial distinction between 'excuses', in which the perpetrator admits the act in question was wrong, but denies full responsibility for it; and 'justifications', in which the perpetrator accepts responsibility for the act, but denies that it was wrong.

This denial may be either conscious or unconscious. Conscious denial is a rhetorical rejection or evasion of the truth or its consequences. As Mary Douglas has argued, it is a 'forensic' strategy in the sense that the accounts in question are aimed at manipulating or deflecting attributions of 'responsibility' or blame away from the person, group or entity doing the denying (Douglas, 1992). Stanley Cohen (1995) later developed the argument that what is being denied may be matters of *fact* (for example, how many people were 'disappeared' by the Pinochet regime); matters of *interpretation* (whether certain actions constitute torture or 'moderate physical pressure'); or the *implications* or consequences of the acts in question (for example, an acknowledgement of the harm done to the victim).

In contrast to these rhetorical forms of denial (lying to others), unconscious forms of denial are expressions of the psychological processes (or 'defence mechanisms') that enable a person to evade or distort the 'claims of external reality' – a form of *lying to one's self*. This denial or disavowal of an external truth is only one element in a larger psychological repertoire for dealing with extreme threat or social injury. Other defences include psychic *numbing*, a form of dissociation involving the diminished capacity or inclination to feel; and *doubling*, the formation of a separate self, specific to the context of atrocity (Lifton and Markusen, 1990). For psychoanalysts, there is an important distinction to be made between this form of unconscious denial or disavowal of *external reality* and the psychological process whereby the demands of *internal* desires are 'repressed' from a person's consciousness.

Evaluation

Stanley Cohen's recent work on denial sharpens the distinction between conscious 'rhetorical' forms of denial and the forms of denial which involve unconscious processes that serve to disavow or block out the claims of external reality. An additional focus of Cohen's work on the denial of responsibility is the extension of the analysis of denial by individuals to include collective forms of denial, such as a denial of human rights violations by *representatives of the state*. In principle, there is no reason why this approach to 'denial' could not be applied to analysis of the motivational accounts offered by the perpetrators of other forms of crime – for example, the white collar crime of insider trading or the corporate criminality of transnational corporations involved in the dumping of toxic waste. Researchers working in these areas will confront the problem of accounts that are driven by economic and other interests rather than personal deceits. Criminologists and criminal lawyers working on issues of denial in the future will face the continuing challenge of avoiding reducing the issue to the play of discourses rather than the expression of specific interests and personal responsibility.

Ruth Jamieson

Associated Concepts: corporate crime, defiance theory, human rights, neutralization (techniques of), state crime

Key Readings

Cohen, S. (1995) *Denial and Acknowledgement: The Impact of Information About Human Rights Violations*. Jerusalem: The Hebrew University of Jerusalem, Centre for Human Rights.
Douglas, M. (1992) *Risk and Blame*. London: Routledge.
Lifton, R.J. and Markusen, E. (1990) *The Genocidal Mentality*. London: Macmillan.
Scott, M. and Lyman, S. (1968) 'Accounts', *American Sociological Review*, 33 (10): 46–62.
Sykes, G.M. and Matza, D. (1957) 'Techniques of neutralization: a theory of delinquency', *American Sociological Review*, 22: 664–70.

DESISTANCE

Definition

Although 'desistance from crime' is a relatively unambiguous concept, it has been very difficult to operationalize in criminological research. To 'cease and desist' any activity is to stop doing something (to cease) and refrain from repeating it again (to desist). Hence, individuals who are at one point engaged in a pattern of criminal pursuits could be said to 'desist from crime' when they cease this involvement and, importantly, abstain from additional behaviours that are deemed to be illegal. Like the colloquial term 'going straight' or 'going legit', desistance should not be seen so much as an event or state, but rather as a process or an ongoing work in progress. One *goes* straight. One does not talk about having *turned* legit or having *become* legit – the 'going' is the thing. As such, desistance is an unusual dependent variable for criminologists to model, because it is not an event that happens but rather the sustained *absence* of a certain type of event (crime) occurring. This definitional distinction has acute implications because the study of desistance as the ability to *maintain* an abstinence from crime, in the face of life's obstacles, might be wholly unrelated to the initial cause for *ceasing* that behaviour in the first place.

Distinctive Features

Desistance from crime, although obviously related to the more familiar concept of 'offender rehabilitation', was originally used as something like the opposite of this medical model term for reform. In medicine, persons with illnesses who are able to recover without treatment are said to have experienced 'spontaneous remission' or a 'natural recovery'. Likewise, the term 'desistance' (originally deemed 'spontaneous desistance') was intended to distinguish the so-called 'natural' self-change process undergone by an offender (who was perhaps never caught and punished) from the process experienced by someone who was formally treated and reformed by the criminal justice system. One either desists 'naturally' (i.e., on one's own accord) or else one is rehabilitated through formal treatment or reform. More recently, however, this distinction has largely been forgotten or ignored as criminology has moved away from its medical model roots. Both the image of rehabilitation, conjuring doctors in white lab coats curing sick offenders, and the related idea of desistance as a biological process similar to puberty, rest on presumptions about the nature of criminality that are no longer sustainable.

Today the word desistance is used almost exclusively as a behavioural concept, intended to describe a widespread pattern of criminal activity and inactivity identified in the longitudinal study of criminal careers. One of the important insights of the criminal career studies of the 1970s and 1980s is that, despite stereotypes of 'born criminals', the vast majority of the individuals we call 'offenders' engage in crime for a relatively short proportion of their lives. Typically, street crimes such as burglary, assault and vandalism are associated with youth, as is apparent in the well-known 'age-crime curve' or the relationship between age and criminal behaviour. For example, Figure 5 shows that in the year 2000, 19-year-old males in England and Wales had a rate of offending that was 50 or more times higher than the rate for men over the age of 50.

There are many explanations for this pattern, replicated across several generations and in multiple contexts. Some young people involved with crime will spend much of their adult lives incarcerated, which will not allow them the chance to commit conventional crimes; others will die young (as we know that offenders have much higher mortality rates than non-offenders); and others will simply figure out ways of avoiding detection by the criminal justice system while continuing to offend. However, a large portion of one-time offenders will simply desist from criminal behaviours and adopt conventional lifestyles where these activities would be incongruous. We know this from a number of sources, but primarily from prospective longitudinal research following cohorts of

offenders across time, and retrospective life histories of former offenders. It has been estimated from such research that as high as 85 per cent of young people involved in crime are likely to have desisted by the time they reach the age of 28, although this number could never be calculated perfectly.

There are a number of social processes found to be associated with individuals' desistance from crime in empirical studies. In particular, research has focused on the correlation between desistance and stable employment (including military service), and strong personal relationships (especially marriage and parenthood). More recently, researchers have sought to uncover more cognitive or motivational factors that might correspond with periods of abstinence from crime. These include measures of self-efficacy, personal shame and the adoption of pro-social labels. The best-known correlate of desistance, however, is ageing itself. Indeed, the relationship between age and criminal behaviour is so strong that a long-standing explanation for desistance is based on biological maturation and physical deterioration over time. More recently, Laub and Sampson's (2001) theory of informal social control has become the most widely tested and supported theory for accounting for desistance. They argue that desistance is largely the result of social bonds developed in adulthood. Attachments in young adulthood (especially to a spouse or a career) provide an individual with 'something to lose' by offending.

Evaluation

As simple as the above definition of desistance appears, the study of desistance has been riddled with definitional problems and confusions. In fact, Laub and Sampson (2001: 8) argue that 'A clear and precise definition of desistance cannot be developed that is separate from a clear and precise research question' and further conclude that, 'Developing a definition of desistance for the sake of having a definition is not worth the effort.' Originally, the term was used to describe groups of subjects in probabilistic models of offending

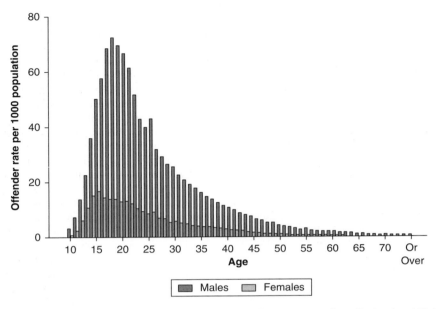

Figure 5 *Recorded offender rates per 1000 relevant population by age-year and sex, England and Wales, 2000 (from Bottoms et al., 2004)*

career trajectories, and in this context it was unproblematic to talk about finding evidence of 'desisters, persisters and innocents' (Blumstein et al., 1985) in one's longitudinal data set. However, it is far more difficult to apply the term to an actual individual.

The most frequently voiced problem is that unlike some more predictably habitual behaviours (such as smoking, heroin usage, etc.) it is difficult to distinguish between desistance from crime and a mere pause between criminal behaviours. For example, suppose a person steals a car on a Friday morning and then abstains from criminal activity for the rest of the day. Is that desistance? And is it desistance if the person does not steal another car for a week? A month? A year? David Farrington warns that even a five-year or ten-year crime-free period is not a guarantee that offending has ceased. Most researchers who use the term 'desistance' imply that this is a permanent break with criminality. Yet, such permanence can only be determined retrospectively – presumably after the ex-offender is deceased – and hence is hardly a practical condition for research purposes.

Some clarification may be found by pilfering from the literature on criminal aetiology. A half century ago, Edwin Lemert introduced considerable clarity into the debate on the origins of deviance by differentiating between two, categorical phases in this developmental process: primary deviation and secondary deviation. Primary deviation involved the initial flirtation and experimentation with deviant behaviours. Secondary deviation, on the other hand, is deviance that becomes 'incorporated as part of the "me" of the individual' (Lemert, 1951: 76) – that is, criminality was a core aspect of the person's identity. Primary and secondary deviation had distinctly different causes according to Lemert, and his real interest was less on why some people initially experimented with primary deviance (as this was highly common) and more on why some of those individuals graduated into secondary deviation.

This same framework might clarify some issues in the study of desistance. Perhaps there are (at least) two, distinguishable phases in the desistance process: primary and secondary desistance. Primary desistance would take the term 'desistance' at its most basic and literal level to refer to any lull or crime-free gap in the course of a criminal career or secondary deviant. Bottoms and colleagues (2004: 370) refer to the *Shorter Oxford English Dictionary* definition of the verb 'to desist' and note that alongside 'to cease or stop' it also includes 'forbear, refrain, abstain'. They conclude, 'We do no violence to ordinary language if we include significant crime-free gaps within the criminological concept of desistance'. However, because every secondary deviant experiences a countless number of such pauses in the course of a criminal career, primary desistance would not be a matter for much theoretical interest.

The real interest, instead, would be on secondary desistance: the movement from the behaviour of non-offending to the assumption of the role or identity of a 'changed person'. In secondary desistance crime not only stops, but also 'existing roles become disrupted' and a 'reorganization based upon a new role or roles will occur' (Lemert, 1951: 76). Indeed, recent research (Burnett, 2004; Maruna, 2001) provides compelling evidence that long-term desistance does involve identifiable and measurable changes at the level of personal identity or the 'me' of the individual.

Shadd Maruna

Associated Concepts: criminal careers, developmental criminology, deviance, labelling, life course theories of crime, recidivism, rehabilitation, restorative justice, social control

Key Readings

Blumstein, D.P., Farrington, D.P. and Moitra, S. (1985) 'Delinquency careers: innocents, desisters, and persisters', in M. Tonry and N. Morris (eds), *Crime and Justice: An Annual Review of Research*, vol. 6: 187–219. Chicago: University of Chicago Press.
Bottoms, A., Costello, A., Holmes, D., Muir, G. and Shapland, J. (2004) 'Towards desistance: theoretical underpinnings for an empirical study', *The Howard Journal of Criminal Justice*, 43 (4): 368–89.

Burnett, R. (2004) 'To re-offend or not to re-offend? The ambivalence of convicted property offenders', in S. Maruna and R. Immarigeon (eds), *After Crime and Punishment: Pathways to Offender Reintegration*. Cullompton, Devon: Willan.
Farrall, S. (2002) *Rethinking What Works with Offenders: Probation, Social Context and Desistance from Crime*. Cullompton, Devon: Willan.
Laub, J.H. and Sampson, R.J. (2001) 'Understanding desistance from crime', in M. Tonry (ed.), *Crime and Justice: A Review of Research*, vol. 28. Chicago: University of Chicago Press.
Lemert, E. (1951) *Social Pathology*. New York: McGraw-Hill.
Maruna, S. (2001) *Making Good: How Ex-Convicts Reform and Rebuild Their Lives*. Washington, DC: American Psychological Association Books.

DETERMINISM

Definition

There is no easy definition of the term 'determinism'. Honderich (1993) describes three meanings of the term, each with its own subtle shifts and variations. Alongside its use with reference to small particles in physics, determinism can be used as an opposite to free will, or it can be used in a more restricted sense to mean that human action is subject to causal laws. In a more general sense, as used here, determinism can be taken in the sense of inevitability: once the antecedents to an event are understood, so the prediction of future similar events becomes possible.

Distinctive Features

Bertrand Russell's (1961) *A History of Western Philosophy* traces the concept of determinism back to 440 BC and the philosophers Leucippus and Democritus. As the basis of their philosophical stance, known as atomism, they argued that nothing happens by chance, that everything is explicable by natural laws. In a position akin to much modern science, the atomists said that science should be empirical, seeking to discover the natural laws by which to understand the universe. Not all philosophers agreed with this view and, from Socrates, Plato and Aristotle onwards, the debate has continued.

In the field of human behaviour, including criminal behaviour, the match is made between, on the one hand, determinism, and free will on the other. If determinism holds that behaviour is predictable (once the laws governing behaviour are eventually understood), so free will takes the contrary stance: no matter what the antecedents might be at the point of acting, individuals could, had they wished, have acted differently than they did.

What might determine human behaviour? There are many levels of explanation, ranging through genetic, psychological, social and political theories. Regardless of whether the antecedents are said to be inside the person or in the environment (or a combination of the two), human action is a function of its antecedent conditions. Such antecedent conditions may be unique to the individual; nonetheless it is these conditions that determine behaviour. Explanations of behaviour then move beyond the concepts of freedom and dignity (Skinner, 1971).

In thinking about criminal behaviour, the issue of determinism is of importance. If behaviour is determined, then this directly challenges the principles of free will, responsibility and choice, the principles upon which many systems of justice are based. At both a philosophical and scientific level the issues are complex (Alper, 1998) – it seems unlikely that the debate started by the atomists is likely to be resolved in the foreseeable future.

Clive Hollin

Associated Concepts: biological criminology, free will, individual positivism, positivism, prediction studies, sociological positivism

Key Readings

Alper, J.S. (1998) 'Genes, free will, and criminal behavior', *Society, Science, and Medicine*, 46: 1599–1611.
Honderich, T. (1993) *How Free Are You? The Determinism Problem*. Oxford: Oxford University Press.
Russell, B. (1961) *A History of Western Philosophy*, 2nd edn. London: George Allen and Unwin.
Skinner, B.E. (1971) *Beyond Freedom and Dignity*. New York: Knopf.

DETERRENCE

Definition

A philosophy of punishment that aims to prevent criminal activity through the development and application of effective and efficient sanctions. It involves demonstrating to both the citizenry and the reasoning criminal that the pains and losses associated with apprehension and punishment will overshadow the possibility of criminal gain or profit.

Distinctive Features

Utilitarian or rational choice theories of human nature posit that individuals are responsible for their actions and will naturally indulge in behaviours that will bring them maximum benefits and goods and minimize risks and costs. For Cesare Beccaria (1738–94) and Jeremy Bentham (1748–1832) the overriding purpose of their work was to provide the criminal justice system with a unified philosophy. They concluded that the role of the criminal law was to promote the wellbeing of the community and it did so when it deterred the commission of crime and minimized the severity of the crimes committed. Because it is natural that human beings will violate the law if they are allowed to do so, in order to prevent crime, society must make the punishments for criminal behaviour greater than the pleasures derived from the successful completion of criminal acts. Deterrence requires three key elements:

- The certainty of apprehension, conviction and punishment.
- The severity of the punishment to be greater than the potential benefits of the criminal act.
- The clarity of the punishment to ensure that the offender is in a position to make the link between her/his punishment and her/his criminal behaviour.

Deterrence assumes two principal forms and both of these are supposed to make it clear that crime does not pay. General deterrence is aimed at influencing the total population, with any future or potential criminal activity being prevented by the universal threat and fear of punishment. Specific deterrence is targeted at the known offender to ensure that this individual is deterred from further involvement in criminal activity. The ultimate form of individual deterrence is the death penalty. Although positivism replaced deterrence theory during the first half of the twentieth century, it re-emerged in the aftermath of 'nothing works' in the form of rational choice and routine activity approaches to crime control.

Critics of deterrence focus on its limited conception of human beings and human action. They argue that we need to develop a considerably more sophisticated theory of human behaviour which explores the internal and external checks on why people do or do not engage in criminal activity. This theory must also recognize that there are a bewildering number of motivational states, rational and irrational, that lead to the commission of criminal acts. We also need to research the complexities of communication and understanding. It is evident that many petty criminals are not capable of accurately balancing the costs and benefits of crime before the commission of the act. It is also the case that many young males who become involved in street fights with other young men do not think about the consequences of their actions either for themselves or others. Deterrence theory has also been criticized because it fails to think through the consequences of what it is proposing for offenders. Many offenders are driven to re-offending because, as a result of being processed by the criminal justice system, they have no alternative. The labelling process and 'naming and shaming' effectively close off the possibility of 'going straight'.

Eugene McLaughlin

Associated Concepts: rational choice theory, routine activity theory, situational crime prevention

Key Readings

Grasmick, H. and Bursik, R. (1990) 'Conscience, significant others and rational choice: extending the deterrent model', *Law and Society Review*, 24: 837–61.

Klepper, S. and Nagin, D. (1989) 'The deterrent effect of perceived certainty and severity of punishment revisited', *Criminology*, 27: 721–46.

Matravers, M. (ed.) (1999) *Punishment and Political Theory*. Oxford: Hart Publishing.

Piliavin, I., Gartner, R., Thornton, C. and Matsueda, R. (1986) 'Crime, deterrence and rational choice', *American Sociological Review*, 51: 101–19.

Scarre, G. (1996) *Utilitarianism*. London: Routledge.

DEVELOPMENTAL CRIMINOLOGY

Definition

The defining feature of developmental criminology is its focus on offending in relation to changes over time in individuals and their life circumstances, with most research being focused in practice on childhood and youth. Developmental criminologists are concerned with questions of *continuity and change* in behaviour, including the onset of and desistance from offending and patterns of offending over time.

Distinctive Features

Developmental criminology has its roots in mainstream criminology and positivist social science, and studies the relationship between biological, psychological and social factors and offending across the life course, from conception to death. A foundation assumption is that the 'baggage' people carry from the past – the continuing effects of earlier experiences such as a happy childhood or sexual abuse – will affect the ways they behave in the present. Thus developmental criminologists reject traditional approaches that emphasize *between-group* differences in favour of a study of *within-individual* changes in offending, in relation to changes in many other factors.

Developmental criminology has been dominated by quantitative methods that aim to measure the relationships between developmental processes and offending. A strong emphasis has been on the use of longitudinal research, with repeated measurements to determine correlations between *risk factors* such as abuse or poverty and subsequent offending. Famous studies include the Pittsburgh Youth Study in the USA and the Cambridge Study on Delinquent Development in the UK.

An early influence in developmental criminology was Cyril Burt and his study of adolescent offending in the 1920s. Since then interest in developmental processes in offending has expanded. A major question in the 1980s was the relationship between *age* and *offending*. The claim that age simply matures people out of crime appeared to be supported by the general tendency for offenders to reduce their rate of offending as they got older. It was argued that some people are more prone to commit crimes than others, particularly because their biological makeup, or family socialization in the first few years of life, had failed to build within them a sufficiently strong capacity for impulse control or self-control. This *propensity* to offend, it was claimed, would not change over the life course, with crime-prone individuals committing more crime at all ages.

Developmental critics of this view argued that crime trajectories or pathways, known as *criminal careers*, were far more varied than this simple model suggested, and that it was necessary to have separate models for exploring such processes as age of crime onset, participation levels, frequency, duration, and desistance from crime, recognizing the different influences at various life phases and stages of criminal careers. Social and psychological factors after the early years, including peer influences and parenting practices, exerted strong effects, with a failure to exercise self-control being only one risk factor, albeit a fundamentally important one.

In the 1990s developmental criminology took the idea of risk factors further and developed the *risk and protective factors paradigm*. While risk factors were associated with an increased probability of a negative outcome, protective factors were thought to buffer the effects of risk factors, helping to make people more *resilient* in the face of adversity. This approach was imported from public health, which had shown (for example) that smoking, fatty diets and a lack of exercise increased the risk of heart disease. Developmental criminologists have used this paradigm to explore many problems, including the relationship between the early onset of problem behaviour and future offending. Longitudinal research has identified relationships between a large number of risk factors and future offending. While causal pathways are complex and prediction at the individual level problematic, there is strong evidence that as a group those children and young people with *multiple risk factors* are more likely to be offenders in the future.

Evaluation

Developmental criminology has made a major contribution to our understanding of the relationship between offending and a wide range of factors that vary across the life course. Even in its most technical and quantitative forms it has provided an alternative to punitive approaches that emphasize use of the criminal justice system and long prison terms to control crime, and it has placed psychological and social factors back on the research and policy agenda. While there is much debate over the relationship between the psychological and the social, developmental criminology provided a timely reminder that offending must be located in its social context. For example, whatever their limitations in contributing to an understanding of underlying processes, risk factors direct attention towards the importance of poverty and family adversity in explaining offending. Developmental criminology therefore provides strong support for the argument that a non-punitive response which strengthens families and communities is fundamental to the prevention of crime.

Despite a tendency to marginalize the relationship between research and practice, and to see policy development as separate from 'science', many developmental criminologists have initiated a close working relationship with policy makers and practitioners. They have, for example, been active in promoting and developing early prevention programmes that aim to 'get in early', often in the first few years of life, to forestall the development of crime and associated problems such as substance abuse or school exclusion. For example, in the 1990s, programmes that aimed to address levels of risk and protection in local communities, such as *Communities that Care,* were introduced in a number of countries. These use randomized controlled trials and quasi-experimental evidence of 'what works' to help policy makers and practitioners tackle local social problems. Another example of policy engagement is the use the risk and protection model to influence youth justice policy. Not only has this model influenced the development of youth crime prevention strategy; it has also shaped – for better or worse – the way offenders are assessed in terms of risk, especially in the UK.

Developmental criminology could make a more constructive policy contribution if several problems were addressed. First, some policy makers have taken the research finding that at the aggregate level there is a strong degree of continuity in anti-social behaviour from childhood to youth, to mean that risk factors can be used to identify and intervene at an early age in the lives of 'risky individuals or families'. The problem here is that while there is a strong statistical relationship between early anti-social behaviour and future problems there is also a large number of *false positives*, with about half the children typically *not* going on to have problems.

Second, developmental criminologists tend to see the relationship between offending and non-offending as unproblematic, having little to say about the role of the state in defining what is 'criminal'. This lacuna is exacerbated by policy makers misunderstanding the evidence about the continuities in anti-social behaviour produced by developmental criminologists, which in practice has led to the stigmatization and labelling of those children and families identified through new batteries of tests.

Third, while developmental criminology does recognize social context its focus tends to be limited to the influences of friends and family and sometimes school. Consequently developmental criminology has had little to say about the wider influences on life course outcomes, such as the global impact of restructured labour markets on national and local employment opportunities.

Finally, developmental criminology has been too uncritical of government policies, failing to recognize that major risk factors for offending can be embedded unintentionally in new programmes when these fail to comprehend the complex realities of the lives of children and young people, especially those who are growing up in disadvantaged communities.

Ross Homel and Alan France

Associated Concepts: criminal careers, desistance, life course theories of crime, longitudinal study, risk factor research

Key Readings

Farrington, D. (2002) 'Developmental criminology and risk focused prevention', in M. Maguire, R. Morgan and R. Reiner (eds), *The Oxford Handbook of Criminology*, 3rd edition. Oxford: Oxford University Press.

Farrington, D. and Jolliffe, W. (2009). 'A systematic review of the relationship between childhood impulsiveness and later violence', in M. McMurran and R.C. Howard (eds), *Personality, Personality Disorder and Violence*. New York: Wiley.

France, A. and Homel, R. (ed.) (2007) *Pathways and Crime Prevention: Theory, Policy and Practice*. Cullompton: Willan.

France, A. and Utting, D. (2005) 'The paradigm of "risk and protection focused prevention" and its impact on services for children and families', *Children and Society*, 19: 77–90.

Homel, R. (2005) 'Developmental crime prevention', in N. Tilley (ed.), *Handbook of Crime Prevention and Community Safety*. Cullompton: Willan.

Sampson, R.J. and Laub, J. (2005) 'A life-course view of the development of crime', *The Annals of the American Academy of Political and Social Science*, 602: 12–45.

DEVIANCE

Definition

Deviance is a twentieth-century sociological concept intended to designate the aggregate of social behaviours, practices, acts, demeanours, attitudes, beliefs, styles or statuses which are culturally believed to deviate significantly from the norms, ethics, standards and expectations of society. It emerged in the USA around 1937, within the context of Roosevelt's New Deal, as a solution to the problem of how sociologists in an emergent welfare state were to summarize categorically such matters as delinquency, mental and physical disability, criminal behaviour, drug abuse, cultural rebellion, a sustained dependency upon state benefits, street-level political opposition, intellectual and artistic radicalism, homosexuality, and the behaviour of Native American populations – without insulting but yet implying the value of both psychiatric and sociological explanations of these phenomena as forms of sociopathy. Social deviance refers to that which is censured as deviant from the standpoint of the norms of the dominant culture. It is an effect of the bio-politics of social-democratic welfare capitalism.

Distinctive Features

Social deviance is a broader concept than criminal behaviour, referring to a range of social phenomena which the dominant culture has stood against either in principle or in practice. As such, it is intertwined with the dominant culture – the very identity and historical formation of which are defined, driven and sustained by what it censures as social deviance. As a defining feature of a dominant culture and a reflection of divisions in a political economy, social deviance is a pivotal aspect in the constitution of society. Society's norms and virtues are defined, partly, by their opposition to its enemies' sins and vices. It is therefore seen as legitimate for the agencies of social control, and the state as a whole, to violate the liberty of those who are held by those agencies to violate the rights and principles of others or of the state itself.

Without that differential in authoritative backing, there is often little in the physics of the respective behaviours which would differentiate them. It is the significance we attribute to behaviours which locates them within the moral order of virtue, deviance, criminality, insanity or evil. How an act, such as a killing, for example, is perceived within the dominant culture depends more upon our historically shaped principles of morality and the circumstances of its execution than upon any behavioural feature. Killing could be described as a heroic act in war, a sign of evil or madness when perpetrated upon a stranger, a crime of passion in a domestic relationship, an act of mercy in the case of euthanasia, or as tortious negligence in industrial situations.

The concept of deviance is distinct from that of mere difference in that the former contains the implicit likelihood of possible authoritative intervention or sanction. Difference in modern society is respected as a right: deviance is always liable to be penalized or regulated. Deviance is a culturally unacceptable level of difference which is subject to constant suspicion and surveillance from social control agencies. Difference is seen to contribute to the vitality and creativity of modern capitalist society, whereas deviance always holds a threat to the social fabric.

Evaluation

Many social scientists today feel that the concept of deviance has run its historical course or at least has lost its cutting edge. Until the 1970s, the sociology of deviance focused on the social processes whereby certain acts, individuals or groups were targeted for social censure, stigmatization, exclusion or punishment. That study advanced criminology away from the naive idea that crimes were unambiguous acts of evil committed by born criminals. It served a social-democratic movement which highlighted the social roots of misbehaviour, thus placing the blame more upon society than the individual, and raising important questions about dominant social norms, the dangers of criminalization, the impartiality of policing, the neutrality of justice, and the counter-productiveness of punishment.

At the beginning of the new millennium, however, social scientists cynically believe that moral judgements are always made from a standpoint of partisan interest as well as general principle and that they are therefore profoundly relative to the culture or period within which they are embedded. Events in the twentieth century, such as the Holocaust, have given many an awareness of the horrors that can be involved in scapegoating censured social groups. In addition, globalization, mass communications, travel and mobility have resulted in a greater moral tolerance in a highly differentiated, multicultural world – who is to say what is now deviant? Consequently, all moral judgements are now seen as questionable in principle, not just those pertaining to areas of ambiguity. Indeed, any lack of ability to challenge a moral judgement would be taken as a negative sign regarding its authority. In a depoliticized age, the power of authority to define and control popular morality and culture has been reduced. Deviance could be anything within a multicultural pluralism and has therefore lost its significance as a social issue. Society has advanced to the point where a condescending sensitivity to insulting the urban poor has been supplanted by critiques of social censure and of political authority itself. The core meaning and purpose of the concept of social deviance has thus been eroded. When norms lose their authority, authority loses its norms.

What concerns politicians and social scientists at the beginning of a new century are two issues that co-exist and interrelate in a constant tension: (1) to locate, understand and create areas of social agreement which might constitute the basis of social censure and control for a more healthy, secure and peaceful society; and (2) to expose, criticize and explain social norms and systems of social control which are discriminatory, hypocritical and oppressive in order to enable a society where its members are allowed to develop their positive capacities to the full. Authority is trying to regain its moral power, and moral critique is trying to expose authority. The continuing harsh reality of poverty, inequality, oppression, misinformation and ill-health on a global scale means that both these utopian concerns face massive challenges.

Colin Sumner

Associated Concepts: crime, delinquency, governmentality, labelling, moral panic, penality, penology, social censure, social control, social exclusion, stigma

Key Readings

Becker, H. (1963) *Outsiders*. New York: Free Press.

Goffman, E. (1968) *Stigma*. Harmondsworth: Penguin.

Lemert, E. (1951) *Social Pathology*. New York: McGraw-Hill.

Matza, D. (1969) *Becoming Deviant*. Englewood Cliffs, NJ: Prentice-Hall.

Sumner, C.S. (1994) *The Sociology of Deviance: An Obituary*. Buckingham: Open University Press.

Young, J. (1999) *The Exclusive Society: Social Exclusion, Crime and Difference in Late Modernity*. London: Sage.

DEVIANCY AMPLIFICATION

Definition

The process whereby the media, police, public and political reaction to non-conformity acts not to control deviancy but has the obverse reaction of increasing it.

Distinctive Features

Leslie Wilkins (1964) first used the term 'deviation amplification' to explore the relationship between levels of tolerance/intolerance and the reinforcement of deviant identities. He noted how societies that had developed an intolerant response to deviancy tended to define more acts as criminal and took more formal action against criminals. This in turn led to the increased alienation of deviants, more crime by deviant groups, and a corresponding affirmation of intolerance of deviants by conforming groups. The production of intolerance is subject to a 'positive feedback loop', in which the identification of and reaction to deviancy becomes self-perpetuating. The further an individual is defined as having moved away from the cultural norm the more they are likely to behave in a nonconformist fashion. As a result Wilkins argued that deviancy control would be best achieved by building social systems that could tolerate difference and minimizing the number of persons who were defined as deviant.

The concept of deviancy amplification has clear resonances with many of the propositions of a labelling approach in which the key factor in deviancy creation is believed to be social reaction rather than individual behaviour. In Britain, Jock Young (1971b) applied the concept in his participant observation study of marijuana users in Notting Hill, London, in the late 1960s. He showed how the relatively harmless social activity of marijuana smoking was transformed into a serious social problem through the combined reactions of the mass media, the police and the public. Through sensational reporting, users were portrayed by the media as sick, promiscuous and dangerous outsiders. During 1967 such stereotypes inflamed popular indignation. Media pressure forced the police to take more direct action by increasing surveillance and rates of arrest. For the drug users what was once a peripheral activity became a symbol of their difference and a key part of their defiance of perceived social injustices. Police activity acted to amplify the extent and symbolic importance of drug usage for the users themselves. Moreover as drug taking was driven underground it moved from being a low key, low profit activity to one organized by a 'criminal underworld' and practised in an even more secretive fashion. In this way social reaction amplifies deviance in both mythical and actual terms. A vicious spiral of escalation ensues.

The concept was also used by Stan Cohen in his (1972) study of the moral panic associated with the Mods and Rockers in Britain in the mid-1960s. Here once again it was argued that relatively minor scuffles between groups of youths were exaggerated by media reportage and magnified by subsequent police and judicial targeting. And once again their deviance was initially amplified through a social reaction which in turn produced an actual amplification in real levels of deviancy as the Mods and Rockers took on aspects of their new publicly defined personas.

Evaluation

Together with the labelling approach, the concept of deviancy amplification draws attention to the unintended consequences of public perceptions, police actions and social reaction in general. It reveals how processes of reaction are also processes of invention and creation. The concept has been most commonly applied to explain escalations in expressive forms of deviancy. Its wider applicability to other less publicized forms of rule-breaking are less clear. It may remain the case that in other instances (for example, domestic violence) it is a *lack* of negative social reaction (intolerance) which provides the climate for its continuation. The extent to which a real amplification of deviance is driven by its public identification also remains questionable – and probably unknowable. A complex of motivations may underlie the development of deviant careers, of which social reaction might play a relatively small part.

John Muncie

Associated Concepts: deviance, labelling, moral panic, social reaction

Key Readings

Cohen, S. (1972) *Folk Devils and Moral Panics*. London: MacGibbon and Kee.
Wilkins, L.T. (1964) *Social Deviance*. London: Tavistock.
Young, J. (1971a) 'The role of the police as amplifiers of deviancy, negotiators of reality and translators of fantasy', in S. Cohen (ed.), *Images of Deviance*. Harmondsworth: Penguin.
Young, J. (1971b) *The Drug Takers: The Social Meaning of Drug Use*. London: Paladin.

DIFFERENTIAL ASSOCIATION

Definition

Initially developed by Edwin H. Sutherland (1883–1950), the concept of differential association is an attempt to account for the acquisition and maintenance of criminal behaviour in terms of contact, or an association, with particular environments and social groups.

Distinctive Features

Much of the very early research and theory concerned with the causes of crime had focused attention on the individual characteristics of the offender: these individual factors included genetic and biological functioning, psychological factors and psychiatric status. During the 1920s and 1930s a group of researchers, including Clifford R. Shaw and Henry D. McKay, at the University of Chicago, began to challenge the view that explanations for crime were to be found at an individual level. The significant contribution of the Chicago School was the advancement of the thesis that crime was brought about not by individual factors but was instead a product of social forces.

As criminologists' attention turned toward social factors, the particular role of social organization and disorganization in explaining crime came to prominence. A broad position evolved that people, perhaps young people in particular, living in parts of cities that were characterized by social disadvantage and disorganization were at a greatly increased risk of participating in delinquency. Further, once a neighbourhood becomes a focus for a delinquent culture, then the possibility arises that through the cultural transmission of delinquent values other young people will be drawn into that same crime. In a sense, these emerging sociological theories shifted the pathology away from the individual and onto the social structure.

During the 1930s Sutherland spent part of his academic career at the University of

Chicago, working alongside the researchers who developed a sociological theory of crime. However, Sutherland's own contribution was in part driven by a strain that was evident in the data collected by the Chicago researchers. While formulating a cogent theoretical perspective based on social disorganization, the data also spoke of a social cohesion and organization at the centre of criminal activity. For example, it was difficult to argue that white collar crime was a product of social disorganization.

Sutherland took a broad perspective, advocating that crime itself was a socially defined construct, with the power to define crime held by certain influential sections of society. It was therefore not the case that he ascribed to a view of crime as a product of individual psychopathology. However, he did not lose sight of the individual: he was concerned to understand how crime was transmitted through generations, and how a given individual was drawn into crime. The mechanism for cultural transmission was seen to be learning, such that criminal behaviour would be learned in the same way that any other behaviour will be learned. Sutherland argued that the answer to the next question – how criminal behaviour is learned – lay in understanding how social influences impact on the individual. Specifically, each individual has a *differential association* with other people who are more or less disposed towards delinquency.

As an explanatory concept of the impact of differential associations, Sutherland invoked the notion of a 'definition': those individuals with more contact with other people favourably disposed towards crime would themselves develop definitions favourable to crime, and vice versa. A definition towards crime would indicate not only learning the skills necessary to commit an offence, but would also incorporate the attitudes and moral values that supported criminal activity. It is important to note that Sutherland is not suggesting that the association has to be with criminals, rather that the association is with people who might either encourage crime or fail to censure criminal acts.

As the theory developed in sophistication, Sutherland set out a number of postulates:

1 Criminal behaviour is learned.
2 Learning takes place through an association with other people.
3 The main setting for learning is within close personal groups.
4 Learning includes both techniques to carry out certain crimes and attitudes and motives that are supportive of committing crime.
5 Learning experiences – differential associations – will vary in frequency and importance for each individual.
6 The processes involved in learning criminal behaviour are no different from those required when learning any other behaviour.

Evaluation

With the articulation of this position as Differential Association Theory, Sutherland offered perhaps the first integrated social psychological account of crime. He then continued to refine his ideas throughout his writings, and after his death his colleague Donald Cressey continued the work (e.g., Sutherland, 1939, 1947; Sutherland and Cressey, 1974). Sutherland's views are remarkable in that they anticipate much of what was to follow in both psychology and criminology. The theory is clearly sociological in its portrayal of powerful social forces as defining the nature of crime. However, with its concern for the individual, it is also psychological in orientation. The proposition that learning takes place via associations within social groups and intimate relationships is evident in contemporary social learning theory and in social structure theories in criminology. The view that each individual's unique learning experiences will lead to the acquisition of specific skills and cognitions fits with contemporary learning theory. Indeed, offenders' cognitions in the form of rational choice and decision making have become a focus for much debate in the recent literature. Finally, Sutherland's view of the normality of the learning that leads to criminal behaviour is in accordance with the many contemporary theorists who would reject explanations of crime based on individual psychopathology.

Sutherland's theory does leave many questions unanswered. How does learning occur? What exactly are the social conditions that lead to learning criminal skills and attitudes? And at an individual level, how do these skills and attitudes function? Sutherland did not have the empirical base from which he could begin to answer such questions, but he still set an agenda for future generations of researchers.

Clive Hollin

Associated Concepts: appreciative criminology, Chicago School of Sociology, conditioning, differential reinforcement, interactionism, rational choice theory, social learning theory

Key Readings

Sutherland, E.H. (1939) *Principles of Criminology*. Philadelphia, PA: Lippincott.
Sutherland, E.H. (1947) *Principles of Criminology*, 5th edn. Philadelphia, PA: Lippincott.
Sutherland, E.H. and Cressey, D.R. (1974) *Principles of Criminology*, 9th edn. Philadelphia, PA: Lippincott.

DIFFERENTIAL REINFORCEMENT

Definition

In learning theory the concept of reinforcement refers to the relationship between a behaviour and the outcomes it produces. Attempts to understand criminal behaviour in terms of its outcomes are called differential reinforcement.

Distinctive Features

Sutherland's concept of differential association highlights the importance of learning in attempts to understand criminal behaviour. In the 1950s such ideas were being developed in criminology, whilst within mainstream psychology there were significant advances in the development of theories of learning. In particular, B.F. Skinner's work on the principles of operant conditioning had demonstrated the relationship between behaviour and its consequences (Skinner, 1938, 1969). His experimental research showed that the environmental consequences that follow a specific behaviour will act either to increase or decrease the probability of that behaviour happening again in the future. When a behaviour produces consequences that the individual finds rewarding and the frequency of that behaviour is increased, it is said to be *reinforced*. Alternatively, a behaviour that produces outcomes that the individual finds aversive and which therefore act to decrease the rate of behaviour is said to be *punished*. (In the language of operant conditioning, the term 'punishment' simply means that a behaviour decreases in frequency.)

The principles of reinforcement were applied to criminal behaviour, as an extension of differential association theory. They offered a means, consistent with learning theory, to account for the way in which offending could be both acquired and maintained (Burgess and Akers, 1966). Jeffery (1965) suggested that criminal behaviour can be viewed as operant behaviour: that is, within the context of the associations that an individual experiences, criminal behaviour is acquired and maintained by its reinforcing consequences. Further, extending the principles of operant learning, criminal behaviour will occur when the environment signals that a criminal act is likely to produce rewards. To understand why a person commits a crime, it is necessary to understand that individual's learning history. The task of understanding an individual's learning history means understanding the rewarding (and punishing) consequences of the criminal behaviour for the individual concerned. It is necessary, therefore, to understand not only the person but also their environment which provides the setting for criminal acts.

The setting conditions for crime operate at two levels: first, conditions of the type known to be precursors to persistent offending; second, the immediate situational cues which signal that a criminal act is likely to produce rewarding consequences. With regard to the former, this might include individual factors, such as poor school attainment, family and peer relationships, and social disadvantage, such as low family income and poor housing.

The importance of immediate setting events has been increasingly recognized over the past few years. For example, houses may be targeted for burglary because they offer an easy opportunity, such as an unlocked door or an open window; or because of certain design features, such as thick trees or high hedges, that will hide the criminal from observation and detection; or for the reason that goods such as televisions and video recorders are easily observed, making the property an attractive target. This situational analysis of the environment in which crimes occur has informed both understandings of criminal behaviour and situational crime prevention strategies to reduce crime.

Moving to the consequences of criminal behaviour, in acquisitive crimes such as burglary and embezzlement, the rewards are plainly financial and material gains. Such gains can be *positively reinforcing* in that they produce material outcomes that the offender finds rewarding. Alternatively, the gains can be *negatively reinforcing* in that they allow the offender to avoid the aversive situation of having no money. The link between unemployment and crime would serve as a broad example of how offending might be related to the need to avoid an unwanted financial and social situation. As well as tangible, material rewards, criminal behaviour can also produce social rewards such as peer group status and esteem.

Jeffery also noted that criminal behaviour can produce aversive consequences, such as a loss of liberty and disrupted intimate relationships, that can have a punishing (in the learning theory sense of the word) effect on behaviour. Overall, for each and every individual it is the historical balance of reinforcement and punishment that determines the likelihood of criminal behaviour when the opportunity presents itself. (For a case study applying behavioural analysis to a complex set of criminal behaviours see Gresswell and Hollin, 1992.)

Evaluation

As the research on processes of learning matured, two crucial issues emerged. First, the complexity of people's lives means that it is impossible to know their full learning history. Thus, there can never really be a complete understanding of any behaviour, criminal or otherwise. A behavioural analysis of an individual's criminal behaviour will always be limited by the boundaries of the available information. Second, in adopting operant conditioning as an explanatory framework, differential reinforcement falls prey to the criticism that it does not consider what happens inside the individual.

Clive Hollin

Associated Concepts: conditioning, differential association, rational choice theory, situational crime prevention, social learning theory

Key Readings

Burgess, R. and Akers, R. (1966) 'A differential association-reinforcement theory of criminal behavior', *Social Problems*, 14: 128–47.

Gresswell, D.M. and Hollin, C.R. (1992) 'Towards a new methodology for making sense of case material: an illustrative case involving attempted multiple murder', *Criminal Behaviour and Mental Health*, 2: 329–41.

Jeffery, C.R. (1965) 'Criminal behavior and learning theory', *Journal of Criminal Law, Criminology, and Police Science*, 56: 294–300.

Skinner, B.F. (1938) *The Behavior of Organisms: An Experimental Analysis*. New York: Appleton-Century-Crofts.

Skinner, B.F. (1969) *Contingencies of Reinforcement: A Theoretical Analysis*. Englewood Cliffs, NJ: Prentice-Hall.

DISASSOCIATION

See: Desistance; Neutralization (techniques of); Subculture

DISCOURSE ANALYSIS

Definition

A generic term covering a heterogeneous range of social science research methods which are concerned with the activities present in recorded talk and their relationship to other texts (for example, official statements on policies and practices). It is concerned with 'the way versions of the world, of society, events and inner psychological worlds are produced in discourse' (Potter, 1997: 146).

Distinctive Features

Discourse analysis is a perspective on social life which combines theoretical ideas and analytical orientations from various disciplines, such as linguistics, psychology and sociology. It shares many of the features of conversational analysis in that it is concerned with the ways in which people ascribe meaning to routine social interactions through talk. However, discourse analysis differs from conversational analysis in a number of aspects (Silverman, 1993). It deals with a wider range of social science concerns (such as gender relations and social control) and, consequently, does not eschew the use of theoretical frameworks. It also uses a variety of written, as well as spoken, 'utterances', especially in relation to the analysis of institutional talk. Finally, it does not require the same degree of mechanistic precision in the analysis of transcripts.

The concept of 'discourse' developed as a reaction against both positivistic epistemologies seeking scientific 'truths' and relativistic perspectives on knowledge which claimed that the process of knowing is ineluctably contradictory, uncertain and contingent (Worrall, 1990). It sought to identify the mechanisms whereby 'truths' are socially constructed through talk and, despite (or because of) an underlying incoherence, become the accepted (and, therefore, powerful) version of events. According to Foucault (1972) discourse is the key to power. Power, he argues, is not the overt domination of one group by another but the acceptance by all that there exists a reliable, smooth and coherent 'text' underlying all the apparent paradoxes of life. This process of reconstructing paradox as coherence is the fundamental project of discourse.

Analysis of discourse involves the deconstruction of coherence to reveal the underlying paradox and expose the absence of that which is represented as being present. For example, one way of ensuring the continuity of discourse is to demarcate its boundaries by employing 'practices of exclusion'. Such practices might include the prohibition of certain topics or explanations on grounds of 'irrelevance' (for example, poverty as an explanation of crime), the disqualification of certain individuals from being authorized speakers (for example, victims of crime in the courtroom), and the rejection of certain statements as illegitimate (for example, a sex offender claiming that his offence 'just happened').

In order to analyse discourse one has to ask questions not just about the content of discourse but also about its author (who says it?), its authority (on what grounds?), its audience (to whom?), its object (about whom?), and its objective (in order to achieve what?). Discourse analysis is particularly interested in the way in which rhetoric and argument are organized in talk and texts so as to undermine alternative or oppositional versions.

Evaluation

Potter (1997: 147) says that 'a large part of doing discourse analysis is a craft skill, more like bike riding or chicken sexing than following the recipe for a mild chicken rogan josh'. The main difficulty in defining discourse analysis is that it covers a wide range of activities, from linguistic analysis (akin to conversational analysis) to postmodern analysis of the relationship between the construction of knowledge and power (Lyon, 1999). In some of its variations it would not be recognized as a research 'method' at all by many social scientists. Despite these criticisms, discourse analysis has played an important role in encouraging a reflexive and critical approach to the conventional wisdom, which passes for knowledge in penal policy and the criminal justice system. It has exposed the inconsistencies and contradictions which are rendered coherent in institutional and routine talk about crime and criminals.

Anne Worrall

Associated Concepts: conversational analysis, deconstruction, documentary analysis, postmodernism

Key Readings

Burton, F. and Carlen, P. (1979) *Official Discourse*. London: Routledge and Kegan Paul.
Foucault, M. (1972) *The Archaeology of Knowledge*. London: Tavistock.
Lyon, D. (1999) *Postmodernity*, 2nd edn. Buckingham: Open University Press.
Potter, J. (1997) 'Discourse analysis as a way of analysing naturally occurring talk', in D. Silverman (ed.), *Qualitative Research: Theory, Methods and Practice*. London: Sage.
Silverman, D. (1993) *Interpreting Qualitative Data: Methods for Analysing Talk, Text and Interaction*. London: Sage.
Worrall, A. (1990) *Offending Women: Female Lawbreakers and the Criminal Justice System*. London: Routledge.

DISCRETION

Definition

The power conferred on criminal justice professionals to use their judgement to decide what action to take in a given situation. This includes the decision to take no action. Discretion is officially delegated within the criminal justice system and not limited to one decision point. Because it extends to include all points of decision making and encompasses procedures and working methods, it flows back and forth throughout all parts of the criminal justice system.

Distinctive Features

Discretion is one of the most contentious issues in criminal justice because the professionals involved at each stage of the criminal justice process enjoy a considerable degree of mandated flexibility in the decisions they can make about the processing of individual cases. It is the day-to-day discretionary actions of police officers, prosecutors, defence lawyers, judges, and prison and probation officers that lubricate the criminal justice system and ensure that 'justice' is discharged. Discretion provides criminal justice professionals with the space both to engage in discriminatory activities and to subvert policies that they do not agree with.

There is wide agreement that the establishment of consistent criminal justice policies and the fair and equal treatment of all individuals, irrespective of their class, gender or race, requires the regulation of discretionary powers.

Particular attention has focused on the discretionary powers of police officers because they are the 'gatekeepers' to the criminal justice system, and unlike many other organizations, discretionary power is located primarily with the lowest-ranking employees. The police role requires discretionary power because officers are required to deal with a vast range of laws, incidents and forms of behaviour and make critical decisions. The source of police discretion lies with the legal powers they are given, the nature of the criminal law they have to enforce, the context within which police work takes place, and the limitations on resources. However, the location of a considerable degree of unregulated autonomy at the bottom of the organization poses serious problems for supervisors. Police officers can use their discretion to discriminate for or against sections of the community, through either an under- or an over-enforcement of the law. The injudicious, provocative and abusive application of police powers triggered serious confrontations between the police and minority ethnic communities in the USA and the UK during the 1990s.

As a result of judicial judgements, community complaints about misconduct, miscarriages of justice, and an increasing number of expensive civil actions, police forces have paid considerably more attention to structuring the discretionary powers of officers. This has resulted in:

- Training programmes to equip officers to use discretion in a more professional manner.
- The creation of ethical principles and guidelines governing the whole organization.
- Codes of practice and internal circulars to limit and/or guide stop and search, interrogation, the use of deadly force, and the response to domestic violence and racist violence.
- Strategies to raise the visibility of officers' work practices.
- The establishment of internal and external review bodies.

These strategies are premised on the principle that discretion is an inescapable part of police work. However, there are many who believe that the problem of police discretion will not be resolved until discretionary powers such as stop and search are abolished or meaningful complaints systems and modes of democratic accountability are implemented.

Eugene McLaughlin

Associated Concepts: 'broken windows', criminal justice, discrimination, disparity, disproportionality, net widening, social control, zero tolerance

Key Readings

Galligan, D.J. (1990) *Discretionary Powers: A Legal Study of Official Discretion.* Oxford: The Clarendon Press.
Hawkins, K. (ed.) (1992) *The Uses of Discretion.* Oxford: The Clarendon Press.

Ohlin, L.E. and Remington, F.J. (1993) *Discretion in Criminal Justice: The Tension Between Individualization and Uniformity.* Albany: State University of New York Press.
Vizant, J.C. and Crothers, L. (1998) *Street-Level Leadership: Discretion and Legitimacy in Front-Line Public Service.* Washington, DC: Georgetown University Press.
Walker, S. (1993) *Taming the System: The Control of Discretion in Criminal Justice 1950–90.* Oxford: Oxford University Press.

DISCRIMINATION

Definition

Discrimination consists of unfavourable treatment based on a person's sex, gender, 'race', ethnicity, culture, religion, language, class, sexual preference, age, physical disability or any other improper ground. It limits the economic, social and political opportunities of the individual or group discriminated against. In some contexts discrimination has been legally enforced (for example, *apartheid* in South Africa). In many other contexts discrimination exists *de facto*, in spite of laws intended to prevent its occurrence.

Distinctive Features

Discrimination includes behaviour ranging in severity from aversion and avoidance to harassment and violence. It includes insulting, patronizing or disrespectful behaviour, and the refusal to offer employment (or pay fair wages), to provide housing or medical treatment, or to provide a commercial or social service. Discrimination directly restricts civil liberties such as freedom of movement and association. It can also take the form of harassment, attack, exclusion and expulsion. In its most extreme form, discrimination has led to mass murder. Some theorists emphasize an investigation of the 'life form' of discrimination and its roots in local histories. Others emphasize the effects of discrimination in creating disadvantage and limiting the life chances of those discriminated against. Poverty, unemployment, ignorance, crime, increased infant mortality and a shortened life expectancy have all been shown to be consequences of discrimination. Racial discrimination has also been one of the most prominent explanations for the over-representation of black people among arrestees and in-prison populations.

A distinction can be made between direct and indirect discrimination. Among the best examples of *direct discrimination* are those that have been enshrined in national or state legislation such as the Jim Crow laws in the USA. These laws enforced segregation in education and public transport and also prohibited sexual relationships across the 'colour-line'. In some places African Americans were denied the right to vote and, as a consequence, to serve on juries or gain equal access to justice. In South Africa, until the *apartheid* regime ended in 1990, blacks were not allowed to vote or travel without restriction. Similarly, restrictions on women's ability to own property, to vote and so on have been in place in many countries. An explicit ban on the employment of openly homosexual people in the police or military is another example of direct discrimination. Such legal restrictions have obvious and wide-ranging consequences for fairness and social justice.

These *de jure* forms of discrimination are easy to identify and criticize as unjust. Even when there are no laws promoting or requiring discrimination, however, people are often directly excluded or singled out for unfavourable treatment. In many criminal justice agencies (including police, prisons and the courts) explicit, overt and direct discrimination has led to informal restrictions on the recruitment and promotion of women, ethnic minorities and other social groups. Discrimination also contributes to explaining why there are often marked inequalities in service provision (Brown, 1997). Sometimes discriminatory practices will persist even in the face of laws or policies designed to eliminate discrimination. This *de facto* discrimination can be the result of covert activity – that

which is intentional, but hidden – but can also result from indirect discrimination.

Indirect discrimination refers to treatment that might be described as 'equal' in a formal sense between different groups, but is discriminatory in its *actual effect* on a particular group. The 'minimum height' requirement for police officers in some jurisdictions is an example of indirect discrimination. Women and people from some ethnic groups are less likely to be able to meet the minimum requirement even though height is irrelevant to the job of being a police officer. This requirement, irrespective of its intent, clearly has the *effect* of restricting job opportunities for some groups, and may, therefore, be considered discriminatory.

Sometimes indirect discrimination will occur knowingly, but also covertly, in order to exclude women, homosexuals or people from ethnic minority communities; however, there are many other instances where such exclusion appears to be neither conscious nor deliberate. For example, few criminal justice agencies provide services for non-English speakers in the UK or the USA. Although it is probably not the intent of these organizations specifically to exclude non-English speakers, this is, in fact, what happens and as such it can be seen as having an indirect discriminatory effect.

Discrimination is closely tied up with the concept of *prejudice*: ideas that identify particular groups as 'inferior' or 'a problem'. The expression of prejudiced opinions and the use of negative stereotypes are often found to accompany discriminatory practice. Such prejudices (as racism, sexism and homophobia) are frequently explicit. In some criminal justice occupations, women and people from ethnic and other minorities will be seen by the dominant group of white men as inferior and less able to do the job (in both front-line and managerial contexts) and will find their employment prospects affected as a result. For example, in Britain, some male police officers have strongly resisted the idea of women joining the police service in numbers. When they were employed, certain male officers felt that women should be kept 'in their proper place' and away from 'real' policework (Brown, 1997). The experience of abusive and discriminatory practices in the workplace and the so-called 'glass ceiling' to career advancement has led to many employees taking legal action against employers in criminal justice agencies.

Evaluation

Studies of discrimination in action in the criminal justice process have suggested that this occurs under certain conditions. Where the law is permissive, individual discretion wide, and where there is a lack of guidelines as to how a decision should be taken, decision making is often based on subjective judgements. For example, police officers have the power to stop and search a person of whom they have 'reasonable suspicion', which is an ambiguous and ill-defined concept. In such instances of wide discretion and autonomy, and where the cultural norms support particular kinds of stereotypes and prejudices, the results are frequently discriminatory. It has been shown that police officers use colour as a criterion for stop and search and that black people are much more likely to be stopped than would be expected given their numbers in the general population. Where decisions and how they are reached are not monitored, and where accountability is weak, discrimination can go unchecked.

The right to equality before the law and protection against discrimination has been central to the conceptions of basic human rights that underpin the formation of the United Nations and the European Union. Protection against discrimination is recognized in Article 7 of the Universal Declaration of Human Rights, and in Article 14 of the European Convention on Human Rights. These call for fundamental rights and freedoms to be secured 'without discrimination on any grounds such as sex, race, colour, language, religion, political or other opinion, national or social origin, association with a national minority, property, birth or other status'. The international conventions on the elimination of all forms of discrimination against women and against racial discrimination are more stringent. These require governments to review national and local policies, and to 'amend, rescind or nullify' any laws or regulations which have the effect of creating or perpetuating discrimination. There is also a duty to promote tolerance and equality of opportunity (Banton, 1996).

Legislation based on these international principles can be found in many countries. This focuses on the concepts of anti-discrimination (for example, anti-racism/anti-sexism/anti-homophobia), equal opportunities or affirmative action. In the USA, the Civil Rights Act 1963 prohibited discrimination against blacks and other minorities in respect of voting, employment and the use of public accommodations. The Fair Housing Act 1968 also prohibited property companies from discriminating when seeking buyers for houses. Similarly, in Britain, the Race Relations Acts of 1965 and 1968 prohibited direct discrimination on the grounds of 'race' and ethnicity, and the 1976 Race Relations Act extended the law to prohibit indirect discrimination. Similar legislation has prohibited discrimination against disabled people and against women. The Race Relations (Amendment) Act 2000 applied these principles for the first time to public services, including the police.

The concept of discrimination is helpful to understand the processes by which the life chances of less powerful individuals and groups are shaped by responses to them by the powerful. It contributes to understanding how, for example, women and people from ethnic minority communities make up a disproportionately small number of the ranks of criminal justice professions (especially those at the top, such as chiefs of police and judges). It helps to explain why the culture of these professions is often hostile – in both language and practice – towards particular groups (such as women, gay people, disabled people and those from ethnic minority communities). It also helps to explain why the protections of the criminal justice process are so often described as unsatisfactory by members of these excluded groups.

The notion of anti-discriminatory practice is a perspective that acknowledges the existence and impact of 'race', gender and homophobic stereotyping, prejudice and their echo in direct and indirect discrimination. From this perspective, positive action is required to eliminate discrimination actively and promote equality of opportunity.

Ben Bowling

Associated Concepts: criminal justice, criminalization, discretion, disparity, disproportionality, human rights, police bias, social justice

Key Readings

Banton, M. (1996) *International Action Against Racial Discrimination.* Oxford: The Clarendon Press.
Bowling, B. and Phillips, C. (2000) *Racism, Crime and Justice.* London: Pearson.
Brown, J. (1997) 'Equal opportunities and the police service in England and Wales: past, present and future possibilities', in P. Francis, P. Davies and V. Jupp (eds), *Policing Futures.* London: Macmillan.
Kleg, M. (1993) *Hate, Prejudice and Racism.* Albany, NY: State University of New York Press.

DISPARITY

Definition

The concept of 'disparity' is most clearly associated with sentencing and the practice of giving different sentences for similar offences, but it also has wider relevance in terms of offenders and victims being treated differently or unequally throughout the criminal justice system when their circumstances are similar.

Distinctive Features

Discoveries of disparity in the treatment of offenders in the criminal justice system strike at the heart of the ideal that justice is abstract and that all are equal before the law. Whilst disparity is concerned more with differences in process than differences in outcome, it is often used interchangeably with 'discrimination' and most pointedly concerns 'equal treatment'. Indeed, most people appear to believe that fairness necessarily involves treating 'like cases alike'. But equal treatment involves at one extreme the impartial application of existing rules and procedures, regardless of the outcome (procedural justice), and at the other, the idea that any policies or procedures that have the effect of punishing a higher proportion of one social group than another are unjust, and that law and policy should be adjusted so as to achieve equal outcomes (substantive justice). Techniques for reducing disparity include: judicial self-regulation (with courts of appeal and the like), statutory sentencing principles (as in penal codes), numerical guideline systems (as in the Minnesota system – with clear classifications of offences and categories of relative gravity), and mandatory sentences (prescribed maximum and minimum penalties) (Ashworth, 1998).

Calls to eradicate disparity have included calls for equal treatment, but this is not unproblematic. Following critiques of the sentencing of women for example, both in principle and practice, 'equal' has come to mean 'like men'. As punishment has become increasingly more severe in England and Wales, the USA and elsewhere, 'equal treatment' with men is far from desirable – let alone 'just', some would argue – and so the quest for equal treatment is increasingly questioned.

In the USA, Tonry (1996) has revealed that the success of sentencing guidelines in various states has led to increased imprisonment of women as the disparities between sentencing females and males have been reduced. Indeed, this process of 'levelling-up' in order to reduce sentencing disparities is not uncommon. The 'split the difference' policy of California is rather unusual, however, as it involves a lowering of sentences for men and a raising of sentences for women.

In jurisdictions where there are sentencing guidelines rather than rigid systems of mandatory sentencing, the move towards consistency, equality and proportionality of punishment to crime has meant that mitigating circumstances, such as child care or family responsibilities, have ceased to be available. Thus the call for 'equal treatment' has been replaced by a call for 'appropriateness'. That is, it is argued that what is required is that circumstances appropriate to each person should be considered regardless of assumptions about gender-based and other stereotypical perceptions of 'needs'(Hudson, 1996).

Evaluation

The concept of disparity is often confused with, as well as used interchangeably with, 'discrimination'. Whereas disparity concerns the consistency with which criteria are applied to cases, discrimination, when properly understood, refers to the use of illegitimate criteria. For instance, race is a prime example of a criterion that has been recognized as illegitimate. However, the concepts are closely intertwined. A good deal of research has been carried out to measure both disparity and discrimination, though much of this has been statistical in nature, with obvious limitations. First, there is an assumption that disparity or discrimination can be proved or dismissed through the use of sophisticated statistical analysis. Second, it ignores the more dynamic aspects of decision making – the significance of appearance and demeanour, prejudices revealed in attitude rather than in specific decision, and the interaction between defendants and officials. Third, such research has often focused on a single process or moment in decision making, and on a single factor (for example, race or gender), when a number of factors may be relevant in combination. Equally, treating 'like cases alike' in terms of outcomes (sentencing outcomes for instance) can mask processual differences. But the real problem is that 'disparity' is an empty category that can be filled only by reference to some standard, and in principle the standard could be set by any criteria.

Loraine Gelsthorpe

Associated Concepts: discrimination, disproportionality, racialization

Key Readings

Ashworth, A. (1998) 'Four techniques for reducing disparity', in A. von Hirsch and A. Ashworth (eds), *Principled Sentencing: Readings on Theory and Policy*. Oxford: Hart Publishing.
Daly, K. (1994) *Gender, Crime and Punishment*. New Haven, CT: Yale University Press.
Hudson, B. (1996) *Understanding Justice*. Buckingham: Open University Press.
Tonry, M. (1996) *Sentencing Matters*. New York: Oxford University Press.

DISPLACEMENT

See: Defensible space; Rational choice theory; Repeat victimization; Situational crime prevention; Surveillance

DISPOSITIONAL THEORIES

Definition

An alternative means of describing positivist and some interactionist theories. Its key characteristic is to argue that because of certain biological, psychological or sociological conditions some people are born with or come to acquire a *disposition* to behave in a criminal manner. A 'dispositional bias' is at its strongest in positivism but is also present in those interactionist and labelling theories which maintain that the labelling of people as deviant cements a deviant identity and predisposes them to commit further criminal acts. An alternative to dispositional theory can be found in rational choice theory.

John Muncie

Associated Concepts: criminal careers, deviancy amplification, individual positivism, labelling, positivism, sociological positivism

DISPROPORTIONALITY

Definition

The extent to which something appears to be inappropriate or 'out of proportion' in relation to something else. The term has been used in criminology to describe a disparity, or imbalance, in patterns of crime and the administration of criminal justice.

Distinctive Features

It is common to describe a situation where an individual or a group is privileged or disadvantaged in comparison to another as disproportionate. Five examples illustrate the usage of the term.

1 *Disproportionality in punishment.* The penological notion of proportionality is central to just desert theories of sentencing (von Hirsch, 1998). A sentence of the court could be described as disproportionate if a person convicted of a minor offence were sentenced to a long prison term or if a judge or magistrate failed to take into account mitigating circumstances. Disproportionality in sentencing can also be identified at the group level. For example, Hood's (1992) study of Crown Courts in the English Midlands found that black people were disproportionately given custodial sentences in comparison to whites, even once all the legally relevant variables had been taken into account. This study also indicated that where a custodial sentence was given, the average sentence length was longer for black and Asian defendants, in comparison with their white counterparts.

2 *Disproportionality in the use of police powers.* The use of a power – such as that to stop and search under s.l of the Police and Criminal Evidence Act in the UK – can be described as disproportionate if it is used excessively on specific social groups. For example, police statistics show that black people in London are about five times as likely to be stopped and searched in comparison with white people. The term has also been used in human rights jurisprudence to describe an imbalance in the intrusiveness of a police power – such as planting a listening device – in comparison with the seriousness of the crime being investigated.

3 *Disproportionality in imprisonment.* There is a disproportionately large number of black people in the prison population in Britain, in comparison with their numbers in the general population: while there are 176 white people in prison per 100,000, there are 1,245 black people in prison per 100,000 (cf. Tonry, 1994). The obvious question that arises from these statistics is why the British criminal justice system imprisons such a greater proportion of the black population than the white population. Among the possible explanations are a disproportionate risk of being arrested, convicted or sentenced to custody, or disproportionately long prison sentences. Disproportionate rates of imprisonment could also reflect rates of offending among the black population.

4 *Disproportionality in victimization and offending.* Evidence from victimization surveys indicating that people from ethnic minorities suffer a level of victimization that exceeds that of white people can be described as 'disproportionate victimization'. The term can also be used to describe unexpectedly high actual or supposed 'crime rates' among, for example, black people. In this usage, 'disproportionality in offending' is a rival explanation to 'discrimination in criminal justice' for disproportionate imprisonment rates (Russell, 1998: 46).

5 *Disproportionality in employment in the criminal justice professions.* Statistical evidence shows that many fewer women and people from ethnic minority groups are employed in criminal justice agencies, especially in more senior ranks, than would be expected

on the basis of their numbers in the population. This appears – on the face of it – to be the result of discrimination on the part of employers, and there is certainly evidence that such discrimination does occur. However, this imbalance may also be explained by legitimate factors, such as a lack of suitably qualified applicants or an unwillingness to apply for reasons of preference for other occupations.

Evaluation

Disproportionality is a slippery concept, not least because it has subtly different meanings depending on the context in which it is used. The example of the 'race and crime debate' – where the term is frequently used – can serve as an illustration of the various competing definitions.

There is more or less universal agreement that black people are more likely than white people to be stopped, searched, arrested and imprisoned. The question on which the 'race and crime' debate has turned is whether this disproportionality – found in the 'outcomes' of the criminal justice process – is the result of discrimination (at one or more points in the process), a disproportionate involvement by black people in offending, or a combination of both of these. Further questions are also raised regarding how the disproportionately high rates of unemployment, poverty, exclusion from school and the concentration of black people into urban areas impact on their experiences of crime and criminal justice. These uses of the term are subtly distinct from the penological notion of proportionality, referring to the extent to which punishment and crime are commensurate. The definitions coincide when it can be shown that the punishment of black people is not only disproportionate in comparison to their numbers in the population, but also unduly harsh given the nature of their offending.

Identifying disproportionate outcomes of the criminal justice process is a necessary but not sufficient step towards establishing discrimination. In civil rights jurisprudence, disparities in the treatment of women and people from ethnic and other minorities can be taken as *prima facie* evidence of discrimination which can be tested by assessing the extent to which differences can be explained by legitimate factors. Where disparities are shown to be unjustified, the discriminatory practices that create and sustain them may be ruled unlawful and the complainants entitled to some redress.

Ben Bowling

Associated Concepts: discrimination, disparity, just deserts, penology, police bias, racialization, victimology

Key Readings

Bowling, B. and Phillips, C. (2001) *Racism, Crime and Justice*. London: Pearson.
von Hirsch, A. (1998) 'Proportionate sentences: a desert perspective', in A. von Hirsch and A. Ashworth (eds), *Principled Sentencing: Readings on Theory and Policy*, 2nd edn. London: Hart Publishing.
Hood, R. (1992) *Race and Sentencing*. Oxford: Oxford University Press.
Russell, K. (1998) *The Color of Crime*. New York and London: New York University Press.
Tonry, M. (1994) 'Racial disproportion in US prisons', *British Journal of Criminology*, 34: 97–115.

DISPUTE SETTLEMENT

See: Informal justice; Redress; Restorative justice

DIVERSION

Definition

The process of keeping offenders and other problem populations away from the institutional arrangements of criminal justice or welfare.

Distinctive Features

Diversion has its roots in what Stanley Cohen (1985) termed the 'destructuring moves' of the 1960s. Its orientation toward an alternative procedural rationale grew out of a radical critique of the penal welfare strategy and was closely associated with measures of decarceration (away from prison), delegalization (away from the state) and deprofessionalization (away from the expert). Diversion subsequently emerged as a dominant trend in juvenile justice reform. Short of rejecting penal sanctions completely, proponents of diversion in juvenile justice advocated the development of initiatives to keep juveniles out of court, custody and residential care. Their general aim was to remove or minimize the juveniles' penetration into the justice system. For critics of treatment-type interventions, increased professional services were seen either as failing to reform the delinquent or as morally unacceptable. Social work professionals redefined their mission in terms of 'leaving the kids alone'. In the process, social sciences arguments (especially from the labelling perspective) were rediscovered which suggested that the process of arrest, trial and conviction can have potentially damaging effects of stigmatization.

In a parallel debate, diversion fitted in with demands for a 'return to justice' from the liberal justice lobby (Morris et al., 1980). Their central arguments were that due process safeguards had been undermined by the rise of individualized treatment in juvenile justice. The expectation was that, by re-establishing values of proportionality, procedural justice and the predictability of legal administration, the extent of penal intervention would also be reduced. Similar 'just deserts' arguments have since been adopted to support the use of police cautioning outside the formal court system as the proportionate response to minor forms of law breaking or to offences committed by persons of low culpability (such as the old and the mentally ill).

Evaluation

Diversionary initiatives (especially alternatives to formal court processing) have proliferated in most Western juvenile justice systems. They are frequently state-sponsored and administered or controlled either by officials (such as the police) or community-based agencies. Because of its definitional ambiguity, diversion has developed in different directions at different times and has come to have a variety of meanings in terms of policies and programmes. In particular, the distinction between 'diversion from' and 'diversion to' has been a major concern in juvenile justice literature. In this latter version of diversion as a referral to alternative programmes, the paradox is that more, rather than fewer, juveniles ended up being subject to new forms of community-based intervention.

Diversion can also mean keeping the younger and less delinquent population away from a career of crime through early identification and treatment. The expansion of delinquency prevention initiatives can thus generate an inflationary spiral in the processing of delinquency cases, leading to greater regulation in the lives of young people and their families (Klein, 1979). Furthermore, critics argued that diversion has sometimes been conflated with a crime control ideology. In the United States, intensive programmes such as 'boot camps', which were originally promoted as an alternative measure to divert offenders who would otherwise be sentenced to long-term incarceration, are increasingly being used as a sentencing option in their own right for less serious offenders.

Wider developments of managerialism in criminal justice in the 1990s have meant that criminal justice officials supported diversion out of the practical need for a rationalization of resources and the establishment of an efficient crime management apparatus.

Diversion of cases in preliminary phases is now part of the state's strategy for 'defining deviance down' to adapt to high crime rates and increased caseloads in most Western criminal justice systems (Garland, 1996).

Maggy Lee

Associated Concepts: bifurcation, community sentences, crime prevention, decarceration, decriminalization, just deserts, juvenile justice, labelling, managerialism, net widening, radical non-intervention, social control

Key Readings

Cohen, S. (1985) *Visions of Social Control: Crime, Punishment, and Classification.* Cambridge: Polity Press.

Garland, D. (1996) 'The limits of the sovereign state – strategies of crime control in contemporary society', *British Journal of Criminology*, 36 (4): 445–71.

Klein, M. (1979) 'Deinstitutionalization and diversion of juvenile offenders: a litany of impediments', in N. Morris and N. Tonry (eds), *Crime and Justice: An Annual Review of Research*, vol. 1. Chicago: University of Chicago Press.

Morris, A., Giller, H., Szwed, E. and Geach, H. (1980) *Justice for Children.* London: Macmillan.

Pratt, J. (1986) 'Diversion from the juvenile court', *British Journal of Criminology*, 24 (2): 81–92.

DOCUMENTARY ANALYSIS

Definition

The detailed examination of documents with a view to making assertions about some aspect of the social world, for example, the social or historical context in which the documents were produced, the social meanings which they transmit, the effects of such meanings on social groups, and the social control function of documents.

Distinctive Features

A wide range of documents has been used in social research, including life histories, diaries, newspapers and magazines, stories, essays, official documents and records, web pages, and research reports. Such documents may be made up exclusively of the written word or they could also include statistics, as in a report of crime trends.

The life history is similar to a biography or autobiography and is a means by which an individual provides a written record of his or her own life in his or her own terms. It can include a descriptive summary of life events and experiences and also an account of the social world from the subject's point of view. The use of newspapers has been central in what is usually referred to as media analysis. Media analysis has several interests, one of which is an examination of the way in which stereotypes of categories of people or types of action are created, reinforced and amplified with wide-ranging consequences for those people and actions. For example, newspapers have been used to examine the portrayal of folk devils and also the creation and career of the label and stereotype of the 'mugger' in the British press.

Researchers can make use of essays or other writings which are already in existence or solicit such writings as part of their research design. For example, Cohen and Taylor's (1972) examination of the subjective experiences of imprisonment and strategies of psychological survival among long-term prisoners was in part founded on an analysis of essays and poems and topics suggested by Cohen and Taylor themselves. Official documents, for example reports of public inquiries, provide valuable data for the analysis of official definitions of what is defined as problematic (for example, public disorder), what is viewed as the explanation of the problem, and what is deemed as the preferred solution. Apart from documents at a societal or macro level, there are other official documents at an institutional or micro level which can prove just as important in the disposal and destination of individuals, for example, offenders. These are organizational records, such as probation reports, which define what is, or is not, problematic about individuals, which put forward explanations for behaviour and actions, and which record decisions relating to outcomes. Such individual records are not insulated from official documents operating at a societal level in so far as there is often a close connection between the formulation of concepts, explanations and solutions at one level and such formulation and application at another.

Evaluation

The validity of any document is dependent on its authenticity (whether it is original and genuine), its credibility (whether it is accurate), its representativeness (whether it is representative of the totality of documents in its class), and its meaning (what it is intended to say) (Scott, 1990). What is more, any evaluation of documentary analysis must consider the way in which it is influenced by broad theoretical approaches and the types of research questions posed by these approaches. For example, the positivist approach to documents – sometimes also known as content analysis – assumes that there is a correspondence between the manifest content of documents and their meaning: documents are representations of what they mean. Researchers using this approach analyse the manifest content of documents to ask questions such as: What are the characteristics of the content? What inferences can be made about the causes and generation of the content? What inferences can be made about the effects of communication?

By way of contrast, the interpretative approach starts from the assumption that different meanings can be attributed by different individuals to the same manifest content. It would, for example, be interested in the varying ways in which defendants, prosecutors, judges and jurors make sense of documents placed before a court of law and with what consequences.

A critical approach to documentary analysis is concerned with how and when certain kinds of documents come to be treated and accepted as 'knowledge' and with the social control functions of such knowledge. In this way, critical analysis emphasizes the close connection between documents and the exercise of power. One variant of this critical approach to documents is discourse analysis, which has been associated with Michel Foucault.

Victor Jupp

Associated Concepts: content analysis, discourse analysis, folk devil, positivism, stereotyping

Key Readings

Cohen, S. and Taylor, L. (1972) *Psychological Survival: The Experience of Long-Term Imprisonment.* Harmondsworth: Penguin.

Jupp, V. and Morris, C. (1993) 'Traditions in documentary analysis', in M. Hammersley (ed.), *Social Research: Philosophy, Politics and Practice.* London: Sage.

Scott, J. (1990) *A Matter of Record: Documentary Sources in Social Research.* Cambridge: Polity Press.

DOMESTIC VIOLENCE

See: Family crime; Victimology; Violence

DRIFT

See: Subculture

DUE PROCESS MODEL

Definition

A 'due process' model or perspective emphasizes the need to administer justice according to legal rules and procedures which are publicly known, fair and seen to be just.

Distinctive Features

In a 'due process' model of criminal justice the main function of the criminal courts is to act as an impartial arbitrator of conflicts arising between the state and its citizens. Central to this perspective are the presumption of innocence, the restraints of arbitrary power, and the inviolability of legal rules and procedures. Such procedures do not weight the process against the accused or in favour of those in power, but rather seek to guarantee a measure of judicial equality to all parties: hence the absolute need to abide by strict and formal procedures, to ensure that adherence to 'due process' results in a smooth-running, fair and impartial system. Other key elements (legal safeguards) in a 'due process model' might be described as follows: arrested persons must be informed as to what the charges are and, where relevant, why they are going to court; there are clear standards of proof (with the plaintiff or prosecution bearing the onus of proof); there are extensive rules which determine what is allowable or not as legal evidence (with 'hearsay evidence', crudely translated as 'gossip', being admissible only under certain conditions); and with each party being given the opportunity to tender evidence before the court (and jury) to cross-examine the other party so as to clarify matters or raise objections. In addition, within a 'due process model', judicial proceedings are normally conducted in open court so as to avoid situations like the Inquisition, where 'justice' is arrived at behind closed doors with few public checks and balances upon judicial power. Herbert Packer, who offered an incisive account of both a 'due process' model and a 'crime control' model in 1964, suggests that whilst the crime control model resembles an assembly line, the due process model looks very much like an obstacle course – with successive stages being designed to present formidable impediments to carrying the accused any further along the process. Whilst 'justice must be seen to be done' in the case of minors there may be some limitations on this procedure, with special 'juvenile' or 'youth courts' being held behind closed doors so as to protect them from public gaze. Also, there may be exceptions to the rule of 'open court' when it is thought appropriate, especially in sensitive or difficult situations, to hear testimony 'in camera' (behind closed doors, with bans on publishing the proceedings). Broadly speaking, however, the institutional processes associated with 'due process' are designed to protect a citizen's rights.

The concept of 'due process' has its origins in the Classical School of criminology, which itself was reacting against punishment under the *ancien régime* of eighteenth-century Europe which was both arbitrary and harshly retributive, dominated by capital and corporal penalties. As a protagonist of the Classical School, jurist and philosopher Cesare Beccaria (1738–94) published *Dei Delitti e delle Pene* (1764) [On Crimes and Punishments], which provided a thorough and searching critique of the criminal justice systems of Europe. Beccaria, along with others in the Classical School, called for reform, for clarity in the law and 'due process' in criminal procedure, combined with a certainty and regularity of punishment.

In England, the due process approach is often associated with the attitudes of the legal profession, particularly those involved in defence work, and with the aims of such organizations as Liberty. The concept has been brought to bear in a number of areas within the criminal justice system where there has been concern about a lack of fairness and openness in decision-making processes. For example, there have been criticisms of the lack of 'due process' safeguards associated with the system of parole ever since its inception. By this is meant that there have been criticisms about the secretive nature of the decision-making processes, a lack of accountability, and a lack of attention to offenders' rights in the whole process. The concept has been similarly employed to describe procedural irregularities in decision-making processing that affects cautions and prosecutions, with evidence to suggest that some people might be given cautions where there is insufficient evidence to convict or where there is no admission of guilt (see Wasik et al., 1999, Chapter 2).

Evaluation

The concept of 'due process' has been usefully employed in critiques of criminal justice practice in recent years, particularly in England with regard to the lack of procedural safeguards in police interviews, the use of cautions, legal representation, parole decisions, prisoners' rights and the use of the Crown Court (with adult-style criminal proceedings) for juveniles.

Whilst the concept of due process may be useful as a representation of 'the ideal', setting out how the system *ought to be*, there are those who would argue that 'the reality', that is, *how the system is*, may be so far removed that the 'ideal' becomes increasingly difficult to achieve with the result that the criminal justice process finds it harder and harder to function efficiently. In this case, complexity and high standards may militate against justice.

It has also been argued that procedural justice (due process) is a far cry from substantive justice and that really it is substantive justice (that is, justice which relates to specific human rights aims or to penological aims such as abolitionism, restorative justice, rehabilitation and deterrence) which should be of central importance. Formal legalism – mere adherence to rules and adoption of legal safeguards – does not in itself make a system just.

Loraine Gelsthorpe

Associated Concepts: classicism, crime control model, disproportionality, just deserts

Key Readings

Hudson, B. (1996) *Understanding Justice*. Buckingham: Open University Press.
Packer, H. (1964) 'Two models of the criminal process', *University of Pennsylvania Law Review*, 113: 1–68.
Wasik, M., Gibbons, T. and Redmayne, M. (1999) *Criminal Justice: Text and Materials*. London: Longman.

E

ECO-CRIME

Definition

Acts of environmental harm and ecological degradation – illegal and/or harmful behaviour including threatening, damaging or destroying the natural environment. It is a term often used synonymously with 'green crime' or 'environmental crime'.

Distinctive Features

As a legal category, eco-crime has been defined as 'an unauthorised act or omission that violates the law and is therefore subject to criminal prosecution and criminal sanction' (Situ and Emmons, 2000: 3). Many such violations are reflected in the growing number of domestic laws as well as international environmental protocols, treaties and conventions that provide legal mandates which prohibit a range of activities identified as hazardous and deleterious to global ecosystems. For example, UNICRI (the United Nations Interregional Crime and Justice Institute) divides these internationally recognized crimes against the environment into five groups including: the illegal dumping of domestic waste; the trafficking and dumping of toxic waste and nuclear materials; deforestation, environmental pollution and indigenous dislocation; the illegal trade in ozone-depleting substances; and the illegal trade in, and poaching of, endangered species. Moreover, UNICRI acknowledges that there are other crimes against the environment that are not included in their brief, but are covered by international environmental law such as the destruction or vandalism of sites of national heritage; the contamination of food and the environments in which it is produced; the theft of indigenous genetic resources; and the contamination of freshwater resources (see Soyland, 2000).

Other legal categories of eco-crime are directed towards actions that violate laws whilst attempting to protect the environment. In other words, eco-friendly protest groups that sabotage or destroy agricultural and chemical sites in the name of conservation and ecological preservation have been referred to as 'eco-militants' or 'eco-terrorists'. For example, the FBI defines eco-terrorism as 'the use or threatened use of violence of a criminal nature against innocent victims or property by an environmentally-oriented, subnational group for environmental-political reasons, or aimed at an audience beyond the target, often of a symbolic nature'. This is what Lynch and Stretetsky (2003) refer to as the 'corporate perspective' of green crime: a perspective that identifies the ways in which corporations are perceived as victims of those that disrupt their operations and production.

That said, the growing body of international environment treaties is continually repositioning notions of environmental terrorism within acts of state and corporate criminality and neglect. Moreover, debates about international security since September 11, 2001, have defined the potential use of biological and chemical warfare by organized terrorist networks as 'eco-terrorism'. Consequently, the word eco-crime has various socially constructed meanings. It is also a term used to describe acts of environmental harm not necessarily covered in legal statute, including the actions of governments. As a result, environmental harm, constructed from various eco-philosophical perspectives, extends the definition of eco-crime beyond legal codes to licensed or lawful acts of ecological degradation committed by states and corporations. For example, Westra (2004: xv) writes:

> Assaults on humans, whether perpetrated with bare hands or with instruments of violence, are crimes. If the deprivation of necessary ecological integrity, either by encroachment and manipulation of the wild, or inquination and pollution on inhabited areas is a present and constant threat to human health and function, ultimately to human life, then too is an assault, therefore a crime that must be viewed, treated and punished accordingly. The fact that in present day legal infrastructure it is not so treated represents an additional moral 'crime' in itself.

Westra's work extends the definition of eco-crime beyond the ecological degradation to human health, global security and justice. She suggests that eco-crimes such as 'regulatory offences' that are committed by governments and corporations in pursuit of economic advantage or progress are 'attacks on the human person'. Therefore, eco-crimes should be viewed as human rights violations as they deprive citizens of the freedoms and liberties expressed in various international covenants. Moreover, Westra argues that eco-crimes are not only a violation of one's right to a healthy environment but also a direct assault on the person. For example, the exploitation and appropriation of genetic resources and biodiversity from developing countries have for many years been referred to as 'bio-piracy' or 'eco-cide'. Not only is it deleterious to the environment, but Westra's analysis would also argue that it is an assault on the person as it deprives the individual from fully expressing his/her social, cultural and economic rights – as such, it is an act of violence.

Evaluation

Eco-crime is both a legal and social construct. The diversity of subject matter covered under both international and national environmental law, and within notions of environmental harm, has necessitated the integration of diverse expertise and knowledges including criminology. Within criminological studies, debates about eco-crime have emerged within discourses on state and corporate crime or 'crimes of the powerful' and within developing debates of 'green and environmental criminology' (Lynch and Stretetsky, 2003). In this sense 'environmental criminology' does not refer to examining the spatial distribution of offences and explaining the spatial distributions of offenders – this is a separate criminological enterprise with its origins in social ecology, in particular Burgess's zonal theory of city development. Lynch and Stretetsky's use of the term 'environmental criminology' relates to crimes and harms against the environment – a lexicon explored within 'green criminology'.

Green criminology, first coined by Lynch in 1990, is a useful paradigm for analysing both sociological and legal definitions of 'eco-crime'. It provides an umbrella under which to theorize and critique the emerging terminology related to environmental harm. Carabine et al. (2004: 28) identify that green criminology, in its 'early stage of development has four main tasks: (a) to document the existence of green crimes in all their forms and to evolve basic typologies and distinctions such as that between primary and secondary green crimes; (b) to chart the ways in which the laws have been developed around this area, and to assess the complications and political issues generated; (c) to connect green crimes to social inequalities; and (d) to assess the role of green social movements (and their counter-movements involved in a backlash) in bringing about social change.'

Green criminology inspects diverse narratives and disciplines and provides an interface with social movements and green politics. It seeks to explore issues of environmental harm by utilizing a range of analytical tools in the production of a knowledge that is theoretical, empirically grounded and politically active. For example, discourses in environmental justice invoke theoretical perspectives in 'eco-feminism', 'eco-Marxism' and 'red–green social movements' to examine eco-crime within notions of harm and oppression.

Reece Walters

Associated Concepts: corporate crime, crime, crimes against humanity, green criminology, human rights, social harm

Key Readings

Carabine, E., Iganski, P., Lee, M., Plummer, K. and South, N. (2004) *Criminology: A Sociological Introduction.* London: Routledge.

Lynch, M. (1990) 'The greening of criminology: a perspective for the 1990s', *The Critical Criminologist*, 2: 11–12.

Lynch, M. and Stretetsky, P. (2003) 'The meaning of green: contrasting criminological perspectives', *Theoretical Criminology*, 7 (2): 217–38.

Situ, Y. and Emmons, D. (2000) *Environmental Crime: The Criminal Justice System's Role in Protecting the Environment.* Thousand Oaks, CA: Sage.

Soyland, S. (2000) *Criminal Organisations and Crimes Against the Environment.* Turin: UNICRI.

Westra, L. (2004) *EcoViolence and the Law – Supranational Normative Foundations of Ecocrime.* Ardsley, NY: Transnational Publishers Inc.

EDGEWORK

See: Carnival (of crime); Cultural criminology; Postmodernism

ELECTRONIC MONITORING

Definition

The process by which offenders' movements or whereabouts may be checked for the purpose of enforcing a curfew or court order. Most systems in current use involve the fitting of a small electronic device, or 'tag', on the ankle or wrist of the offender and checking their compliance with the conditions of a curfew or house arrest by using a static monitoring unit at the offender's home. Developing systems include computer-aided voice recognition to allow checks from different locations, GSM locator systems using the mobile telephone infrastructure, and GPS (ground position by satellite) technology to provide continuous checks on their movement and location. These last two are as yet untested except in small-scale projects. All have the same aim – to offer some spatial control short of the total separation imposed by custody.

Distinctive Features

Electronic monitoring in criminal justice systems started in 1984 in the USA as a means of enforcing house arrest. Early pilot projects grew fairly rapidly – there were 30 of these within two years – and by 1988 over 3,000 offenders were being tagged. The early years were, however, dogged by technical problems, unrealistic expectations and poor outcomes. Although designed to reduce both prison populations and criminal justice costs, the generally low-risk offenders on whom they were made, coupled with the ability to detect breaches of the order at any time, led to significant net widening. A ten-year summary of experience by the National Institute of Justice in Washington concluded that, all too often, both costs and prison populations had risen.

Nevertheless, continued experimentation and development covered bail enforcement, 'front door' schemes (as a sentencing option for the courts, either on its own or in conjunction with another community penalty), and 'back door' schemes (as a condition of an early release from prison). Canada, Australia and Singapore (where it was extensively used as part of a home release programme for drug addicts) were all early users; England and Wales, Sweden and the Netherlands started different types of applications in 1995. Much of Western Europe now has, or is planning for, pilot projects to test its usefulness.

England and Wales are set to be two of the largest users. A 'back door' home detention curfew scheme for prisoners serving up to four-year sentences started in January 1999 and curfew orders as a sentence of the courts became available from December 1999. Jointly, they should produce about 35,000 orders per year. They followed a substantial pilot project over four years (Mortimer and May, 1997). In most jurisdictions, though, tagging remains a small-scale sentencing option – the USA had about 77,000 monitored offenders at any one time in 1998, compared with 1.7 million in prison and 3.6 million on probation or parole.

Evaluation

Providing electronic monitoring to low risk offenders has been found to increase recidivism rates and further increase costs. It is cost effective when used on moderate and high-risk offenders and coupled with appropriate interventions that target specific criminogenic factors. The evidence is that electronic monitoring is more effective when combined with other rehabilitative programmes (Evans, 1996). It is also most effective as a short-term option, 'buying time' for other community options, including treatment programmes, to take effect. Compliance rates have been found to fall steeply after three months (Whitfield, 1997).

The most successful outcomes have been demonstrated in Sweden, where a carefully targeted 'front door' scheme to replace prison sentences of up to three months has, over three years, reduced the prison population by 25 per cent and saved an estimated 150m krona. Targeting remains the key issue if electronic monitoring is to develop, long term, as a viable community-based sentencing option – although its future as a device for controlling prison numbers through 'back door' schemes is probably more certain. All too often, electronic monitoring has been used as a simple punishment or for offenders other than those for whom it was designed – people whose movements are linked to their offending. Critics see it as redolent of excessive state control and

part of the increasingly stringent apparatus of criminal sanctions, while supporters view it as a way of reducing prison populations and costs without increasing risks. The dangers, as well as the opportunities offered by new technologies, will continue to need careful assessment.

Dick Whitfield

Associated Concepts: community sentences, net widening, social control, surveillance

Key Readings

Evans, D. (1996) 'Electronic monitoring: APPA testimony to Ontario Standing Committee on Administration and Justice', *Perspectives*, Fall: 8–10.

Mortimer, E. and May, C. (1997) *Electronic Monitoring in Practice*, Research Study no. 177. London: Home Office.

Nellis, M. (2009) 'Surveillance and confinement: explaining and understanding the experience of electronically monitored curfews', *European Journal of Probation*, 1 (1): 41–65.

Whitfield, D. (1997) *Tackling the Tag: The Electronic Monitoring of Offenders*. Winchester: Waterside Press.

EMERGENCY LEGISLATION

Definition

Laws introduced following the suspension of, or departure from, legal normality when either a state of emergency is declared or is assumed to exist. These typically involve the pervasive violation of human rights.

Distinctive Features

States of emergency occur with remarkable frequency throughout the world and at any one time a large proportion of the world population will be subject to emergency legislation. Once introduced, it often has a permanency which belies its nomenclature. International law, in particular human rights law, however, lays down standards to govern the use of emergency legislation. Generally, for example, where such standards apply, the threat must be proximate and the use of the powers limited spatially, but these criteria are largely ignored.

Both totalitarian and democratic regimes resort to this form of law (see for example Amnesty International, 1999), notwithstanding that they may be signatories of international human rights treaties. In totalitarian or military regimes the introduction of emergency powers and the suspension of the legal safeguards for the protection of the citizen have frequently permitted security forces to resort to anonymous arrests, secret detentions, torture, disappearances and extra-judicial killings. In democratic regimes the violation of human rights is generally less but nevertheless involves a fundamental derogation from the rule of law, permitting arbitrary arrest, detention without trial, and widespread restrictions on the freedom of movement and expression. For example, the United Kingdom – a signatory to international human rights treaties – introduced emergency legislation in Northern Ireland in 1973, replacing other special powers (Farrell, 1986) which had been in existence since the state was established in 1921. It involved expanded powers of arrest, detention without trial, and jury-less courts (Ni Aolain, 1996). Emergency legislation, even in democratic regimes, is often accompanied by 'dirty tricks' and secret wars and the use of state-directed or 'independent' pro-state death squads (McLaughlin, 1996: 287). States that resort to emergency legislation will typically deny that any abuses have occurred and devise a number of techniques of denial (Cohen, 1993). In addition, the appearance of legitimacy and justification can be lent to the laws concerned, and the violations of rights they allow, by an explicit declaration of a state of emergency in accordance with specific human rights law instruments which the state concerned has ratified.

Evaluation

Emergency legislation is an important concept because of its prevalence throughout the world. It has, however, been little studied by criminologists. Political crimes committed under it have largely been ignored in traditional texts. In addition, there has been very little analysis of the form of criminal justice which is established by emergency legislation or the patterns of abuse which occur. As a result, generalizations about criminal justice systems have at best been partial or at worst a caricature of the reality.

Paddy Hillyard

Associated Concepts: human rights, political crime, the state, state crime

Key Readings

Amnesty International (1999) *Annual Report 1999.* London: Amnesty International Publications.

Cohen, S. (1993) 'Human rights and crimes of the state: the culture of denial', *Australian and New Zealand Journal of Criminology,* 28 (1): 87–115.

Farrell, M. (1986) *The Apparatus of Repression: Emergency Legislation.* Derry: Field Day Publications.

International Commission of Jurists (1983) *States of Emergency: Their Impact on Human Rights.* Geneva: International Commission of Jurists.

McLaughlin, E. (1996) 'Political violence, terrorism and crimes of the state', in J. Muncie and E. McLaughlin (eds), *The Problem of Crime.* London: Sage.

Ni Aolain, F. (1996) 'The fortification of an emergency regime', *Albany Law Review,* 59 (4): 1353–87.

EMOTIONS (OF CRIME)

Definition

The study of particular emotions associated with crime – such as shame, fear, anger, contempt, disgust or excitement – has long roots, particularly in psychology and the sociology of deviance. The focused interest in, and systematic research of, the emotional dimension of crime and punishment are, however, of a fairly recent date. The current sociological interest in, analysis of, and reflection upon emotions of crime do not only result from theoretical developments within criminology or within the sociology of deviance; they also point to broader social and cultural developments.

Distinctive Features

In his *Seductions of Crime*, Jack Katz (1988), inspired by the older work of George Herbert Mead, argued for the sociology of deviance and for criminology to complement their field of aetiological enquiry by paying attention to the immediate 'foreground factors' of criminal activities, i.e., the 'seductions and compulsions' that are inherent in those activities and in the interactions and micro-dynamics leading up to them. Those foreground attractors will often attract or compel offenders who find themselves in particular situations to more or less gradually build themselves up towards criminal offences or acts of transgression. Too much of criminological theory and research, according to Katz, had previously focused, one-sidedly, on 'background factors' such as offenders' material and social conditions or their psychological development and life-course events. This, in Katz's view, had prevented criminology from really understanding what it was that would lead offenders to offend. Unlike other theories that equally focused on the immediacy of the criminal event – such as opportunity theory, rational choice theory or routine activities theory – Katz's was about the emotional and sensual dimension of crime. For criminology to grasp the real 'magic in the criminal's sensuality' and motivation, it needed to understand how offenders, in and through the often stylized aesthetics of particular criminal acts, would try to mobilize and/or overcome certain 'moral emotions' such as 'humiliation, righteousness, arrogance, ridicule, cynicism, defilement and vengeance' (1988: 4–9). The most appropriate way to grasp the motivational 'magic' of the 'badass', the 'hardman',

the 'cold-blooded' killer or the white collar criminal, Katz argued, was to read minutely the emotionality, aesthetics and moral sensuality (the 'seductions and compulsions') that are at play in criminal acts or transgressions.

Katz's book opened up a new avenue for sociological research and reflection on the issue of the emotions of crime. It coincided with a growing interest in the import of particular emotions such as fear, anger, resentment, vindictiveness or hate in more visceral public reactions to crime that had been marked, since about the middle of the 1970s, by ever-rising levels of punitiveness, particularly in the USA and the UK. John Braithwaite's (1989) text (on *reintegrative shaming*) appeared at about the same time as Katz's book. He suggested how the non-stigmatizing use and manipulation – during 'restorative justice' conferences – of emotions, and particularly of shame in offenders, could support reconciliatory, reintegrative, or even community-building efforts. As a result Braithwaite's book provided further impetus, within the criminological community, for the study of emotions of crime, conflict (whether interpersonal, ethnic or social), reconciliation and 'peacemaking'. This would continue throughout the 1990s and on into this century (see for example de Haan and Loader, 2002). The role and place of emotions and 'emotional work' in criminal justice institutions, professions and cultures is now an emerging research topic.

A marked interest in emotions can also be witnessed beyond criminology. To a certain extent this interest redresses an imbalance that had hitherto existed in much academic writing. However, it also seems to reflect social and cultural developments in what one might call an *emotional age*. In our 'neo-tribal' age, claims the French theorist Michel Maffesoli (1996), rational calculation and the regularities of institutional life are gradually giving way to what he calls a 'Dionysian', or uncontrolled, spontaneous, sensuous sociality. Against a backdrop of crumbling institutional boundaries, of life-course predictability being replaced with the contingency of events and moments of *ad hoc* experience and choice, of a wild consumerism that fills the vacuum left by the waning of both tradition and structured modernity, emotions and sensuality are becoming much more predominant in social life. Where once the formalized and structured regularity and continuity of institutional life (in impersonal bureaucracies, for example) were able to store emotional and moral energy, or at least hold its flow in check, this energy is now gradually being released in an age when individuals increasingly find themselves in situations where they need to make choices, not in the least with regards to their sense of self and identity. In an age of hyper-consumerism, of unrelenting motion, and of never-ending 'seductions and compulsions', *e-motion* emerges at and accompanies every event through which individuals (including the 'badass', the 'hardman' and the 'cold-blooded' killer) construct their moral sense of self or consume themselves an identity. What is notable here is that many of those events, in an age of 'blurring boundaries', are about exploring, establishing or maintaining boundaries of self and identity. In light of this, it is probably no coincidence that, according to Katz, the stylized aesthetics, emotional attractions and passionate compulsions experienced and expressed in particular acts and transgressions can allow offenders to negotiate or '[play with] the line between the sense of themselves as subject and object, between being in and out of control, between directing and being directed by the dynamics of the situation' (1988: 8). This negotiation and play, in turn, will tend to reinforce the emotional charge of the criminal experience.

This quotation brings us to the ever-growing body of predominantly US-based literature on 'edgework' that has emerged in the wake of Katz's book. 'Edgework' refers to emotionally-charged and adrenaline-fuelled acts and transgressions (motorcycle racing, base jumping, and other risky or even criminal transgressions), where individuals will deliberately attempt to reach and negotiate the physical 'edge' of daring and endurance, hoping to be able to thus arrive beyond social strictures and 'reflective consciousness' and to attain, through the mastery of their senses and emotions, a certain degree of 'self-actualization' (Lyng, 2004: 362). In an age when many seem to be obsessed with 'risk'

and its 'control', this should perhaps come as no surprise. The focus in much of this strand of enquiry is once again on the emotional, sensuous and aesthetic dimensions of particular acts and events. The emphasis on the importance of the body and the senses in social interaction, and as a location of discipline, domination and subversion, is particularly notable here.

Evaluation

Katz's call to complement sociological theorizing and research on crime with a focus on the emotional, sensual and aesthetical dimension of criminal acts and events was both timely and very welcome. It has inspired a growing body of literature on the role and place of emotions in crime and on the importance of emotional life for an adequate understanding of individual and collective reactions to crime. However, situated largely within a methodological context of phenomenological 'thick description', much of this literature tends to remain on a descriptive level. Recently however a number of strands of criminological enquiry have emerged that could provide the theoretical space as well as the empirical tools to connect, on the one hand, ethnographic descriptions of the emotional 'foreground' dynamics of criminal acts and events with, on the other, 'background' factors such as social and cultural conditions and individual biographies. One of those strands is to be found in Tony Jefferson's psychoanalytically inspired (2002) outline for a psychosocial criminology where the emotional life of crime is linked with biographical narrative. Another of those strands can be distinguished in what goes under the name of 'cultural criminology'. Cultural criminologists tend to read the emotions of crime, transgression and 'edgework' as part and parcel of practices that are deeply enmeshed in culturally shared constructions of meaning and schemes of interpretation.

Ronnie Lippens

Associated Concepts: carnival (of crime), cultural criminology, new deviancy theory, psychoanalytic criminology

Key Readings

Braithwaite, J. (1989) *Crime, Shame and Reintegration*. Cambridge: Cambridge University Press.

de Haan, W. and Loader, I. (eds) (2002) Special Issue of *Theoretical Criminology*, issue 6(3), *On the Emotions of Crime, Punishment and Social Control*. London: Sage.

Jefferson, T. (2002) 'For a psychosocial criminology', in K. Carrington and R. Hogg (eds), *Critical Criminology: Issues, Debates, Challenges*. Collumpton: Willan.

Katz, J. (1988) *Seductions of Crime*. New York: Basic Books.

Lyng, S. (2004) 'Crime, edgework and corporeal transaction', *Theoretical Criminology*, 8 (3): 359–75.

Maffesoli, M. (1996) *The Time of the Tribes*. London: Sage.

ENVIRONMENTAL CRIMINOLOGIES

See: *Chicago School of Sociology; Eco-crime; Geographies of crime; Green criminology, Situational crime prevention; Social ecology*

ESSENTIALISM

Definition

This concept has been used in various ways in the philosophy of the social sciences. Essentialists believe that it is possible to establish the truth of a scientific theory and arrive at total explanations by identifying the essence or the reality that lies behind the appearance of a phenomenon. The concept also refers to the assumption that human beings possess indispensable qualities or characteristics which classify their true nature. An essence is a reality fixed in an originating moment and applies to both the inherent, innate properties of an individual human being and the abstract universal governing the type to which all examples conform.

Distinctive Features

In criminology there has been a remarkable tendency to essentialize crime and the relationship between class and crime; gender and crime; race and crime; and social structure and crime. Essentialism also has a critical place in common-sense conversations about crime and criminality and provides the basis for the construction of stereotypes and the marking out of differences such as criminal and non-criminal; normal and abnormal; and deviant and non-deviant.

Essentialist ways of thinking are challenged by post-structuralists and postmodernists who stress that 'truth' and 'reality' are contingent, contestable, historical, relational, provisional and plural in nature, and demand that we interrogate the power relations inherent in the act of naming. In criminology, it was interactionist or labelling approaches that first challenged essentializing theories.

Eugene McLaughlin

Associated Concepts: biological criminology, interactionism, Marxist criminologies, personality theory, positivism, postmodernism, post-structuralism, stereotyping

ETHNIC CLEANSING

See: Crimes against humanity; Genocide; State crime

ETHNOGRAPHY

Definition

The study of small groups of people and of micro social situations and contexts. The emphasis is usually on explanations based on understanding the ways in which individuals interpret and socially construct their world.

Distinctive Features

Ethnography has its roots in the social anthropology of the late nineteenth century and early twentieth century and literally means the description (*graphy*) of cultures (*ethno*). Social anthropologists studied the institutions, beliefs and customs of pre-industrial societies, mainly in Africa, the Pacific and the Americas. The main forms of fieldwork were observations of cultural groups in their natural habitat and 'talking' to members of these groups. The commitments and methods of social anthropologists were adapted by sociologists to the study of subcultural groups within the fast advancing industrial, urban society of the twentieth century. For example, the Chicago School of urban sociology advocated the detailed examination of small groups and subcultures within a complex urban context by seeking to examine actions and events as if they were 'anthropologically strange'. They produced detailed qualitative accounts of the underside of Chicago, for example a delinquent boy's own story: *The Jack Roller* (Shaw, 1930). Such accounts stood alongside quantitative analyses of the city, usually in the form of 'mappings' of its social ecology, for example by using indices such as delinquency rates. Ethnographic accounts provided description of the subcultures within particular ecological areas or 'zones'.

Ethnography continues to play an important role in criminological research, especially when linked to theoretical perspectives such as new deviancy, interactionism, labelling and appreciative criminology. As a research style it is especially suited to such perspectives because of their emphasis on interactions, social meanings and constructions, labelling and stereotyping, as well as to explanations based on these.

A number of methodological commitments are associated with ethnographic research. First, there is a focus on studying the social world from the perspectives of the individuals being studied. It is emphasized that social scientific explanations should be based or 'grounded' (Glaser and Strauss, 1967) in the everyday perspectives of everyday people rather than in the pre-constituted and abstract theories of social scientists. Second, it is assumed that various individuals and categories of individuals can hold different perspectives. A social context comprises several perspectives, each of which will be equally valid for the people who hold these. There is, then, no single objective reality: rather there is a multiplicity of realities and the role of the ethnographer is to capture and describe these. Third, social perspectives (and the social meanings, definitions, labels and stereotypes which comprise them) cannot be separated from social interactions. Indeed they are the very substance of interactions. For this reason ethnographers pay particular attention to observing the ways in which people interact in social contexts. Fourth, there is a belief that such observation should be naturalistic, that is, that everyday people should be studied interacting in what for them are everyday situations, and as they would normally and naturally do so. Therefore, ethnographic research is often covert rather than overt, so as not to disturb the social context which is being examined.

The ethnographic tradition has refused to link itself to any particular form of data collection. It rejects fixed protocols as to how data should be collected and analysed. However, the main sources of data include unstructured interviews (for example, life histories and narrative interviews), documents and forms of observation. Participant observation is often cited as being central to ethnographic research, although other forms of unstructured observation are used. Participant observation also involves the collection of findings by participating in the social world of those being studied: taking on some role in the social group, or on its margins, and observing, reflecting upon and interpreting the actions of individuals in that group.

The close involvement of the researcher in what they are studying can mean that they will have a major impact on the findings and the conclusions derived from them. Therefore, in order to assess their validity it is important for that researcher to reflect upon and report their role in all stages of the research. This is known as reflexivity.

Evaluation

There are key issues regarding the validity of criminological research based on ethnography. One concerns whether a researcher can provide an accurate account of a social context as opposed to a personal interpretation. Related to this is the issue of reliability, that is, whether different researchers would produce the same account and reach the same conclusions. Further, there is the danger that the emphasis on small-scale contexts inhibits the extent to which conclusions can be generalized from such contexts. Much depends on their representativeness and typicality.

These issues apart, ethnography has made an important contribution to criminology in terms of providing an appreciative and humanistic dimension, opening up explanations based on empathy and subjective understanding, and in making visible the 'underside' of the social world in a way that would not be made possible by the more formal methods of social surveys and experimentation.

Victor Jupp

Associated Concepts: appreciative criminology, Chicago School of Sociology, convict criminology, cultural criminology, interactionism, labelling, new deviancy theory, participant observation, reflexivity

Key Readings

Ferrell, J. and Hamm, M. (eds) (1998) *Ethnography at the Edge: Crime, Deviance and Field Research.* Boston: Northeastern University Press.

Glaser, B. and Strauss, A.L. (1967) *The Discovery of Grounded Theory.* Chicago, IL: Aldine.

Hammersley, M. (1992) *What's Wrong With Ethnography?* London: Routledge.

Hammersley, M. and Atkinson, P. (1995) *Ethnography: Principles in Practice,* 2nd edn. London: Routledge.

Hobbs, D. and May, T. (eds) (1983) *Interpreting the Field: Accounts of Ethnography.* Oxford: Oxford University Press.

Shaw, C.R. (1930) *The Jack Roller.* Chicago: University of Chicago Press.

EUGENICS

See: Genetics

EVALUATION RESEARCH

Definition

The form of policy research devoted to assessing the consequences (intended and unintended) of either a set of existing policies or a new policy programme. It has a particular focus on the measurement of the extent to which stated goals and objectives of policies and programmes are being, or have been, met.

Distinctive Features

This is a broad body of research findings which is focused on testing and measuring 'what works' in terms of the outputs and outcomes of initiatives and programmes of intervention and policy innovation in criminal justice and crime control. Most evaluative research is sponsored by the bodies who themselves are responsible for the particular programme or innovation. It is often 'in house' in character and is generally based on short-term funding. By the end of the twentieth century the evaluation industry had grown substantially. The question of the effectiveness of the myriad of measures employed to reduce crime and criminality came to occupy the centre of policy debates in many Western criminal justice jurisdictions.

And yet the problem remains as to how the meaning of effectiveness can be adequately pinned down. The development of a renewed interest in 'what works' is, for some, heartening following the years of pessimism in criminology engendered by Martinson's influential (1974) evaluation that 'nothing works' in rehabilitation programmes for offenders.

Evaluation

Much evaluation research has been criticized by criminologists for being compromised by its dependency on the sponsorship of the very agencies whose work it is asked to evaluate. However, it should not be inferred from such criticisms that independent, academic evaluation research is flawed *per se* and insignificant to both criminology and the policy process. In Tilley's (2000) view, 'What evaluations can offer is a way of winnowing over a period of time what works in producing varying outcomes, at least for a while, for whom and in what circumstances.' At its worst, much evaluation research is short-term in character, poorly funded, often undertaken by inadequately trained employees of one of the agencies implicated in the programme concerned, and characterized by severe technical difficulties. The lack of adequate and proper evaluations in criminal justice and crime reduction is widely recognized and remarked on by academic commentators. As Nick Tilley (2000) notes, there are many areas of uncertainty in this body of work. In particular, the 'industry' around evaluation is described by Tilley as an 'evaluation jungle' in which there are dangers, pitfalls and difficulties, and the risk of becoming lost in thickets. The rhetorical power of evaluation is substantial, and hard(-looking) evidence can be effective in eliciting resources. Most commissioners of evaluation research want the 'facts', but facts do not speak for themselves in research and they are often contested. As noted earlier, much evaluative research is tied to the 'apron strings' of the sponsor, is often 'in house' in character, and normally based on short-term funding. All these factors mitigate against its success as academically credible research.

It is important to distinguish 'in-house' audits from detached and 'scientific' research-based evaluations. Other difficulties are associated with independent evaluations of programmes. Most of those involved in the programme (bar the independent evaluator) are characterized by a strong success imperative and will be looking for good news. And independent and objective evaluation is attractive not least for the external credibility it brings. Negative or sober findings and uncertain and nuanced narratives of achievement from academic evaluations – which

have been the norm – are likely to result in tears from those who are committed to the programme in question. To add to the potentially tangled terrain of evaluation research, it is vital to recognize that academic evaluators also have their own agendas which may not serve the policy and practice purposes of evaluation (such as pursuing their own academic research interests rather than those of the commissioning agency).

The attractions of evaluation research to both the public and policy makers lie in its concern with discovering just what works and what doesn't in specific contexts and processes. Indeed, the case for systematic evaluations of crime control and reduction initiatives may be said to be taken as given. It is difficult to argue with efforts to reduce crime in the most efficient, effective and economical fashion. Indeed, all those who are engaged professionally in criminal justice and crime prevention would doubtless wish to know whether their work is having a real impact. None of those involved in the work of crime reduction and criminal justice would wish to spend their time, money, effort, and indeed their whole careers achieving little or nothing. Furthermore, given the broader backdrop of a managerialized 'audit culture' that is increasingly at work in criminal justice systems, with its emphasis on the monitoring of measurable outputs, it is unlikely that the pressure on public agencies to measure effectiveness through evaluation audits will diminish.

It is worthwhile to note that both crime and crime control are not 'closed systems'; instead there are both exogenous and endogenous sources of change in these 'open systems' which undermine the predictability of future effectiveness on the basis of past effectiveness (Tilley, 2000). Modesty in what evaluation research may offer policy makers and practitioners in criminal justice would appear necessary. It is widely recognized by criminologists that, however objective, academic evaluations cannot provide the sole basis for deciding on policy and practice. Policy and practice are necessarily the site for contested value positions about which the evaluator has no authoritative opinion.

Gordon Hughes

Associated Concepts: action research, actuarialism, administrative criminology, experimental criminology, experiments, managerialism, 'what works'

Key Readings

Martinson, R. (1974) 'What works? Questions and answers about prison reform', *Public Interest,* 35: 22–54.

Pawson, R. and Tilley, N. (1997) *Realistic Evaluation.* London: Sage.

Sherman, L., Gottfredson, D., MacKenzie, D., Eck, J., Reuter, P. and Bushway, S. (1997) 'Preventing Crime: What Works, What Doesn't, What's Promising'. A Report to the US Congress, available at http://www.ncjrs.org/works/index.htm

Tilley, N. (2000) 'The evaluation jungle', in K. Pease, S. Ballintyne and V. McLaren (eds), *Key Issues in Crime Prevention, Crime Reduction and Community Safety.* London: IPPR.

EXPERIMENTAL CRIMINOLOGY

Definition

Experimental Criminology '... offers experimental and quasi-experimental research in the development of evidence based crime and justice policy; spans an array of scientific disciplines ... and promotes advancement of the science of systematic reviews and experimental methods in criminology and criminal justice' (*Journal of Experimental Criminology*). A primary locale for the practice of experimental criminology is the Campbell Collaboration on Crime and Justice, which produces systematic reviews of evidence. There is also an Academy of Experimental Criminology and an Experimental Criminology Division of the American Society of Criminology; while the Jerry Lee Foundation sponsors research centres in experimental criminology at the

University of Pennsylvania, the Institute of Criminology (University of Cambridge), and the Australian National University. There is a considerable overlap of key personnel across these institutions, suggesting a network of researchers engaged in common purpose.

Distinctive Features

The institutions of experimental criminology are of relatively recent origin but nevertheless suggest a concerted scientific enterprise, whether in terms of epistemological foundations, ontology and practical purposes, appropriate methodologies, or disciplinary institutions. On all these counts, the appurtenances of experimental criminology resemble those of other distinctive movements in science, past and present.

The purpose of experimental criminology is avowedly pragmatic – to discover 'what works' in the control, treatment or prevention of crime. Its origins can be traced back to widely perceived crises in the effectiveness of state criminal justice institutions emerging during the 1970s. In reaction, James Q. Wilson argued that criminology should abandon its preoccupation with being a science of the causes of crime, since measures based on its findings were neither feasible nor desirable for the government or public at large. Instead, criminology should become a policy science whose purpose should be to evaluate the tools that governments typically have at their disposal, in order to bring about greater efficiency and effectiveness in the delivery of criminal justice, primarily through the key institutions of the police, the courts and prisons (Hope, 2010).

The apparent success of the Cochrane Collaboration in the field of medicine and health care encouraged the founding protagonists of experimental criminology in their belief that a change in policy and practice could be brought about by assembling evidence of sufficient scientific rigour on a convincing scale of generality – an approach to policy making generally termed 'evidence-based' (Sherman, 2009). With experimental criminology, scientific rigour is to be achieved by research methods that seek to maximize their 'internal validity' (that is, where we can be sure that research results are a genuine product of the method that produces them); internal validity will then underwrite the assessment and selection of effective crime control measures. Experimental criminology rests on the assumption that the most superior method for ensuring internal validity is the *Randomized Controlled Trial* (RCT), which is seen as the 'gold standard' of research design.

The efficiency of state criminal justice institutions is to be maximized by targeting high-risk offenders, crime targets or places (i.e., those that seem to contribute 'disproportionately' to the incidence of crime), using research methods that would enable accurate predictions of their crime risk in advance of crime occurrence – the prospective, longitudinal research design being regarded as the most internally valid method upon which to base such predictions (Sherman, 2007).

In order to ensure the generalization from particular 'trials' of policy measures (that is, to maximize their 'external validity'), experimental criminology has also borrowed the method of *systematic review* from the Cochrane Collaboration. For example, the findings of completed studies are collated for review, and then rated according to the *Maryland Scientific Methods Scale* (MSMS), a qualitative heuristic that gives higher ratings the more a study's method resembles the paradigmatic RCT design. Studies are then grouped according to the kind of intervention, practice or policy measure they are evaluating, with conclusions on the efficacy of particular policies and practices then being based on an average of the scores that individual studies in a particular group attain on the MSMS. Less frequently, systematic reviews also use quantitative methods, such as aggregating the findings from individual studies on a particular type of policy intervention in order to estimate the average likely size of the effect of an intervention.

Evaluation

Notwithstanding experimental criminology's practical intent, it cannot evade scrutiny of the bases upon which it makes causal statements, especially since it asserts a scientific basis for its claim-making. Just as criminology itself is liable for the way it makes statements about the 'causes of crime', so experimental criminology is liable for the way it makes causal statements about the likely effects of crime control policies and practices. Whereas criminology proper has contributed to an understanding of criminal justice as a system that institutionalizes processes of selection, labelling and deviancy amplification (called *criminalization*), so the bias of experimental criminology towards evaluating criminal justice institutions leads to a bias towards promoting criminalization, even though it purports to do otherwise. As a science, when evaluated in terms of the counterfactual process of criminalization, experimental criminology reifies the teleological selection bias of the criminal justice system (Hope, 2010).

When confronted with the question of how to prevent crime, the bias towards criminal justice institutions will lead experimental criminology towards selecting from amongst the range of current institutional responses, rather than considering radically new approaches or alternatives to criminal justice. For example, it has converted the idea of *restorative justice* from an extra-judicial approach to dispute resolution into a sentencing disposal (Sherman, 2009). While it may be able to draw on comparative evidence (from its systematic reviews) about the relative efficacy of, say, policing versus imprisonment, it cannot say anything about alternative ways of preventing crime that are based upon premises that differ from deterrence, the common denominator of these institutions and the basis on which their effects have been made commensurate and comparable (Durlauf and Nagin, 2011). Consequently, experimental criminology ends up endorsing the processes of criminalization, since these are the practical solutions adopted by criminal justice institutions in light of the impracticality of delivering the quality and quantity of punishment required by the doctrine of deterrence (cf. Berk et al., 2009).

The teleological bias of experimental criminology towards criminal justice is further reinforced by its methodology. In order to implement randomization, the 'gold standard' of the RCT requires the strict control of subjects. Such levels of control are most likely to occur in institutional settings that can secure the constrained, coercive participation of subjects, such as courts and corrections, and least likely to occur in interventions predicated on the collective, voluntary participation of citizens. It follows that the systematic reviews of experimental criminology favour criminal justice interventions and negate efforts to reduce crime in civil society settings (Sherman et al., 2002), largely because RCTs are much more feasible in criminal justice than in community settings. Further, since the RCT design is methodologically cumbersome in its handling of social and collective processes, it will often be unable to capture complex social development in community settings, such as the growth of collective efficacy in informal social control, or will rule them out as 'confounds', even when these are crucial to the integrity of the intervention.

Because the RCT research design seeks to model average (mean) effects, neither can it handle easily the heterogeneity inherent in the social world, which produces a differential effect of state criminal justice on its subjects. A range of ostensibly similarly designed RCT experiments focusing on the arrest of the perpetrators of domestic violence came up with a variety of effects amongst their subjects. Subsequent analysis apparently discovered a heterogeneity in subjects' responses according to background and personal circumstances, which was subsequently explained by a supposed latent disposition to 'defiance' distributed differentially amongst the population of domestic violence perpetrators (Sherman, 1992). Nevertheless, this reinterpretation is *post hoc* inductive and thus risks committing the fallacy of 'affirming the consequent'.

Similarly, experimental criminology defines so-called crime occurrence 'hotspots' as objects of intervention on the basis of records of police response (Sherman, 2009). Hotspots are thus selected after police officers have been called to these repeatedly, albeit without them realizing the true extent of their corporate engagement with these places. Thus the process of selecting hotspots confounds the reasons why crime might concentrate in these with the reasons why police officers will concentrate their efforts on particular locations. So long as the police exercise discretion in how incidents are dealt with (and so long as the public exercise discretion in what they report to the police), the counterfactual of criminalization implies that the two 'causes' of hotspots cannot be assumed to be the same. Likewise, crime hotspots that do not come overtly to police attention may be overlooked, or may alter their 'temperature' spontaneously without police attention.

Finally, notwithstanding the risk to policy making of erroneous evidence, experimental criminology is nevertheless alluring, particularly to policy makers 'trapped' into delivering their electoral mandates. The apparent certainty deriving from its scientific aura, combined with the lengthy time-horizon over which results are to be expected, will allow policy makers to extract political capital from being seen to be 'doing good' in the here-and-now, without entailing much of a hostage to fortune aspect.

Tim Hope

Associated Concepts: crime science, evaluation research, longitudinal study, 'what works'

Key Readings

Berk, R., Sherman, L., Barnes, G., Kurtz, E. and Ahlman, L. (2009) 'Forecasting murder within a population of probationers and parolees: a high stakes application of statistical learning', *Journal of the Royal Statistical Society, Series A*, 172 (1): 1–21.

Durlauf, S.N. and Nagin, D.S. (2011) 'Imprisonment and crime: can both be reduced?', *Criminology and Public Policy*, 10 (1): 13–54.

Hope, T. (2010) 'Official criminology and the new crime sciences', in M. Bosworth and

C. Hoyle (eds), *What is Criminology?* Oxford: Oxford University Press.

Journal of Experimental Criminology Available at http://www.springer.com/social + sciences/criminology/journal/11292

Sherman, L.W. (1992) *Policing Domestic Violence: Experiments and Dilemmas.* New York: The Free Press.

Sherman, L.W. (2007) 'The power few: experimental criminology and the reduction of harm: The 2006 Joan McCord Prize Lecture', *Journal of Experimental Criminology*, 3: 299–321.

Sherman, L.W. (2009) 'Evidence and liberty: the promise of experimental criminology', *Criminology and Criminal Justice*, 9 (1): 5–28.

Sherman, L.W., Farrington, D.P., MacKenzie, D.L. and Welsh, B.C. (eds) (2002) *Evidence-Based Crime Prevention.* London: Routledge.

EXPERIMENTS

Definition

An experiment is a research study in which the researcher makes a measured intervention or treatment – a manipulation of the independent variable(s) – and observes its effect on a dependent variable, with (ideally) every other possible source of variation in the dependent variable controlled by the design of the study. Where literally *every* other possible source of variation has been controlled, any observed change in the dependent variable *must* be due to the manipulation of the independent variable.

Distinctive Features

Figure 6 illustrates a typical two-group experiment. The upper line represents a group who receive the treatment or intervention, and we shall assume that their experience between time 1 and time 2 is carefully controlled. Their states at time 1 and time 2 are carefully measured, and any change is recorded. A change at time 2 might not be due to the manipulation, however; it might have happened in any case simply from maturation (growing older). We therefore have a second group who are as similar as possible to the first at time 1 and whose experience between time 1 and time 2 is as near as possible the same, except that they do not receive the treatment. If group 1 differs from group 2 at time 2, having been similar at time 1, then the difference must logically be due to the treatment, which is the only difference in the two groups' experiences.

One further check that is generally made is on the operation of chance itself. Because effects are normally probabilistic rather than absolute, a *small* difference between the two groups may not signify more than the operation of chance. That is, if the manipulation had no effect whatsoever, we would still expect group scores not to come out exactly identical but to vary a little. The question is, how large is 'small' or 'very slightly'? In other words, how big does a difference have to be before we pay attention to it? As a decision rule we use statistical techniques based on the mathematics of probability which can specify, given certain assumptions, how likely a given size of difference is to be obtained by chance alone. Arbitrarily we tend to reject the 'null hypothesis' of only chance variation when the odds on obtaining our result by chance alone are as long as one in twenty ($p < 0.05$) or one in a hundred ($p < 0.01$). If the observed result is sufficiently unlikely on one of these criteria it is described as *statistically significant* and accepted as probably reflecting a real underlying difference. (Statistical mathematics is complex but the application of statistical tests is relatively easy, given computer packages to do the calculations for us.) One use of experimental designs is in the evaluation of treatments, policies and institutional changes. To evaluate the effectiveness of a new way of running a prison, for example, one might institute the new regime in one setting and refrain from instituting it in another. If the two settings are very similar, and the inmate groups are also very similar to each other, then differences

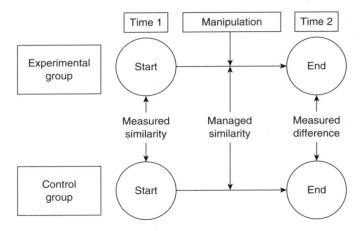

Figure 6 *The design of the ideal experiment*

in inmate behaviour between the two might be taken as probably a result of the innovation (but with considerable reservations, discussed below). Experimental research is seldom used for the study of crime and the causes of crime, because it is generally impossible and always unethical to institute a manipulation of some people's lives and refrain from doing so with others, at random, in order to make observable changes in their behaviour or attitudes. The gross factors known to be linked to crime and disorder – gender, class, material deprivation and unemployment, membership of particular groups or subcultures, perhaps personality variables – are not susceptible to manipulation by the experimenter.

Evaluation

The logic of experimentation is impeccable, but its preconditions can seldom be met. For the experiment to prove causation conclusively, every extraneous factor must be controlled and every variable precisely measured. It is very difficult to control every extraneous factor outside the laboratory (or at all, with human subjects). Real-life experimental evaluations tend to founder on the difficulty of measuring the intervention (the treatment): when something is 'shown to work' it is

generally very difficult indeed to specify precisely what that 'something' is.

Roger Sapsford

Associated Concepts: causation, evaluation research, experimental criminology

Key Readings

Fowles, A.J. (1978) *Prison Welfare: An Account of an Experiment at Liverpool.* Home Office Research Study No. 35. London: HMSO.
Haney, C., Banks, C. and Zimbardo, P.G. (1973) 'Interpersonal dynamics in a simulated prison', *International Journal of Criminology and Penology,* 1: 69–97.
Jupp, V. (1989) *Methods of Criminological Research.* London: Unwin Hyman.

EXTRATERRITORIAL LAW ENFORCEMENT

Definition

Law enforcement activity which extends outward with the boundaries of the state in which the law enforcement agency so engaged is officially headquartered.

Distinctive Features

There are a number of legal principles that give meaning to the idea of 'extraterritorial law enforcement'. The most important of these is the 'territorial principle', which is a concept that reflects an important aspect of sovereignty. Under this principle the state has the authority to act as the sovereign power within its territory. According to Shaw (1997: 458), this 'is the indispensable foundation for the application of the series of legal rights a state possesses'. In the criminological domain it is well accepted that a state should be able to prosecute offences committed, or allegedly committed, on its soil, since territoriality is a logical manifestation of the international state-system which vests power in the authorities representing the individual state's sovereign power. The logical corollary of this is that other states do not have the right to exercise law enforcement powers within the territory of another sovereign state. To do so is to undertake 'extraterritorial law enforcement'. Unless states affected by extraterritorial law enforcement consent to such, it may be considered a violation of state sovereignty.

It is the state's authorities who are responsible for the conduct of law and the maintenance of good order within its territory. Thus all crimes committed (or alleged to have been committed) within the territorial jurisdiction of a state may come before the municipal courts and the accused, if convicted, may be sentenced. This is so even if the accused is a foreign national (with the possible exception of persons who have diplomatic immunity who are normally protected from such actions).

The territorial concept has been modified in certain ways in order that certain anomalies can be answered. Thus territoriality has been extended so as to include crimes where only part of the offence has occurred on a given state's territory. A classic illustrative example would be where a person fires a weapon across an international frontier resulting in someone's death. In such situations both the state where the gun was fired and the state where the death takes place may exercise jurisdiction, but the actual exercise of such powers often depends on where the offender is apprehended. A similar logic might also be applied in cases involving criminal conspiracy where criminal activities are alleged to have occurred in each of two or more countries. This instance is, however, complicated by the fact that 'criminal conspiracy' is not recognized in every jurisdiction.

Advances in communications and travel have transformed the context in which these principles are applied. For example, in Europe the Protocol concerning Frontier Controls and Policing, Co-operation in Criminal Justice and Mutual Assistance relating to the Channel Fixed Link (1991) was established to facilitate joint French–British policing of the Channel Tunnel. Under this Protocol, police, customs and immigration officers may carry out their duties in specified 'control zones' in one another's territory, and on board through trains and at international railway stations. In effect, the Protocol creates a 'reciprocal constitution of sovereign territory in the domain of the other' (Sheptycki, 1998: 62). Under these arrangements each state can claim jurisdiction and apply its own law when it cannot be ascertained with certainty where precisely an offence has been committed. However, it is also the case that the state that first receives the person suspected of having committed such an offence has priority in exercising jurisdiction. Thus, although jurisdiction is primarily territorial, it is not exclusively so. States may enter into arrangements whereby jurisdiction is exercised outside the national territory and whereby jurisdiction by other states is exercised within the territory.

The 'nationality principle' also may affect states' view of criminal jurisdiction. For example, Germany claims jurisdiction over crimes committed by German nationals, notwithstanding that the offence may have been committed abroad. The nationality principle may be useful when proceeding in instances where it is alleged that persons have undertaken foreign travel for the purposes of engaging in criminal activity, for example illicit sexual activity with under-age persons. In the German case, charges may be brought in the 'tourist's' home country and this is, in fact, the only way to proceed since Germany will not extradite its own nationals. According to Shaw (1997), English courts will usually limit such actions to serious cases; treason, murder and bigamy have provided the case law.

The 'passive personality principle' asserts that states may exercise jurisdiction in order to try individuals for alleged offences committed abroad which affect the nationals of the state so claiming. The International Convention Against the Taking of Hostages (1979) allows states to claim jurisdiction in hostage incidents on the basis of the passive personality principle, namely 'if the state considers it appropriate'. Further, the Comprehensive Crime Control Act (1982) extends the jurisdiction of the USA to include '[a]ny place outside the jurisdiction of any nation with respect to an offence by or against a national of the United States' (Shaw, 1997: 468). It seems likely that, as the global fight against terrorism and transnational organized crime develops, so will applications of the passive personality principle.

The 'protective principle' or the 'state security principle' allows states to exercise jurisdiction over 'aliens' (i.e., non-nationals) who have committed, or have allegedly committed, an act abroad that is prejudicial to the security of the state concerned. This principle is justified on the basis that it allows for the protection of the 'vital interests' of the state concerned. However, this is a complicated matter since the alleged perpetrator may not be committing an offence under the law of the country of residence, and an extradition request could be refused on the grounds that the alleged offence is 'political'. The classic case in UK law is *Joyce* v *Director of Public Prosecutions*, which pertained to the infamous pro-Nazi Second World War propagandist Lord Haw-Haw, who was convicted of treason.

In the wake of the *Achille Lauro* incident, the Omnibus Diplomatic Security and Anti-Terrorism Act (1986) provided for jurisdiction over homicide and physical violence outside the USA where an American national was the victim. This legislation combines aspects of both the passive personality principle and the state security principle. Article 6 provides that jurisdiction may be claimed over an offence when a US national has been seized, threatened, injured or killed; or if the offence has been committed in an attempt to compel the US government to do or abstain from doing any act.

On the 'high seas', criminal law enforcement is exclusive to the flag-state of the vessel concerned. The flag-state may give permission to another state's vessels to exercise criminal law jurisdiction, or the captain of a vessel may invite officers aboard, but in the absence of such permission, no vessel may be boarded on the high seas by another country's personnel. Notable exceptions here are cases of piracy and when a vessel has engaged in a 'hot pursuit' from a place within territorial waters.

Evaluation

Extraterritorial law enforcement is frequently contested, even when one of the above principles can be invoked. There are instances where apprehension of a suspect and the exercise of criminal law jurisdiction might be considered illegal, especially when extradition treaties provide for the legal transfer of alleged criminals. The case *US* v *Alvarez-Machain* is one example. The Supreme Court decision in this case suggested that, notwithstanding the existence of an extradition treaty between the USA and Mexico, the unlawful apprehension of a suspect by state agents acting in the territory of another state would not, under American law, be considered a bar to the exercise of jurisdiction. In the UK, the case of *R.* v *Horseferry Road Magistrates Court ex parte Bennet*, the House of Lords declared that, where an extradition treaty exists with the relevant country, 'our courts will refuse to try him if he has forcibly been brought within our jurisdiction in disregard of those procedures by a process to which our own police, prosecuting or other executive authority have been a knowing party' (Shaw, 1997: 480).

James Sheptycki

Associated Concepts: globalization, the state, transnational organized crime, transnational policing

Key Readings

Shaw, M.N. (1997) *International Law,* 4th edn. Cambridge: Cambridge University Press.
Sheptycki, J.W.E. (1998) 'The global cops cometh', *British Journal of Sociology,* 49 (1): 57–74.

EXTROVERSION/ INTROVERSION

Definition

Extroversion may be taken as meaning 'outward turning', as in turning one's thoughts to the world, and introversion as 'inward turning', as in self-contemplation.

Distinctive Features

Carl Jung (1875–1961) used the terms to refer to an outward (extroverted) or inward (introverted) turning of psychic energy. He suggested that this distinction was, indeed, one of the most fundamental aspects of human personality. Sigmund Freud (1856–1939) also drew on the notion of extroversion and introversion in his theories of psychopathology. He saw an outward approach to life as beneficial and contra-indicative of psychopathology, while introversion was seen to be a sign of not-at-all healthy psychic functioning.

Personality theory, most prominent in mainstream psychology from the 1940s through to the 1970s, also used the notion of extroversion/introversion. However, the terms extroversion and introversion were often used to refer to social behaviour, rather than psychic functioning. In particular, the psychometric approach to the measurement of personality identified outgoing, sociable behaviour and inward-looking, withdrawn behaviour as opposite poles of a basic personality type. This personality type was described in detail in the work of Hans Eysenck (1916–97), with Extroversion (E), alongside Neuroticism (N) and Psychoticism (P), as the three basic dimensions of personality (Eysenck, 1959).

Eysenck's work is important because he attempted to connect his basic personality types to other areas of research and theory so as to produce a more complete account of human functioning. In particular, he made connections between physiological functioning (primarily the central and autonomic nervous systems), conditionability in Pavlovian terms, and social development. Simply, he argued that a personality type which combined High E and High N would condition least well; while a LowE–LowN combination would condition most effectively. Eysenck developed this theme to give an account of criminal behaviour based on his theory of personality (Eysenck, 1964, 1977).

The force of his contribution was to present a testable theory of anti-social behaviour. The evidence testing the theory is mixed, with some studies indicating support for this position. However, psychological theories have moved on to become much more environmental in nature, placing a greater emphasis on the role of the social and physical environment in explaining behaviour.

Clive Hollin

Associated Concepts: conditioning, individual positivism, personality theory

Key Readings

Eysenck, H.J. (1959) *Manual of the Maudsley Personality Inventory.* London: University of London Press.
Eysenck, H.J. (1964) *Crime and Personality.* London: Routledge and Kegan Paul.
Eysenck, H.J. (1977) *Crime and Personality,* 3rd edn. London: Routledge and Kegan Paul.

FAMILY CRIME

Definition

An emergent generic term which draws attention to the extent and range of violence and abuse in 'private' domestic life.

Distinctive Features

Historically, one of the major consequences of representing crime as part of the public sphere is that events occurring within the private sphere of the family have been considered to be less serious than 'real crime' and as something distinct from crises of law and order. For example, domestic violence, child abuse and elder abuse have rarely been discussed as part of political and public concerns about the 'problem of crime'. This partiality is also reflected in academic criminology. Relatively few texts discuss child abuse and elder abuse, in particular, except in the context of victimization.

Family violence, understood primarily in terms of cruelty to children, but also involving what was described as conjugal violence, was first identified as a social problem in the late nineteenth century. The public concern at the time was short-lived and did not re-emerge until the second half of the twentieth century. Events outside the family which might be identified as criminal have tended, except in 'extreme' cases, to be seen as normal if they occur within the confines of family relationships. For example, if an adult assaults another in the street, it is likely to be considered a criminal act; but if a man hits his wife at home

this is more likely to be seen as a domestic argument. Equally, if parents hit a child, this may be seen as normal discipline, an understandable reaction to a difficult child, or at worst cruelty, yet infant murders are more common than murders in any other age group.

Since the 1960s different forms of family violence have come to be identified and made more visible: physical abuse and neglect of children in the 1960s, domestic violence in the 1970s, child sexual abuse in the 1980s, and elder abuse in the 1990s. As a result it has been argued that the family is the predominant setting for every form of physical violence: from slaps to torture and murder. Some form of physical violence in the life cycle of family members is so likely that it can be said to be 'almost universal' (Hotaling and Straus, 1980).

By the end of the twentieth century domestic violence in particular had assumed a new visibility. In the UK evidence from victimization surveys revealed that:

- one woman in four experienced domestic violence at some stage in their life;
- two women were killed by current or former partners every week;
- thousands of children witnessed cruelty and violence every day;
- domestic violence accounted for one-quarter of all violent crime.

In contrast, child abuse does not typically appear in victim surveys; estimates of its extent are usually taken from the numbers of children whose names have been placed on child protection registers, but even then they number tens of thousands every year.

Evaluation

As a result there now appears to be a greater agreement that family crime not only exists but is also extensive. However, there remains very little consensus on how such violence and abuse should be understood and tackled. Historically the issue has been seen as primarily a private, welfare or civil, rather than criminal, matter. It remains significant that the first Society for the Protection of Children was only set up in New York in 1871, when a child who was being treated cruelly by her adoptive parents could only be 'rescued' when a judge interpreted that the word 'animal', in the laws against cruelty to animals, might also include children. Similarly from the earliest record, many if not most societies have given the patriarch of the family the right to use force against women and children under his control. The issue of 'legitimate chastisement' is most strikingly illustrated by the 'rule of thumb', which is reputedly derived from the ancient right of a husband to beat his wife with a stick no thicker than his thumb.

Since the 1970s feminist research and campaigning have been pivotal in providing resources for women survivors of male violence and in ensuring that, first, rape and domestic violence and, latterly, child sexual abuse have been firmly placed on the political agenda. Gordon (1989) challenged the idea that state intervention was an intrusion into private matters by asking 'whose privacy' and 'whose liberties' were being violated. Many jurisdictions now recognize domestic violence both as a crime and a police priority. However, the state response to violence against children has been more ambivalent and clouded by notions of child protection rather than criminalizing abusers. Although the corporal punishment of children has been condemned by many Western jurisdictions and by international conventions of human rights, the constitution of 'reasonable chastisement' remains contested. In the UK, for example, there is no single criminal offence of abusing a child.

Strategies to tackle domestic violence are also still presented as part of crime reduction policies rather than in terms of analyses of gender relations or of the nature of families (Saraga, 2001).

A constantly shifting balance between family privacy, support for parental authority, and public recognition of familial violence continues to marginalize the issue of family crime in broader law and order agendas. It remains to be seen how far emergent discourses of human rights will be able to overcome such persistent ambivalence.

Esther Saraga and John Muncie

Associated Concepts: masculinities, radical feminism, sex crime, victimology, violence

Key Readings

Biggs, S., Phillipson, C. and Kingston, P. (1995) *Elder Abuse in Perspective.* Buckingham: Open University Press.

Dobash, R.E. and Dobash, R.P. (eds) (1998) *Rethinking Violence against Women.* London: Sage.

Gordon, L. (1989) *Heroes of their Own Lives: The Politics and History of Family Violence, 1880–1960.* London: Virago.

Hotaling, G.T. and Straus, M.A. (eds) (1980) *The Social Causes of Husband–Wife Violence.* Minneapolis: University of Minnesota Press.

Morgan, J. and Zedner, L. (1992) *Child Victims.* Oxford: The Clarendon Press.

Saraga, E. (2001) 'Dangerous places: the family as a site of crime', in J. Muncie and E. McLaughlin (eds), *The Problem of Crime*, 2nd edn. London: Sage.

FEAR OF CRIME

Definition

Fear of crime is a rational or irrational state of alarm or anxiety engendered by the belief that one is in danger of criminal victimization.

Distinctive Features

Life in complex, highly urbanized societies requires high levels of trust in others, especially strangers, and there is considerable evidence that 'strangers' are a potent source of fear in the public imagination. Particular forms of 'dangerous stranger' crime and/or high levels of crime can have a corrosive effect on everyday life because of the individual and public fear and anxiety they generate. A pervasive fear of crime encourages a physical and psychological withdrawal from the community. It also weakens informal social control systems and undermines the capacity of individuals and communities to respond to the problems that they face. As a consequence, it provides space for further crime and disorder. In addition public faith in the criminal justice system and the capacity of the state to protect its citizens is damaged by fear of crime. This produces public calls for tougher law and order policies and creates the demand for high levels of private anti-crime security and self-protection.

Research suggests that the fear of crime is an ill-defined term that covers a variety of complex worries and anxieties. It relates to an individual's judgement about the amount and nature of crime in society and her/his own neighbourhood. Self-perceived vulnerability is also crucial to levels of individual fear. It also relates to a multitude of anxieties about the pace and nature of social and cultural change. For example, a sense of neighbourhood decline and shifts in racial and ethnic demographics seem to be particular sources of fear and anxiety. Conventional wisdom holds that the members of the public who will be most afraid of crime will be the ones who have been victimized. However, research in a variety of jurisdictions suggests that the relationship between the risk of victimization and fear of crime is not straightforward. Although it is true that among certain sections of the public fear of crime would seem to be out of all proportion to the actual risk of becoming a victim, this general statement about risk needs to be qualified. In-depth research among women in specific localities, for example, suggests

that their fears and concerns are not exaggerated. On the contrary, women have a well-founded and precise understanding of their vulnerability with regard to sexual violence.

Fear of crime can escalate because of: direct experience; secondary knowledge from family, friends and acquaintances; the campaigning work of pressure groups representing victims; police officers and politicians who want to play the law and order card; the activities of private security firms looking for business; and insurance companies protecting their interests. Sections of the news media also have a key role to play in circulating the fear of crime through: over-reporting violent and sexual crimes; adopting personalization and sensationalization techniques; giving intense coverage to, and commentary on, crimes that grip the public imagination; and conducting hardline and alarmist campaigns against particular types of criminals.

Evaluation

For criminal justice policy makers in many jurisdictions, tackling the fear of crime has become a priority. Government-sponsored advertising campaigns have been run in an attempt to persuade the public that many of their fears are irrational. Efforts have also been made to persuade the news media to be more responsible in their crime reporting activities. Situational crime prevention strategies have been used by administrative criminologists to target harden both potential victims and locations. Left realist-inspired local authorities in the UK have developed situational and community-based safety strategies that are intended to protect citizens from the criminal or anti-social behaviour of others and enable them to pursue their lives without the fear of victimization. These strategies specifically take account of the safety needs of vulnerable members of the community. Police forces have also developed aggressive, high-profile operational strategies to shift the burden of fear from potential victims to offenders.

These policy developments and practical initiatives aside, there remains an urgent need to reach a more sophisticated theorization of such concepts as 'fear', 'risk', 'danger', 'security' and 'safety'.

Eugene McLaughlin

Associated Concepts: left realism, moral panic, personal safety, risk, situational crime prevention, victimology

Key Readings

Best, J. (1999) *Random Violence: How We Talk About New Crimes and New Victims.* Berkeley: University of California Press.

Davis, M. (1998) *Ecology of Fear: Los Angeles and the Imagination of Disaster.* New York: Metropolitan Books.

Ferraro, K.F. (1995) *Fear of Crime: Interpreting Victimization Risk.* Albany: State University of New York Press.

Hollway, W. and Jefferson, T. (2000) 'The role of anxiety in fear of crime in everyday life', in T. Hope and R. Sparks (eds), *Crime, Risk and Insecurity: Law and Order in Everyday Life.* London: Routledge.

Lewis, D.A. and Salem, G.W. (1985) *Fear of Crime: Incivility and the Production of a Social Problem.* New Brunswick, NJ: Transaction.

Schlesinger, P. and Tumber, H. (1994) *Reporting Crime: The Media Politics of Criminal Justice.* Oxford: The Clarendon Press.

FEMINIST CRIMINOLOGIES

Definition

Varied analyses using feminist or critical social theories that ask: what is the place of sex/gender in crime and justice? And what is the place of sex/gender in criminological and justice theories?

Distinctive Features

Feminist criminologies challenge the androcentrism (or male-centredness) of the field of criminology and its explanations of crime and justice system practices in varied ways. Taking a broad and inclusive definition of feminist perspectives, two major axes are apparent: one drawing on liberal theory and the other on critical social theory (Daly and Chesney-Lind, 1988).

Liberal feminist criminologies assume that men and women are 'the same' but women are denied opportunities to do the same things as men, including participating in crime. This perspective typically ignores class and racial-ethnic differences among women, and defines gender either as the possession of masculine or feminine attitudes or as role differences between men and women. By contrast, feminist criminologies that draw on critical social theories assume that men and women are both the same and different, and they focus on gender power relations rather than role differences. They also argue that traditional criminological theories are incapable of explaining the relationship of sex/gender to crime or justice system practices. This latter set of feminist criminologies is diverse; it includes scholars who focus exclusively on sex/gender, who are interested in the intersections of class, race and gender, and who analyse sex/gender as an active accomplishment or as a discursive field. They often draw from feminist work outside criminology, including post-structural, post-colonial, critical race, philosophical, discourse and psychoanalytical theories.

Feminist criminologies are new, having emerged in the 1970s inspired by the women's movement. Beginning in the mid-1980s they began to change, reflecting shifts in feminist thought more generally. Recent work attends to differences among women, to the impact of post-structuralist thinking in representing 'women', and to different epistemologies in producing feminist knowledge: empiricist, standpoint and postmodern. Whereas scholars in the 1970s and 1980s focused on depicting 'real women' and 'women's experiences', those in the 1990s became interested in the problems of representing 'women' in light of the discursive power of social, criminological and legal texts to contain sex/gender and women in ways that seemed obdurate to change (Smart, 1995).

During the 1990s, three modes of analysing sex/gender have emerged: class–race–gender, doing gender, and sexed bodies (Daly, 1997). Class–race–gender focuses on the intersections of different social relations on women's (and men's) lives; doing gender (and subsequently doing masculinity) centres on the situations and social practices that produce gender; and sexed bodies focuses on sexual difference and on the relationship of sex and gender as corporeal and cultural categories. During this period there has been increasing interest in portraying women victims and lawbreakers as having choice and agency, rather than depicting women (or girls) as the passive victims of male (or white) oppression (Daly, 1998).

Evaluation

Feminist perspectives in criminology are a very recent development, having only begun to appear in criminology or criminal justice texts in the early 1990s. As a set of perspectives, feminist criminologies make diverse claims about the relationship of sex/gender to crime and justice system practices. There is no one feminist criminology and some would suggest that the term *feminist criminology* should be abandoned. Over the past three decades feminist perspectives in criminology have been applied most frequently to victimization, and especially to family violence and sexual assault. While developed feminist theories of victimization and men's violence toward women have emerged, feminist theories of crime are less evident.

Different sources of field expansion, one beginning with theories of crime and the other beginning with theories of gender, have created different types of knowledge about women, gender and crime. The first follows in the footsteps of traditional criminology and is liberal feminist in orientation; it seeks to devise a comprehensive theory that would explain gender differences in law-breaking (Steffensmeier and Allan, 1996). The second is the province of more critical feminist criminologists, who begin with theories of sex/gender and with studies of women's (and men's) lives and apply this body of knowledge to crime. This group is less interested in devising a comprehensive theory of gender and crime, and more inclined to identify the ways in which sex/gender structures men's and women's life-worlds, identities and thinkable courses of action (Maher, 1997). Future work will likely reflect theory-building preferences that are structured not only by liberal and critical social theories, but also by the theorist's gender.

Kathleen Daly

Associated Concepts: critical criminology, feminist research, hegemonic masculinity, liberal feminism, masculinities, postmodern feminism, radical feminism, sexuality, victimology

Key Readings

Daly, K. (1997) 'Different ways of conceptualizing sex/gender in criminological theories and their implications for criminology', *Theoretical Criminology*, 1 (1): 25–51.

Daly, K. (1998) 'Gender, crime, and criminology', in M. Tonry (ed.), *The Handbook of Crime and Punishment*. New York: Oxford University Press.

Daly, K. and Chesney-Lind, M. (1988) 'Feminism and criminology', *Justice Quarterly*, 5 (4): 497–538.

Maher, L. (1997) *Sexed Work: Gender, Race and Resistance in a Brooklyn Drug Market*. Oxford: The Clarendon Press.

Smart, C. (1995) *Law, Crime and Sexuality*. London: Sage.

Steffensmeier, D. and Allan, E. (1996) 'Gender and crime: toward a gendered theory of female offending', *Annual Review of Sociology*, 22: 459–87.

FEMINIST RESEARCH

Definition

The term 'feminist research' escapes any simple or ready definition. The questions 'What makes research feminist?' and 'Is it possible to speak of feminist methodology/ies or method?' have been the subject of continuing debate since at least the early 1980s.

Distinctive Features

Early debates centred on the assertion that feminist research was 'research about women, by women, for women'. Feminists recognized that women had been marginalized, stereotyped and sexualized in pre/non-feminist research. This 'absence' was first addressed by making women visible as autonomous subjects. However, the far-reaching nature of feminist critique generated complex methodological and epistemological questions to the extent that the feminist research project came to entail more than the simplistic addition of women to existing research agendas.

In criminology this is evident in a body of empirical studies examining women's relation to patriarchal institutions, for example in law, criminal justice and policing. As well as redressing absences in such research, these studies, consistent with feminism, advocated political and policy interventions designed to secure beneficial changes to the circumstances of those found to be experiencing oppression or discrimination. From the outset, feminist research aimed both to understand the nature of patriarchal oppression and to bring about change (Kelly et al., 2000).

Although the 'about women, by women, for women' formulation became something of an orthodoxy in the early 1980s, it has proved inadequate as a definition. Duelli Klein (1983) dismissed the notion that focusing on women as subjects is sufficient to define research as feminist, arguing that without a feminist framework, research about women can perpetuate dominant androcentric assumptions. The formulation was also limiting in its exclusion of research into the operation of male power, patriarchal institutions, men and masculinity, although these issues featured significantly in feminist research agendas. The early formulation also suggested that to be feminist, research had to be conducted by women, although it is clear

from Duelli Klein that the significant factor here is a commitment to feminism. As a result, the assertion that feminist research was 'for women', came closest to identifying what makes research feminist. Defined by Duelli Klein (1983: 90) as '... research that tries to take women's needs, interests and experiences into account and aims at being instrumental in improving women's lives ...', the 'for women' tenet established feminist research as 'women-centred'.

Through its commitments to feminism and a women-centred research practice, feminist research presents a major challenge to the empiricist orthodoxy that social science research should strive for objectivity and be value-free. In relation to criminology, it is revealed that what previously passed as objective was imbued with masculinist misrepresentations of women. Recognizing that scholarship inevitably reflects the conditions of its production, including the gender standpoint of its producers, feminism rejects the possibility of objective knowledge. Rather, the subjectivity of the researcher is acknowledged as significant in the research process. Reflexivity at the personal level is a core methodological principle in feminist research. As Holland and Ramazanoglu (1994: 130) note, a key innovation of feminist research is 'the attempt to grasp the parts that experience, emotion and subjectivity play in the research process, rather than seeing these as weaknesses to be controlled'.

The critique of objectivity extended to research practice. Feminism demonstrated how the aim of objectivity resulted in the objectification of research participants. By contrast, feminist researchers respect participants as the holders of valuable knowledge and experience. Being granted permission to gather and use this knowledge is considered a privilege. In accordance with feminist ethics is the commitment to developing research practices that will ensure that women are not exploited or hurt by the research process. In contrast to the positivist commitment to 'objectivity', the 'women-centred' character of feminist research highlights the importance of subjectivity and meaning. MacKinnon

(1987), for example, makes connections between feminist research, consciousness raising, and the practice of sharing individual and personal experiences. Without a structural and cultural location, subjectivity in itself is not a sufficient basis for theory-building, but when contextualized it represents a significant starting point.

Placing women's experience at the centre of research carries the danger of exclusions in relation to marginalized groups, for example, black and minority ethnic women, lesbians, and those belonging to minority faith groups. The question of 'which women?' must also be interrogated. This point has been emphasized in black feminist critiques and in research that is sensitive to issues of inclusion and exclusion.

Considerable emphasis was initially placed on qualitative methods in order to be sensitive to subjective experience and the meanings accorded to it. This approach also enabled power imbalances between the researcher and research subjects to be more readily negotiated. In fact, by the late 1980s, feminist research was often represented as synonymous with qualitative methodology. However, for feminists involved in activism, awareness of the strategic role of statistics in establishing a case for political intervention meant that quantitative research also became something of a necessary evil. But feminist attempts to develop more 'participant friendly', sensitive and accountable survey practices resulted in some creative innovations. Contrary to some academic representations, feminist research practice has demonstrated that all methods – surveys and discourse analysis, as well as autobiographical accounts and face-to-face interviewing – have been drawn on by feminists.

It is not the research methods that make research distinctively feminist. Rather, what distinguishes feminist research is its feminist commitment to producing research 'for women', the identification of women's experiences as a new empirical resource, and the positioning of the researcher within the research processes. The distinctiveness of feminist research lies at the following related levels of methodology and epistemology:

- Feminist research is explicitly positioned within the feminist project of understanding the nature of women's oppression with a view to ending it.
- Research agenda reflects women's concerns.
- Its underlying theory is feminist, and its practice centres on women's experiences within a framework that acknowledges continuity and difference between women positioned differently in relation to other major power structures, significantly race, sexuality, culture and class.
- Its outcomes are presented accessibly and made available to those for whom they will be useful.
- It recognizes the significance of gender and gender power relations in all dimensions of social life.
- It accepts the importance of subjectivity and the personal experience of the researcher.
- It minimizes or eliminates exploitative relations between researchers and participants.

These principles are embedded in practice at all stages of feminist research, from theorizing the initial problem, its underpinning epistemologies and the data-gathering process, to the writing and publication of outcomes, including a strategic consideration of how to frame the issues and whether and where to publish.

Evaluation

Feminist research is not primarily about methods. It is a theoretical, empirical, interpretative, critical and engaged process, informed by the goal of ultimately eliminating the oppression of women. Acknowledging that feminist work is positioned within a struggle for change does not mean that it is biased, simply subjective and anecdotal. On the contrary, the development of strategies for change requires an accurate naming and analysis of the existing situation or problem. Feminist research aims to produce outcomes that can be verified. Its openness regarding methodological and theoretical assumptions facilitates accountability and criticism. How feminist research is evaluated depends primarily on the standpoint of the reviewer. Those hostile to feminism criticize its overtly political standpoint, its emphasis on subjectivity and a rejection of objectivity, and its lack of a common method. Those more persuaded by feminism evaluate it against its own aims and achievements, including its usefulness in generating change.

Jill Radford

Associated Concepts: critical criminology, critical research, liberal feminism, radical feminism, reflexivity

Key Readings

Duelli Klein, R. (1983) 'How to do what we want to do: thoughts about feminist methodology', in G. Bowles and R. Duelli Klein (eds), *Theories of Women's Studies.* London: Routledge and Kegan Paul.

Holland, J. and Ramazanoglu, G. (1994) 'Power and interpretation in researching young women's sexuality', in M. Maynard and J. Purvis (eds), *Researching Women's Lives from a Feminist Perspective.* London: Taylor and Francis.

Kelly, L., Burton, S. and Regan, L. (1994) 'Researching women's lives or studying women's oppression? Reflections on what counts as feminist research', in M. Maynard and J. Purvis (eds), *Researching Women's Lives from a Feminist Perspective.* London: Taylor and Francis.

Kelly, L., Radford, J. and Scanlon, J. (2000) 'Feminism, feminisms: fighting back for women's liberation', in K. Atkinson, S. Orton and G. Plain (eds), *Feminisms on Edge: Politics, Discourses and National Identities.* Cardiff: Cardiff Academic Press.

MacKinnon, C. (1987) *Feminism Unmodified: Discourses on Life and Law.* Cambridge, MA: Harvard University Press.

FOCUS GROUPS

Definition

A form of interview which involves a number of individuals who will discuss a particular topic under the direction of a facilitator who will promote interactions between individuals and make certain that the discussion remains focused on the topic of interest. The data are not just the outcome of an exchange between the facilitator and the group but also the outcome of interactions between group members.

Distinctive Features

The term 'focus group' is derived from Merton and Kendall's (1946) work on the persuasiveness of wartime propaganda in the USA. Focus groups subsequently became a favoured tool within market research, for example, to examine product imagery. In the 1980s and 1990s they were widely used by social scientists and also by political parties to gather ideas regarding policy formation and presentation.

Social scientists use focus groups in three ways. First, they are used in an exploratory role, as a preliminary to more extensive research. For example, data collected from the groups can be used to identify issues which are crucial to the participants themselves, rather than what social scientists think is important; they may help to devise subsequent research design; and they can assist in the formulation of questions to be used in structured interviews. Second, focus groups can be employed as a method in their own right and as a central part of a research study, for example, to find out about how representatives of a community experience crime victimization and what views they have about strategies for prevention. Third, focus groups can be used to triangulate or support findings from other forms of research. These groups can generate in-depth attitudes, opinions, examples and case studies which are often not obtainable from large-scale but shallow social surveys.

Typically, focus groups will be composed of between four and 12 participants, who will have been selected because they fit some criteria that are relevant to the research topic. Usually an attempt will be made to ensure that the composition of the group is representative of the population to which the researchers wish the conclusions to apply.

The discussion of topics is initiated by a facilitator who starts with introductions and general issues and then moves on progressively to more focused questions. The role of facilitator is not solely to initiate an exchange with group members (as in-depth interviews), but to encourage interactions between group members which will generate data that would not usually be obtained in one-to-one interviews. The advantages of this interactive effect are that group members can be reminded of issues by others in the group; they can generate ideas new to the researcher; and they can give support to each other when discussing sensitive topics. For example, research involving a group discussion on domestic violence with a group of women from refuges found that they were prepared to share information of a personal and harrowing nature because they each had had similar experiences. Once one group member began to talk, others were prepared to join in.

Evaluation

As with all methods of research there is a trade-off between strengths and weaknesses in relation to the topic of research. Focus groups are quicker and cheaper than detailed interviews with an equivalent number of individuals. They provide the depth and flexibility of approach of unstructured interviews and in addition supply insights into the effects of interactions between group members. In addition, group interviews can support individuals when discussing sensitive topics and also facilitate the brainstorming of original ideas. However, a good deal of skill is required of the facilitator in encouraging interactions, managing group dynamics, and keeping the discussion on the central topic. There can also be problems of generalizability, and researchers should exercise caution in making inferences from a focus group and extending these to cover a wider population. This is one of the criticisms levelled at the use of focus groups by political parties to assist in the formulation of policy.

Victor Jupp

Associated Concepts: ethnography, feminist research, triangulation

Key Readings

Kreuger, R.A. (1994) *Focus Groups: A Practical Guide for Applied Research.* Thousand Oaks, CA: Sage.
Merton, R. and Kendall, P. (1946) 'The focused interview', *American Journal of Sociology*, 51: 541–57.
Morgan, D.L. (ed.) (1993) *Successful Focus Groups.* Newbury Park, CA: Sage.
Stewart, D.W. and Shamdasani, D.N. (1990) *Focus Groups: Theory and Practice.* Newbury Park, CA: Sage.

FOLK DEVIL

Definition

A category of persons who become defined as a threat to societal values and interests and the embodiment of 'what is wrong with society'. Folk devils are presented in a stylized and stereotypical fashion by the mass media.

Distinctive Features

The concept of a 'folk devil' is closely associated with Cohen's (1972) analysis of the ways in which confrontations between Mods and Rockers in an English holiday resort were reported in the media. The analysis owes much to the development of interactionist, labelling and new deviancy approaches within criminology during the mid- to late 1960s. These approaches influenced the direction taken in Cohen's empirical work, which was essentially qualitative and ethnographic and involved an examination of the role of the media in reporting the events. His conclusions were that the media played a key role in symbolization in which key symbols, such as lifestyle, are portrayed as different from the norm and in a socially unfavourable light. Within symbolization a word, such as 'Mod', would become symbolic of a certain status, such as delinquent or deviant. Objects, such as distinctive hairstyles and clothing, would symbolize the word, and the objects themselves would then become symbolic of the status, including the emotions attached to the status. Symbolization is thus crucial to the creation of folk devils.

The media would also play an important part in the exaggeration and distortion of events, as well as in making predictions about future events, perhaps elsewhere, which would be likely to be even worse than the exaggerations and distortions. This produced forms of societal reaction to the folk devils, such as greater police vigilance and surveillance and public campaigns to control or prohibit events. With regard to the Mods and Rockers, there was pressure for greater police vigilance and stronger action from the forces of law and order. The police reacted by intensifying foot patrols and operating greater levels of surveillance and interventions in seaside towns, dance halls and fairs, which were seen as potential areas of trouble. It is a fundamental element of Cohen's thesis that such a societal reaction to folk devils will increase rather than decrease subsequent deviance, a process known as deviancy amplification. The public and police will react to folk devils in terms of the images and symbols presented to them by the media. Individuals will then respond accordingly, thereby confirming their status both as deviant and as a threat to what is viewed as normal.

The concept of the 'folk devil' is inextricably linked to another, namely 'moral panic'. The thesis is that societies will go through periods of social change which will instil feelings of uncertainty, fear and threat in their members, and that during such periods folk devils emerge as the symbol and even the cause of what is wrong. There is a middle range explanation for the emergence of folk devils in the media in terms of the need for 'news value' and 'good copy'. However, Cohen's thesis also suggested a much more fundamental explanation in the rapid social change which Britain was undergoing in the 1960s (the decline of traditional working-class communities, increased permissiveness) and the dissipation of ensuing public anxiety by identifying folk devils as scapegoats and as symbols of what was wrong.

Hall et al. (1978) drew on Cohen's work in their analysis of the young-black-mugger-as-folk-devil. Their work was similar to Cohen's in the way in which it identified an increase in street mugging as a socially constructed phenomenon and traced its creation as a moral panic in the media during the 1970s. However, Hall and his colleagues linked the moral panic and the portrayal of young black muggers as folk devils to a crisis in hegemony during an economic recession within a capitalist system. It was argued that the public concern about mugging served to distract attention away from the underlying causes and inherent problems of the increasing economic decline. It thrust social anxieties onto black youths who were perceived as threats to ordinary (often elderly) citizens and to social order on the streets of inner city areas. Also, the threat from young black muggers was used to justify increased and heavier policing and a general drift towards a law and order society. In offering this analysis Hall et al. extended Cohen's thesis by adding a Marxist and critical slant to what was a predominantly interactionist and labelling approach to crime and deviance.

The concept of a 'folk devil' is capable of wide applicability but has been applied most forcefully to the analysis of youth and of youth cultures (although often in couplets such as 'black youth', 'working-class youth', 'inner city youth'). A key reason for this is that young people are treated as a barometer for the current social health of society and as a means of forming a prognosis for its future.

Evaluation

The 'folk devil' is a robust and enduring theoretical concept which has made important contributions to criminology by opening up fruitful lines of theorizing and empirical enquiry. It has facilitated the fusion of valuable aspects of interactionism and labelling theory with those offered by critical criminology and analysis at a social structural level. In doing so it has encouraged enquiries into micro and macro aspects of social life and the interconnections between these. Added to this, more recent applications of discourse analysis within criminology have embraced the concept of the 'folk devil' in terms of addressing which types of people are portrayed as problematic within discourses at different levels of society, why this is so, and to what effect.

Empirical enquiries, especially those based on ethnographic methods, have used the 'folk devil' as a sensitizing device for guiding research. These include documentary analysis of media reports, police reports and public statements by politicians and the judiciary; examinations of the social construction of official statistics and of their role in creating crime waves and moral panics; and observations of the interactions between 'deviants' and law enforcement officers in terms of the application, receipt and amplification of deviant labels. The concept has also had some policy applications, for example in terms of introducing topics on the negative aspects of stereotyping into the education and training of criminal justice personnel and related professions.

Despite these contributions there is a danger that the discourse of the 'folk devil' (as an exaggerated and distorted image which is socially constructed and then used as a scapegoat for some other problems) masks the fact that crime is a reality for those victims who have experienced it and for those who live in fear of it. Such a viewpoint is associated with those who come from a position of criminological realism and who emphasize the need to face up to the reality of crime.

Victor Jupp

Associated Concepts: criminalization, demonization, deviance, discourse analysis, ethnography, gangs, interactionism, labelling, moral panic, new deviancy theory, racialization, scapegoating, social reaction, stereotyping

Key Readings

Cohen, S. (1972) *Folk Devils and Moral Panics: The Creation of Mods and Rockers.* London: MacGibbon and Kee. (London, Paladin, 1973; new edition Martin Robertson, Oxford, 1980.)

Goode, E.R. and Ben-Yehuda, N. (1994) *Moral Panics: The Social Construction of Deviance.* Oxford: Blackwell.

Hall, S., Critcher, C., Jefferson, T., Clarke, J. and Roberts, B. (1978) *Policing the Crisis: Mugging, the State and Law and Order.* London: Macmillan.

Thompson, K. (1998) *Moral Panics.* London: Routledge.

FORENSIC ANTHROPOLOGY

Definition

A broad definition of 'forensic anthropology' might be the study of human variation within a legal context. Practitioners, however, understand the term to mean more specifically the forensic investigation of the skeleton and of partially skeletonized human remains.

Distinctive Features

Forensic anthropology grew as a discipline during the twentieth century, via the application of methods – often termed osteology or physical anthropology – that had been developed for the investigation of archaeological human remains and the study of anatomy for the investigation of crime.

The discipline is most well developed in the United States where the American Board of Forensic Anthropology was founded in 1977. The ABFA was founded: (a) to encourage the study of, improve the practice of, establish and enhance standards for, and advance the science of forensic anthropology; (b) to encourage and promote adherence to high standards of ethics, conduct and professional practice in forensic anthropology; (c) to grant and issue certificates, and/or other recognition, in cognisance of a special qualification in forensic anthropology to voluntary applicants who conform to the standards established by the Board and who have established their fitness and competence thereof; (d) to inform the appropriate branches of federal and state governments and private agencies of the existence and nature of the ABFA and the professional quality of its Diplomates for the practice of forensic anthropology; and (e) to maintain and furnish lists of individuals who have been granted certificates by the Board.

In this way the ABFA aims to make available to the judicial system, and others, a practical and equitable system for readily identifying those persons professing to be specialists in forensic anthropology who possess the requisite qualifications and competence (http://www.csuchico.edu/anth/ABFA/).

Forensic anthropology is well developed in Guatemala and Argentina, where the discipline developed in response to the investigation of political murders by past governments. Practice in the European countries and elsewhere is patchy. There are about 20 practising forensic anthropologists in the UK, for example, where there are about the same number of real forensic anthropology cases – as opposed to archaeological or faunal remains – per annum. This necessitates UK practitioners having to gain experience via training in anatomy or archaeology, for example, and to practise in other countries – most significantly in the investigation of human rights abuses in the Balkans and elsewhere. Forensic anthropology has played a major role in the investigation of such abuses in South America, Africa, Europe and Asia.

In the UK, the Council for the Registration of Forensic Practitioners (CRFP) and the Forensic Science Society professional registration schemes are available for assessing practitioners' competency.

These distinctions highlight the varying demand for forensic anthropologists according to patterns of crime, environment and climate. A city like Los Angeles, for example, has a homicide rate that is many times that of UK cities; the proximity of a sparsely populated desert environment means that bodies are more easily concealed than in a densely populated United Kingdom, and the hot dry climate encourages rapid skeletonization. Furthermore, in the United States, training in archaeology is regarded as a standard requirement of competency for the forensic anthropologist. Forensic anthropology cases are often partially or totally buried, whether they are encountered in routine police work or in mass graves. In the UK, competency in forensic anthropology and archaeology is accredited separately under the CRFP registration system – a situation that has arisen as the result of local influences and, arguably, not as a consequence of the implementation of best practice.

Forensic anthropology is distinct from 'forensic pathology', in which the causes of death and disease processes are investigated more substantially from the whole body (when available), again within a legal context. Many forensic pathologists consider themselves *de facto* forensic anthropologists, and the relative importance of the two disciplines in the investigation of skeletonized or partially skeletonized human remains is still contentious.

In many countries, a specialist dentist – the forensic odontologist – undertakes an examination of the dentition. The extent to which a forensic anthropologist takes responsibility for the analysis of the teeth will therefore vary. The methods of skeletal analysis are standard. They permit the estimation of sex – from the skull and pelvis; of age – mainly from the dentition and pelvis; of height – from the long bones; of build – from the skeleton generally; and of ancestry – mainly from the skull.

It is important to recognize that these features of identification from the skeleton are estimates and not exact determinations. Exact classification from the skeleton is impossible. There is a significant degree of variability in the development and, especially, the ageing processes from individual to individual – due to genetic, cultural, behavioural and environmental factors. Similarly, estimating the time since death is also problematic as this too can vary according to the climate, weather conditions, moisture level, clothing, manner of burial and concealment, and so on. Often the cause of death is to be found in the soft tissues. With the exception of blunt and sharp force traumas, particularly gun shot wounds, there is often no trace of the cause of death on the skeleton.

Forensic anthropology in human identification is therefore often an intelligence tool, providing a broad guide to identity. A process of elimination can then be used to investigate candidate missing persons. In the event of a strong candidate emerging, identity can be confirmed from dental records or DNA. This can be straightforward, as in the case of a closed major fatality incident, such as a plane crash, where there are good *ante-mortem* data regarding the identity of the victims.

The issue of investigative rather than evidential value applies especially to the allied discipline of forensic facial reconstruction. Facial reconstruction is a method for the recreation of facial appearance from the skull by reconstructing the facial soft tissues in clay or by computer, using known average tissue depths at certain landmark sites as guidelines. It is important to note that certain facial features that are significant for recognition – the shape of the eyes and eyelids, the tip of the nose and the lips – are not predicted at all strongly by the skull and are to an extent guesswork. Facial reconstruction can generate a true resemblance of the individual during life, but not an exact likeness. Nevertheless the method does seem to generate leads, with a firm identification in about 50 per cent of cases where no other means of identification are available.

Evaluation

Forensic anthropology is an emergent discipline whose role as a distinctive specialization is now well established – particularly in the United States. Some resistance continues from within Medicine, whose practitioners traditionally hold responsibility for the field, but the case for specialized training and accreditation in forensic anthropology is difficult to argue

against. Accreditation is piecemeal outside the USA, with the regard for the importance of allied skills in archaeology also varying.

As a method, forensic anthropology can often be more valuable as an intelligence tool in the investigation than a method of determining identity or cause of death – this being especially so in the case of a forensic facial reconstruction from the skull. Forensic anthropology has been slow to incorporate more powerful scientific developments, especially DNA profiling, as part of its repertoire. Nevertheless, it has played a key role in the investigation of major human rights abuses and genocides of the twentieth century.

Martin Evison

Associated Concepts: forensic psychology, genocide, human rights

Key Readings

Bass, W.M. (1995) *Human Osteology: A Laboratory and Field Manual.* Missouri, IL: Archaeological Society.
Iscan, M.Y. and Helmer, R.P. (1993) *Forensic Analysis of the Skull.* New York: Wiley-Liss.
Krogman, W.M. and Iscan, M.Y. (1986) *The Human Skeleton in Forensic Medicine.* Springfield, IL: Charles C. Thomas.
Reichs, K.J. (ed.) (1998) *Forensic Osteology: Advances in the Identification of Human Remains,* 2nd edn. Springfield, IL: Charles C. Thomas.
White, T.D. and Folkens, P.A. (2000) *Human Osteology,* 2nd edn. New York: Academic Press.

FORENSIC PSYCHOLOGY

Definition

Forensic psychology involves the application of psychological knowledge to all aspects of the criminal and civil justice system, and therefore encompasses a broad array of topics and methodologies. A common view of forensic psychology is that it is only concerned with the 'criminally insane'. However, although psychopathy and dangerous and severe personality disorder are prominent themes in both research and practice, forensic psychology is equally concerned with the broader spectrum of criminal behaviour, investigation and rehabilitation. Key areas within forensic psychology include: theories of offending that attempt to seek a psychological explanation as to why certain people commit criminal acts, whether these be serious sexual offences or minor theft; offender profiling, which is an investigative technique that makes use of statistical modelling of the behavioural patterns of known criminals to provide details concerning the type of person that may have committed a crime; studies of the techniques and procedures used by police agencies to obtain evidence from witnesses, especially through interviewing and identification procedures; the reliability of witness testimony, the validity of expert testimony and the behaviour of juries in the courtroom; and the rehabilitation of offenders, which is largely based on clinical psychological treatment.

Distinctive Features

A key feature of forensic psychology is its applied nature, with research and theory tending to be directed toward specific criminal justice system policy and practice. It is also a discipline that has both prominent academic and practitioner branches. Forensic clinical practitioners often work within secure psychiatric units concentrating on the assessment and rehabilitation of offenders, although their expert knowledge is also of use to the police, courts and probationary services. To practise in a clinical setting requires extensive clinical training and accreditation, making one distinctive feature of forensic psychology the prominence of national accrediting bodies, such as the British Psychological Society's Division of Forensic Psychology, and the American Board of Forensic Psychology.

It is a discipline that draws on knowledge from many other areas of psychology. As well as the treatment of offenders making use of clinical psychological theory and practice, other areas involve knowledge from cognitive, personality, developmental and social psychology. For example, in studying the role of a witness in the criminal justice system it is necessary to understand their cognitive processes, such as those of perception and memory, that will determine the extent and accuracy of the information the witness can provide, whilst an understanding of the social processes that occur in small groups is crucial when examining jury decision making.

As might be expected from such a broad array of topics, forensic psychology is studied using multiple methodologies and perspectives. These include clinical intervention and case studies, laboratory and field experimentation, psychometric testing, the statistical analysis of offender patterns, interviewing, and qualitative analysis techniques. Although the discipline as a whole can be said to involve a broad array of topics and methodologies, it is often the case that a particular approach will dominate within certain sub-areas: as well as clinical methodologies being prevalent in the treatment of offenders, the scientific, experimental approach tends to be used when studying witnesses, and psychometrics are widely used in developing theories of offending.

Overall, breadth is a key factor that makes forensic psychology a distinct discipline from that of 'forensic psychiatry', although there is undoubtedly a degree of overlap between the two. One key distinction is that forensic psychology seeks to study more of the criminal justice system, notably that pertaining to criminal investigation. However, even within a clinical setting it is possible to distinguish a forensic psychologist from a forensic psychiatrist on the grounds of the therapeutic approach taken.

Although there are many courses available that offer interdisciplinary awards in forensic psychology and criminology, the roots of the two disciplines in psychology and sociology can lead to differences in how similar topics are approached. These differences are perhaps most prominent in theories of offending, with forensic psychologists tending to look more to genetic, cognitive and personality characteristics, whilst criminologists concentrate on broader societal factors. Other distinctions result from differences in methodology, with clinical and experimental approaches featuring far more prominently in forensic psychology.

Evaluation

As forensic psychology is an applied discipline, one way of evaluating its success is to examine its impact on relevant policy, procedures and practice. Such an evaluation reveals considerable international differences. In the USA, psychologists are frequently called as expert witnesses to give evidence on many topics, including the reliability of witnesses, whilst in the UK this is less usual, with expert forensic psychology testimony often being limited to assessments of the mental state of the accused. Arguably, however, forensic psychology has had more of an impact on legislation in the UK, with policy such as the Codes of Practice to the Police and Criminal Evidence Act taking on board the findings of psychological research. The implementation of knowledge gained from forensic psychology can also be seen in many countries around the world within rehabilitation programmes and the procedures used by the police for interviewing witnesses, particularly vulnerable witnesses such as children.

It is also possible to take a more critical stance and evaluate forensic psychology from a criminological perspective. As is generally the case in psychology, forensic psychology does not tend to give a prominent role to broader social issues, and it can be argued that the resulting theories of criminality therefore miss many contributing factors. A possible result of this is that the challenge offered by forensic psychology to the criminal justice system involves the implementation of reasonably minor procedural changes rather than more radical and far-reaching criticisms of the general approach taken.

Graham Pike

Associated Concepts: cognitive behaviourism, forensic anthropology, psychopathy

Key Readings

Adler, J. (ed.) (2004) *Forensic Psychology: Concepts, Debates and Practice.* Cullompton: Willan.

Carson, D. and Bull, R. (eds) (2003) *Handbook of Psychology in Legal Contexts,* 2nd edn. Chichester: Wiley.

Hollin, C.R. (ed.) (2003) *The Essential Handbook of Offender Assessment and Treatment.* Chichester: Wiley.

McGuire, J. (2004) *Understanding Psychology and Crime: Perspectives on Theory and Action* (Crime & Justice Series). Buckingham: Open University Press.

Westcott, H.L., Davies, G.M. and Bull, R. (eds) (2002) *Children's Testimony: A Handbook of Psychological Research and Forensic Practice.* Chichester: Wiley.

Wrightsman, L.S. and Fulero, S.M. (2004) *Forensic Psychology,* 2nd edn. London: Wadsworth.

FREE WILL

Definition

Within the discipline of criminology this concept generally refers to the ability to choose a certain course of action against another, one of which may be regarded as 'deviant'. Although this supposition does not presume that all behaviour is necessarily freely and rationally chosen, it implies that individuals can recognize rules and laws and decide which to obey. To what extent free will exists therefore facilitates discussions surrounding the motives and predictability of human behaviour. Rather than certain acts being determined, either by forces within, or external to, the individual, this allows crime to be viewed as a matter of personal autonomy.

Distinctive Features

The concept of free will has a number of important implications for the study of crime, criminality and penal policy. Within each of these three areas theorists have sought causal explanations, predictive models, and the justification or effectiveness of modes of punishment. As autonomy underpins classicist criminological approaches, and determinism is a central tenet of the contrasting paradigm of positivist criminologies, the notion of freely chosen behaviour is central to many disagreements within the discipline. Indeed, whether criminal acts are freely enacted or externally driven is the crux of this major area of debate. As the legal theorist Herbert L.A. Hart (known for his influential work on jurisprudence) argues, responsibility for most crimes relies upon certain 'mental elements'. Without proof that someone has the knowledge and foresight to predict the consequences of their actions and their potential harm, then although negligence may be shown, criminal responsibility would not. He claims that for legal purposes 'an act is something more than a mere movement of the body: it must be willed' (1963: 41). To claim in the criminal courts, for example, that an individual is responsible and purposive in their actions may invalidate mitigating factors, which may have led to an accusation of murder being reduced to manslaughter. Conversely, if criminal intent or *mens rea* is not proven, if the accused is judged insane, provoked, or claims to have simply acted recklessly, then the concept of autonomous action may be disregarded. Being able to prove that the individual acted within the realm of freedom of choice is therefore linked to notions of justice and legitimacy, not only in theoretical debates but also in case law.

Evaluation

One of the assumptions underpinning the idea that individuals can exercise free will is that society, the law and justice are based upon equality. Individuals within this broadly classicist approach may not be viewed as being free to choose whether to take part in the social contract, but they have faculties of reasoning and access to social justice. The problem with assuming that free

will is enacted by individuals is that structures within society constrain different groups at different times in various ways, although as Bottoms and Wiles (1996: 101) argue, 'it is dangerous to assume that place or design acts as a monocausal variable'. In paraphrasing Anthony Giddens's (1984) work on structuration theory, they propose that although society enforces constraints, '[H]uman subjects are knowledgeable agents ... [who] largely act within a domain of "practical consciousness"' (1996: 102–3). Finally, they quote Marx's famous dictum that human beings 'make history but not in circumstances of their own choosing' to illustrate the difficulties of explaining the constraints and choices surrounding the behaviour defined as criminal.

Similarly, in response to more individualist psychological approaches, in some cases it might be argued that the actor's behaviour was 'involuntary' owing to a number of factors which are difficult to disprove. Instances of this include being subject to compelling internal psychological drives, the addiction to substances such as drugs, extreme provocation, or automatous behaviour such as sleepwalking. More recent work on sociobiology, twin and adoption studies also suggests that 'some factor' (Mednick et al., 1996) is transmitted genetically to children which increases their propensity to commit crime.

Other more recent advocates of this approach are Wilson and Hernstein (1986), who suggest that although individuals are free to choose a course of action that may be criminal, a combination of inherited traits and learned behaviour will influence their choice. Whether the act is outweighed by potentially negative outcomes is therefore influenced, according to this sociobiological approach, by a combination of nature and nurture.

Louise Westmarland

Associated Concepts: classicism, determinism, neo-conservative criminology, rational choice theory, right realism

Key Readings

Bottoms, A.E. and Wiles, P. (1996) 'Explanations of crime and place', in J. Muncie, E. McLaughlin and M. Langan (eds), *Criminological Perspectives*. London: Sage.

Giddens, A. (1984) *The Constitution of Society*. Cambridge: Polity.

Hart, H.L.A. (1963) 'Acts of will and legal responsibility', in D.F. Pears (ed.), *Freedom and the Will*. London: Macmillan.

Mednick, S.A., Gabrielli, W.F. and Hutchings, B. (1996) 'Genetic factors in the etiology of criminal behavior', in J. Muncie, E. McLaughlin and M. Langan (eds), *Criminological Perspectives*. London: Sage.

Wilson, J.Q. and Hernstein, R.J. (1986) *Crime and Human Nature*. New York: Simon and Schuster.

FUNCTIONALISM

Definition

A structuralist perspective which argues that, although crime and deviance are problematic, they must also be understood as 'social facts' and analysed in terms of the possible manifest and latent functions that they perform in enabling the smooth running of the social system as a whole. Hence functionalism distances itself from those criminological perspectives that view crime and deviance as pathological and abnormal.

Distinctive Features

There is a long tradition of functionalist theorizing and explanation across the social sciences. It was introduced into sociology during the nineteenth century and developed and reworked within anthropology. From the 1920s through to the 1950s, the functionalist paradigm dominated North American sociology and the approach was embodied most famously in the work of Talcott Parsons who developed a grand theory of social systems.

Functionalists argue that studying society as if it were a living organism is necessary if we are to understand its major structural institutions and be able to explain human behaviour. Society is viewed as a delicate system where the interdependent parts work in an integrated manner for the common good. Society is deemed to be an independent entity that is greater than the number of individual members. In order to survive and perpetuate itself, society has needs that have to be met and in certain instances these take priority over individual needs. Structures, institutions, practices, roles, values and norms exist because they contribute to the maintenance and proper functioning of society. Functions are assumed to be either manifest (intended) or latent (unintended or unrecognized). If an institution is unable to carry out its functions it will eventually cease to exist and be replaced by new institutional arrangements. According to Percy Cohen (1968: 167), functionalist theorizing is marked by the following basic assumptions:

- norms and values are the basic elements of social life;
- social life involves commitments to agreed norms and values;
- societies are necessarily cohesive;
- social life depends on solidarity and generates harmony;
- social life is based upon reciprocity and co-operation;
- social systems rest on consensus;
- society recognizes power as legitimate authority;
- social systems are integrated and stable;
- social systems tend to persist – conflict is temporary until equilibrium is re-established;
- change is a functional adaptation.

Functionalists such as Daniel Bell and Talcott Parsons were attracted to the study of crime and deviance because in many respects it would provide the ultimate test for their theorizing. However, the social theorist most closely associated with the initial application of functionalist theorizing to crime and deviance was Emile Durkheim. His sociological positivism sought to identify and explain 'social facts': ways of thinking, feeling and acting that a society imposes upon its members to produce order. Even though he did not produce a systematic treatise on the subject, crime and deviance were of interest to Durkheim because his central political project was working out how social cohesion and solidarity could be secured in the face of rapid social and economic change.

Durkheim's contribution to functionalist criminology is two-fold. First, he argued that crime and deviance were normal (social facts) because acts that offend collective norms and expectations existed in all societies and their universal presence pointed to their systemic functionality. For Durkheim, crime and deviance, so long as they were not excessive, were functional because (i) the ritual of punishment is an expressive experience that serves to bind together members of a social group and establish a sense of community, and (ii) they are useful in inaugurating necessary changes and preparing people for change. Even if society discovered the means for eradicating real crimes, it would have to elevate human weaknesses and petty vices to the status of crime. Albert Cohen (1966) built on Durkheim's position by clarifying the various ways that crime and deviance make positive contributions to society:

- deviance cuts through 'red tape';
- deviance acts as a safety valve for societal pressures and discontents and reduces strains;
- deviance clarifies the rules;
- deviance unites the group against the deviant(s) and provides commonality and solidarity;
- deviance defines and heightens conformity and normality;
- deviance acts as a warning signal for defects in society.

A classic example of functionalist theorizing on the positive contribution of crime and deviance to the social order remains Kingsley Davis's controversial analysis of the role played by prostitution in contemporary society. He argues that prostitution exists despite near universal condemnation and prohibition because it enables a small number of women to take care of the sexual needs of a large number of men: 'it is the most convenient sexual outlet for armies and for legions of strangers, perverts, and the physically repulsive in our midst. It performs a role which apparently no other institution fully performs' (1971: 351). Davis intimates that prostitution reinforces the norms and values and equilibrium of the family by providing a safety valve for married men's pent-up sexual frustrations and deviant needs. Hence, it allows the family to be a model of temperance and moderation and certifies the respectability of married women. Prostitution is functional for the women involved, according to Davis, because it enables them to earn more money than they would in other occupations. This led to the conclusion that there will always be a system of social dominance that provides the motive for commercial sex.

Durkheim's second contribution was his theorizing on anomie. He never spelt out how much crime and deviance would be healthy and normal. For him, too little crime and deviance was indicative of an overly regulated society and excessive intolerance, whereas too much crime and deviance lowered the levels of trust and interdependence that were necessary for the survival of society. It is this point that connects across to Durkheim's notion of the anomic society. This is a society in which the rules of behaviour and norms have broken down during periods of rapid social change and economic transition (recession, depression or economic boom). If a gap occurs between what the population expects and what the economic and productive forces of society can deliver, a situation of strain develops that can manifest itself in normlessness or anomie. A state of anomie undermines a society's capacity to exercise social control. Robert Merton (1957) subsequently reworked the concept of anomie in an attempt to illustrate how the USA's social structure exerted pressure on individuals to engage in nonconformist behaviour and could generate dysfunctionality. Durkheim viewed anomie as problematic and associated it with institutional normlessness and abnormality, but for Merton anomie resulted from the incongruity between culturally valued goals associated with the 'American Dream' and the number of legitimate opportunities available to pursue and achieve these goals. The resulting strain and frustration produced five 'modes of adaptation' – conformity, innovation, ritualism, retreatism and rebellion. Not surprisingly, the most common deviant response – innovation – was to be found among the lower classes. Many of the major sociological theories of delinquency are indebted to Merton's reworking of Durkheim's theorizing (as evidenced in sub-cultural theories and variants of control theory, for example).

Evaluation

Functionalist theorizing was attacked during the 1960s and stood accused of teleology and over-determinism. Its obsession with stability, consensus and social order; its emphasis on the self-governing nature of society; and its lack of a theory of power, also laid it open to the charge of being ideologically conservative and supportive of the status quo. Although it fell out of favour, it is possible to find examples of functionalist theorizing and logic across a variety of positivist, structural and materialist criminologies. Elements of what we might describe as a neo-functionalist criminology retain a firm presence in much of North American criminology.

Eugene McLaughlin

Associated Concepts: anomie, determinism, positivism, social control theory, sociological positivism, strain theory, subculture

Key Readings

Cohen, A.K. (1966) *Deviance and Control.* Englewood Cliffs, NJ: Prentice-Hall.

Cohen, P. (1968) *Modern Social Theory.* London: Heinemann.

Davis, K. (1971) 'Prostitution', in R. Merton and R. Nisbet (eds), *Contemporary Social Problems,* 3rd edn. New York: Harcourt Brace Jovanovich.

Durkheim, E. (1964) *The Rules of Sociological Method.* New York: The Free Press.

Merton, R. (1957) *Social Theory and Social Structure.* New York: The Free Press.

Messner, S. and Rosenfield, R. (1996) *Crime and the American Dream.* Belmont, CA: Wadsworth Publications.

GANGS

Definition

The term 'gang' is vague and can be defined in very different ways. For pioneering gang researchers working in Chicago in the early twentieth century, gangs were composed of groups of young people who spontaneously formed and then became unified through conflict (Thrasher, 1927). Today this non-criminalizing way of defining gangs has been replaced by definitions that place criminality at the centre of what a gang is (Klein and Maxson, 2006). Other gang identifiers (many or few) are left to the discretion of the researcher, but can include having a leader, wearing distinguishing colours, or controlling a territory. Such conceptual imprecision means that it is possible to have as many or as few gangs as you wish, depending on the variables contained in the definition used.

Distinctive Features

Historically, gangs were seen as a typically American problem; they did not feature as a subject that commanded a great deal of attention from European criminologists. For most of the postwar period, for example, British criminologists opted to research youth subcultures. This however has now changed. Internationally, researching (a) gang membership, (b) gang typologies, (c) gang activities, and (d) gang intervention programmes has become a hot topic within criminology and this reflects the sensationalized attention 'gangs' receive from the mass media and politicians.

Underpinning the extraordinary rise to prominence of 'the gang' in international criminological research and criminal justice practices can be found a series of contested, if also widely accepted, claims that have been made about them. The first is that what was once a uniquely American problem has crossed the Atlantic to take root in the cities of the UK and Europe. According to this thesis, large organized Americanized gangs are now prevalent in inner city areas. Not only have they arrived, they are also arming themselves with what various commentators like to term ' new weapons of choice'. These include various 'weapon dogs' which they use to 'terrify communities'; 'rape' which they use against 'girlfriends and mothers'; knives and guns which they use to kill each other; and, more recently, public disorder. For example, according to the UK government and the police, gangs were behind the scenes of widespread urban disorder that occurred in August 2011.

For John Pitts (2008), one of the most fervent proponents of a 'gangland UK' thesis, gangs today represent nothing less than the 'new face'of youth crime. They are, he contends, in control of drug markets; they control life in the estates where they are based; and they use violence to compel people to become members. These compulsory gang converts he terms 'reluctant gangsters'. This is a thesis that places 'the gang' at the epicentre of criminal enterprise. It has certainly assumed the status of orthodoxy on the part of the main political parties who have undertaken to suppress gangs by all means available. Where, until recently, the UK had little by way of dedicated gang suppression initiatives, this has changed as a burgeoning gang suppression industry has grown up in order to fight them (Hallsworth, 2011). Given that the UK has little expertise in fighting gangs, the government has looked to the USA and its highly developed gang suppression industry for inspiration. Indeed, as part of its response to the urban disorders of 2011, the coalition government sought policy advice from the architect of USA-style 'zero tolerance' policing, Bill Bratton.

Evaluation

How much of this thesis stands up to critical scrutiny? To begin with it could be observed that the UK has a long distinguished history of collective violence involving young people, a history that contemporary 'gang talk' tends to be in denial of, caught up as it is in the 'infinite novelty' of the present (Pearson, 1983). In a contemporary street world where young people typically associate in groups and where most adopt the *de-facto* uniform of the 'street warrior', establishing when a gang is indeed a gang is by no means an easy feat and it is certainly not an exact science.

Gang identification is particularly complicated because how gangs are imagined and represented in, and stereotyped by, the media and by 'right thinking people' like politicians is often very different from the street worlds where people live out their gang realities (Hallsworth, 2011). In the former category we find 'gang talkers' who will typically imagine the gang as a corporate entity that possesses a complex division of labour and elaborate hierarchy. As ethnographies of gangs in the USA and most recent gang research in the UK appear to show, however, gang life is much more fluid and volatile than this official gang talk suggests (Hagedorn and Macon, 1988; Hallsworth, 2011). Indeed getting your gang recognized by others around you is a social accomplishment that is assiduously worked on by would-be gang members, not least because they often face considerable skepticism on the part of others who may well accuse them of being 'wanabees'.

None of this disputes that entities called gangs exist on the streets of the UK and elsewhere. Indeed, as the American experience has shown, where we find areas of concentrated disadvantage, groups that approximate gangs will take root (see Jankowski, 1991; Brotherton and Barrios, 2004). In the context of the widespread dissemination of a US-based rap culture with its violent aesthetics, the influence of this style with its gang signifiers has certainly made itself felt in the social presentation of the self that many young people adopt. That many would-be rappers mobilize gang imagery in the videos they post on YouTube also helps to confirm the gangland thesis, even though what people do on video and what they do in real life are not necessarily the same.

While it is reasonable to suppose that gang members do use weapons like knives and sometimes guns, engage in the drugs trade and own dogs like pit bull terriers, it could also be noted that other individuals and groups who are not gangs may also carry weapons and use them; that the drug trade is most certainly not controlled by gangs; and that many people who are not gang members choose to own pit bulls or something similar (including the present author). In other words, there is an excess to the violence that is currently attributed to gangs that is not gang related. Unfortunately, by reifying the gang and turning it into a fetish, 'gang talkers' miss such subtlety. Lacking epistemological doubt, they impose on the streets a vision of the gang where this is evoked as literally a 'transcendental evil' that is responsible for every crime. The truth is also most certainly elsewhere.

The lesson to take away from this is that it is important to treat 'gang talk' with caution. Instead of blaming gangs for everything, they need to be studied in relation to the wider street ecology of which they are a part. While any study of this ecology might yield gangs, a more profitable line of enquiry would begin by looking at the wider cultural dynamics of life 'on road' and by also looking at the co-presence within this street world of peer groups who are not gangs and of more organized criminals who do not have such a pronounced street presence.

Simon Hallsworth

Associated Concepts: cultural criminology, moral panic, policy transfer, subculture, zero tolerance

Key Readings

Brotherton, D. and Barrios, L. (2004) *The Almighty Latin King and Queen Nation: Street Politics and the Transformation of a New York City Gang.* New York: Columbia University Press.

Hagedorn, J. and Macon, P. (1988) *People and Folks: Gangs, Crime, and the Underclass in a Rustbelt City.* Chicago, IL: Lake View Press.

Hallsworth, S., (2011) 'Gangland Britain: realites, fantasies and industry', in B. Goldson (ed.), *Youth in Crisis: Gangs Territoriality and Violence.* London: Routledge.

Jankowski, M.S. (1991) *Islands in the Street: Gangs and American Urban Society.* Berkeley: University of California Press.

Klein, M.W. and Maxson, C.L. (2006) *Street Gang Patterns and Policies.* Oxford: Oxford University Press.

Pearson, G. (1983) *Hooligan: A History of Respectable Fears.* London: Macmillan.

Pitts, J. (2008) *Reluctant Gangsters: The Changing Face of Youth Crime.* Cullompton: Willan.

Thrasher, F.M. (1927) *The Gang: A Study of 1313 Gangs in Chicago.* Chicago: University of Chicago Press.

GATED COMMUNITIES

See: Defensible space; Geographies of crime; Situational crime prevention

GENETICS

Definition

A genetics-based criminology concentrates on attempting to identify the biological source or sources of criminal and anti-social behaviour.

Distinctive Features

Genetic determinism, in a variety of forms, has been a constant if largely hidden part of the Western criminological tradition. The best known early genetic approach to criminality was proposed by Cesare Lombroso (1835–1909) as part of his assertion of a positivist criminology that viewed crime as the product of physical and scientifically measurable variables that were beyond the control of the individual. Lombroso developed his theory of 'the criminal type', which depended on the identification of physical characteristics that indicated a biological reversion to a primitive or atavistic stage of evolution. The examination of the skull of a notorious Italian criminal led Lombroso to this discovery: 'At the sight of that skull, I seemed to see all of a sudden, lighted up as a vast plain under a flaming sky, the problem of the nature of the criminal – an atavistic being who reproduces in his person the ferocious instincts of primitive humanity and the inferior animals.' Even though Lombroso subsequently qualified his 'born criminal thesis', the conviction that crime was hereditary generated studies such as those carried out in the USA by Hooton in the 1930s and Sheldon in the 1940s.

It must be noted that the Eugenics movement of the first thirty years of the twentieth century has been largely written out of the history of criminology's flirtation with biology. The origins of Eugenics lie in Darwin's theory of evolutionary progress, and it was defined by its originator, Sir Francis Galton (1822–1911), as 'the study of the agencies under social control that may improve or impair the racial qualities of future generations either physically or mentally'. The Eugenics movement – which both conservatives and progressives adhered to – was obsessed by the fear that those with negative genes, such as for low intelligence, insanity, pauperism and criminality, would swamp the human race. In order to reverse the imminent collapse of Western civilization, this movement argued that the biologically unfit and undeserving should be eliminated or limited in number, and the biologically fit and worthy be encouraged to reproduce. This highly racialized scientific approach to 'social problems as diseases' resulted, in a variety of countries prior to the Second World War, in immigration restrictions, marriage laws, segregation of the mentally and physically handicapped, selective reproduction, and the widespread practice of sterilization. Because the historical research has not been carried out we do not know how many criminologists were involved in the Eugenics movement. Eugenics was ideologically discredited, largely as a result of the Nazis' *Lebensborn* and 'racial self-defence' programmes, which took its core ideas to their logical conclusions.

Human genetics finally emerged as a cleansed discipline in the 1950s and it stayed well away from making pronouncements on controversial social problems such as criminality. This was also the period when sociological explanations of crime were dominant. However, during the 1980s crime was revisited by the sociobiologists and by those researchers who continued to carry out twin and adoption studies. Those presenting papers at controversial conferences on genetics and crime held in the UK and USA during 1995 rejected the search for the 'gene for crime'. However, they also stressed that the research capabilities were now available to enable scientists to untangle the genetic and environmental sources of crime and disorder and identify the temperamental traits and behavioural predispositions that may trigger some individuals to engage in specific forms of criminality and disorder. More recently, there has been renewed speculation that the human genome project will allow scientists to pronounce on the complex ways criminality and disorder are genetically encoded.

Eugene McLaughlin

Associated Concepts: biological criminology, determinism, individual positivism, positivism, racialization

Key Readings

Bock, G.R. and Goode, J. (eds) (1996) *Genetics of Criminal and Anti-Social Behaviour.* Chichester: Wiley.
Burley, J. (1998) *The Genetic Revolution and Human Rights.* Oxford: Oxford University Press.
Jones, S. (1996) *In the Blood.* London: Harper Collins.
Lombroso, C. (ed.) (1911) *Criminal Man According to the Classification of Cesare Lombroso.* New York: Putnam.
Seldon, S. (1999) *Inheriting Shame: The Story of Eugenics and Racism in America.* New York: Teachers College Press.
Wilson, J.Q. and Herrnstein, R. (1985) *Crime and Human Nature.* New York: Simon and Schuster.

GENOCIDE

Definition

Acts organized and committed, in time of peace or war, with the intent to exterminate, in whole or in part, a national, ethnic, racial or religious group. Genocide is distinguishable from all other crimes, including ethnic cleansing, because it is state organized.

Distinctive Features

In 1933, the Polish scholar Raphael Lemkin proposed that an international treaty be agreed to define aggression towards national, ethnic and religious groups as an international crime. In 1944, Lemkin, who was by then an advisor to the United States War Department, coined the term 'genocide' because he believed that the terms 'mass murder' and 'war crimes' were inadequate to the task of describing and explaining what had happened in Nazi Germany. Existing criminal categories could not account for the motive for the crime, that is, acting on the principle that the victim is not human. Lemkin defined genocide as a co-ordinated plan to destroy the essential foundations of the life of national groups, with the aim of annihilating the groups themselves. According to Lemkin, genocide had two phases: first, the destruction of the national pattern of the oppressed group; and second, the imposition of the national pattern of the oppressor. What is significant to note from the original formulation is that physical extermination is only the most extreme form of genocide.

In the aftermath of the Nuremberg war crimes trials, the UN General Assembly adopted a resolution verifying that genocide was the most serious crime against humanity and that it was prohibited under international law irrespective of whether it occurred in peace or war. The 1948 UN Convention on the Prevention and Punishment of the Crime of Genocide defined genocide as 'acts committed with the intent to destroy, in whole or in part, a national, ethnical, racial or religious group'. Genocidal acts include: killing members of the group; causing serious bodily or mental harm to members of the group; deliberately inflicting on the group conditions of life calculated to bring about its destruction in whole or in part; imposing measures intended to prevent births within the group; and forcibly transferring children of the group to another group. The 1948 Convention also outlawed conspiracy to commit genocide, attempts to commit genocide, and complicity in genocide. Crucially, the Convention covers both individual and state responsibility for acts of genocide and imposed a general duty on all signatory states not only to punish but also to prevent and suppress such acts. It ruled that those charged with genocide could be tried by a court in the territory within which the act was committed or by a specially convened international court. To facilitate extradition proceedings between states, genocide was also decreed to be a nonpolitical crime.

As a result of *Realpolitik*, the 1948 Convention settled on a more limited definition of genocide than the one coined by Lemkin. It has been noted, for example, that the categories of 'politically defined groups' and 'economically defined groups' were deliberately omitted from the definition, as was the notion of cultural genocide, namely destroying a group through its compulsory incorporation into a dominant culture. The principle of 'intentionality', which was embedded in the definition, has also been criticized by human rights activists because it allows governments and individuals to argue that their actions were accidental and/or unplanned, happening in the heat of battle.

There was also considerable disagreement about the acts of mass violence that could be covered by the definition. For example, in 1966, the year after General Suharto seized power in Indonesia, the military dictatorship is estimated to have murdered between 500,000 and one million people. After the Indonesian invasion and annexation of East Timor in 1975, an estimated 200,000 out of a total population of 700,000 were killed. During the Khmer Rouge's reign (1975–8) in Cambodia, it is estimated that between one and two million people died in the 'killing fields' as a result of the conditions of state-initiated massacres and prison-based execution programmes. However, the international community argued that these acts did not meet the definition of genocide since both perpetrators and victims were from the same ethnic/racial background. In part the hesitation to define these actions as genocidal also emanated from the desire not to over-use the term and thereby trivialize the nature and meaning of the Holocaust.

In 1993 the first international tribunal was established to prosecute those responsible for committing or ordering serious violations of international humanitarian law, including genocide, in the former Yugoslavia (ITY). A similar tribunal was established in 1994 for Rwanda (ITR) to investigate the murder of 800,000 people, mostly in the Tutsi minority, by the Hutu majority. Both tribunals had to develop rules of procedure and establish principles to define the exact criminal nature of what had happened. In August 1998, the ITR produced a landmark decision in the history of international criminal law when it found Jean Kambanda, Rwanda's former Prime Minister, guilty of the crime of genocide. During 2000 the ITY heard the first charges of genocide to come before it. The indictment of senior officers of the Bosnian Serb army represented a breakthrough in international criminal law because it established that there was evidence that senior politicians and military leaders had planned the massacre of 7,000–8,000 Bosnian Muslims in the UN 'safe haven' of Srebrenica in 1995.

In 1998, 120 nation-states signed a resolution calling for the establishment of a permanent International Criminal Court (ICC) with the power and organizational capacity to investigate and prosecute genocide, war crimes and crimes against humanity. The court came into existence in 2002 but without recognition or ratification by numerous nation-states, including China, India, Israel and the USA. In order to establish its credibility, the new court will certainly have to end the 'culture of immunity' that was the hallmark of the twentieth century and establish punishments that are deemed to be appropriate to such criminality.

Eugene McLaughlin

Associated Concepts: crimes against humanity, critical research, denial, extraterritorial law enforcement, forensic anthropology, hate crime, human rights, obedience (crimes of), political crime, the state, state crime, transnational policing, torture

Key Readings

Ball, H. (1999) *Prosecuting War Crimes and Genocide: The Twentieth Century Experience.* Lawrence, KS: University of Kansas Press.
Destexhe, A. (1995) *Rwanda and Genocide in the Twentieth Century.* New York: New York University Press.
Gourevitch, P. (2000) *We Wish to Inform You that Tomorrow We Will Be Killed With Our Families.* London: Picador.
Honig, J.W. and Both, N. (1996) *Srebrenicia: Record of a War Crime.* Harmondsworth: Penguin.
Jonassohn, K. (1998) *Genocide and Gross Human Rights Violations.* Plymouth: Transaction.

GEOGRAPHIES OF CRIME

Definition

These address the complex of relationships constructed through crime, space and place.

Distinctive Features

Cartographic schools of criminology were established in various European countries during the nineteenth century, most notably in Belgium by Adolphe Quetelet (1796–1874) and in France by A.M. Guerry. Maps were drawn to plot regional patterns of crime, compare rural and urban differences, and survey the relationship between crime and other socioeconomic conditions. In an allied development, in England observational studies were undertaken within the newly industrialized cities by Mayhew and Booth to identify and examine 'criminal areas' such as the 'rookeries' of London. Many of these early surveys were undertaken to further the case for social and moral reform. An ecological approach to the study of urban crime was more fully developed by the Chicago School of social research during the 1920s. The guiding principle of the Chicago School was that cities were living organisms, composed of interconnected parts, and the task of researchers was to understand how each part related to the overall structure of the city and the other parts. The zonal theory of city growth developed by Robert Park and Ernest Burgess enabled them to map the contours of crime more precisely and to offer an explanation as to why crime was concentrated in the zone of transition. Clifford Shaw and Henry McKay used this conceptual framework to construct their path-breaking study of the relationship between juvenile delinquency, gang membership, and urban social disorganization. Versions of the ecological model and methodologies developed by the Chicago School dominated studies of urban crime undertaken between the 1920s and 1960s in cities across the United States and Europe.

As a result of theoretical and methodological developments in the 1980s and 1990s, environmental criminologies have given way to research on how crime is spatialized. A new generation of criminologists from a variety of disciplinary backgrounds became interested in theorizing the complex human public interactions and relationships associated with living in 'the city'. Contemporary spatial approaches to the study of crime can be grouped into four broad research areas:

- Studies concerned with identifying the spatial distribution of crime, criminogenic localities, vulnerable areas, defended spaces and sites of contestation and resistance.
- Studies of how and why the risk of crime victimization is distributed over space, and the differential risks within and between different localities and various sections of the population.
- Studies of how and why the fear of crime is spatialized. This involves analysing the public's perception of where the crime problem is located, and working through their mental mappings of safe and dangerous places.
- Studies of the flow and movement of particular crimes such as drugs and prostitution between different localities and countries.

Evaluation

Geographical research on crime and criminality has continued to play a central role in the development of crime prevention programmes, ranging from situational crime prevention strategies such as target hardening and crime prevention through to environmental design (CPED). The underlying premise of these crime prevention efforts is that the proper design and utilization of the built environment in conjunction with new surveillance technologies can lead to a reduction in the fear and incidence of crime and an improvement in the quality of urban life. *De facto* spatial policing is also taking place through the privatization of public space and the development of gated or 'crime-proof' communities. Sophisticated crime mapping techniques such as geographic information systems (GIS) are also a logical, if controversial, outcome of spatial research into crime 'hotspots' (places where according to a

variety of statistics the opportunities for certain forms of crime are highest). GIS consist of specialist database management systems, spatial analysis packages and sophisticated computer mapping systems which facilitate 'geocoded' proximity analysis, spatial clustering analysis and spatial correlation procedures. It is these features that have made GIS an invaluable tool not only for mapping crime 'hotspots' but also for analysing crime trends and managing criminal investigations.

Eugene McLaughlin

Associated Concepts: Chicago School of Sociology, defensible space, fear of crime, situational crime prevention, social ecology, surveillance, victimology

Key Readings

Cohen, J. (1941) 'The geography of crime', *Annals of the American Academy of Political and Social Sciences*, 217: 29–37.

Fyfe, N. (2001) *Geography of Crime and Policing*. Oxford: Blackwell.

Grescoe, T. (1996) 'The geography of crime', *Geographical Magazine*, 9: 26–7.

Hirschfield, A., Brown, P. and Todd, P. (1995) 'GIS and the analysis of spatially referenced crime data: experiences in Merseyside UK', *International Journal of Geographical Information Systems*, 9 (2): 191–210.

Longley, P.A., Goodchild, M., Maguire, D. and Rhind, D.W. (1999) *Geographical Information Systems*. London: Wiley.

McLaughlin, E. and Muncie, J. (1999) 'Walled cities: surveillance, regulation and segregation', in S. Pile, C. Brook and G. Mooney (eds), *Unruly Cities*. London: Routledge.

GLOBAL CRIMINOLOGY

Definition

The term 'global criminology' denotes an evolving body of work which seeks to examine the value of criminology for understanding the scope and complex nature of globalization and transnational interconnectedness. The term cannot be taken to imply that criminology as a social science has become global in its scope. Rather it indicates methodological, theoretical and ethical attempts to move criminological scholarship beyond the established national boundaries.

Distinctive Features

Globalization itself is by no means a novel phenomenon, but has long historic antecedents and has been described as a key feature of modernity. However, due to the growing technological, economic, cultural and other social developments, we have in recent decades witnessed an intensification of cross-border connections. Global perspectives within criminology aim to examine the nature of these interconnections as they pertain to the studies of crime, punishment and social control. Seeking to develop a more globally conscious research imagination, global perspectives tend to be based on a more or less explicit critique of the predominant ethnocentric outlook within criminology and the so-called methodological nationalist framework (Aas, 2007). They challenge the assumption about nation-states as containers of social processes and demand transcendence of the traditional, inward-looking, analytical and conceptual frameworks which are principally based on nation-states (Sassen, 2007).

Transnational perspectives within criminology point out that many of the contemporary security challenges have become transnational rather than being simply international, and demand a simultaneous view of global, national and local levels. Local harms and security issues are often a product of a long chain of geographically dispersed and unbounded events and actions, where global economic flows are intertwined with environmental issues, cultural struggles and the politics of everyday security and peace. The spatially distributed nature of contemporary threats is partly captured by Ulrich Beck's concept of the 'world risk society' which, despite what is commonly assumed, does not

arise from the fact that everyday life has generally become more dangerous. It is not a matter of the increase, but rather of *de-bounding* of uncontrollable risks (see Beck in Aas, 2007).

Thematically, criminological studies of transnational connections take up a number of topics. In addition to the historically well-established field of transnational organized crime, the past three decades have seen a growing interest in issues of comparative justice, migration and evolving systems of policing, as well as in topics such as human rights, environmental crime and justice, terrorism, genocide and crimes against humanity, peace-building, and transitional justice. Through its international outlook, global criminology examines the emergence of the international criminal justice institutions and the mechanisms for the global governance of crime (Crawford, 2011). Particularly in our post-9/11 climate, the issues of transnational crime have moved centre stage in global and national political and security debates (Findlay, 2008). We are thus witnessing an intensification of international, state-sponsored law enforcement and criminal justice missions, in addition to a growing private market of transnational security consultants and companies (Bowling, 2010). Several observers have also noted a blurring of the traditional boundaries between internal and external security, policing and military tasks, and ultimately also between crime control and warfare.

It should be noted however that global perspectives within criminology examine more than the obviously transnational categories, such as international terrorism, the International Criminal Court or international police and justice missions – issues which seem to be safely placed outside of or above the nation-state. More importantly, they turn their focus on processes which cut across the established categories of the national and local and attempt to discover how globalization processes can be both 'rooted and rootless', embedded in local (or better, 'glocal') settings and performed by situated actors. The impact of the intensified migratory flows on criminal justice is therefore to be found not only in the renewed salience of human trafficking and smuggling, but also in the growing ethnic diversity of local neighbourhoods and the changing compositions of the national prison populations, as well as in the expanding use of deportation and immigration detention. Globalization therefore entails not only openly global phenomena, but also demands that attention is paid to local and national nuances, processes and adaptations. Nor does global interconnectedness necessarily mean convergence and sameness. To take crime policy as an example, an analysis of penal policy transfers reveals that how internationally exported policies such as 'zero tolerance' travel can by no means be predicted from the outset; instead these need to be examined in the national context. Zero tolerance can mean very different policing practices when applied in New York, Oslo, London or Mexico City (Aas, 2007).

Evaluation

One of the challenges for transnational perspectives is that a by now thriving criminology of globalization has not necessarily implied globalization of criminology as a discipline. Criminology is still by and large a discipline of the West, whereby most of its research and publishing activities are located in the countries of the global North, particularly in the USA and the UK. This global inequality in the field of knowledge production raises a question about how well equipped criminology's theoretical and analytical arsenal is to capture and analyse Southern realities. Critics have therefore pointed out that criminology's theoretical perspectives may be misleading when applied universally, on a global level, just as Western crime models have been critiqued for their harm-producing effects when exported transnationally (Bowling, 2010). It remains to be seen how transnational criminology will address the inequalities and asymmetries inscribed into the discipline and whether it will evolve into a truly global field of study.

Katja Franko Aas

Associated Concepts: comparative criminology and criminal justice, corporate crime, cybercrime, eco-crime, genocide, globalization, human trafficking, post-colonial criminology, terrorism, transnational organized crime, transnational policing, war crimes

Key Readings

Aas, K.F. (2007) *Globalization and Crime*. London: Sage.
Bowling, B. (2010) *Policing the Caribbean: Transnational Security Cooperation in Practice*. Oxford: Oxford University Press.
Crawford, A. (ed.) (2011) *International and Comparative Criminal Justice and Urban Governance: Convergence and Divergence in Global, National and Local Settings*. Cambridge: Cambridge University Press.
Findlay, M. (2008) *Governing through Globalized Crime: Futures for International Criminal Justice*. Cullompton: Willan.
Sassen, S. (2007) *A Sociology of Globalization*. New York: Norton.
Sheptycki, J. and Wardak, A. (2005) *Transnational and Comparative Criminology*. London: Glasshouse.

GLOBALIZATION

Definition

A widely, but often loosely, used term which usually implies an increasing homogeneity of national economics, politics and culture. Such convergence is assumed to be driven in the main by international flows of de-regulated capital, information and people, and dominated by multinational, neo-liberal economics and technologies.

Distinctive Features

There appears to be a widely held view that in the twenty-first century the world is changing faster than ever before. Both academically and popularly many of these changes are considered to be associated with 'globalization'. Put simply, goods, money and information, as well as crime, pollution, drugs and disease, now routinely travel the world, and that world appears to be more interconnected: events and decisions made in one part will have repercussions throughout the rest. Global multi-national corporations and financial markets now seem to provide the economic, political and cultural parameters within which we live. The sovereignty of individual nation-states and the authority of traditional social institutions also seem to be increasingly redundant in the face of such powerful forces (Nelken, 1997).

Despite widespread acceptance of such notions, the meaning and implications of globalization remain subject to intense debate. The concept is often used interchangeably with other competing macro-concepts such as *transnationalization* (the dissolving of national boundaries), *supranationalization* (transcending national limits), *internationalization* (exchanges of capital and labour), *universalization* (the spread of information and cultural phenomena worldwide), *neo-liberalization* (the removal of regulatory barriers to international exchange/transfer), *Westernization* (standardization driven by advanced industrial economies), *Anglo-Americanization* (homogenization, driven by a USA/UK alliance), or indeed *modernization* (the diffusion of managerial economics). Disputes also emerge over the question of whether globalization is anything new at all, or simply a modern version of *colonization*. The power of globalization as an analytical concept appears seductive but also dangerous and flawed. It is seductive because it seems to offer some valuable means through which sense can be made of macro-shifts in economics, politics and culture; it is flawed and dangerous because it encourages the tendency to deliver reductionist and economistic readings of social change such that the endless expansion of unregulated capitalist relations appears unchallengeable (Yeates, 2001).

Can it then be expected to help us in any way to understand contemporary transformations in crime and crime control? An emergent and growing fear is that global flows of money, people and information are providing the perfect conditions and opportunities for organized crime to flourish. Criminal enterprises such as the Sicilian Mafia, Chinese triads, Colombian drug cartels, the mafias of Russia and eastern Europe, the Jamaican Yardies and so on are assumed to have made widespread profits in human rights violations, such as the trafficking of drugs, animals, arms and humans, as well as in international pornography and prostitution and computer fraud. A vision of criminality out of control has burgeoned since 9/11 and particularly with the threat of international terrorism. The idea that crime no longer has any boundaries is widespread, as is the notion that the criminal-law enforcement practices of individual nation-states are no longer able to contain it. Transnational organized crime, it is contended, requires an equally transnational policing and criminal justice response.

Globalization implies two interrelated transformations that are of particular interest to those studying systems of criminal justice. First, criminal justice policies are converging world-wide (and particularly so across the Anglophone global North). The necessity of attracting international capital and of fighting international crime compels governments to adopt similar economic, social and criminal justice policies. Second, such homogenization appears to be underpinned by a fundamental shift in state/market relations whereby neo-liberal conceptions of the 'free market' driven by multi-national corporations encourage the formulation of policies based less on principles of accountability, welfare protection and social inclusion, and more on social inequality, deregulation, privatization and authoritarianism. The American-led 'war on drugs' and 'war on terror' are often taken as prime examples of such international developments.

Evaluation

Understanding the role of globalization in processes of international and national criminal justice reform is in its infancy. But it is already clear that the argument that criminal justice has become a global product can only be sustained at the very highest level of generality. Globalization inevitably draws our attention to macro-political and economic determinants. The dangers of over-generalization and neglect of local variance abound. First, globalization is not one-dimensional. International policy transfers, international criminal courts and United Nations conventions and treaties may offer some progressive alternatives to a free market multi-national globalization. Economic globalism speaks of the import, largely US-inspired, of neo-liberal conceptions of community responsibilization backed by an authoritarian state. However, legal globalism, largely UN-inspired, unveils a contrary vision of universal human rights delivered through social democracies. Second, the idea that global capital is hegemonic and capable of transforming all that it touches is both essentialist and determinist. There are discrete and distinctive ways in which neo-liberalism finds expression in conservative and social democratic *rationalities* and in authoritarian, retributive, human rights, responsibilizing or restorative *technologies* (O'Malley, 2002). The effect of globalization is neither uniform nor consistent. Diversity in criminal justice reform warns against any attempt to imply homogeneity. Rather the global is only realized in specific localities and it is through these that it will inevitably be reworked, challenged and contested. The key issue to be addressed may not be how globalization is producing uniformity but how it is activating diversity (Nelken, 1997).

Individual nation-states are undoubtedly being challenged by global processes, but analysis at the level of the nation-state may also be limited and limiting. Regional governments, federated states, international cities and multiple forms of community governance all suggest alternative visions of statehood and citizenship and offer alternative routes of access to decision making on social and economic issues. As Robertson (1995) and Bauman (1998) have tried to capture in the notion of 'glocalization', global neo-liberal pressures are always mediated, and can only be realized through local identities and sensibilities. Globalization can only ever be one amongst many influences on policy and even then its influence may push and pull in diverse ways *at the same time*. Global/national/local are not exclusive entities: the key issue is how they interact and are experienced differently in different spaces and at different times.

Because the concept of globalization has been applied predominantly to transformations in western and Anglophone countries, our understanding of global processes (and the role of criminology in making sense of such transformations) might itself also be considered to be peculiarly ethnocentric (Chan, 2000). Further work in this area needs to be carefully attuned to ongoing processes of multiplicity (as well as uniformity), divergence (as well as convergence) and contingency (as well as determinism), not only in understanding global crime and criminal justice but also in examining the role of criminology in perpetuating particular criminological ideas. Acknowledging hybridity and recognizing multiple lines of invention, contestation and contradiction are some of the key challenges facing future global criminological research.

John Muncie

Associated Concepts: global criminology, governance, human rights, human trafficking, policy transfer, state crime, terrorism, transnational organized crime, transnational policing

Key Readings

Bauman, Z. (1998) *Globalisation: The Human Consequences*. Cambridge: Polity.

Chan, J. (2000) 'Globalisation, reflexivity and the practice of criminology', *Australian and New Zealand Journal of Criminology*, 33 (2): 118–35.

Nelken, D. (1997) 'The globalisation of crime and criminal justice', *Current Legal Problems*, 50: 251–77.

O'Malley, P. (2002) 'Globalising risk? Distinguishing styles of neo-liberal criminal justice in Australia and the USA', *Criminal Justice*, 2 (2): 205–22.

Robertson, R. (1995) 'Glocalisation: time-space and homogeneity-heterogeneity', in M. Featherstone, S. Lash and R. Robertson (eds), *Global Modernities*. London: Sage.

Yeates, N. (2001) *Globalisation and Social Policy*. London: Sage.

GOVERNANCE

Definition

The concept of governance is regarded as having a number of uses in contemporary political theory to signify 'a change in the meaning of government, referring to a *new* process of governing; or a *changed* condition of ordered rule; or the *new* method by which society is governed' (Rhodes, 1997: 46, emphasis in original). In criminological thought, governance has been used to signify changes in the control of crime and to acknowledge other cognate objects of control such as incivility, harm, safety and security.

Distinctive Features

The principal feature of this concept, for both its advocates and critics, is its break with state-centred thinking about the exercise of political power. Power is not possessed by a sovereign, as in Thomas Hobbes' image of Leviathan's sword, to be wielded over civil society. Preference is given to a Machiavellian conception of political authority as the tenuous, unresolved outcome of struggles between coalitions of public and private, formal and informal, actors. These struggles are rooted in the central paradox of power: when actors possess the potential to govern they are not powerful because they are not actually governing, but neither are they powerful when they seek to govern because they are dependent on others to carry out their commands (Clegg, 1989: 201ff). From this paradox certain implications follow for the process, condition and method of governing problems such as crime and for the re-definition of objects of control.

The recognition of this paradox implies a new process of governing through negotiation, bargaining and other relationships of exchange rather than through command, coercion or normative appeals for support. In order to accomplish and sustain political authority, would-be sovereigns have to appreciate their 'power-dependence' on other actors and recruit and retain sufficient supporters to maintain a governing coalition

(Rhodes, 1997: 8–9). A criminological exemplar of this is the attempt to control crime through partnerships of statutory, commercial and voluntary organizations (Crawford, 1997). The multi-agency approach has accompanied official recognition of the limits to the state's capacity to reduce crime, in particular the insufficiency of criminal justice and the consequent need to enrol expertise and resources from non-state actors including the 'responsibilization' of private citizens for their own security (Garland, 2001).

Governance has also been used to describe a changed condition of rule in advanced liberal polities in which power is exercised through 'self-organizing, inter-organizational networks' as contrasted with the mechanisms of command and control through bureaucracies (Rhodes, 1997: 15, 47). Polities, it is argued, are consequently fragmenting into a plurality of competing centres of power with no single actor able to exercise overall control across a given territory. For some commentators, this fragmentation has reached such an intensity that it represents the emergence of a new 'post-Westphalian' political order in which sovereign states can no longer be regarded, as in the Treaty of Westphalia (1648), as having exclusive authority within their own geographical borders. In criminological thought, the notion of 'security networks' has been proposed as an alternative to policing and criminal justice in order to acknowledge both the devolution and privatization of functions previously undertaken by statutory agencies and the *concurrent* existence of private governments, from corporations through to vigilante groups and indeed criminal organizations, who seek to exercise control over certain populations (Johnston and Shearing, 2003). From this perspective, the Westphalian image of the sovereign state has always been a misrepresentation of the actual practice of governing. A more anthropological conception identifies the omnipresent plurality of competing orders or 'nodes of governance' rather than any neat correspondence between a single sovereign authority and a national geographical territory (Johnston and Shearing, 2003: 145–51).

The post-Westphalian condition of governance is one in which the diverse contexts of control, the multifarious governable places in which power is exercised, are recognized (Smandych, 1999). This has important implications for comparative criminology which has tended to treat the contexts of crime and control as synonymous with the national cultures and institutions of criminal law enforcement. Nodal governance entails an understanding of the organization of control within different territories, such as sub-national localities and regional governments, or in supra-national realms such as the European Union. It also focuses attention on cross-border territories such as those instituted by the North American Free Trade Area (NAFTA) or the Eurozone. Recognition is given as well to private governable places such as shopping-malls, commercial aircraft, religious communities and the extra-territorial cyberspace. Appreciating the diverse spatial scales at which control is organized implies sensitivity towards the different temporalities of governance. For example, the electoral cycles for municipal, regional and national assemblies are not coterminous in many polities and this often generates competing mandates and conflicts between national, sub-national and, in Europe, supra-national authorities of varying political persuasion. Such contextual factors are of concern to criminology when explaining the different pace of reform and the transferability of innovations in strategies of control. They alert criminological thought to the geo-histories of control and how these are shaped by the political, economic and cultural trajectories of different governable places (Stenson and Edwards, 2003).

Beyond any belated recognition of limits to the sovereign nation state, the post-Westphalian condition entails real changes and innovations in the methods of governing. To attenuate the problem of power-dependence in a fragmented polity and further consolidate governing coalitions, would-be sovereigns will experiment with techniques for governing at a distance. The exemplar of this in contemporary administration is the use of performance indicators to engineer compliance with set objectives. Performance management replaces direct command and control with the discipline of episodic audits, the outcomes of which can result in various, often fiscal, rewards and penalties. In these terms the offer of financial support and threat of withdrawing such support will act as a bargaining tool for retaining the membership of certain actors within a network. In this way, national authorities can drive through reforms to police, probation and prison services and to their interrelationship with cognate policy actors, such as health professionals, education authorities, housing managers and employment agencies.

The idea of 'joined-up' government to attack multi-faceted and complex problems, such as youth offending through multi-agency partnerships employing a broad spectrum of social policy interventions, represents a definite break with the methods of modern public administration. It challenges the specialization of government into discrete areas of functional expertise and, in so doing, defines new objects of governance. Youth offending, for example, ceases to be defined only in terms of 'criminality' and subject to the expertise of criminal justice professionals; it also becomes a problem of education and health as well as, in the argot of the New Labour administration in Britain, one of 'social exclusion' and 'anti-social behaviour'.

Evaluation

Such processes of re-definition or 'problematization' reflect the core insight of governmentality studies with which the concept of governance has an affinity: that governors have to render their objects thinkable as a prerequisite of governing them (Smandych, 1999). To this end the new processes, methods and changed condition of governing implied by governance also act to redefine the scope of criminological enquiry beyond that artefact of criminal law, 'crime', and towards other notions of order and well-being. In turn, and insofar as 'harm', 'safety' or 'security' are defined as the objects of control, in which conventional notions of crime are submerged, criminology itself is challenged as a means of understanding order and justice by other intellectual instruments, such as political science, sociology, anthropology, risk management and social policy.

Discussion of the concept of governance and its impact on the study of crime and control emphasizes the political character of criminology. Notions of harm, safety, incivility, security and so on are not simply competing labels signifying the same thing. They embody certain normative judgements and interests in how the human condition and threats to it should be understood. It is to be expected, therefore, that this discussion entails controversy over the meaning and consequences of governance for crime control.

Central to current arguments over governance is the continued relevance of sovereign power. It may be that sovereignty is being reformulated rather than simply delimited or even superseded by nodal governance (Garland, 2001; Johnston and Shearing, 2003; Stenson and Edwards, 2003). Polities are constituted through relations of power-dependence, because of the paradoxical nature of power, but it is equally implausible to argue that state executives can never intervene effectively within their geographical territories or that they do not continually struggle with constraints upon the scope of such intervention: 'there is "asymmetric interdependence" ... Fragmentation and centralization coexist. There is a persistent tension between the wish for authoritative action and dependence on the compliance and actions of others' (Rhodes, 1997: 15). Exploring this tension – how it generates dilemmas and contradictions in the accomplishment of control and drives the politics of law and order beyond the relatively narrow confines of criminal justice – provides a critical challenge for, and to, criminological thought.

Adam Edwards

Associated Concepts: governmentality, multi-agency crime prevention, policing, responsibilization, risk

Key Readings

Clegg, S. (1989) *Frameworks of Power*. London: Sage.
Crawford, A. (1997) *The Local Governance of Crime: Appeals to Community and Partnerships*. Oxford: Clarendon Press.
Garland, D. (2001) *The Culture of Control*. Oxford: Oxford University Press.
Johnston, L. and Shearing, C. (2003) *Governing Security: Explorations in Policing and Justice*. London: Routledge.
Rhodes, R.A.W. (1997) *Understanding Governance: Policy Networks, Governance, Reflexivity and Accountability*. Buckingham: Open University Press.
Smandych, R. (ed.) (1999) *Governable Places: Readings on Governmentality and Crime Control*. Aldershot: Ashgate.
Stenson, K. and Edwards, A. (2003) 'Crime control and local governance: the struggle for sovereignty in advanced liberal polities', *Contemporary Politics*, 9: 203–17.

GOVERNMENTALITY

Definition

The term applies to the characteristically 'modern' form of government that governs each individual and the 'population' through apparatuses of security (police, courts, health and welfare departments, etc.). It also refers to an approach that focuses on the intellectual, linguistic and technical ways in which phenomena are constituted by government as governable problems. It is primarily in the latter sense that governmentality has a place in criminology.

Distinctive Features

Studying social relations from the point of view of governmentality means focusing on governance as a mentality or rationality of rule, stressing that phenomena have to be intellectually and linguistically represented as a certain kind of problem in order for them to be governed. For example, Simon

(1997) has argued that American society is increasingly being 'governed through crime', as more and more matters are represented as problems of 'criminality' and its effects, to be governed through criminal justice, crime prevention and so on. In turn, governmentality characteristically examines how such 'problematizations' are linked to practicable techniques for achieving their government. For example, crime is said to be more and more governed through risk. This marginalizes therapeutic or punitive techniques for governing offenders, and valorizes such techniques as crime prevention, offender incapacitation and victim compensation and 'empowerment' (O'Malley, 1998). Governmentality thus focuses on questions of how government is planned as a practical exercise. Typical research has examined such issues as: how are the nature of offenders and the mainsprings of crime re-imagined when we move from welfare states to neo-liberal government? How is this change linked to changes in the types of sanction that are deployed to deal with crime? What new 'problems' of crime emerge – for example: how to make potential victims more active in securing themselves and their property against crime. And how to make police more 'responsive' to public demands for security.

Governmentality also assumes the dispersal of governance in contemporary societies. 'The state' becomes merely one site – or, rather, a complex of sites – in which government is located. Governmentality work has examined how the government of crime is practised, not simply by police and the criminal justice 'system' but also by the insurance industry, communities, potential victims, shopping centre managers and so on. Such work, it can be witnessed, avoids explanation, especially where this reduces government to a reflex of some other force, such as class interests or post-modernity. Rather, government is seen to be 'assembled' from available intellectual and material resources – and so is regarded as humanly contingent rather than theoretically determined. Governmental accounts are also characterized by a refusal

to subject government to critique, rather seeing such evaluation as internal to government itself. These characteristics reflect a methodological suspension or denial of truth judgements – for understanding how government 'makes up' its truths is a key object of analysis. Governmentality denies an accessible 'real truth' from which critique and explanation are mounted.

Evaluation

Governmentality is an influential but still inchoate approach and there are debates among its adherents about its nature and purpose (O'Malley et al., 1997). Consequently, commenting upon its strengths and shortcomings is subject to dispute. However, on the positive side, it has provided original and incisive analyses of the government of crime, especially as this is related to risk techniques and neo-liberal politics. Perhaps this is because it breaks away from highly abstract theorizations and focuses instead on detailed configurations of rule. Perhaps too it is because the refusal to engage in critique has generated a kind of non-committed analytic that has opened up many new insights. However, these possible sources of strength are also its most criticized features.

One of the most contentious features is its focus on the 'ideal knowledges' or mentalities of governance, rather than on 'what actually happens'. For many critics of this aspect of governmentality, it is 'essential to explore the real practices and processes in which these programs and rationalities and technologies are selectively and sometimes unexpectedly used, with all their compromised formations and unintended effects' (Garland, 1997). For some governmentality writers, however, this descends into a familiar, realist, sociological terrain, one that is unlikely to provide the resources to think beyond what already exists and – perhaps ironically – to destabilize rule. For others, however, this exercise may be essential, as part of the process of understanding government's key characteristic of failure.

Another contested feature is governmentality's rejection of 'critique'. Some criticize governmentality because it does not allow commentators to identify how malfunctioning institutions can be reformed, how authorities' explanations of crime are wrong, how and why programmes fail and so on (e.g. Garland, 1997). One response would argue that this criticism fails to escape the problematic of government – for like government, it sets for itself the task of making us into something else, to govern us better, on the basis of a superior regime of truth. This process of displaying the truth claims of government, and their contingent nature, is the operation of a 'diagnosis' that displaces critique within governmentality. Diagnosis focuses on the question of 'how not to be governed thus?', rather than on that of 'how can we best be governed?' Whether this is nihilistic, or promotes the contestation of government, is the key evaluative issue; but it involves a political rather than methodological choice.

Pat O'Malley

Associated Concepts: discourse analysis, governance, managerialism, post-structuralism, risk, security, social constructionism

Key Readings

Dean, M. (1999) *Governmentality: Power and Rule in Modern Society*. London: Sage.

Garland, D. (1997) '"Governmentality" and the problem of crime', *Theoretical Criminology*, 1: 173–214.

O'Malley, P. (ed.) (1998) *Crime and the Risk Society*. Aldershot: Dartmouth.

O'Malley, P., Weir, L. and Shearing, C. (1997) 'Governmentality, criticism, politics', *Economy and Society*, 26: 501–17.

Rose, N. (1999) *Powers of Freedom*. Cambridge: Cambridge University Press.

Simon, J. (1997) 'Governing through crime', in G. Fisher and L. Friedman (eds), *The Crime Conundrum: Essays on Criminal Justice*. Boulder, CO: Westview Press.

GREEN CRIMINOLOGY

Definition

The term 'green criminology' emerged in the early 1990s to describe a critical and sustained approach to the study of environmental crime. Green criminology broadly refers to the study by criminologists of environmental harms (that may incorporate wider definitions of crime than those provided in strictly legal definitions), environmental laws (including enforcement, prosecution and sentencing practices), and environmental regulation (systems of civil and criminal law that are designed to manage, protect and preserve specified environments and species, and to manage the negative consequences of particular industrial processes).

Distinctive Features

The key focus of green criminology is environmental crime. This is conceptualized in several different ways within the broad framework of green criminology. For some writers, environmental crime is defined narrowly within strict legal definitions – it is what the law says it is. For others, environmental harm is itself deemed to be a (social and ecological) crime, regardless of legal status – if harm is done to environments or animals, then this ought to be considered a 'crime' from the point of view of the critical criminologist.

The kinds of harms and crimes studied within green criminology include the illegal trade in endangered species (such as, for example, the trade in exotic birds or killing of elephants for their ivory tusks), the illegal harvesting of 'natural resources' (such as illegal fishing and illegal logging), and the illegal disposal of toxic substances (as well as the pollution of air, land and water). Wider definitions of environmental crime extend the scope of analysis to consider harms associated with legal activities such as the clearfelling of old growth forests and the negative ecological consequences of new technologies such as the use of genetically modified organisms in agriculture (e.g., a reduction to biodiversity through the extensive planting of GMO corn). Recent work has considered the criminological aspects of climate change, from the point of view of human contributions to global warming (e.g., carbon emissions from coal-fired power plants) and the criminality associated with the aftermath of natural disasters (e.g., incidents of theft and rape in the wake of Hurricane Katrina in New Orleans).

Environmental victimization is considered from the point of view of transgressions against humans, specific bio-spheres or environments, and nonhuman animals. This is conceptualized in terms of three broad areas of analytical interest: *environmental justice* (where the main focus is on differences within the human population: social justice demands access to healthy and safe environments for all, and for future generations); *ecological justice* (where the main focus is on 'the environment' as such, and where to conserve and protect ecological well-being, for example forests, is seen as intrinsically worthwhile); and *species justice* (where the main focus is on ensuring the wellbeing of both species as a whole, such as whales or polar bears, and individual animals, which should be shielded from abuse, degradation and torture).

There are several ways in which one can analyse issues pertaining to environmental regulation and the prevention of environmental harm. One approach is to chart the existing environmental legislation and provide a sustained socio-legal analysis of specific breaches of the law, the role of environmental law enforcement agencies, and the difficulties and opportunities of using criminal law against environmental offenders. Another approach places the emphasis on social regulation as the key mechanism to prevent and curtail environmental harm, including attempts to reform existing systems of production and consumption through a constellation of measures and by bringing non-government and community groups directly into the regulatory process. A third approach presses the need for transnational activism, with the focus on fundamental social change. What counts is engaging in strategies that will challenge the dominant authority structures and those modes of production that are linked to environmental degradation and destruction, negative transformations of Nature, species decline and threats to biodiversity. Social movements are seen to be vital in dealing with instances of gross environmental harm.

The development of green criminology has led to new interests, new conceptualizations and new techniques of analysis. This is because there is an increasing acknowledgement of environmental problems and the relevance of this to traditional criminological concerns with social injury and social regulation. There is also greater awareness of the inter-connectedness of social and environmental issues; for example, matters relating to poverty, health, indigenous people's rights, the exploitation of non-human nature, corporate business wrongdoing, state corruption and so on are seen in many instances to be inseparable. In addition, there is recognition of the need for multi-disciplinary approaches to the study of environmental harm, involving co-operation between different 'experts', including those with a traditional and experiential knowledge that is associated with culture and livelihood (such as indigenous peoples, and farmers and fishers), as well as a sensitivity towards ideas and research generated in intellectual domains such as the law, police studies, political science, international relations, zoology, biology, philosophy, sociology and chemistry.

These kinds of observations and interrelationships are forcing a re-think of the social and natural universe, and a re-conceptualization of the relationship between humans and Nature in ways that give greater weight to the non-human when it comes to assessing issues such as environmental harm. In practical terms, this translates into new and over-lapping domains of consideration within green criminology itself: hence the concern with transgressions against humans, environments and animals.

Evaluation

Green criminology has emerged in the last twenty years as a distinctive area of research, scholarship and intervention. It is distinctive in the sense that it has directed much greater attention towards environmental crime and harm than mainstream criminology and has heightened awareness of emergent issues, such as the problems arising from the disposal of electronic waste (e-waste) and the social and ecological injustices linked to the corporate colonization of Nature (including biopiracy and the imposition of GMO crops on developing countries).

While the link between and among green criminologists is the focus on environmental issues, important theoretical and political differences are nonetheless becoming more apparent over time. For example, some would argue that green criminology must necessarily be anti-capitalist and exhibit a broad radical orientation. Others, however, would construe the task as one of conservation and natural resource management within the definitional limits of existing laws. Still others would promote the idea that the direction for such research should be global and ecological, and that new concepts need to be developed that will better capture the nature and dynamics of environmental harms in the twenty-first century.

Typically there are differences within green criminology around issues pertaining to the distinction between 'harm' and 'crime'. These differences do not stem solely from disputes over the legal/illegal divide however. There are also profound disagreements with regard to victimization and varying conceptions of justice. For instance, there may be differences *within* a particular area of work, such as debates over 'animal rights' versus 'animal welfare' in the case of concerns about species justice. There are also disagreements in terms of priorities, values and decision making *between* particular areas of green criminology. This is evident, for example, in debates over multiple land-use areas. This kind of dispute can involve those who would argue that human interests should come first (from the perspective of environmental justice), or that specific ecological niches be protected (from the perspective of ecological justice), even if some animals have to be killed or removed from a specific geographical location. From the point of view of species justice, however, big questions can be asked regarding the intrinsic rights of animals and the duty of humans to provide care and protection for nonhuman species.

The hallmark of green criminology, regardless of this diversity of opinion and plurality of views, is that proponents argue that criminology ought to take environmental crimes seriously, and in doing so should rethink how it does what it does, and how it might conceptualize the relevant issues. It is interesting in this respect that a number of prominent criminologists are now utilizing their expertise from mainstream areas of criminology (e.g., situational crime prevention, general strain theory) to study environmental issues specifically, such as the illegal trade in elephant tusks and social problems arising from climate change. Green criminology is not only expanding in its own right, but also simultaneously there is a greening of criminology more generally.

Rob White

Associated Concepts: animal abuse, corporate crime, crime, critical criminology, eco-crime, social harm

Key Readings

Beirne, P. and South, N. (eds) (2007) *Issues in Green Criminology: Confronting Harms Against Environments, Humanity and Other Animals.* Cullompton: Willan.

Gibbs, C., Gore, M., McGarrell, E. and Rivers III, L. (2010) 'Introducing conservation criminology: towards interdisciplinary scholarship on environmental crimes and risks', *British Journal of Criminology,* 50: 124–144.

Kangapunta, K. and Marshall, I. (eds) (n.d.) *Eco-Crime and Justice: Essays on Environmental Crime.* Turin: United Nations Interregional Crime and Justice Research Institute (UNICRI).

Lynch, M. and Stretesky, P. (2003) 'The meaning of green: contrasting criminological perspectives', *Theoretical Criminology,* 7 (2): 217–238.

Sollund, R. (ed.) (2011) *Global Harms: Ecological Crime and Speciesism.* New York: Nova Science Publishers.

White, R. (2009) *Environmental Crime: A Reader.* Cullompton: Willan.

HATE CRIME

Definition

A criminal act motivated by hatred, bias or prejudice against a person or property based on the actual or perceived race, ethnicity, gender, religion, disability or sexual orientation of the victim. The naming of 'hate crime' as a public problem has been the result of a successful cross-over campaign involving anti-racist, gay and lesbian rights, women's rights and disabilities' rights groups.

Distinctive Features

In jurisdictions where it is recognized, certain criminal acts, if perpetrated because of hatred, hostility, bias or negative attitudes towards the group or collectivity to which the victim is perceived to belong, are defined as hate crimes. Hence, a hate crime encompasses racist crime, sex crime, homophobia, anti-Semitism and sectarianism, and links across to ethnic cleansing and genocide. Levin and McDevitt (1994) argue that hate crimes tend to be motivated either by: thrill-seeking; reacting to the visible presence of 'outsiders' or 'others'; or an ideological motivation. A particular focus for those campaigning for hate crime legislation has been the violent words and actions of organized extreme right-wing political groupings. In a variety of jurisdictions, for example, white supremacist neo-Nazi groups stand accused of using a variety of media outlets to advocate race wars and a cleansing of those defined as having deviant lifestyles (Hamm, 1993).

In the USA high-profile cases, such as the murder of James Byrd Jr. in Jasper, Texas, and Matthew Shepard in Laramie, Wyoming, in October 1998, focused the news headlines on 'hate crime'. During the 2000 election, a campaign by Renee Mullins, the daughter of James Byrd Jr., interrogated George Bush on where he stood on the issue of hate crime, reinforcing demands for stronger legislative action. Such was the political potency of the issue that during the 2001 election debates both Al Gore and George Bush openly committed themselves to supporting the principle of 'hate crime' legislation. Discussions of 'hate crime' have also entered the mainstream of US popular culture through novels such as Richard Dooling's *Brain Storm*, a special edition of *South Park*, and various heated discussions on chat shows. The Internet has also provided anti-hate crime campaigners in the USA with new ways of mobilizing support and interacting with the formal news media. For example, HateCrime.org, as part of its campaign to ensure that anti-gay violence was highlighted in national hate crime legislation, encouraged supporters to write to the editors of the nation's main newspapers and provided a direct link to these publications. Special police units have been established and hate crime laws have been passed by many states in the USA which enable the establishment of data collection systems to track the incidents of hate crimes reported to the authorities and/or to increase the punishments set for criminal actions motivated by hate (see Jacobs and Potter, 1998; Gerstenfeld, 2003).

In the UK, the term 'hate crime' materialized in policy discourse as a result of the

Metropolitan Police's response to the highly critical findings of the official inquiry into the racist murder of Stephen Lawrence. The establishment of the Racial and Violent Crimes Task Force (CO24), lay advisory groups and borough-based Community Safety Units (CSUs) created a fresh dialogue between the police and those groups and communities who had complained that they were under-protected and particularly vulnerable. Initially the Met concentrated on 'race hate crime', with John Grieve, the Director of CO24, declaring war against the racists. The no-warning nail bomb attack in Soho in London during April 1999 by David Copeland, a self-declared neo-Nazi, resulted in calls for tough new penalties for anti-gay 'hate crimes'. As a result a new squad dedicated to fighting homophobia was established. The discovery that the majority of incidents being referred to the new CSUs were incidents of domestic violence widened the definition of 'hate crime' used by CO24. On 8 June 1999 the first co-ordinated 'hate crime' arrests of racist offenders took place in early morning raids in South London.

To raise public awareness about the realities of 'hate crime' in London, a high-profile media campaign ran initially through autumn 1999 and early 2000. Victim-centred advertisements and leaflets informed Londoners that: 'Racist crime, domestic violence, hate mail, homophobic crime are hate crimes. They hurt. They're illegal. They can be stopped. Contact your local Community Safety Unit. We're based at a police station in your area and are specifically trained to deal sensitively with victims of hate crime.' Further publicity for anti-'hate crime' initiatives in London was garnered on the first anniversary of the publication of the Stephen Lawrence Inquiry report. In March 2001, as part of a month-long campaign aimed at 15- to 25-year-olds, cinemas screened advertisements informing audiences that 'all hate crime is illegal and can be stopped'. BBC2 also broadcast a 'hate crime' documentary highlighting the work of the CSUs. To hammer home the point, on 20 March that same year, London's news media informed listeners

that the Metropolitan Police had arrested more than 100 people during a series of dawn raids aimed at tackling 'hate crime' in the capital. The alleged offences ranged from racially aggravated threats to kill and homophobic harassment, to the publication of racist and homophobic material, domestic violence and rape. And Londoners were assured by reporters who had taken part in the 'March Against Hate Initiative' (part of 'Operation Athena') that the Met had 'taken out' some of the worst extremists operating in the capital.

In October 2001, a £250,000 advertising campaign was launched by the Metropolitan Police to discourage young people from committing race hate crimes. Advertorials were placed in youth magazines to support television advertisements featuring some of the country's best-known pop stars. Nationally, the release of a very detailed ACPO guide to 'Identifying and Combating Hate Crime' in September 2000 represented another significant step in mainstreaming the term. The guide stressed that 'hate crime' would be a priority not just for the Metropolitan Police but also for all police forces because it was 'exceptionally pernicious and damaging to individuals and communities'.

In 2004, UK police forces began the process of forging a policy on the sensitive question of whether 'crimes of honour' (or 'honour crimes') in certain minority communities constitute a hate crime. These crimes range from threatened or actual emotional and physical violence to confinement, rape and murder and are so called because women are perceived to have acted in a way that has dishonoured their family and the wider community. It can manifest itself in being seen with a man in public, refusing to participate in a forced marriage, demanding a life that is independent of the wishes of the family, committing adultery, seeking a divorce or 'encouraging' rape. The fundamental sense of shame seems to be premised upon the notion that the family cannot control its members. Police and prosecutors are faced with considerable difficulties in investigating these crimes, and have no real sense of whether this form of criminality is widespread. Accurate figures are difficult to compile because most of these crimes go unreported or are denied. An 'honour killing' is often the result of a collective decision by a family and may be sanctioned or understood by the wider community and justified by a particular understanding of a religious code. Women in the family and the community are unlikely to co-operate with the police as they have a key role in the everyday regulation of the honourable behaviour of other women and in enforcing the self-respect of the family. In terms of how best to conceptualize 'crimes of honour' there is also a difference of opinion. For some campaigners this is a form of criminality that is specific to particular patriarchal communities where women are legally and culturally subordinated to men. For others, crimes of honour are best understood as part of a continuum of patriarchal violence against women that cuts across cultures, traditions and religions.

Evaluation

Anti-hate campaigners have argued that hate crimes need to be acknowledged in criminal legislation as different because they inflict distinctive harms upon their victims as well as on society. A 'hate crime' is uniquely destructive and unsettling because a victim is deliberately targeted because of a core characteristic of her/his identity and it is intended to terrorize not just the immediate victim but also entire communities. For them, hate crime legislation must be seen as an important part of the ongoing process of identifying and articulating the values and ground rules of vibrant, safe, multicultural societies, including a public recognition and affirmation of the right to be different. Hate crime, in all its many manifestations, strikes at the diversity upon which multicultural societies thrive, denying the right to self-identity and self-determination and imposing a subordinate/inferior/less-than-human status on the victim and her/his community/group. In addition, there is every possibility that the perpetrators of hate crimes are involved in other forms of criminality and that hate crime

hotspots are locations characterized by communal tensions and social problems that need to be addressed (Chakraborti, 2010; Kelly and Majhan, 1998).

The concept of hate crime has come under heavy criticism from conservative and liberal commentators in both the USA and the UK on the grounds that it will be used by minority groups to censor and criminalize those who oppose multiculturalism and positive discrimination. According to Jacobs and Potter (1998), the willingness and ability of minority interest groups to distort and exaggerate the available statistics have enabled them not just to determine but also to dominate the terms of the public debate in the USA and trigger a 'moral panic' about the existence of a hate crime 'epidemic'. Through sensationalist headlines, alarmist articles and an uncritical repetition of the 'epidemic' claims of these interest groups, the news media 'accepted, reinforced, and amplified the image of a nation besieged by hate crime, despite the absence of any reliable evidence to support that claim and in the face of much evidence to contradict it' (1998: 50). Jacobs and Potter also vehemently disagree with demands for increased penalties for hate crime and ask why it is that only particular groups are able to claim special protection. They are also concerned by what they see as the willingness of liberals and radicals to support measures such as sentence enhancement for these crimes because this inevitably feeds into the nation's ever-tougher approach to crime and punishment. They think that, however well intentioned, hate crime legislation will do more social harm than good for the following reasons. First, campaigning for the eradication of discrimination in public life is quite different from transforming the average unthinking criminal into an 'equal opportunities' offender. Second, the latest extension of the civil rights/affirmative action agenda will politicize the crime problem and corrupt the core principles of criminal law and rules of evidence. Finally, the fragmentation of criminal law into various offender/victim configurations such as race, gender, religion and sexual orientation will inevitably heighten tensions and reinforce prejudices and mutual suspicions. Hence, at a deeper level, this politically correct legislation will contribute to the further 'Balkanization' of American society because every conceivable minority group will be encouraged to lobby for recognition as victims of hate crime. Their main conclusion is that hate crime legislation should be repealed and generic criminal laws enforced impartially and without prejudice. This would ensure that American society returns to a situation where crime is a social problem that unites all law-abiding citizens and the fight against crime enhances social solidarity.

Eugene McLaughlin

Associated Concepts: ethnic cleansing, genocide, police bias, racialization, violence

Key Readings

Chakraborti, N. (2010) *Hate Crime: Concepts, Policy, Future Directions*. Cullompton: Willan.
Gerstenfeld, P.B. (2003) *Hate Crimes: Causes, Controls and Controversies*. London: Sage.
Hamm, M.S. (1993) *American Skinheads: The Criminology and Control of Hate Crime*. New York: Praeger Press.
Jacobs, J. and Potter, K. (1998) *Hate Crimes: Criminal Law and Identity Politics*. Oxford: Oxford University Press.
Kelly, J.R. and Majhan, J. (eds) (1998) *Hate Crime: The Global Politics of Polarisation*. Carbondale, IL: Southern Illinois University Press.
Levin, J. and McDevitt, J. (1994) *Hate Crimes: A Study of Offender Motivation*. Boston, MA: Northeastern University Press.

HEDONISM

Definition

The pursuit of pleasure, sometimes considered as the subordination of reason to the play of desires and the attractions of the senses. Hedonism is also associated with risk-taking and excitement in criminality.

Distinctive Features

Hedonism is fundamental to the formation of classical criminology, especially in the work of Bentham (1823) and Beccaria. Defined as the desire to maximize pleasure and minimize pain, it was assumed to be the underlying mainspring of human behaviour. The rational choice criminal was imagined as weighing up the balance of pleasures and pains likely to result from the commission of a crime. Where this 'felicity calculus' indicated a positive balance of pleasures, criminal offending would result. As such, the assumption of hedonism underlies most punitive penology that is geared towards deterrence. Bentham, himself, developed tables for the infliction of punishment based on the principle that the net calculus of pain had only marginally to outbalance the sum of pains. This principle, in turn, played a key intellectual role in the assault on the 'excessive' punishments of the eighteenth century.

By the 1930s, much academic criminology had dispensed with such thinking, arguing that few people lead such calculating lives, that most crimes are spontaneous acts of irrationality, and that many criminals are constitutionally incapable of performing the calculation of pleasures and pains. Despite this the model of hedonistic behaviour persisted, albeit transformed. As crime increasingly came to be regarded as a pathology, hedonism too was pathologized – re-created as an inability to govern the desire for pleasure and excitement. This pathology was theorized as a cause of crime in a multitude of ways by positivist sociology and psychology.

Sociologically, hedonism was understood in Victorian terms as a universal, animalistic quality that socialization had to overlay with discipline. The middle classes were understood as 'normal' precisely because of such self-government: 'deferred gratification' became the norm against which hedonism was pathologized. Predictably, weak socialization emerged early on as a cause of crime, and 'broken' and 'inadequate' working-class families were identified as failing to implant the necessary norms and techniques of self-discipline. More broadly, the breakdown of social control in the chaotic environment of inner city 'transitional zones' was seen as giving young people excessive licence for their hedonistic desires. Other, cultural, theories of hedonistic pathology associated the boring, mundane and routine conditions of lower-class life with the emergence of criminogenic 'focal concerns' such as the search for 'excitement' or 'thrills' (Miller, 1958). As such models had trouble accounting for the gendered nature of working-class crime, subsidiary accounts suggested that the close familial governance of young women's (sexualized) hedonism gave women fewer opportunities to offend, and resulted in domesticated desires that immunized them against offending in later life (Cohen, 1954).

While most of these models linked crime to hedonism via social pathologies, the nexus is also found in psychological approaches. Thus Eysenck (1964) identified criminality especially with extroversion (outgoing impulsiveness) and neuroticism (behavioural instability). Extroverts, because of lower response thresholds in the brain's reticular formation, are said to require stronger stimuli to achieve excitation, and to respond weakly to rewards (pleasures) and punishments (pains). Therefore, they seek strong stimuli and learn conformity more slowly, and thus – it is argued – are more likely to commit crime. The familiar criminological formula of weak moral control coupled with a strong desire for excitement is thereby retained, but the felicity calculus – the hedonistic attempt to achieve surplus pleasure over pain – has been translated into a neuro-psychological function of the brain.

More recently, this association between crime and excitement has been revived but taken in new directions (e.g., Bell and Bell, 1993). For example, rejecting rational choice models, Katz (1988) has argued that criminology has underestimated crime's emotional attractions. These extend hedonism beyond mere 'pleasures' to include other sources of excitement (righteous slaughter, sneaky thrills, doing stick-ups) that allow the subject to emotionally transcend the mundane nature of modern existence. Ironically, Katz's work, like most traditional sociological criminology, assumes a pathology (this time in the nature of modernity) that gives rise to a pressure to offend 'hedonistically'.

Such anti-rationalist developments coincide with the return of the rational choice felicity principle – embedded in the models of situational crime prevention and risk management that have become characteristic of *fin de siècle* administrative criminology. For the moment, at least, the latter has proven more influential.

Evaluation

Hedonism has proven almost impossible to avoid as an element in modernist (or with Katz, postmodernist) criminology – perhaps because the binary of pain and pleasure is so central to post-Enlightenment thought. It appears almost everywhere that rational choice models are deployed and, as with Katz or Eysenck, even where they are rejected. This suggests that hedonism is a category that can only be evaluated in relation to its particular criminological uses. For example, in some accounts it is limited because it is gendered (women's hedonism is sexualized), it is 'classed' (working-class hedonism is pathological and criminogenic), and it is 'aged' (youthful hedonism is virtually taken for granted as criminogenic). However, hedonism is also fundamental to the abstract and universal 'rational choice' criminology that ignores the causal impact of class, age and gender. Perhaps only those criminologies – for example, Marxist – that deny the category of human nature may escape this.

Pat O'Malley

Associated Concepts: carnival (of crime), cultural criminology, deviance, extroversion/introversion, free will, risk, subculture

Key Readings

Bell, N. and Bell, R. (eds) (1993) *Adolescent Risk Taking*. London: Sage.

Bentham, J. (1823) *An Introduction to the Principles of Morals and Legislation*. London: Pickering.

Cohen, A. (1954) *Delinquent Boys*. Glencoe, IL: The Free Press.

Eysenck, H. (1964) *Crime and Personality*. London: Routledge and Kegan Paul.

Katz, J. (1988) *The Seductions of Crime*. New York: Basic Books.

Miller, W. (1958) 'Lower class culture as a generating milieu of gang delinquency', *Journal of Social Issues*, 14: 5–19.

HEGEMONIC MASCULINITY

Definition

The set of ideas, values, representations and practices associated with 'being male' which is commonly accepted as the dominant position in gender relations in a society at a particular historical moment.

Distinctive Features

In an imaginative lateral shift, Bob Connell (1987, 1995) plucked the concept of hegemony from its original class setting in order to try to understand gender relations. Where Gramsci had sought to understand how a dominant class manages to legitimate its rule in societies characterized by class inequality, Connell set himself the task of understanding how an unequal gender order manages to reproduce itself: how hierarchies of dominance and subordination among men and between men and women come to be commonly accepted at any particular historical moment. The idea of hegemonic masculinity as the culturally dominant form of masculinity was the answer he proposed, which, following Gramsci, he saw as always historically contingent and contested. Hence, there are always subordinate masculinities. Given the widespread cultural ascendancy of hetero-sexuality, the idea of homosexual masculinities as subordinate is unsurprising. Given the long-standing, well-nigh general subordination of women, those masculinities that can be represented somehow as close to femininity will also be rendered subordinate.

In addition, Connell talks of 'complicit' and 'marginalized' masculinities. The former refer to those large numbers of men who do not themselves practise the hegemonic version of masculinity but do not challenge it either; they are its 'complicit' beneficiaries. Marginalized masculinities result from the interplay of gender with other structures such as class and race. Given the relations of domination/subordination between ethnic groups, for example, the masculinities of such subordinate groups will always be subject to the authority of the hegemonic masculinity of the dominant group, which has the power to marginalize or to authorize admission to the hegemonic project. Certain black US athletes, for example, may be 'authorized' exemplars of hegemonic masculinity, though this has no effect on the social authority of black men more generally.

Since Connell's original introduction of the term in the late 1980s, the idea of hegemonic masculinity has become almost ubiquitous in attempts to think through relationships among men, crime and masculinities. Perhaps the most common finding is how depressingly often hegemonic masculinity is implicated in the commission of crime and its control, a finding which testifies both to the strength and to the weakness of the concept.

Evaluation

Connell's introduction of the term 'hegemonic masculinity' has inspired and influenced the whole range of contemporary writings on men and masculinity, including that currently being conducted within criminology. The strength of its appeal lies in its ability to recognize the diversity of men's lives, something that the early feminist writings on male violence failed to do, but without losing sight of the importance of power. The idea of power structuring relations among men has, for example, enabled the relationship between particular crimes and men's specific positions in gender/race/class hierarchies to be explored, something Messerschmidt does in *Masculinities and Crime* (1993). It also permits analysis of organizations and cultures as well as individual men since hegemonic masculinity, like hegemony generally, is not just a personal matter but is also deeply embedded in institutional life across the society as a whole; hence the re-examinations of a variety of criminal justice institutions to reveal the masculinities embedded within them (Walklate, 1995). A final strength is the importance it attaches, in true Gramscian fashion, to contestation. Since hegemony is essentially about defending the indefensible – class inequality for Gramsci, gender inequality for Connell – it is always liable to challenge; it is never fixed nor absolute. Sometimes, only when it gets challenged by subordinate masculinities, in, for example, the idea of gay marriages or gay parenting, is hegemonic masculinity's commonly accepted, 'taken-for-grantedness' revealed for what it is: in this case, the imposition of one kind of sexuality, heterosexuality, through all kinds of powerful institutions from the Church to the State, as the common sense of the age, the norm, the culturally exalted, the ideal.

Despite the subtlety of Connell's theorizing, emphasizing the importance of diversity, power, institutions and practice, and the greater gender awareness it has undoubtedly promoted within criminology, problems remain. There is a tendency to deploy the term 'masculinity' as if it referred simply to a list of 'manly' attributes – competitive, aggressive, a risk-taker, strong, independent, unemotional, and so on – a tendency which, if anything, is heightened once the term 'hegemonic' is added, given the usual considerable overlap between the list and some cultural norm, ideal or stereotype of masculinity. (Students asked to write down what they understand by masculinity will tend to come up with very similar lists of 'hegemonic attributes'.) Within criminology, this has led

to an accentuation of the negative dimensions of these features in order to make the connections between masculinity and crime (and criminal justice), and to ignore the more positive, caring dimensions underpinning, for example, the father who protects and provides. Messerschmidt's (1993) catalogue of criminals may all be doing masculinity *differently,* depending on their place in gender, race and class relations, but they are all doing *bad* not good. Moreover, in reducing hegemonic masculinity to a set of traits or characteristics the notion is rendered static and not the subject of constant contestation, as Connell's theoretical usage would suggest. However, the problem here may well reside partly in the original notion since, even though Connell talks of a range of subordinate masculinities, hegemonic masculinity is always used in the singular. In other words, is there only ever one hegemonic strategy at any given historical moment, as Wetherell and Edley (1999) ask, or is hegemonic masculinity a much more contingent notion, one that is always dependent on context? If this is the case, it poses a far more complex series of questions in understanding how masculinities and crimes are related than has been attempted hitherto.

A final problem is the oversocialized view of the male subject that users of the concept have generally taken, despite Connell's (1995) insistence that the depth and complexity of Freud's study of the Wolf Man constituted a challenge to all subsequent researchers interested in masculinity. Several writers have reiterated the importance of not ignoring the psychic or subjective dimension of masculinity, even though they have done so from very different theoretical traditions, and none of them is advocating a return to classical Freudianism (Jefferson, 1994; Wetherell and Edley, 1999). To the extent that some of these strictures are taken seriously, we can expect more complex and sensitive accounts of the relationships among men, masculinities and crime to emerge. However, we would do well to listen to Sandra Walklate (1995) when she warns us not to allow our interest in masculinity to obscure the role of other explanatory variables. Whilst hegemonic masculinity may well be implicated in certain crimes on certain occasions, expecting it to provide all the answers would be a serious mistake.

Tony Jefferson

Associated Concepts: critical criminology, feminist criminologies, hegemony, Marxist criminologies, masculinities

Key Readings

Connell, R.W. (1987) *Gender and Power.* Cambridge: Polity Press.
Connell, R.W. (1995) *Masculinities.* Cambridge: Polity Press.
Jefferson, T. (1994) 'Theorizing masculine subjectivity', in T. Newburn and E.A. Stanko (eds), *Just Boys Doing Business?* London: Routledge. pp. 10–31.
Messerschmidt, J.W. (1993) *Masculinities and Crime.* Lanham, MD: Rowman and Littlefield.
Walklate, S. (1995) *Gender and Crime.* London: Prentice-Hall/Harvester Wheatsheaf.
Wetherell, M. and Edley, N. (1999) 'Negotiating hegemonic masculinity: imaginary positions and psycho-discursive practices', *Feminism and Psychology,* 9 (3): 335–56.

HEGEMONY

Definition

An unequal relationship between the ruling class (or alliance of classes) and the subordinate classes within a given social order which is based on authority or leadership achieved through the production of consent rather than through the use of coercion or force.

Distinctive Features

One of the earliest uses of the term 'hegemony' appears in the writings of Lenin in the phrase 'hegemony of the proletariat'. Then it had the narrow meaning of political leadership within a class alliance, specifically the need for proletarian leadership in any alliance with the peasantry. In the writings of the Italian Marxist Antonio Gramsci (1971), the term achieves a far broader reach. Specifically, he expanded its meaning to include moral and intellectual leadership across society as a whole. He developed the idea as a way of conceptualizing how, in the aftermath of the Russian Revolution and the First World War, the industrial capitalist democracies of Western Europe and the USA managed to avoid the proletarian uprisings predicted for them by classical Marxism. Without ever abandoning the Marxist idea of the centrality of classes and class struggle, his key insight was that successful class rule entails the creation – through alliances, concessions, compromises and new ethico-political ideas and projects – of a collective will which was not narrowly class-based but had popular, national appeal. In short, a class wishing to become hegemonic had to 'nationalize' itself, had to become a 'popular religion'.

When such a 'national-popular' consensus is achieved, the dominant classes can be said to be ruling hegemonically: through authority or leadership rather than coercion or force. However, such an achievement is always fragile and temporary since it is contingent upon an ever-changing set of economic, political and ideological conditions, including, crucially, the constant challenges from the subordinate classes, whose goal, according to Gramsci, should be to win over the people to adopt an alternative hegemonic project. Consequently, the achievement of hegemony in a particular historical moment, or conjuncture, could be followed by more coercive, less hegemonic moments: new legislation, tougher policing and, *in extremis*, the use of the army, to deal with dissent, unrest, conflict and, at worst, civil war.

Within criminology, Stuart Hall and colleagues used this Gramscian notion of hegemony to underpin their attempt, in *Policing the Crisis* (1978), to understand the state's response to mugging in the 1970s. One of the early examples of Marxist criminology in Britain, *Policing the Crisis* argued that the hegemony enjoyed by the ruling alliance in Britain in the 1950s entered into crisis in the 1960s as the conditions underpinning the postwar social democratic settlement proved impossible to sustain. Challenges to the existing consensus arose on multiple fronts, around issues to do with youth, drugs, sexual mores, race, women, students, industrial relations, crime and Northern Ireland. By the 1970s, the conditions for successful hegemonic rule had collapsed, signalled by an election-winning law and order crusade, new laws, the tougher policing of all kinds of protest and unrest, the entry of the army into Northern Ireland, and internment. Set within this context, the crackdown on mugging in 1972–3 by the police and the judiciary, to the accompaniment of media headlines and sermonizing editorials, was symptomatic of the collapse of hegemony. As one among several moral panics, the 'mugger' became a convenient folk devil, or scapegoat, for the new, more troubled and conflictual times.

Evaluation

The biggest single problem with Gramsci's concept of hegemony was its attempts to move beyond a class reductionist understanding of the reproduction of capitalism without ever losing sight of the concept's fundamental basis in economic class relations. This meant hanging onto the fact that for a class to become hegemonic it must move beyond its narrow class interests and construct a broad-based ethico-political project, whilst never overlooking the fact that hegemony had *necessarily* also to be 'economic'. For Chantal Mouffe (1979), one of Gramsci's most sympathetic commentators, this meant that only the two fundamental classes (bourgeoisie/proletariat) could be hegemonic and ultimately, since only the proletariat had an interest in finally ending exploitation, only a working-class hegemony could become genuinely successful. This lingering reductionism haunts her own attempt to work up Gramsci's concept of hegemony from the 'practical state' in which he left it in *The Prison Notebooks*. Having first established Gramsci's non-reductive conception

of ideology; then the way elements within a hegemonic project must divest themselves of their class origins if they are to be capable of nationalizing themselves; and, finally, the importance of disarticulation-rearticulation to an ideological struggle (rather than the confrontation of different, opposed, class-based world-views) – she is forced to confront what it is that unifies the hegemonic project in a way that ensures its class character. At that point she suggests that this unity is supplied by the 'hegemonic principle' and that this is always class-based.

Despite this difficulty, at the level of theory, of how to 'think' the structural basis of concepts without lapsing into structural determinism (a difficulty common to a whole raft of concepts in these post-structuralist/postmodernist times), when used to make sense of particular conjunctures, hegemony remains one of the most useful of Marxist concepts. Deployed by Stuart Hall (1988), it enabled a series of insightful and prescient readings of the rise and popular appeal of Thatcherism and the new right in the UK. Against those who stressed Thatcher's luck in becoming Britain's longest-serving Prime Minister this century and pulling off an unprecedented transformation of the face of modern Britain, Hall always saw Thatcherism as something more profound – as a hegemonic project, albeit one based on a contradictory combination of nostalgic morality, ruthless modernization, authoritarian leadership and populist common sense. If 'Blairism' then became the new common sense of the age, it was certainly inconceivable without the 'regressive modernization' and 'authoritarian populism' which Hall unerringly identified as typifying the project that was Thatcherism.

Tony Jefferson

Associated Concepts: authoritarian populism, Birmingham 'school', communitarianism, critical criminology, folk devil, hegemonic masculinity, Marxist criminologies, masculinities, moral panic, new criminology, radical criminologies, scapegoating, social reaction, the state

Key Readings

Gramsci, A. (1971) *Selections from the Prison Notebooks*. London: Lawrence and Wishart.

Hall, S. (1988) *The Hard Road to Renewal*. London: Verso.

Hall, S. and Jefferson, T. (eds) (1996) *Resistance Through Rituals*. London: Hutchinson.

Hall, S., Critcher, C., Jefferson, T., Clarke, J. and Roberts, B. (1978) *Policing the Crisis*. London: Macmillan.

Mouffe, C. (1979) 'Hegemony and ideology in Gramsci', in *Gramsci and Marxist Theory*. London: Routledge and Kegan Paul. pp. 168–204.

HIDDEN CRIME

Definition

At one level this refers to specific acts of crime which are not recorded in official crime statistics. At another level it refers to categories of crime which are either not represented in official statistics or significantly under-recorded. Sometimes it is also referred to as invisible crime.

Distinctive Features

Official statistics are known to massively under-record the true extent of crime. The reasons for this are numerous but one significant factor is that police rely heavily on victims and witnesses to report crime, and on occasions they will choose not to do so. The gap between the true extent of crime and crime recorded in statistics is known as the 'dark figure of unrecorded crime'. Estimates of this gap can be obtained by comparing official crime statistics with results derived from victim surveys (whereby individuals are asked if they have recently been the victim of a crime, and if so, whether they reported it to the police) and from self-report studies (whereby individuals are asked whether they have recently committed crimes and whether they were subsequently charged with the offence). The extent of hidden crime can vary according to the category of the crime but it is known to exist to some degree in relation to all such categories. Even in relation to so-called conventional crimes – for example street crimes, car crimes and house burglary – a certain proportion will remain hidden.

Outside of so-called conventional crimes there are other types which, because of their nature, are not represented in official statistics or are massively under-represented. The range here includes, first, crimes committed by employees against organizations for which they work, such as using an organization's facilities illegally and stealing work-based materials for personal use. Second, there are crimes perpetrated by organizations against their employees, including breaches of health and safety regulations resulting in workplace injuries, illnesses, accidents and sometimes deaths. A third example is fraudulent behaviour, including the use of another's money for personal or organizational gain without their knowledge or consent, and the use of 'sleaze' money to change the course of events, such as in political life or in the field of sport and leisure. Fourth, the range encompasses hitherto neglected green crimes, including the pollution of the environment by industrial organizations and the smuggling of endangered species and products produced from them. A fifth category can be given the generic title 'cybercrime'. This includes computer crimes such as hacking, the illegal appropriation of image and likeness, and the use of the Internet in order to sell drugs, to publish obscene materials, or to advertise services in relation to paedophilia.

Seven features of hidden or invisible crimes can be identified (Jupp et al., 1999). First there is *no knowledge,* namely there is little individual or public knowledge that the crime has been committed. The ingenuity of the fraudster, the complexity of the act, and the lack of knowledge and vigilance can all conspire to render a crime invisible. Even where individuals are aware that an act or event has taken place, it can be taken for granted, as normal rather than criminal. For example, workers in hazardous industries may see themselves as doing a difficult job rather than as victims of illicit health and safety practices. A second feature is that there are *no statistics,* that is, official statistics will fail to record or classify the crime. This may be because victims are unaware a crime has been committed, or they may treat the crime as normal and not something to be reported, or they may be frightened or intimidated, or they may be unwilling to report the crime to the police because it is something in which they have colluded. Even where an action or event is reported to the police the complexity of some crimes, especially those relating to financial transactions, together with the ingenuity and specialist knowledge of those carrying them out, will often mean that the police are unable to satisfy themselves that a crime has been perpetrated and can therefore be recorded as such.

A third feature of hidden crime is that of *no theory,* that is, criminologists and others have neglected to explain the crime, its existence and its causes. Criminology has been heavily influenced by studies of sections of the population which are most visible in official crime statistics and by explanations which can be cast in terms of individual pathology. In the main, hidden crimes do not fit into these categories. Also, the sheer diversity of hidden or invisible crimes and of the sites at which they are committed – at the workplace, on the Internet, in the financial marketplace – probably militates against the development of any comprehensive theory of such crimes.

Fourth, hidden crime is characterized by *no research.* There are a number of reasons for this; for example there are the mutually reinforcing effects of the paucity of knowledge, statistics and theory in relation to invisible crimes. Further, there are practical aspects to conducting a social enquiry which will restrict the feasibility and possibility of researching invisible crimes. One of these relates to access. There will often be parties who will have vested interests in relation to withholding information about their activities – parties who by one means or another will be able to exercise their power to deny researchers access to data with which to formulate and support conclusions. In the absence of such data either the research is not carried out or it is carried out by means that are not typically found in standard texts on research methods. Where the latter occurs investigators are open to the often-unjustifiable criticism of being non-scientific and biased.

Fifth, there is the characteristic of *no control,* that is, there are no formal or systematic mechanisms for the control of such crimes. This can be a result of blurring the boundaries between what is legitimate and illegitimate, because of the complexity of many crimes, for example fraud, and also because of the diffusion of offenders. Further, where crime is international, especially in the context of increasing globalization and fewer barriers between nation-states, the possibility of detection, let alone prevention and control, is made more difficult. Sixth, hidden crimes are characterized by *no politics,* that is, such crimes as breaches of the health and safety legislation do not typically appear as a significant part of the political agenda. Much greater emphasis is placed on conventional and street level crimes and on law and order campaigns to combat them. Finally, there is *no panic,* that is, hidden crimes are not constituted as moral panics and their perpetrators are not portrayed as folk devils. There is a close connection between the formulation of the political agenda and the construction and amplification of moral panics and folk devils in the media. There has been increased awareness of financial irregularities, 'sleaze' and breaches of food safety regulations, but these are invariably portrayed as scandals which are exposed rather than examples of sustained deviant or criminal activity. They are often treated as 'one-offs', and the fault of particular individuals at particular times, rather than as deep-seated structural problems.

Evaluation

The above features help provide a means for categorizing and characterizing a wide range of acts and events that remain invisible in everyday life. Moreover, when combined, such features constitute a template with which to assess their relative invisibility. The elements making up this template (knowledge – statistics – theory – research – control – politics – panic!) can be viewed as independent of one another but there is also the potential for interaction and mutual reinforcement. For example, ignorance of victimization (no knowledge) often leads to non-recording in official statistics (no statistics), which in turn can have consequences in terms of under-theorizing (no theory), a lack of policy making at the government level (no politics), and scant consideration by the popular media (no panic).

Particular acts or events do not necessarily exhibit all of the above features and nor will they exhibit them to the same degree at any given point in time. The relative invisibility of particular acts and events and their subsequent recognition and identification as crimes will depend on whether the template fits (do the elements apply?), the degree to which it fits (to what extent does it apply?), and the power of interactive effects (to what extent do the elements reinforce one another?).

Victor Jupp

Associated Concepts: art crime, corporate crime, crime, cybercrime, family crime, official criminal statistics, self-reports, social harm, state crime, victim surveys, white collar crime

Key Readings

Box, S. (1992) *Power, Crime and Mystification.* London: Routledge.
Davies, P., Francis, P. and Jupp, V.R. (eds) (1999) *Invisible Crimes: Their Victims and Their Regulation.* London: Macmillan.
Jupp, V.R., Davies, P. and Francis, P. (1999) 'The features of invisible crimes', in P. Davies, P. Francis and V.R. Jupp (eds), *Invisible Crimes: Their Victims and Their Regulation.* London: Macmillan.

HISTORICAL METHODS

Definition

In the last third of the twentieth century social historians increasingly turned their attention towards questions of crime and criminal justice institutions. Their principal aim was not to develop a better understanding of crime but rather to use the examination of crime and criminal justice as a means for broadening and deepening the understanding of past societies and of change through time.

Distinctive Features

The work grew out of the new social history of the 1960s and the fascination with 'history from below' that was typified by the work of E.J. Hobsbawm, George Rude and E.P. Thompson. Initially the approach was rooted in a class-conflict perception of society. It was believed that an analysis of criminal justice records would bring the historian closer to the voices of those who seemed to have been generally ignored by historians. Much of the early work focused on periods of major economic upheaval, such as the eighteenth and early nineteenth centuries when, it was assumed, much 'crime' in the form of rioting and the appropriation of property was, in fact, a response to new concepts of private property, to new work practices, and to new systems of payment for labour. More recently, and thanks largely to the growth of women's history, there has been a shift away from class to gender perceptions. This has tended to shift the focus away from property offences to interpersonal violence while, at the same time, generating questions about, first, the gender perceptions of agents of the criminal justice system, and second, the extent to which notions of gender, and in particular masculinity, have fostered aspects of criminality.

The historian's general concern with change through time has resulted in much work on the way in which different forms of criminality were constructed at different moments, notably the construction of the image of the juvenile delinquent, as well as that of the 'dangerous' and subsequently 'criminal' classes. A changing perception of the criminal during the nineteenth century has also been charted, from morally inferior to mentally deficient. Much of the early work had a strong statistical basis, with several historians constructing their own data from quarter sessions and assize records. The judicial statistics for the nineteenth century have been carefully assessed in conjunction with other social data to suggest, and subsequently to explain, a general levelling out of theft and violence during the Victorian and Edwardian periods. These conclusions have, however, been challenged by the suggestion that, from the mid-nineteenth century, the Treasury was imposing restrictions on the activities of the police and the courts through strict cash limits.

The concept of 'social crime' was developed to explain offending such as poaching, smuggling and wood theft, which, in many instances, had a considerable community sanction. But it has also been challenged as being too slippery to explain very much, especially since in some instances both poaching and wood theft were undertaken to meet the demands of the market, while eighteenth-century smuggling was often a large-scale capitalist enterprise. The analysis of offending in the workplace, both pre-industrial and industrial, has thrown up similar complexities, and the early hypothesis of property crime as a response to industrialization and the capitalization of industry is now looking very tattered. Unfortunately, the extent to which such economic developments fostered white collar crime has been far less extensively researched.

Evaluation

The historian's desire to read and assess sources created by the agents of the criminal justice system has fostered new explorations of these agents and the institutions to which they belonged. There has, in consequence, been significant new work on the origins and development of police organizations and prisons – though the work of Michel Foucault and others has been an equally important intellectual stimulus here. There have also been important explorations of the impact of, and interrelationship between, social norms and legal norms in police practice, as well as in the decision making of both prosecutors and the courts.

Clive Emsley

Associated Concepts: critical criminology, moral economy, social constructionism

Key Readings

Arnot, M.L. and Usborne, C. (eds) (1999) *Gender and Crime in Modern Europe.* London: UCL Press.

Emsley, C. (1996) *Crime and Society in England, 1750–1900,* 2nd edn. London: Longman.

Emsley, C. and Knafla, L.A. (eds) (1996) *Crime History and Histories of Crime: Studies in the Historiography of Crime and Criminal Justice in Modern History.* Westport, CT: Greenwood Press.

Robb, G. (1992) *White-Collar Crime in Modern England: Financial Fraud and Business Morality 1845–1929.* Cambridge: Cambridge University Press.

Taylor, H. (1998) 'Rationing crime: the political economy of criminal statistics since the 1850s', *Economic History Review,* LI: 569–90.

Wiener, M.J. (1990) *Reconstructing the Criminal: Culture, Law and Policy in England, 1830–1914.* Cambridge: Cambridge University Press.

HUMAN RIGHTS

Definition

Human rights is an extremely difficult concept to define, not least because it is constantly being re-defined to suit changing circumstances. Many authors writing in this field find it easier to offer an extensive list of rights that can illustrate what it is to be defined as 'human'. If we follow the basic United Nations' definition, human rights are the rights an individual accrues because s/he is a human being. Human rights are held by all human beings equally and universally and are inalienable and indivisible. An individual cannot be denied these rights any more than s/he can be denied the status of 'human being'. Human rights are also interdependent and part of a complementary framework. A more expansive definition of human rights refers to those basic standards without which the individual cannot live with dignity. To violate someone's human rights is to treat that individual as though s/he were not a human being. In claiming these rights, each of us accepts the responsibility not to breach the human rights of others and to support those whose rights are being contravened or denied.

Distinctive Features

The evolution of international human rights is sometimes divided into periods denoting 'first' and 'second' generation rights. First generation rights refer to concepts developed in particular historical and philosophical eras and include famous documents such as the American Declaration of Independence and the French Declaration of the Rights of Man and of the Citizen. Second generation rights refer to more recent Declarations which began after the First World War, and partly as a result of the Russian Revolution, and most significantly these include the charter of the United Nations following the Second World War. The resulting European Convention of Human Rights eventually led to the formalization of constitutional rights in the UK through the Human Rights Act, 1998. In a discussion of this progress, Lester and Clapinska argue that 'the universality of human rights has been recognised by the United Nations as inherent in the very nature of human beings, an essential part of their common humanity' (2000: 63). The rights that these documents proclaim are intended to protect the individual from the power of the state and, in international arenas, to promote human rights across international

boundaries. Fundamental rights range from the right to life and freedom from torture, to the rights of free speech, political freedom and worship. In addition there are rights surrounding the administration of the law, such as the right to a fair trial (including legal representation and various conditions whilst awaiting trial), the presumption of innocence, and humane punishment if convicted.

For criminologists, human rights are often about challenges to the laws of the state, basic freedoms, and to some extent the internationalization of various rights and standards of protection for citizens. As the introduction of the Human Rights Act into the UK Constitution in 2000 illustrates, the way lawyers argued cases has had to change fundamentally. This is because although the Act does not change domestic law, and the judiciary still maintain their independence, there is now legally enforceable protection against the misuse of public powers. In the case of the police, for instance, as Neyroud suggests, the Human Rights Act 'brought both a new language to policing and a new decision-making calculus' (2003: 585).

Another area of interest for criminologists is the sphere of state crime and the enforcement, or more usually non-enforcement, of international conventions on war crimes, torture and the process of criminalization of certain groups who may be labelled political offenders or terrorists. As these groups often pose fundamental challenges to the state, debates about what is crime, and which individuals or groups are criminalized and for what reason, will once again arise. This has become more pertinent following the events of 9/11 and the subsequent US 'war on terror', where human rights' violations are alleged to have been perpetrated in the aftermath of war, for example by using the term 'combatants' rather than 'prisoners' to describe captives, and making 'emergency' changes to the terrorism legislation.

Within the discourse of human rights, according to Stan Cohen (1996), there are state crimes which are rightly classed as 'gross' violations. He argues that there are acts committed by regimes, which include genocide, mass political killings, state terrorism and torture, and disappearances which in terms of criminology would be defined as murder, rape, espionage, kidnapping and assault. Defining an agreed concept of human rights is problematic, he argues, however, because the values underpinning these declarations will vary according to a group's or state's definition. Freedom fighters become terrorists when they endanger the social order, and enemies of the state can later become democratically elected leaders. Despite these problems Cohen argues that human rights has become a dominant narrative and an important issue for criminologists, especially through the growth of victimology surrounding the abuse of women and children.

Evaluation

Although the measures listed in declarations of human rights are designed to protect the individual from the state, and sometimes from other nations' actions, such as in times of war, in effect there are few enforceable international laws. A number of seemingly influential bodies have rules of engagement and supposed co-operation, such as the United Nations Declaration of Human Rights and the European Court of Human Rights, but the 'rhetoric' of human rights is not supported by the power to prevent states committing crimes. It appears that these fundamental laws about human conduct are being left to independent human rights organizations, such as Amnesty International, to highlight behaviour by nation states that consistently violates the rights of their own citizens. Furthermore, only states who are signatories to treaties such as the European Convention on Human Rights can be held accountable to their aims. Hurwitz argues that clauses such as 'national security, public safety or territorial integrity' (1981: 139) are often used to avoid implementing such laws.

Louise Westmarland

Associated Concepts: denial, genocide, globalization, social harm, the state, state crime, torture

Key Readings

Brysk, A. (ed.) (2002) *Globalization and Human Rights*. Berkeley: University of California Press.
Cohen, S. (1996) 'Human rights and crimes of the state: the culture of denial', in J. Muncie, E. McLaughlin and M. Langan (eds), *Criminological Perspectives*. London: Sage.
Hurwitz, L. (1981) *The State as Defendant*. London: Aldwych.
Lord Lester of Herne Hill and Clapinska, L. (2000) 'Human rights and the British Constitution', in J. Jowell and D. Oliver (eds), *The Changing Constitution* (5th edn). Oxford: Oxford University Press.
Neyroud, P. (2003) 'Policing and ethics', in T. Newburn (ed.), *Handbook of Policing*. Cullompton: Willan.

HUMAN TRAFFICKING

Definition

Refers to the trading and systematic movement of people by various means, potentially involving a variety of agents, institutions and intermediaries. It typically involves coercion, deception and/or the exploitation of those who are moved within or across borders.

Distinctive Features

Trafficking of persons has been described as a form of 'new slavery in the global economy' (Bales, 1999). Its growth has been linked to repression, war, civil conflict, social inequalities and/or a lack of access to resources and employment opportunities in some of the world's poorest and most unstable regions. The wider development of criminal networks in trafficking (e.g., of human organs, drugs, firearms) is the context in which the growth of human trafficking has become a highly profitable commercial enterprise. Women and children are particularly vulnerable to human trafficking and other forms of forced migration because of the feminization of poverty and their marginalization and disenfranchisement in society. Women are mainly trafficked in order to work in the sex and entertainment industries, forced into sweatshop labour, kept in domestic servitude, or taken for marriage in destination countries. Children may be kidnapped, trafficked and sold for labour in the agricultural or informal economic sectors or as soldiers.

There is no single internationally accepted definition of trafficking. Some definitions stress the elements of force and coercion in trafficking whilst others emphasize the migratory aspects or business dimensions of the activity. Historically, trafficking in persons was defined for the first time within a Convention of the United Nations in 1949, mainly in relation to the procuring, enticing or leading away of a woman by coercion for the purpose of prostitution. Since then, there have been moves to broaden the understanding of trafficking to include other forms of exploitation (sexual exploitation, forced labour or services, servitude, the removal of organs) and to address the human rights of those who are trafficked. Even if and where trafficking is associated with prostitution, the argument is that it is not sex work *per se* which should be the focus but the way in which it is organized and the conditions under which women have to work. The range of trafficking harms may include high risks to personal safety, debt bondage, abuse at the hands of other migrants, intermediaries or criminal organizations and, in the case of sexual abuse, exposure to sexually transmitted diseases and reproductive illnesses.

There are three main stages to the trade in persons: the recruitment of irregular migrants; their movement to countries of transit and destination; and the control of migrants once their journey has ended. Different intermediaries or crime groups may be involved in each of these stages, some of which are more organized than others. They fall on a continuum ranging from freelance criminals or entrepreneurs providing a single service (for example, transportation, fake documents) and loose confederations of agencies striding legal and illegal ventures, to highly structured criminal organizations controlling the trafficking process from start to finish. Many individuals involved in the transnational business of human trafficking do not fit the image of the conventional criminal. They include (semi-)legitimate migration brokers, labour recruitment agents and other service providers in hidden economies in countries of transit and destination. Significantly, critics have pointed out that human trade would not thrive as it does in particular regions if public officials, responsible for the oversight of immigration and custom services, did not co-operate with traffickers or smugglers.

Evaluation

The fight against human trafficking as a form of transnational crime has become a major topic of official concern at an international level. Whilst most states or groups of states have approached the problem from a crime control perspective, less attention has been given to considering why irregular migrants would engage with traffickers in the first place. One argument is that given the increasing curtailment of legal migratory opportunities, human trafficking and smuggling have become the only viable means of entry into Fortress Europe and other destination countries for many migrants. Seen in this light, it seems counter-productive for state authorities to 'rescue' trafficked persons from their situation and simply return them to their country of origin, often to the same conditions from which they originally fled. Indeed, some critics have questioned the distinction between trafficking and smuggling (and between those who are taken across borders against their will and those who voluntarily take part in the move). Green and Grewcock (2002) have argued that this artificial distinction between trafficking and smuggling extends to state understandings and treatment of persons who are trafficked (as victims deserving of sympathy though still subject to return) and those who engage the service of a smuggler (as unambiguously undeserving).

International responses to human trafficking and the development of specific anti-trafficking initiatives reflect the conflicting agendas and priorities raised by this issue.

Whilst there is obvious concern to protect victims and to prevent the abuses of trafficking, the overall debate is dominated by state concerns about how to control the growth of asylum and irregular migration. Official discourses of a 'war' against human trafficking tend to regard all those who cross borders without authorization as a threat to state sovereignty, economic prosperity and social order, and to provide justifications for increasingly punitive, covert and extra-legal measures of policing, regulation and exclusion. State measures of control have ranged from blanket border enforcement, visa policies, carriers' liability legislation and sanctions against employers of undocumented migrants, to finger printing, radar surveillance, detention and the expulsion of alien 'others'. Many of these punitive sanctions and border enforcement practices have been highly contentious and ineffective, and arguably they only serve to push a greater percentage of human traffic into the hands of exploitative crime networks and drive up the costs of irregular migration.

Maggy Lee

Associated Concepts: globalization, human rights, transnational organized crime, transnational policing

Key Readings

Bales, K. (1999) *Disposable People: New Slavery in the Global Economy*. Berkeley: University of California Press.

Green, P. and Grewcock, M. (2002) 'The war against illegal immigration: state crime and the construction of a European identity', *Current Issues in Criminal Justice*, 14: 87–101.

Kelly, L. (2002) *Journeys of Jeopardy: A Review of Research on Trafficking in Women and Children in Europe*. IOM Migration Research Series No. 11. Geneva: IOM.

Kyle, D. and Koslowski, D. (eds) (2001) *Global Human Smuggling: Comparative Perspectives*. London: Johns Hopkins University Press.

Lee, M. (2010) *Trafficking and Global Crime Control*. London: Sage.

Shelley, L. (2010) *Human Trafficking: A Global Perspective*. New York: Cambridge University Press.

INCAPACITATION

Definition

A justification for punishment which maintains that the offender's ability to commit further crimes should be removed, either physically or geographically. In certain societies incapacitation can take the form of rendering criminals harmless through the removal of offending limbs (for instance, hands in the case of thieves), whilst in others the banishment of criminals to confined spaces, like prisons, curtails the possibilities for offending behaviour. The death penalty is the starkest form of incapacitation.

Distinctive Features

In contrast to other justifications of punishment, such as rehabilitation, the logic of incapacitation appeals to neither changing the offender's behaviour nor searching for the causes of the offending. Instead it advocates the protection of potential victims as the essence of punishment, as opposed to the rights of offenders. Many contemporary criminal justice strategies currently subscribe to the doctrine of incapacitation. In part, this is because it fills the void created by the collapse of rehabilitation and the associated argument that 'nothing works' in the 1970s, but also because it claims to offer a means of social defence through removing offenders from society and thereby eliminating their capacity to commit further crimes.

Examples of current criminal justice sentencing policy that are informed by the logic of incapacitation would include the 'three strikes and you're out' penalty and selective incapacitation, both of which will usually involve long periods of incarceration. One of the distinguishing features of these approaches is that they are concerned with identifying offenders or groups of offenders who are likely to commit future crimes on the basis of the risk, or likelihood, of offending. The argument is that a small number of offenders are responsible for a significant proportion of the crime in certain areas and if these individuals or groups were imprisoned then this would have a pronounced effect on the local crime rate. It is recognized that research carried out by the Rand Corporation in the USA provided the intellectual origins for contemporary incapacitative sentencing policies (see Greenwood, 1983). More generally, the doctrine of incapacitation has become the main philosophical justification for imprisonment in countries that subscribe to the notion that 'prison works', as it takes many persistent and serious offenders off the streets and thereby, it is claimed, reduces the crime rate (Murray, 1997).

Evaluation

Incapacitation is essentially a strategy of containment – and is frequently justified through a form of moral reasoning known as utilitarianism, which maintains that the financial and social benefits will outweigh the costs of an ever expanding prison population. The model for this approach is what is known as the American 'prison experiment', where there has been a dramatic growth in the prison population over the past thirty years. For instance, in 1970 there were 196,000 prisoners in state and federal prisons in the United States, but by the mid-1990s the state and federal prisons were holding over 1.1 million prisoners on any given day (Currie, 1996).

An influential attempt to think through these changes is provided by Malcolm Feeley and Jonathan Simon (1992). Their argument is that a 'New Penology' has risen at the expense of an 'Old Penology'. For them, the 'Old Penology' was preoccupied with such matters as guilt, responsibility and obligation, as well as diagnosis, intervention and treatment of the individual offender, whereas they would claim the 'New Penology' is radically different and actuarial in orientation as it is concerned with techniques for identifying, classifying and managing groups that have been sorted by their levels of dangerousness. The aim is not to intervene in offenders' lives for the purposes of ascertaining responsibility or rehabilitating them. It is instead a strategy of managing dangerousness, and incapacitation is part of this broader, apolitical displacement of individualized discipline and rehabilitation.

Critics of incapacitation, like Elliot Currie (1996), argue that whilst this strategy might have had some effect on the crime rate this effect is distressingly small in relation to the huge costs involved. At best it can be argued that the effect of this massive experiment with imprisonment on the crime rate has been modest. For instance, whilst the overall crime rate declined by 3 per cent between 1993 and 1996 in the United States, it still remains at a very high level – with a homicide rate seven times that of England and Wales (Young, 1999). However, what is more alarming is the clear racial dimension to this strategy of containment, to the extent that one in nine African American males aged 20–29 is in prison, whilst a staggering

one in three is either in prison, on probation or on parole (Mauer, 1997).

These figures raise fundamental ethical and moral questions about the nature of US society and the dangers posed by the wholesale importation of the incapacitation doctrine. For it is clear that the 'experiment' has been funded by diverting public expenditure away from welfare and towards prisons, whilst the level of violence, particularly among the young and disadvantaged, continues to decimate life in many North American cities. Incapacitation as a penal policy amounts to little more than the 'warehousing' of prisoners, since there is scarcely any recognition of the human character of the offender and nor are the reasons for offending addressed in any fundamental way, as this is viewed as a pointless exercise.

Eamonn Carrabine

Associated Concepts: actuarialism, capital punishment, crime control model, deterrence, penality, penology, rehabilitation, retribution, social defence theory

Key Readings

Currie, E. (1996) *Is America Winning the War on Crime and Should Britain Follow its Example?* London: NACRO.

Feeley, M. and Simon, J. (1992) 'The New Penology: notes on the emerging strategy of corrections and its implications', *Criminology*, 30 (4): 449–70.

Greenwood, P. (1983) 'Controlling the crime rate through imprisonment', in J.Q. Wilson (ed.), *Crime and Public Policy.* San Francisco, CA: Institute for Contemporary Studies.

Mauer, M. (1997) *Intended and Unintended Consequences: State Racial Disparities in Imprisonment.* Washington, DC: The Sentencing Project.

Murray, C. (1997) *Does Prison Work?* London: Institute for Economic Affairs.

Young, J. (1999) *The Exclusive Society.* London: Sage.

INCARCERATION

Definition

The process of confining and segregating deviant populations into specialist institutions for the purposes of punishment, treatment or care.

Distinctive Features

The eighteenth century marked a decisive moment in the history of social control in Northern Europe, as imprisonment became the dominant means of dealing with undesirable conduct and the preferred form of punishment. Up until this point the two main purposes of imprisonment were, first, to hold in custody those awaiting trial or the execution of a sentence, and second, to coerce fine defaulters and debtors into making good their misfortune. Whilst custody could be used for punishment, it was primarily used for detention, and makeshift structures – like fortresses, castles, cellars and town gates – were deployed for this purpose. Instead the main forms of punishment were primarily corporal and included execution, mutilation, branding, whipping, and other forms of public shaming (such as the use of stocks and pillories).

However, as feudal systems of existence began to break down with the advent of mercantile capitalism and there were significant population migrations from rural areas to burgeoning towns and cities – as dispossessed peasants and labourers were forced to become urban scavengers – there emerged innovative responses to the anxieties provoked by this upheaval. From the 1500s galley slavery, transportation, bridewells and workhouses came to complement conventional forms of corporal punishment, as a means of distinguishing the 'deserving' poor from the 'undeserving' poor and fuelling the colonial expansion.

Nevertheless, it is the Enlightenment that gave birth to incarceration as the generalized response to crime and deviance, as opposed to the myriad public spectacles of suffering, and it proposed the architecture of segregation as the sole means of manufacturing virtue and communicating deterrence. But this was not an isolated event as whole populations became subject to processes of incarceration; not only were thieves consigned to prisons, but also the mad became subjected to asylums, children were introduced to schools, workers came to exchange their labour power in factories, and the ill began to be treated in hospitals.

The question that needs to be answered is why did incarceration become the dominant response to crime from the end of the eighteenth century? Up until the 1970s the explanation would have been that imprisonment represents an enlightened, humanitarian, progressive response over the barbarism of earlier epochs. This Whig view of history emphasized how early forms of punishment, based on vengeance, irrationality and cruelty, had been replaced by informed, professional and expert intervention and would celebrate the zeal of benevolent reformers in explaining why contemporary penal systems exist. However, this interpretation has been widely challenged by a range of 'revisionist' histories of the 'Great Incarcerations' (Cohen, 1985).

The earliest work that looked behind the rhetoric of reformers and asked why particular punishments would gain prominence during certain historical periods is provided by Rusche and Kirchheimer (1968). Their argument is informed by a Marxist understanding of social relations and highlights relationships between the form of punishment and the economic requirements of particular modes of production. For instance, they argue that prisons emerged with the advent of industrial capitalism as a means of creating a submissive and regulated workforce. Their account has been criticized for the way in which it provides a one-dimensional explanation of penal relations that prioritizes the significance of the labour market at the expense of other factors. A more sophisticated account is Ignatieff's (1978) analysis of the birth of imprisonment. He rejects economic functionalism and argues that incarceration was a response to the crisis in class relations wrought by the

Industrial Revolution, as it served to establish the legitimacy of the law and was understood as one element within a larger vision of securing popular consent in an increasingly unequal, class-divided society.

However, the most influential 'revisionist' history of imprisonment is Foucault's *Discipline and Punish* (1977), as he argues that the emergence of the prison does not mark a more humanitarian form of punishment. Instead, it represents an attempt to punish more efficiently and extensively in order to create a disciplined society, through the techniques of surveillance, classification and examination perfected in the new institutional spaces (e.g., Bentham's Panopticon). The originality of Foucault's argument lies in the importance he attaches to the relationship between power and forms of knowledge. The emergence of the prison is but one instance of the dispersal of new forms of knowledge and his project is to examine how domination is achieved and how individual subjectivity is socially constructed. The prison has always been a failure, as it does not reduce crime, yet the reason why it persists is because it stands at one end of a continuum in which surveillance and regulation have become normalized throughout society. Foucault employs the phrase 'carceral archipelago' to describe the chain of institutions that stretch out from the prison to imply that Western liberal democracies are intimately bound up with forms of oppression.

Evaluation

Whilst 'revisionist' histories continue to be influential, a number of critics have found fault with the way in which all social relations have been described in the language of domination, oversimplifying complex processes and overstating the instrumental aspects of punishment at the expense of the social support commanded by condemnation (Garland, 1990). Moreover, there is a failure to consider the punishment of women, which problematizes thinking on the role and development of incarceration. For instance, why women are more likely to be treated as 'mad' rather than 'bad' poses questions that conventional and revisionist histories are unable to answer.

Eamonn Carrabine

Associated Concepts: carceral society, decarceration, historical methods, normalization, panopticism, social control, transcarceration

Key Readings

Cohen, S. (1985) *Visions of Social Control.* Cambridge: Polity Press.
Foucault, M. (1977) *Discipline and Punish: The Birth of the Prison.* Harmondsworth: Penguin.
Garland, D. (1990) *Punishment and Modern Society: A Study in Social Theory.* Oxford: Clarendon Press.
Ignatieff, M. (1978) *A Just Measure of Pain: The Penitentiary in the Industrial Revolution.* London: Macmillan.
Rusche, G. and Kirchheimer, O. (1968) *Punishment and Social Structure.* New York: Russell and Russell (originally published 1939).

INDIVIDUAL POSITIVISM

Definition

A theoretical approach that views crime as being generated primarily by forces located within the individual. This usually takes one of two forms. A criminal predisposition is to be found either in biologically given constitutional factors or in the psychological make-up of particular individuals.

Distinctive Features

A key defining characteristic of individual positivism is that the fundamental predisposition to crime lies in the individual. Crime is determined by innate genetic or physiological incapacities or by inadequate child-rearing practices in dysfunctional families.

In the early twentieth century several attempts were made to isolate the key physiological characteristics of known criminals. Goring (1913) studied more than 3,000 male prisoners in and around London and compared them with various control groups of non-prisoners. Using correlational analysis he found that criminals tended to be shorter in height and weigh less. He explained such differences with reference to notions of 'inbreeding within a criminal class' which generated a lineage of mental deficiencies within certain families. Such correlations of body build and behavioural tendencies became their most sophisticated in the work of Sheldon (1949). His analysis suggested that the shape of the body correlated with individual temperament and mental well-being. Analysing and comparing 200 boys in a reformatory in Boston with 4,000 students, he concluded that most delinquents had a body shape made up of well-developed muscles and an athletic appearance. Their personalities were strong, active, aggressive and sometimes violent.

The earliest attempts to isolate a genetic cause of criminality involved analyses of the family trees of known criminals. Dugdale (1910), for example, traced more than 1,000 descendants of the Jukes – a New York family who were infamous for their involvement with criminality and prostitution – and found 280 paupers, 60 thieves, 7 murderers, 140 criminals and 50 prostitutes. He concluded that 'undesirable' hereditary characteristics were passed down through families. Criminal families tended to produce criminal children. Criminals were born not made. Evidence from the Cambridge study in Delinquent Development in the 1970s continued to suggest that crime did indeed run in families. This study noted that of 397 families half of all convictions were concentrated in just 23. Convictions for one family member were strongly related to convictions for each other family member. Three-quarters of convicted mothers and convicted fathers had a convicted child.

More rigorous research directed at isolating a genetic factor has been carried out with twins and adoptees. These have concluded that children's behaviour is more similar to that of their biological parents than to that of their adoptive parents. Mednick concluded that some factor was transmitted by convicted parents which would increase the likelihood that their children, even after adoption, would be convicted for criminal offences (Mednick et al., 1987). Further research has since examined a wide range of bio-chemical factors (such as hormones, testosterone, adrenalin and blood sugar levels) in attempts to isolate an individual causal factor in the generation of deviant, anti-social, criminal or violent behaviour. However, most current research in this tradition would not claim that biological make-up alone can be used as a sufficient explanation for crime. Rather, some biological factors may generate criminality, but only when they interact with certain other psychological or social factors. Nevertheless this type of research continues to attract significant research funding and publicity.

Another form of individual positivism, often termed the 'psychogenic school', has shifted the focus of analysis away from biologically given constitutional factors and towards more dynamic mental processes. Psychologists and psychiatrists have attempted systematically to associate particular personality traits with criminal behaviour. Much of this has depended on the construction of performance tests, personality scales and measurements of intelligence. From these a wide range of traits has been singled out as being indicative of delinquent and criminal propensities. These include extroversion, defiance, suspicion, a low IQ, excitability and impulsiveness (Eysenck, 1964). Farrington (1996) details numerous risk factors including: being the child of a teenage mother, an impulsive personality, low intelligence and a poor performance in school, harsh or erratic parental discipline and parental conflict, as well as peer group influences and socio-economic status.

Evaluation

Individual positivism formed the bedrock of criminological studies for the first half of the twentieth century and regained importance in the 1990s. For some, because of advances in our knowledge of genetic structures, it offers a way forward in understanding a criminality which is free from a multitude of complicating social variables. For others it is little more than a dangerous political gambit to segregate those who are deemed to be physically or emotionally unfit. From within psychology, positivism has been attacked for its lack of attention to processes of human cognition and social learning in which individuals are viewed as capable of self-reflection and self-development, rather than as beings who will simply act upon pre-given determinants. Whilst individual positivists tend to characterize deviant behaviour as pathological, it has also been argued that deviancy is a meaningful behaviour pattern which only becomes undesirable when judged and labelled by others. There are two major limitations to those theories which attempt to replicate the principles of scientific determinism. First, the more that criminological research has developed, the more the number of variables thought to be important in crime has increased. Even if such variables were capable of adequate measurements, controlling for their relative effect is probably impossible. This leads to sampling variations between studies so that results are always difficult to replicate. A long list of correlations tends to be produced which, though interesting in themselves, will shed no light on the question of causation. Second, psychological research may be capable of unearthing more and more variables, but it then usually attempts to explain crime with reference to some existing psychological theory which is designed to account for some psychological abnormality.

Nevertheless, theories based on individual positivism continue to have a widespread popular and political appeal. Notions of parental neglect, 'bad blood' and psycho-pathology all have their roots here. The search for the causes of crime by identifying a criminal type or a criminal personality will continue because of the general reluctance to believe that criminality is in any way 'normal'.

John Muncie

Associated Concepts: biological criminology, causation, conditioning, correlational analysis, determinism, dispositional theory, genetics, personality theory, positivism, risk factor research, somatotyping

Key Readings

Dugdale, R. (1910) *The Jukes*. New York: Putnam.

Eysenck, H.J. (1964) *Crime and Personality*. London: Routledge and Kegan Paul.

Farrington, D. (1996) *Understanding and Preventing Youth Crime*, Social Policy Research Findings No. 93. York: Joseph Rowntree Foundation.

Goring, C. (1913) *The English Convict*. London: HMSO.

Mednick, S., Moffit, T. and Stack, S. (eds) (1987) *The Causes of Crime: New Biological Approaches*. Cambridge: Cambridge University Press.

Sheldon, W. (1949) *Varieties of Delinquent Youth*. New York: Harper.

INFORMAL JUSTICE

Definition

Informal justice refers to a variety of initiatives that are intended either to overcome the major limitations of formal criminal justice processes or replace the criminal justice system.

Distinctive Features

During the 1960s and 1970s socio-legal scholars campaigned for a move away from the formal criminal justice system and dependence on state-centred forms of law towards alternative forms of dispute resolution. Considerable attention was paid to the applicability of non-Western practices and the need to do justice differently. Amongst more radical writers, efforts were made to locate or imagine forms and processes of socialist justice that were built on different principles from those operating in Western capitalist societies. No single model of informal justice was developed but their common features included the advocacy of non-formal, non-adversarial, non-conflictual procedures and greater levels of direct community participation. The purpose of informal justice was defined as arbitration, mediation, reconciliation, reparation and restoration, and would require decentralization, delegalization, deprofessionalization and deregulation. A critique of informal justice soon appeared, pointing, for example, to the potential for reactionary and very coercive forms of community or popular justice. But perhaps more significant were evaluations of a variety of initiatives that suggested that 'alternatives' rather than replacing formal practices were in fact being added on to the existing unreformed system. The results were a blurring of the boundaries between formal and informal, the expansion of the overall system of social control, and the creation of new forms of unaccountable governance. The remnants of the heated debates about informal justice now take place in relation to the possibilities for alternative forms of policing – dispute resolution and peacemaking initiatives and, perhaps most significantly, restorative justice projects. Those who are wary of the whole idea of 'informal justice' continue to focus on the logical outcome of such a process – spontaneous or organized vigilantism where self-appointed 'guardians' will mete out justice. Lynchings in the southern states of the USA, 'burning tyre' justice in the townships of South Africa, and punishment beatings in Northern Ireland can all be cited as disturbing examples of informal justice.

What is perhaps equally significant are ongoing examples of 'community justice' where specific types of dangerous or threatening offenders are, in the absence of decisive actions from the criminal justice system, hounded from neighbourhoods.

Eugene McLaughlin

Associated Concepts: abolitionism, community justice, peacemaking criminology, redress, restorative justice

Key Readings

Abel, R. (ed.) (1982) *The Politics of Informal Justice,* vols. 1 and 2. New York: Academic Press.

Cohen, S. (1985) *Visions of Social Control.* Cambridge: Polity Press.

Findlay, M. and Zvekic, U. (1988) *Analysing Informal Mechanisms of Crime Control: A Cross-Cultural Perspective.* Rome: UNSDRI.

Matthews, R. (1988) *Informal Justice.* London: Sage.

Merry, S.E. and Milner, N. (1993) *The Possibility of Popular Justice: A Case Study of Community Mediation in the United States.* New Brunswick, NJ: Rutgers University Press.

Pavlich, G.C. (1996) *Justice Fragmented: Mediating Community Disputes Under Postmodern Conditions.* London: Routledge.

INSTITUTIONAL RACISM

Definition

Institutional racism refers to the processes – intentional and unintentional – by which criminal justice agencies will systematically discriminate against certain social groups on grounds of race or ethnicity.

Distinctive Features

In their seminal (1967) text *Black Power: The Politics of Liberation in America,* Stokely Carmichael and Charles V. Hamilton distinguished between individual and institutional racism. They defined individual racism as overt acts carried out by individuals which would cause death, injury and/or the violent destruction of property. Classic examples of individual racism would include white people driving out black people from a particular neighbourhood or arson attacks on black people's property. Institutional racism they argued was 'less overt, far more subtle, less identifiable in terms of specific individuals committing the acts' (1967: 4). It was equally, if not more, damaging in terms of its consequences as individual acts of racism. Because of its pervasive and insidious nature, they held that it was institutional racism that denied black people proper welfare provision, health care amenities, education and access to proper jobs, and also trapped them in slum tenements where they were exploited by landlords and loan sharks. And in terms of its outcomes institutional racism was remarkably similar to colonialism.

Carmichael and Hamilton used the term to present a devastating 'Black Power' critique of white liberal attitudes towards 'race' in the USA, arguing that although institutional racism 'relies on the active and pervasive operation of anti-black attitudes' because it originates 'in the operation of the established and respected forces in the society' it receives less attention and public condemnation. Institutional racism is maintained and perpetuated not just by the procedures and practices of white institutions but also through indifference, inertia and ignorance on the part of the white masses and officials. This was to lead them to make two primary conclusions. First, that it was institutional racism that lay at the root of the alienation of black people and caused a multitude of oppressive conditions resulting in serious disturbances in black neighbourhoods. When these neighbourhoods exploded it was the residents who were characteristically blamed for the criminality, and in due course experts would be appointed to prepare 'authoritative' reports which would typically refuse to address this deep-seated institutional racism. Second, race relations policies based on inclusion, assimilation and the adoption of white middle-class values tended only to incorporate black people into their own institutionalized oppression.

Evaluation

Because of its origins and its radical critique considerable efforts were made to discredit the value of the term by an insistence amongst many social scientists that it was too sweeping and ill-defined and thus this made it difficult for race relations bodies to 'prove' intention and causation. However, its potency for activists lay in its insistence that racism had to be addressed at an institutional or systemic level rather than concentrating the effort on identifying individual racists. Carmichael and Hamilton had also provided an intriguing explanation for how racism could persist in organizational settings despite the existence of official legislation geared towards the removal of discriminatory practices and equality of opportunity.

In the sphere of criminal justice in a variety of jurisdictions, a heated debate took place concerning the extent of racial discrimination, particularly the disproportionate application of discretionary police powers to black communities and the over-representation of young black men in the prison population. Black community groups insisted that institutional racism was at work, with young black men receiving less favourable treatment at every stage between arrest and conviction. The cumulative effect was their disproportionate representation in the prison population. Community groups were also critical of the manner in which the criminal justice system discriminated against black victims of crime and the serious under-representation of black people in criminal justice agencies. However, official explanations, such as those articulated by Lord Scarman in his report into the inner city riots in the UK in 1981, rejected allegations of institutional racism, focusing instead on the criminal tendencies of young black men and the overtly racist actions of a minority of frontline police officers.

In the UK, the controversial and unresolved issue of institutional racism resurfaced during the official inquiry into the racist murder of Stephen Lawrence in South London in 1993. To the consternation of the Metropolitan Police, the inquiry team concluded that the police investigation 'was marred by a combination of professional incompetence, institutional racism and a failure of leadership by senior officers'. The final report also provided the UK government with an official definition of institutional racism: 'the collective failure of an organization to provide an appropriate and professional service to people because of their colour, culture or ethnic origin. It can be seen or detected in processes, attitudes and behaviour which amount to discrimination through unwitting prejudice, ignorance, thoughtlessness, and racist stereotyping which disadvantage minority ethnic people' (1999: paragraph 6.34). The report emphasized that there had to be an unequivocal recognition and acceptance of the problem of institutional racism and commitment to a fundamental organizational change. The government established an ambitious programme of reform to ensure that the policies, procedures and practices of the criminal justice agencies would be consciously and actively anti-racist and would also promote racial fairness and equality. Whether this momentum for change will be sustained and the reform programme realized is open to question. As yet, there is little evidence that the criminal justice agencies have any understanding of how their policies and procedures and practices turn out to be 'racialized'. However, what is truly remarkable is that as a result of the Stephen Lawrence inquiry report, a version of a concept first coined by 'Black Panthers' now stands as the accepted centre of the race relations strategy of the UK criminal justice system.

Eugene McLaughlin

Associated Concepts: criminal justice, discretion, discrimination, disproportionality, police bias, racialization

Key Readings

Carmichael, S. and Hamilton, C.V. (1967) *Black Power: The Politics of Liberation in America.* London: Jonathan Cape.
Scarman, Lord (1981) *The Brixton Disorders, 10–12 April 1981.* London: HMSO.
Stephen Lawrence Inquiry (1999) *Report of an Inquiry by Sir William MacPherson of Cluny.* London: HMSO.

INTEGRATIVE CRIMINOLOGY

Definition

An interdisciplinary approach to understanding crime and crime control which incorporates at least two disciplinary (or non-disciplinary) bodies of knowledge. This incorporation of criminologies and other bodies of knowledge should ideally aspire to encompass any and all data, theories and methods that would shed light on the production of crime, criminals and social control, including the field of criminology itself.

Distinctive Features

Unlike single perspectives or disciplinary approaches within criminology that assume crime and crime control are the products of primarily biological, psychological, economic, political, social or cultural factors, the emerging integrative paradigm argues that criminological knowledge should incorporate analyses that assimilate the realities from each of these areas of enquiry. Integrative criminology also assumes that the study of the causes or aetiology of crime and the study of the control or regulation of criminals are not separate but related phenomena. Together, these areas of criminology constitute the integrative parts of the whole of crime and social control. Thus, in order to understand criminals, crime control and prevention, or criminology, criminologists should not only study each of these in relationship to the other, but also do so as these are connected with other bodies of interdisciplinary knowledge such as cultural, media and gender/sex studies. Finally, integrative criminology endeavours to provide analyses that will link the various bodies of knowledge that focus on the connections between the aetiology of crime, the behaviour of criminals, and the policies and practices of crime control.

C. Ray Jeffery made one of the earliest explicit cases for integration in his (1990) textbook *Criminology: An Interdisciplinary Approach.* In this work he argued that criminology had to integrate various bodies of knowledge from biology, psychology, sociology, law and other fields. Subsequently, he has argued that what is required is an integration of both a theory of crime and a theory of criminal behaviour. In order to accomplish this, Jeffery has maintained that criminology has to develop an interdisciplinary theory of behaviour and then apply it to the explanations of crime and criminal behaviour. At present the study of crime and crime control, or of crime and justice, reveals an assortment of integrative strategies (Barak, 1998a).

Integrating criminologies are expressed in a myriad of ways that may include merging the goals and objectives within or across the traditional and non-integrative approaches of classical, positivist and critical criminologies. Basically, however, there are three kinds of integrative approaches that may be adopted: (1) disciplinary perspectives that connect various explanations of crime and crime control from within one field of study, operating up and down, such as sociology, psychology or anthropology; (2) multidisciplinary perspectives that partition the subject matter of crime and crime control into levels of analysis that are explained by different disciplines, operating side by side, such as sociology, psychology and anthropology; and (3) interdisciplinary perspectives that integrate crime and crime control, operating as holistic-interactive analyses, which incorporate the full range or varieties of knowledge from such diverse fields as the social sciences, natural sciences and the humanities.

Essentially, there are two kinds of integrative criminology taking place today: 'modernist' and 'postmodernist' (Barak, 1998b). Both types of synthesis call for a conceptual integration. However, modern forms emphasize the centrality of theory in scientific endeavours and the construction of 'causal models', while postmodern forms emphasize the ever-changing voices of plurality that provide meaning for the local sites of crime, justice, law and community, and the construction of reciprocal, interactive or dialectical models of 'causality'. In comparison, the modern approaches are more concerned with integrating theories while the postmodern approaches are more concerned with integrating knowledges. Rather than pursuing the cause–effect predictions of theoretical integration within one or between a few disciplines like the modernists, postmodernists are developing explanatory models of crime and crime control that integrate the entire group of interdisciplinary knowledges.

An important distinction between the various models of integration hinges on the scope or range of deviance and criminality addressed by a specific approach. Usually, the causal logic of integrative theorization tends to be a composite of causal relationships taken from other theories that combine elements from social ecology theory, social learning theory, social control theory and subcultural theory. For example, Elliott et al.'s (1985) integrated macro-micro theory of delinquency and drug use contends that social disorganization, strain and inadequate socialization cause a weakening of conventional bonding and a strengthening of delinquent bonding, which then result in delinquent behaviour.

Other modernist formulations such as the social process-micro models tend to emphasize the integration of kinds-of-people explanations of human behaviour. For example, Wilson and Herrnstein (1985) have proposed an eclectic, social, learning-behavioural choice formulation that relies on both positivist determinism and rational free will. This model of theoretical integration combines factors involving human agency, individual action and social process, while it omits considerations of social organization and culture. A third type of modernist integration includes the social structural-macro models, such as Quinney's (1977) structural theory which argues that all criminal activities are class-specific. In this formulation, the contradictions of capitalist development will result in two interconnected sets of crime: the crimes of 'domination and repression' committed by the capitalists and agents of crime control and the crimes of 'accommodation and resistance' committed by workers and ordinary people.

Finally, there are the postmodernist efforts at integration. These argue that crimes are recursive productions, that is, routinized activities which cannot be separated from historically and culturally specific discourses and structures that have attained a relative stability over time and place. For example, Henry and Milovanovic's (1996) constitutive criminology argues such discourses of difference and structured inequality will become courses of social action where criminals and crime-fighters alike represent excessive investors in the accumulation and expression of power and control. Similarly, Gregg Barak's *Representing O.J.: Murder, Criminal Justice, and Mass Culture* (1996) argues that in order to understand the reactions of different groups of Americans to the O.J. Simpson trial, for example, an integration of the legal and cultural factors, such as the social and psychological group experiences that have helped to shape various peoples' attitudes and perceptions of crime and justice, must be adopted.

Evaluation

Although the field of criminology has always formally identified itself as an interdisciplinary exercise, most of its theoreticians and practitioners have worked primarily from narrow disciplinary frameworks. Hence, integrative or interdisciplinary criminology represents a challenge to the more traditional disciplinary approaches applied by the majority of criminologists. As an emerging paradigm within criminology, integration is relatively new, so the jury is still out and the verdict pending. A number of criminologists today are sceptical of the ability of integrative criminology to deliver on its promises and possibilities. Some criminologists, such as Travis Hirschi, have already concluded that integrative criminology does not work and will not succeed. On the other hand, some criminologists, like John Braithwaite, believe that integration is the only way to proceed.

Gregg Barak

Associated Concepts: constitutive criminology, interactionism, social constructionism, social learning theory

Key Readings

Barak, G. (1996) *Representing O.J.: Murder, Criminal Justice, and Mass Culture.* New York: Harrow and Heston.
Barak, G. (ed.) (1998a) *Integrative Criminology.* Aldershot: Ashgate.
Barak, G. (1998b) *Integrating Criminologies.* Boston, MA: Allyn and Bacon.
Elliott, D.S., Huizinga, D. and Ageton, S. (1985) *Explaining Delinquency and Drug Use.* Beverly Hills, CA: Sage.
Henry, S. and Milovanovic, D. (1996) *Constitutive Criminology.* London: Sage.
Jeffery, C.R. (1990) *Criminology: An Interdisciplinary Approach.* Englewood Cliffs, NJ: Prentice-Hall.
Quinney, R. (1977) *Class, State, and Crime.* New York: David McKay.
Wilson, J.Q. and Herrnstein, R.J. (1985) *Crime and Human Nature.* New York: Simon and Schuster.

INTERACTIONISM

Definition

A theoretical approach which focuses on interactions between individuals as symbolic and linguistic exchanges and as means of creative action. It views the social world as the product of such interactions. Sometimes this theoretical approach is also referred to as symbolic interactionism.

Distinctive Features

Interactionism is part of a broad strand of theorizing in the social sciences which seeks to integrate notions of purposeful and meaningful action with explanations of social phenomena such as crime and deviance. The writings of Max Weber were influential in building social meanings into theory but the specific formulation of symbolic interactionism emerged and developed during the inter-war years, mainly at the University of Chicago and principally as a result of the work of the social psychologist George Herbert Mead. Mead did not systematically produce his theoretical ideas in written form. The published material is a compilation of lectures and notes and as a result there are a number of contradictions and areas for clarification in terms of the fine detail (Mead, 1934). However, his general thesis is as follows. Animal behaviour is largely determined and characterized by stimulus–response. Human behaviour, on the other hand, is flexible and dynamic and has the potential for creativity. An individual forms a concept and image of him- or herself ('the self') by interacting with others and developing a reflexive awareness of how he or she is viewed by others. This is made possible through the significant symbols that people share. Human language is made up of symbols and it is through these that individuals can communicate meaningfully. This is what is known as symbolic interactionism. It is by such communication that the individual takes on the perspective of others and learns to act accordingly towards them and others. However, there is also an element of the self which has the potential for rejecting or changing the perspectives of others and for acting spontaneously and creatively.

Mead was especially interested in the development of 'the self' and in child development. These interests were encased in a general theoretical framework and set of insights which influenced other theorists, not just in social psychology but also in sociology (for example, Herbert Blumer, who made significant contributions in the 1960s). These insights were in turn transferred and applied to a wide range of forms of social interaction, including those associated with crime and deviance.

Interactionism is not a grand theory in the sense of a set of integrated propositions. Rather, it is a framework which offers a set of assumptions about the nature of social action, the nature of the social world, and relationships between them. It also comprises a set of key concepts. The main assumptions are that human action is characterized by free choice, flexibility and dynamism. It is forever changing according to types of interaction and types of context. Forms of social action are formed, adapted, refined or changed in interactions with others in micro-social contexts. Social order in such contexts and in society in general is not fixed and external, but the product of such interactions. Social order is also not consensual; rather it is a plurality of perspectives, values and norms. Key concepts here include 'interaction', 'meaning', 'social learning', 'negotiation', 'process', 'stereotyping', 'labelling' and 'career'.

The interactionist framework and the assumptions and concepts which comprise it provide a basis for seeking explanations of social phenomena (such as crime) which typically are non-positivist. Instead, explanations are cast in terms of processes and interactions rather than predispositions, pathologies, determinants and causes, especially where these are seen as located in the individual. Interactionism also provides a basis for empirical enquiry, often using the methods and practices of ethnography. Ethnography has a particular affinity with interactionism because both of these share an interest in 'capturing the actor's point of view' and also because methods such as participant observation are especially suited to the study of social interactions. The use of ethnographic enquiry, guided by interactionist concepts, to study criminal subcultures is sometimes referred to as appreciative criminology.

The interactionist perspective has influenced criminological thinking at various junctures since its emergence from the symbolic interactionism of the 1930s. It was particularly influential as part of the radical reaction, in the 1960s and early 1970s, towards the dominance of positivism in criminology. It was typified by the labelling approach to deviance which emphasized that deviance is what people label as such. It encouraged many lines of enquiry. These included foci on: crime as the outcome of social interaction; crime as the result of negotiated processes involving rule violators and control agents as definers; changing definitions of crime in law enactment; police discretion in the enforcement of the law; crime as a meaningful act; and the consequences of being labelled deviant, for example in terms of further deviancy amplification.

Evaluation

An important element of social interaction is the exercise of power. Interactionists are interested in power, for example in the ways in which some categories of people are able to make deviant labels 'stick' and others are unable to cast them off. One of the challenges of interactionist-inspired criminological enquiry has been the ability to demonstrate successfully how the exercise of power in micro-social contexts has its source in wider, structural power inequalities in society. This requires criminologists to produce a synthesis of theorizing and empirical enquiry at micro and macro levels.

The contribution of the interactionist strand within criminology has been to challenge positivist approaches, with their emphasis on causality, by raising definitional issues (who gets labelled as deviant?) and by encouraging a focus on control agents as generators of crime (who does the labelling?). It has also produced a rich vein of ethnographic studies of deviant subcultures, criminal justice agencies and processes of social control.

Victor Jupp

Associated Concepts: appreciative criminology, ethnography, labelling, new deviancy theory, social learning theory

Key Readings

Becker, H. (1963) *Outsiders: Studies in the Sociology of Deviance.* New York: The Free Press.
Blumer, H. (1969) *Symbolic Interactionism.* Englewood Cliffs, NJ: Prentice-Hall.
Mead, G.H. (1934) *Mind, Self and Society.* Chicago: University of Chicago Press.
Sumner, C. (1994) *The Sociology of Deviance: An Obituary.* Buckingham: Open University Press.

J

JUST DESERTS

Definition

The proposition that the principles of proportionality, due process, determinant sentencing and non-discretional decision making should be the central elements of systems of criminal justice.

Distinctive Features

The principles of 'just deserts' in sentencing are usually compared with those of rehabilitation, treatment or welfare. In the 1970s liberal lawyers and civil libertarians in the USA were becoming increasingly critical of rehabilitative sentencing. They argued that the 'need for treatment' acted as a spurious justification for placing excessive restrictions on individual liberty, particularly for young women, which were out of proportion either to the seriousness of the offence or to the realities of being in 'need of care and protection'. Indeterminate sentencing schemes, notably in California, meant that the length of sentence was at the discretion of an Adult Authority (parole) board rather than a judicial body. Time in prison rested on psychological assessments of how far an offender had 'improved' rather than with reference to the actual crime committed. As a result minor offenders could serve longer sentences than those convicted of more serious offences, particularly if they declined the 'offer' of treatment. In a series of prison riots, most notably at Attica, a key grievance

was the indeterminacy and lack of proportionality in sentencing. Probation, social work and welfare judgements were viewed as a form of arbitrary and discretional power. Many offenders, it was argued, were subjected to apparently non-accountable state procedures and their liberty was often unjustifiably denied (American Friends Service Committee, 1972).

In the field of juvenile justice it was similarly argued that the investigation of social background was an imposition: that social work involvement not only preserved explanations of individual pathology, it also undermined young persons' right to natural justice. Young people were placed in double jeopardy – sentenced for their background as well as for their offence – and as a result their movement up the sentencing tariff was often accelerated (Morris et al., 1980).

In the wake of these criticisms a new justice-based model of corrections emerged. Its leading proponent in America, von Hirsch (1976), proposed that the following principles be reinstated at the centre of criminal justice practice:

- proportionality of punishment to crime, or the offender is handed a sentence that is in accordance with what the act deserves;
- determinacy of sentencing and an end to indeterminate, treatment-oriented sentences;
- an end to judicial, professional and administrative discretion;
- an end to disparities in sentencing;
- equity and protection of rights through due process.

The idea of punishing the crime, not the person, had clear attractions for those seeking an end to the abuses of discretional power.

Evaluation

However, this liberal critique also coalesced with the concerns of traditional retributivists that rehabilitation was a 'soft option'. For them tougher sentencing would also enable criminals to get their 'just deserts'. For this reason Clarke (1985) maintained that the staking out of 'justice' as a strategy for reform is always liable to allow proponents of law and order to recruit the arguments of 'natural justice' for their own ends, although the former is more concerned with retribution and the latter with judicial equality and consistency. Within the political climate of the 1980s notions of 'just deserts' and 'antiwelfarism' were indeed politically mobilized by the right. The language of 'justice and rights' was appropriated by one of 'self responsibility and obligation'. Accordingly, Hudson (1987, 1996) has argued that the 'just deserts' or 'back to justice' movements that emerged in many Western jurisdictions in the 1980s were evidence of a 'modern retributivism' rather than necessarily heralding the emergence of new liberal regimes and sentencing policies.

John Muncie

Associated Concepts: disproportionality, due process model, natural justice, rehabilitation, retribution

Key Readings

American Friends Service Committee (1972) *Struggle for Justice.* New York: Hill and Wang.
Clarke, J. (1985) 'Whose justice? The politics of juvenile control', *International Journal of the Sociology of Law,* 13 (4): 405–21.
von Hirsch, A. (1976) *Doing Justice: The Choice of Punishments.* New York: Hill and Wang.
Hudson, B. (1987) *Justice Through Punishment.* London: Macmillan.

Hudson, B. (1996) *Understanding Justice.* Buckingham: Open University Press.
Morris, A., Giller, H., Geach, H. and Szwed, E. (1980) *Justice for Children.* London: Macmillan.

JUSTICE

See: *Actuarialism; Crime control model; Criminal justice; Due process model; Informal justice; Just deserts; Managerialism; Natural justice; Popular justice; Restorative justice; Social justice*

JUVENILE JUSTICE

Definition

At its simplest 'juvenile justice' is the subdivision of criminal justice that focuses specifically on law, policy and practice in respect of child 'offenders'. For the purposes here a child means 'every human being below the age of eighteen years', as provided by the United Nations Convention on the Rights of the Child (United Nations General Assembly, 1989, Article 1). Up until the late nineteenth century, children who transgressed the criminal law were exposed to the same 'justice' systems as adults and faced identical penalties. During the latter half of the century, however, judicial processes, court systems and correctional institutions designed primarily for adults were increasingly regarded as being unsuitable for children. Such recognition was underpinned by a dualistic conceptualization of childhood, whereby 'juvenile delinquents' were perceived not only as 'precocious threats' requiring *correction* but also as 'vulnerable victims' in need of *protection*.

Distinctive Features

The Illinois Juvenile Court Act 1899 established the first court in the world (in Chicago, USA) specifically for 'neglected' and/or 'delinquent' children. Furthermore, whilst the Act fell short of providing child 'offenders' with a complete dispensation from punishment, it nonetheless emphasized rehabilitation, introduced protective practices and procedures, and instituted the formal separation of juvenile and adult justice systems. Essentially this model – whereby care/welfare/rehabilitative imperatives and control/justice/punitive priorities must co-exist, however awkwardly – came to characterize juvenile justice systems internationally. Specialist juvenile courts and justice systems were established in Britain (1908), France and Belgium (1912), Spain (1918), the Netherlands (1921), Germany (1922) and Austria (1923). By 1931, a League of Nations' study found that separate juvenile justice systems existed in 30 countries and since that time similar systems have been established in many more countries throughout the world (UNICEF, 1998). Despite the internationalization of juvenile justice, however, the concept defies a clear-cut definition, not least because it is pitted with tensions and contradictions: it 'exists as a function of the child care and criminal justice systems on either side of it, a meeting place of two otherwise separate worlds' (Harris and Webb, cited in Goldson et al., 2002: 120). The extent to which juvenile justice systems emphasize the 'caring ethos of social services' and the 'neo-liberal legalistic ethos of responsibility and punishment', or attempt to 'hybridize' both, is temporally and spatially contingent (Muncie and Hughes, 2002: 1). In other words, juvenile justice laws, policies, practices and system formations not only change over time (the temporal dimension); they also vary from one country or state to another (the spatial factor) (Goldson and Muncie, 2012). In short, juvenile justice systems are dynamic and ever-changing sites of contestation and change, the settlements of competing and/or intersecting conceptual features. Six such features are particularly significant and inform, to a greater or lesser extent, juvenile justice throughout the world.

First there is *welfare*. The principles that children should be protected from the full weight of 'adult' criminal justice, and that interventions should address both 'needs' and 'deeds', underpin the concept of welfare in juvenile justice. Such ostensibly benign imperatives also attract some critique, however. Conservative critics argue that the primary function of juvenile justice should be to *control* child 'offenders' rather than *care* for them. Welfare is thus presented as being too lenient and 'soft on crime'. Alternatively, critical criminologists, children's rights advocates and radical juvenile justice practitioners question the legitimacy of imposing wide-ranging interventions on the basis of 'need' and also challenge individualized notions of rehabilitation and treatment. They argue that attempts to transmit welfare through juvenile (criminal) justice systems often produce more harm than good. The same commentators also contend that uninhibited professional licence and discretionary judgements undermine children's right to justice.

Second is *justice*. This principle emphasizes the significance of proportionality. It claims that the legal rights of child 'offenders' must be secured and safeguarded through due process and legal representation. Formal intervention is conceived primarily in terms of 'restrictions of liberty' that must be limited to the minimum necessary in accordance with the severity/gravity of the offence, as distinct from the perceived needs of the child. Custodial sentencing should be strictly reserved for the most serious offences only and for the shortest possible time.

Third we have *informalism*. This concept is underpinned by a range of theoretical perspectives, practical propositions and destructuring impulses that combine to challenge the legitimacy of formal juvenile justice systems. Informalist perspectives claim that juvenile justice processes stigmatize children by applying criminogenic 'labels'. Such 'labelling', it is argued, is not evenly applied and is instead mediated through the structural divisions of class, 'race' and gender. Furthermore, it is argued that labelling triggers a negative 'social reaction' which, in turn, will have enduring and spiralling consequences. Informalism shifts the primary focus away from juvenile crime towards the problematization of the juvenile justice apparatus itself. Although informalism has never been comprehensively applied, some of its core contentions have influenced justice-based approaches as outlined above.

Fourth is *rights*. There is a range of international standards, treaties, rules and conventions that inform juvenile justice. Of particular note in this respect are: the United Nations Standard Minimum Rules for the Administration of Juvenile Justice (the Beijing Rules, 1985); the United Nations Guidelines for the Prevention of Juvenile Delinquency (the Riyadh Guidelines, 1990); and the United Nations Rules for the Protection of Juveniles Deprived of their Liberty (the JDL Rules, 1990). Perhaps most important of all here is the United Nations Convention on the Rights of the Child, which has – with some exceptions, most notably that of the USA – been adopted by countries throughout the world more quickly and more comprehensively than any other international convention in history.

Fifth there is *responsibility*. The concept of responsibility is most clearly expressed in juvenile justice with regard to the age of criminal minority, otherwise known as the age of criminal responsibility. This relates to the age at which a child is held to be fully accountable before criminal law: the point when a child's act of transgression can be formally processed as a 'crime'. There is no clear international standard regarding the age at which children can reasonably be deemed to be criminally responsible. Although the Beijing Rules (see above) provide that the age of criminal responsibility 'shall not be fixed at too low an age level, bearing in mind the facts of emotional, mental and intellectual maturity', there are significant variations across the world: from age 7 (including Australia, Barbados, Ghana, Hong Kong, Kuwait and the Lebanon) to age 18 (including Belgium, Colombia, Luxembourg, Panama and Uruguay).

Sixth we have *punishment* and *institutionalization*. Throughout the history of juvenile justice, and despite the varying forms that juvenile justice systems take, nation-states have always reserved the power to punish child 'offenders' and have ultimately expressed this through the practices of institutional containment. In the final analysis – and although rates of child incarceration do indeed vary across time and place – the locked institution is the linchpin of juvenile justice systems.

Evaluation

The range of international socio-legal instruments that apply to juvenile justice – either directly (as in the case of the Beijing Rules, the Riyadh Guidelines, the JDL Rules, and the United Nations Convention on the Rights of the Child), or more indirectly in respect of generic human rights standards – is an indicator of its global significance. It is ironic, therefore, that juvenile justice systems throughout the world regularly compromise, if not flagrantly violate, the human rights of child 'offenders'.

Formal ratification of the United Nations Convention on the Rights of the Child obliges the government of each 'State Party' to submit periodic reports (usually every five years) to the United Nations Committee on the Rights of the Child, which is based in Geneva. The Committee then considers the detail of such reports, together with other evidence submitted by non-governmental organizations (NGOs), and assesses the extent to which national laws, policies and practices are consistent with the international provisions of the Convention. The track records of State Parties in respect of juvenile justice is amongst those areas most frequently criticized by the Committee, which has expressed its concerns in almost 70 per cent of cases (UNICEF, 1998).

The attitude that a society takes to child 'offenders' – children who invariably see out their childhood within adverse social-structural conditions – is an important indicator of its core values and principles and its commitment to the wider social justice project. The burgeoning influence – in North America and Western Europe in particular – of penal policies that emphasize intolerance, punitivism and incapacitation does not bode well for either the realization of progressive social justice systems in general, or juvenile justice systems in particular, in advanced capitalist societies.

Barry Goldson

Associated Concepts: delinquency, diversion, due process model, human rights, informal justice, just deserts, net widening, social justice

Key Readings

Goldson, B. and Muncie, J. (2012) 'Towards a global "child friendly" juvenile justice?', *International Journal of Law, Crime and Justice,* 40 (1): 47–64.

Goldson, B., Lavalette, M. and McKechnie, J. (eds) (2002) *Children, Welfare and the State*. London: Sage.

Muncie, J. and Goldson, B. (eds) (2006) *Comparative Youth Justice*. London: Sage.

Muncie, J. and Hughes, G. (2002) 'Modes of youth governance: political rationalities, criminalization and resistance', in J. Muncie, G. Hughes and E. McLaughlin (eds), *Youth Justice: Critical Readings*. London: Sage.

UNICEF (1998) *Innocenti Digest: Juvenile Justice*. Florence: UNICEF.

United Nations General Assembly (1989) *The United Nations Convention on the Rights of the Child*. New York: United Nations.

L

LABELLING

Definition

A sociological approach to understanding crime and deviancy which refers to the social processes through which certain individuals and groups classify and categorize the behaviour of others. On this basis labelled individuals are stereotyped to act in certain ways and are responded to accordingly. Such reaction tends to reinforce a self-conception as deviant and has the unanticipated consequence of promoting the behaviour that it is designed to prevent.

Distinctive Features

Unlike traditional approaches which assume that the causes of crime and deviance lie either within individual offenders themselves or within their socio-economic circumstances, the labelling approach argues that criminological analysis should begin with how people come to be defined as deviant and then examine the implications that such definitions hold for future offending behaviour. The approach is widely associated with the work of Howard Becker (1963), who famously claimed that deviance is not inherent in any action, but is created when rules and sanctions are applied to behaviour considered to be 'offending'. Behaviour only becomes deviant when it is labelled as such. Traces of such an approach can be found throughout the nineteenth century. The penal reformer and utilitarian philosopher Jeremy Bentham, for example, argued that certain social reactions to crime – the

unreformed prison – are more likely to promote offending than curtail it. Henry Mayhew, the social commentator, considered that overzealous policing was a significant factor in the creation of juvenile delinquency in the mid-nineteenth century. Such themes are widely repeated in the perennial claim that prisons are 'colleges of crime' and that they cement 'criminal careers'. In the 1930s Frank Tannenbaum (1938) argued that deviance was created through a process of social interaction. Whilst a majority will commit deviant acts only a minority will come to be known as deviant. The known deviant is then targeted, identified, defined and treated as such even though their behaviour may be no different from those who have not been so identified. As a result certain people will 'become deviant' through the imposition of social judgements on their behaviour: they *become* the very essence of what is being complained of. In the 1950s Edwin Lemert further refined the approach by distinguishing between primary and secondary deviation. He argued that primary deviance is often a temporary waywardness and perpetrators have no conception of themselves as deviant. Secondary deviance is created through the reaction of others to the initial deviance. Through name-calling, stereotyping and labelling, a deviant identity is established and confirmed. Often deviants will resolve this personal crisis by accepting their deviant status and by reorganizing their lives accordingly. They will become more, rather than less, deviant. Lemert's conclusion that *social control causes deviancy* was a crucial turning-point in the development of a radical criminological imagination that has flourished since the 1960s.

A fully fledged labelling approach emerged through the work of Howard Becker, Kai Erikson and John Kitsuse in the 1960s. For each, the key to understanding the origins of deviance lay in the reactions of a social audience rather than in the behaviour of an individual actor. It is the audience who determine whether or not any behaviour comes to be defined as deviant. A number of studies were published in the 1960s and 1970s which revealed the processes of *becoming* a marijuana smoker, a prostitute, a homosexual, a prisoner and so on. In each of these it was the stigma attached to the label that was considered pivotal in informing future behaviour patterns. Defined as 'outsiders', it is such groups that come to epitomize what is considered to be criminal. A self-fulfilling prophecy ensues. Criminality is continually sought only in those identified as criminal. And the power of the label of 'criminal' ensures that 'criminal careers' are exacerbated.

To counter this process, labelling theorists argue that only a diminution or the absence of an official reaction is able to reduce offending significantly. When no stigma, ostracism or exclusion is applied to a deviant act then delinquent 'careers' will not be established. In contrast to reactive 'get tough' approaches, decriminalization and a radical non-interventionism are called for.

By focusing on the processes whereby behaviour comes to be criminalized and by adopting a relatively non-judgemental or appreciative stance to primary deviance, labelling opened up whole new areas of interest in criminology, in which the concepts of stigma, social reaction and control were to become pivotal. Through labelling, the traditional behavioural question – why do they do it? – was subordinated to a more critical line of enquiry – who defines another as deviant, for what purposes, and with what implications for future deviant activity?

Evaluation

Labelling continues to offer an important challenge to traditional criminological approaches.

By focusing on definitional issues it is able to reveal how the concepts of 'crime' and 'deviance' are not universally agreed upon, but are instead socially constructed, contingent and contestable. By drawing attention to the role of social reaction (and law and order enforcement in particular), it warns of the ways in which criminal justice may cause that which it has been designed to curtail. However, a number of radical authors have subsequently argued that the logic of labelling is limited when employed without any analysis of the social and political structures and inequalities in which such labels are constructed and upheld. Labelling fails to explain *why* it is that only *some* behaviours come to be defined in a historical and political context as deviant whilst others do not. A key question – whose law and whose order is being protected? – was notably overlooked. As a result, some critical criminologists in the 1970s argued that the insights of labelling needed to be wedded to a Marxist model of society and the state. Only then could the subjective encounters of social reaction and social control be viewed as objective social processes that were set in particular social formations. As a result, labelling has been critiqued as merely offering an *approach* and not meeting the requirements for a fully worked-up criminological theory.

A different critique offered by positivist criminologists focuses on the lack of serious attention that labelling gives to primary deviance. By concentrating on such 'victimless' crimes as drug taking, homosexuality and so on, it has failed to recognize sufficiently the fundamental deviance attached to other 'serious crimes' such as murder, robbery and institutional violence. In addition, it has been suggested that the origins of a 'deviant identity' lie not in the processes of social reaction but in local community and neighbourhood settings. The multiple sources and differential impacts of a range of negative labels are likely to be far more complex than that which was offered by the labelling perspective of the 1960s.

John Muncie

Associated Concepts: criminal careers, deviancy amplification, interactionism, radical criminologies, radical non-intervention, social constructionism, social reaction

Key Readings

Becker, H. (1963) *Outsiders: Studies in the Sociology of Deviance.* New York: The Free Press.

Erikson, K.T. (1966) *Wayward Puritans: A Study in the Sociology of Deviance.* New York: Wiley.

Kitsuse, J. (1962) 'Societal reaction to deviant behaviour', *Social Problems,* 9: 247–56.

Lemert, E. (1951) *Social Pathology.* New York: McGraw-Hill.

Plummer, K. (1979) 'Misunderstanding labelling perspectives', in D. Downes and P. Rock (eds), *Deviant Interpretations.* Oxford: Oxford University Press.

Tannenbaum, F. (1938) *Crime and the Community.* New York: Colombia University Press.

LEFT IDEALISM

Definition

A sociological approach to crime and punishment whose roots lie in Marxist and neo-Marxist theory. This requires taking the problem of crime seriously while also critically analysing the processes of criminalization, social construction and state power, which contribute to making crime and the responses to it a complex social process. Therefore academic research should be critical and interventionist, built on analysing the wider structures of power that reproduce the social divisions underpinning the social order of contemporary capitalist democracies.

Distinctive Features

Left idealism sits on the critical wing of criminology and is often contrasted with left realism. Both perspectives have their roots in the early 1970s and the shift towards a Marxist-oriented approach to the understanding of crime and deviance. In 1975 Jock Young argued in his influential essay 'Working Class Criminology' (in Taylor et al., 1975) that critical criminology was fragmenting into a number of distinct strands, two of which he identified as realism and idealism. By the mid-1980s the rise and consolidation of the New Right led realists such as Kinsey, Lea, Matthews and Young to call for a reappraisal of the role of criminology. In particular, they demanded that criminologists should reject the idealization of the criminal and the utopian romanticism they identified as central to idealist thought. Instead, they argued that criminologists should take crime and the fear of crime seriously, especially its impact on the powerless.

However, those labelled as idealists did not accept Young's argument:

> The critics of the new realists ... reject their categorization as left idealists and argue forcefully that their interventionist work within critical criminology has responded to the realities of life under Thatcherism. Further, they challenge new realism on its misreading of history, under-theorization both of the structural contradictions under advanced capitalism and the advanced capitalist state form and its rule of law, and on its essentially superficial approach to the complexities of crime, crime control and the criminal justice process. (Sim et al., 1987: 39)

Thus British idealists such as Gilroy, Hillyard, Bunyan, Scraton, Sim and Gordon not only rejected a label which was, and is, identified with them, they also highlighted a series of key theoretical and political distinctions between their conceptualization of politics and criminology and that propounded by Young and his colleagues.

First, contrary to the theoretical 'straw man' that realists had established, those labelled as idealists did not see the state as a homogeneous entity incapable of change. This 'crude and simplistic' caricature (van Swaaningen, 1997: 201) seriously underestimated the idealist position that the state was a contingent and contradictory set of institutions. Critical criminologists should therefore exploit these contradictions through research, whose results should be made available to those groups struggling to reform and radically change the criminal justice system. This 'criminology from below' (Sim et al., 1987: 7) resulted in a range of interventionist work in Britain throughout the 1970s and 1980s around prisons, the police, Northern Ireland, violence against women, institutionalized racism and deaths in custody. Like abolitionists, idealists understood political action as a hegemonic process which involved analysing the state both as a coercive set of institutions and as a site where dominant ideas could be fought over, challenged and resisted. Consequently, they supported community groups involved in official and unofficial inquiries into the operation of different criminal justice institutions to ensure that state definitions of 'truth' did not prevail and that alternative accounts from below were not marginalized. This remained a key aspect of left idealism in the 1990s.

Second, idealists maintained that crime and public concerns about it were complex phenomena which needed to be unpacked and understood. The realist's 'undifferentiated and abstract view of crime' was:

> Theoretically and politically problematic not only because it allows the already elastic concept of crime to become a catch-all category but also because it presents an idealized view of the working class community as a 'homogeneous group united by its fear of crime despite the everyday divisions of gender, race, craft, income and employment'. (Gilroy and Sim, cited in Sim et al., 1987: 45)

Third, they argued that the state was concerned with the reproduction of an unequal social order rather than, as in the case of the police, offering a 'service' to the powerless. This did not mean that its institutions defended processes of domination in every instance, but that wider structures of power played a central role in the construction of criminal justice policies and the deployment of state personnel. Finally, like the abolitionists, they contended that the state's response to crime should be deconstructed and replaced with an alternative set of democratically embedded policies and practices. This position

contrasted with that of the realists, who 'with their focus on the beginning of the "penal chain" (crime prevention and the police) ... nearly forgot where this chain ends: in punishment' (van Swaaningen, 1997: 200).

Evaluation

Left idealism remains a central strand in critical criminological praxis. While the charge of utopianism is still levelled at them, idealists would say that the events of the 1990s have only underlined the strength of their thesis. The consolidation of the New Right, particularly in the UK and the USA in the first half of the decade, coupled with an intensification in the authoritarian capabilities of the state, illustrates and reinforces their view that while crime should be taken seriously the state's primary focus is on the maintenance and reproduction of a social order that remains deeply divided along the faultlines of social class, gender, 'race', age and sexuality.

At the same time the moral panics around juvenile crime, single parents, asylum seekers and drug users during the decade illustrate how discourses surrounding conventional definitions of crime and deviance can still be mobilized ideologically to reproduce structures of domination and subordination. The election of New Labour in the UK in 1997, many of whose ideas on law and order can be traced back to left realism, reinforced the idealist argument still further. While idealists would not support the sociologically reductionist position which contends that Labour has abjectly followed the policies of previous Conservative administrations, they would contend that many of the government's policies on law and order are built on a further consolidation of state power. This consolidation includes: a range of new powers for state servants; an ideological construction of particular groups as criminalistic and deviant; a failure to confront the issue of the democratic accountability of state institutions; and a reluctance to deal with crimes committed by the powerful, for example, in terms of deaths at work and in custody. As Sumner (1990: 3) notes, tying theory and research to a social democratic agenda means that 'there is a grave danger of running into the cul-de-sac of a social democratic, parochial reformism which is not so far away from neo-positivist, administrative criminology'.

Realists maintain that idealists still conceptualize the state as a homogeneous entity which operates at all times and in all places for the benefit of those in power. Idealists would make two responses to this point. First, it remains necessary to scrutinize the state sociologically, its lack of democratic accountability and the institutional and personal accumulation of power that has underpinned its development since the beginning of the nineteenth century. Indeed, the trend towards post-structuralist and postmodernist thought in the social sciences has led to the state being airbrushed out of academic analysis. The state should therefore be brought back in as a focus for research and theorizing. This can be done without it degenerating into a reductionist and instrumental view of state power.

Second, idealists would contend that the interventionist work of the 1970s and 1980s, built on exploiting the contingencies and contradictions in the state, continued into the 1990s. In a range of areas including deaths in custody, health and safety at work, violence against women, and state behaviour in Northern Ireland, idealist academics have continued to work with community groups and others to change laws and state practices. Additionally, in the UK they have provided support for, and worked with, groups involved in major political issues such as the Hillsborough disaster and the Stephen Lawrence Inquiry. They would also maintain that they have had an influence not only on the public and political debate but, in working with particular pressure groups, have also been instrumental in helping to achieve changes in the law, for example, around inquest procedures affecting deaths in custody.

In terms of future developments, idealists would argue for *greater* utopianism in social and criminological theory and that their alternative definition of crime and punishment remains central to their overall vision of a society devoid of the hierarchies of power that limit human capacities and capabilities. They would

also agree with Stan Cohen that the choice for academics is not necessarily between scepticism and realism 'but to show in concrete situations where intellectual subversion might or might not lead'. For Cohen this 'raises questions of strategy, tactics and alliances'. It follows on from this that criminology has to try to satisfy:

> *triple* loyalty: first an overriding obligation to honest intellectual inquiry itself (however sceptical, provisional, irrelevant and unrealistic); second, a political commitment to social justice; and third (and potentially conflicting with both), the pressing and immediate demands for short-term humanitarian help. We have to appease these three voracious gods. (Cohen, 1998: 118–22; emphasis in original)

Roy Coleman and Joe Sim

Associated Concepts: abolitionism, critical criminology, critical research, hegemony, left realism, the state

Key Readings

Cohen, S. (1998) 'Intellectual scepticism and political commitment: the case of radical criminology', in P. Walton and J. Young (eds), *The New Criminology Revisited*. Basingstoke: Macmillan.

Pearce, S. and Tombs, S. (1992) 'Realism and corporate crime', in R. Matthews and J. Young (eds), *Issues in Realist Criminology*. London: Sage.

Ryan, M. and Ward, T. (1986) 'Law and order: left realism against the rest', *The Abolitionist*, 22 (2): 29–33.

Sim, J., Scraton, P. and Gordon, P. (1987) 'Introduction: crime, the state and critical analysis', in P. Scraton (ed.), *Law, Order and the Authoritarian State*. Milton Keynes: The Open University Press.

Sumner, C. (1990) 'Introduction: contemporary socialist criminology', in C. Sumner (ed.), *Censure, Politics and Criminal Justice*. Buckingham: The Open University Press.

Taylor, I., Walton, P. and Young, J. (eds) (1975) *Critical Criminology*. London: Routledge.

van Swaaningen, R. (1997) *Critical Criminology: Visions from Europe*. London: Sage.

LEFT REALISM

Definition

A school of criminology which emerged initially in Britain in the early 1980s as a response both to the punitive and exclusionary policies of conservatism and to the utopianism of New Left radical criminologies.

Distinctive Features

Left realist criminology, as its name implies, is radical in its criminology and realistic in its appraisal of crime and its causes. It is radical in that crime is seen as an endemic product of the class and patriarchal nature of advanced industrial society. It is not a cosmetic criminology of an establishment sort which views crime as a blemish that with suitable treatment can be removed from the body of society, which is, in itself, otherwise healthy and in little need of reconstruction. Rather it suggests that it is within the core institutions of society (its relationships of class and of gender) and its central values (such as competitive individualism and aggressive masculinity) that crime arises. Crime is not a product of abnormality but of the normal workings of the social order. In addition, it is realistic in that it attempts to be faithful to the reality of crime. This involves several tasks: realistically appraising the problem of crime; deconstructing crime into its fundamental components (the square of crime); critically examining the nature of causality; being realistic about the possibilities of intervention; and above all, fully understanding the changing social terrain in which we now live.

The particular political space in which left realism emerged was in the mid-1980s. The juxtaposition came with the emergence of conservative – 'neo-liberal' – governments in many Western countries that pursued an overtly punishment-oriented approach to crime control. At the time a liberal/social democratic opposition was on the defensive. The neo-liberals actively pointed to the rise in the crime rate and entered vigorously into law and order campaigns on behalf of 'the silent majority', holding offenders responsible for their actions and advocating punishment as the solution. The New Left position, which had its origins in the libertarianism of the 1960s, tended to resemble a mirror image of the right: namely, it denied or downplayed the level of crime, portrayed the offender as a victim of the system, and stressed a multiculturalism of diversity and struggle where radicalism entailed the defence of the community against the incursions of the state, and in particular those of the police and the criminal justice system. What was necessary was a criminology which could navigate between these two currents: which took crime seriously but was also radical in its analysis and policy.

It was, therefore, no accident that two key realist texts were published in the mid-eighties: *What Is to be Done About Law and Order?* (by John Lea and Jock Young) in 1984 in Britain, and *Confronting Crime* (by Elliott Currie) in 1985 in the United States, whilst the first realist crime survey was carried out in 1985 by the Canadian Brian Maclean.

The evocation to 'take crime seriously' involved realists in large-scale local victimization studies directly and 'democratically' asking people about their problems with crime and their assessment of police effectiveness. These surveys, frequently funded by radical local councils, pointed both to the greater burden of crime on the poor, ethnic minorities and women and the extent of police abuses and inefficiency. Later surveys were widened out to include white collar crime and domestic violence (Mooney, 2000). In Britain such work has had a considerable impact on the re-orientation of Labour Party policies towards a heightened concern with crime control issues. Although such quantitative work has become identified with realism, the need for qualitative research to make sense of the findings and provide clues to causality is constantly stressed.

A fundamental task of left realism is to deconstruct the concept of crime. It notes that crime is inevitably the product of action and reaction and that the failure of previous criminologies is that they have problematized one component and ignored the other. Thus positivism focuses on crime and tends to take its definition for granted, whereas constructionism (that is, labelling theory, abolitionism and much of critical criminology) problematizes the way in which crime is defined and constructed yet tends to ignore crime itself. The left realist critique argues that explaining crime necessitates a double aetiology of action and reaction and a corresponding denial of any essence of crime. Rather crime is viewed as a concept that constantly changes over time and varies according to the perspective held by different groups. It occurs in the interrelationship between *offender* and *victim* within the varying definitional flux of *formal* and *informal* systems of control (Young, 1992). (Hence the *square of crime* between these four points.)

Realism stresses the need to seek the causes of crime but is critical of any positivistic notion of a mechanistic nature. A key causal concept is relative deprivation, which encompasses both the subjective and material nature of discontent. Such an emphasis on *both* the subjective and objective dimensions of human action is mirrored throughout realist analysis. Therefore just as it is stressed that the causes of crime cannot be reduced to material deprivation alone, the fear of crime cannot be understood as merely a reflection of risk rates, and the rate of imprisonment cannot be simply correlated with crime rates, for all of these processes involve human evaluation and reflection upon material circumstances. And because of this double nature, the opposite reduction is equally invalid: for material inequality is the basis of crime; the fear of crime cannot be dissociated from the risk of crime; and levels of punishment cannot be discussed without resorting to the crime rates.

Realism is an integrated theory synthesizing theoretical traditions (particularly subcultural theory and labelling theory) and fusing them together within a socialist feminist framework that stresses class and gender inequality (see Mooney, 2000).

Intervening to control crime is a central concern, involving multi-agencies and occurring at different points in the natural history of a specific crime. Social crime prevention is stressed although situational crime prevention and deterrence from the criminal justice system play minor backing roles. The ultimate task is to make fundamental changes in the social order whilst at the same time intervening on a day-to-day basis to protect the public and push reform onwards. As with all radical politics the central problem is to remain committed to change without being merely utopian, and to be immediately effective without being simply technocratic and pragmatic.

Evaluation

Left realism has in the last decade moved away from a polemical position that stressed the need for radicals to take crime seriously and towards the foundation of an integrated theory that attempts to synthesize the major strands of criminological thought. What is now necessary is the development of a sociology that relates to the transition to late modernity and a politics that is in dialogue with contemporary feminist and social democratic theory. A start has been made in this direction, but much exacting and exciting work remains to be done.

Jock Young

Associated Concepts: fear of crime, left idealism, neo-conservative criminology, relative deprivation, social crime prevention, victim surveys

Key Readings

Currie, E. (1985) *Confronting Crime.* New York: Pantheon.
Currie, E. (1998) *Crime and Punishment in America.* New York: Metropolitan Books.
Lea, J. and Young, J. (1984) *What Is to be Done About Law and Order?* Harmondsworth: Penguin.
Lowman, J. and Maclean, B. (eds) (1992) *Realist Criminology.* Toronto: University of Toronto Press.
Mooney, J. (2000) *Gender, Violence and the Social Order.* London: Macmillan.

Young, J. (1992) 'Ten points of realism', in J. Young and R. Matthews (eds), *Rethinking Criminology: The Realist Debate.* London: Sage.
Young, J. (1999) *The Exclusive Society.* London: Sage.

LIBERAL FEMINISM

Definition

Liberal feminism was the first of the theoretical feminist perspectives, developed in the 1920s from the work of Mary Wollstonecraft and J.S. Mill, and it greatly influenced the 'first wave' of modern Western feminism. Its emphasis is very much on the *equality* of men and women, especially with regard to their moral and intellectual characteristics, and thus liberal feminists have argued for social and political changes to the educational and legal framework which they see as constraining women. In the sphere of criminal justice studies, liberal feminism has had a powerful impact on analyses of equity and discrimination.

Distinctive Features

Liberal feminism has claims to be the oldest and the original feminist theory, with its roots both in eighteenth-century Enlightenment thinking and the American Revolution (Banks, 1981). While the French Revolution did little to advance the emancipation of women, the intellectual ferment of ideas which it provoked inspired debate in Britain and America which did challenge the status quo, in which women had effectively no political rights. In 1792, Mary Wollstonecraft published *A Vindication of the Rights of Woman* in which she challenged notions of female inferiority and insisted that there should be equal educational opportunities for women with men and employment for single women. In 1869, J.S. Mill's *On the Subjection of Women* took up similar arguments in support of the contemporary campaigns for female enfranchisement: 'the legal subordination of one sex to the other – is wrong in itself ... and that it ought to be replaced by a principle of perfect equality'.

The American Declaration of Independence inspired the statement of feminist principles that emerged from the Seneca Falls Convention in 1848. This event, which marked the founding of organized feminism in the USA, laid claims to sexual equality and equal rights for women alongside men.

Thus both the early feminist writers and the campaigners whom they inspired relied on an individualist notion of equality and on comparing women with men. Campaigns focused on a formal recognition of females as free and equal individuals who could enjoy full legal and civil rights to vote, to enter into contracts, and gain an education and membership of professions. Much effort in the USA and Britain went into lengthy struggles to gain the vote, and indeed sometimes, as in certain US states, before all of the male population had been enfranchised. Nevertheless, their insistence on rights-based claims to enfranchisement proved successful in the early twentieth century in Australia and New Zealand and afterwards in Britain and the USA.

In the later twentieth century a second wave of feminism flourished which had notably different aims. Nevertheless, there are clear links between this phase and the earlier one, chiefly via the modern version of liberal feminism. The central notion remains that of removing barriers and constraints to achieving equality. Equal rights and equal opportunities are key issues: sex discrimination must go; there must be more women in politics and positions of power, and in senior posts in industry and commerce; and sex stereotyping in the media, education and public attitudes should be combated (Dale and Foster, 1986). The US's National Organization of Women, and Britain's Equal Opportunities Commission, are institutional examples of liberal approaches to women's rights.

In criminology, liberal feminists demonstrated many instances of the inequitable treatment of girls and women: for example, the extra penalties incurred by 'wayward' girls in the USA or the more limited options available in prisons for women. However, some research has indicated that women may be less severely sanctioned than men, and equalizing punishment (for example, through strict sentencing guidelines) may lead to the harsher, male norm being imposed (Chesney-Lind and Faith, 2000).

Evaluation

Liberal feminists have sought to play down biological differences between the sexes and to argue that women can achieve equality with men. These views have been criticized for ignoring structural differences between the power positions of men and women, especially in the family, and also for offering strategies that relate mainly to the interests of white middle-class women and not to those of black or working-class women. This criticism has had a particular relevance for criminology (Daly and Stephens, 1995) since women (and men) from some minorities are heavily over-represented in offender populations.

Campaigns mounted by first wave feminists to ensure the entry of women into policing, the legal and correctional professions were ultimately successful, although their representation remains low in many countries. Nor has this small female presence achieved the significant changes that earlier reformers had hoped for (Chesney-Lind and Faith, 2000). Critics of liberal approaches have argued that institutions such as the law and the state are too imbued with patriarchal assumptions and sexist practices to enable real progress to occur. However while liberal feminism clearly has its limitations, it has still had an influence and impact on much subsequent thinking and has provided the basis for later and more radical perspectives. Regarding the latter Eisenstein (1981) had contended that, because of its 'self-contradictory nature', liberal feminism logically leads to the development of much more radical approaches.

Frances Heidensohn

Associated Concepts: discrimination, feminist criminologies, radical feminism

Key Readings

Banks, O. (1981) *Faces of Feminism.* Oxford: Martin Robertson.
Chesney-Lind, M. and Faith, K. (2000) 'What about feminism? Engendering theory-making in criminology', in R. Paternoster and R. Bachman (eds), *Explaining Criminals and Crime: Essays in Contemporary Criminological Theory.* Los Angeles, CA: Roxbury.
Dale, J. and Foster, P. (1986) *Feminists and State Welfare.* London: Routledge.
Daly, K. and Stephens, D. (1995) 'The "Dark Figure" of criminology: towards a black and multi-ethnic feminist agenda for theory and research', in N. Rafter and F. Heidensohn (eds), *International Feminist Perspectives in Criminology.* Milton Keynes: Open University Press.
Eisenstein, Z. (1981) *The Radical Future of Liberal Feminism.* London: Longman.
Wollstonecraft, M. and Mill, J.S. (1929) *The Rights of Women,* and *The Subjection of Women* (ed. G. Catin). London: Dent.

LIFE COURSE THEORIES OF CRIME

Definition

Life course theory refers to analytical perspectives which study the cumulative effects of static and dynamic features of social contexts on people's lives, e.g., their development and behavioural continuity (see Elder, 1998; Elder and Shanahan, 2006). The life course refers to a sequence of socially-embedded, age-graded events and roles that connect life phases (Elder and Shanahan, 2006: 667). Life course criminology is the study of these events and roles (transitions and trajectories) and their relation to stability and change in crime involvement.

Distinctive Features

In the last twenty years, with the advent of a number of large-scale, longitudinal studies, life course criminology and related developmental theories 'have become one of the liveliest and most prominent areas of research in the field' (Osgood, 2005: 602; see also Farrington, 2005). However, to date relatively few criminological theories, and even fewer empirical studies, have taken a truly life course perspective on the explanation of crime.

Unlike developmental theories that study the life span or life cycle as an unfolding sequence of roles (typically linked to the reproductive cycle, e.g., child, young adult, spouse, parent) which occurs regardless of context, life course explanations of crime suggest that people's crime involvement is continually activated, sustained and changed by their social contexts (e.g., their exposure to different kinds of people and/or environments under different circumstances; Elder and Shanahan, 2006; Sampson and Laub, 1997).

Life course theory posits four key principles (Elder, 1998; Elder and Shanahan, 2006):

1 *The principle of historical time and place*: a person's life course is embedded in and shaped by the historical times and places he/she experiences during his/her lifetime.
2 *The principle of timing in life-stages*: the impact of an event on a person's development depends on when that event occurs in the person's life.
3 *The principle of linked lives*: social and historical influences are expressed through a person's network of interdependent relationships.
4 *The principle of human agency*: people help determine their life course through the choices they make in relation to the opportunities and constraints presented by social and historical circumstances.

These principles highlight the fact that people's lives unfold, socially and biologically, within a dynamic socio-historical context that plays a crucial role in determining how people feel, think and act (in other words, people of different ages and different social circumstances will be differentially affected by social and historical events during their lifetime; Elder, 1998).

The life course is characterized by social pathways, or trajectories, which represent long-term patterns of behaviour, such as crime involvement (Sampson and Laub, 1997). These patterns are distinguished by a sequence of transitions that will arise from life events (for example, the transition to unemployment following job loss). Trajectories and transitions then interact to generate turning-points, or changes, in a person's life course, which may impact behaviour (e.g., unemployment may interact with a trajectory involving minor crime involvement which may initiate more serious offending; see Elder and Shanahan, 2006; Sampson and Laub, 1997).

Importantly, socio-historic forces shape these pathways – while people have self-selective capacities (agency) through which they can partially determine how they adapt to life events, these are contingent upon relevant opportunities and constraints (Elder, 1998; Laub et al., 2009). And while social selective pressures may be significantly implicated in people's exposure to opportunities and constraints, chance will also play a part (Laub et al., 2009).

Social change and behavioural development are interrelated through processes known as 'linking mechanisms' (Elder and Shanahan, 2006: 689–91). One linking mechanism concerns the process by which a person's life-stage affects his/her experience of life events and how equipped he/she is to adapt successfully. Another is the process by which *situational imperatives* (behavioural demands or requirements, e.g., due to resource limitations or commitments) of the circumstances a person encounters constrain his/her behaviour and expression of agency. A related mechanism is *control cycles*, the process by which changes in the balance between expectations and resources affect a person's sense of agency. A final mechanism is the *accentuation dynamic*, the process through which transitions feed back against a person's life history and influence his/her characteristics and behaviour.

These linking mechanisms embody one of the major strengths of life course theories of crime – that they not only recognize the importance of personal and circumstantial (e.g., social, environmental and contextual) factors for explaining people's crime involvement, but also draw attention to the fact that these interact. Different people respond differently to life events as a consequence of their life stage, previous trajectories and agency. Although different life course theories of crime address this interaction, and its role in crime to greater and lesser degrees, it is a feature which sets life course theories apart from more static life cycle theories.

Another feature which sets life course theories apart is the fact they are equally capable of addressing behavioural change and stability. They see stability as being driven by dynamic, reinforcing processes (e.g., cumulative or reciprocal processes which sustain behavioural outcomes), not just stable traits (which often become the focus of uniform life cycle theories, e.g., Gottfredson and Hirschi's self-control theory) (Sampson and Laub, 1997). Change is always possible and driven by the interaction between personal and/or circumstantial changes (e.g., changes in agency or beliefs, and/or socio-economic circumstances or social networks, respectively, typically as a result of life events which create transitions and turning-points in life course trajectories).

Methodologically, life course theories are challenging to test due to the breadth of data (personal and contextual) they require over time. A driving force behind the rise of life course theories of crime over the past decades has been the emergence of large-scale longitudinal studies. Longitudinal data, spanning all the life stages, are critical for comprehensively testing life course theories. Techniques for analysing life course data are accordingly complex, as they need to statistically model, and relate, social and behavioural pathways over time. Trajectory analysis has become a popular technique for identifying life course patterns (e.g., Nagin, 2005). However, many such analyses summarize general trends (Osgood, 2005) and therefore, like other taxonomies, may falsely imply qualitative differences between groups of people and hence different explanations for their patterns of crime.

Evaluation

Although complex and challenging to test, life course theories of crime are extremely valuable for bringing together many disparate elements of criminological and related social and psychological theories, and looking at human development and life experiences as a whole, embedded within their social and historical context.

One shortcoming of such theories (and related research) is that many focus on correlates of crime and prediction as opposed to explanation. Considering the complexity of life course theories and the number of potentially important variables, this is one way to begin to identify which of these may be important. However, in order to understand which variables actually lead to continuity or a change in criminal behaviour across the life course, criminologists need to identify which factors are causes and the causal processes through which they affect behaviour against a backdrop of personal characteristics and experiences, previous trajectories and sociohistorical circumstances.

Another current limitation of life course approaches to the explanation of crime (empirically as well as theoretically) is the use of taxonomic methods to categorize different kinds of people or pathways. Taxonomies of offenders suggest different causes for different people's crimes; taxonomies of trajectories create artificially rigid pathways which may not take into account factors such as agency, chance and the interaction between people and their social circumstances. In some ways taxonomic approaches simplify the task of studying complex and infinitely variable subjects such as people and social pathways; in others, however, they only complicate it. An important ongoing debate in criminology is whether or not there can be one explanation for all acts of crime (i.e., a general theory), or whether different kinds of offenders and/or different kinds of offences require different explanations (i.e., because they involve different causal processes; see Osgood, 2005, for a discussion). A third explanatory framework (most often seen in interactive explanations of crime; e.g., Wikström, 2005) is often overlooked – that all acts of crime can be explained by the same causal process but may reflect differing content.

Recognition of the centrality of the interaction between people and social contexts in the explanation of crime is perhaps the most vital aspect of criminological life course theories. Most criminological theories are predominantly person or environment oriented, and even those which purport to address both will often hinge their explanation of crime on either people or environments; hardly any will adequately address their interaction and how it leads to crime (but see for example Wikström, 2005). Life course theories of crime place this interaction at the centre of their analytical framework. People must make choices about their actions, but will not do so in a social vacuum; action choices will depend upon the circumstances (e.g., motivation, opportunities and constraints). One person will act differently under different circumstances, and different people will respond differently to the same circumstances. To study this interaction across the life course requires multilevel, longitudinal data, which are difficult and expensive to acquire, but may provide a richer empirical basis for understanding the causes of crime (i.e., how people become involved in crime, why they persist, and why they desist).

Kyle Treiber

Associated Concepts: developmental criminology, longitudinal study, prediction studies

Key Readings

Elder, G.H., Jr. (1998) 'The life course as developmental theory', *Child Development*, 69: 1–12.

Elder, G.H., Jr and Shanahan, M.J. (2006) 'The life course and human development',

in R.M. Lerner (ed.), *Handbook of Child Psychology Volume 1: Theoretical Models of Human Development*. Hoboken, NJ: Wiley. pp. 665–715.

Farrington, D.P. (2005) 'Integrated developmental and life-course theories of offending', *Advances in Criminological Theory*, Volume 14. London: Transaction.

Laub, J.H., Sampson, R.J. and Sweeten, G.A. (2009) 'Assessing Sampson and Laub's life-course theory of crime', in F.T. Cullen, J.P. Wright and K.R. Blevin (eds), *Taking Stock: The Status of Criminological Theory* (*Advances in Criminological Theory*, Volume 15). London: Sage. pp. 313–33.

Nagin, D.S. (2005) *Group-Based Modelling of Development*. Cambridge, MA: Harvard University Press.

Osgood, D.W. (2005) 'Making sense of crime and the life course', *Annals of the American Academy of Political and Social Science*, 602: 196–211.

Piquero, A. and Mazerolle, P. (2001) *Life-Course Criminology: Contemporary and Classic Readings*. Canada: Wadsworth/Thomson Learning.

Sampson, R.J. and Laub, J.H. (1997) 'A life-course theory of cumulative disadvantage and the stability of delinquency', in T. Thornberry (ed.), *Developmental Theories of Crime and Delinquency: Advances in Criminology Theory*, Volume 7. London: Transaction. pp. 133–62.

Wikström, P.-O.H. (2005) 'The social origins of pathways in crime: towards a developmental ecological action theory of crime involvement and its changes', in D.P. Farrington (ed.), *Integrated Developmental and Life-Course Theories of Offending* (*Advances in Criminological Theory*, Volume 14). London: Transaction. pp. 211–46.

LONGITUDINAL STUDY

Definition

A form of study in which observations are collected from the same people at different, sometimes key, points in their lifetime, often with a view to studying personal or individual development. Variants are sometimes also known as cohort studies and panel studies. In both cases there is repeated contact with the same individuals over a period of time.

Distinctive Features

With longitudinal cohort studies a sample is drawn from a particular 'cohort' which is defined by membership of a particular group or category of individuals, such as those born in a particular week or year, children entering school at the same time, or offenders sentenced to imprisonment at the same time. The same sample members are contacted at regular intervals and over a much longer period of time than is typical of other forms of survey. In this respect, longitudinal surveys are prospective designs (studying people as they develop) rather than retrospective designs (collecting observations about people's backgrounds retrospectively). Although it is not a necessary feature of longitudinal cohort studies, there is often an emphasis upon describing and explaining personal development, the progression of life events, and the onset of behavioural patterns or physical illness. Sometimes these descriptions and explanations are used as a basis for making predictions about changes in other but similar types of people, for example predictions about the kinds of people who are likely to embark on and pursue criminal careers.

Longitudinal surveys have been utilized in a wide range of areas, for instance psychiatry, paediatrics, child development, and health. In criminology such surveys are associated with studies of the causes of delinquency and crime as typified by the Cambridge Study in Delinquent Development. In 1961 a sample of 411 working-class boys, aged about 8 years old, was selected from the registers of six state primary schools in an area of London. Girls were not included in the sample. The sample members were contacted at regular intervals up until the age of 21 and a subsample of these were interviewed. Finally, all sample members were contacted when they were 32 years old to examine which of them had continued a 'life of crime' into adulthood and why. Five key factors relating to the boys when they were 8–10 years old were identified as being statistically related to subsequent delinquency. These were a low family income, a large family size, parents with a criminal record, low intelligence, and poor parental child-rearing practices (West, 1982). Six predictors of offending in later years, up to the age of 32, were also identified. These were poverty, poor parenting, family deviance, school problems, hyperactivity/impulsiveness/attention deficit and anti-social behaviour (Farrington, 1989).

The strategy of analysis used to explain delinquency and subsequent criminal careers owes much to the logic of the comparative method. At the point at which two subgroups were identified within the sample – those 'delinquent' and those 'non-delinquent' – these groups were compared along a range of variables in order to examine which were the best predictors of differences between them (in effect asking the question 'which factors do the delinquents share in common which are not shared to the same extent by the non-delinquents?'). This form of analysis is not only comparative but also multivariate, in so far as a number of variables are introduced in order to explain the variables 'delinquency' and 'subsequent criminal careers'. These are not only explanatory variables but also predictors of delinquency and crime. Such predictors provide the basis for suggesting policy initiatives, such as introducing training in child-rearing methods for parents.

Although the distinction is not precise, panel studies differ from cohort studies in so far as they are based on representative samples of the population to be studied rather than cohorts based on birth or a particular entry point (for example, admission to a prison).

Longitudinal studies can also vary according to the period of time over which data are collected from the cohorts or panels. In addition there may be variations in the frequency of the intervals between data collection points (sometimes known as 'sweeps'). Birth cohort studies can often extend over a lifetime, and because they are usually interested in maturation and development (for example, of a criminal career) they will collect data over longer time intervals than are typical for panel studies.

Evaluation

The strengths of longitudinal designs are as follows. First, unlike one-shot cross-sectional designs, longitudinal research is not dependent on the collection of retrospective data in seeking to relate past experiences to present day attitudes and actions. It can collect a wide range of data about a wide range of variables at different stages in an individual's life. Second, the collection of data at the stages in an individual's life to which they relate reduces the invalidity associated with the collection of retrospective data (for example, inaccuracies of memory). Third, longitudinal studies can focus on individual development and provide direct evidence of the time-ordering of variables which gives credence to causal inferences that link contemporary attitudes and actions to previous backgrounds, experiences and events.

On the negative side, however, longitudinal surveys are very costly and they produce their results very slowly, especially those relating to the later stages of development. Also, there is always a risk that members will change as a result of being part of the study, perhaps by responding in ways that they believe are expected of them. What is more, the sample runs the risk of being seriously depleted by drop-out over the years, something known as 'sample attrition'. A further problem is that variables about which data are collected at early stages may not anticipate

theoretical developments at a later stage, with the result that crucial data relevant to such developments may not have been collected. This is sometimes referred to as the problem of 'fading relevancy'. A much more fundamental critique is of the causal and positivist assumptions of such surveys. Critical criminologists, for example, would argue that in placing an emphasis on the causal agents in the early lives of individuals they distract attention from contemporary inequalities and oppressions and also do not address 'crimes of the powerful'.

Victor Jupp

Associated Concepts: causation, cohort studies, comparative method, cross-sectional design, developmental criminology, positivism, prediction studies, sampling

Key Readings

Farrington, D. (1989) 'The origins of crime: the Cambridge Study of Delinquent Development', in *Research Bulletin*, Home Office Research and Planning Unit, no. 27: 29–33.

Magnusson, D. and Bergman, L.R. (eds) (1990) *Data Quality in Longitudinal Research*. Cambridge: Cambridge University Press.

Magnusson, D., Bergman, L.R., Rudinger, G. and Torestad, B. (1990) *Problems and Methods in Longitudinal Research*. Cambridge: Cambridge University Press.

Robins, L. and Rutter, L. (1990) *Straight and Devious Pathways from Childhood to Adulthood*. Cambridge: Cambridge University Press.

West, D.J. (1982) *Delinquency: Its Roots, Careers and Prospects*. London: Heinemann.

M

MANAGERIALISM

Definition

A set of governmental knowledges, techniques and practices which aim to fracture and realign power relations within the core agencies of the criminal justice system in order to transform the structures and reorganize in a cost-effective manner the processes of both funding, delivering and imagining criminal justice.

Distinctive Features

Managerialism, or to be more specific, 'New Public Managerialism' (NPM), is a set of post-bureau-professional knowledges, practices and techniques drawn from a wide variety of sources (reinventing government, new public administration, new wave management, human resource management, postmodern organizational theory). In its cultural projection and discursive meaning, NPM is a hybrid theoretical and political construction. Its purpose is to fracture and realign relations of power within public sector organizations in order to transform the structures and reorganize the processes for both funding and delivering quality public services. NPM mechanisms and techniques have been deemed to be crucial to driving the managerialization of all aspects of the formulation and delivery of public services in an era of the smaller state. Taken together, they represent the post-neo-liberal means through which both

the public sector and the state are to be managerialized so that they are performance-oriented. Proponents of the NPM paradigm on both sides of the Atlantic sought to transcend neo-liberalism in a bid to reinvent and revitalize notions of the public sector and the public service ethos at the end of the twentieth century. Indeed, it is important to note that their potency and influence were based upon the fact that the approach they were promoting challenged the neo-liberal 'there is no alternative' privatization of the public sector.

The UK has been in the vanguard of managerial reform of the public sector, and it is possible to identify two waves of managerialization that have enveloped the criminal justice system. Under successive New Right administrations (1979–97), the managerial reform of criminal justice was progressed through the quasi-marketization of certain criminal justice functions and the responsibilization of individuals and communities. The overall purpose of the first wave of managerialization was to create a cost-effective, efficient and unified criminal justice system that would work within nationally agreed sets of guidelines and standards to reduce the crime rate and the fear of crime to 'acceptable' levels.

The second wave of managerial reform has been enacted through New Labour's belief that the capacities of the state must be 'modernized' so that it can manage and regulate rather than being submerged by the social, cultural and economic changes wrought by the 'new global order'. New

Labour's long-term programme of renewal and reform acknowledged that the New Right's managerial reform process of the late 1980s and early 1990s was a necessary act of modernization that improved productivity and delivered better value for money and enhanced quality of service. A new wave of NPM has attempted to entrench 'performance management' across the public sector. In the case of the criminal justice system, 'modernization' has involved the establishment of consistent and mutually reinforcing aims and objectives; the installation of a 'what works' and 'best practice' culture; the development of an evidence-based approach to the allocation of resources; the institutionalization of performance management to improve productivity; and the establishments of multifunctional, multi-agency 'partnerships'.

Thus, the UK has witnessed the intensification of the NPM disciplines of efficiency, effectiveness and economy that were already working their way, albeit unevenly, through the various parts of this intricate policy environment. In certain vital respects, further managerial reform is necessary if the contradictions and tensions generated by the Conservatives' uneven and differentiated public sector reform project are to be 'resolved'. Virtually every Home Office policy document stresses that 'modernization' will be achieved through constant priority and target setting, auditing, monitoring, evaluation and inspection. Criminal justice professionals have had to realize that the capacity for audit and inspection will be developed to assess the performance of the criminal justice system as a whole and to provide assurance that it is operating economically and efficiently as well as achieving its aims and objectives effectively.

Evaluation

There is considerable disagreement about what is driving managerialism not just in the UK but also in many other advanced Western polities. Managerialization, for certain commentators in the UK and Australia, is a relatively autonomous public sector reform process that needs to be analysed on its own terms. For others, it is linked directly to the hegemony of neo-liberal and neo-conservative forms of crime control – for example, the privatization of core criminal justice functions, the commodification of security, and the rise of actuarial justice. Yet others have attempted to understand managerialism through the broader theoretical prism of governmentality studies. Somewhat surprisingly, given the origins of the key ideas, US criminologists have not theorized the appearance of the new public management in the criminal justice system. A primary focus has been the increasingly central role of the commercial security corporations in the delivery of core criminal justice functions. However, Feeley and Simon (1994) did note that a 'paradigm shift' was taking place in the US criminal justice process. The old system was framed by concepts such as personal guilt, responsibility and punishment, as well as the diagnosis, intervention and treatment of individual offenders. The new penology was 'actuarial' in nature. The central aim was not intervention in the lives of offenders for the purpose of determining responsibility and an appropriate punishment. Actuarial techniques would be used to identify, classify and manage groups and subgroups sorted by levels of actual dangerousness and potential risk and threat. The new practices of actuarial justice included risk classification, incapacitation of the offender, preventive detention, profiling and surveillance. They would also neutralize or restructure older penal-welfare knowledges and practices. Feeley and Simon were careful not to attribute actuarial justice to neo-liberal or neo-conservative crime control policies, arguing that it also had its roots in the liberal due process model. However, they did note that in broader political terms it was not a coincidence that actuarial justice emerged at the same time as US public policy moved away from the idea of a welfare state and towards identifying a dangerous permanent 'underclass' that could only be managed or 'warehoused' in ghettoes and prisons rather than eliminated.

What is significant here is that it has taken so long for a viable post-managerialist vision of criminal justice to be articulated by critics. During 2002–3 we witnessed the first concerted backlash against New Labour's seemingly relentless managerialization of criminal justice. For critics, New Labour's pursuit of managerial reform was intimately linked to declining levels of public confidence and trust in government, and increasing levels of public dissatisfaction with criminal justice agencies. New Labour insisted that driving up standards from the centre via directives, targets, inspections and audits had been necessary during the first administration because the New Right had undermined the institutional capacity of the public sector as well as 'community capacity'. However, there was acceptance that this 'command and control' model of governance and resource allocation was not delivering the desired long-term changes. The 'steel trap' of managerial audit and inspection had generated too many detailed performance indicators and targets that as a result had stifled diversity, creativity and innovation. New Labour stood accused of creating a hyper-regulatory, over-commanding managerial state that had done nothing to reverse declining levels of public confidence in the crime control capacities of the state. Critics argued that there needed to be a 'cultural shift' to create diversity in provision and consumer choice, provide criminal justice agencies with more control over budgets, and allow the freedom to purchase services from the most appropriate provider. There was also a renewed discussion about the viability of communalizing criminal justice.

Eugene McLaughlin

Associated Concepts: actuarialism, administrative criminology, crime science, governance, neo-conservative criminology, racial profiling, risk

Key Readings

Braithwaite, J. (2000) 'The new regulatory state and the transformation of criminology', *British Journal of Criminology*, 40: 222–38.

Clarke, J. and Newman, J. (1997) *The Managerial State*. London: Sage.

Feeley, M. and Simon, J. (1994) 'Actuarial justice: the emerging new criminal law', in D. Nelken (ed.), *The Futures of Criminology*. London: Sage.

James, A. and Raine, J. (1998) *The New Politics of Criminal Justice*. London: Longman.

McLaughlin, E. and Murji, K. (2001) 'Lost connections and new directions', in K. Stenson and R. Sullivan (eds), *Crime, Risk and Justice*. Cullompton: Willan.

McLaughlin, E., Muncie, J. and Hughes, G. (2001) 'The permanent revolution: New Labour, New Public Management and the modernization of criminal justice', *Criminal Justice: The International Journal of Policy and Practice*, 1 (3): 301–18.

O'Malley, P. (1997) 'Policing, politics and postmodernity', *Social and Legal Studies*, 6 (3): 363–81.

MARXIST CRIMINOLOGIES

Definition

A variety of criminological perspectives that draw on the Marxian tradition in sociological theory in order to explicate the dimensions of crime and its control that revolve around class, power and the state.

Distinctive Features

Some social theorists have argued that Marxist criminology is not possible – strictly speaking – because Marxism, as a form of theoretical system, specifies its own objects of analysis (such as 'the mode of production', 'class relations', 'alienation', 'ideology', 'hegemony') and thus subsumes the analysis of crime under much more general concerns

(Bankowski et al., 1977). The bulk of Marx's vast corpus of work did not concern itself with crime. However, it is still possible to discover something of his perspective on crime and its control. In his early journalism Marx wrote an extended essay based on the Proceedings of the Sixth Rhine Assembly debates on The Law on Thefts of Wood which was published in the German paper *Rheinische Zeitung* in October of 1842. In this article, he discussed how the peasants living in the Rhine Valley had had taken away their traditional right to gather fallen wood (a primary source of fuel for cooking and heating) as the framework of the old feudal form of law was redrafted in line with the needs of the emergent order of industrial capitalism. This is an example of criminalization, which contemporary criminologists would clearly recognize, and it had negative consequences for those at the bottom end of the 'class structure'.

'Property is Theft' is an aphorism frequently associated with Marx. In truth that maxim was Proudhon's (*La propriété, c'est le vol*) – Marx was seldom so pithy. Still, that sort of revolutionary rhetoric, and the sympathies which it represented, were vigorously articulated during the recrudesence of student rebellion of the late 1960s. May 1968 seemed to symbolize the possibility of revolutionary change in affluent Western societies and in that moment many academics who had been inspired by, or were instrumental in developing, the sociology of deviance were galvanized into a radical mode of enquiry that drew heavily on the Marxian tradition. There are many examples of work carried out in this vein. They all exhibit a concern to illuminate the 'class dimensions' of power insofar as these relate to instances of crime and crime control. Within this perspective, the 'capitalist order' itself is held to be criminogenic, and the crime panics that emerge from time to time are analysed as being attempts at the orchestration of a public consensus (in Marxian terms, 'hegemony') by the police, the media, the judiciary, and other elements of the 'state–corporate apparatus': this not only deflects public concern away from the central contradictions of capitalism (which

emanate from the 'wage–capital relation'), but also serves to provide a justification for ratcheting up the power of the system of social control which, perversely, contributes to the intensification of the conditions that produced the crime phenomena in the first place. This reasoning was employed to considerable effect in *Policing the Crisis* (Hall et al., 1978), which remains one of the seminal contributions of British criminology. Focusing on a 'mugging panic' in London during the early 1970s, the denouement of their argument was that, because crime is one of the few symbolic sources of unity in an increasingly divided and embittered class society and, moreover, because the traditional elements of consensus (especially the deference to authority, the trappings of class power and the threat of external enemies) were exhausted – bringing the 'hegemony of the state' under threat – the 'war against crime' becomes the primary source of re-legitimation. The state's main concern, so the argument goes, is to define the elements of the crisis of capitalism away. The crisis is depicted in such a way that images of deviants (criminals, industrial dissidents, ethnic minorities, drug-takers, youth, welfare scroungers, political deviants, etc.) are foregrounded. Thus confusion is created and the working class come to mis-recognize their enemy. The crisis is deflected on to youth, crime and race, and away from capitalist class relations.

Evaluation

One of the earliest attempts to situate the study of crime within a Marxian problematic can be found in the work of Willem Bonger, but these works have had little lasting influence and were dismissed by latter progeny as 'not so much the application of a fully fledged Marxist theory as they are a recitation of a "Marxist catechism" in an area which Marx had left largely untouched' (Taylor et al., 1973: 222). The 'new criminologists' of the 1970s attempted to synthesize a 'fully social theory of deviance' and they did so very much through Marx's preferred style of intellectual labour. *The New Criminology* is largely a work of critique; the first eight chapters of the book are given over to a sustained criticism of liberal criminology, positivism, ecological and anomie theories, labelling theory, interactionism and phenomenology, classical Marxism (including the writings of Marx, Engels and Bonger), and, lastly, conflict theory. This *tour d'horizon* of early and mid-twentieth-century criminological thinking remains a useful summary, even if the theoretical predilections of its authors are not widely shared. In the final chapter a 'synthesis' is presented which tries to salvage useful elements of the theories that preceded 'the new criminology'. Briefly, this synthesis argues that it is axiomatic that capitalism is criminogenic and that a society based on 'socialist diversity' is the only social formation that, in principle, holds out any possibility of being crime-free. For the criminologist then, the goal should be the demise of capitalism and the transformation of society to one of socialist diversity. Anything else, by definition, implicates the criminologist in 'correctionalism', that is: the coercive use of the criminal sanction to 'correct' behaviour on a personal basis when the roots of crime lie in the social structural inequalities of wealth and power. Their later work (Taylor et al., 1975) was not a significant departure from this line, but in it Jock Young did lay the basis for the argument that working-class control over policing should be greatly extended, an idea that presaged the school of left realism.

In *What Is to Be Done About Law and Order?* (Lea and Young, 1984/1993) 'left realists' were to argue that the fatal flaw in Marxist approaches to criminology had been their failure to offer any realistic solutions to crime, other than emphasizing 'changing the social order'. But Marxist-based criminologies do not succumb to realist criticisms so easily. Steven Box (1983: 3) pointed out that 'official crime' was real enough and that 'a radical criminology which appears to deny this will be seen as naive and rightly rejected', but 'before galloping off down the "law and order" campaign trail, it might be prudent to consider whether murder, rape, robbery, assault and other crimes focused on

by state officials, politicians, the media and the criminal justice system do constitute the major part of our real crime problem.' He suggested that 'maybe they are only one crime problem and not *the* crime problem'. The clue to 'understanding most serious crimes', Box argued, 'can be located in power, not weakness, in privilege, not disadvantage, in wealth, not poverty'. Further, in another early contribution to the radical perspective, William Chambliss's (1978) work *On the Take: From Petty Crooks to Presidents* charted the social composition of racketeering in Seattle, showing that the 'hidden hands' in American organized crime were also leading lights within the political and economic elite. Extensive field work allowed Chambliss to piece together the links between front-line operators and the shadowy entrepreneurs who ultimately controlled the crime networks: key personnel in the police force, the legal profession, business, local government and the prosecutor's office. Writing in the late 1970s, Chambliss was able to assert that these connections extended to the highest office in the land. Presidents Nixon and Johnson were said to have had substantial dealings with men 'whose business profits derived at least in part from illegal business'. Evidence of the pervasive connections between the 'underworld' and the 'upper world' of the capitalist order seemed ample enough to indicate that criminality was indeed an endemic feature of American capitalism.

Criminologists who follow the lead of Durkheim might maintain that Marxist analyses represent an unnecessary narrowing of concern to the criminogenic properties of capitalist society; 'crime is a normal social fact', it is a feature of *any* social order. Those who wish to draw on insights from the Marxist tradition might argue in turn that, in the contemporary period when free-market liberalism has become hegemonic (to use a Marxist term) globally, this narrowing is not so much the product of theoretical blinkers (that is, the result of idealist assumptions), but rather is the realistic basis on which criminology must inevitably build. In this regard it would do to cite W.G. Carson's *The Other Price of Britain's Oil* (1982). His book took as its starting point the unacceptable level of fatal and non-fatal accidents that occurred during the United Kingdom's scramble to develop its offshore oil and gas reserves. Carson was moved to remark that it was conditions in the capitalist world economy that could 'explain why successive governments would opt to get their hands on the newfound wealth of the Continental Shelf as rapidly as possible and at almost any cost'. It was only by seeing the development of Britain's petroleum extraction industry in the context of global capitalism that 'the troubles endured by those who have been killed or injured in the North Sea can be viewed in terms of the "historical change and institutional contradiction" which earned them anything more than a coincidental place in 'the course of world history'.

The crimes of the powerful remain a significant blindspot for conventional criminology. Yet if there is any sense in the notion that 'property is theft', there is much criminological work to be done. A significant new frontier is being opened up through the institution of intellectual property. Patent law has been extended in such a way as to allow the ownership of DNA and other biological materials. It has become possible for multinational corporations to 'own' DNA sequences. 'Biopiracy' is a term that has been given to the practices of some companies who have asserted the right of ownership over genetic materials taken from living organisms (Manning, 2000). If the roots of Marxist criminologies can be said to lie in the article on The Law on Thefts of Wood, it would seem that the crimes of capitalist accumulation continue to provide fertile ground for critical scholarship in this field.

James Sheptycki

Associated Concepts: conflict theory, corporate crime, criminalization, critical criminology, labelling, left realism, new criminology, new deviancy theory, radical criminologies

Key Readings

Bankowski, Z., Mungham, G. and Young, P. (1977) 'Radical criminology or radical criminologist?', *Contemporary Crisis,* 1 (1): 37–51.

Box, S. (1983) *Power, Crime and Mystification.* London: Tavistock.

Carson, W.G. (1982) *The Other Price of Britain's Oil.* New Brunswick, NJ: Rutgers University Press.

Chambliss, W. (1978) *On the Take: From Petty Crooks to Presidents.* Bloomington, IN: Indiana University Press.

Greenberg, D. (1980) *Crime and Capitalism.* Palo Alto, CA: Mayfield Publishing Company.

Hall, S., Critcher, C., Jefferson, T., Clarke, J. and Roberts, B. (1978) *Policing the Crisis: Mugging, the State and Law and Order.* London: Macmillan.

Lea, J. and Young, J. (1984/1993) *What Is to be Done About Law and Order?* Harmondsworth: Penguin.

Manning, P.K. (2000) 'Policing new social spaces', in J.W.E. Sheptycki (ed.), *Issues in Transnational Policing.* London: Routledge.

Taylor, I., Walton, P. and Young, J. (1973) *The New Criminology.* London: Routledge and Kegan Paul.

Taylor, I., Walton, P. and Young, J. (eds) (1975) *Critical Criminology.* London: Routledge and Kegan Paul.

MASCULINITIES

Definition

Variable sets of ideas, values, representations and practices associated with 'being male' which structure relations among men as well as between men and women, and produce effects on individuals, organizations and cultures.

Distinctive Features

The traditional idea of masculinity (in the singular) as a set of psychological attributes was developed to understand differences between the sexes. In its classical psychoanalytic variant, naturally bi-sexual infants are precipitated into sexed identities through the difficulties of coping with the entry of the father into the mother–child dyad. Rather than continue an unequal struggle to take the place of the father, boy children, fearful of the potentially castrating father, forsake their desire for the mother and settle for becoming like the father (and hence the culturally masculine he embodies) through identifying with him (which, for Freud, was a difficult and never-completed process). The social psychological variant married research into differences between the sexes (which always found remarkably few) with role theory (how social positions, like father, get reproduced), to produce the idea of male and female sex-roles (or masculinity and femininity), the successful learning of which ensures the cultural reproduction of sexual difference.

Second wave feminists concerned with understanding the oppression of women introduced the importance of power, the idea that the key difference between men and women was the greater power men systematically enjoyed. When the spotlight was turned specifically on violence, and the maleness of the perpetrators was noticed and named, the notion of masculinity began to enter criminology's field of vision. Men's violence against women was seen as part of the system of male power and a key to its reproduction – hence explaining why domestic violence and rape were often not taken seriously. The early interest in male psychology, whether based in biology, early relationships or the social learning of sex-roles, had shifted to an interest in the social structures of male domination (or patriarchy). This provided the basis for a less individually-based understanding of masculinity, but the conception of masculinity informing the work (where there was one) was still a singular one.

The emergence of feminist-inspired, gender-aware historical and ethnographic work on men revealed not only the diverse forms masculinity has taken over time and cross-culturally, but also the co-existence of different forms of masculinity within particular cultures; thus was born the idea of masculinities. And, just as power affects the relations between men and women and masculinity/femininity, so it was seen to affect relations among masculinities. Masculinities were argued to be 'structured in dominance', with the most powerful (or valued), culturally speaking, in any given social order, being 'hegemonic'.

In attempting to understand the complex, contradictory and uneven nature of male domination and thus move beyond the reductiveness of the idea of 'the structure of patriarchy', certain feminist writers had begun to posit several structures underpinning gender relations, each with their own specific forms of oppression and particular historical trajectory. Building on this idea, Connell (1987, 1995), the most influential contemporary writer on masculinities, suggested the existence of three distinct but interrelated structures: labour (to do with work and the division of labour); power (to do with authority, control, coercion and violence); and cathexis (to do with sexuality, emotional relationships and desire). None of these was accorded primacy and all were to be understood as the outcome of practice (albeit always taking place within structured, or constrained, situations). Collectively, the product of these manifold structured practices at any given time was the historical pattern of gender relations: the 'gender order'.

Within criminology, Messerschmidt (1993) has developed these ideas and applied them to thinking about crime. He utilizes Connell's notions of a tripartite structure of gender relations and hegemonic and subordinated masculinities, as well as the importance of practice. In addition, he addresses the structures of race and class by conceptualizing all structures as implicated simultaneously in any given practice, and practice as situationally constrained by the need to 'account' for our actions to normative conceptions (of appropriate gender/race/class conduct). In different situations class, gender or race 'accounting' may be more or less salient. Within this schema, crime becomes a resource for certain men in certain situations for accomplishing masculinity. Its salience for particular men as such a resource will depend on other resources at their disposal, which, in turn, will be a product of their position in class, gender and race relations and the sorts of situations they find themselves in.

Evaluation

Freud thought the concept of masculinity was one of the most 'confused' in science. Unfortunately, pluralizing the term has not eliminated all confusions. In particular, there is a constant tendency to elide men and masculinities, to reduce the latter to lists of attributions, what men do ('take risks', compete, etc.) or should do (be strong, stoical, etc.), as opposed to what women do/should do, rather than use the term consistently in relational terms: as places within gender relations that *only* exist in contrast to femininities – no femininities, no masculinities. No doubt this attributional tendency stems in part from our desire to concretize, to turn abstract relations into definable objects, as well as from the sorts of observable differences between men and women which we encounter daily.

One development of a strictly relational approach has been to see masculinity purely as an ideology developed to help people make sense of the continuation of sexual inequality in an age of formal equality (MacInnes, 1998). Others, like Collier (1998), influenced by debates about embodiment, have attempted to develop relational accounts in a way that puts back the 'sexed' body, but without reverting to a biological essentialism. The relentlessly sociological nature of most contemporary accounts has reawakened an interest in the psychological dimension of masculinity, influenced this time by post-structuralism and the 'object relations' school of psychoanalysis (Jefferson, 1997). Critics of Messerschmidt's attempts to explain the 'doing' of all kinds of crime, from varieties of work-based crime to diverse forms of street crime, as different ways of 'doing' masculinity, have begun to question whether this key idea of his is always *necessary* to explain a particular crime, and, more generally,

whether it is *sufficient* as an explanation of *any* crime. The idea of masculinity as a key concept in understanding why most crimes are committed by men was an exciting, post-feminist development. Whether the spate of new writings this idea has generated can surmount the many theoretical confusions intrinsic to it, time alone will tell.

Tony Jefferson

Associated Concepts: feminist criminologies, hegemonic masculinity, hegemony, psychoanalytic criminology, radical feminism

Key Readings

Collier, R. (1998) *Masculinities, Crime and Criminology.* London: Sage.
Connell, R.W. (1987) *Gender and Power.* Cambridge: Polity Press.
Connell, R.W. (1995) *Masculinities.* Cambridge: Polity Press.
Jefferson, T. (1997) 'Masculinities and crimes', in M. Maguire, R. Morgan and R. Reiner (eds), *The Oxford Handbook of Criminology,* 2nd edn. Oxford: The Clarendon Press.
MacInnes, J. (1998) *The End of Masculinity.* Buckingham: Open University Press.
Messerschmidt, J.W. (1993) *Masculinities and Crime.* Lanham, MD: Rowman and Littlefield.

MEDIATION

See: Reparation; Restorative justice

MENTORING

Definition

Mentoring has a long history which can be traced back to the ancient Greeks. According to Homer's epic poem *The Odyssey*, Odysseus entrusted Mentor to act as guardian and tutor to his only son, Telemachus. In essence, mentoring is generally thought of as a relationship between an older, more experienced mentor and an unrelated young protégé. The mentor provides guidance, instruction and encouragement with the aim of developing the competence and character of his or her protégé. While such relationships may develop in a variety of settings, mentoring has come to provide a key focus for work with disaffected young people.

Distinctive Features

Mentoring may take place within the context of naturally occurring relationships, but the term itself has generally come to be used to describe formalized versions of this type of relationship. Formal or 'artificial' mentoring is generally thought of as a relationship between two strangers, instigated by a third party, who intentionally matches the mentor with the mentee according to the needs of the younger person as a part of a planned intervention or programme. Formal mentoring typically concentrates on young people who, for varying reasons, are considered to be 'at risk' – whether this is because of disruptive behaviour, non-attendance at school, learning difficulties, offending, or contact with the criminal justice system and/or substance use.

As a response to youth disaffection, formal mentoring was pioneered largely in the United States. One of the earliest and most influential mentoring programmes was established in 1904 by Ernest Coulter, a court clerk from New York City. Big Brothers Big Sisters of America (BBBSA), as it has come to be known, claims to be one of the biggest mentoring programmes in the world. BBBSA targets young people with 'associated risk factors', including residence in a single-parent home or a history of abuse or neglect, and seeks to pair them with an unrelated adult volunteer. The adult and young person agree to meet between two and four times a month for at least one year, with an average meeting lasting approximately four hours. The programme is not aimed at specific 'problems'; rather it focuses on developing the 'whole person' (Tierney et al., 1995).

While formal mentoring has much more recent origins in the United Kingdom, it has quickly become very popular. The Dalston Youth Project (DYP) was one of the first mentoring programmes to be established in this country and was set up in 1994 by Crime Concern in the London borough of Hackney. The DYP targets disaffected young people and seeks to build their skills and confidence through a one-to-one mentoring relationship with an adult volunteer, alongside a structured education and careers programme. Its stated aims are to reduce youth crime and other at-risk behaviour; to help at-risk young people back into education, training and employment; and to enable community members to get involved in solving community problems through volunteering.

The DYP is widely considered to have been a successful project and, within two years of being set up, was cited as an example of good practice by the Audit Commission. In 1996, a survey conducted by the National Mentoring Network found over 4000 people acting as mentors to pupils in more than 400 educational establishments (Skinner and Fleming, 1999). Mentoring was given a further boost by the rise of New Labour, fitting comfortably with the new government's emphasis on social inclusion, civic renewal and community responsibility. In recent years, mentoring has benefited from considerable government support across a wide range of areas including education and skills, youth justice and homelessness. By 2000, the Youth Justice Board had funded almost 100 mentoring schemes and the Home Office had also become a significant funder of local mentoring programmes.

Although highly fashionable, mentoring has faced a number of criticisms. One of the main difficulties with this approach is pinning down precisely what it is. Developing a clear definition is complicated by the fact that mentoring practices vary and may include one or more of the following: facilitation, coaching, buddying, befriending, counselling, tutoring, teaching, life-styling and role-modelling.

Added to this definitional difficulty, mentoring lacks a strong theoretical base. According to Kate Philip (2000), the classical model of mentoring rests on an uncritical acceptance of traditional developmental theories about youth. She also argues that this model makes gender-bound assumptions about family and organization and tends to neglect structural features of poverty and exclusion. These criticisms are reflected in her conclusion that the classical model of mentoring is highly individualistic (it has as its heart a relationship that is essentially private and isolated from young people's social environments), is highly gendered (privileging white male experience), and pays relatively little regard to the young person's stated needs. Other commentators have noted that the way in which mentoring may be expected to bring about changes in young people's attitudes, behaviours or life-styles is far from clear. In view of these limitations, they suggest that mentoring has been under-theorized (Newburn and Shiner, 2005).

Evaluation

In an age of supposed 'evidence-based' practice, mentoring rests upon very insecure foundations. There is surprisingly little evidence as to the effectiveness of this approach, which has come to prominence due largely to its common-sense appeal. Mentoring has been subject to relatively little research, and that which has been conducted has generally failed to meet even the most basic criteria of evaluative rigour. Only a handful of independent evaluations have been published and, although some have been reasonably rigorous, others have been limited by their scale and design.

This is not to say that mentoring is without merit, however, simply that it has been inadequately evaluated. Many young people talk positively about having had a mentor and some of those evaluations which have been conducted have yielded some positive results. An evaluation of Big Brothers Big Sisters of America reported substantial benefits for participants in relation to drug and alcohol use, violent episodes and school attendance (Sherman et al., 1998). The largest and most robust evaluation of mentoring in Britain to date also pointed to some positive outcomes – specifically in relation to engagement in education, training and work, although not in relation to offending (Newburn and Shiner, 2005).

Even with these encouraging findings there remains too little information for adequate policy making. The evidence, on balance, is equivocal, and mentoring can best be described as 'promising' (Sherman et al., 1998). Under these circumstances the priority is for more research, not more unevaluated programmes. Without strong evidence of its efficacy, mentoring may fall victim to the whims of fashion, fading from view just as quickly (and inexplicably) as it came to prominence.

Michael Shiner

Associated Concepts: community crime prevention, crime prevention, evaluation research, responsibilization, risk, social exclusion, 'what works'

Key Readings

Newburn, T. and Shiner, M. (2005) *Dealing with Disaffection: Young People, Mentoring and Social Inclusion.* Cullompton: Willan.

Philip, K. (2000) 'Mentoring: pitfalls and potential for young people', *Youth and Policy*, 67: 1–15.

Sherman, L., Gottfredson, D., MacKenzie, D., Eck, J., Reuter, P. and Bushway, S. (1998) *Preventing Crime: What Works, What Doesn't, and What's Promising: A Report to the United States Congress.* Washington, DC: National Institute of Justice.

Skinner, A. and Fleming, J. (1999) *Mentoring Socially Excluding Young People: Lessons from Practice.* Manchester: National Mentoring Network.

Tierney, J.P., Grossman, J.B. and Resch, N.L. (1995) *Making a Difference: An Impact Study of Big Brothers Big Sisters.* Philadelphia, PA: Public/Private Ventures.

MORAL ECONOMY

Definition

The concept of the moral economy, in the context of criminal offending, was developed by E.P. Thompson as a means of analysing and explaining eighteenth-century crowd action.

Distinctive Features

Dissatisfied with social tension charts and the reductionist argument that food shortages and high prices led to hunger which, in turn, led to food riots, Thompson looked for the notions that legitimated rioting in the eyes of the participants, the communities that supported them, and the authorities who, for much of the eighteenth century, gave them a measure of licence. He concluded that the men and women in the crowds were motivated by beliefs that they were defending customs or traditional rights. They were not entirely helpless or hopeless, but sensed that they had some power to help themselves and ensure food of decent quality at a fair price. Eighteenth-century rioters rarely took food without payment of some kind, and they would destroy grain or bread to punish a double-dealing farmer, miller or baker, rather than simply taking them. For much of the century, landed gentry, casting middlemen as profiteering interlopers, were sympathetic to such crowds. A gradual change began with the increasing acceptance of Smithian economics, particularly the importance of the freedom of the marketplace, towards the end of the century, and specifically by a government fearing itself threatened by a radicalism that appeared to advocate French revolutionary models.

Evaluation

Criticism was levelled at Thompson's concept of the moral economy, in particular for its failure to appreciate nuances in Adam Smith's work and the way in which the market worked. Twenty years on Thompson replied with his customary panache and Swiftian wit. During those two decades, as well as subsequently, the idea of the moral economy was also developed by those who were more sympathetic to his perspective, perhaps most significantly by David Arnold and John Bohstedt. The former traced similar patterns of rioting to that of eighteenth-century England in early twentieth-century India, while the latter described how eighteenth-century rioting might be construed as 'community politics'. According to Bohstedt, horizontal and vertical relationship networks within communities were brought into play at different moments of crowd action, and with different results depending on a community's structure. In 1985, following the Broadwater Farm riots in London, Bohstedt published a letter in *The Times* suggesting how these disturbances also needed to be considered in such terms. No historian can now approach crowd action without some acknowledgement of the moral economy concept, yet, as Mark Harrison has warned, there is danger in the way in which crowd and riot have often been conflated in social history and in seeking to impose a moral economy legitimation to every riot. Disorders, he has insisted, on occasions looked backward to traditional rights for legitimacy while on others they looked forward to a vision of how society might be in the future, but they could also be spurred on by demands to meet changing expectations.

Clive Emsley

Associated Concepts: historical methods, Marxist criminologies, primitive rebellion, social justice

Key Readings

Arnold, D. (1979) 'Looting, grain riots and government policy in South India, 1918', *Past and Present*, 84: 111–45.

Bohstedt, J. (1983) *Riots and Community Politics in England and Wales, 1790–1810*. Cambridge, MA: Harvard University Press.

Harrison, M. (1988) *Crowds and History: Mass Phenomena in English Towns, 1790–1835*. Cambridge: Cambridge University Press.

Thompson, E.P. (1991) *Customs in Common*. London: Merlin Press.

MORAL PANIC

Definition

A disproportional and hostile social reaction to a condition, person or group defined as a threat to societal values, involving stereotypical media representations and leading to demands for greater social control as well as creating a spiral of reaction.

Distinctive Features

Since it appeared in the title of Cohen's (1972) book, the term 'moral panic' has been ubiquitous in criminology and the sociology of deviance. Its many uses to characterize social reaction are too numerous to catalogue here but include media coverage of youth, sex, drugs, juvenile crime, single parents, child abuse and diseases of humankind and animals (such as HIV/AIDS, as well as BSE or 'mad cow' disease).

Cohen's work on the moral panic around Mods and Rockers in Britain examined media coverage in the 1960s and the pronouncements of various authorities or experts who defined the 'youth problem' as a symptom of the state of society and social decline. He used the analogy of a disaster to identify various stages of social reaction. The inventory involved taking stock of what happened, a time at which media descriptions and definitions were crucial since they were the main source for most people's information. Cohen categorized the media inventory of Mods and Rockers in three parts: first, the media exaggerated the numbers involved, the extent of the violence and the amount of damage caused. Distortion of the events was multiplied by the use of sensational headlines and the adoption of a dramatic reporting style, especially in the use of words such as 'orgy of destruction', 'mob' and 'siege'. Second, the media coverage contained many predictions that there would be more conflict and violence. Third, Cohen argued that this coverage served to re-code or to symbolize deviance through associating the word 'Mod' with particular expressions of style such as clothes and hairstyles. Symbolization leads on to sensitization so

that other events that may otherwise have been seen as isolated or unconnected ones are linked into a pattern and understood as symptomatic of the same underlying malaise. Both processes produce an increase in social control responses and Cohen saw this control culture as containing three common elements:

- *Diffusion,* in which events in other places are interconnected with the initial event.
- *Escalation,* in which there are calls for 'strong measures' to counter the threat.
- *Innovation,* referring to increased powers for the police and courts to deal with the threat.

Various moral entrepreneurs who call for action to be taken against the outbreak of lawlessness will usually also proclaim that the current controls are inadequate. As Cohen showed, entrepreneurs will exaggerate the problem in order to make local events seem to be of pressing national concern and an index of the decline of morality and standards. The stepping-up of controls leads to further marginalization and stigmatization of deviants which, in turn, leads to more calls for action, more police action and so on, until we have a deviancy amplification spiral. Cohen's analysis located the nature and extent of reaction to Mods and Rockers to the social context of Britain in the 1960s. In particular, ambivalence about social change in the postwar period, the new affluence and freedom of youth cultures and their apparent rejection of traditional forms of incorporation such as work and families are used to contextualize the panic.

The social context of moral panics was developed by Hall et al.'s (1978) analysis of the social reaction to 'mugging' or street crime. Working within a Marxist framework, they argued that mugging achieved the prominence it did because its themes of 'race', crime and youth meshed with or crystallized political and economic shifts in the 1970s. Economically, this was a period of crisis in Britain. Politically, Britain's standing in the world was continuing to decline and, domestically, trade unions, left wingers and the welfare state were blamed for much of the state of 'sick Britain'. New racial discourses were emerging that identified blacks as part of the problem of British society. Concerns about sexual permissiveness and a lack of controls on young people were also carrying on from earlier times. In this climate racialized crime statistics were used to draw attention to the problem of disproportionate amounts of street crime committed by young blacks and drove discourses for more law and order to stem the rising tide of crime and to protect innocent victims. Hall et al. argued that this moral panic underscored the development of authoritarian populism in Britain in the 1970s.

Moral panics have been seen as inevitable and periodic occurrences for societies undergoing a reaffirmation or re-definition of moral boundaries. Functionalism has been a recurring feature of moral panic theory, even in its radical applications. In a crude version the reaction is seen as akin to a form of mass delusion where the public is 'duped' into panicking. This tends to overstate the extent of social consensus and assume a straightforward correspondence between the intentions of an elite and outcomes. In seeking to move beyond this, Goode and Ben-Yehuda (1994) distinguish between three theories or approaches. The grassroots model is where a panic originates with the general public and expresses a genuinely felt, even if mistaken, concern about a threat. The elite-engineered approach is where an elite deliberately and consciously generates concerns and fears. The interest-group theory is where rule-creators and moral entrepreneurs launch crusades for controls. Goode and Ben-Yehuda have distilled five key characteristics of a moral panic:

- disproportionality of reaction;
- concern about the threat;
- hostility to the objects of the panic;
- widespread agreement or consensus that the threat is real;
- volatility, that is, moral panics are unpredictable in terms of scale and intensity.

Evaluation

A moral panic entails simplification, stigmatization and heightened public feeling about an individual, group or event. Calling this a moral panic draws attention to exaggerated and distorted media coverage and the ways in which it may be seen as symbolizing diffuse social anxieties in particular conjunctures. A wide battery of arguments has been raised against the conceptualization and utilization of moral panics as a way of capturing social reaction. Criticizing Hall et al. (1978) in particular, left realism maintains that crime and the fear of crime should be taken seriously and not dismissed as 'just' an expression of media overreaction or panic. Waddington (1986) also took issue with the empirical basis of *Policing the Crisis*. He argued that, contrary to the view presented in that book, mugging was rising, and questioned the view that the media coverage was disproportionate. Waddington, as well as others, then asked what a 'proportionate' reaction would be. The scale of media reaction can rarely be measured or judged in terms of either proportionality or seriousness, as the highly uneven coverage of wars around the world indicates. This therefore casts doubt on one of the central tenets of moral panics.

Problems have also been identified with the use of the concept of moral panic to capture reactions to diverse themes or issues. There is a problem in reducing all episodes of overreaction to the catch-all notion of 'panickiness'. A more detailed understanding of different types of social reaction, as well as the very different conditions that seem to constitute moral panics, has been called for. Watney (1987), for example, questioned those who used it to characterize media and policy reactions to HIV/AIDS. He argued that moral panic theory was unable to deal with the entire field of representations because it operated by creating a distinction between exaggerated media representations and the 'reality' of a particular issue, with the latter being treated as standing outside the field of representations. Furthermore, there is a problem with the implicit or explicit contrast between the 'irrational' panic and the supposedly 'rational' analysis of it.

McRobbie and Thornton (1995) also argued that the idea of moral panic needs to be rethought in an environment with multiple media outlets and where folk devils are accustomed to presenting alternative frameworks for understanding or explaining an issue or problem. Moral panics, they added, have become routine, not exceptional. In an environment where there may be an institutionalized need for the media to generate 'good stories', moral panics can easily become part of a promotional culture that 'ironically' uses sensationalism for commercial purposes.

Karim Murji

Associated Concepts: authoritarian populism, Birmingham 'school', deviance, deviancy amplification, folk devil, labelling, left realism, Marxist criminologies, new deviancy theory, social constructionism, social reaction, stereotyping

Key Readings

Cohen, S. (1972) *Folk Devils and Moral Panics.* London: MacGibbon and Kee. (New edition Oxford, Martin Robertson, 1980.)
Goode, E. and Ben-Yehuda, N. (1994) *Moral Panics: The Social Construction of Deviance.* Oxford: Blackwell.
Hall, S., Critcher, C., Jefferson, T., Clarke, J. and Roberts, B. (1978) *Policing the Crisis.* London: Macmillan.
McRobbie, A. and Thornton, S. (1995) 'Rethinking "moral panic" for multi-mediated social worlds', *British Journal of Sociology,* 46 (4): 559–74.
Waddington, P.A.J. (1986) 'Mugging as a moral panic: a question of proportion', *British Journal of Sociology,* 32 (2): 245–59.
Watney, S. (1987) *Policing Desire: Pornography, Aids and the Media.* London: Methuen.

MULTI-AGENCY CRIME PREVENTION

Definition

A planned, co-ordinated response by several social agencies to the problems of crime and incivilities. The movement to multi-agency prevention implies that probation/corrections services, education, employment, family services, health and housing, private bodies such as charities and business, and at times the 'community', as well as the police, all have a role to play in crime prevention.

Distinctive Features

Such initiatives are, for the most part, elements of a 'top-down', managerialist project emanating from neo-liberal states in the past two decades of the twentieth century. This project has also involved the 'local delivery' of crime prevention by means of multi-agency partnerships between statutory agencies, private business and, at times, 'community' initiatives in various 'watch' schemes. In both the academic literature and in policy circles, the terms 'multi-agency' and 'community' crime prevention are often used interchangeably. This is understandable on a number of counts. First, the term 'community' retains its feel-good factor and is thus a useful legitimating, rhetorical device in crime prevention discourses. Second, and less cynically, some multi-agency prevention initiatives have sought to adopt a *social* crime prevention approach and attempt to involve members of local communities in their work. However, the key feature to multi-agency crime prevention is that it is chiefly a 'top-down', neo-corporatist strategy from both central and local state regimes.

Multi-agency crime prevention now has the status of a taken-for-granted 'fact of life' in the crime control business across many contemporary states. Popular examples of such multi-agency interventions across the world include both local government- and privately-run CCTV initiatives, play/sports schemes during school holidays, activity-based projects with (potential) young offenders, educational projects on drugs, and so on. However, the exact contours of multi-agency crime prevention, not to mention the 'success' of such approaches, remain somewhat unclear. It is impossible to discuss multi-agency crime prevention, or what is increasingly termed 'community safety', without engaging in a debate about the changing modalities of state power in relationship to civil society and 'the public'. Indeed, notions of 'local' and 'central' state are becoming increasingly problematic with the rise of what is often termed 'governance at a distance'. This development is well illustrated by the example of state power being exercised through indirect rather than direct agency, as in the fad for local, preventive 'partnerships against crime'. In this new era the responsibility for setting up and running multi-agency crime prevention initiatives at the local level is increasingly put out to 'tender', inviting bids from rival competitors.

Alongside the emotionally expressive politics of popular punitiveness, the discourse of managerialism has come to play an increasingly important part in the restructuring of criminal justice in most mature capitalist democracies. The managerialist discourse suggests that the organization and co-ordination of public services are best realized by means of the processes of marketization and the replacement of professionals and bureaucrats by managers. It assumes that better management will prove an effective and economical solution for a wide range of economic and social problems. Indeed it has come to affect the organization and operational work of the police and other agencies of criminal justice and prevention in novel and unprecedented ways. In most multi-agency crime prevention initiatives a managerialist ethos is increasingly coming to the fore, as evidenced in the obsession with 'mission statements', 'performance indicators', measurable 'objectives', 'customer surveys', 'audits' and 'evaluation' and so on, all of which reflect the governmental pressure to be able to count 'what works' in crime and disorder reduction.

Evaluation

Supporters argue for the superiority and success of such corporate and managed approaches over traditional, single-agency prevention approaches. However, academic research has been more circumspect about the success of multi-agency partnerships in crime reduction, highlighting the lack of clarity and conflict about shared goals between the participating agencies, and limited, tangible evidence of successful outcomes (Graham and Bennett, 1995). Research has also pointed to the centrality of power differentials between the major agencies involved and the importance of sectional differences within existing communities 'subject' to such multi-agency co-operation. Furthermore, the conceptual boundaries of multi-agency social crime prevention are particularly vague, encompassing a diversity of schemes under the label. Despite or perhaps because of this 'catch-all' quality to such initiatives, the appeal of multi-agency crime prevention partnerships across contemporary states, when faced both by growing rates of crime and disorder and declining trust in traditional crime control responses, is unlikely to wane in the foreseeable future.

Gordon Hughes

Associated Concepts: community crime prevention, community safety, crime prevention, evaluation research, governance, managerialism, realist criminologies, situational crime prevention, social crime prevention

Key Readings

Crawford, A. (1997) *The Local Governance of Crime.* Oxford: The Clarendon Press.
Graham, J. and Bennett, T. (1995) *Crime Prevention Strategies in Europe and North America.* New York: Criminal Justice Press.
Hughes, G. (1997) 'Strategies of crime prevention and community safety in contemporary Britain', *Studies on Crime and Crime Prevention,* 5: 221–44.
O'Malley, P. and Sutton, A. (1997) *Crime Prevention in Australia: Issues in Policy and Research.* Sydney: Federation Press.
Pearson, G., Blagg, H., Smith, D., Sampson, A. and Stubbs, P. (1992) 'Crime, community and conflict: the multi-agency approach', in D. Downes (ed.), *Unravelling Criminal Justice.* London: Macmillan.

MULTIVARIATE ANALYSIS

Definition

The explanation of variation in a dependent variable using more than one independent/explanatory variable. It has three main uses:

1 determining the overall effect of several independent variables on a dependent one;
2 determining the *independent* effect of one variable on another, controlling for the overlapping effects of other variables;
3 statistical control of alternative explanations for the observed effect, for example, control for sampling inadequacies.

Distinctive Features

A (zero-order) correlation coefficient estimates the amount of variation in a dependent variable which is 'explained' by a single independent variable. A multiple correlation coefficient shows the amount 'explained' by a number of variables taken together. (In statistics 'explanation' means adequate prediction; it does not necessarily imply, and certainly does not prove, the identification of a causal mechanism.) A variant of the correlational technique is *partial correlation*, which establishes the amount of variation in a dependent variable explained by an independent one with the effects of one or more other variables held constant – the *independent* effect of the independent variable on the dependent one. Techniques such as multiple regression (see below) allow us to establish the minimum number of variables needed to make as good a prediction of the dependent variable's values as can be achieved with the information that has been collected – the point at which adding more variables to the prediction yields no new information. They also allow us to assess the effect of leaving a given variable out of the prediction – by how much the proportion of variance explained falls – and so to establish the independent effects of each variable and its share in the overall prediction.

The simplest multivariate procedure is tabular analysis as illustrated in Table 1. The first four rows show the relationship between age and criminal conviction for the total sample, and we can see that older people in this mythical sample are less likely than younger people to be convicted during the next year:

Table 1 *Age, gender and previous convictions in a mythical survey*

Convictions during next year	Total	Age Younger (%)	Older (%)	
Total sample				
None	2450	55.0	75.0	$\chi^2 = 195.62$, $p < 0.001$
One	600	17.5	15.8	$\varphi = 0.31$
Two	480	17.5	12.6	
More than two	270	10.0	3.9	
Males				
None	1000	40.0	60.0	$\chi^2 = 159.94$, $p < 0.001$
One	500	30.0	22.0	$\varphi = 0.40$
Two	480	17.5	12.6	
More than two	270	10.0	3.9	
Females				
None	1450	83.3	76.3	$\chi^2 = 63.30$, $p < 0.001$
One	100	5.0	5.6	$\varphi = 0.25$
Two	200	15.0	10.5	
More than two	150	10.0	5.6	

75 per cent of older people have no such convictions, compared with 55 per cent of younger people, and 10 per cent of younger people have more than two convictions but only 3.9 per cent of older people. The χ^2 figure on the right is a measure of how far the pattern in the table departs from a random one, and $p < 0.001$ indicates that the relationship is statistically significant – there is less than one chance in a thousand of obtaining a departure as extreme as this by chance alone. Φ is a correlation coefficient, a measure of the strength of the relationship. The remainder of the table looks at males and females separately. We may note that:

1 women have fewer convictions than men – many more of them have none at all;
2 the relationship of age and conviction rate is significant for both genders; but
3 the ϕ coefficient is much smaller for women than for men, suggesting that the relationship with age is much stronger for men than for women.

Tabular analysis is the easiest kind of multivariate analysis to interpret. However, it is relatively crude and insensitive and it also becomes very cumbersome when dealing with more than three or four variables. Other commonly encountered varieties of multivariate analysis include:

• Multiple regression, which combines the effects of different variables into a single predictor of a dependent variable, making allowance for their overlap. Statistics generally produced are the multiple correlation and its statistical significance, the significance of each component variable's contribution, and estimates of their independent effects (beta coefficients). Multiple regression needs an interval or ratio-level variable as the dependent variable (one where it makes sense to talk about some values as being twice or half others – like money or age or number of previous convictions). Dichotomies (variables with only two values – such as gender) or interval/ratio variables may be used as independent variables.
• Discriminant function analysis, which works in a similar way to multiple regression but will allow categorical variables (e.g., type of crime) as dependent variables.
• Analysis of variance works on categorical independent variables and on an interval/ratio dependent one. It provides an estimate of each variable's independent contribution to the explanation of variance and a similar estimate for each interaction effect (each combination of variables working together).
• Logistic regression permits the sophisticated prediction of categorical variables, combining the strengths of discriminant function analysis, analysis of variance and tabular analysis, but it is sometimes difficult to interpret.

All of these methods, adapted to different kinds of data, are used for the same purposes: to assess the overall effect of several variables on a dependent variable; to assess the independent effect of variables that may be related to each other as well as to the dependent; and/or to control for alternative explanations to the one proposed.

Evaluation

Caution should be applied when interpreting multivariate analyses, however.

• Most of such analyses work by first taking account of the variable which explains the greatest amount of variation, and then of the variable that explains the greatest amount of what is left, and so on. The effect of the first variable is therefore sometimes exaggerated because all of the overlap with other variables is attributed to it.
• It is always possible that apparent causal relationships are in fact spurious and due to the effect of some other variable which has not been measured. Statistical control is never as effective in eliminating alternative explanations as control by the design of the study.

- While correlation is necessary for causation, it is not sufficient. There is always a tendency in these analyses to move from prediction to causal explanation, and this is seldom appropriate without additional evidence and argument which cannot be supplied by the analysis itself.

Roger Sapsford

Associated Concepts: causation, correlational analysis, experiments, prediction studies

Key Readings

Hood, R. (1992) *Race and Sentencing.* Oxford: The Clarendon Press.
Sapsford, R.J. (1999) *Survey Research.* London: Sage.

N

NATURAL JUSTICE

Definition

A concept of natural justice emphasizes the basic principles necessary to ensure fairness in legal proceedings; principles of justice deriving from the nature of humanity; and principles of justice which would obtain in a state of nature and which are independent of social relationships.

Distinctive Features

Natural justice entails practical applications in law of principles to ensure procedural fairness, in civil as well as criminal proceedings. That is, that no one should be the judge in their own cause; and that no one should be condemned without representation.

The first principle has led to procedural rules about vested interests and about the independence of the judiciary; the second mandates a right to legal representation, if necessary paid for by the state.

Is it illogical or nonsensical to describe formally constituted laws as 'unjust'? Officials enforcing pass and residence laws in apartheid South Africa were applying laws enacted by the recognized legislative body, but this did not make the laws 'just'; similarly rules affecting the treatment of Jewish people in Nazi Germany were passed by parliamentary process and so were 'laws', but we would none the less have no hesitation in describing these as 'unjust'. It follows, therefore, that there must be some quality of 'justice' which is not simply that which is prescribed by law; a quality which can act as a standard by which existing laws and legal systems can be assessed.

Philosophers from the ancients onwards have pondered the essence of natural justice. To be natural, justice must be derived from characteristics that all persons have in common and must not be derived from the culture and institutions of particular societies; to be natural, justice must be based on characteristics that persons have independent of their status, relationships or individual biographies. Aristotle thought natural justice was revealed by universality: all known societies have some common laws, for example a law of murder. Religious philosophers, such as St Thomas Aquinas, have seen natural justice as a reflection of the wisdom of God; modern religious theorists have pointed to the common elements in all the major faiths as revealing the divine source of natural justice.

Secular theories have sought the origin of natural justice in the nature of human beings and have nominated *reason* as the characteristic possessed by all human beings simply by virtue of being human. Humans possess reason and they seek to pursue their own goals. Since the eighteenth century, natural justice theories based on irreducible human characteristics have usually been formulated as rights theories. These have been expressed in idealistic proclamations such as the United States' Declaration of Independence in 1776 and the French Declaration of Rights in 1789. More recently, after the Second World War the founding of the United Nations was marked by the Universal Declaration of Human Rights and echoed by the European Convention on Human Rights. Most declarations of rights are embellishments on the common elements of 'life, liberty and the pursuit of happiness'.

Evaluation

Theories of natural justice have been unfashionable for several decades. Awareness of the differences in societies' conceptions of rights and justice led to the rise of 'relativism' in social science and 'legal positivism' or 'legal realism' among legal theorists. These perspectives emphasize the social embeddedness of moral rules and the role of legislators and judges in defining justice for any society. In legal theory there is perhaps not so much distance between natural justice and legal positivism positions as there is between relativists and universalists in social science. The best-known contemporary theorist of natural justice, Finnis (1980), places importance on the context and interpretation, while Hart (1994), a leading legal realist, says that valid legal systems must necessarily contain some minimum content of natural law.

Natural justice is undergoing a revival in the form of an increased adherence to human rights theory and politics. A desire to help those living under oppressive regimes has led a championing of the claims of human rights against the inviolability of sovereignty; feminists and those seeking to remove discrimination against ethnic and religious minorities have also drawn on the idea of human rights. Even communitarian theorists and critics of 'cultural imperialism' would acknowledge the necessity of a universal commitment to fundamental human rights.

Barbara Hudson

Associated Concepts: communitarianism, human rights, social justice

Key Readings

Dworkin, R. (1977) *Taking Rights Seriously.* London: Duckworth.

Finnis, J. (1980) *Natural Law and Natural Rights.* Oxford: Oxford University Press.
Hart, H.L.A. (1994) *The Concept of Law,* 2nd edn. Oxford: Oxford University Press.
Reiman, J. (1990) *Justice and Modern Moral Philosophy.* New Haven, CT: Yale University Press.
Sandel, M. (1998) *Liberalism and the Limits of Justice,* 2nd edn. Cambridge: Cambridge University Press.

NEO-CONSERVATIVE CRIMINOLOGY

Definition

Neo-conservative criminology treats criminality as one of a group of social pathological phenomena, the prevalence of which is due to the corrosive influence of the liberalist modern culture. In terms of criminal justice policy neo-conservative criminology is oriented, on the one hand, towards the preservation of traditional values and norms, and on the other, towards the promotion of a technocratic rationality that decouples the control of crime from its social and economic aetiology.

Distinctive Features

The term 'neo-conservative criminology' signifies the existence of a close causal relationship between specific theoretical positions on crime and crime control and the neo-conservative political convictions of their authors. The main exponent of neo-conservative criminology is the American James Q. Wilson – a political scientist who has nevertheless greatly influenced criminal justice policy through his widely read writings (for example, he co-authored along with George Kelling (1982) the influential theory of Broken Windows) and his numerous advisory roles during the Reagan and Bush administrations.

Neo-conservative criminology does not amount to a criminological theory. It should rather be understood as a specific application of a broader social engineering perspective that utilizes theoretical, and particularly applied, knowledge in the service of the functional exigencies of the state and the economy. Whilst according to neo-conservative political thought the economic, technical and managerial achievements of modernity should be safeguarded and further extended, the same does not apply to its ethical and cultural components. Indeed modernist culture, with its emphasis on 'subjective value orientations' and 'expressive self-realization', is held out as undermining the motivational requirements of an 'efficient economy and a rational state administration', namely the individual's willingness to achieve and to obey (Habermas, 1989). In place of such a subversive modernist culture, neo-conservatives ask for a revival of tradition and call for 'courage for the past' in the state, schools and family.

The functional logic which lies behind their justification of traditionalism in terms of its beneficial effects for the system can also be discerned in certain other central features of neo-conservative thinking. Neo-conservatives urge the state to withdraw to activities it can effectively control – so as to lessen legitimation problems. Moreover, they also recommend a greater detachment of administration from public will-formation so as to minimize the burden of democratic participation on controversial issues concerning socio-political goals.

The influence of neo-conservative political thinking can be easily traced in the specific understanding of crime and deviance that is characteristic of neo-conservative criminology. The latter elevates the moral culture of a society to a key (if not *the* key) variable for the explanation of long-term changes in the levels of criminality and disorder. A central proposition of neo-conservative criminology is that the propensity of people to commit crimes will vary in accordance to the extent to which they have internalized a commitment to self-control. This in turn depends on the level of a society's investment in promoting self-control (through its socialization mechanisms) as well as on the (not necessarily unchangeable) genetic and biological characteristics of individuals which will determine the effectiveness

of the conditioning process in specific cases. Existing high levels of criminality and disorder are thus causally linked to the weakening strength of the sources of social authority, namely family, schools, religion and so forth, and even more so to the corrosive influence of the surrounding culture which 'emphasizes rights rather than rightness of behaviour' and which celebrates self-expression – to the point of self-indulgence – instead of promoting self-control and self-restraint.

In view of the detrimental effects of this expressive individualism, neo-conservatives attempt to redefine what properly constitutes the private sphere. Forms of behaviours and individual choices that have broader social ramifications cannot, in their opinion, be treated as wholly private matters, but instead call for a public response. The use of drugs, disorderly behaviour, and specific choices concerning the family structure (single mothers, and the ways in which children are raised) should accordingly not be dealt with on the basis of the liberal principle of moral neutrality but require an affirmative moral stance. Hence we have witnessed strong neo-conservative opposition to the decriminalization of 'victimless crimes', their espousal of a 'zero tolerance' approach to disorderly behaviour, their proposals for introducing specific disincentives for single mothers, and so on.

The rather comprehensive conception of the good which this neo-conservative stance embodies reflects 'a healthy appreciation of tradition', that is, the need to exploit those traditional values and institutions on which the public order and stability of the social and economic structure depend.

However, the 'functional traditionalist' streak of neo-conservative criminology should not allow us to overlook its strong technocratic orientation which is apparent in its attempts to rationalize the administration of the criminal justice system. Efficiency and effectiveness in the pursuit of clearly prescribed and realistic goals is the main, if not the sole, criterion for choosing from alternative policies of crime control. If the curbing of drug use is the goal, then one should concentrate on those drug users who 'can be saved' at a lower cost (namely, first time users). To 'avoid wasted resources and dashed hopes', attention should, moreover, be focused on those areas 'where the public order is deteriorating but not unreclaimable', as well as on the careful selection of high-risk repeat offenders 'for arrest, prosecution and incarceration'.

However, as Wilson, who authored the above quotes, points out, existing criminological theories are generally of little use when specifying the precise points and methods of an effective intervention. Being preoccupied with causal analysis (with the identification of the root or ultimate causes of crime), these theories draw our attention to factors that cannot be changed at all or those that can only be changed with great difficulty. The development of reasonable policy alternatives is instead thought to require 'patient trial and error, accompanied by hardheaded and objective evaluations' (Wilson, 1985: 253–4). The implicit identification of social and policy analysis with policy making entails a shift of focus away from the pursuit of the 'utopian' goal of tackling the root causes of crime and towards the achievement of 'marginal gains' (gains that are compatible with the existing constraints of the contemporary social and economic system).

Evaluation

Neo-conservative criminology undoubtedly contributes to the rationalization of the criminal justice system. It does so by placing a heavy premium on the efficient handling of urgent 'policy' problems and by advocating a kind of social analysis that is of direct relevance to the resolution of such problems. However, the instrumental type of (applied) analysis that they advocate leaves no room for a serious probing of the normative questions involved in the development of criminal justice policy. 'Political' policies tend to be treated as managerial ones and to be evaluated in terms of their effectiveness with respect to certain goals: namely those goals that are derivable from factual 'needs' and are thus essentially beyond choice.

The tendency, furthermore, of neo-conservative criminology to clearly demarcate causal analysis from policy analysis and policy making results in a lowering of expectations with regard to crime prevention and control, to engage in the pursuit of marginal gains primarily through a fight against symptoms and the abandonment of attempts to tackle the root causes of crime. The extent to which the latter is necessary or unavoidable remains an open question. Attempts to remove the root causes of criminality are portrayed by neo-conservative criminology as utopian in view of a variety of more or less 'objective' biological, social, economic, political and technical constraints. However, many of these constraints may themselves be manufactured and thus in principle solvable. Causal analysis can direct our attention towards possible new fields of intervention and change, which policy-related research, in being inextricably linked – as it is – to the requirements of the policy maker, is bound to exclude from its agenda.

Finally, the selective attention paid by neo-conservative criminology to the moral culture of contemporary society as a major cause of existing levels of crime, as well as an appropriate field of intervention, is open to serious criticism. The importance attached to culture as a causal factor – largely on the basis of speculation rather than firm evidence – is dictated by the same functional logic which runs throughout neo-conservative writings. Modernist culture is examined by the neo-conservatives solely from the point of view of its functional role as an element of the 'pattern maintenance' of the system. But attempts to restore traditional values and norms are themselves utopian. Traditional (familial) values (to take only one example) cannot be restored without 'turning back the clock of modernization' (for example, by undoing the social, political and economic processes which have historically led to a change in the female role and family relationships). As has succinctly been pointed out, 'precisely the fact that today tradition must be invoked shows that it has lost its power' (Horkheimer, 1974, cited in Habermas, 1989: 44).

A significant question is, moreover, raised concerning the extent of the legitimation of the particular normative preferences of neo-conservative criminology. The functional understanding and use of values does not necessarily provide the legitimation for these being imposed on society's members. There must also be other morally and philosophically valid reasons for attempting the refurbishment of fading values.

Tonia Tzannetakis

Associated Concepts: actuarialism, administrative criminology, 'broken windows', managerialism, rational choice theory, realist criminologies, situational crime prevention, underclass, zero tolerance

Key Readings

Habermas, J. (1989) *The New Conservatism.* Cambridge: Polity Press.
Wilson, J.Q. (1985) *Thinking about Crime.* New York: Vintage.
Wilson, J.Q. (1991) *On Character: Essays by James Q. Wilson.* Washington, DC: A.E.I. Press.
Wilson, J.Q. and Herrnstein, R.J. (1985) *Crime and Human Nature: The Definitive Study of the Causes of Crime.* New York: Simon and Schuster.
Wilson, J.Q. and Kelling, G. (1982) 'Broken windows', *Atlantic Monthly,* March: 29–38.
Young, J. (1994) 'Incessant chatter: recent paradigms in criminology', in M. Maguire, R. Morgan and R. Reiner (eds) *The Oxford Handbook of Criminology.* Oxford: The Clarendon Press. pp. 69–124.

NET WIDENING

Definition

The processes whereby attempts to prevent crime and develop community-based corrections act to expand the criminal justice system and draw more subjects into its remit.

Distinctive Features

In the 1970s diversion became a widely acclaimed strategy for reducing the numbers of offenders, and particularly young offenders, appearing in court and thereby avoiding the stigma and labelling that resulted from judicial processes.

Sentencing alternatives such as probation and community supervision were also intended to reduce the use and cost of custody. However, it has been repeatedly found that while these 'alternatives' have burgeoned, so have prison populations. Moreover, the very existence of apparently benign and welfare-based options has increased the numbers subject to some form of official, rather than informal, intervention. In California, for example, increasing the proportion of offenders placed on probation was encouraged by providing state funds (a subsidy) to the counties for not committing cases to state institutions. However, Lerman's (1975) assessment of the subsidy programme found that many probationers were subsequently placed in custody for probation violations. Moreover, those not recommended for probation were receiving longer sentences. He suggested that the creation of new 'diversionary' measures achieved no long-term decarceration and ultimately expanded the numbers subject to various forms of official surveillance and detention. This resulted not just from court-room decisions but also from an increased willingness on the part of social workers to use their discretionary power to intervene on the offenders' behalf. A Canadian study, which examined the effects of community corrections programmes introduced in Saskatchewan from 1962 to 1979, concluded that not only had these failed to reduce the size of the prison population, they had also actually resulted in a three-fold increase in the proportion of persons under formal state control. Similarly, the National Evaluation of the Deinstitutionalization of Status Offenders project in the USA reported that the programmes were so clearly biased towards heightening the intake of less serious offenders that many more had been caught up in the referral network than if the project had not been established.

Stanley Cohen (1979) described such processes as 'thinning the mesh' and 'widening the net'. Allied to his wider 'dispersal of discipline' thesis, Cohen contended that as control mechanisms are dispersed from custody into the community they penetrate deeper into the social fabric. A blurring of boundaries between the deviant and non-deviant and between the public and the private occurs. A 'punitive archipelago' is expanded as new resources, technology and professional interests are applied to an increasing number of 'clients' and 'consumers'. Entrepreneurs are drawn into the control enterprise in search of profits. Communities are mobilized to act as voluntary control agents in their own right. But, throughout, the prison remains at the heart of the system. The rhetoric of diversion and community camouflages what is really going on. Instead, alternatives to prison and crime prevention policies fail to reduce the reach of criminal justice and tend to draw more people into the mesh of formal control:

- Petty or 'potential' delinquents are subject to more intrusive and disguised control in the name of diversion or prevention.
- As the soft end of the system appears more and more benign, so the hard core appears more hopeless and becomes a target for such policies as selective incapacitation.
- Whole populations are subjected to further and subtler involvement in the business of social control. They are made the object of preventive social control before any deviant act has taken place.

For Cohen (1985: 37) and Austin and Krisberg (1981) the real effect of diversion and decarceration is to increase the reach and intensity of state control:

- The criminal justice system expands and draws more people into its reach (net widening).
- The level of intervention, involving individualized treatment and indeterminate sentencing, intensifies (net strengthening).

- Institutions are rarely replaced or radically altered but supplemented by new forms of intervention (different nets).

Evaluation

These readings of criminal justice reform have been challenged in various ways as one-dimensional, unduly pessimistic and nihilistic. Indeed Cohen's (1985) later reflection on this 'nothing works' mentality concedes that the intentions of 'doing good' are not automatically misguided. Specific policies at particular times may have a positive and progressive effect – that there remains some possibility 'for realizing preferred values'. He eventually argues for a slightly different reading of net widening which would allow for a 'sensitivity to success (however ambivalent)'. McMahon (1990: 144) also points out that the concept only directs attention towards expansionary trends and draws attention away from 'any moderation of penal control which may have taken place and from the superseding of some previous forms of penal control by preferable ones'. Nevertheless, the concept continues to serve as a reminder of the unintended consequences of some criminal justice reform, particularly when that reform is couched in terms of 'zero tolerance', the need for early (pre-criminal) intervention, or as acting in the 'best interests' of others.

John Muncie

Associated Concepts: bifurcation, carceral society, community corrections, decarceration, diversion, juvenile justice, social control

Key Readings

Austin, J. and Krisberg, B. (1981) 'Wider, stronger and different nets: the dialectics of criminal justice reform', *Journal of Research in Crime and Delinquency*, 18 (1): 165–96.

Cohen, S. (1979) 'The punitive city: notes on the dispersal of social control', *Contemporary Crises*, 3 (4): 341–63.

Cohen, S. (1985) *Visions of Social Control.* Cambridge: Polity Press.

Lerman, P. (1975) *Community Treatment and Social Control.* Chicago: University of Chicago Press.

McMahon, M. (1990) 'Net-widening: vagaries in the use of a concept', *British Journal of Criminology*, 30 (2): 121–49.

NEUTRALIZATION (TECHNIQUES OF)

Definition

A distinctive set of justifications that enables individuals to drift away temporarily from the normative rules and values of society and engage in delinquent behaviour. This social psychological 'social control' perspective was developed by Gresham Sykes and David Matza in order to challenge overly deterministic, positivistic subcultural theories of crime which denied agency and rationality.

Distinctive Features

Delinquents, according to Sykes and Matza, rather than forming a subculture that stands in opposition and antagonism to the dominant social order, 'drift' in and out of deviant activity. The division between 'deviant' and 'respectable' is not hard and fast, and delinquents are conceived of as choice-makers who move between and have to negotiate these two interconnected worlds. The proof of this is the fact that delinquents often voice a sense of guilt and/or shame about their actions; frequently convey their respect for law-abiding citizens; and regularly draw the line between those who can be victimized and those who cannot. Delinquents are not immune to the demands of the dominant social order; are not delinquent all of the time; and do not necessarily conceive of themselves as criminals.

Because they are intimately connected to a normative value system that is flexible and provides 'qualified guides for action', delinquents can develop a set of techniques or rationalizations to neutralize and temporarily suspend their commitment to these values and construct the freedom to engage in deviant acts to cope with the moral dilemmas posed by their actions, as well as to retain their self-esteem and non-criminal self-image. For Sykes and Matza, learning the following techniques of neutralization lessens the effectiveness of social controls and enables the individual to become delinquent or justify her/his delinquency:

1 The denial of responsibility ('I did not mean to do it').
2 The denial of injury ('No one was hurt').
3 The denial of the victim ('She started it').
4 The condemnation of the condemners ('They are just as bad').
5 The appeal to higher loyalties ('I was helping my friends').

These techniques assert the rightfulness and normality of the behaviour and are extensions of commonly accepted motivational accounts that are in use in everyday life. Matza subsequently incorporated this thesis into his 'drift' theory of juvenile delinquency, proposing that the techniques of neutralization are the means by which individuals will gain an 'episodic release' from established moral constraints and then drift into and out of delinquency.

Evaluation

There have been remarkably few empirical evaluations of neutralization theory. The thesis has been developed generally by Agnew (1994) whilst Coleman (1994) has reworked it conceptually in the context of researching white collar criminality. Stan Cohen (1993) has provided criminology with one of the most innovative applications of Sykes and Matza's techniques in his argument that they are present in official state discourses concerning human rights violations and state crime. Critics of Sykes and Matza, such as Katz (1987), continue to insist that certain types of committed criminals have different values and that neutralization is unnecessary. There is also still a major debate about whether delinquents and criminals engage in neutralization (before the event) or an *ad hoc* rationalization (after the event).

Eugene McLaughlin

Associated Concepts: appreciative criminology, defiance theory, rational choice theory, subculture

Key Readings

Agnew, R. (1994) 'The techniques of neutralization and violence', *Criminology*, 32: 555–79.
Cohen, S. (1993) 'Human rights and crimes of the state', *Australian and New Zealand Journal of Criminology*, 26 (2): 97–115.
Coleman, J.W. (1994) *The Criminal Elite: The Sociology of White Collar Crime.* New York: St Martin's Press.
Katz, J. (1987) *Seductions of Crime: Moral and Sensual Attractions in Doing Evil.* New York: Basic Books.
Matza, D. (1964) *Delinquency and Drift.* New York: Wiley.
Sykes, G.M. and Matza, D. (1957) 'Techniques of neutralization: a theory of delinquency', *American Sociological Review*, 22: 664–70.

NEW CRIMINOLOGY

Definition

A form of radical criminology which first came to fruition in the UK in the early 1970s. It was designated 'new' because of its then novel attempt to fuse an interactionist approach to deviance focusing on personal meaning with a structural approach grounded in the analysis of political economy, class relations and state practices. It is widely cited as marking the beginnings of a critical criminology.

Distinctive Features

The term originates from a book of the same name authored by Ian Taylor, Paul Walton and Jock Young and published in 1973. It was the product of discussions and developments inspired by the National Deviancy Conference established in 1968 as a forum for critical analysis. Much of the book is a sustained critique of classical and positivist criminologies as well as of interactionism, labelling and classical Marxism. A final chapter, however, attempts a synthesis of several of these different theoretical traditions under the rubric of a fully social theory of deviance. The new criminology advocates that such a theory must include the connections between:

- *the wider origins of the deviant act* (the economic and political contingencies of advanced industrial society);
- *the immediate origins of the deviant act* (the interpretation and meaning given to deviance by individuals);
- *the actual act* (the rationality of individual acts and the social dynamics surrounding them);
- *the immediate origins of social reaction* (the contingencies and conditions crucial to the decision to act against the deviant);
- *the wider origins of deviant reaction* (the political and ideological concerns of the state);
- *the outcome of the social reaction on the deviant's further action* (the conscious decisions made by an individual to respond to sanctions);
- *the nature of the deviant process as a whole* (the necessity to integrate all elements of the deviant process while being alive to the conditions of social determination and self-determination).

However, *The New Criminology* was not only an attempt to develop the parameters of an adequate criminological theory; it was also designed to promote a form of radical politics. Its insistence that inequalities and divisions in material production and ownership are intrinsically related to the social factors producing crime brought notions about the possibility of a crime-free society to the fore: a society based on principles of socialist diversity and tolerance. The intention, then, was also to construct the parameters of a radical praxis. Any criminology not committed to 'the abolition of inequalities of wealth and power' was bound to be ultimately reducible to the interests of the economically and politically powerful. Above all, the new criminology sought to illustrate how crime was politically and economically constructed, through the capacity and ability of state institutions within the political economy of advanced capitalism, to define and confer criminality on others. The study of crime could no longer be compartmentalized in a world of pathologies, deviances and otherness, but was to be used as a means through which the exploitative machinations of the state could be exposed. The new criminology opened a door through which valuable insights could be made not into crime *per se*, but into how society worked, how the social order was maintained, and how such order could be subjected to political challenge.

Evaluation

This politicization of criminology was in many ways a logical extension of the critical questioning of social science and its role in research, teaching and policy making that had emerged in the 1960s. Becker (1967) brought such questioning directly into criminology and the sociology of deviance by asking social scientists: 'Whose side are you on?' Social science in general, and individual positivism in particular, were charged with lending the state a spurious legitimacy, and functioning as little more than a justification for oppressive power. What the new criminology managed to achieve was a radical reconstitution of criminology as part of a more comprehensive sociology of the state and political economy, in which questions of political and social control took precedence over behavioural and correctional issues. By the mid-1970s such reflections on the construction of crime became pivotal in the

formulation of a *critical criminology*. When the task of criminology was defined as one of creating a society 'in which the facts of human diversity are not subject to the power to criminalize' (Taylor et al., 1973: 282), it was clear that it was being transformed from a science of social control into a struggle for social justice.

Such critical analysis was indeed influential in arousing interest in an analysis of the role of the law in capitalism, in particular spawning a series of revisionist histories of the relationships between what counted as 'crime', class position and systems of punishment. Such complexities could not be addressed, for example, by an uncritical adoption of the economic and material determinism of Marxism. A major stumbling block in the synthesis of Marxism, interactionism and labelling was that the concerns of criminology and its continuing observance of the concept of 'crime' did not represent a theoretical field of study within Marxism. Rather crime is an ideological category generated by state agencies and intellectuals. For many Marxist scholars the new criminological agenda was limited because there could be no such thing as a Marxist criminology. Retaining the concept of crime as the key referent inevitably laid open the possibility of collusion with state-sponsored definitions of undesirable behaviours. It was noticeable too that the new criminology retained a gender-specific mode of analysis and failed to encompass the then emergent field of gender studies or to include any reference to women and crime in its analysis. From a left realist perspective, subsequently developed by one of the original authors of the new criminology, it was further claimed that the pursuit of structural change and tolerance of diversity were idealist and utopian. A lack of political pragmatism and failing to be policy prescriptive would offer little practical help to those on the receiving end of repressive control systems or to those members of the working class who suffer most from the effects of everyday criminal actions. Nevertheless the new criminology's programme of focusing on agency and structure, and on the micro as well as the macro social world, arguably created a vital space from which a whole range of critical, feminist and left realist positions could subsequently emerge.

John Muncie

Associated Concepts: critical criminology, left idealism, left realism, Marxist criminologies, new deviancy theory, radical criminologies

Key Readings

Becker, H. (1967) 'Whose side are we on?', *Social Problems,* 14 (3): 239–47.
Taylor, I., Walton, P. and Young, J. (1973) *The New Criminology.* London: Routledge.
Taylor, I., Walton, P. and Young, J. (eds) (1975) *Critical Criminology.* London: Routledge.
Walton, P. and Young, J. (eds) (1998) *The New Criminology Revisited.* Basingstoke: Macmillan.

NEW DEVIANCY THEORY

Definition

A theoretical position which emphasizes micro-sociological explanations of the ways in which deviance is generated in interactions between individuals and law enforcement agents, with particular reference to the process of labelling and deriving from symbolic interactionism.

Distinctive Features

New deviancy theory emerged in the 1960s and early 1970s as part of a radical response to the positivist domination of criminology. It attempted to recover the 'meaning' in human behaviour that was denied in positivism. It had a number of influences and strands including interactionism (derived from George Herbert Mead's writings on symbolic interactionism), labelling theory and the ethnographic tradition of social research.

The main features of new deviancy theory are as follows. There is an emphasis on social action as free, creative and spontaneous, rather than something which is determined by individual predispositions or by external and all-constraining social reality. Social interactions, institutions and structures do have a limiting influence on individuals but at one and the same time they are the constructions of these individuals. Individuals and categories of individuals have the capacity to bring their own meanings to interactions, institutions and structures and there is the potential – indeed, certainty – that there will be a multiplicity of meanings and interpretations. Social order is therefore characterized by plurality rather than a naturally occurring consensus. Different groups and sections of society will have their own norms and values and there may be conflict between these. Such conflict may be characterized by the exercise of power by one group over another in order to impose its value system. This may be done via repressive institutions such as the police and the penal system and more subtly by ideological apparatus such as the media.

The influence of labelling theory within new deviancy can be seen in terms of conceptions of what is, and is not, crime and deviance. A favoured dictum is that crime and deviance are that which is labelled as such. This can happen at a societal level in terms of law enactment and the definitions in legislation of certain kinds of acts as 'criminal', and it can also happen at street level in terms of the ways in which law is enforced by individual police officers. The latter involves a consideration of the meanings officers attach to others' actions and of the ways in which they lie within or outwith the law, as they interpret it, and in the particular circumstances of the time.

New deviancy theory does not have a conception of crime as a distinct and separate phenomenon which is perpetrated by a category of people who are 'criminals'. Nor does it explain the criminality of such people by reference to individual predispositions to crime or other causal determinants. Rather, crime is ubiquitous and criminals are evenly distributed across society. In order to explain crime and its distribution and to understand how and why categories of people become criminal it is necessary to examine definitional and labelling processes. For new deviancy theorists this involves a focus on agents of social control and the institutions of criminal justice and not a sole preoccupation with the offender and his or her antecedents. In this endeavour key concepts from interactionist perspectives are enlisted, such as 'meaning', 'social definition', 'label', stereotype', 'social reaction' and 'deviancy amplification'.

Methodologically, new deviancy typically employs ethnographic methods of research on the grounds that they are much more compatible with such concepts. Ethnographic research can facilitate direct and natural observation of interactions between would-be offenders and law enforcers and can employ unstructured methods of interview and documentary analysis to uncover the meanings, labels and stereotypes employed in the everyday practices of criminal justice personnel.

Policy implications of new deviancy flow from the assumption that there can be a plurality of equally valid perspectives: that crime is what is labelled as such and that social reaction and social control are what generate crime. Such implications can include increased tolerance of the diversity and plurality of cultural values and forms of action in society: the official debunking of popular but inaccurate stereotypes of crime and criminals; the decriminalization of certain forms of action; and non-intervention in events and actions on the part of control agencies.

Evaluation

The contributions of new deviancy theory are numerous. For example, in its emphasis on interactions, labelling and social construction it offers a reminder that crime is a social concept rather than something which is 'fixed' and 'given'. It also encourages an examination of definitional issues both in law enactment *and* in the enforcement of law and criminal justice personnel. Methodologically it provides an alternative perspective on official crime statistics to that provided by positivist approaches. This perspective encourages a view of crime statistics as the outcome of criminal justice policies and practices rather than valid indicators of the 'true' extent of crime.

One key danger to adopting a new deviancy framework is that of treating the notion of the social construction of crime as a universal 'covering law' (that is, one which covers or explains all forms of action deemed to be criminal). There are certain kinds of crimes, such as rape and paedophilia, where individual pathologies are likely to have a great deal of credence as explanations. What is more, the victims of these and other crimes are unlikely to take kindly to offences committed against them being treated as mere social constructions (within which the *offender* may be treated as the victim). The critique that new deviancy theory fails to face up to the fact that crime, and the fear of crime, are experienced as a reality by many, tends to come from those who advocate realist criminological thinking.

Victor Jupp

Associated Concepts: deviance, ethnography, interactionism, labelling, radical criminologies, social constructionism

Key Readings

Becker, H. (1963) *Outsiders: Studies in the Sociology of Deviance.* Glencoe, IL: Free Press.

Sumner, C. (1994) *The Sociology of Deviance: An Obituary.* Buckingham: The Open University Press.

Young, J. (1990) 'Thinking seriously about crime: some models in criminology', in M. Fitzgerald, G. McLennan and J. Pawson (eds), *Crime and Society: Readings in History and Theory.* London: Routledge in association with The Open University Press. pp. 248–310.

NEWSMAKING CRIMINOLOGY

Definition

The processes whereby criminologists use mass communication for the purposes of interpreting, informing and altering the images of crime and justice, crime and punishment, and criminals and victims.

Distinctive Features

Gregg Barak (1988) first used the term 'newsmaking criminology' to explore the relationships between the study and production of crime news and the interaction by criminologists and others involved in the processes of mass communication. Like students of crime and media generally, students of newsmaking criminology are concerned with the degrees of distortion and bias in the news, or with the distance between the social reality of crime and the newsmaking reality of crime. Like other analysts of the news media, newsmaking criminologists are similarly interested in seeing that the news media 'tell it like it is', and better yet, 'like it could be' or 'like it should be', based on an informed scientific view of crime and justice (Barak, 1994).

The concept of newsmaking criminology refers to criminologists' conscious efforts and activities in interpreting, influencing or shaping the presentation of information or of 'newsworthy' items about crime and justice. Newsmaking criminology attempts to demystify images of crime and punishment by locating these within the context of all illegal and harmful behaviour; it strives to affect public attitudes, thoughts and discourse about crime and justice so as to affect social policies of crime control; and it encourages criminologists to find their public voices and to come forth and share their knowledge of crime and justice as creditable spokespeople. In short, newsmaking criminology is about analysing, participating and ideally impacting on the mass-mediated, socially constructed and collectively consumed images of crime and justice. Several styles of newsmaking criminology have been identified, including: (1) disputing data; (2) challenging journalism; (3) self-reporting; and (4) confronting media (Henry, 1994). Each of these styles possesses strengths and weaknesses for newsmaking criminologists. As newsmaking criminology continues to develop, its strategies have been fine-tuned (Barak, 1996) and its methods expanded. For example, as the World Wide Web grows in the dissemination of mass communication, it is changing the manner in which we both offer and seek information on a daily basis. Today, news groups, political organizations, criminal justice agencies, criminology associations and individual criminologists all make use of the Web in order to influence and shape public knowledge and attitudes about crime and justice (Greek, 1997; Greek and Henry, 1997).

Evaluation

The ultimate value of newsmaking criminology still remains to be seen. In terms of criminologists having a strong influence over the social construction of crime and justice, this appears to vary by nation-state and the role of public intellectuals in particular societies. At the same time, newsmaking criminology has already raised the consciousness of criminologists about the processes of newsmaking and about their interactive roles with the mass-mediated images of crime and justice, whether these are in the areas of researching, teaching or newsmaking *per se*.

Gregg Barak

Associated Concepts: constitutive criminology, crime news, cultural criminology, social constructionism

Key Readings

Barak, G. (1988) 'Newsmaking criminology: reflections on the media, intellectuals, and crime', *Justice Quarterly*, 5 (4): 265–87.

Barak, G. (ed.) (1994) *Media, Process, and the Social Construction of Crime: Studies in Newsmaking Criminology*. New York: Garland.

Barak, G. (1996) 'Media, discourse, and the O.J. Simpson trial: an ethnographic portrait', in G. Barak (ed.), *Representing O.J.: Murder, Criminal Justice, and Mass Culture*. Guilderland, NY: Harrow and Heston.

Greek, C. (1997) 'Using the Internet as a newsmaking criminology tool'. Paper presented at the annual meeting of the American Society of Criminology, San Diego.

Greek, C. and Henry, D.B. (1997) 'Criminal justice resources on the Internet', *Journal of Criminal Justice Education*, 8: 91–9.

Henry, S. (1994) 'Newsmaking criminology as replacement discourse', in G. Barak (ed.), *Media, Process, and the Social Construction of Crime: Studies in Newsmaking Criminology*. New York: Garland.

NORMALIZATION

Definition

Implicit in this term is the idea of the normal. Whilst the normal has meaning in statistical terms it is inflected with ideas of what is traditional and cultural. It conflates what *is* with what ought to be. A normal distribution suggests a spread around the mean but it also predicts values at and beyond standard deviations either side of the mean. Thus a standardized deviance is expected yet normal comes to be associated with the 'mean'. A conservative might speak of normalization meaning a return to order after a temporary and unexpected disorder. A radical take on the same process might emphasize the price paid by the 'normalized'. Military humour mixes the two in the abbreviation SNAFU – Situation Normal, All Fucked Up!

Within criminology, theoretical usage of the term is derived from Foucault's '*dispositifs de normalisation*'. However, the term is also used in a variety of contexts, including in the debate about whether drug use has become normalized or in describing attempts to bring prison regimes into line with human rights outside the prison.

Distinctive Features

For Foucault (1975) the disciplines of psychiatry, medicine and criminology produce knowledge about and exercise power over the subject. That power may sometimes be to incarcerate or exclude but it works most effectively when internalized and acted upon by the self-policing, docile body – bio-politics. We know it is 'normal' to be sane, non-criminal, heterosexual, slim, hardworking and so on. It is this knowledge as much as – and often more than – the power that renders the subject docile. However, just as the disciplines produce rather than simply attempt to repress deviance as a category, they also create resistance. Thus the 'criminal' and the 'homosexual' are brought into being. Their resistance may take the form of denying that they are deviant through 'techniques of neutralization' or by embracing and flaunting the disciplinary norms – for example, via black pride, gay pride.

In a self-report study of criminologists and criminal justice practitioners, Robinson and Zaitzow (1999) found that 66 per cent reported driving under the influence of alcohol or drugs at some time and 35 per cent within the previous year. Only slightly fewer (60 per cent) had used illegal drugs at some time, with 27 per cent reporting recent use. One-third had bought drugs and 11 per cent admitted to selling them. Thus crime can be seen to be normal: as statistically expected and measurable. However, it is more arguable whether crime is normalized. It is from this position of complicity that criminologists have, for example, engaged in the debate – with politicians and practitioners – about whether drug use in society or amongst young people has become normalized.

Evaluation

In the past Britain may have waged war with China to force the opium trade upon them, but today – like the USA – it sees itself as waging a war on drugs. Or at least this is the official line. Shiner and Newburn (1999) open their discussion of the issue by noting the furore in January 1997 over the comments of a number of pop stars about drug use. Noel Gallagher, of the UK rock group Oasis, declared in the *New Musical Express* (29 January 1997) that 'the majority of people in this country take drugs ... like getting up and having a cup of tea'. This confirms the claim of Parker et al. (1995) that for young people taking drugs has become the norm and that non-drug-taking can be seen as deviant. Yet Shiner and Newburn draw on UK and US data to argue convincingly that whilst drug taking was common amongst young people it was not the norm and that substantial numbers continue to 'say no to drugs' and disapprove of their use.

However, it could be argued that Shiner and Newburn accept too readily the distinction between legal and illegal drugs and fail to take sufficient account of cultural aspects. Using figures for both prescribed and over-the-counter medicines it is possible to argue that there is a cultural expectation of using a 'pill for every ill' amongst the entire population. In this scenario tea, coffee, alcohol, Prozac, ecstasy and aspirin are all utilized to get people through their everyday life. Moreover, popular culture and the media are saturated with references to drug use and culture. For instance, a certain bicycle advertisement punningly asks, 'What's he on?'

The debate about the normalization of drugs often turns on definitional issues about what is *or should count as* normal. Similarly, the argument for the normalization of prison regimes (Feest, 1999) or of policing (Mulcahy,

1999) assumes the normality of the comparator being used. Thus, in a carceral society – returning to Foucault – can we simply compare regimes inside prison with those obtaining outside? Is the policing, say, of London normal enough for that of Belfast to be compared to it?

Nic Groombridge

Associated Concepts: deviance, neutralization (techniques of), pathology

Key Readings

Feest, J. (1999) 'Imprisonment and prisoners' work: normalization or less eligibility?', *Punishment and Society*, 1 (1): 99–107.

Foucault, M. (1975) *Surveiller et punir.* Paris: Gallimard.

Mulcahy, A. (1999) 'Visions of normality: peace and reconstruction of policing in Northern Ireland', *Social and Legal Studies*, 8 (2): 277–95.

Parker, H., Measham, F. and Aldridge, J. (1995) *Drugs Futures: Changing Patterns of Drug Use amongst English Youth.* London: Institute for the Study of Drug Dependency.

Robinson, M.B. and Zaitzow, B.H. (1999) 'Criminologists: are we what we study? A national self-report study of crime experts', *The Criminologist*, 24 (2): 1, 4, 17–19.

Shiner, M. and Newburn, T. (1999) 'Taking tea with Noel: the place and meaning of drug use in everyday life', in N. South (ed.), *Drugs: Cultures, Controls and Everyday Life.* London: Sage.

OBEDIENCE (CRIMES OF)

Definition

Harmful acts committed by a subordinate in obedience to the orders of a superior.

Distinctive Features

Explanations of 'crimes of obedience' took on renewed significance as a result of the return of ethnic wars and genocide in the late twentieth century. The International Criminal Tribunals for the Former Yugoslavia and Rwanda established in the 1990s continue to grapple with issues of individual responsibility and obedience to orders, as did the Nuremberg Tribunal before them.

In the immediate aftermath of the Second World War, social scientists also sought explanations for crimes of obedience, as represented, in particular, by the Holocaust, through an analysis of the personality traits of the perpetrators. Perhaps the most notable work in this area was Theodore Adorno's analysis of the 'authoritarian personality' in the 1950s. In later analysis, however, by Hannah Arendt (1964) and Stanley Milgram (1974), the focus shifted towards the social processes that enabled such crimes rather than the psychological predispositions of individual perpetrators.

In a series of laboratory experiments, Milgram (1974) found that a majority (65 per cent) of apparently normal people could be induced to harm others if instructed to do so by a person in authority. In these experiments, Milgram investigated the willingness of research subjects, who had been asked to play the role of a 'teacher' in a learning experiment, to administer what they were told would be painful electric shocks to another subject on the instructions of the person in charge of the experiments. Despite apparent evidence that the pain administered was becoming progressively more severe and dangerous, the majority of the research subjects ('teachers') were prepared to continue administering shocks when urged to do so by the authority. Milgram found that the greater the distance between the research subjects giving the shocks and the 'victims', the greater was their willingness to obey instructions to continue. Conversely, the greater the distance between the research subject and the 'authority', the less was their willingness to continue.

Milgram described the research subjects who obeyed orders to inflict pain on others as having entered an 'agentic state', one in which, upon entering the experimental authority system, they had relinquished their sense of personal responsibility for their harmful actions by transferring responsibility to their superiors. Importantly, according to Milgram, this was a function not of individual propensities so much as a specific social condition explicable in terms of a culturally generated deference to authority.

Arendt (1964), writing about the Nazi war criminal Adolf Eichmann, argued that it becomes possible (though not inevitable) for ordinary people to do evil when the wrongdoing is 'banalized' – that is, when it is made routine and morally neutral. More recently, in their work on war crimes in Vietnam, Kelman and Hamilton (1989) argued that crimes of obedience are more likely to be committed where there has been a 'weakening of moral restraint'. Kelman (1995), in his later work on the social context of torture, suggested that this weakening of moral restraints against wrongdoing is brought about by three interrelated social processes that simultaneously *authorize* (the harm is sponsored, expected or tolerated by those in authority) and *routinize* the harmful acts and also *dehumanize* their victims. The process of authorization is one in which the situation is redefined in such a way that normal moral principles do not apply and the individual is 'absolved of the responsibility for making moral choices'. The process of routinization structures the (harmful) action so that there is no opportunity for raising moral questions or making moral decisions. Finally, the process of dehumanization ensures that the 'perpetrator's attitudes towards the victim become structured in such a way that it is neither necessary nor possible for him to view his relationship with the victim in moral terms' (Kelman, 1995: 29–32).

Evaluation

Social scientific work on 'crimes of obedience' is important for the way it highlights the different social contexts and social processes that are associated with the production of what otherwise might simply be dismissed (and therefore not explained) as immoral, evil or pathological acts. In his writing on the Holocaust, for example, Zygmunt Bauman has emphasized the inescapable importance of understanding the processes through which immoral regimes are institutionalized and given a 'normal' authority (Bauman, 1989). Thomas Scheff's work on emotions, nationalism and war is a good example of a social scientist trying to make sense of the ways in which ethnic division, rage, humiliation and the cultural devaluation of the fate of individual human beings may combine to produce the conditions of genocide and other war crimes (Scheff, 1993). The laboratory-based experimental work conducted by Milgram did not in itself identify – and did not try to identify – any of these processes or the factors that influenced the behaviour of the 35 per cent of his subjects who refused to obey.

Milgram's 'agentic state' model of obedience failed also to explain the temporal dimension of obedience. People are often caught up in sequences of demands for obedience, in which the degree of harm escalates from one moment to the next. Once they have committed their first crimes of obedience, they may be trapped into continuing to obey.

Overwhelmingly, the concept of a crime of obedience has been applied to activities conducted in circumstances of war. There is, of course, no reason in principle why the concept might not be applied, to useful analytic effect, in many other areas of human life that are of interest to students of crime – for example, in respect of the collective collusion required of middle-range employees in large corporations when undertaking systematically fraudulent activity or crimes against the environment. The exploration of the utility of the concept in these areas will be an important future task both for criminal lawyers involved in specific litigation and for social scientists involved in the analysis of 'criminal behaviour' in these areas, as much as in respect specifically of crimes committed in circumstances of war.

Ruth Jamieson

Associated Concepts: genocide, social control theory, state crime, torture, war crimes

Key Readings

Arendt, H. (1964) *Eichmann in Jerusalem.* Harmondsworth: Penguin.

Bauman, Z. (1989) *Modernity and the Holocaust.* Cambridge: Polity Press.

Kelman, H.C. (1995) 'The social context of torture: policy process and authority structure', in R. Crelinson and A. Schmid (eds), *The Politics of Pain.* Oxford: Westview Press.

Kelman, H.C. and Hamilton, V.L. (1989) *Crimes of Obedience.* New Haven, CT: Yale University Press.

Milgram, S. (1974) *Obedience to Authority.* New York: Harper & Row.

Scheff, T. (1993) *Bloody Revenge: Emotions, Nationalism and War.* Boulder, CO: Westview Press.

OFFENDER PROFILING

Definition

Refers to a range of techniques in which clues to the likely characteristics of an offender are gleaned from a careful consideration of the way in which a crime or series of crimes is carried out. Offender profiling thus usually refers to the process by which all the available information about a crime, a crime scene and a victim is used in order to make predictions as to the type of person most likely to have committed the crime. It is most commonly used in cases of serious sexual assault and sexual murder, which tend to be the cases in which there is a significant interaction between victim and offender. Offender profiling is also referred to as 'psychological profiling' and 'statistical profiling' and covers aspects such as 'crime scene analysis'. Those working in profiling usually have a psychological background, although some psychiatrists and specially trained law enforcement personnel have also taken on this role.

Distinctive Features

Offender profiling has been the subject of a large number of well-known films (e.g., *The Silence of the Lambs* and *Manhunter*) and television series (e.g., *Cracker, Profiler* and *C.S.I*). As such, many readers will feel that they already know what is involved in the process of profiling. However media representations often give a misleading impression as to what the technique involves. Such portrayals tend to depict profilers as relying a great deal on intuition and hunches whereas in reality this is rarely the case.

Profiling can in fact take a number of different forms and there is often disagreement between different schools of profilers and between individual profilers as to what the technique should involve. At the core of this disagreement is a debate as to whether profiling should be seen as an art or a science. Those profilers who have emerged from the FBI's Behavioral Support Unit have tended to see what they do as an art or a craft in which experience plays a large part. However, the opposing view, put forward most forcibly by the British academic David Canter, is that profiling should be seen as a scientific endeavour in which the principles of psychological research and analysis are applied to an investigation.

Profiling first emerged as a result of work carried out at the FBI's Behavioral Support Unit (now known as the Investigative Support Unit) at Quantico, Virginia, USA (Hazelwood and Burgess, 1987; Ressler et al., 1988). Early workers based there examined a number of high profile serial sexual homicides in the USA and assembled as much information as possible about the people who carried out such attacks. What emerged was the view that this type of crime was carried out by two distinct 'types' of offenders: 'organized' and 'disorganized'. As the label suggests, organized offenders typically showed a great deal of planning and took steps to avoid detection. By contrast, disorganized offenders tended to carry out unplanned, random attacks with little thought given to avoiding detection. Perhaps most interesting was the view that these two types of offender had significantly different personality characteristics. For example, organized offenders were said to be intelligent, socially skilled, and invariably to be living with a partner. By contrast, disorganized offenders were typically of low intelligence, sexually and socially inept, and often to have experienced a severe form of mental illness.

The FBI's early work was helpful in solving a number of high profile cases in the USA. A close focus upon the selection of the victim, and the way in which the crime was carried out, gave investigators additional information, which was sometimes useful in directing the course of an investigation. While the goal of profiling is never to name the perpetrator for the police, by identifying the characteristics that an offender is most likely to possess, investigators might be encouraged to pursue certain lines of enquiry rather than others.

The FBI sought to identify other ways in which offenders might be classified. For example, in examining the primary motive behind rapists' behaviour, they suggested that four 'types' could be identified. These were labelled power-reassurance, power-assertive, anger-retaliatory, and anger-excitement. The view here was that a careful examination of the way in which the crime was committed would reveal useful information about the primary motive underlying the attack. Furthermore, such understanding would help to identify the likely characteristics of an offender.

Whilst such classifications make for interesting reading, concerns have been raised over the reliability and validity of the FBI's work. The fact that their theories have rarely if ever been put to scientific test has set off alarm bells in the minds of many psychologists. Foremost amongst the critics has been the British psychologist David Canter. Canter's psychological training has meant that he approaches the area of profiling in a somewhat different way from that of the FBI. In fact, in order to distance himself from the work of others, he calls his approach *investigative psychology* (Canter, 1994).

Unlike the FBI, Canter uses scientific method in his work on offending. In studying sexual assault he has adapted a technique known as Smallest Space Analysis (SSA) to identify specific characteristics that can be associated together and types of offender behaviour that are distinctive. He has developed a number of hypotheses including the Circle Hypothesis. This states that when a circle is drawn around all the crimes committed by an individual, there is a very high probability that the offender will live within that circle. Further refinement of this theory has enabled Canter to make predictions as to the area within the circle where the offender is most likely to live. This type of research is generally referred to as geographic profiling (Canter, 2003).

Evaluation

There is no doubt that offender profiling has the potential to be an extremely useful tool in helping to solve certain types of crime. However, it is also true to say that this potential has not always been reached. The failure of some profilers, especially those from the FBI school, to subject their methods and theories to scientific evaluation means that progress has not been as rapid as one might have hoped. Fundamental disagreements between individual profilers about how profiling is carried out have also meant that a great deal of time and effort has been wasted in rubbishing others' views rather than in developing a cohesive approach.

Given the public interest in the subject of profiling, it is perhaps surprising to learn that relatively little research has been carried out to evaluate its effectiveness. What research is available has tended to paint a rather negative picture, with investigators reporting that, in many cases, the profile supplied was not particularly helpful in solving a crime. However, there are a number of reasons why such views should not be taken as proof that profiles are not actually very useful (Ainsworth, 2001: 178).

Providing that a scientific approach to profiling is adopted in the future, there seems little doubt that techniques will develop and improve to a point where they can be of genuine help in solving certain types of serious crime.

Peter B. Ainsworth

Associated Concepts: crime science, forensic psychology, serial killing

Key Readings

Ainsworth, P.B. (2001) *Offender Profiling and Crime Analysis*. Cullompton: Willan.

Canter, D. (1994) *Criminal Shadows: Inside the Mind of the Serial Killer*. London: HarperCollins.

Canter, D. (2003) *Mapping Murder: The Secrets of Geographic Profiling*. London: Virgin Books.

Hazelwood, R.R. and Burgess, A.W. (1987) *Practical Aspects of Rape Investigation: A Multidisciplinary Approach*. New York: Elsevier.

Jackson, J.L. and Bekerian, D.A. (eds) (1997) *Offender Profiling: Theory, Research and Practice*. Chichester: Wiley.

Palermo, G.B. and Kocsis, R.N. (2005) *Offender Profiling*. New York: Charles C. Thomas.

Ressler, R.K., Burgess, A.W. and Douglas, J.E. (1988) *Sexual Homicides: Patterns and Motives*. New York: Lexington.

OFFICIAL CRIMINAL STATISTICS

Definition

Statistical data compiled by the police and the courts and routinely published by governments as indices of the extent of crime.

Distinctive Features

Most countries annually collect data which are a count of the volume of particular categories of crime as recorded by the police. In the USA data are submitted voluntarily by local police departments to the FBI and published as *Uniform Crime Reports*. In the UK similar statistics are produced by the Home Office (*Criminal Statistics England and Wales* and the biannual *Statistical Bulletins*). Each of these includes data on offences (from which trends in crime over time are charted) and on offenders who have eventually been found guilty or cautioned (from which details of the sex and age of offenders are derived).

The first national crime statistics were produced in the early nineteenth century in France (by Quetelet in 1842). In England and Wales crimes recorded by the police have been published since 1876 and in the USA this has happened since 1930. Both of these latter countries have witnessed a dramatic rise in the crime rate since the mid 1950s, with the only sustained fall occurring since the mid- to late 1990s. A similar long-term upward trend has been a feature of most Western democracies, with the notable exception of Switzerland (Maguire, 1997: 159).

Breaking down this overall rate into *offence groups* reveals that the 'crime problem' is predominantly one of crimes against property (theft, burglary, criminal damage) and above all theft of, or from, vehicles. Crimes of violence appear to be small in comparison. Turning to the data on *offenders*, it is first notable that their numbers are dramatically lower than the total number of offences recorded. Whilst some of this disparity may be attributable to those committing more than one offence, it is clear that in the vast majority of cases nothing is officially known about those responsible (Coleman and Moynihan, 1996: 43; Maguire, 1997: 173). The data on 'known offenders', however, produce a picture of the 'typical offender' as male and young. For example, in England and Wales the official criminal statistics have consistently found that over 80 per cent of offenders are male and almost half are under the age of 21.

Criminologists have long debated the reliability of these statistical measures. Self-evidently they only measure those offences reported to and recorded by the police. As a result these basic data are now regularly added to by nationwide victim surveys. In 1972 the US Bureau of the Census began collecting information about rates of victimization by asking random samples of the population to recall crimes committed against them in the past year. In 1982 Britain followed this lead with its own *British Crime Survey* (BCS). Both in the USA and in Britain it was consistently revealed that only about 50 per cent of crime is in fact reported to the police.

Evaluation

The official criminal statistics do not provide any straightforward answers to questions about how much crime, how many criminals and how many victims. The 'true facts' of crime are probably unknowable as they depend not only on what we define as crime but also on the *validity* of the statistical measures used, no matter how these are produced. Most academic analysts, the media, politicians and the public rely on official statistics as 'hard facts', but they are both partial and subjectively constructed.

- In the USA the *Uniform Crime Report* distinguishes between index crimes and non-index crimes. It constructs crime trends by tabulating eight index crimes – those the FBI believes to be the most serious. The list does not include fraud, embezzlement, offences against the family or children, drug abuse, vagrancy and so on. In England and Wales the official statistics do not include offences recorded by the British Transport Police, the Ministry of Defence Police and the UK Atomic Energy Authority Police, who collectively record about 80,000 offences per year (Maguire, 1997: 149). Tax evasion (recorded by HM Revenue and Customs) and VAT evasion (recorded by HM Revenue and Customs) will only appear in official criminal records if they are subsequently brought to court.

- Crime statistics are based on those crimes reported to and subsequently recorded by the police. But some offences may not be reported because of ignorance that a crime has been committed (for example, tax evasion, computer fraud); because there appears to be no victim (for example, certain drugs offences, prostitution, sexual offences between consenting adults, illegal abortion); because the victim is powerless (for example, child abuse); because of ambivalence towards or distrust of the police (for example, certain youth cultures); because the offence may be considered trivial (for example, thefts from work, vandalism, minor shoplifting, brawls); because the victim may be concerned that the offence will not be taken seriously (for example, some cases of rape); or because the victim has no faith that the police will act to protect his or her interests (for example, racial intimidation and harassment). Measurements of crime rest initially and critically on the extent to which the public perceives and interprets behaviour as 'criminal' (Walker, 1983: 292).
- Not all offences reported are recorded as such by the police. The amount of resources available to the police and courts is limited, and thus subjective and/ or administrative decisions are made concerning which crimes to act against. It is only recorded crime which enters the official statistics. Walker (1983: 286) notes that, although the police in England and Wales have a statutory obligation to record crimes, considerable discretion remains about whether it is considered sufficiently serious to warrant their attention. Violent

disputes between neighbours or members of a family, for example, may be classified as 'domestic – advice given' and the alleged 'offence' not recorded. Similarly, how a recorded offence is classified by the police – as 'theft from a person' or 'robbery'; as 'burglary, no loss' or 'vandalism'; as 'wounding' or 'common assault' for example – will affect the rate at which certain crimes appear to be committed. Problems inherent in recording, and variations due to local police 'targeting', will also affect our understanding of the extent of particular crimes.

- Changes in law enforcement and in what the law counts as crime also preclude much meaningful discussion over the extent of historical increases and decreases in crime. Legislative changes may mean that existing categories are redefined, thus rendering historical comparison meaningless. Some increases in crime can be artificially constructed solely by their economic and administrative circumstance: inflation provides a perfect example of such a bias. The law is not index linked and so acts of criminal damage, officially defined in England and Wales as damage exceeding £20 in value, shot up from 17,000 in 1969 to 124,000 in 1977. Inflation thus shifted many thousands of previously trivial incidents of damage into the more serious crime bracket.
- Changes in police practices, priorities and politics will also have a dramatic effect on such headline statistics as 'crimes recorded by the police'. What is remarkable for example about long-term historical trends in crime rates in England and Wales is their consistently low level during the nineteenth and early twentieth centuries followed by a consistent doubling in every decade (except the 1950s) until the 1990s. By examining police inspectorate and committee reports at the time, Taylor (1998) argues that the increases in crime between 1914 and 1960 can be largely accounted for by senior police officers 'playing the crime card' in order to improve their establishment. By recording large numbers

of minor property offences which were traditionally 'cuffed' (not recorded) chief constables were able to persuade their police authorities to increase funding. The crime rate is then more a reflection of police lobbying and politics than of criminal behaviour.

- Changes in the number of arrests, trials and sentences may not represent actual changes in the amount of crime, but rather changes in the *capacity* of the criminal justice system to process individual cases. Increases or decreases in the number of police, judges, courtrooms and prison places will inevitably affect these statistics. More police, more judges and more prisons appear to have an almost infinite capacity to increase the amount of officially recorded crime. This is partly because there is an ever-present and unlimited well of unrecorded criminal behaviour which can be tapped into when and if the political will and the resources for law enforcement are sufficiently activated. It is also because there exists a huge potential to perceive and redefine actions as 'crimes' as the technological ability to implement forms of mass surveillance increases.

Collectively, such processes of data collection inevitably mean that notions of crime waves and of perpetual increases in offending have to be interpreted with extreme caution. Nevertheless, the pictures they create of crime, criminals and offending remain some of the key means through which academic, political, media and public knowledge is gained. Official statistics cannot be dismissed as simply meaningless. They can provide valuable insights into police and court definitions of crime and the operation of social, legal and organizational constraints and priorities. They cannot, however, be expected to aid our understanding of the 'independent entity of crime' because, by its nature, no such fact exists.

John Muncie

Associated Concepts: crime, hidden crime, self-reports, victim surveys

Key Readings

Coleman, C. and Moynihan, J. (1996) *Understanding Crime Data*. Buckingham: Open University Press.

Maguire, M. (1997) 'Crime statistics, patterns and trends: changing perceptions and their implications', in M. Maguire, R. Morgan and R. Reiner (eds), *The Oxford Handbook of Criminology*, 2nd edn. Oxford: Clarendon.

Taylor, H. (1998) 'The politics of the rising crime statistics of England and Wales 1914–1960', *Crime, History and Societies*, 2 (1): 5–28.

Walker, M.A. (1983) 'Some problems in interpreting statistics relating to crime', *Journal of the Royal Statistical Society, Series A*, No.146, part 3: 282–93.

OPPORTUNITY THEORY

Definition

An approach to explaining criminal behaviour that sees crime as a function of the characteristics of situations that offer the opportunity, to those inclined to take it, to benefit from an illegal act.

Distinctive Features

Historically, theories of crime took either a 'dispositional' stance, with a focus on the individual offender, or a 'sociological' approach, with an emphasis on the social conditions associated with crime. A rather different approach began to emerge following the work of Cohen and Felson (1979) and the advent of 'routine activities theory'. The core of this theoretical approach is that crime will occur when three elements combine: a specific situation (i.e., a time and location), a target, and the absence of effective guardians. This combination then provides the *opportunity* for successful offending.

The beginnings of views about crime based on routine activities and opportunity are to be found in research broadly concerned with the environmental correlates of crime. These studies examine the specific environmental conditions that might account for patterns of crime. For example, rising numbers of burglaries can be explained by the greater proportion of empty houses as more people go out to work leaving their homes unguarded and offering the opportunity for undetected crime. Similarly, it can be seen that more street parking leads to higher rates of car theft; street violence is more likely in dimly lit areas of towns and cities; and the probability of vandalism to property is increased when there is no one with direct responsibility for the safety of buildings and utilities.

The concept of opportunity began to come under increasing scrutiny, with various dimensions of the three critical elements being described in the literature. With respect to the target, Bottoms and Wiles (1997) note the importance of 'target attractiveness'. Target attractiveness has several dimensions: financial value is obvious, but other factors such as being simple to sell and easily transported can be important in making a target attractive. It is also the case, of course, that the same target will not be equally attractive to all potential offenders.

The critical elements of the situation might, as Bottoms and Wiles (1997) suggest, be seen in terms of 'accessibility'. Accessibility refers to the physical qualities of the situation such as visibility, ease of access and lack of observation at the scene of the crime. The latter factor, lack of observation, may be linked with the third dimension of opportunity, the absence of a responsible guardian. A reasonable guardian may, for example, be a neighbour, an official such as a car park attendant, or a police officer.

In considering accessibility and guardianship, it is difficult to disentangle the environment and the individual. For example, an individual might need specialist knowledge to recognize the environmental cues that signal an attractive target. Thus burglars may be aware of cues, such as a type of lock or window catch, that will signal easy entry to a property. Similarly, a guardian may be present but it is the guardian's perceived effectiveness that is the critical dimension with respect to the potential offender's decision making and eventual actions.

As the concept of opportunity is stretched to include a wider range of factors, so the associated models of crime become more complex. Clarke (1995) presents a model of the opportunity structure for crime that incorporates such diverse elements as socio-economic structure, perception, physical environment and information processing. Such deepenings also begin to overlap with the view, reminiscent of classicism, of criminals as motivated by self-interest. Owing more to economics than human science, the basis of human action is seen in terms of 'expected utility'. A quotation from van den Haag illustrates this approach in its most stark form: 'I do not see any relevant difference between dentistry and prostitution or car theft, except that the latter do not require a license ... The frequency of rape, or of mugging, is essentially determined by the expected comparative net advantage, just as is the rate of dentistry and burglary' (1982: 1,026).

Like an accountant reckoning a balance sheet, the offender considers the net gains and losses then, as it were, moves into the market to make a profit. The offender is seen as a rational decision maker, as a 'reasoning criminal', with personal benefit a prime motivation for crime. This theme of the criminal as a rational decision maker was developed to significant effect by Cornish and Clarke (1986). They are clear that while social factors, such as family and peer group, may be part of an individual's growing up to be involved in crime, the 'event decision' – the making of a rational choice – at the point of committing the offence, is critical.

Evaluation

The development of concepts such as opportunity, routine activities and rational decision making has had a profound practical impact on the form of situational crime prevention (Clarke, 1992). This approach to crime prevention takes the broad approach that by changing elements of the situation, such as target availability and levels of surveillance, it is possible to impact significantly on the opportunities for crime and the offender's decision making. There are criticisms of this approach at theoretical and practical levels, particularly with regard to the rationality of some offending and the issue of displacement. However, there is little doubt that the overall approach has taken criminological theory into new areas of research and practice.

Clive Hollin

Associated Concepts: classicism, crime science, defensible space, free will, geographies of crime, rational choice theory, routine activity theory, situational crime prevention, surveillance

Key Readings

Bottoms, A.E. and Wiles, P. (1997) 'Environmental criminology', in M. Maguire, R. Morgan and R. Reiner (eds), *The Oxford Handbook of Criminology,* 2nd edn. Oxford: Clarendon.
Clarke, R.V. (ed.) (1992) *Situational Crime Prevention: Successful Case Studies.* New York: Harrow and Heston.
Clarke, R.V. (1995) 'Situational crime prevention', in M. Tonry and D.P. Farrington (eds), *Building a Safer Society: Strategic Approaches to Crime Prevention.* Chicago: University of Chicago Press.
Cohen, L.E. and Felson, M. (1979) 'Social change and crime rate trends: a routine activities approach', *American Sociological Review,* 44: 588–608.
Cornish, D.B. and Clarke, R.V. (eds) (1986) *The Reasoning Criminal: Rational Choice Perspectives on Offending.* New York: Springer-Verlag.
van den Haag, E. (1982) 'Could successful rehabilitation reduce the crime rate?', *Journal of Criminal Law and Criminology,* 73: 1,022–1,035.

ORGANIZED CRIME

Definition

This concept emerged first in the United States in the 1920s but is now used internationally, for example, by the United Nations and G8 countries, as shorthand to describe a range of serious crimes that are deemed especially difficult to control. It may be defined as the ongoing activities of those collectively engaged in production, supply and financing for illegal markets in goods and services.

Distinctive Features

There are two main analogies employed in the description and analysis of organized crime: the market and government. In the first, a distinction is commonly drawn between 'ordinary' criminals, even if in gangs, whose crimes are 'predatory' – that is, concerned with the illegal redistribution of already existing wealth – and criminal organizations committing 'enterprise' crime: the production and distribution of new, though illegal, goods and services (Naylor, 1997). This is not a hard and fast distinction: the more opportunistic the criminal organization, the more likely it is to be involved in both types of crime.

This basic idea of 'enterprise' crime is central to most contemporary accounts of the concept, both official and academic, but crucially different approaches emerge once analysis proceeds. In the official discourse, criminal enterprises will *penetrate* an otherwise lawful business, thus undermining and corrupting it, for example, offering counterfeit supplies or protection including threats. Such activities do happen but they represent only a partial account. A fuller examination of the interaction between organizations and markets shows that under certain conditions the relationship between legal and illegal organizations is *symbiotic.* For example, the study of corporate crime examines the extensive illegal behaviour of organizations that are formally legal. Similarly, Smith (1980) develops a model of enterprises being situated on a spectrum between legality and illegality and explains how the interaction of entrepreneurs and customers leads to 'stratified market-places' – for example, entrepreneurs may prefer to borrow money from a bank but, if unable to do so, may go to a loan shark.

Overall, the enterprise model is at the heart of the common metaphor of the criminal 'firm'; for some, however, what is particularly significant about criminal organizations including, for example, the Mafia, is not their marketplace activities so much as their 'governmental' behaviour. At one level, this may reflect attempts by criminal organizations to corrupt government in general, for example, through contractual bid-rigging and law enforcement in particular, paying-off police, prosecutors and judges for favourable decisions. However, more fundamentally, criminal organizations have been characterized as threatening the state's monopoly of functions such as coercion, protection and extraction (Naylor, 1997: 15–16). These functions are all central to the legitimacy claims of modern states, and to the extent that other organizations deploy violence, offer protection and benefits and extract 'taxation', then they may be seen as challenging that central claim. Post-Soviet Russia is seen as one example of this. Indeed, taking a longer historical view, the struggles between rivals to establish monopolies can be viewed as the central feature of 'state-making' (Tilly, 1985).

Evaluation

Considerable controversy has surrounded the use of this concept, much of it centring on the nature and extent of the organization of crime. Work carried out for the US President's Crime Commission in the 1960s presented the Italian-American Mafia as the core manifestation of organized crime; specifically that it resembled a corporate *hierarchy* with the associated features of rank and division of labour. Critics argued that this image resulted from researchers' over-reliance on files and other evidence from a law enforcement community that was anyway predisposed to describe their targets in the same hierarchical

terms as they themselves were organized. Alternative models that are built more on the idea of *networks* – for example, those based on families, or more broadly, friends and business connections (e.g., Hobbs, 1998) – are a more accurate depiction.

Further impetus has been given to this controversy by the identification of transnational organized crime as a major problem during the 1990s. The reasons for this are clear: the end of the Cold War and the collapse of the former regimes of the Soviet bloc have seen a reorientation not just of security intelligence agencies and military forces but also of academic departments of international relations towards the analysis of 'new' security threats. Coinciding as this has with the era of globalization, the result has been an outpouring of official concern at national and international levels that organized crime is not just a 'serious problem' but that it actually constitutes a threat to national security. Further, the threat is normally presented as if it were primarily an *external* one in much the same way as 'ordinary' crime is normally represented as crimes of 'the other'. Therefore the discussion surrounds 'Russian-', 'Asian-', 'Nigerian-organized crime' and so on, and unreliable estimates of the values of cross-border crime are often given. Actually, more careful analysis indicates that crime remains predominantly local in origin and that it is carried out by national citizens.

Thus, great care must be taken with use of the concept: organized crime is an issue on which governments feel strongly the need to reassure insecure populations that 'something can be done' and there is consequently much rhetoric about 'wars' on crime and drugs. In reality, organized criminality is so deeply embedded within the operation of domestic and global markets that the most that can be achieved is to somewhat ameliorate its most damaging effects.

Peter Gill

Associated Concepts: art crime, corporate crime, critical criminology, extraterritorial

law enforcement, globalization, Marxist criminologies, state crime, transnational organized
crime, white collar crime

Key Readings

Abadinsky, H. (1997) *Organized Crime,* 5th
edn. Chicago, IL: Nelson-Hall.
Galeotti, M. (2007) *Global Crime Today: The
Changing Face of Organised Crime.* London:
Routledge.
Hobbs, D. (1998) 'Going down the glocal',
The Howard Journal of Criminal Justice, 37
(4): 1–19. (See also other articles in this
special edition.)
Naylor, R.T. (1997) 'Mafias, myths and markets',
Transnational Organized Crime, 3 (3): 15–30.
Smith, D. (1980) 'Paragons, pariahs and pirates',
Crime and Delinquency, 26 (July): 45–57.
Special Issue on Transnational Crime (1998)
*International Journal of Risk, Security and
Crime Prevention,* 3(2).
Tilly, C. (1985) 'War making and state mak-
ing as organized crime', in P. Evans (ed.),
Bringing the State Back In. Cambridge:
Cambridge University Press.

P

PANOPTICISM

Definition

A theoretical concept associated with the French philosopher Michel Foucault (1977). Foucault uses Jeremy Bentham's eighteenth-century design for a prison – the Panopticon (which was never actually built) – as a starting point from which to analyse the general 'exercise of power' in society as a whole.

Distinctive Features

The central feature of Bentham's unused prison design for the Panopticon was visibility and inspection. In the words of Foucault (1977: 200):

> We know the principle on which it [i.e., the Panopticon] was based: at the periphery, an annular building; at the centre, a tower; this tower is pierced with wide windows that open onto the inner side of the ring; the peripheric building is divided into cells, each of which extends the whole width of the building; they have two windows, one on the inside, corresponding to the windows of the tower; the other, on the outside, allows the light to cross the cell from one end to the other. All that is needed, is to place a supervisor in a central tower and to shut up in each cell a lunatic, a patient, a condemned man, a worker or a pupil. By the effect of backlighting, one can observe from the tower, standing put precisely against the light, the small captive shadows in the cells of the periphery. They are like so many cages, so many small theatres, in which each actor is alone, perfectly individualized and constantly visible. The panoptic mechanism arranges spatial unities that make it possible to see constantly and to recognize immediately. In short, it reverses the principles of the dungeon; or rather of its three functions – to enclose, to deprive of light and to hide – it preserves only the first and eliminates the other two. Full lighting and the eye of a supervisor capture better than darkness, which ultimately protected. Visibility is a trap.

In a chapter entitled 'Panopticism', Foucault argues that institutions other than prisons begin to use the same forms of power – visibility and inspection – to exercise control in factories, schools, hospitals and so on. The Panopticon 'must not be understood as a dream building; it is the diagram of a mechanism of power reduced to its ideal form; its functioning, abstracted from any obstacle, resistance or friction, must be represented as a pure architectural and optical system: it is in fact a figure of political technology that may and must be detached from any specific use' (1977: 205).

Despite using the Panopticon as a historical metaphor for the seventeenth and eighteenth centuries, the application of the theoretical principles of the disciplinary power of visibility, and the idea that inspection or observation affects behaviour which Foucault develops, have numerous contemporary resonances. In particular, the increasing use of closed circuit television (CCTV) in our cities, in both public and private spaces, has precisely the same disciplinary functions that Foucault suggested lay at the heart of the Panopticon, and is linked to the idea of the 'carceral society'.

Evaluation

What makes Foucault so interesting and challenging is his almost poetic use of language. Like a true poet or philosopher he makes connections between seemingly unconnected events. Alternatively, what makes him frustrating is his failure to cite sources and his endless willingness to push his materials beyond the point at which they can be sustained. Panopticism benefits and suffers from these strengths and weaknesses in almost equal measure. It should be remembered, for example, that Bentham's design was never accepted and the Panopticon never built. On the other hand, as a basis for analysing our contemporary preoccupation with security surveillance, panopticism offers many interesting insights.

David Wilson

Associated Concepts: carceral society, electronic monitoring, penality, penology, surveillance

Key Readings

Bozovic, M. (ed.) (1995) *The Panopticon Writings of Jeremy Bentham.* New York: Verso Press.
Foucault, M. (1977) *Discipline and Punish: The Birth of the Prison.* London: Allen Lane.

PARTICIPANT OBSERVATION

Definition

The collection of information through active participation in the social world that is under study.

Distinctive Features

Pioneered by the Chicago School of Sociology in the 1920s, the key aim of participant observation is to view the social world, as far as possible, from the actor's own point of view. Typically this involves becoming part of the group under study, learning its culture and observing its behaviour. The key aim is to gain access to the meanings that actors themselves make of their own personal and social situations. It facilitates data collection on situations as they occur rather than in artificial situations (as in experimental research) or through constructs of reality provided by the researcher (as in survey research). The promise is held that such observations can help to make sense of behaviour that may appear to be irrational and paradoxical to those 'on the outside'. As a result, it is most closely associated with interactionism and appreciative forms of criminology. The participant observer becomes immersed 'in the field' by emphasizing:

- the study of groups in their natural surroundings, with the minimum of disturbance;
- empathy and understanding;
- the direct observation of interactions and in particular the meanings they have for participants;
- descriptions in terms of the everyday understandings of actors in a situation.

Gold (1969) distinguished four forms of such research – 'observer-as-participant', 'participant-as-observer', 'the complete observer', and 'the complete participant'. In full participant observation, the researcher identifies an area worthy of study and enters the field without much preconception about what is to be found. Typically the observer also conceals their identity as a researcher from those being studied.

In the 1960s and 1970s the development of explicitly anti-positivist approaches to the study of crime and deviance, for example in labelling and new deviancy theory, provided the political and theoretical inspiration for what was arguably the heyday of participant observation research. Polsky's (1971) research into poolroom hustlers in New York and Parker's (1974) study of a group of male 'street kids' in Liverpool came closest to Gold's notion of 'complete participant' – in that their position as researcher as well as participant was often indistinguishable. Both carried out their research covertly and, in order to gain trust, engaged in deviant activities themselves – a position that some ethnographers have described as having 'gone native'. However, each also provided invaluable insights into the complexity of subcultural codes and behaviour that previous researchers had been unable to, or had failed to, acknowledge. As a result each was also able to offer a damning critique of 'orthodox' research masquerading as 'science'.

On the other hand, participant observation has also been used to improve understandings of the internal workings of the criminal justice system, as in Holdaway's (1983) study of the British police. This work was carried out covertly and was able to reveal the extent to which police work was framed by the everyday meanings and definitions that officers themselves had constructed to make sense of their role and the people that they policed.

Fully developed, covert participant observation research is necessarily time-consuming, difficult, long-term and potentially risky, and can in some circumstances raise serious ethical questions. It is probably no surprise, in a criminology that had by the 1990s become dominated by technicist, evaluative and administrative concerns, that such research has become increasingly rare. But it remains one of the few means by which a humanization of the subjects of criminological research can be achieved.

John Muncie

Associated Concepts: appreciative criminology, Chicago School of Sociology, ethnography, interactionism, new deviancy theory, research ethics

Key Readings

Adler, P.A. (1993) *Wheeling and Dealing: An Ethnography of an Upper Level Drug Dealing and Smuggling Community.* New York: Columbia University Press.

Burgess, R.G. (1984) *In the Field.* London: Unwin Hyman.

Gold, R. (1969) 'Roles in sociological field observation', in G. McCall and J. Simmons (eds), *Issues in Participant Observation.* London: Addison-Wesley.

Holdaway, S. (1983) *Inside the British Police.* Oxford: Blackwell.

Parker, H. (1974) *View from the Boys.* Newton Abbot: David and Charles.

Polsky, N. (1971) *Hustlers, Beats and Others.* Harmondsworth: Penguin.

PATHOLOGY

Definition

Within bio-medical discourse (the study of disease; by extension and common usage) the abnormal (that which is not normal), an unhealthy deviation from the norm, degenerate. For those who follow individualistic explanations of crime, pathology will be located in the individual at the level of genes, hormones or the psyche. For sociologists, the pathology might be located in the family, peer-group, area or social formation.

Distinctive Features

Durkheim (1964 [1895]) devoted a chapter to the 'Normal and the Pathological'. However, the greater part of his discussion was given over to bio-medical analogy. Moreover the term 'morbidity' was sometimes used – again emphasizing the organicism of his argument. Famously, Durkheim used suicide to illustrate the utility of sociological method even in the most seemingly individual act. Similarly, he claimed, 'If there is any fact whose pathological character appears incontestable, that fact is crime. All criminologists are agreed on this point. Although they explain this pathology differently.' He then proceeded to make his oft-quoted claim about crime being normal (even amongst a 'society of saints'). However, he allowed some crime to be pathological. He acknowledged that a person could commit crime for individual pathological reasons *and* sociologically that a rate of crime may be pathologically higher than that predicted for social types and levels of society. This too he called morbidity or abnormal. However, contrary to the general positivism of his arguments, he also recognized – and foreshadowed the labelling perspective – 'that, among these divergences, there are some with a criminal character. What confers this character upon them is not the intrinsic quality of a given act but that definition which the collective conscience lends them' (1964 [1895]: 70).

It is a mark of the extent to which sociological criminology has advanced that Durkheim's claim that all criminologists agree on the pathological character of crime strikes the modern reader as odd. Durkheim was able to overturn the narrow bio-medical definition of pathology and give it a sociological face. However, despite his influence 'pathology' has not usually been the nomenclature favoured by those who followed in his footsteps. It can be argued that it appears in various disguises in the sociology of deviance, such as differential association, social disorganization and strain. It might also be argued that some positivistic readings of both Marxism and feminism see class society and patriarchy as pathological or responsible for the 'pathologies' of the working class or of men.

Evaluation

It can be argued that pathology no longer has any place in sociology. However, as psychopathology, it has once again been elevated to prime importance in criminal justice discourse and popular cultural representation – note the character of Hannibal Lecter in *Silence of the Lambs* – as an explanation of crime. Sumner (1994) claims that the field of study Durkheim opened up was killed off in 1975, and proposes replacing deviance with censure as the field of study. In this, the term 'pathology', including psychopathology, can be seen as the censure of the different by those with the power to define it. This can be seen in Durkheim's terms as functional – in labelling terms as misguided or counterproductive – or in Foucauldian terms as productive. The disciplines of medicine and the psy-sciences employ the nexus of power/knowledge to produce – and offer to control – pathology, as they have done with madness, crime and sexual dissidence.

Administrative criminology has sought to side-step the issue of pathology within the individual or society but replaces it with the fear or risk of others' pathology, which is to be managed. In this way the gated community might be seen as a *cordon sanitaire* and security guards as white blood corpuscles and T-cells mobilizing to neutralize pathogens. 'Sterilizing' urban spaces in the nineteenth century was the job of the 'new police'. Now it falls to the Martian ray of CCTV. Staying with the medical metaphor, society seems uncertain whether to swallow up (a cannibalistic response) or vomit out (a bulimic response) the pathologized 'other' (Young, 1999).

Nic Groombridge

Associated Concepts: demonization, deviance, individual positivism, normalization, psychopathy, sexuality, social censure, sociological positivism

Key Readings

Durkheim, E. (1964 [1895]) *The Rules of Sociological Method.* London: The Free Press of Glencoe.

Lemert, E. (1972 [1967]) 'Forms and pathology of drinking in three Polynesian societies', in *Human Deviance, Social Problems and Social Control.* Englewood Cliffs, NJ: Prentice-Hall. pp. 218–33.

Sumner, C. (1994) *The Sociology of Deviance: An Obituary.* Buckingham: The Open University Press.

Young, J. (1999) *The Exclusive Society: Social Exclusion, Difference and Crime in Late Modernity.* London: Sage.

PEACEMAKING CRIMINOLOGY

Definition

The study of the processes and ways of relating that leave people safer, more trusting and less guarded with others. The science and art of weaving people, including those called 'offenders' and 'victims' in conventional 'war-making' criminology, into social networks secure from violence. Peacemaking criminology is the opposite of the prevailing 'war-making' paradigm in criminology, which is the science and art of identifying, isolating and subduing offenders or would-be offenders.

Distinctive Features

Like all spiritual, religious, political or cultural traditions, all social science, including criminology, can be divided into two competing paradigms on how to belong in social order. The war-making paradigm presupposes that we are born ignorant and need to learn to obey instruction from our properly constituted earthly superiors, from whose might right is made. In this paradigm the key dependent variables are negative – such as crime, violence, criminality, punishment, deterrence and risk. In the peacemaking paradigm social relations become stronger and richer insofar as they are built on mutual respect. Dependent variables in a peacemaking paradigm are positive, such as compassion, love, empathy, respect, dignity, mutuality and trust.

Within the peacemaking paradigm, punishment itself is presumed to be a social problem rather than a social solution. It is common to see those identified as doing peacemaking criminology belonging to corollary groups. Some, for example, draw upon Gandhian principles of non-violence. Some, including those who note that 'penal servitude' is the one kind of 'slavery' explicitly allowed by the Thirteenth Amendment to the United States Constitution, call themselves 'penal abolitionists'. Some advocate 'restorative' or 'transformative' rather than 'retributive justice'.

Some call for 'compassion' in Buddhist terms, others for 'love' and 'mercy' in Judaeo-Christian-Muslim terms. Traditional ways of responding to personal and structural violence, from indigenous peoples around the world, are especially prominent in peacemaking literature and in criminal justice practice, as in the New Zealand parliament's adoption of the Maori practice known worldwide today as family group conferencing; in Canadian sentencing circles; or in the growing Anglo legal recognition of, and admiration for, the Navajo peacemaking court in the United States.

Criminologists who are drawn towards peacemaking commonly report that their spirits are lifted by studying what people value in others and how to elicit what we like from each other, in contrast to the despair and discouragement that they had come to feel when studying what it is we want people not to do and how to get people to stop doing things. It feels better to learn how to get what we do want and what we value in others than to learn how to crush human miscreants.

Whether secular or deist, peacemaking criminology is explicitly concerned with the spiritual attitude we bring to bear in our social relations, while war-making criminology tends to embrace the Enlightenment dualism between spiritual value and social fact-making. Much peacemaking criminology is critical of value neutrality in retributive criminology. Indeed, one theory of the causes of violence and punitiveness, notably as stated by the renegade German psychoanalyst Alice Miller, is that all violence and punishment will presuppose a personal dissociation of one's feelings from one's actions. When you pull the switch to punish a transgressor, your feeling for the transgressor's suffering is cut off by messages from authority figures as to what you *ought* to do to the offender for some higher good. In peacemaking criminology there is no higher good than empathy; or as some, such as the US war resister A.J. Muste and the criminologist Richard Quinney, have put it, 'peace is *the* way'. In radical feminist terms, in peacemaking criminology, power over others is violence itself; building a safe community relies on power sharing and participatory democracy.

Evaluation

The three main criticisms of peacemaking criminology are that it is not a theory, that it is impractical, and that it is privileged.

Peacemaking criminology is not a theory. As with retribution, peacemaking is more an attitude or definition of the situation. On the other hand, peacemaking criminology includes theories of how peace is made.

Practicality is a paradigmatic matter. Peacemaking criminology is not prophecy. Peacemaking theory only purports to predict whether people will be safer or more at risk as a result of this or that intervention, not whether people will actually do what makes them safer. There is in peacemaking criminology a rich body of empirically-tested propositions as to what brings people together or separates them.

The realist criticism is that peacemaking criminology is concocted by people who do not understand just how bad oppression is, the urgency of supporting those who even take up arms to resist and subdue their oppressors, nor the progress that has been made through militant class struggle. Other than prisoners, it is by and large true that peacemaking criminologists and their critics are privileged. This issue recurs in all our theological and political debates over whether to be hard-hearted or to let our hearts bleed.

Some texts have taken to calling 'peacemaking criminology' a 'school'. In recent history, 'peacemaking' became an operative word in criminological circles when the title of an edited book – *Criminology as Peacemaking* – caught on after its publication in 1991. Criminologists who say they are doing 'peacemaking' encompass a wide range of criminological individualists, which surely includes those who would be loath to accept the definition of 'peacemaking' set forth here. In peacemaking criminology, as in everyday life, it pays us not to take for granted that we know any criminologist by the label 'peacemaking' alone.

Hal Pepinsky

Associated Concepts: abolition, anarchist criminology, human rights, labelling, restorative justice, social reaction

Key Readings

Anderson, K. and Quinney, R. (eds) (2000) *Erich Fromm and Critical Criminology: Beyond the Punitive Society.* Urbana, IL: University of Illinois Press.
Consedine, J. (1999) *Restorative Justice: Healing the Effects of Crime.* Lyttleton, NZ: Ploughshares Press.
Fuller, J.R. (1998) *Criminal Justice: A Peacemaking Perspective.* Boston, MA: Allyn and Bacon.
Miller, A. (1990) *For Your Own Good: Hidden Cruelty in Child-Rearing and the Roots of Violence.* New York: Noonday Press.
Morris, R.M. (1993) *Penal Abolition: The Practical Choice.* Toronto: Canadian Scholars' Press.
Pepinsky, H.E. and Quinney, R. (eds) (1991) *Criminology as Peacemaking.* Bloomington, IN: Indiana University Press.

PENALITY

Definition

A term introduced from the French *pénalité* and owing its current salience primarily to the influence of Foucault. It designates not only the institutions and agencies composing the penal system but also their surrounding economic, political, intellectual and cultural conditions.

Distinctive Features

Use of the term 'penality' is often intended to strike a conscious difference from the traditional concerns either of normative penal theory on the one hand or the instrumental and pragmatic preoccupations of conventional penology on the other. Whereas the former is devoted to a discussion of the proper aims of penal action (their basis in legal theory, their moral implications, their coherence) and the latter has historically been taken up with ameliorating penal institutions and refining their effectiveness, 'penality' denotes an attempt to historicize penal questions and to situate these in terms of their sociological and political connections and surrounding conditions. Thus, in an important early instance of the English-language use of the term, Garland and Young argued that conventional penology had become 'marginal to any attempt actually to explain the nature of the penal system' (1983: 5). In place of such descriptive, meliorist and politically compromised exercises, they proposed a more intellectually ambitious enterprise which would reconceive the penal realm as a 'specific *institutional site* ... traversed by a series of different social relations' (1983: 21).

Although the translation of Foucault's *Discipline and Punish* was the single event that gave the greatest impetus to such attempts at reconsideration, the social analysis of penality in fact has much longer and more extensive intellectual antecedents. These flow in part from the legacies of Durkheim, whose social theory reserved an important place for punishment among the ritual affirmations of social solidarity. His influence is also visible, if sometimes more remotely, in the work of anthropologists such as Mary Douglas and of historical sociologists such as Kai Erikson. Such studies made available an awareness that practices for the maintenance and application of conduct norms and rules and for the imposition of sanctions, censures and blame were culturally and historically variable and specific. They thereby also facilitated a recognition that the penal arrangements so familiar to the citizens of contemporary Western societies might similarly be subjected to a more sceptical and critical appraisal.

A comparable shock of 'defamiliarization' resulted from the appearance of a number of 'revisionist' histories of penal systems and institutions, especially prisons. The foundational text here is unquestionably Rusche and Kirchheimer's *Punishment and Social Structure* (first published in 1939 and influentially republished in 1968). Rusche and Kirchheimer's basic contention, flying in the face of much

philosophical effort to distil the proper or intrinsic nature of punishment, was that 'there is no such thing as punishment, but only concrete systems of punishment'. This thesis might be taken as a motto for the revisionist historians. Whatever their differences (for example the explicitness of their debt to Marxist theory or to specific varieties thereof), the latter had in common a concern to locate the development of the 'modern' form of penitentiary imprisonment, around the turn of the eighteenth and nineteenth centuries, to the emergence of industrial capitalism, and the deployment of penal power by the state to the management of the conflictual social relations over which it presided (see Garland, 1990: Chapters 4 and 5).

In this context, the primary distinctiveness and originality of Foucault's contribution lay not so much in his view of the broad outlines of chronology, nor even in any particular new empirical discovery, but rather in his anatomization of the styles and techniques of penal discipline that were characteristic of modernity. Foucault saw the prison not as *sui generis* but rather as standing within a continuum of disciplinary institutions (schools, hospitals, workhouses, barracks) whose common aspect was the minute regulation of daily conduct and whose object lay not merely in the suppression or subjugation of the unruly but rather in the positive production of 'docile yet capable bodies'. In Foucault's account, the emergence of modern penality is unintelligible without reference to the new varieties of specialist knowledge (such as psychology, psychiatry, social statistics and epidemiology) that provided its classifications, and that guided, supported and authorized its strategies of intervention – its 'discursive practices' (see Garland, 1990: Chapter 6; Howe, 1993: Chapter 3).

In subsequent work, elements of each of these conceptual resources have been revised and put to diverse uses. For example, David Garland in *Punishment and Welfare* (1985) traces the emergence of a form of penality characteristic of twentieth-century welfare states and especially the development of hybrid forms of 'welfare sanction'. Pat Carlen in *Women's Imprisonment* (1983) identifies the modes of discipline specific to the carceral control of women. Jonathan Simon in *Poor Discipline* (1993) follows the rise, decline and re-engineering of parole and the supervision of offenders. Adrian Howe (1993) proposes a thoroughgoing feminist re-evaluation of penality in terms of the multiple modes of discipline governing the lives of girls and women. Garland (1990) offers an ambitious synthesis which accommodates not only the long-standing preoccupations with the powers of the state and the Foucauldian concern with the 'micro-physics' of penal practice, but also a wider interest in the place of the penal in modern culture and especially in its expressive and emotive aspects.

Evaluation

In view of the complexity and scale of contemporary penal systems, their endless changeability (yet the obdurate and intractable nature of many of their central problems) and the intense political controversy and sensitivity that surround them, the social analysis of penality has become a necessary and highly active field of criminological enquiry. The emergence of new modes and techniques, for example around the assessment and calculation of risk, in conjunction with some ostensibly very old themes in populist political rhetoric, together with the grossly unequal weight of penal action that falls on specific sections of the population – especially along the fault-line of race (Wacquant, 2000) – makes for a penal landscape that demands a continuous effort of understanding and critical evaluation.

Richard Sparks

Associated Concepts: carceral society, governmentality, penology, risk, social control

Key Readings

Carlen, P. (1983) *Women's Imprisonment*. London: Routledge and Kegan Paul.
Foucault, M. (1977) *Discipline and Punish*. London: Allen Lane.

Garland, D. (1985) *Punishment and Welfare*. Aldershot: Gower.
Garland, D. (1990) *Punishment and Modern Society*. Oxford: Oxford University Press.
Garland, D. and Young, P. (eds) (1983) *The Power to Punish*. Aldershot: Gower.
Howe, A. (1993) *Punish and Critique: Towards a Feminist Analysis of Penality*. London: Routledge.
Rusche, G. and Kirchheimer, O. (1968) *Punishment and Social Structure*. New York: Russell and Russell.
Simon, J. (1993) *Poor Discipline*. Chicago: University of Chicago Press.
Wacquant, L. (2000) 'The fourth peculiar institution: the prison as surrogate ghetto', *Theoretical Criminology*, 4 (3): 377–90.

PENOLOGY

Definition

A term which (although arguably in less common usage now than formerly) covers the application of clinical, managerial or social scientific methods or expertise to the disciplined study and evaluation of penal institutions, especially prisons.

Distinctive Features

In its older and narrower sense 'penology' designates the attempt to reform or rationalize penal conditions and regimes so as to maximize their corrective effectiveness. In recent times (roughly since the middle of the twentieth century), its sense has broadened to include any form of systematic enquiry into the characteristics of penal systems – including, at its radical edge, arguments for their abolition.

It is conventional, and probably appropriate, to date the inception of modern penological thinking from the reform projects undertaken by John Howard, Jeremy Bentham and others from the late eighteenth century onwards. Mention of these two very different thinkers, the former an impassioned advocate of Christian charity and the latter a utilitarian rationalist, betrays a duality that has since recurred many times in the historical development of penology between motivations grounded in humanitarian magnanimity or the desire for the religious reformation of the offender, and those directed more instrumentally at the refinement of techniques of behavioural control. To the extent that these ambiguities attended the birth of penology it is unsurprising that the subsequent activities of penologists have often produced ambiguous, hybrid and sometimes perverse or contradictory results, as historians of the subject have often demonstrated (see for example Ignatieff, 1978; McGowen, 1995). It suffices here only to note that the particular histories of prison architecture and disciplinary regimes, as well as the minutiae of medico-psychiatric services, religious observance, diet and other aspects of the material infrastructure and social relations of penal institutions, are largely unintelligible without reference to the intellectual inputs of the various penologies that have successively informed them. In that penology has been throughout most of its history a reform-minded subject with practical goals, it has been characterized by the repeated inventiveness (and as often the repeated failures) of projects for the improvement, if not indeed the utopian perfectibility, of prisons and other penal arrangements.

For much of the twentieth century two major foci of penological effort are apparent. The first is the monitoring of variations in sentencing and of the manipulation of penal regimes (both in prisons and in non-custodial settings) for evidence of their impact on offending and reoffending, whether on grounds of rehabilitation, deterrence or incapacitation. In the hands of its more sophisticated practitioners (for example Norval Morris, Michael Tonry, or Franklin Zimring and Gordon Hawkins for the United States; Nigel Walker or Anthony Bottoms for the United Kingdom), this concern necessarily shades into legal theory and the philosophy of punishment. If penology has a disciplinary identity which is distinguishable from these normative and theoretical matters it lies in its rigorous application of empirical procedures. For a representative survey of work in these traditions see von Hirsch and Ashworth (1998).

The second major focus of enquiry is the systematic study of penal institutions themselves – their social organization, routines and characteristic relationships; the experience of confinement and of custodial or supervisory work; the recurrent problems of imprisonment (riots, violence, suicide and self-harm); and, more especially in the last three decades, questions of discriminatory or disparate treatment on grounds of race, gender and age. Such work arguably enjoyed a heyday in the middle decades of the twentieth century when the prison aroused the fascination first of functionalist (Clemmer's 'prison community', Sykes's 'society of captives') and later of symbolic interactionist (Goffman's 'total institutions') sociologies (see Sparks et al., 1996: Chapter 2, for a short survey).

The subsequent relative decline both of therapeutic penology and of prison sociology, especially in the United States, would seem to flow in large part from a diminished confidence, increasingly evident from the 1970s onwards, in the capacities of penal interventions to reduce reoffending (the so-called 'loss of the rehabilitative ideal', or in its more extreme formulation the 'nothing works' position). For many observers this coincides with a shift, again most pronounced in the United States, towards primarily incapacitative rationales for punishing or, more critically understood, a move towards a 'warehousing' approach to imprisonment. These developments are summed up by Garland (1990) as constituting a 'crisis of penal modernism'. The irony for penology is that whereas the latter developments tend to increase the scale of imprisonment this is met by a reduced intensity of scholarly interest in what goes on in prisons, or more generally in the lives and fates of offenders, beyond that of a merely supervisory concern with risk management and case-processing (for an account of the outworkings of this view see Simon, 2000).

Evaluation

Penology has not, however, come to a complete stop. For its more practically oriented practitioners there is now both a sense that 'nothing works' always was an over-reaction and a resurgent interest (albeit in a more modest but more technically sophisticated vein) in 'what works?'. For others there is also the sobering awareness that however much penologists have historically claimed to stand on the progressive side of every engagement, the subject cannot evade its complicity in or responsibility for the disciplinary apparatuses erected in its name and especially their regressive consequences for stigmatized and dispossessed people.

Richard Sparks

Associated Concepts: deterrence, incapacitation, incarceration, penality, rehabilitation

Key Readings

Garland, D. (1990) *Punishment and Modern Society.* Oxford: Oxford University Press.
von Hirsch, A. and Ashworth, A. (eds) (1998) *Principled Sentencing: Readings on Theory and Policy,* 2nd edn. Oxford: Hart Publishing.
Ignatieff, M. (1978) *A Just Measure of Pain.* Harmondsworth: Penguin.
McGowen, R. (1995) 'The well-ordered prison: England, 1780–1865', in N. Morris and D. Rothman (eds), *The Oxford History of the Prison.* Oxford: Oxford University Press.
Simon, J. (2000) 'The "society of captives" in the era of hyper-incarceration', *Theoretical Criminology,* 4 (3): 285–308.
Sparks, J.R., Bottoms, A.E. and Hay, W.T. (1996) *Prisons and the Problem of Order.* Oxford: Oxford University Press.

PERSONAL SAFETY

Definition

The daily, often taken-for-granted, routines that human beings engage in as a way of feeling safer at home, on the street and in the workplace.

Distinctive Features

The concept is primarily associated with the radical feminist response to the fear of crime debate. Radical feminists argue that that debate constructs a passive image of (female) victims of crime and renders their fears irrational by pursuing an understanding of criminal victimization which focuses on the threat posed by random violence from a stranger. The radical feminist response to the fear of crime, however, focuses attention on the threat of danger from people (men) who are known, and consequently is concerned to understand how women (and men) manage danger in their routine everyday lives. Hence a concern with the active construction of strategies for the management of personal safety. It is a concept that emphasizes the active participation by individuals in their everyday lives rather than presuming that human beings are passive recipients of events that just happen to them. Work informed by this concept has demonstrated that men and women adopt different languages of personal safety. For example, women's strategies are much more likely to be informed by the threat of sexual danger, whilst men's strategies are much more likely to be informed by the threat of physical danger, though the subsequent experience of vulnerability can be felt in very similar ways. In addition, age and sexuality also appear to contribute to individual personal safety strategies.

Evaluation

This concept constituted an important interjection into the fear of crime debate and has contributed to a more careful and considered approach to understanding the way in which crime routinely impacts upon the everyday life of individuals. It challenges the image of the individual paralysed by the fear of crime and encourages an understanding of the ways in which people manage what they know may or may not happen to them. In particular it has contributed to an appreciation of understanding women as experts in their own safety as well as the difficulties of separating the public from the private – the fear of the unknown from the fear of the known.

As a concept it has become absorbed by the crime prevention literature, in which setting it has lost some of its feminist resonance. Nevertheless, as an idea, it does encourage practitioners to work with an active rather than a passive image of the human being.

Sandra Walklate

Associated Concepts: community safety, crime prevention, fear of crime, left realism, radical feminism, victimology

Key Readings

Goodey, J. (1997) 'Boys don't cry; masculinities, fear of crime, and fearlessness', *British Journal of Criminology,* 37 (3): 401–18.

Stanko, E. (1990) *Everyday Violence: How Women and Men Experience Sexual and Physical Danger.* London: Pandora.

Stanko, E. (1997) 'Safety talk: conceptualizing women's risk assessment as a "technology of the soul"', *Theoretical Criminology,* 1 (4): 479–99.

Walklate, S. (1998) 'Excavating the fear of crime: fear, anxiety or trust?', *Theoretical Criminology,* 2 (4): 403–18.

PERSONALITY THEORY

Definition

A central feature of mainstream psychology. The term 'personality' is generally taken to refer to a relatively stable set of distinguishing psychological characteristics. It is the combination of such features that defines a particular type of personality. Personality theory is therefore concerned with understanding the constituents of personality, its development and, ultimately, its measurement.

Distinctive Features

The core of personality theory lies in attempting to understand the behavioural variance that can be ascribed to factors internal to the person, as opposed to the effects of the environment. Thus, personality can be thought of as the stable structure and pattern of an individual's thoughts and feelings which, in turn, are related to distinctive styles of behaviour. Personality theorists might look for basic dimensions, or *types*, of personality that can be ascribed to distinctive psychological factors such as beliefs or emotions. The idea of types of personality is not new: Hippocrates, for example, described four basic types of temperament as Sanguine (Optimistic), Melancholic (Depressed), Choleric (Irritable) and Phlegmatic (Calm).

If, as personality theory suggests, there are particular personality *types*, then what are the constituents of the type? Some personality theorists argue that *traits* are the building blocks of a personality type. A consistent grouping of particular traits is then said to constitute a type. For example, a personality test might show that an individual has scored highly on the traits of competence, self-discipline, dutifulness and reliability. This grouping of traits might then be said to define a conscientious type of personality.

The distinction between a type and a trait can be thought of as the distinction between a category and a dimension. Gordon Allport (1897–1967) summed it up in a comment that a person can be said to *have* a trait but to *fit* a type.

As in any broad theoretical approach, personality theorists differ in their views about the distinctions between traits, the nature of types, and the complex biological and psychological processes that must be involved. From the standpoint of criminology, it is the personality theory of Hans Eysenck (1916–97) that is of greatest interest.

Eysenck's theory is, in essence, a control theory, beginning from the perspective that everyone has the potential to behave in a criminal manner: the issue is why does everyone not commit crimes? In other words, what are the forces that *control* the common propensity to crime? Eysenck (1959) defined two personality types, *extroversion* (E) and *neuroticism* (N); later work (Eysenck and Eysenck, 1968) described a third dimension,

313

psychoticism (P). Each of these basic types is conceived as a continuum, with most people falling in the middle range, and, it follows, with comparatively few people at the extremes of each scale. Extroversion runs from high (extrovert) to low (introvert); similarly neuroticism runs from high (neurotic) to low (stable); and this is also the case with psychoticism.

Eysenck's theory of personality proposes that, principally through our genetic endowment, we are born with cortical and autonomic nervous systems that will directly affect our ability to learn from, or more properly *condition* to, environmental stimuli. Biologically, the extrovert is cortically *under*-aroused and so seeks stimulation to maintain cortical arousal at an optimal level. The extrovert will display traits such as being impulsive, seeking excitement and social contact, and being assertive. The introvert is cortically *over*-aroused and tries to avoid stimulation to keep arousal down to a comfortable level: introverts are characterized by a quiet, reserved demeanour. In terms of conditioning, that is, learning by Pavlovian conditioning or association rather than operant conditioning, the theory maintains that extroverts condition less efficiently than introverts.

Neuroticism, sometimes called emotionality, is said to be related to the functioning of the autonomic nervous system (ANS). Individuals at the high extreme of this continuum are characterized by a very labile ANS, which causes strong reactions to any unpleasant or painful stimuli: high N individuals display moody, anxious behaviour. Low N individuals have a very stable ANS and so display calm, even-tempered behaviour even when under stress. As with E, N is also linked with conditionability: high N leads to poor conditioning because of the vitiating effects of anxiety; low N leads to efficient conditioning. Each individual will manifest both E and N and, as conditionability is related to levels of E and N, it follows that stable introverts (Low N–Low E) will condition best; stable extroverts (Low N–High E) and neurotic introverts (High N–Low E) will be at some mid point; while neurotic extroverts (High N–High E) will condition least well.

The third personality dimension, psychoticism (P), is less well formulated than E and N: while maintaining a genetic basis for P, its biological basis has not been described in detail. P consists of traits such as a preference for solitude, a lack of feeling for others, sensation-seeking, toughmindedness and aggression.

The relationship between personality and crime has been further described and refined (for example Eysenck, 1977; Eysenck and Gudjonsson, 1989). But the principal assumption informing the theory remains that children learn to control anti-social behaviour through the development of a 'conscience': this conscience, Eysenck maintains, is a set of conditioned emotional responses to environmental events associated with the anti-social behaviour. For example, a child who misbehaves receives a parental reprimand, the fear this brings is associated with the anti-social act, and over time this conditioning determines that child's level of socialization. The speed and efficiency of social conditioning will mainly depend upon the individual's personality in terms of E and N. As the High E–High N combination leads to poor conditionability then such individuals will be least likely to learn social control and therefore, it is predicted, will be over-represented in offender populations. Conversely, Low E–Low N would lead to effective socialization, so that these individuals would be predicted to be under-represented in offender groups. The remaining two combinations, High E–Low N and Low E–High N, fall at some intermediate level and so would be expected in both offender and non-offender groups. The third personality dimension, P, is also argued to be strongly related to offending, particularly with crimes that involve hostility towards other people.

Evaluation

Eysenck's theory of crime (or more properly *anti-social behaviour*) has generated a great deal of empirical research. The broad position is that there is unanimous support for the contention that offenders will score highly on P; the majority of studies show that offender samples score highly on N; and the evidence is mixed for E. In seeking to account for the discrepant findings for E, Eysenck suggested that E might be split into two components, Sociability and Impulsiveness, with only the latter related to offending. A study by Eysenck and McGurk (1980) confirmed that an offender sample scored higher than a non-offender sample on Impulsiveness, with no difference between the two samples on a measure of Sociability.

Evidence in support of the theory is presented in a study by McGurk and McDougall (1981), who conducted a cluster analysis of the P, E and N scores of 100 delinquents and 100 non-delinquent college pupils. The analysis showed four personality clusters in each group: both groups contained Low E–High N and High E–Low N clusters, but the clusters predicted to be related to criminal behaviour (High E–High N and High P–High E–High N) were indeed found in the delinquent sample alone. The Low E–Low N group, which the theory would predict to be highly socialized, was found only in the non-delinquent group. However, not all studies using cluster analysis have produced such clear findings.

The weight of empirical evidence lends some support to Eysenck's thesis that there is a relationship between personality (as he defines it) and crime. A number of reservations, as Eysenck acknowledges, need to be made. The theory does not explain all crime and, with its concentration on the high and low extremes of the personality types, is clearly not applicable to all offenders. Further, one of the theoretical bases of the theory, the link between classical conditioning and socialization, remains to be established satisfactorily. Still further, the theory demands acceptance of a trait theory of personality which is only one of a number of ways of conceptualizing personality, and one that has come under fierce attack from proponents of other theoretical approaches to understanding human behaviour.

Clive Hollin

Associated Concepts: biological criminology, conditioning, extroversion/introversion, psychopathy, social control theory

Key Readings

Eysenck, H.J. (1959) *Manual of the Maudsley Personality Inventory.* London: University of London Press.

Eysenck, H.J. (1977) *Crime and Personality,* 3rd edn. London: Routledge and Kegan Paul.

Eysenck, H.J. and Eysenck, S.B.G. (1968) 'A factorial study of psychoticism as a dimension of personality', *Multivariate Behavioural Research* (Special Issue): 15–31.

Eysenck, H.J. and Gudjonsson, G.H. (1989) *The Causes and Cures of Criminality.* London: Plenum Press.

Eysenck, S.B.G. and McGurk, B.J. (1980) 'Impulsiveness and venturesomeness in a detention centre population', *Psychological Reports,* 47: 1299–306.

McGurk, B.J. and McDougall, C. (1981) 'A new approach to Eysenck's theory of criminality', *Personality and Individual Differences,* 2: 338–40.

POLICE BIAS

Definition

The majority of police forces world-wide claim as their mandate preventing crime, bringing law breakers to justice, maintaining the peace and protecting the community. Many pledge to discharge their duties with integrity, respect human rights obligations, treat all sections of the community equally, and deploy only minimum force. However, evidence emanating from North America, Latin America, South Africa, Indonesia, Australia and across the European Union indicates that racial minorities are still at the forefront of discriminatory and abusive policing practices.

Distinctive Features

There are a number of distinctive but interrelated allegations of racially biased police practices that are divided into the over-policing of racial and ethnic minorities and under-policing in relation to the specific law and order needs of these minorities. Allegations of over-policing relate to the discriminatory use of police powers when dealing with members of racial minorities, particularly in relation to the powers of surveillance, traffic stops, street frisks, arrest, detention, investigation and resorting to the excessive use of force. As well as incidents of individual harassment, minority communities have complained about the 'racial profiling' of certain crime categories, saturation policing by specialist police squads, and incursions on cultural and political events, as well as immigration raids. Well-publicized incidents emanating from the USA in the late 1990s dramatized how routine policing in minority neighbourhoods could tip over into extremely coercive and violent forms of social control. New York, during the 1990s, acquired a global reputation for pioneering 'zero tolerance' policing practices that targeted petty crime, low-level disorder and incivility, on the grounds that these were indicators of potentially serious criminal behaviour. The spectacular drop in the official crime rate resulted in 'zero tolerance' policing being exported to Europe and Australia. However, while the crime rate plummeted, the intensive policing practices associated with 'zero tolerance' strained the already frayed relationship between the NYPD and the city's racial minorities. Two incidents provoked a nationwide discussion on the desirability of letting the police off the leash in sensitive multi-racial contexts. In August 1997 it become known that Abner Louima, a Haitian immigrant, was brutalized by white police officers after an altercation outside a nightclub. As this high profile case was making its way through the courts, in February 1999 Amadou Diallo, an unarmed Guinean immigrant street vendor, was shot dead by four white undercover officers from the pro-active Street Crime Unit. What was particularly controversial was the fact that the police officers had fired 41 bullets, with a total of 19 hitting the young African immigrant. In Los Angeles,

during 1999, it was also established that a core group of officers of the Rampart Division of the LAPD were responsible for beating and shooting suspects, fabricating evidence, planting incriminating evidence, and rigging crime scenes in order to entrap suspects. This turned into the biggest police scandal in the history of the LAPD. These sensational revelations were extremely damaging for the police force because they struck at the heart of the force's anti-gang crime fighting methods in some of the city's poorest and most ethnically dense streets. The Rampart scandal revealed a new level of criminality and coined a new criminal justice concept: the gangster cop. In New York and Los Angeles the common complaint voiced was that certain communities were living in fear of the police as well as criminals.

As a result of what they perceive to be constant harassment and discrimination, across a variety of jurisdictions, significant sections of these communities, particularly young people, have become alienated from the police. The ultimate manifestation of the near complete breakdown of the police–community relationship is the anti-police riot. Riots in the UK during the 1980s and in France during the 1990s were precipitated by what were perceived to be heavy-handed police actions in minority neighbourhoods. The USA watched in shock as the most serious riot of the postwar period engulfed South Central Los Angeles, claiming 54 lives and causing millions of dollars' worth of damage. Triggered by the acquittal of four white police officers for the brutal beating of Rodney King, the ferocity of the May 1992 riots indicated the depth of anger, frustration and despair that existed in minority communities. For many respectable community leaders the verdict represented a final loss of faith by African Americans in the fairness of the criminal justice system. It also suggested that white middle-class America was willing to condone the systematic police brutalization and mistreatment of minority populations.

The second facet of racially discriminatory policing relates to the alleged refusal by the police to provide an adequate response to minority community needs. Their critics would claim that responding to the needs of residents in crime-ridden ghettos and inner cities is a lower police priority than responding to the needs of respectable neighbourhoods. For the sake of maintaining public order the police have virtually abandoned certain neighbourhoods. Such a 'hands off' policy effectively leaves these neighbourhoods in the hands of local criminals. Critics also claim to have identified a consistent pattern in the response of the police to racist crimes, that is, the lack of an effective response; a reluctance to prosecute; the definition of such crimes as non-racist; and treating the victim as the criminal and reacting harshly to community self-protection measures. With the recent upsurge of right-wing extremism across the European Union and the increasing seriousness of attacks on guest workers, refugee camps and immigrant communities, the apparent lack of police protection has become a major cause for concern. This lack of intervention stands in stark contrast to over-policing that racial minorities claim they are normally subjected to. In the UK, the murder of black teenager Stephen Lawrence by a gang of young white men in April 1993 propelled the issue of how the police responded to racist crime to the centre of the public debate. A public inquiry was established to examine why the Metropolitan Police had failed to bring the killers to justice and to make recommendations to ensure that such a miscarriage of justice did not happen in future. The report of the inquiry chaired by Sir William Macpherson was published in a blaze of publicity in February 1999. To the consternation of the Metropolitan Police it concluded that the police investigation was characterized by a combination of professional incompetence, institutional racism and a failure of leadership by senior officers. As a result, UK police forces were required to overhaul their approach to the recording, investigation and prosecution of racist crime and ensure that their work practices met the requirements of specific communities. In the USA, during the 1990s, pressure groups began to demand an effective police response

to violence and intimidation directed at minority communities. As a result of prolonged campaigning, federal, state and local authorities began to recognize the category of 'hate crime'. New categories of criminal behaviour and corresponding sentencing guidelines were established and police forces, in certain parts of the country, established specialized investigative units to concentrate on the perpetrators of hate crimes. Similar campaigns to pass 'hate crime' legislation have also been established in Australia and Europe.

Evaluation

Various explanations have been forwarded to account for problematic relations between the police and racial minorities. The orthodox police position tends to deny the problem of racial harassment and discrimination. Police representatives also continue to argue that the real source of the problem is the over-representation of certain racial groups in the criminal statistics. Thus it is suggested that the criminality of certain communities results in proactive policing practices, and in the 'war against crime' there will be casualties. They also point to the anti-police attitudes that are entrenched in these communities. Complaints about harassment and discrimination are interpreted by many police officers as attempts to undermine both the efficiency of anti-police operations and force morale. As far as rank and file police officers are concerned, they are required by law to exercise their powers and they also have a right in the fight against crime to use force where necessary. More enlightened senior officers would argue that the problem of racial prejudice lies in the attitudes of a minority of individual officers rather than the institution. They would also acknowledge that the racist attitude of one officer can destroy the quality of service and non-discriminatory efforts of the rest of the police force. From this perspective, the screening of applicants should be tightened; the psychological testing of potential recruits must be improved; the training in community and race relations should be extended; recruiting practices must be overhauled to ensure that each force is representative of the community they serve; the supervision of frontline officers needs to be intensified; and community outreach programmes should be established.

However research, primarily from the USA and the UK, suggests that racially discriminatory policing is not just the prerogative of a few 'rotten apples'. In the aftermath of the Los Angeles riots there were numerous news reports indicating that, in certain US police forces, racist attitudes were widespread among officers. The alternative explanation argues that the source of this conflictual relationship lay with the police mandate and the structural position of racial minorities. From the late 1960s, it is argued, there has been a fundamental shift as tough law and order tendencies emerged both in the USA and the UK. Those who have suffered most from this reordering of criminal justice policies have been racial minorities. They no longer have any core role to play within the new economic order and are suffering in a disproportionate manner from structural unemployment, the effects of cutbacks in welfare, and urban disinvestment. They are to all intents and purposes politically and socially powerless, existing on the margins of the reconstituted edifice of citizenship. Within this context a potent ideological connection has been made between 'race' and crime and this has provided the *raison d'être* for the introduction of aggressive policing tactics. Racial minorities have been criminalized and scapegoated, and white support has been mobilized for 'the thin blue line'. Related to this perspective is the observation that police forces have utilized news media scares to foster an image of a crisis-ridden threatened society in which racial minorities are responsible for an inordinate amount of predatory criminal activity. As a result, police forces have been able to demand more autonomy and resources in order to be able to meet the challenges of this purported crisis. The police, on this account, have actually contributed to the sense of racial crisis.

From this perspective, suggestions for improving police training and race relations courses, recruiting minority officers and making racism a disciplinary offence will not work because the source of the problem is structural not individual. Racism is institutionalized in the police. The charge of 'institutional racism' has been vehemently denied by police forces in the USA and the UK and by various official inquiries into controversial police actions. However, in the UK, in the first years of the new century, the terms of the debate have changed as a result of the finding that 'institutional racism' played a central role in the inability of the Metropolitan Police to bring the murderers of Stephen Lawrence to justice.

Police forces in the UK have acknowledged the problem of 'institutional racism' and committed themselves to implementing a reform programme that will enable them to become anti-discriminatory public services and ensure that officers do not engage in inappropriate language and behaviour or perpetuate stereotypes. Critics remain sceptical about the ability and willingness of police forces to instigate the policies needed to root out racist and abusive officers and dismantle the 'blue wall of silence'. They argue that external pressure needs to be exercised to force change upon police forces and to monitor the functioning of reforms. In the USA, Human Rights Watch has recommended that federal aid should go only to those police departments that can demonstrate they are taking tangible steps to respect human rights and curb police abuse. The organization also supports the creation and strengthening of civilian review agencies, establishing early warning systems to identify and track officers who are the subject of repeated complaints, and creating a special prosecutors office to pursue cases against police officers accused of criminal conduct.

Eugene McLaughlin

Associated Concepts: institutional racism, racial profiling, racialization, zero tolerance

Key Readings

Cannon, L. (1999) *Official Negligence: How Rodney King and the Riots changed Los Angeles and the Los Angeles Police Department*. Boulder, CO: Westview Press.

Davis, M. (1999) *Ecology of Fear*. New York: Metropolitan Books.

Holmes, M.D. and Smith, B.W. (2008) *Race and Police Brutality*. New York: SUNY Press.

Human Rights Watch (1998) *Shielded From Justice*. New York: Human Rights Watch.

Ioimo, R., Tears, R.S., Leslie A., Meadows, J., Becton, B. and Charles., M.T. (2007) 'The Police View of Bias-Based Policing', *Police Quarterly*, 10 (3): pp. 270–287.

Miller, J.G. (1997) *Search and Destroy*. New York: Cambridge University Press.

POLICING

Definition

The most influential definitional starting-point in sociological discussions of 'policing' is that of Egon Bittner (1975: 39) who claimed that the most distinctive characteristic of 'the police' is that they are 'a mechanism for the distribution of situationally justified force in society'. However, more recently Johnston and Shearing (2003: 9) have argued that as a result of the radical pluralization of the policing function we should adopt the concept of 'governance of security' to encompass 'programmes for promoting peace in the face of threats that arise from collective life'.

Distinctive Features

Definitions of policing which emanate from within police institutions tend to reduce the police function to two main elements: crime control and order maintenance – the oath taken by British constables specifically refers to the prevention of crimes and the preservation of the peace. Empirical studies of the tasks carried out by police officers consistently suggest that the control of crime takes up only a minority of their time. Maintaining order is a better description for much of what they do, with the caveat that this is often carried out in private rather than public and is often as likely to involve the police acting in a social service role rather than as law enforcers.

Policing necessarily involves the exercise of discretion, often in situations where (in contrast to other points in the prosecution process) there are no clear-cut legal guidelines on the correct action to take. Hence it is paradoxically true that one thing that defines policing is the deliberate *non-enforcement* of the law when to do so would threaten to compromise the authority of the officer(s) concerned.

Bittner made it clear that in the vast majority of instances the 'ability to use force' definition ought not to be taken as implying that violence was used in most, or indeed many, police–public interactions. Nevertheless, the police's ability to use force if they deem it necessary structures all kinds of encounters with the public. It also, inevitably, involves the assertion by police officers of control over public space and their implicit demand that the public must respect their authority.

'Policing' is a task which has always been carried out by more people than those specifically labelled as 'police', which in the Common Law countries has tended to be synonymous in popular thought with those officers who have sworn an oath to act in a legal capacity as constables. The increasing *de facto* reliance on private security forces (in the shape of 'bouncers') for order maintenance, in addition to their more accustomed role in dealing with crime in the shape of private security guards, has made this fact more apparent. It has also been rendered more relevant by the recent growth in the UK of various kinds of 'community support officers' and other civilians employed by police forces to carry out roles which were once traditionally the province of sworn officers.

Contemporary developments in the theorization of policing have mainly taken the form of attempting to account for the relative decline of the monolithic 'public-service' or state-centred model of policing, in favour of the emergence of a 'post-Keynsian' (O'Malley and Palmer, 1996) or 'late modern' (Johnston,

2000; Johnston and Shearing, 2003) form of policing. The former version is characterized by the co-operation between police institutions and voluntarily-mobilized community groups, driven by a broader societal shift from a 'welfare liberal' to a 'neo-liberal' model of the state. The latter gives more weight to the influence of risk-oriented thinking which is the product of an endogenous process of development within organizations. Loader (2000) has identified several categorizations of policing which are set to continue to expand at the expense of traditional 'policing by government'. These are 'policing through government', where the state employs private police; 'policing above government', dealing with the pooling of police power in bilateral relationships and international bodies such as the European Union; 'policing beyond government', covering the expanding private security industry; and 'policing below government', which defines various citizen and community initiatives.

Evaluation

In each of Loader's categories the state remains the ultimate arbiter of violence and thus Bittner's original definition remains apposite. The definition considered here looks at narrowly-defined policing. The collective policing (and self-policing) of behaviour, especially among peer groups and in public spaces, could also make a claim to be included as one of society's most important mechanisms of self-control. Yet theoretical models that proclaim power is everywhere mean it is difficult to define where it is concentrated significantly; hence is it better to accept the narrow definition offered above, which necessarily centres around institutions, than attempt to collapse all exercise of authority into the definition of 'policing'.

Johnston (2000) sees the theoretical conflation of the function of policing with the institution labelled 'the police' as an error, given the historically temporary nature of the state's monopoly of force: yet the reach of traditional police forces was never as total, nor their claim to authority as uncontested by

other institutions, as many theorists assume. The concentration in much criminological literature on changes, largely tending towards more 'post-structuralism' in the exercise of crime control and order maintenance policing, needs to be balanced by an appreciation of the continuing role played by police forces in preserving the integrity and power to act of the state and its institutions. The first duty of any police *force* is to protect 'the state, whose coercive arm they are' (Waddington, 1999: 64).

Chris A. Williams

Associated Concepts: 'broken windows', community policing, governance, police bias, private policing, problem oriented policing, racial profiling, transnational policing, zero tolerance

Key Readings

Bittner, E. (1975) *The Functions of the Police in Modern Society: A Review of Background Factors, Current Practices, and Possible Role Models.* New York: Aronson.
Jason-Lloyd, L. (2003) *Quasi-Policing.* London: Cavendish.
Johnston, L. (2000) *Policing Britain: Risk, Security and Governance.* Harlow: Longman.
Johnston, L. and Shearing, C. (2003) *Governing Security: Explorations in Policing and Justice.* London: Routledge.
Loader, I. (2000) 'Plural policing and democratic governance', *Social and Legal Studies,* 9 (3): 323–45.
O'Malley, P. and Palmer, D. (1996) 'Post-Keynsian policing', *Economy and Society,* 25 (2): 137–55.
Waddington, P.A.J. (1999) *Policing Citizens: Authority and Rights.* London: UCL Press.

POLICY TRANSFER

Definition

In its most deterministic reading, the idea of policy transfer implies the wholesale movement of various crime control strategies that have been developed in one jurisdiction and then imported and adopted by others. This suggests something of a global convergence of criminal justice. In a more relativist version it is acknowledged that any such transfer is always subject to 'local' conditions and translations. Here the sensitizing concepts become those of policy networks, 'flows' and divergence, rather than those of a hegemonic jurisdiction, 'transfers' and convergence.

Distinctive Features

The possibility of Anglo-American convergence of social, economic and criminal justice policy tends to dominate the literature on transfer. Although the cross-national movement of policy ideas and political rhetoric is of course by no means new, some political scientists have argued that the USA has become a major source of inspiration for welfare reform in the UK, particularly since the 1980s. This includes 'welfare to work', internal markets in public services, privatization, and any number of 'early intervention' programmes (see for example Dolowitz and Marsh, 2000).

Latterly numerous authors have remarked upon a similar trend affecting British criminal justice (Jones and Newburn, 2007). In England and Wales since the mid-1990s, zero tolerance policing, night curfews, electronic tagging, mandatory minimum sentences, drugs czars, the naming and shaming of young offenders, community courts, private prisons, Chicago-style policing based on neighbourhood focus groups, strict controls over parents and, for a short period in the 1990s, boot camps, have all in some form surfaced in England, having originated in the USA.

A straightforward reading of such a development might be that it is only 'natural' for nation states to look worldwide in efforts to discover 'what works' in preventing crime and to reduce reoffending. But it is also clear that particular lines and directions of transfer involve political choice and strategic decision making. In Britain for example the incoming Labour government of 1997 shifted its ideological

and policy attention away from Western Europe and towards the USA. From this Garland (2001) has been able to trace the emergence of a similar 'culture of control' in both countries. Wacquant (1999) has also noted how law and order talk directed at 'youth', 'problem neighbourhoods', 'incivilities' and 'urban violence' came to increasingly dominate the political and media landscape of the USA in the 1990s. Significantly, he has argued, this 'talk' was also in the process of gradually permeating European public debate such that it had begun to provide the framework for any broader political discussions of justice, safety, community and so on. Wacquant has detailed how various neo-conservative think tanks, foundations, policy entrepreneurs and commercial enterprises in the USA were able to valorize the diminution of the social or welfare state (in the name of neo-liberal economic competitiveness) and the expansion of a penal or punitive state (in order to deal with the economically excluded). He has noted how this mentality 'originates in Washington and New York City, crosses the Atlantic to lash itself down in London, and, from there, stretches its channels and capillaries throughout the Continent and beyond ... [such that] one discerns a solid consensus taking shape between the most reactionary segment of the American Right and the self proclaimed avant-garde of the European "New Left" ...' (Wacquant, 1999: 322, 333). Indeed the export of penal policies from the USA to other advanced industrial economies is a notable feature of twenty-first century penality. Certainly, aspects of zero tolerance policing (France, Australia, Germany, Brazil, Argentina, Ireland), curfews (Belgium, France, Scotland), electronic monitoring (Singapore, Canada, Australia, Sweden, the Netherlands, Scotland), 'scared straight' programmes (Italy), mandatory sentencing (Western Australia, Northern Territories) and pre-trial detention as a 'short, sharp, shock' (Germany, the Netherlands, France) now have a presence in many jurisdictions.

However strong the evidence for the transfer of American punitive policies, it is also clear that criminal justice in numerous western and non-Western jurisdictions has been informed by contra penal trajectories such as those derived from the import of restorative justice conferencing pioneered in New Zealand and Australia. Critics of the 'inevitable' hegemony of US-inspired neo-liberal punitiveness would point out countervailing tendencies at work in numerous justice systems across the world, as expressed for example in various forms of family group conferencing in Australasia, in healing circles in Canada, and in community peace committees in South Africa. In 2002 the United Nation's Economic and Social Council urged all states to adopt the universal principles of restorative justice, including non-coercive offender and victim participation, confidentiality and procedural safeguards. There is also an increasingly important role being developed by the United Nations and the Council of Europe in harmonizing policy in accord with the principles of human rights rather than populist punitiveness (Muncie, 2005).

These examples indeed suggest that there is some remarkable global criminal justice policy travel, but also that this occurs along several dimensions and proceeds in various directions. The transfer of policy is clearly not one directional or one dimensional.

Evaluation

It is vital to note that whilst policy transfer may help to set some parameters of reform it does not necessarily dictate the precise forms of national or local criminal justice policy that are adopted. Newburn (2002) and Nellis (2000), for example, have explored in detail the role of 'agency' in the formulation and implementation of specific policies. Their research has revealed important differences in substance and significant differences in the processes through which policy is reformed and implemented. Newburn (2002) finds that the concept of zero tolerance associated with the New York policing reforms of the early 1990s, although widely praised in the UK, has barely survived its import. The strategies adopted by the NYPD were only employed in some minor experiments in mainstream British policing. Its impact has been more on the level of political rhetoric, fuelled by cross-party commitments in the UK to develop more punitive-sounding policies that can be widely perceived as being 'tough on crime'. Similarly, Nellis's (2000) analysis of the trans-Atlantic transfer of electronic monitoring from the USA to England (but also to Singapore, some Australian states, Sweden and the Netherlands) makes clear that the terms 'inspiration' and 'emulation' rather than 'copying' best describe the processes involved.

The act of transfer might then be better described as *policy learning* or *policy translation*. The simple, deliberate transfer of complete policies, laws and practices from one jurisdiction to another is virtually unachievable. The effects and outcomes vary greatly according to jurisdiction and also to the local circumstances in which they are applied. Differences in legislative frameworks and institutional architecture inhibit a direct transplantation of policies and deeply embedded differences in history, tradition and culture may prevent even a partial replication. These lines of enquiry suggest that policy transfer is never direct and complete but is partial and mediated through national and local cultures (which are themselves changing at the same time).

Nevertheless the logic of assuming we can learn 'what works' from others remains politically seductive. We can expect governments facing 'perpetual crises' of law and order to continually seek 'quick fixes' based upon whatever evaluative and experimental work seems to have been 'successful' elsewhere. Such 'fixes' however may be short-lived and partial unless equal or greater acknowledgment is given to the impact of national policy environments and localized practice cultures (Muncie, 2005; Stenson and Edwards, 2004). In this context it is also imperative to remind ourselves always that policy as rhetoric, policy as codified, and policy as activated and practised on the ground are rarely the same thing – and that each of these will have their own material effects.

John Muncie

Associated Concepts: comparative criminology and criminal justice, evaluation research, global criminology, globalization, human rights, restorative justice, transnational policing, 'what works', zero tolerance

Key Readings

Dolowitz, D. and Marsh, D. (2000) 'Learning from abroad: the role of policy transfer in contemporary policy making', *Governance*, 13 (1): 5–24.

Garland, D. (2001) *The Culture of Control*. Oxford: Oxford University Press.

Jones, T. and Newburn, T. (2007) *Policy Transfer and Criminal Justice: Exploring US Influence over British Crime Control Policy*. Maidenhead: Open University Press.

Muncie, J. (2005) 'The globalization of crime control: the case of youth and juvenile justice', *Theoretical Criminology*, 9 (1): 35–64.

Nellis, M. (2000) 'Law and order: the electronic monitoring of offenders', in D. Dolowitz (ed.), *Policy Transfer and British Social Policy*. Buckingham: Open University Press.

Newburn, T. (2002) 'Atlantic crossings: policy transfer and crime control in the USA and Britain', *Punishment and Society*, 4 (2): 165–94.

Stenson, K. and Edwards, A. (2004) 'Policy transfer in local crime control: beyond naïve emulation', in T. Newburn and R. Sparks (eds), *Criminal Justice and Political Cultures: National and International Dimensions of Crime Control*. Cullompton: Willan.

Wacquant, L. (1999) 'How penal common sense comes to Europeans: notes on the transatlantic diffusion of the neo-liberal doxa', *European Societies*, 1 (3): 319–52.

POLITICAL CRIME

Definition

Political crime has been defined in a number of different ways but, apart from a broad definition which sees all crime as political, most seek to make a distinction between political crime and ordinary crime because of either the different *motivations* or *ideology* of the individuals involved or the different *context* in which the crime takes place.

Distinctive Features

All crime is political in the sense that it is a violation of the criminal law, which itself derives from a political process and defends some value system. Two early materialist proponents of this position, who have been much neglected by criminologists, were Godwin and De Sade (Jenkins, 1984). Godwin rejected all claims that could be made in favour of the state and criminal law and De Sade argued that the criminal law was developed to safeguard property, much of which the powerful had acquired themselves through violence and theft. Property was simply theft. Radical criminology also considered that crime was political in the sense that the processes of 'crime-creation are bound up in the final analysis with the material basis of contemporary capitalism and its structures of law'. Most writers, however, make a distinction between political crime and ordinary crimes because there are important differences in form, context and motivation.

There are a number of definitions that emphasize the *conviction* or *motivation* of the actor. Schafer (1971, 1974), for example, distinguished between the convictional and the conventional criminal. The former commits crime because he or she is convinced about the truth or justification of their own altruistic beliefs. Hagan (1997) defines political crime as criminal activity which is committed for ideological purposes rather than by private greed or passion. He provides a list of different types of motivation and examples of individuals who expressed these: sociopolitical (Robin Hood), religious (Martin Luther), moral or ethical (anti-abortion activists), science (Copernicus or Galileo), and political causes (Nathan Hale, Benedict Arnold). For Hagan, political crime can take two forms: crime by the government or crime against the government. But others argue (for example, Turk, 1982) that political crime should not also include crimes committed by the state.

Closely related to the debate about the definition of political crime is the question of how those who commit these types of offence should be treated when punished. The activities of both the Fenians and the Suffragettes, who both broke the law for political objectives, led to considerable discussion in the late nineteenth and early twentieth centuries over whether political offenders should have special status in prison. Anglo-American law, in general, has, since the early twentieth century, consistently refused to allow a distinction to be made between political and ordinary criminals (Radzinowicz and Hood, 1981).

One exception was the granting of the special status category to prisoners in Northern Ireland under emergency legislation in 1972. When the government tried to abolish it, IRA prisoners went on hunger strike in 1980/81. The then Prime Minister of the United Kingdom, Mrs Thatcher, expressed the government's position in the now famous aphorism: 'A crime, is a crime, is a crime.' In short, no crimes can have political origins and no criminal would be recognized as a political criminal. Notwithstanding this position, subsequently an official government inquiry into the emergency legislation acknowledged a distinction that most people made in Northern Ireland between political criminals and those who were euphemistically described as 'ordinary decent criminals'.

Evaluation

The concept of political crime, however defined, is a key notion in criminology. As Schafer (1974: 8, 22) has pointed out, it is 'pivotal to the understanding of criminology and the whole normative system of society.' It has been a relatively neglected concept. Few criminology textbooks discuss it or provide historical or contemporary examples. Yet the concept challenges a number of taken-for-granted assumptions about crime and its causes. To begin with, it challenges definitions of crime that assume crime to be a relatively unproblematic concept possessing some ontological reality. Events or activities that are defined as criminal are only one set

of a range of harms captured in criminal law. A notion of political crime draws attention to the politics involved in deciding what should or should not be embraced by the criminal law. Second, the concept draws attention to the fact that crime and criminal behaviour are not always negative phenomena. Many people will commit crimes for altruistic purposes, just as people will choose to give blood, and as a direct result of their activities many progressive reforms have been introduced. Third, when defined in terms of the illegal activities of states or governments, it forces a comparison between the extent of harm from political criminals and 'ordinary decent criminals'. In many regions of the world the harm produced through state crime is far greater than through ordinary crime. One problem, however, with the concept when defined in terms of motivation is its relativity. A political criminal today may be a government minister tomorrow.

Paddy Hillyard

Associated Concepts: crime, emergency legislation, genocide, human rights, new criminology, primitive rebellion, radical criminologies, social harm, the state, state crime

Key Readings

Hagan, F.E. (1997) *Political Crime: Ideology and Criminology.* Boston, MA: Allyn and Bacon.

Jenkins, P. (1984) 'Varieties of Enlightenment criminology: Beccaria, Godwin, de Sade', *British Journal of Criminology*, 24 (2): 112–30.

Radzinowicz, L. and Hood, R. (1981) 'The status of political prisoners in England: the struggle for recognition', *The Virginia Law Review*, 65 (8): 1421–81.

Schafer, S. (1971) 'The concept of the political criminal', *Journal of Criminal Law, Criminology and Police Science*, 62 (3): 380–7.

Schafer, S. (1974) *The Political Criminal: The Problems of Morality and Crime.* New York: The Free Press.

Turk, A. (1982) *Political Criminality.* London: Sage.

POPULAR JUSTICE

See: Informal justice

POSITIVISM

Definition

A theoretical approach that emerged in the early nineteenth century which argues that social relations and events (including crime) can be studied scientifically using methods derived from the natural sciences. Its aim is to search for, explain and predict future patterns of social behaviour. In criminology it straddles biological, psychological and sociological disciplines in an attempt to identify the key causes of crime – whether genetic, psychological, social or economic – which are thought to lie largely outside of each individual's control.

Distinctive Features

The key characteristic of positivism is an application of the methods of the natural sciences to the study of social behaviour. It has generally involved the search for cause and effect relations that can be measured in a way that is similar to how natural scientists observe and analyse relations between objects in the physical world. Positivism does not concern itself with the abstract and the unproven, but with the tangible and quantifiable. Through gaining 'objective' knowledge about how behaviour is determined by physiological, psychological and environmental conditions, it is assumed that most social problems can be understood and treated by using the 'positive application of science'.

Whilst it is difficult to identify the precise moment when a positivist criminology emerged, one of the first attempts to apply positivist principles to crime emerged through the work of French and Belgian statisticians in the 1820s. Adolphe Quetelet, for example, found that crime and crime rates, rather than being random and unpredictable, were remarkably constant. He inferred that crime seemed to obey the same law-like irregularities as physical phenomena. However, it is widely assumed that a modern *scientific* criminology began with the advent of a criminal anthropology associated with the work of the Italian physician Cesare Lombroso in the 1870s. By studying the body shapes of executed criminals, Lombroso attempted to prove scientifically that those who broke the law were physically different from those who did not. Such notions were in direct contrast to the prevailing judicial doctrine that was grounded in principles of neo-classicism, one which maintained that, with few exceptions, behaviour was a matter of free will and individual choice. People broke laws because they anticipated that the benefits would outweigh any losses. They acted largely out of hedonism, choosing behaviour that was pleasurable and avoiding that which would give pain. For much of the eighteenth and nineteenth centuries this meant that no defences of criminal acts could be entertained. The arrival of Lombroso's theory remained a significant challenge to the judicial orthodoxy, for if criminality was determined by factors other than rational choice then surely it made little sense to punish offenders – their condition should instead be treated.

By the early 1920s the development of a criminological science – positivism – was to become influential not only in physiology, but also in medicine, psychiatry, psychology and sociology. Offending began to be thought of as being determined by biological and/or cultural antecedents and it was no longer viewed as simply self-determining. By searching for the specific causes (or aetiology) of criminal behaviour, positive criminology assumes that criminality has a peculiar set of characteristics. Accordingly, most research of this type has tried to isolate key differences between criminals and non-criminals. Some theorists have focused on biological and psychological factors, thus locating the sources of crime primarily within the individual, and bringing to the fore questions of individual pathology and abnormality. This approach is central to individual positivism. In contrast, sociological positivism argues that the key causative factors lie in the social contexts external to the individual. Here crime is more a matter of social pathology.

Evaluation

Many of the basic principles of positivism came to be questioned during the 1960s. In particular positivism was criticized for:

- denying the role of human consciousness and meaning in social activity;
- assuming that there was an underlying consensus in society, of which crime was a key violation;
- presenting an over-determined view of human action;
- equating crime with *under*-socialization or social *dis*-organization rather than accepting the validity of different forms of socialization and social organization;
- ignoring the presence and relevance of competing value systems, cultural diversity or structural conflict.

Nevertheless, positivism has maintained a strong presence in contemporary criminological studies. Since the 1970s work has continued on examining the role that genetic structures play in determining patterns of individual behaviour – including crime. Evidence from the Cambridge Study in Delinquent Development has suggested that crime runs in particular families. Poor parenting, low intelligence, hyperactivity and antisocial behaviour have been cited as key predictors of future criminality. Similarly, research on the long-term trends in crime has concluded that property crime increases at times of economic depression whilst personal crime increases at times of economic prosperity. Positivism also retains a popular and political appeal (in both its individual and sociological variants) because of a general reluctance by governments to accept that crime lies beyond their control. However, it also remains the subject of controversy. Some

would argue that the use of the scientific method remains superior to conjecture or polemic, but such methodology carries no automatic guarantee of uncovering the 'truth'. Inaccurate assumptions, misinterpretations, the misapplication of findings and inadequate measures for testing can all conspire to produce not only misleading but also dangerous conclusions. Assumptions are likely to be made about exactly which factors, from a myriad of the potentially relevant, are worthy of study. In this, the selection of particular variables will depend on *a priori* assumptions that the scientist holds about the nature of human behaviour. Positivist modes of study tend to discover various *correlations* between crime and extraneous conditions but can rarely if ever claim to have specified any direct *causes*. Above all, the concept of crime is accepted uncritically.

John Muncie

Associated Concepts: biological criminology, causation, determinism, dispositional theories, genetics, individual positivism, rehabilitation, sociological positivism, somatotyping

Key Readings

Ferri, E. (1901) *Criminal Sociology*. Boston, MA: Little, Brown.
Lombroso, C. (1876) *L'Uomo Delinquente*. Milan: Hoepli.
Lombroso, C. (1913) *Crime: Its Causes and Remedies*. Boston, MA: Little, Brown.
Quetelet, A. (1842) *A Treatise on Man*. Edinburgh: Chambers.

POST-COLONIAL CRIMINOLOGY

Definition

At its most simple, the term 'post-colonial' refers to the historical period after colonialism; it is linked to anti-colonization and decolonization.

A much broader conceptualization of the term would include analysis of the ongoing relationship between the colonial and post-colonial and the signalling of new ways of thinking which have emanated from heterogeneous sources. In this sense the post-colonial is both a condition and a space. Although at the time of writing there is no fully fledged post-colonial criminology, there is a convincing case for such an emergent field of study.

Distinctive Features

The concept 'post-colonial' is most fully developed in the humanities and it refers to the interdisciplinary work of a body of scholars such as Edward Said, Gayatri Spivak and Homi Bhabha, who are involved in a political project of both remembering and promoting new forms of literature from those countries colonized by European imperial powers, particularly England. These new and not so new literatures have the vital role of challenging and disrupting the Western sense of where the 'centre of important things' lies. They also analyse what was left behind in terms of the cultural residues of race and empire. Hybridity, subaltern, interstices, otherness, alterity, double awareness, in-betweenness, rootedness and diaspora are among the key words that mark out the complexities of post-colonial analysis. The post-colonial is vitally important for understanding the shifting cultural relationships between different parts of a thoroughly globalized world. As a mode of critique and challenge, it provincializes much of what passes for general theory and points to its Eurocentricism.

So what work would a post-colonial criminology do? Its initial work would consist of:

- analysing criminology's historical complicity in techniques of colonial governance;
- exposing its practices of interiorization and exteriorization;
- revealing the racialized subjects and categories constructed within and through criminological discourses;
- centring what has been denied, ignored and marginalized;

- working within or in relation to non-European and non-Western criminological 'writings from elsewhere';
- identifying and inscribing what has been silenced by 'the canon' and 'founding gestures' of Western criminology;
- reinterpreting the 'classics' of Western criminology through the application of post-colonialism's key concepts and methodologies;
- acknowledging that the point of departure for understanding Western criminal justice practices might be 'elsewhere';
- producing alternative conceptualizations of 'self-evident' issues;
- deploying strategic essentialism to generate new oppositions;
- formulating discourses of resistance to neo-colonial criminological practices.

Evaluation

Post-colonialization would involve the rethinking and rewriting of criminology's past and present with the overall intention of decolonizing the disciplinary space. This involves interrogating Western criminology not only from the outside but also from within. In the case of 'British' criminology this would involve problematizing its unacknowledged core English identity and reference points. Reading a contemporary post-colonial criminology one would, for example, be conscious of the plurality of cultural meanings attached to words such as 'crime', 'criminal', 'state', 'law and order', 'culture' and 'justice'.

Eugene McLaughlin

Associated Concepts: constitutive criminology, postmodernism, post-structuralism

Key Readings

Chambers, I. and Curtis, L. (eds) (1996) *The Post-Colonial Question: Common Skies and Divided Horizons.* London: Routledge.
Gilroy, P. (1986) *There Ain't No Black in the Union Jack.* London: Hutchinson.

Hall, S., Critcher, C., Jefferson, T., Clarke, J. and Roberts, B. (1978) *Policing the Crisis: Mugging, the State, and Law and Order*. London: Macmillan.

Shohat, E. (1992) 'Notes on the "postcolonial"', *Social Text*, 31/32: 99–113.

Spivak, G. (1993) *Outside in the Teaching Machine*. London: Routledge.

Sumner, C. (1986) *Crime, Justice and Underdevelopment*. Aldershot: Gower.

POSTMODERN FEMINISM

Definition

A strand of feminism informed by postmodernism, post-colonialism and post-structuralism which rejects the notion of the essentialist 'woman' by arguing that the term is culturally constructed in relation and opposition to 'man' and can be deconstructed and reconstructed due to its fluidity.

Distinctive Features

Influenced by post-structuralist theorists such as Derrida and Foucault, postmodern feminists reject not only the notion of 'woman' but also patriarchy and women's subordination. Also referred to as 'post-feminism', this term is misleading, however, as it is often used by the media to define a period of time when feminism is no longer deemed relevant.

Postmodern feminism rejects binary opposites, for example male/female, objectivity/subjectivity, by arguing that concepts are culturally constructed in relation to one another and are therefore unstable. The production of knowledge is questioned and claims to objectivity and the notion of a universal 'truth' are rejected. Postmodern feminists have criticized standpoint theorists by claiming that neither women nor men can ever have total knowledge as all knowledge is partial and situated, and while all standpoints are conflicting none of these are privileged (Haraway, 1991).

Criticisms of postmodern feminism come most strongly from radical feminists who hold that destroying the concept 'woman' will result in less collective activism. There is also concern that postmodern feminism is too 'academic' and will further widen the gap between feminist activists and academics resulting in a form of elitist feminism. It is also accused of dressing up in philosophical (male?) language what feminism has been saying for years – for example, the questioning of 'malestream' knowledge and claims to objectivity originated from other strands of feminism in the early 1980s. These criticisms, along with the rejection of the existence of patriarchy, have led some feminists to classify postmodern feminism as part of the growing backlash against feminism.

Evaluation

Few feminist criminologists accept postmodern feminism as being useful in its entirety, although it is also worth noting that intellectual autobiographies are increasingly offered in an acknowledgement that a researcher's work to some degree will reflect who and what they are. The notion that 'woman' is culturally created through power and language draws parallels with feminist objections to how women are portrayed in court in sexual assault cases. However, the influence that postmodern feminism had in recognizing this is debatable.

While postmodern feminism has been useful in terms of theory, it has limited use in view of the key aims of second-wave feminism, and although epistemological debates have been widely accepted it remains the case that few feminists are able to accept a feminism without sisterhood – a feminism without 'women'. Until criminology is ready to depart from 'modernity' and embrace 'the postmodern', there is little future for a postmodern feminism within criminology or vice versa.

Nicole Westmarland

Associated Concepts: deconstruction, post-colonialism, postmodernism, post-structuralism, radical feminism

Key Readings

Barrett, M. (2000) 'Postfeminism', in G. Browning, A. Halcli and F. Webster (eds), *Understanding Contemporary Society: Theories of the Present*. London: Sage.

Brooks, A. (1997) *Postfeminisms – Feminism, Cultural Theory and Cultural Forms*. London: Routledge.

Haraway, D.S. (1991) *Simians, Cyborgs and Women: The Reinvention of Nature*. London: Free Association Books.

Riley, D. (1988) *Am I That Name? Feminism and the Category of 'Women' in History*. New York: Macmillan.

Smart, C. (1990) 'Feminist approaches to criminology, or postmodern woman meets atavistic man', in A. Morris and L. Gelsthorpe (eds), *Feminist Perspectives in Criminology*. Milton Keynes: Open University Press.

Young, A. (1996) *Imagining Crime*. London: Sage.

POSTMODERNISM

Definition

Postmodern theory in criminology arose in the early 1990s out of the disenchantment with modernist and Enlightenment thought. It privileges non-linear developments, orderly disorder, extreme sensitivity to initial conditions, disproportionate effects, fractal geometry, chance factors, contingency, irony, local knowledge, the decentred subject and the effects of language in the constitution of the subject. It situates its critique and suggestions for reconstruction, or transpraxis, in political economy.

Distinctive Features

Postmodern thought can be traced to French theorists in the 1970s and 1980s. Several of these formed the kernel of the first wave: Baudrillard, Cixous, Deleuze, Derrida, Foucault, Guattari, Irigaray, Kristeva, Lyotard, Moi. Many were influenced by Nietzsche and more recently by Jacques Lacan, a revisionist Freudian who integrated the works of Benveniste, Jakobson, Kojeve, de Saussure, Strauss and topology theory. He was to give Freud's early work a linguistic spin (the 'unconscious structured like a language'). Second wave theorists who emerged in the late 1980s and 1990s have since applied this body of theory to law, criminology, cultural and media studies, and clinical and literary criticism.

Postmodern thought differs from modernist thought along several dimensions (see Milovanovic, 1997).

- *Society and social structure.* Modernist thought, such as typified by the works of Durkheim, Parsons and Luhmann, privileges order, stability, linear developments, equilibrium and homeostatic analysis. Postmodern analysis privileges order *and* disorder (orderly disorder), far-from-equilibrium conditions, non-linear change, chance, indeterminacy, contingency and irony. Rather than rigid structures such as bureaucracies, postmodern analysis privileges 'dissipative structures' which are very sensitive and responsive to their environment.

- *Social roles.* Modernist thinkers often rely on a Parsonian notion of the person whereby s/he is seen as a role player on various stages, reading specific scripts. Through socialization one is cast into various roles. For postmodernists, roles are unstable constructions; a person is always a role-maker.

- *Subjectivity/agency.* Modernists celebrate the notion of the individual (the centred subject) best typified in *Cogito, ergo sum.* This is the conscious, determining, reflective, rational and unitary person, epitomized in the notion of the juridic subject, the 'reasonable man in law'. Postmodernists offer the idea of the decentred subject, a person who is less in control and more located in various languages and what they allow.

- *Discourse.* Modernist thought assumes language is neutral; it is but an instrument for use in verbalizing a person's desire. Postmodernists argue that discourses are rather linguistic co-ordinate systems, and language is always already populated with voices. It is never a neutral medium.

- *Knowledge.* Modernist thought privileges global knowledge and foundational truths that can be arrived at through the scientific method. Postmodernists see knowledge as always partial, fractured, fragmented and contingent. They focus on Pathos (suffering, struggle, overcoming) rather than Logos (logic and rationality).
- *Space/time.* Modernist thought situates itself in Newtonian physics of space and time and in Euclidean geometry. Linearity, stasis, determinism and stability are privileged. Postmodernists on the other hand hold up quantum mechanics, non-Euclidean geometry, topology theory, fractal geometry, 'striated space' and the irreversibility of time, among others.
- *Causality.* Modernist thought privileges determinism, linear causality and the inherent potential for discovering all laws of nature. Postmodernists, however, say 'God plays dice'. Quantum and chaos theories indicate the centrality of chance and indeterminacy as well as disproportionate effects.
- *Social change.* Modernists assume a linear development in historical change, whether Hegelian (Absolute Spirit), Marxian (dialectical materialism), Weberian (rationalization) or Durkheimian (a Darwinian-driven division of labour). Postmodernists identify non-linear change, orderly disorder, continuity and discontinuity as existing side by side, singularities which are moments in which accurate understanding breaks down, and disproportionate effects (small changes may have large, unanticipated results).

The emerging perspective has several prominent threads, some of which have been integrated and some not.

- *Discourse analysis.* The most significant form has been Lacanian psychoanalytic semiotics. It assumes the interconnectedness of the subject and discourse. The subject of desire finds her/his co-ordinates of being in various discourses which 'speak the subject'. Lacan has offered the notion of the decentred subject in a static form (Schema L) and in more dynamic forms (Graphs of Desire, Schema R, Schema I, Borromean Knots). In criminology, discourse analysis is important for realizing how various social realities get constructed and how some become more stable and privileged. In postmodern society a new reality has been constructed through the media, the 'hyper-real', which has become the co-ordinate for social action.
- *Chaos theory.* Chaos theory has offered several novel conceptualizations that challenge modernist ideological constructions. These offer the notion of attractors (points toward which dynamic systems tend), iteration (continuous feedback loops that lead to disproportionate effects), a sensitive dependence on initial conditions (small changes may, after iteration, produce disproportionate and unexpected results), fractal geometry (in-between dimensions exist beyond the integer space that is privileged in modernist thought), far-from-equilibrium conditions (dynamic states that refuse closure) and dissipative structures ('structures' that are extremely sensitive to initial conditions, which take on only tentative, contingent stable forms, and are always in the process of becoming). Criminological theory has seen several recent approaches applying these conceptualizations (see the collection of essays in Milovanovic, 1997).
- *Catastrophe theory.* This approach, pioneered by Thom (1975), argues for discontinuities appearing in otherwise continuous systems. It provides a topology of various generic forms of catastrophe, depending on the number of variables that are relevant. It also identifies bimodal behaviour in each at the 'fold' region, which represents discontinuous change. For an application to explain 'seductive' forms of crime ('edgework') see Milovanovic (1996) and for insights on developing alternative conflict resolutions see Milovanovic (1999).
- *Topology theory.* Perhaps least understood, topology is referred to as a 'rubber maths'.

Only recently, perhaps through Lacan's extensive use, has it begun to emerge in situating behaviour on more complex, interacting planes for expository purposes. It is more useful as a discovery principle that indicates some insight on complex dynamics. For an application in explaining nonmaterial forms of crime see Milovanovic (1996) and for general theorizing in criminology see Arrigo (1998).

Two approaches have been at the cutting edge in integrating various of these threads into criminology:

- *Constitutive criminology.* Constitutive theory argues for the interconnectedness of phenomena and co-production in the manifestation of phenomena. It offers the notion of COREL sets in indicating historical specificities of configurations of coupled iterative loops that have often unexpected effects. Thus alternative notions of 'cause', 'harms', 'reduction' and 'repression' have been conceptualized.
- *Postmodern feminism.* Several theorists have spearheaded postmodern analysis in criminology and law. They have offered an 'ethical feminism' as opposed to a hate politics, 'contingent universalities' and new understandings of the subject in law, textual constructions of the female offender, and concepts for a social justice.

Evaluation

Postmodern criminology began to bloom in the late 1990s. Early forms (prior to 1990) were heavily criticized for their nihilism, fatalism and relativism, and best identified in battle cries for a 'reversal of hierarchies' and 'anti-foundationalism'. This is called the 'nihilistic form of postmodernism'. More mature forms are 'affirmative postmodernism', which is rooted not in reaction-negation dynamics but in a Nietzschean call for the affirmative. This is called transpraxis; in other words, not just a reaction and criticism (negation) directed towards what is, but also visions for a possible better society that are

offered simultaneously. At a minimum, postmodernist thought has ushered in considerable debate in criminology on re-thinking causation, subjectivity, responsibility and forms of organization. The work that is now appearing is beginning to integrate the various dimensions of postmodern analysis and apply these to difficult issues in criminology. More recently, critical race theory has also begun to utilize and develop the conceptual tools provided by postmodern theorizing.

Dragan Milovanovic

Associated Concepts: chaos theory, constitutive criminology, cultural criminology, deconstruction, discourse analysis, integrative criminology, postmodern feminism, post-structuralism, praxis, psychoanalytic criminology, virtual criminology

Key Readings

Arrigo, B. (1998) 'Theories of crime and crimes of theories: on the topological construction of criminological reality', *Theory and Psychology*, 8 (2): 219–53.

Henry, S. and Milovanovic, D. (1996) *Constitutive Criminology.* London: Sage.

Milovanovic, D. (1996) 'Postmodern criminology', *Justice Quarterly*, 13 (4): 567–609.

Milovanovic, D. (1997) *Chaos, Criminology and Social Justice.* New York: Praeger.

Milovanovic, D. (1999) 'Catastrophe theory, discourse, and conflict resolution', in B. Arrigo (ed.), *Social Justice/Criminal Justice.* Belmont, CA: Wadsworth.

Thom, R. (1975) *Structural Stability and Morphogenesis.* Reading, MA: Benjamin.

POST-STRUCTURALISM

Definition

Post-structuralism refers to a variety of theoretical perspectives that succeeded structuralism in France. Indebted to Nietzsche's critique of reason and rationality, post-structuralists look for the tensions and contradictions and the irrational in discursive formations. In criminology, post-structuralism remains most closely associated with the work of Michel Foucault.

Distinctive Features

Structuralism originated in the linguistic studies of language undertaken by Ferdinand de Saussure (1857–1913). It was subsequently taken up by Lévi-Strauss, Lacan and Althusser who applied structural-linguistic concepts to the humanities and social sciences in an attempt to construct a more coherent mode of analysis. Structuralists favoured holistic forms of analysis that characterized phenomena in terms of parts and wholes, defining structure as the interrelation of parts of a common system. Revealing the underlying codes, rules and functions that organized phenomena into a social system was the purpose of structuralist analysis. Structuralists believed in objectivity, logic, unity, coherence, self-sufficiency, rigour and truth, and claimed social scientific status for their theorizing. In doing so they rejected humanist approaches such as phenomenology and existentialism, with their stress on the subject and subjectivity. Meanings are constituted not by conscious subjects but by relations among the parts of a system. Criminology has always been home to structuralist approaches such as structural functionalism and structural Marxism. Both of these share a belief in their social scientific ability to identify the underlying causes that generate particular patterns of criminal behaviour, and emphasize materiality and the primacy of structure over agency. Although French structuralist debates had little impact on criminology, Althusser's writings on scientific Marxism – with its emphasis on structural causality – and his reading of ideology did resonate within left-wing criminology in the UK in the late 1970s.

Post-structuralism is both a reaction against and a complication of structuralist insights and can be found in the work of writers such as Derrida, Foucault, Deleuze and Kristeva. Post-structuralists question the assumption that systems are self-sufficient structures and that theorists can somehow position themselves outside and independent from that which they are analysing. For post-structuralists there is no 'outside' position (whether in language or politics) from which to critique. The world, rather than existing separate from the ways we talk about it, is constructed in discourse. Post-structuralists also challenge the structuralist claim to scientific status, preferring to view science as a discourse that is constituted through and embodies the social relations of power that underpin its claims to truth. It is worth noting that the post-structuralists are also dismissive of structuralism's claims to clarity, opting for a mode of address and argumentation marked by density, impenetrability, ambiguity and incoherence. Post-structuralism not only re-centres the subject – it also constructs a subject that is fragmentary and contradictory. Consequently, it stresses the importance of differences over unity. As a result of post-structuralism's anti-essentialism, greater attention was paid to theorizing subjectivity, agency and power. Post-structuralism has had a major influence on feminist and postmodernist theorizing.

Derrida developed deconstruction as a method for destabilizing and decentring modern philosophy's claims to truth. Deconstruction involves looking at a system, examining how it has been built, and then identifying the keystones and defining angles that support its structure. By moving the component pieces around, one can free oneself from the authority and logics of the system. In its analysis of texts, deconstruction identifies the key processes of signification, looking for the incoherences, instabilities and ambivalences within texts, locating the traces of oppositional elements, and reversing the normal patterns of interpretation. Deconstruction is radically disruptive because it first of all reverses and then seeks to replace 'natural' oppositions such as nature/culture, male/female and object/subject. For Derrida these oppositions are restrictive substitutes for thinking.

Post-structuralism impacted on criminology via Michel Foucault's anti-realist and anti-essentialist *Discipline and Punish* (1977). In this book he presented not a history but an 'archaeology' or 'genealogy' of the transformation of the notion of punishment and the birth of the prison. Foucault's intention was to lay to rest those congratulatory histories of the modern prison which told a story of progress, reform and enlightenment. For Foucault, what was significant in the transformation of a mode of punishment that depended on the infliction of bodily pain and public theatrical spectacle, to one organized around incarceration, regulation, surveillance and a reformation of the mind, was not whether it was better or more humane but how it represented the reorganization of disciplinary knowledge/power. In his view the techniques and rationales embedded in Bentham's proposed 'Panopticon' – surveillance, classification, examination – were the embodiment of this shift to a new modality of control. The prison was but one representative institution of the carceral society where disciplinary power/knowledge was exercised within a multitude of institutional practices. Foucault's analysis of the prison also provides us with an answer to the question of why the new model prison failed to reform offenders. Discussions that focus on the 'success' or 'failure' of the prison are inappropriate. The prison cannot fail because 'it is not intended to eliminate offences, but rather to distinguish them, to distribute them, to use them'.

Evaluation

A post-structuralist Foucauldian perspective on the constitution of power/knowledge has provided criminologists with a vital set of conceptual tools for analysing official texts across a wide range of criminal justice settings and for undertaking histories of the present. The work of feminists writers such as Vikki Bell (on incest), Carol Smart (on law) and Alison Young (on postmodern criminology) signifies the intellectual power of post-structuralist ideas.

Eugene McLaughlin

Associated Concepts: deconstruction, discourse analysis, essentialism, panopticism, postmodern feminism, postmodernism, social control

Key Readings

Bell, V. (1993) *Interrogating Incest: Feminism, Foucault and the Law.* London: Routledge.

Berman, A. (1996) *From the New Criticism to Deconstruction: The Reception of Structuralism and Post-Structuralism.* Urbana, IL: University of Illinois Press.

Foucault, M. (1977) *Discipline and Punish.* Harmondsworth: Penguin.

Smart, C. (1995) *Law, Crime and Sexuality.* London: Sage.

Young, A. (1995) *Imagining Crime.* London: Sage.

PRAXIS

Definition

Praxis refers to the link between theory and practice, and the struggle that exists in all intellectual movements to transform existing (oppressive or marginalizing) societal conditions into meaningful reflection, action and change. It is a complicated and intricate phenomenon because it entails a re-constitution of culture, institutions, relationships and social interaction, such that a more humane, emancipatory climate of pro-social civic life prevails. Moments of praxis, then, redirect our entire way of being from the alienating constraints of identity politics towards the unifying dynamics of a pluralistic society. Self-determination, intentionality, sociality and creativity are cornerstones of praxis and the new social order it endorses.

Distinctive Features

The notion of praxis has its roots in the work of Karl Marx. Marxism is a dialectical and historical theory of human progress that responds to the economic and social problems associated with (advanced state-regulated) capitalism. For Marx (1868) praxis was that moment in which 'the free development of each [was] the free development of all'. According to Marxist thought, praxis is a political and economic effort designed to change the conditions that give rise to psychological alienation and social oppression. Indeed, during the period in which Karl Marx lived and wrote, people were alienated from their labour, from their fellow workers, and from themselves. Under such conditions, change was necessary and inevitable. The source of this change was a blend of scholarly enquiry and political action; namely, praxis.

Others have contemporized Marx's notions on praxis and applied his insights in different social science contexts. For example, the dialogical and liberation pedagogy of Paulo Freire (1985: 50) calls for *conscientization*. The purpose of conscientization is for the oppressed to 'exercise the right to participate consciously in the socio-historical transformation of their society'. Freire was particularly interested in how the oppressed (such as the poor, the illiterate, the disenfranchised) could function as cultural revolutionaries. The key to transformation is reflection and dialogue in which the subjugated speak 'true words' about themselves, about the conditions in which they live, and about the necessary and inevitable process by which change (an alternative, emancipatory reality) can materialize.

Feminists, especially Marxist and socialist feminists, have appropriated Marx's notion of praxis. Both claim that the conditions in which women find themselves are related to the state of 'malestream' praxis and the culture of patriarchy and capitalism. Women's liberation is rooted in transforming the sexual division of labour and reconstituting society's notions of masculinity, femininity, competition, hierarchy and production. Feminist praxis entails endorsing such interventions as consciousness-raising, connectivity, the primacy of relationships, and 'the personal is political'.

Postmodernists have further refined the Marxist notion of praxis by utilizing the concept of 'transpraxis.' Transpraxis retains the Marxist conviction that theory and practice need to be linked to produce change; however, it also addresses the role of language in such transformations. Transpraxis involves the dialectics of linguistic struggle in which the new, reconstituted order does not recreate conditions of alienation and oppression. It is a deliberate and affirmative attempt not to reverse hierarchies but, instead, to affirm those who victimize, marginalize and criminalize while also renouncing their victimizing, marginalizing and criminalizing practices. Transpraxis is an effort to validate the act of resistance. The key to transpraxis is found in speech, words, grammar and how we talk about (and then act upon) emancipation.

Evaluation

Praxis (or transpraxis) symbolizes efforts to alter and improve the conditions in which people live, work and engage others. Critical and radical criminology have been more closely linked with the Marxist notion of praxis. Socialist feminist criminologists have similarly relied upon the Marxist concept, infusing it with a sensitivity to gender politics. Postmodern criminologists (particularly constitutive criminologists) have also appropriated the idea of transpraxis in their explanation of crime, criminals and criminal behaviour.

Bruce Arrigo

Associated Concepts: constitutive criminology, critical criminology, feminist criminologies, Marxist criminologies, political crime, postmodernism

Key Readings

Eisenstein, Z. (ed.) (1979) *Capitalist Patriarchy and the Case for Socialist Feminism.* New York: Monthly Review Press.
Freire, P. (1972) *Pedagogy of the Oppressed.* New York: Herder and Herder.
Freire, P. (1985) *The Politics of Education.* South Hadley, MA: Bergin and Garvey.
Henry, S. and Milovanovic, D. (1996) *Constitutive Criminology: Beyond Postmodernism.* London: Sage.
Marx, K. and Engels, F. (1845–6) *The German Ideology.* New York: International Publishers.
Marx, K. (1868) *Capital,* 3 vols. New York: International Press.

PREDICTION STUDIES

Definition

The aim of prediction studies is to find the variables (risk factors) that most accurately predict the likelihood of offending (or more usually) reoffending. It is held that knowledge of accurate predictors of offending is both important theoretically and practically valuable, as, for example, in informing parole decisions.

Distinctive Features

Prediction studies are characterized by two elements: first, a definition of the *criterion* of concern; second, an identification of the *predictors* (or risk factors) for the specified criterion. For example, prediction studies may be concerned with the specific criterion of *violent* offending by males. The aim of the research therefore would be to find the specific predictors of male violent offending. There are two types of predictors: *static* predictors are risk factors that cannot change, such as criminal history, family background and employment record; *dynamic* predictors are risk factors that can change, such as level of drinking, employment or relationships.

There are also two main styles for conducting prediction studies. *Actuarial prediction* seeks to statistically analyse data gathered across a range of potential predictors in order to identify those predictors that perform best in predicting the given criterion. *Clinical prediction* relies on individuals, teams or case conferences to make predictions as to the likelihood of future offending. The generally accepted position, dating from Meehl's seminal (1954) text, is that statistical prediction is superior to clinical prediction.

Attempts at predicting risk can have various outcomes, each of which will have very different implications for those involved. Strong predictors for a given criterion will produce high levels of *true positive* and *true negative* outcomes. In other words, the predictors will correctly predict either the occurrence or absence of the criterion. These 'true'

outcomes, positive and negative, are known as 'hits'. A *false positive* outcome arises when the presence of the predictors indicates the outcome will occur but it does not arise; while a *false negative* refers to the situation when, in the absence of predictors, the criterion of risk actually does occur. 'False' outcomes are generally called '*misses*'.

The first attempts at a prediction of reoffending were made by criminologists in the 1920s (e.g., Burgess, 1928). These mainly relied on the measurement of a range of potential static risk factors for reoffending, typically information gleaned from demographic and criminological records, followed by statistical calculations to determine those factors that best predicted the outcome (that is, recidivism). This tradition has continued into more recent times with the development of several actuarial prediction instruments based on static factors for use with general offender populations.

Examples of actuarial scales used to predict offending include the California Base Expectancy Scale, the Salient Factor Scale and the Offender Group Reconviction Scale. The Salient Factor Scale, developed and refined in studies conducted within the US Parole Commission, is an actuarial scale that contains only static risk factors. It is a six-item checklist that produces a score from 0 to 10 points: the higher the score, the lower the likelihood of reconviction, with bands of scores used to categorize risk. Hoffman (1994) reported a long-term follow-up of the Salient Factor Score on three samples of prisoners released from prison and concluded that the scale had retained its predictive accuracy over the seventeen-year period in which the various samples of offenders were released.

While prediction scales based on static factors can be accurate, by definition they cannot give any indication of a change in risk. However, the new generation of 'risk-need' scales have been designed to include dynamic as well as static risk factors. For example, the Level of Supervision Inventory-Revised (LSI-R) is completed through file review and interview, and assesses a range of risk factors, including 'static' factors such as previous convictions and 'dynamic' factors such as alcohol problems and employment. The pattern of scores identifies specific areas of offender need (to inform service providers), while the total score can be translated into a risk band for future offending (Andrews and Bonta, 1995). The empirical evidence supporting the LSI-R as a measure of risk and needs is strong: Gendreau et al. (1996) concluded their review of predictors of adult recidivism with the view that the LSI-R was the current measure of choice.

Evaluation

It is plain that in risk assessment the stakes can be high for all concerned: in working with offenders, the assessment of risk can influence sentencing decisions, the type of disposal, the appropriate level of security, parole, a breach of probation order, and the level and intensity of interventions. Research aiming to produce a valid and reliable method to estimate the likelihood of an individual reoffending depends on measurement of two variables. The first necessity is for an accurate measurement of offending; the second is for an accurate measurement of the predictors of risk, whatever these may be, for the type of offence under consideration. It is plain that there is considerable room for error in the measurement of these variables. It follows that any scales produced should be sufficiently tried and tested in order to be as robust as possible.

Clive Hollin

Associated Concepts: evaluation research, risk, risk factor research, 'what works'

Key Readings

Andrews, D.A. and Bonta, J. (1995) *LSI-R: The Level of Supervision Inventory-Revised.* Toronto: Multi-Health Systems.

Burgess, E.W. (1928) 'Factors determining success or failure on parole', in A.A. Bruce, A.J. Harno, E.W. Burgess and J. Landesco (eds), *The Workings of the Indeterminate Sentence Law and the Parole System in Illinois.* Springfield, IL: Illinois State Board of Parole.

Gendreau, P., Little, T. and Goggin, C. (1996) 'A meta-analysis of predictors of adult offender recidivism: what works', *Criminology,* 34: 401–33.

Hoffman, P.B. (1994) 'Twenty years of operational use of a risk prediction instrument: the United States Parole Commission's Salient Factor Score', *Journal of Criminal Justice,* 22: 477–94.

Meehl, P.E. (1954) *Clinical Versus Statistical Predictions: A Theoretical Analysis and a Review of the Evidence.* Minneapolis, MN: University of Minnesota Press.

PRIMARY DEVIATION

See: Labelling; Social reaction

PRIMITIVE REBELLION

Definition

In Eric Hobsbawm's original (1959) formulation, primitive rebellion is defined as a form of social movement or social agitation that is 'pre-political' in the sense that the protagonists 'have not yet found, or only begun to find, a specific language in which to express their aspirations about the world'.

Distinctive Features

Primitive rebellion as used by Hobsbawm referred to 'pre-political' social agitation in the nineteenth and twentieth centuries, particularly millenarianism, labour sects, the city mob, the Mafia and the 'social bandit'. It is in relation to social banditry, and his related notion of 'social crime', that this work on primitive rebellion has produced the most impact on criminology. Hobsbawm himself restricted social banditry to peasant societies, on the grounds that it was a backward-looking protest, one that fought for a traditional vision of a just world while having next to no organization and being 'totally unadaptable' to modern social movements. In his later treatment of social banditry (Hobsbawm, 1969) he developed this view to stress that social banditry may operate as a surrogate for a social movement through its symbolic representation of peasant discontents. In this way, many 'less than ideal' bandits have been raised to the status of social bandit, simply because they provided the poor with their only available overt symbols of resistance.

The notion of primitive rebellion proved attractive to conflict and class oriented radical criminologists of the 1960s and 1970s, particularly those sharing Hobsbawm's Marxist leanings. Thus, Australian work focusing on the 'Kelly Outbreak' of the 1880s developed the nexus between crime and class struggles over land, locating the critical feature of social banditry in the social support that the rural poor provided for bandits – not just food, shelter and information, but also their non-cooperation with the authorities. Such work confirmed Hobsbawm's views that when organized political movements emerged to take up the cause of the downtrodden, social bandits would be deprived of their conditions of existence (O'Malley, 1979).

Bringing together rebellion and political 'primitivism', not only in the form of social banditry but also in the category of the urban 'mob', provided a foundation for criminologists and historians seeking to understand crime among the poor and minorities. Such work focused on social crime in the eighteenth and nineteenth centuries, including poaching, smuggling, Luddism, haystack burning, and other crimes interpreted as upholding the old 'moral economy' and traditional rights of the poor. It sought to give a voice to poor criminals whose offences were related to resisting the egregious exploitation associated with early capitalist development. Much of this work echoed Hobsbawm's caution that such criminals would not simply appear as heroic and attractive, but often as bloody, reactionary and barbarous as well. Even so, the characterization of contemporary urban street crime as a primitive rebellion and 'social crime' by some criminologists in the 1970s led to others becoming highly critical of tendencies that 'romanticized' hoodlums and thugs.

Nevertheless, an recent attempt has been made to revive this line of analysis. Citing the emergence of new, urban 'dangerous classes', their exclusion from capitalist relations, and their participation in alternative economies, Lea (1999) has suggested that Hobsbawm's notions of primitive rebellion and social crime may once again enter criminological currency.

Evaluation

Primitive rebellion sensitized a generation of social historians and critical criminologists to the nexus between popular crime and politics, by broadening the notion of politics to include the expressions of the inchoate and ignorant and by linking these to 'criminal' acts of resistance where criminal law operated as a means of oppression. Equally important, it provided a vital stimulus for developing a critical historiography within criminology. The historical analyses associated with E.P. Thompson and his colleagues, that owed much to Hobsbawm's pioneering work, remain one of the most lasting, scholarly and elegant contributions to criminology. Such work added considerable sophistication to a radical criminological theory that had become prone to a rather literal and unsubtle translation of Marxist theory. However, the concept of primitive rebellion has occupied a limited and diminishing place in criminology in the past two decades and it seems unlikely that it will recover the high profile it held during the 1970s. Its decline can probably be linked to the crystallization of anti-romanticism into left realism during the 1980s. Additionally, the current theoretical environment has rather turned its back on class oriented accounts and related forms of radical theory – in particular Marxist theory. Nevertheless, especially if Hobsbawm's own cautions about romanticism are heeded, this primitive rebellion still seems to promise much for analysis of the inchoate politics of some forms of contemporary crime among the underclass and the excluded. Its implications for feminist criminology have yet to be explored.

Pat O'Malley

Associated Concepts: critical criminology, left idealism, Marxist criminologies, moral economy, political crime

Key Readings

Hay, D., Thompson, E. and Linebaugh, P. (eds) (1975) *Albion's Fatal Tree: Crime and Society in Eighteenth Century England.* London: Allen Lane.
Hobsbawm, E. (1959) *Primitive Rebels: Studies in Archaic Forms of Social Movement in the 19th and 20th Centuries.* Manchester: Manchester University Press.
Hobsbawm, E. (1969) *Bandits.* Harmondsworth: Penguin.
Lea, J. (1999) 'Social crime revisited', *Theoretical Criminology,* 3: 307–26.
O'Malley, P. (1979) 'Class conflict, land and social banditry: bushranging in nineteenth century Australia', *Social Problems,* 26: 271–83.
Thompson, E. (1977) *Whigs and Hunters: The Origins of the Black Act.* London: Allen Lane.

PRIVATE POLICING

Definition

A growing body of criminologists have been critical of a tendency within the discipline to conflate the term 'policing' with the work of the public police (e.g., Johnston and Shearing, 2003), seeking to take account of the growing prominence of other agencies within this sphere and particularly that of private security. No precise definition for the term 'private policing' can be offered, due to the definitional complexities associated with both the concept of 'privateness' and the activity of 'policing' (see Jones and Newburn, 1998; Wakefield, 2003). It has typically been the case, however, that in those literatures making

reference to 'private policing' within their title or text, the focus rests on the staffed, uniformed sector of the private security industry which supplies security officers to protect distinct territorial areas.

Distinctive Features

Internationally, the private security industry has grown remarkably in size and profile. The reasons for this include growing safety concerns within organizations and among private individuals; the expansion of privately controlled, publicly accessible urban developments such as the shopping mall, business complex or gated residential community; and an increasing tendency for public and private sector organizations to contract out their noncore services including security roles.

The expansion of private security has been part of a process duplicated in many countries, whereby the primacy of the public police has begun to diminish with the proliferation of alternative service providers. Bayley and Shearing have, controversially, gone so far as to postulate that developed democratic societies have reached a new historical era within policing. They have argued that 'Modern democratic countries such as the United States, Britain and Canada have reached a watershed in the evolution of their systems of crime control and law enforcement. Future generations will look back on our era as a time when one system of policing ended and another took its place' (1996: 585). Their pluralist analysis of policing has been developed further by Johnston and Shearing, who favour the term 'security governance' over that of 'policing' and portray this activity as now being 'the collective responsibility of networks of commercial and non-commercial "partners"' (2003: 141) rather than just that of the public police. The division of labour in policing, and specifically the boundaries of public and private policing, continue to be a key focus of policing scholars, and Jones and Newburn (1998) offer a helpful analytical framework based around the sectoral, spatial, legal, functional and geographical divisions between policing agencies.

Key to understanding the nature and objectives of private policing is an appreciation of the functions of private security officers. Shearing and Stenning (1981) emphasized how, for security personnel, there was no legally defined public duty to act in furtherance of the public interest, in contrast with the requirements upon the public police. In keeping with this association with private interests is their preventative approach, oriented towards the protection of assets and a maximization of profits, and with an emphasis on 'loss prevention' as opposed to 'crime prevention'. In an analysis of the wide range of tasks undertaken by security personnel within three publicly accessible leisure venues, Wakefield (2003) identified six broad functions. These were 'housekeeping' (helping to maintain the fabric of buildings and the safe running of the venues), 'customer care', 'preventing crime and anti-social behaviour', 'enforcing rules and administering sanctions' (when visitors failed to comply with the required behavioural standards for the venues), 'responding to emergencies and offences in progress', and 'gathering and sharing information' (documenting information and evidence about activities and incidents, sometimes for disclosing such to other policing agencies).

Another important dimension to studying private policing is the issue of accountability within the private security industry. It has repeatedly been alleged in literature on the industry's accountability mechanisms that these provisions are weak and insufficient when compared with those applying to the public police, although most critiques have only focused on the legislative constraints and regulatory mechanisms related directly to the security industry. One exception has been that undertaken by Stenning (2000), who identified a number of legal protections that extended beyond the various mechanisms for the statutory and/or self-regulation of the private security industries in different countries. He argued that public authorities tended to be more willing to prosecute private security personnel than police officers for breaches of criminal laws (e.g., the use of excessive force); that civil suits (e.g., for false arrest, false imprisonment or negligence) against security personnel or organizations have tended to be more successful than those brought against the police; and that employment law, contractual liability (including insurance contracts) and marketplace accountability have also provided checks on the practices of private security. One might add to this list of formal structures the management practices and disciplinary mechanisms that are adopted within security companies and corporations' in-house security departments – namely, private systems to deter or punish wrongdoing by managers and staff (see Wakefield, 2003). Continuing research on the regulation and accountability of private security is needed, including attention being given to the inter-agency policing partnerships – both formal and informal – in which security personnel often become involved.

Evaluation

The appropriate boundaries of public and private policing, and the rightful place of private security within policing, remain a topical area for criminological debate. While critics of private security often focus on its underlying profit motive in order to argue that it cannot operate for the public good in the same way as a state-funded police force, the increasing status of private security has proven difficult to stem. Johnston and Shearing's (2003) 'nodal model' of security governance reflects their recognition that the pluralization of policing has been an irreversible effect of governmental transformations in Western industrial democracies. Wakefield (2003) argues for a refocusing of policing scholars' attention, one that shifts away from the respective roles of the many policing bodies and moves towards the legislative and policy context in which policing activities take place. She views the surveillance-oriented and exclusionary strategies that are becoming more and more prevalent within both public and private policing styles as being issues for greater concern, as these impact adversely on citizens' human rights and civil liberties as societies become increasingly preoccupied with the management and elimination of risk.

Alison Wakefield

Associated Concepts: actuarialism, governmentality, policing, risk, security, surveillance

Key Readings

Bayley, D.H. and Shearing, C.D. (1996) 'The future of policing', *Law and Society Review*, 30 (3): 585–606.
Johnston, L. and Shearing, C. (2003) *Governing Security: Explorations in Policing and Justice*. London: Routledge.
Jones, T. and Newburn, T. (1998) *Private Security and Public Policing*. Oxford: Clarendon.
Shearing, C.D. and Stenning, P.C. (1981) 'Modern private security: its growth and implications', in M. Tonry and N. Morris (eds), *Crime and Justice: An Annual Review of Research*, Vol. 3. Chicago: University of Chicago Press.
Stenning, P. (2000) 'Powers and accountability of private police', *European Journal on Criminal Policy and Research*, 8: 325–52.
Wakefield, A. (2003) *Selling Security: The Private Policing of Public Space*. Cullompton: Willan.

PRIVATIZATION

See: Managerialism

PROBATION

Definition

Supervision of offenders in conditions of freedom by designated officers of the court (sometimes called probation officers or community corrections officers). Nowadays regarded as an 'alternative to prison', though, historically, it has been viewed as an 'alternative to punishment'.

Distinctive Features

Probation emerged towards the end of the nineteenth century as a reaction against the austere uniformity of penal institutions. Rooted in humanitarian concerns for the poor and a growing awareness of the contaminating influence of imprisonment, it represented a move towards the individualization of sentencing – tailoring the punishment to the needs of individual offenders. The underlying assumption was that criminals would benefit from developing close relationships of trust with law-abiding citizens who would use their experience, wisdom and professional training to reclaim and rehabilitate them. The role of the probation officer was to offer advice and guidance on social problems such as employment, money and accommodation, as well as counselling for personal and relationship problems. Some jurisdictions (including England and Wales) even expected the probation officer to 'befriend' the offender.

According to Hamai et al. (1995) the concept of probation appears to imply four key elements in most countries where it exists: selection (following an assessment that the offender is 'suitable'); a conditional suspension of punishment (or, more commonly, nowadays, of imprisonment); personal supervision; and finally, guidance and/or treatment. Beyond that basic definition, probation may mean many different things depending on the social and economic framework within which it has to function.

Offenders are selected for probation via a process of assessment by a probation officer who will advise, or write a report for, the sentencing court. Probation orders require offenders to maintain contact with their supervising officer and to tell their supervisor about changes in their circumstances. Failure to comply with these conditions constitutes a breach of the probation order and an offender can then be re-sentenced, usually to a period of imprisonment.

Evaluation

Historically, probation has been orientated towards the welfare of offenders, and probation officers have been required to undergo training as social workers. With the demise of the rehabilitative ideal in the 1960s and 1970s, however, traditional approaches to probation were discredited (Brownlee, 1998; Worrall, 1997). Critics with socialist views on welfare provision argued that traditional probation was patronizing and coercive, pragmatists pointed out that it simply did not 'work', and those of a conservative persuasion held that it was too lenient and should be replaced by more punitive sentences. As a result, probation supervision has been increasingly 'strengthened' by the addition of various conditions, mainly relating to where an offender is required to live, the persons with whom s/he may associate, and the 'programmes' s/he is required to undertake.

The nature of probation intervention has also changed. Personal counselling, based on psychotherapeutic approaches, has been replaced by cognitive-behavioural programmes, based on social learning theory. Rather than attempting to change the whole personality or circumstances of an offender, cognitive-behavioural programmes focus on specific unacceptable behaviours and seek to modify these by correcting distortions in the way an offender will think about their crime. Offenders are required to accept full responsibility for their actions (instead of blaming their victims or their circumstances), empathize with the victims of their offences, and expand their repertoire of responses to those situations that have previously triggered a criminal response. Programmes cover a range of specific problem behaviours such as anger management, drunken driving and sex offending.

These programmes collectively form the 'What Works?' agenda. The etymology of this phrase lies in a famously pessimistic remark made in 1974 by the criminologist Robert Martinson to the effect that 'nothing works' in penal interventions. The disillusion which followed this conclusion (supported by research findings at the time) led to a loss of confidence in probation which was to last until the early 1990s when the 'discovery' of cognitive-behavioural programmes (initially in North America) gave rise to a series of conferences entitled 'What Works?' (McGuire, 1995). This phrase then caught the imagination of politicians and professionals with the result that today it has come to dominate probation intervention in the English-speaking world. Evaluation research gives some cause for cautious optimism in respect of the effectiveness of such programmes in reducing reoffending (see Vennard and Hedderman, 1998), but critics have argued that the current enthusiasm for the cognitive-behavioural approach should not result in the neglect of other provision such as basic literacy skills and social skills. Nor should the wider social problems that may lead people into crime be overlooked.

Anne Worrall

Associated Concepts: community corrections, community sentences, evaluation research, rehabilitation, social learning theory, 'what works'

Key Readings

Brownlee, I. (1998) *Community Punishment: A Critical Introduction.* Harlow: Addison-Wesley Longman.

Hamai, K., Ville, R., Harris, R., Hough, M. and Zvekic, U. (1995) *Probation Round the World: A Comparative Study.* London: Routledge.

McGuire, J. (1995) *What Works? Reducing Reoffending.* Chichester: John Wiley.

Ruggiero, V., Ryan, M. and Sim, J. (eds) (1995) *Western European Penal Systems: A Critical Anatomy.* London: Sage.

Vennard, J. and Hedderman, C. (1998) 'Effective interventions with offenders', in P. Goldblatt and C. Lewis (eds), *Reducing Offending: An Assessment of Research Evidence on ways of Dealing with Offending Behaviour,* Research Study 187. London: Home Office.

Worrall, A. (1997) *Punishment in the Community: The Future of Criminal Justice.* Harlow: Addison-Wesley Longman.

PROBLEM ORIENTED POLICING

Definition

Problem oriented policing is a deceptively simple and sensible idea. It requires police forces to analyse the problems that they are routinely called upon to deal with and devise more effective ways to respond to them.

Distinctive Features

Problem oriented policing was first developed by Herman Goldstein in the late 1970s and represents an attempt to persuade the police that it is in their interests to adopt a different operational philosophy. He was critical of the traditional incident-driven policing strategies, where the organization responds to individual calls for assistance as they happen and attempts to cope with that demand. Officers or their colleagues repeatedly revisit the same localities and social settings to deal with the repetitive, all too predictable behaviour of individuals and groups. This is demoralizing for officers, a waste of organizational resources, and unsatisfactory for members of the public. Goldstein is also critical of police work, which concentrates on law enforcement and crime control. The majority of incidents with which police officers have to deal are non-criminal in nature and police methods should reflect this fact. The prioritization of the law enforcement function disproportionately influences the operational practices, structure, training and recruitment policies of police forces. It can also compound rather than resolve problems because it leads police officers to think that the solution to the problems they face is more legal powers. For Goldstein, police forces need to accept that good police work requires the development of the most effective means for dealing with a multitude of troublesome situations. Equally crucially, these means will very often, but not always, require the invocation of criminal law.

The reactive, law enforcement-based model of police work should be replaced by proactive 'bottom-up' approaches which emphasize getting to grips with the underlying conditions that create the problems police officers have to deal with. They can do this because many of the incidents that take up police time are recurring rather than random in nature. Police forces should analyse patterns of crime incident clusters to identify their underlying causes and problems and formulate appropriate responses. To do so requires disaggregating vague and overly general categories such as 'crime', 'disorder', 'violence' and so on into particular problems. It is not good enough to break these down into 'robbery', 'theft', 'assault', for example, because these concepts are framed by the criminal law. There should be as detailed a breakdown of problems as possible from the outset and an identification of their key characteristics (location, time, participants' behaviour and so on). In addition, information should be gathered from a range of police and non-police sources. Only then can specific plans and imaginative strategies be developed to reduce or eradicate these recurring problems. In this way police officers will concentrate not on organizational matters but the ends for their police work and the quality of the police product. Problem-solving policing is more rewarding for officers and enables the organization to manage the demands made upon it more effectively because police work is geared towards resolving the root causes of related problems.

Evaluation

In many respects problem oriented policing makes common sense, and yet for police forces to embrace this model, it requires them to engage in a fundamental re-examination of what they do and why and how they do it. It also requires police officers, at all levels of the organization, to focus on the substantive outcomes of police work and stop thinking of themselves as law enforcement officers. Forces have to commit themselves to addressing complex and sensitive problems and harms that are normally overlooked or ignored by officers. In addition it asks that officers are trained in problem-solving techniques and empowered to work with and be accountable to local communities. Forces must also develop reliable incident data in a form that is open to an external evaluation and public discussion.

Eugene McLaughlin

Associated Concepts: 'broken windows', community policing, geographies of crime, situational crime prevention, zero tolerance

Key Readings

Brodeur, P. (1998) *How to Recognize Good Policing: Problems and Issues.* London: Sage.

Eck, E. and Spelman, W. (1987) *Problem Solving: Problem Oriented Policing in Newport News.* Washington, DC: US Department of Justice, National Institute of Justice.

Goldstein, H. (1977) *Policing a Free Society.* Cambridge, MA: Ballinger.

Goldstein, H. (1979) 'Improving policing: a problem-oriented approach', *Crime and Delinquency,* 25: 236–58.

Goldstein, H. (1990) *Problem-Oriented Policing.* New York: McGraw-Hill.

Leigh, A., Read, T. and Tilley, N. (1998) *Brit Pop II: Problem Oriented Policing in Practice,* Police Research Series, Paper 93. London: Home Office.

PROPORTIONALITY

See: Discrimination; Disparity; Disproportionality; Due process model; Just deserts

PSYCHOANALYTIC CRIMINOLOGY

Definition

This neologism is misleading if it is taken to designate a discrete sub-genre of criminological scholarship. In this sense no such entity as psychoanalytic criminology exists. However, it is possible to talk of the vicissitudes of relationships between psychoanalysis and criminology over the past century.

Distinctive Features

We can make a start here by reversing the two terms that together compose the neologism. Criminological psychoanalysis? Psychoanalysis has always been criminological. In making this claim, I have in mind the dynamic role accorded to criminal wishes and fantasies within the broad spectrum of psychoanalytic theories of mental processes. For instance, the psychoanalytic terms pertaining to neurosis convey a primitive and talionic penal code within the unconscious. Psychoanalytic theory makes no qualitative distinction between normal and pathological, and its account of the character of human subjectivity attributes significance to the traces of unconscious taboos and violent wishes and fantasies that persist throughout life. These are seen in phenomena such as the dream, parapraxes and the losing of objects. There is a conception of human nature or identity within every criminological theory or philosophy of punishment, however implicit. Psychoanalysis challenges these in various ways.

Relationships between psychoanalysis and criminology are not reducible to the study of the emotional aspect of offending behaviour and of punishing. Psychoanalysis presents criminology with a number of epistemological questions. Clearly the psychoanalytic appreciation of methodological rigour is quite different from that favoured by empirical criminology. A psychoanalyst would contend that the happy analysis of an isolated dream fragment can reveal far more than a large-scale survey on delinquency. Further, psychoanalysis problematizes the relationship between fantasy and reality.

Freud's brief 1916 insight, 'Criminals from a sense of guilt', presented his reflection on the dynamic role of mental conflict in the origins of criminality. This piece suggested a wholly new approach in criminology and penology. So how far has this been developed?

Writing about France, Laurent Mucchielli (1993) argued that the history of connections between psychoanalysis and criminology has been marked by suspicion. Yet for a time aspects of psychoanalytic thought exercised a major influence within British criminology. What can be made of this difference?

Over the past century, psychoanalysts have been prominent among those arguing for the reform of criminal law and penal policy; for example, British psychoanalysts gave testimony to the Royal Commission on Capital Punishment of 1952. These activities were informed by a literature on the unconscious motivations of legal punishment, which foregrounded the aggression and ambivalence of subjective investments in punitive practices. A general statement of this view is of the order of: 'Punishment of the criminal is punishment of something which the individual feels to be present in themself.'

Psychoanalysis accords a central place to gender and sexuality in its exploration of the psyche. From the early days, analysts held up the significance of troubles with masculinity to the origins of men's criminality. A recent example of this kind of scholarship can be seen in Tony Jefferson's (1996) use of Kleinian concepts such as projection to think about the case of Mike Tyson in terms of the relationship between the constitution of black masculine subjectivity and the crime of which the boxer was convicted.

An understanding of the contemporary as the locus of a 'risk society' or 'actuarial society' has recently attained prominence in theoretical criminology. An alternative way of looking at this question of our actuality employs the idea of an affective society. Such a picture is offered by Hollway and Jefferson (1997), who employ a psychoanalytic conception of anxiety to think about the fear of crime, and by Mark Watson (1999), in his essay on the paranoiac structure of police discourse. Key respects in which the subject of a society construed as affective differs from the subject of a risk society include the retrospective temporal orientation of the former and his/her emotional and unconscious reflexivity,

which predominates over the cognitive and rational.

Evaluation

Psychoanalytic thought exercised a considerable influence upon the British criminology of the inter-war and post-war periods (Valier, 1998). In the sphere of penal practice, probation became reconceived as a process of emotional re-education, and the role of the probation officer therein that of caseworker. From the 1970s onwards, radical, conflict and feminist criminologies with a commitment to political critique denounced the psychoanalytic study of the criminal as positivistic, normative and biologically deterministic. The rejection of the rehabilitative ethos in penality under the aegis of the slogan 'nothing works' also contributed to the falling from favour of psychoanalytic thought in criminology. The extent to which psychoanalysts had engaged from the outset upon a complex and sometimes heated debate concerning the ethics of their practice and the efficacy of their techniques was overlooked, as was the profound disagreement between different genres of psychoanalysis.

Over the past century there have been many contentious debates among psychoanalysts. The expulsion of various individuals from particular circles of affiliation and professional bodies, as well as the emergence of rival schools of thought and of clinical practice, have been a lasting manifestation of the degree of divergence. In addition to division pertaining to institutional structures and doctrinal preferences, the proliferation of different cultures of psychoanalysis influenced by local sociopolitical contexts has been marked.

The most intentionally provocative and self-consciously political culture of psychoanalysis emerged in France with the impetus of the 'return to Freud' undertaken by Jacques Lacan. Lacan repeatedly differentiated his work from the genre of American ego-psychology, which emphasized the adaptation to dominant socio-cultural structures and mores. In his address to the second international congress on criminology of 1950, he asserted that 'the denunciation of the morbid Universe of the misdeed cannot have for its corollary, nor for its aim, the ideal of an adaptation to a reality without conflicts' (Lacan, 1984: 24). He emphasized the emotional ambivalence occasioned by the dialectical negativity by which the ego is formed through an identification with the other. Two of his earliest works discussed the cases of certain criminal women. His doctoral thesis of 1932 described the case of Aimée, who had attempted to stab a famous actress. Lacan rejected organic explanations of psychosis and saw her act as springing from conflicts within her personality. Her delusional system had turned these conflicts into external persecutors. The wish behind the delusions was one of unconscious self-punishment. This was followed by a paper on the Papin sisters, two maids who had murdered their employers in 1933. Lacan's reflection on these criminal cases was crucial to the elaboration of his concepts of the imaginary and the mirror phase, the latter theorizing the alienation that resides at the heart of all human subjects and initiates in an act of self-misrecognition.

Lacanian thought has now exercised considerable influence in areas such as literary and cultural criticism. There is a rich literature extant which employs psychoanalytic thought in analysis of the plethora of visual and literary representations of crime and punishment with which we are daily confronted.

The psychoanalytic understanding of the criminal cannot be simply condemned as a correctionalist, normalizing discourse. A more nuanced account of the kinds of psychoanalysis taken up by criminology, and of the changes to classical technique thought necessary for the treatment of criminals, as well as an engagement with the extensive critical literature on many aspects of psychoanalysis, are prerequisites to any assessment of relationships between psychoanalysis and criminology. Further, the comfortable assimilation of psychoanalytic thought into criminological theory is both unlikely and undesirable. For this eventuality to take place, a considerable domestication of psychoanalysis would have to occur.

Claire Valier

Associated Concepts: hegemonic masculinity, masculinities, postmodernism, risk, sexuality

Key Readings

Hollway, W. and Jefferson, T. (1997) 'The risk society in an age of anxiety: situating the fear of crime', *British Journal of Sociology*, 48 (2): 255–66.

Jefferson, T. (1996) 'From "little fairy boy" to "the complete destroyer": subjectivity and transformation in the biography of Mike Tyson', in M. Mac an Ghaill (ed.), *Understanding Masculinities: Social Relations and Cultural Arenas.* Buckingham: Open University Press.

Lacan, J. (1984) 'Psychanalyse et criminologie. Résumé', *Ornicar*, 31: 23–7.

Mucchielli, L. (1993) 'Le sens du crime: histoire des r(apports) de la psychanalyse à la criminologie', in L. Mucchielli (ed.), *Histoire de la criminologie française.* Paris: L'Harmattan.

Valier, C. (1998) 'Psychoanalysis and crime in Britain during the inter-war years'. The British Criminology Conferences, Selected Proceedings. Electronic journal available at the website of the British Society of Criminology: http://www.britsoccrim.org/volume1/012.pdf

Watson, M. (1999) 'Policing the affective society: beyond governmentality in the theory of social control', *Social and Legal Studies*, 8 (2): 227–52.

PSYCHOPATHY

Definition

A collection of personality traits, including a lack of remorse and guilt, irresponsibility, impulsiveness, pathological lying, manipulativeness, shallow affect, egocentricity, glibness, superficial charm, and a failure to learn from punishment (Cleckley, 1976). Although these traits may be associated with criminal behaviour, psychopathy and offending are not necessarily linked.

Distinctive Features

Despite the list of personality traits that are characteristic of psychopathy, there is no universally accepted definition of the construct. Similar constructs are described in the *Diagnostic and Statistical Manual of Mental Disorders*, 4th edition (DSM-IV; American Psychiatric Association, 1994) and the *International Classification of Disease*, 10th edition (ICD-10; World Health Organization, 1992). DSM-IV has Anti-social Personality Disorder, and uses behavioural rather than personality traits as diagnostic criteria. Dissocial Personality Disorder is the ICD-10 equivalent to psychopathy, and its diagnostic criteria are similar to Cleckley's list of characteristics.

In an attempt to operationalize the concept of psychopathy, and make assessments more reliable, Robert Hare developed the Psychopathy Checklist-Revised (PCL-R; Hare, 1991). Based on Cleckley's criteria, the PCL-R is a 20-item clinical rating scale completed through interview and file information, with scores of 30 and above indicating psychopathy. In Hare's own words, psychopathy as assessed by the PCL-R is defined as '... a constellation of affective, interpersonal, and behavioural characteristics, including egocentricity, impulsivity, irresponsibility, shallow emotions, lack of empathy, guilt or remorse, pathological lying, manipulativeness, and the persistent violation of social norms and expectations' (Hare, 1996).

Initially, the PCL-R was seen to be composed of two factors: one concerning the interpersonal and emotional facets of psychopathy, and the other reflecting the anti-social lifestyle components of psychopathy. More recently three hierarchical factors have been found by Cooke and Michie (2001), with the first reflecting an arrogant and devious interaction style, the second representing affective deficits, including a lack of remorse and empathy, and the third reflecting a behavioural style characterized by impulsivity and irresponsibility. These three factors are highly inter-correlated and form the general factor of psychopathy. Further analyses by Hare (as cited in Hemphill and Hart, 2002) have shown an additional fourth factor of anti-social behaviour. There is a high correlation between Anti-social Personality Disorder and high scores on the PCL-R (i.e., high levels of psychopathy), although the prevalence among forensic populations of high PCL-R scores (15–30 per cent) is much lower than that of Anti-social Personality Disorder (50–80 per cent).

The exact relationship between psychopathy and criminal behaviour is not fully understood, although it is clear that the presence of psychopathic characteristics is highly associated with offending. Furthermore, among those offenders who score highly on the PCL-R there are typically high levels of criminality and violence, and high PCL-R scores are highly predictive of both general and violent reoffending. A consideration of the factors of the PCL-R can usefully show how psychopathic characteristics may influence criminal behaviour. The factor representing an *arrogant and devious interaction style* highlights the need by psychopathic individuals to be of high status, which may be satisfied through committing offences. Having a devious interaction style can also facilitate certain types of crime. The *affective deficits* of the second factor could perhaps increase the likelihood of offending through the lack of constraints usually exerted by feelings of guilt, remorse and empathy. Emotional volatility is also contained within this factor, offering an explanation for increased violence among psychopathic individuals. The third factor relating to *irresponsible and impulsive behaviour* can lead psychopathic individuals to commit offences through impulsiveness, boredom and a lack of planning before they act.

In England and Wales the relationship between offending and psychopathy has also been confused by use of the term 'psychopathic disorder' in the Mental Health Act 1983, which was defined as 'suffering from a persistent disorder or disability of the mind which results in abnormally aggressive or seriously irresponsible conduct' (McMurran,

2001: 467). However, while there is an overlap between 'psychopathic disorder' and psychopathy the two are not the same construct.

The characteristics of psychopathic individuals have led many practitioners to believe that psychopaths are extremely difficult to treat or even 'untreatable'. Indeed, most definitions of psychopathy make mention of their inability to learn from experience or punishment. This resistance to treatment leads to high levels of attrition from treatment programmes and can disrupt treatment for other prisoners or patients in a group setting. Along with the manipulative nature and interpersonal style of psychopaths, management of this client group can be extremely difficult for staff. While this population undoubtedly present problems within the treatment arena, there is a growing view that part of the problem is that we have yet to discover the most appropriate treatment method for psychopaths (Lösel, 1998). Recent discussions in this area have proposed that using the attributes of psychopaths to the advantage of treatment methods and goals may be one way to help improve their engagement in treatment (Hemphill and Hart, 2002).

Evaluation

One major problem with psychopathy is the lack of an agreed definition or system for assessment. A further issue with the DSM-IV system is its use of behaviours as proxies for personality traits. While this has allowed for the increased reliability of assessments of Anti-social Personality Disorder, it may also reduce the construct validity. The PCL-R, although a standardized instrument, has also been criticized, as there is still a reliance on clinical judgement. A second issue with psychopathy, which is linked to the use of behaviours as criteria for diagnosing Anti-social Personality Disorder, is the disparity in the prevalence of Anti-social Personality Disorder and high PCL-R scores in forensic populations. By using behavioural criteria such as assaults, that may or may not reflect the underlying personality traits linked to psychopathy, the DSM-IV criteria have been criticized for confounding Anti-social Personality Disorder with general criminality.

Emma J. Palmer

Associated Concepts: criminal careers, pathology, personality theory

Key Readings

Cleckley, H. (1976) *The Mask of Sanity* (5th edn). St. Louis, MO: Mosby.

Cooke, D.J. and Michie, C. (2001) 'Refining the concept of psychopathy', *Psychological Assessment*, 13 (2): 171–88.

Hare, R.D. (1991) *The Hare Psychopathy Checklist-Revised*. Toronto: Multi-Health Systems.

Hare, R.D. (1996) 'Psychopathy: a clinical construct whose time has come', *Criminal Justice and Behaviour*, 23: 25–54.

Hemphill, J.F. and Hart, S.D. (2002) 'Motivating the unmotivated: psychopathy, treatment, and change', in M. McMurran (ed.), *Motivating Offenders to Change: A Guide to Enhancing Engagement in Therapy.* Chichester: Wiley.

Lösel, F. (1998) 'Treatment and management of psychopaths', in D.J. Cooke, A.E. Forth and R.D. Hare (eds), *Psychopathy: Theory, Research and Implications for Society.* Dordrecht: Kluwer Academic.

McMurran, M. (2001) 'Offenders with personality disorders', in C.R. Hollin (ed.), *Handbook of Offender Assessment and Treatment.* Chichester: Wiley.

PUBLIC CRIMINOLOGY

Definition

With the rapid academic expansion of Anglo-American criminology since the mid-1990s it could be assumed that criminologists would have a central role to play in criminal justice policy development, public debate and political decision making. However, criminologists from a variety of perspectives began to voice their concerns about both the rapid fragmentation of the discipline into 'camps' and a noticeable decline in the public engagement with and use of criminological analysis and research findings. These observations coalesced into deliberations about the public status of criminology, in particular about why criminologists were having such a scant, discernible impact on the public debate and how they could play an influential role in public deliberations about crime and crime control.

Distinctive Features

In their recent analysis of the different ways of 'doing' criminology Loader and Sparks (2010) have identified the following ideal types of criminologist: scientific expert; policy advisor; observer-turned-player; social movement theorist; and the 'lonely prophet'. However, it is more in keeping with the rationale of this dictionary to distinguish between different criminological perspectives.

Sociological Criminology Garland and Sparks (2000) provide us with a sociological understanding of the question of academic criminology's problematic relationship with public policy and public debates. The collective experience of having to adjust to the threat posed by living in a late modern environment disordered by crime and delinquency has generated high levels of crime consciousness and a punitive public mood. As a result, the categorizations that a generation of post-war criminologists took for granted have been undermined by the politicization of crime fears, victim-oriented criminal justice policy shifts, and the marketization of crime control and the delivery of criminal justice services.

For Garland and Sparks, criminologists have had to confront the embarrassing fact that in a society saturated with 'crime talk', they have the utmost difficulty in communicating with politicians, policy makers, practitioners and the public. Criminological reasoning is now mediated and contested by interest groups, activists and a multitude of institutional actors and public opinions. And

added to this, criminologists are alienated from late modern political culture because crime, policing and punishment are polarizing electoral issues. However, the cultural centrality of crime is 'an opportunity for criminology to embrace a more critical, more public, more wide-ranging role' (2000: 201). To do so, criminologists will have to demonstrate a reflexive understanding of 'the way that crime is experienced, represented and regulated' (2000: 202) and the changing political culture.

Critical Criminologies For Jock Young (2003) late modern criminology is fragmented and characterized by a multitude of new voices as a result of the collapse of boundaries over who is authorized to speak about crime and on what terms. And this democratization has impacted on the institutional knowledge base for policy making, politics and public opinion in unpredictable ways. From the 1980s onwards, right realist and administrative criminologists did manage to construct a lucrative policy base by working within the groove of an increasingly punitive criminal justice system. Carefully cultivated relationships with the news media, public commentators and political networks allowed them to redefine the terms of the debate about criminal justice policy and social policy. And Young insists that even in the most hostile of political and ideological circumstances, it is critical criminology that is required to act as a counter-voice to free market and neo-conservative punitive crime control practices.

For Hillyard et al. (2004: 385) the answer has to be for the critical criminologist to continue to 'conduct rigorous, challenging and socially relevant research that will alleviate rather than exacerbate problems caused by conventional crime, while simultaneously confronting the social harms generated by the powerful'. To this end the criminologist is first and foremost someone who works on the injustices of the criminal justice process. At this point it is important to note the impact that feminist criminologists have had in placing the needs of victims of violence on the criminal justice agenda. Policy makers have been compelled to recognize and try to deal more sensitively with issues such as domestic violence, sexual harassment and sexual crimes (and, in general, to acknowledge the role of gendered, racial and class-related biases in criminal justice practices).

Cultural Criminologies For Ferrell et al. (2008) the starting-point is understanding the mass-mediaization of criminological knowledge in order to engage actively with popular culture and the news-media. Despite the overwhelming presence of crime and criminal justice topics in media news and popular culture, criminologists have not usually been the key source on whom journalists will rely. On the contrary, most sections of the media will choose to draw disproportionately on the expert status and public authority of uniformed criminal justice professionals and criminal lawyers. This communication gap then results in public perceptions of crime that are not founded in criminological analyses and research data. A central task for criminologists is to convince journalists and reporters that they have important analyses and research findings to discuss. A proactive media presence will require criminologists to skill themselves in how the 'old' and 'new' media work and to recognize opportunities for intervening in a decisive manner in myriad public debates. One important implication of the cultural criminological critique is that the next generation of criminologists will need to be educated in the latest scholarship and technical practices of journalism and communication and new media studies. For cultural criminologists the ability to intervene in decisive public debates and carve out new public space means that the media matter. 'Doing' cultural criminology is closely related to how sophisticated criminologists can become in understanding, and participating in, a dynamically evolving range of mass-media forums.

Administrative Criminologies The problem from this perspective is how the discipline's lack of relevance and practical 'real world' impact relates to the unaddressed structural weaknesses of the evidence base. It has a credibility problem. The discipline has not offered expert users convincing research findings on offences, offenders, victims and their interconnections that would allow it to guide policy making. Criminologists – as applied social scientists – have to become methodologically sophisticated through the utilization of innovative research designs, the rigorous analysis of research data and conduct of replication studies, the diversification of funding streams, and the enhanced regulation and oversight of professional practice and standards. For others criminology has to develop into a policy science. Sherman (2005) argues for a technically sophisticated 'experimental criminology' that relates directly to the world of practitioners, aiming to provide them with 'what works' choices. For Clarke (2004) criminology must become an applied 'crime science' whose core task is to explain crime (rather than criminality) and how crime is committed (rather than why it is committed). It must also be dedicated to developing effective crime control strategies.

Evaluation

The debate about the public role and responsibilities of criminology has produced an interesting set of discussions about:

- how we should conceive of criminology as a discipline;
- what the objectives of criminology are;
- what it is that makes criminological analysis credible;
- what the responsibilities of the criminologist are.

At the core of this public criminology debate is the vexed relationship between knowledge, power and action. As is evident throughout this dictionary, there are many ways to 'do' criminology. There would seem to be broad agreement that criminologists have a professional duty to participate in the public sphere of politics and policy making. However, to what end and how this is to happen are disputed. Should the purpose of criminological deliberations and research be producing policy recommendations for effective crime control or the broader goal of reducing social injustice and enhancing human rights? In certain contexts of course there is not a necessary conflict between these different goals. However, in others the choice is stark. Equally importantly, criminologists need to keep in mind that they have ethical and professional responsibilities that must always mediate their desire to leave the 'ivory towers' of academia. This requires the maintenance of a suitable distance from the institutions of criminal justice and the polity.

Eugene McLaughlin

Associated Concepts: administrative criminology, crime science, critical criminology, cultural criminology, feminist criminologies, newsmaking criminology, realist criminologies, social harm, 'what works'

Key Readings

Clarke, R.V. (2004) 'Technology, criminology and crime science', *European Journal of Criminal Policy and Research*, 10 (1): 55–63.
Ferrell, J., Hayward, K. and Young, J. (2008) *Cultural Criminology: An Invitation.* London: Sage.
Garland, D. and Sparks, R. (2000) 'Criminology, social theory and the challenge of our times', *British Journal of Criminology*, 40 (2): 189–204.
Hillyard, P., Sim, J., Tombs, S. and Whyte, D. (2004) 'Leaving a "stain upon the silence": contemporary criminology and the politics of dissent', *British Journal of Criminology*, 44 (3): 369–90.
Loader, I. and Sparks, R. (2010) *Public Criminology*. London: Routledge.
Sherman, L.W. (2005) 'The use and usefulness of criminology: Enlightenment justice and its failures', *ANNALS, AAPSS* 600: 115–35.
Young, J. (2003) 'In praise of dangerous thoughts: a review essay', *Punishment and Society*, 5 (1): 97–107.

PUBLIC OPINION

Definition

Refers to the expressed views of members of the general public which are typically gathered via polls and surveys. These are most frequently associated with assessing the extent of public support for political parties and their policies, but they are also commonly used to gauge public attitudes toward a range of social issues and current affairs including crime and criminal justice.

Distinctive Features

Opinions are expressed to pollsters and researchers in a range of ways: by telephone, in face-to-face interviews or by interactive polling over the internet, for example, and in response to a variety of question formats and stimuli. Opinion polls or surveys carried out by specialist organizations (such as MORI) and academic researchers often aim to measure the views of a representative sample of the general public by using techniques such as random or quota sampling, while more respectable organizations are more likely to qualify their findings when this has not been achieved. Others, typically tabloid newspapers and television programmes, will rely upon self-selecting samples; their readers or viewers, for example, will be invited to express their support for (or their dissent from) a given view or position.

Public opinion polls provide valuable copy for the print and broadcast media, and reports of their findings are widely read by politicians and policy makers. Understanding the role of the media in not only 'reflecting' public opinion but also in shaping it is of pivotal importance for making sense of criminal justice policies and penal politics. The media provide key sources of information, but, as Indermaur and Hough (2002: 202) note, 'they do this in a particular way, reflecting the commercial (or quasi-commercial) pressures to retain their audiences and thus their revenue'. As such, media interests can be regarded as actors in their own right, as well as vehicles through which politicians, interest groups and 'the public' are able to convey themselves and their viewpoints to each other. Through the media, each group acquires its knowledge of the others' views and standpoints. This is particularly the case for politicians and 'policy elites' because their sense of distance from 'public opinion' makes them particularly receptive to the 'window' into 'public opinion' offered by the media (Indermaur and Hough, 2002: 204; see also Hancock, 2004).

Some writers have argued that during the 1980s and 1990s politicians and policy makers did not take into account or understand public opinion sufficiently and, equally, members of the public tended to be ill-informed about crime or criminal justice matters and processes. As a consequence, there 'was the potential for misunderstanding, distortion, misinterpretation and misinformation in both directions' (James and Raine, 1998: 65). More recently, however, governments have tried to furnish the public with more information about crime and criminal justice and sought to develop the tools they use to gather and reflect public opinion and experiences. The frequency and size of the British Crime Surveys, for example, have increased so that the survey now takes place annually in England and Wales and the sample has been extended to include interviews with 40,000 people aged 16 or over. Use of other ways of gathering and reflecting public opinion on crime and criminal justice matters is greater than ever in the current period, as testified to in the proliferation of focus groups, 'consultation' exercises and other forms of public participation in crime policies and criminal justice at a local and national level. These methods for gathering 'public opinion' are, however, still likely to remain 'unrepresentative' of the general population.

Public opinion remains more often invoked than understood. That is, sentencers, politicians, practitioners, penal reformers and criminologists – writing from a variety of perspectives and with the benefit of a greater or lesser degree of informed research – are still apt to make assessments about what the

public will or will not tolerate where penal policy and criminal justice disposals are concerned. Governments in the UK and USA, for example, have justified harsher penalties, more austere regimes and the removal of rights from suspects, defendants and prisoners on the grounds that they are satisfying public opinion. There is a tendency for commentators to view the public as an undifferentiated mass. Moreover, studies which explore *differences* and *divisions* in public opinion (and the conditions that give rise to them) remain relatively undeveloped.

Evaluation

A number of researchers have questioned the adequacy of the tools commonly used to assess and measure public responses; ordinary people may 'frame' questions of crime and justice differently to policy makers and pollsters (Doble, 2002). Durham (1993) has offered several reasons why the validity of findings from many public opinion polls and surveys should be treated with caution: the highly specific nature of the stimulus used to invoke a response from an interviewee; the respondent's lack of familiarity with the scenario in question; the time constraints of the interview; questions about the respondent's understanding of vignettes; and the impact of their own ideological position. Respondents may not have spent much time prior to the interview, or are unable to spend sufficient time during it, to consider the issues in detail. They might also modify their views about crime and punishment when they are given more information. As a consequence, reservations will arise concerning the extent to which there are 'solid opinions in the minds of citizens regarding appropriate punishment for crime' (Durham, 1993: 8). Members of the public participating in surveys are often unable to offer responses that reflect their complex, nuanced and perhaps ambiguous views about crime and punishment.

More sophisticated criminological studies will employ research methods that can uncover the extent to which public opinion is multifaceted or uncertain. They will concern themselves with assessing the range and strength of public attitudes, and they have demonstrated that, given the opportunity to think through some of the issues, people will respond with more sophisticated, reasoned and less punitive responses (see for example Applegate et al., 1996; Cullen et al., 2002; and Doble, 2002 – cited in Hancock, 2004). Providing the public with more information about criminal justice, sentencing and so on can have a positive impact on public opinion – and when members of the public have been accorded a greater opportunity to think through criminal justice issues, positive effects concerning the ways in which people understand, evaluate and assess the criminal justice system have followed (Mirrlees-Black, 2002).

Lynn Hancock

Associated Concepts: crime news, punitiveness, social survey, victim surveys

Key Readings

Doble, J. (2002) 'Attitudes to punishment in the US – punitive and liberal opinions', in J.V. Roberts and M. Hough (eds), *Changing Attitudes to Punishment*. Cullompton: Willan.

Durham, A. (1993) 'Public opinion regarding sentences for crime: does it exist?', *Journal of Criminal Justice*, 21(1): 1–11.

Hancock, L. (2004) 'Criminal justice, public opinion, fear and popular politics', in J. Muncie and D. Wilson (eds), *The Student Handbook of Criminal Justice and Criminology*. London: Cavendish.

Indermaur, D. and Hough, M. (2002) 'Strategies for challenging public attitudes to punishment', in J.V. Roberts and M. Hough (eds), *Changing Attitudes to Punishment*. Cullompton: Willan.

James, A. and Raine, J. (1998) *The New Politics of Criminal Justice*. London: Longman.

Mirrlees-Black, C. (2002) 'Improving public knowledge about crime and punishment', in J.V. Roberts and M. Hough (eds), *Changing Attitudes to Punishment*. Cullompton: Willan.

PUNISHMENT

See: Capital punishment; Convict criminology; Penality; Penology

PUNITIVENESS

Definition

The Concise Oxford Dictionary defines punitive as 'inflicting or intending to inflict punishment'. This definition, however, does not take us very far. While all forms of punishment contain some degree of punitiveness, punishment can also be justified in terms of rehabilitation, incapacitation and general deterrence. A slightly more precise definition of 'punitive' is offered by Stanley Cohen (1994) who suggests that the main attribute of a punitive stance is that it involves the infliction of pain, harm and suffering on individuals in a coercive but impersonal manner by specialist, often legally empowered, agencies.

Distinctive Features

Taking this definition as a starting-point it would seem that the distinguishing feature of punishment, which is designed to be punitive, is that it is essentially retributive and vengeful and directed at the individual legal and moral subject. In general, punitive forms of punishment are seen to be those which arise principally as a response to wrongs that have occurred in the past, rather than those forms of punishment which are justified in terms of their preventing future offending.

To describe a sanction as punitive implies that it involves a degree of excess above the norm. Being punitive, therefore, is not just the dissemination of 'just deserts' but also suggests a form of response that goes beyond that which is deemed appropriate or necessary. In its more extreme forms it includes the expression of vengeance and cruelty, where the objective is to take delight or satisfaction in the pain and suffering of others.

In recent years a growing number of criminologists have suggested that crime control policies have become more punitive. Some see this development as largely a top-down process whereby manipulative politicians develop tough crime control measures, either because they believe they will reduce crime or because they are certain that by advocating such measures they will increase their support and improve their chances of re-election (Bottoms, 1995). On the other hand, there are those who see the development of increasingly punitive policies as a product of the hardening of public attitudes. In both accounts the media are frequently portrayed as playing a key role in fuelling public anxieties by sensationalizing crime-related issues and creating a climate of fear and anxiety.

Since crime control has historically had a substantial coercive and punitive component it becomes necessary to identify exactly what has changed in recent years and what constitutes the apparent surge in punitiveness. One central point of reference in the Anglo-American literature, at least, has been the substantial increase in the prison population. The development of mass incarceration in America, whereby prison is increasingly used as the sanction of a first rather than a last resort, is widely seen as an outcome of the adoption of more punitive policies. Closely related to the rapid increase in the prison population has been the development of tougher sentencing policies in the form of mandatory and determinate sentences. Probably the most commonly referenced development in sentencing policy in this context is the 'Three Strikes and You're Out' legislation which was introduced in America in the mid-1990s. The combined effect of these new sentencing policies, it has been suggested, has been to increase the average length of sentence with the consequence that people are now spending more time in prison.

It is not only that the prison population has grown and that the average length of sentence has increased significantly over the past two decades. John Pratt (2000) has argued that new forms of punishment are emerging which are more ostentatious and also involve more extreme forms of shaming and stigmatization. Similarly, Jonathan Simon (2001) points to the spread of boot camps and supermax prisons in America and argues that we are witnessing the intensification of different forms of punishment involving greater degrees of cruelty and vindictiveness that are 'painful, vengeful and destructive of the penitent body as well as life chances'. He believes that we are increasingly 'governing through crime' while punishment has become a kind of 'therapeutic theatre' in which the offender publicly expresses their feelings of pain and shame.

Other examples which have been seen to indicate the development of a more punitive stance are the adoption of zero tolerance policing policies and the 'spreading of the net' of social control involving the criminalization of activities, such as forms of disorder and anti-social behaviour, that had previously been held to be outside the remit of the criminal justice system.

Explanations for the development of this 'punitive turn' vary, but for a number of commentators the growth in more punitive attitudes is a consequence of the demise of welfarism; the shift away from rehabilitation as the main justification for punishment; the fragmentation of our late modern society; the decline in community cohesion and informal controls; the 'death' of the family; the changing experience of crime; the rise of neo-liberalism; and the advent of the 'risk society'. Some or all of these factors are widely viewed as creating a more punitive climate and/or accounting for the decrease in tolerance amongst the public and politicians.

Evaluation

It is apparent when we examine these accounts that many of the developments which are presented as examples of punitiveness, such as shaming and the new forms of managerialism, are not punitive in the sense that they are principally designed to inflict pain and suffering on individuals. Indeed, according to some accounts, forms of shaming are seen to be an alternative to punitive interventions (Braithwaite, 1989).

For others the new types of punishment that have emerged are not so much expressions of punitiveness but instead represent the expression of a more diverse, volatile and in some cases contradictory system of punishment (O'Malley, 1999). In fact many of the forms of punishment which are presented as examples of the 'punitive turn' are not strictly punitive but may, for example, involve the relatively low key forms of regulation associated not so much with the infliction of pain on individuals but with the management and administration of groups and collectivities. Arguably, many of the most significant forms of regulation that have emerged in recent years are not those which involve shaming, stigmatization or the marking of the penitent body, rather they require the use of surveillance and monitoring techniques which are concerned less with public demonstrations of shame and moral approbation and more with the behavioural and spatial control demanded in monitoring the movements of 'problem populations'.

The suggestion that increased punitiveness is able to explain the major shifts in criminal justice policy in contemporary society can be called into question. A number of late modern societies, such as those in Canada and Ireland, do not seem to be experiencing a 'punitive turn', and research on public attitudes, sentencing policy and imprisonment in these countries suggests that, rather than being an endemic feature of contemporary society, punitiveness – inasmuch as it is increasing – may not be an international development but instead a function of American exceptionalism (Meyer and O'Malley, 2005).

Roger Matthews

Associated Concepts: authoritarian populism, crime control model, crime news, incarceration, net widening, public opinion, social control, tolerance, zero tolerance

Key Readings

Bottoms, A. (1995) 'The philosophy and politics of punishment and sentencing', in C. Clarkson and R. Morgan (eds), *The Politics of Sentencing Reform*. Oxford: Clarendon Press.

Braithwaite, J. (1989) *Crime, Shame and Reintegration*. Cambridge: Cambridge University Press.

Cohen, S. (1994) 'Social control and the politics of reconstruction', in D. Nelken (ed.), *The Futures of Criminology*. London: Sage.

Meyer, J. and O'Malley, P. (2005) 'Missing the punitive turn? Canadian criminal justice, "balance" and penal modernism', in J. Pratt, D. Brown, M. Brown, S. Hallsworth and W. Morrison (eds), *The New Punitiveness*. Cullompton: Willan.

O'Malley, P. (1999) 'Volatile and contradictory punishment', *Theoretical Criminology*, 3 (2): 175–96.

Pratt, J. (2000) 'Emotive and ostentatious punishment', *Punishment and Society*, 2 (4): 417–39.

Simon, J. (2001) 'Entitlement to cruelty: Neo-Liberalism and the punitive mentality in the United States', in K. Stenson and R. Sullivan (eds), *Crime, Risk and Justice*. Cullompton: Willan.

Q

QUEER THEORY

Definition

Queer theory or, in activist parlance, simply 'queer', is a short-hand for gay, lesbian, bisexual and transgendered experience applied to literature, politics, the arts and social sciences; it presents a challenge to both homophobic heterosexism and to affirmative homophilic theories of homosexuality. Applied to crime and criminal justice it exposes the heterosexism of criminal justice practice and of much criminological theory *and* the homoeroticism of its focus on the bodies of young men. The early fusion of criminology and sexology also placed women criminals both outside the law and outside the heterosexual norm.

Distinctive Features

To be or to render odd – queer theory perversely both resists and invites a variety of definitions. Definitions vary depending on whether these are given by activists or academics. Part of the argument is in respect of identity politics – the possibility or desirability of a gay or lesbian movement, culture, sensibility, standpoint or perspective – and part is concerned with the debate about modernism and postmodernism. Healy's summation that 'Queer was lesbian and gay politics catching up with postmodernism' (1996: 175) addresses both aspects. The academic roots of queer theory lie in the humanities, but Seidman (1996) convincingly argues for the relevance to sociology, and Groombridge (1999) points out its significance to criminology and the sociology of deviance. An activist queer politics addressing discrimination on grounds of sexuality or reactions to AIDS may employ direct action which might offend public sensibilities and break the law. Metaphorically it may also seek to bash the gay-bashers through 'camp' and 'drag'.

Its activist roots noted the white, middle-class, Western orientation of gay and lesbian politics and lifestyles which appeared to exclude other identities, much as women of colour and lesbians had noted the exclusionary appeal of feminism to 'sisterhood'. Moreover, academic commentators, drawing on Foucault, noted the disciplinary (even transgressive) features of identities and lifestyles. Psychology, sexology and criminology had for a long time insisted – sometimes by silence – on the normality of heterosexuality and the pathology of other sexualities. Gay activism and human rights campaigners were able to secure some rights for gays and lesbians but did so by insisting on a foundational gay identity (of choice or disposition). Queer theory threatens the stability of both a foundational gay and straight identity by insisting on the fluidity and performativity of identity. The fluidity of queer theory – like much postmodernism – threatens to violate the modernist theories of normative heterosexuality and those of an oppositional homosexuality.

Thus while an empirically-minded and sympathetic researcher might seek to understand homosexuality, a gay or lesbian one may wish to document and understand homophobia. A polemical inversion could perhaps call homophobia deviant or seek its criminalization. This can be seen in the pressure apparent in some jurisdictions to accept or widen the ambit of 'hate crime' legislation. A gay standpoint might want to take such empirical work and campaign around it in the same way that radical feminism attempted to do with research by women on women and for women. Campaigns against homophobic violence and the use of the 'gay-panic defence', but for equal ages of consent, can be seen in this light. The logic of queer theory, however, is that you need not be homosexual in practice or identity to be queer. While this makes political mobilization more difficult it should also be remembered that you don't have to be gay to suffer homophobia. 'Doing' masculinity often involves the rejection of the feminine and the queer. Thus many men operate under the fear of being thought queer just as the fewer openly gay men operate under the fear of being bashed. The political task facing all men is to remove the distal fear of being called a 'poof' or 'faggot' and the proximate fear of being bashed like one. While gay liberation is specifically aimed at improving the lot of gay men and lesbians, queer theory opens up the possibility of a wider liberation.

Evaluation

Although the queer take on sexualities (hetero, homo, bi and transgendered) could be sociologically and criminologically productive (as argued above), there is little evidence outside of socio-legal studies that queer theory has made progress in the social sciences in the same way it has in the humanities. Moreover, given the disputes over definition and applicability (whether being gay is essential or merely helps), it seems likely that any further progress will be uneven. However, homosexuality has haunted criminology from the pathologizing positivism of Lombroso to the appreciative ethnographies of the sociology of deviance. A radical victimology and an increasingly criminal justice practice have recognized attacks on the 'gay community' but still require the 'victim' to 'out' themselves to receive due recognition. Given the limited extent to which criminology has embraced feminism it seems that any serious consideration of sexualities as important to criminology – whether purely empirical, standpoint or queer – may take decades. However, without such consideration, even apparently simple issues – like what we mean by the expressions 'going straight' and 'bent copper' – will elude criminology. Queer theory seeks to find the odd within the normal or render the normal odd, as in the mention of 'straight' and 'bent' above. It is this sort of sub(per)version that will render it unpalatable to the criminological mainstream. Moreover, queer practice and culture – camp to kitsch – has long predated the turning towards theory and may, like some feminisms, wish to keep its distance from criminology.

Nic Groombridge

Associated Concepts: deviance, hate crime, hegemonic masculinity, masculinities, normalization, pathology, postmodernism, sexuality

Key Readings

Groombridge, N. (1999) 'Perverse criminologies: the closet of Doctor Lombroso', *Social and Legal Studies*, 8 (4): 531–48.
Hart, L. (1994) *Fatal Women: Lesbian Sexuality and the Mark of Aggression*. London: Routledge.
Healy, M. (1996) *Gay Skins: Class, Masculinity and Queer Appropriation*. London: Cassell.
Seidman, S. (ed.) (1996) 'Introduction', *Queer Theory/Sociology*. Oxford: Blackwell.
Stychin, C. (1995) *Law's Desire: Sexuality and the Limits of Justice*. London: Routledge.
Tomsen, S. (1997) 'Was Lombroso a queer? Criminology, criminal justice and the heterosexual imaginary', in G. Mason and S. Tomsen (eds), *Homophobic Violence*. Sydney: The Federation Press, Australian Institute of Criminology.

R

RACIAL PROFILING

Definition

Racial profiling refers to police interventions that depend on the race, ethnicity or national origin, rather than the actual behaviour of an individual, or on verifiable information that leads the police to a particular individual who has been identified as having been engaged in criminal activity. In the USA, the debate about racial profiling initially concentrated on whether the disproportionate stopping of African American and Hispanic motorists by law enforcement officers was motivated by racial stereotyping or the consequences of their criminality. In the aftermath of 9/11 the debate about racial profiling has shifted towards the policing and surveillance of Muslim communities.

Distinctive Features

One of the unique features of policing is that rank-and-file officers exercise the greatest amount of discretion in the organization. It is the police constable who makes the most important decisions relating to force policy and who is the 'gatekeeper' who determines which persons will enter the criminal justice system. Attempts to control such discretion are complicated by the fact that officers work in situations that are not readily amenable to direct supervision. It has been accepted that police officers must make many discretionary decisions in the course of their working day. The police have always informally profiled individuals that they believe to be 'suspicious' or 'usual suspects' that are known to them. Therefore it is no great surprise that some of these assessments could be influenced by racial and ethnic as well as other stereotypes. While the police exercise of discretion has long been a source of debate and controversy, developments in the 1980s granted officers even more autonomy in making decisions on whom to stop, search and arrest (Harris, 2002a).

Although most obviously associated with policing, profiling was originally formulated to help apprehend drug couriers attempting to enter the USA. The Drug Enforcement Administration (DEA) developed a number of 'personal indicators' that seemed, from the agency's routine enforcement experiences, to be associated with an increased likelihood of being a drug courier. Among the indicators were speaking Spanish; entering the USA on flights originating in certain Central and South American countries; being young; having purchased the airline ticket for cash; and planning to stay only a short time in the USA. Many young Hispanic travellers claimed that they were being unfairly targeted and harassed and that the war on drugs had been transformed into a war on minorities. The DEA's Operation Pipeline subsequently trained state and local police officers to employ drug courier profiling across the nation's highways. In addition, key Supreme Court decisions sanctioned an increase in police discretion in relation to stop and search practices.

The campaign against racial profiling and police misconduct coalesced around highway stops. The case of four young black and Hispanic men who were fired upon by two white New Jersey State Troopers in April 1998 received high profile news-media attention. According to the young men they were minding their own business and were on their way to college basketball trials in North Carolina. The state troopers insisted that they stopped the van because it was speeding and opened fire because they sensed that the vehicle had been deliberately put into reverse in order to run them down. This focused attention on the allegation that the New Jersey State Police were targeting visible minority motorists in an attempt to deter highway drug trafficking. The state troopers were subsequently found guilty of falsifying their traffic stop reports to conceal the fact that they were stopping a high percentage of visible minority drivers. An official investigation by the New Jersey Attorney General's office concluded that state troopers had proactively engaged in racial profiling along the New Jersey Turnpike.

Although the racial profiling debate has tended to concentrate on 'Driving While Black', police actions based on racial profiling can take a number of forms. African American and Hispanic accounts of disparate treatment at the hands of various police officers included being stopped for being 'in the wrong car'; being stopped and questioned for walking through 'the wrong neighbourhood' at the 'wrong time of day'; and perceived harassment as a result of zero tolerance street policing practices (Davies, 2001; Harris, 2002a).

Evaluation

The overwhelming response from police departments was that, contrary to the assertions of pressure groups, racial profiling or racial bias was not a widespread phenomenon. The evidence for its existence was largely anecdotal and it was being used by anti-police campaigners to make police officers and citizens more race conscious in their encounters, thereby heightening distrust. Others defended the practice by arguing that profiling was not racist: certain visible minorities were disproportionately represented amongst those arrested and imprisoned and it was only sensible that police officers working in particular neighbourhoods should focus on these groups. In addition, it was perfectly reasonable for officers to legitimately look out for a suspect of a particular race or ethnicity if a crime victim or witness description of an offender positively identified such characteristics. From this perspective the debate about racial profiling was diverting attention from the very real criminal victimization problems facing certain neighbourhoods (Ramiez et al., 2000).

Regardless of the practical police arguments in support of racial profiling, the practice has been widely condemned as being contrary to basic constitutional principles and as acting as a crude substitute for evidence-based police-work. Racial profiling has been defined as 'affirmative action in reverse' (Davies, 2001). First, the police are licensed to use existing criminal statistics to justify an intensification of police focus on certain minorities which results in more arrests, thereby reinforcing the beliefs upon which racial profiling by law enforcement agents is based. Second, racial profiling is unacceptable because it weakens the public's confidence in the police, thereby decreasing police–citizen trust. When law enforcement practices are perceived to be biased, unfair or disrespectful, minority communities will be less willing to report crimes, participate in or support anti-crime activities, give evidence and act as witnesses at trials or serve on juries.

Campaigners insisted that the goal was not to sack individual police officers but to eradicate a system of policework premised on institutionalized racial stereotyping. This spurred a series of policy responses: the use of race as a primary basis for stopping and searching citizens was embargoed; the rules about what constitutes 'reasonable suspicion' were tightened; diversity training for officers was introduced; departmental policies were analysed for evidence of institutional racial bias; early warning systems designed to alert supervisors to problem officers and practices were established, as were new mechanisms for filing complaints by citizens who believe they have been unfairly stopped/searched by the police (Ramiez et al., 2000). There have also been demands for the use of video and audio recording and tracking systems to observe and make real-time records of police actions, as well as concerted attempts to collect data on the decision-making processes of police officers in traffic stops. However the gathering of such data is highly problematic, not least because there was no proper benchmark or demonstrator to compare stops. There were, for example, attempts to make officers record what they perceived to be the race, ethnicity or nationality of each driver they stopped without consulting the driver, but the categories constructed and deployed by the police departments bore little resemblance to the multi-ethnic and racial complexities of a metropolitan USA (Rodriguez, 2001). In addition certain forces co-operated with researchers who used covert methodologies to identify racially-biased practices amongst highway patrol officers.

The 9/11 attacks triggered a significant shift in the public debate in the USA about racial profiling (Harris, 2002b). In September 2003 the *New York Times* reported that the majority of Americans polled, including visible minorities, were willing to sanction more intensive security screening checks, closer surveillance and 'threat profiling' for those of Middle Eastern appearance. As Jason L. Riley (2001: 17) put it:

> Of the 22 suspects on the FBI's 'most wanted' list of international terrorists, all are Arabic, all are practitioners of Islam and all come from known state incubators of terrorism in the Middle East. Not 'some' of them or a 'disproportionate number' of them. All of them. Those numbers indicate that any sensible domestic effort to expose terrorist cells would include concentrating on particular groups in particular communities associated with a particular culture. To ignore the fact that America's enemies in this war share a faith and ethnicity – and that their actions, by their own reckoning, are ethnically and religiously inspired would be self-deluding and foolish.

However, law enforcement agencies warned about the dangers of crude religious and ethnic 'threat profiling', arguing that if Arab American communities were alienated as a result of overzealous law enforcement actions it would make the 'war on terrorism' unwinnable.

Eugene McLaughlin

Associated Concepts: discrimination, institutional racism, offender profiling, police bias, racialization, terrorism

Key Readings

Davies, N. (2001) 'The slippery slope of racial profiling', *ColorLines: Race, Culture, Action*, December.

Harris, D. (2002a) *Profiles in Injustice: Why Racial Profiling Cannot Work*. New York: The New Press.

Harris, D. (2002b) 'Racial profiling revisited: just common sense in the fight against terror?', *Criminal Justice*, Summer: 36–41.

Ramiez, D., McDevitt, J. and Farrell, A. (2000) *A Resource Guide to Racial Profiling Data Collection Systems: Promising Practices and Lessons Learned*. Washington, DC: Department of Justice.

Riley, J. (2001) 'Racial profiling and terrorism', *Wall Street Journal*, 24 October.

Rodriguez, G. (2001) 'Who are you? When perception is reality', *New York Times*, Section 4, 3 June, pp. 1/5.

RACIALIZATION

Definition

The process by which a particular group, or its characteristics or actions, is identified as a collectivity by its real or imagined phenotypical characteristics or 'race'. More broadly, it refers to the ways in which social structures and ideologies become imbued with 'racial' meanings.

Distinctive Features

The concept of racialization emerged from historical work which shows that the idea of 'race' is a social construction that appeared at a particular time in European history and, since then, has been used to refer to divisions of the world's population in terms of supposedly fixed biological characteristics. In contrast, racialization draws attention to the ways in which ideas about 'race' have been and continue to be constructed, maintained and used as a basis for exclusionary practices. In its more general sense, the concept of racialization refers to cultural or political processes or situations where 'race' is invoked as an explanation or a means of understanding. Thus suggestions of distinctly 'Irish', 'Italian' or 'Jewish' forms of criminal activity and association could be understood as instances of racialization. A more specific usage analyses the ideological processes through which 'race' is given significance.

Examples of racialization in criminology include:

- the role of the media and authorities, such as the police, in defining street crime or 'mugging' – as well as 'steaming' and 'wilding' – as activities that are characteristic of young black men;
- the police's continuing use of racialized statistics on street crime to mount media campaigns against any diminution in their powers, such as stop and search;
- analysis of discourses of 'race', crime and nation in which criminality is seen as distinguishing black people of African and Caribbean origins as 'other' and as standing outside the boundaries of 'Britishness';
- accounts of 'black crime' and public disorders that rely on 'culturalist' explanations such as a matriarchy, the lack of a father/authority figure, or most crudely, a simple disrespect for English traditions of civility;
- racialization within fields of social policy – including education, employment and crime – that have variously served to construct the 'problem of black youth';
- the connections between 'race' and place that underlie police racializations of particular communities and areas (or 'symbolic locations');

- racialization and criminalization as twinned processes in the development of disciplinary strategies of governance and policing;
- the stigmatization of particular black subcultural styles;
- the identification and construction of particular groups, activities and commodities, for example connections between crack-cocaine and 'yardies' or 'posses';
- media and police constructions of a distinctively 'Asian' criminality;
- racialization within organizations and occupational cultures;
- the racialization of 'whiteness' through ideas of a white criminal underclass or 'white trash';
- the demonization of 'Islamic terrorists';
- racialization as a process of visualization, by which the beating of Rodney King by Los Angeles police officers, for example, could be redefined as a situation where he was seen as endangering the police.

Evaluation

Unlike the term 'race relations', racialization always highlights the constructed nature of 'race'. It shifts the focus of attention away from black people towards questions about how racialization structures and defines social relations. Connections between 'race' and, among many other things, locality, masculinity and sexuality could all be developed further. The contingent and constructed nature of 'race' implies that other constructions are possible, though the extent to which some associations endure indicates how deeply rooted racialization is. The multiplicity of racial constructions traversing their way across biology, culture, politics and nationality also indicates how flexibly racialization can operate.

Karim Murji

Associated Concepts: criminalization, demonization, institutional racism, police bias, social constructionism, stereotyping, stigma

Key Readings

Butler, J. (1993) 'Endangered/endangering: schematic racism and white paranoia', in R. Gooding-Williams (ed.), *Reading Rodney King/Reading Urban Uprising*. New York: Routledge.

Gilroy, P. (1987) *There Ain't No Black in the Union Jack*. London: Hutchinson.

Hall, S., Critcher, C., Jefferson, T., Clarke, J. and Roberts, B. (1978) *Policing the Crisis: Mugging, The State and Law and Order*. London: Macmillan.

Keith, M. (1993) *Race, Riots and Policing: Lore and Disorder in a Multi-racist Society*. London: UCL Press.

Solomos, J. (1988) *Black Youth, Racism and the State*. Cambridge: Cambridge University Press.

Webster, C. (1997) 'The construction of British "Asian" criminality', *International Journal of the Sociology of Law*, 25: 65–86.

RADICAL CRIMINOLOGIES

Definition

There is no single radical criminology. The term is used to delineate a series of distinct theoretical positions whose main common characteristic is one of anti-positivism. Rather than viewing crime as determined by individual or social pathology, radical criminologies assume humans are active agents in the construction of their own biographies. They are more concerned with discovering the meaning of criminal behaviour than they are with trying to isolate its specific causes.

Within the broad classification of 'radical criminology' there is a diverse range of theories that contest the behavioural questions posed by positivist criminologies. Crime is to be found less in particular individual characteristics and environmental conditions and more in relations of power and selective processes of criminalization. In labelling theory this is expressed in terms of a 'society' that creates rules. Within Marxism and critical criminology it is expressed in terms of 'a capitalist state' that has the power to criminalize those behaviours it deems 'threatening'. In some feminist perspectives it is expressed in the social construction of 'hegemonic masculinities' within patriarchal societies. All such notions have shifted the criminological agenda away from popular ideas about causation.

John Muncie

Associated Concepts: critical criminology, cultural criminology, feminist criminologies, interactionism, labelling, Marxist criminologies, new criminology, new deviancy theory

RADICAL FEMINISM

Definition

Radical feminism offers a systematic analysis of the nature of women's oppression, including the ways in which it is sustained through law and criminal justice processes. Its aim is not only to understand male dominance and the control of women and children, but also to end this. It defines what have been named variously as 'violence against women', 'sexual violence' and 'gender violence' as key elements in the power relations of patriarchy: that is, the maintenance of male power and control over women and children. Sexual violence has become a central concept in radical feminist theory, and women throughout the world have organized in a variety of ways to highlight, respond to, and campaign against it.

Distinctive Features

- Its central foci are male supremacy, men and masculinity as structured through the power relations of patriarchy: this is a universal social formation, characteristic of almost all known societies. Its analysis locates women's oppression in patriarchy – a systematic expression of male domination and control over women which permeates all social and political and economic institutions. Patriarchal oppression is conceptualized as fundamental and pervasive. Crossing public and private spheres, it impacts at the level of the state, law, culture and religion and reaches into the intimacy of the home, family and sexuality.

- Often conceptualized solely in terms of gender relations, radical feminism recognizes that, based on a familial model of power, patriarchy is also defined by generational gender power relations. In the traditional notion of 'rule by the father', its gender dimension facilitates an understanding of the power of men over women and its generational element – power hierarchies between men, between women, and over children. The generational dimension of patriarchy further provides a framework for understanding difference and change through time, at both societal and individual levels. This accords dynamism to the concept of patriarchy, enabling analysis of continuity, difference and change through time and between and within societies.
- Radical feminism is a women-centred theoretical perspective and political practice constructed by and for women, inspired by the Women's Liberation Movement of the 1970s. As a politics of resistance radical feminism, through the notion of 'praxis', insists that theory and activism are inseparable. As well as theorizing sexual violence (MacKinnon, 1987; Kelly, 1988) it has also been at the forefront of activism, as has been demonstrated in England by Women's Aid, the Rape Crisis Federation and campaigning groups like Justice for Women.
- Radical feminism is broadly based. Within it there exists a range of concerns and controversies adding to its richness. For example, while most radical feminist analysis holds a social constructionist position in relation to human nature, there are traces of biologistic arguments in early accounts (for example, Firestone's (1970) *The Dialectic of Sex* and Brownmiller's (1975) *Against Our Will*). The diversity of radical feminism is also illustrated by its range of concerns, which include sexuality, health, education, language and the facilitation of autonomous women's spaces, women-centred culture and women's communities in rural and city areas.
- Through its focus on the victimization of women and children, radical feminism has significantly impacted on criminology – by exposing the extent of victimization and by improving police and criminal justice treatment of female survivors of violent relationships and rape. It has also informed criminology and jurisprudence through its analysis of law as a patriarchal institution reflecting and reproducing male dominance. Man-made law is exposed as shaped by male norms and interests and structured around the situations and circumstances that they, rather than women, commonly encounter. Through its failure to effectively sanction male sexual violence or provide protection for women and children, the law acts as a form of male control. MacKinnon (1987) developed the analysis beyond the substance of law to include as well its style, form, ritual and language. The law creates an illusion of fairness and impartiality to mask its inherently masculinist nature.

Evaluation

For complicated reasons that are ultimately linked to its critique of male power there are difficulties in the representation of radical feminism. As a politics of resistance it is virtually unrecognizable in academic accounts, where it is often presented as an American phenomenon that is little changed since the 1970s. Its critique of heterosexuality as an institution predicated upon patriarchal gender power relations, enforced by sexual violence and the stigmatization of alternatives to sexual relationships with men (Rich, 1980), has also resulted in its being defined primarily in terms of lesbian separatism.

It is frequently claimed that radical feminism is based on an ahistorical and universalist model of patriarchy. While this may be true of some early US radical feminist theory, recent writings have been more nuanced to reflect difference, change and historical specificity (Radford et al., 2000).

Of specific relevance to criminology, radical feminism has been criticized for constructing women as 'victims'. This is misplaced. Radical feminism rejects the concept of 'victim' for that of 'survivor', while not denying the reality of victimization (Kelly, 1988). More recent writings recognize both concepts as problematic at the level of identity, as each is defined by unchosen experiences of violence. Radical feminism accords agency to women and men. At an individual level it recognizes that men are responsible for their own actions and the diversity of resistance, coping and survival strategies adopted by women. The presence of a vital radical feminist activism against male violence further highlights the power of women's agency.

A more difficult question relates to radical feminist strategies that are concerned with the law as a site (albeit one of many) for the struggle for change. Radical feminism identifies the law and criminal justice as patriarchal institutions, complicit in the oppression of women and children, and identifies sexual violence as a defining characteristic of patriarchal societies. Yet it also campaigns for changes in the law within a patriarchal social order. This may appear to be contradictory. However, radical feminism holds that the law is too significant an institution to neglect. For example, tens of thousands of individual women by necessity must resort to the law annually in order to make best use of the limited protection it offers. Politically, struggles through the law in campaigns for gender justice can play a significant awareness-raising role and at times can secure some beneficial changes. Nevertheless, radical feminism is not unaware of the limits or ironies of reformism. Whereas sociological theory has perceived the irresolvable tensions between working for long-term structural change and short-term reform, more creative approaches to this dilemma have been explored by radical feminism. Consequently, rather than adopting simplistic reformism, radical feminist strategies have more in common

with a transformative approach to the law – that is, one that involves the transformation of male categories and concepts to address women's experiences.

Radical feminist interventions in relation to violence against women are definitively one of the more successful areas of feminist practice:

> At the very least, their efforts have provided support for tens of thousands of women throughout the world and brought this issue into the public arena from which it cannot now be removed. This has provided a vehicle for change within institutions of the state as well as within wider society. Perceptions, discourses and reactions have all been challenged. (Dobash and Dobash, 1992: 298)

Nevertheless, radical feminism's achievements do not represent a non-controversial model of linear development or progress. Patriarchy has not been overthrown and violence against women has not been eliminated. The law and criminal justice systems are still effectively failing to sanction or prosecute this violence or accord effective protection to those women and children who have been victimized. The radical feminist project has not yet been concluded.

Jill Radford

Associated Concepts: family crime, feminist criminologies, feminist research, hegemonic masculinity, liberal feminism, violence

Key Readings

Dobash, R.E. and Dobash, R.P. (1992) *Rethinking Violence Against Women.* London: Sage.
Hester, M., Kelly, L. and Radford, J. (eds) (1996) *Women, Violence and Male Power.* Buckingham: Open University Press.
Kelly, L. (1988) *Surviving Sexual Violence.* Cambridge: Polity Press.
MacKinnon, C. (1987) *Feminism Unmodified: Discourses on Life and Law.* Cambridge, MA: Harvard University Press.

Radford, J., Friedberg, M. and Harne, L. (eds) (2000) *Women, Violence and Strategies for Action: Feminist Research, Policy and Practice*. Buckingham: Open University Press.
Rich, A. (1980) 'Compulsory heterosexuality and lesbian existence', *Signs*, 5 (4): 631–60.

RADICAL NON-INTERVENTION

Definition

A criminal justice strategy that advocates a minimalist approach to instances of law-breaking in order to reduce the range and depth of state intervention. The least amount of criminal justice processing as possible is viewed not only as humanitarian but also as being effective in preventing the development of criminal careers. Tolerance is preferred to moral indignation.

Distinctive Features

The phrase 'radical non-intervention' has been widely attributed to Edwin Schur. It is the logical policy implication of a labelling approach to understanding crime and deviance. If, as labelling theorists suggested, social reaction does not prevent offending and instead establishes deviant identities and careers, then the reach of the reaction should be reduced. If state intervention causes crime and is a significant agency in the creation of the crime, problem, then steps must be taken to limit its powers. In particular, Schur (1965) argued that a range of 'victimless crimes' should be removed from the remit of criminal law. Drug use, gambling, juvenile status offences (truancy, promiscuity), pornography and so on, it has been argued, may be undesirable, but tackling them with the full weight of the law is not only expensive, it is also generally ineffective. Criminalizing drug users, for instance, not only creates new classes of criminals; it may also drive them to commit further offences to support their habits,

encourage the development of organized crime and law enforcement corruption, and redirect resources away from health and treatment programmes. In short, the removal of many troubling behaviours from criminal law sanction has the potential to be a highly effective measure of crime reduction.

Radical non-intervention (and the labelling approach in general) grew in popularity during the 1960s and was in part a reflection of the emergent distrust of institutional intervention that developed throughout that decade. It has had a profound impact on social policy (Empey, 1982). A series of measures – decriminalization, diversion and deinstitutionalization – designed to limit the extent of the state's intrusion into offenders' lives have been implemented to varying degrees and with varying success in most Western criminal justice systems.

John Muncie

Associated Concepts: decriminalization, diversion, juvenile justice, labelling, tolerance, victimless crime

Key Readings

Empey, LaMar T. (1982) *American Delinquency: Its Meaning and Construction*, 2nd edn. Chicago, IL: Dorsey Press.
Schur, E.M. (1965) *Crime Without Victims*. Englewood Cliffs, NJ: Prentice-Hall.
Schur, E.M. (1974) *Radical Non-intervention: Rethinking the Delinquency Problem*. Englewood Cliffs, NJ: Prentice-Hall.

RATIONAL CHOICE THEORY

Definition

The starting-point for rational choice theory is that offenders seek an advantage for themselves by their criminal behaviour. This entails them making decisions about various alternatives. These decisions are rational within the constraints of time, ability and the availability of relevant information.

Distinctive Features

Rational choice theory is the perspective on offender behaviour which underpins situational crime prevention. Ronald V. Clarke is the leading proponent both of the theory and the situational prevention approach with which it is consistent. Demonstrating that crime could be distributed *as if* offenders were rational (Mayhew et al., 1976) predated the full presentation of the theory (Cornish and Clarke, 1986) by almost a decade. The Clarke and Cornish view dealt both with a person's initial decision to become involved in crime, and the decisions leading up to a crime, with the general decision to commit the offence having been made. The theory has been used more in its second area of application, with the 'choice-structuring' properties of pre-crime situations being the topic of most research in this tradition. Ways of thinking about choice-structuring properties are focusing increasingly on 'offending scripts'.

Rational choice theory has many similarities with routine activity theory. The latter concentrates on the necessary conditions for a crime to occur, namely the convergence in time and place of a motivated offender and a suitable victim in the absence of a capable guardian (Felson, 1997). The two perspectives hold in common a focus on the crime event. They are both concerned with how the press of circumstances shapes individual acts (rational choice) or acts of a particular class (routine activities). Rational choice theory appears to make no differential predictions that would allow a critical test against routine activity. Routine activity theory supposes that, in the aggregate, trends will look as if there were (limited) rationality at the individual level. What rational choice theory adds is twofold. First, a more precise exploration of what counts in people's heads as capable guardianship and victim suitability. And second, offender-specific departures from presumptive rationality, and

thereby a theoretical platform for offender profiling.

Since Ron Clarke and Marcus Felson are now frequent collaborators, we may see these theories being consolidated. Indeed, the process has already begun and their collaboration is increasingly concerned with ethical issues in crime control (Clarke and Felson, 1993). The more explicit application of rational choice theory to the practice of offender profiling would almost certainly prove fruitful.

Evaluation

Rational choice theory frees us from considering pathologies of offender motivation. It should find favour with many of those opposed to the demonizing of offenders as 'different'. It enables rationality to be applied to the design, distribution and maintenance of products and services to limit their vulnerability to crime (the essence of situational prevention), because the behaviour of rational offenders is predictable by other rational people in possession of the same information. One effect has been research in which offenders are questioned about their precautions and methods while offending, research which has proved remarkably fruitful.

It has been suggested (Trasler, 1993) that rational choice theory is more applicable to crime for gain than to 'expressive' crime. Arguably the theory is also liable to criticism on grounds of circularity, in that the choice-structuring properties nominated by offenders are deemed rational in the absence of a precise awareness of situations in which there may have been less risky and more profitable alternatives to hand. Thus, from a distance and without any counter-evidence, rationality is inferred wrongly. No such attack has yet been mounted in print.

Ken Pease

Associated Concepts: administrative criminology, crime science, neo-conservative criminology, opportunity theory, routine activity theory, situational crime prevention

Key Readings

Clarke, R.V. and Felson, M. (eds) (1993) *Routine Activity and Rational Choice*. London: Transaction.

Cornish, D. (1994) 'The procedural analysis of offending and its relevance to situational prevention', in R.V. Clarke (ed.), *Crime Prevention Studies 3*. Monsey, NY: Criminal Justice Press.

Cornish, D. and Clarke, R.V. (eds) (1986) *The Reasoning Criminal: Rational Choice Perspectives on Offending*. New York: Springer-Verlag.

Felson, M. (1997) *Crime and Everyday Life*, 2nd edn. Thousand Oaks, CA: Pine Forge Press.

Mayhew, P.M., Clarke, R.V., Sturman, A. and Hough, J.M. (eds) (1976) *Crime as Opportunity*, Home Office Research Study No. 34. London: HMSO.

Trasler, G. (1993) 'Conscience, opportunity, rational choice and crime', in R.V. Clarke and M. Felson (eds), *Advances in Criminological Theory*. New Brunswick, NJ: Transaction.

REALIST CRIMINOLOGIES

Definition

In contemporary criminology, realist theorizing is most closely associated with the rejection of utopian solutions to crime and the advocacy of pragmatic policies to pursue crime reduction. It originally surfaced as a right-wing critique of sociological positivism and radical criminologies in the USA in the mid-1970s which maintained that it was fruitless to search for the causes of crime and that sole attention should be returned to designing effective measures of crime control. A left-wing variant subsequently developed in Britain in the mid-1980s in order to formulate social democratic policies that would both take crime seriously and implement accountable programmes of crime control. Realist criminologies, of whatever ideological persuasion, are primarily concerned with developing responses to a perceived intensity in

the public's fear of crime – notably of street crime, violence and burglary.

John Muncie

Associated Concepts: administrative criminology, crime prevention, crime reduction, deterrence, fear of crime, left idealism, left realism, neo-conservative criminology, relative deprivation

REASSURANCE POLICING

See: 'Broken Windows'; Community policing; COMPSTAT; Zero tolerance

RECIDIVISM

Definition

Recidivism is concerned with the reconviction rates for offenders released from custody. Such rates are generally used to test whether a term of imprisonment can reduce future reoffending; whether different programmes undertaken within prison contribute towards reoffending; or whether other forms of community-based punishment are more effective at reducing further reoffending.

Distinctive Features

The most typical form of recidivist rate measures the proportion of offenders who have been reconvicted within a two-year period following release. However, this measure has to be used with some caution, as for example, it will reflect only those offences that have been reported, recorded and successfully prosecuted. Figures from a variety of criminal justice systems demonstrate that being sent to prison is likely to be related to future reoffending. For example, *Prison Statistics – England and Wales, 1997* (Home Office, 1998: 156) reveals that of all the prisoners who were discharged in 1994,

56 per cent were reconvicted within two years. This figure can be further broken down to demonstrate that women showed the lowest rate of reconviction, with 46 per cent reconvicted within two years, whereas young offenders had the highest rates of reconviction, with 75 per cent reconvicted within a two-year period.

The high rates of reconviction of young offenders sent to prison were given formal recognition by a government Green Paper in England and Wales entitled *Punishment, Custody and the Community,* which stated that with regard to young offenders even a short period of custody was likely to confirm them as 'criminals', particularly if they acquired new criminal skills from more sophisticated offenders. They see themselves labelled as criminals and are likely to behave accordingly (Home Office, 1988: 2.15).

Recidivist rates have thus also been used to affirm Robert Martinson's originally rather pessimistic analysis of the effectiveness of treatment programmes for the rehabilitation of offenders. Despite Martinson himself reassessing his evidence more favourably, the analysis gave rise to the infamous view that 'nothing works' in terms of treatment programmes within prisons.

None the less, while it is clear that prisons stigmatize rather than re-socialize offenders, attempts have also to be made to prevent them from further de-socializing offenders, and therefore to provide opportunities in prison for education, work and to accept self-responsibility. As a consequence, and prompted by research in Canada into the impact of 'cognitive skills' training on recidivist rates, a new debate has begun to consider 'what works' in a penal setting (Correctional Service of Canada, 1996). Research into 'what works' in reducing further offending would suggest that the following principles apply:

- That the greater the seriousness of both the offending and risk of reoffending, the more intensive and extensive any treatment programme should be.
- That any programme should target the needs of offenders which are directly related to their offending.

- That programmes encouraging the participation of offenders are more effective.
- That once a programme has been started it should be completed as planned and its results evaluated.

This has meant that specific programmes have been introduced within a variety of penal settings to help offenders overcome problems with, for example, drugs and alcohol, or to improve their educational or social skills. These interventions can be taken further and are sometimes targeted at specific types of offenders; in England and Wales, for example, a specific programme has been introduced to deal with sex offenders. Great claims are made for some of these programmes, and a Home Office research study, entitled *Reducing Reoffending,* suggests that 'larger percentage point reductions in recidivism (typically around 20 per cent of points lower than control groups) have been reported' (Goldblatt and Lewis, 1998). However, of late, concerns have also been expressed as to whether forcing prisoners to engage in treatment programmes presents other ethical problems.

More promisingly, research into the efficacy of HMP Grendon in England – which accepts only volunteers and operates as a therapeutic community – has also recently indicated some success in relation to recidivist rates (Marshall, 1997). This suggested that reconviction rates for those prisoners who stayed at HMP Grendon for at least 18 months were lower by as much as one-fifth to one-quarter, based on a prediction of the likely number of future offences which would have been committed by the group under consideration had they not gone to Grendon. This predictive use of recidivist rates is becoming increasingly common.

While most figures demonstrate that going to prison is likely to be related to future offending, they also demonstrate that noncustodial sanctions – whilst substantially cheaper – are not much better at reducing the likelihood of future reoffending (cf. Kershaw et al., 1999). What this suggests is that sentencing decisions, whether these are to incarcerate or punish in the community, have little to do with those factors that influence offending behaviour.

Evaluation

Recidivism is clearly related to being sent to prison. Except in certain circumstances prison stigmatizes rather than rehabilitates and as such any sentencing decision should be based on factors other than the possible beneficial consequences of a period of imprisonment. Some positive interventions can be offered to prisoners who have been incarcerated. The key word here is 'offered', and ethical considerations – such as the desirability of forcing prisoners to engage in treatment by, for example, making this a condition for early release – having rarely featured in the 'What Works?' debate should be more clearly acknowledged.

David Wilson

Associated Concepts: desistance, evaluation research, incarceration, prediction studies, rehabilitation, reparation

Key Readings

Correctional Service of Canada (1996) *The Impact of Cognitive Skills Training on Post Release Supervision among Canadian Federal Offenders*. Ottawa: Correctional Service of Canada.

Goldblatt, P. and Lewis, C. (eds) (1998) *Reducing Reoffending*, Research Study No. 187. London: Home Office.

Home Office (1988) *Punishment, Custody and the Community*, cm 424. London: HMSO.

Home Office (1998) *Prison Statistics – England and Wales, 1997*, cm 4017. London: HMSO.

Kershaw, C., Goodman, J. and White, S. (1999) *Reconviction of Offenders Sentenced or Released from Prison in 1995*, Home Office Research Findings No. 101. London: HMSO.

Marshall, P. (1997) *A Reconviction Study of HMP Grendon Therapeutic Community*, Home Office Research Findings No. 53. London: HMSO.

REDRESS

Definition

According to the *Concise Oxford Dictionary*, 'redress' can mean: to put right or in good order again; to remedy or remove trouble of any kind; to set right, repair, rectify something suffered or complained of like a wrong; to correct, amend, reform or do away with a bad or faulty state of things; to repair an action; to atone for a misdeed or offence; to save, deliver from misery, to restore or bring back a person to a proper state, to happiness or prosperity, to the right course; to set a person right by obtaining or (more rarely) giving satisfaction or compensation for the wrong or loss sustained, teaching, instructing and redressing the erroneous by reason (Sixth Edition, 1976: 937).

Distinctive Features

This seemingly 'obsolete' concept carries with it an elaborate set of different meanings which is why the notion of 'redress' provides such a useful alternative to the key concepts of both 'punishment' and 'crime'. Traditional criminological discourse and, more specifically, deterrence theory support the myth of a direct causal relationship between crime and punishment. The complex notion of 'redress' offers a perspective in which problematic events, normally calling forth punitive intervention by the criminal justice system, are not automatically subsumed under universalistic categories, but rather established through a process of understanding and creative response. As such, the notion of 'redress' can be seen as part of a more comprehensive 'replacement discourse' 'that begins the deconstruction of crime and crime control, the correction of corrections and the ultimate criminal justice policy that denies itself' (Henry and Milovanovic, 1994: 130).

Evaluation

Advantages of the notion of 'redress' are, briefly:

- that it includes almost every conceivable reaction to an event – individual, collective – which causes material or immaterial harm;
- that it implies a response is mandatory, without pre-defining the event as a crime, an illness or whatever;
- that it invites analysis of the event before deciding on or choosing a proper response;
- that as a concept with ancient origins, it invokes a consideration of historical and anthropological forms of dispute settlement and conflict resolution for possible clues to rational forms of response.

To claim redress is merely to assert that an undesirable event has taken place and that something needs to be done about it. It carries no implications concerning what sort of reaction would be appropriate and nor does it define reflexively the nature of the initial event. Since it invites an open discussion about how an unfortunate event should be viewed and what the appropriate response ought to be, it can be viewed as a rational response *par excellence*. It puts forth the claim for a procedure rather than for a specific result. Punitive claims already implied in defining an event as a 'crime' are opened up to rational debate. Thus, to advocate 'redress' is to call for 'real dialogue' (Christie, 1982) at every level of 'crime' control proceedings.

In this way, the notion of 'redress' is put forward in order to reconceptualize the familiar concepts of 'crime' and 'punishment' and generate a critical and constructive alternative to the politics of crime, punishment and penal reform. It is an approach which is ambitious and modest at the same time. The politics of 'redress' tries to combine principles of generalizability and universality with those of contextuality, solidarity and care – not as a blueprint, but as a perspective and a commitment, enabling criminology to liberate itself from the punitive logic of exclusion.

Willem de Haan

Associated Concepts: abolitionism, constitutive criminology, peacemaking criminology, restorative justice, shaming

Key Readings

Christie, N. (1982) *Limits to Pain*. Oxford: Martin Robertson.
de Haan, W. (1990) *The Politics of Redress: Crime, Punishment and Penal Abolition*. London: Unwin Hyman.
Henry, S. and Milovanovic, D. (1994) 'The constitution of constitutive criminology: a postmodern approach to criminological theory', in D. Nelken (ed.), *The Futures of Criminology*. London: Sage. pp. 110–33.
van Swaaningen, R. (1997) *Critical Criminology: Visions from Europe*. London: Sage.

REFLEXIVITY

Definition

The process of monitoring and reflecting on all aspects of a research project from the formulation of research ideas through to the publication of findings and, where this occurs, their utilization. Sometimes the product of such monitoring and reflection will be a reflexive account which will be published as part of the research report.

Distinctive Features

Although important in all areas of social research, reflexivity has an especial role in ethnography in which the investigator is close to the subjects and to the data. What is more, the whole process of formulating ideas, collecting observations, analysing and reaching conclusions is part of the role of the investigator *vis-à-vis* those who are the objects of enquiry. It is for this reason that ethnographers see reflexivity as part of research in its own right and not as a collection of afterthoughts on how a project has been accomplished.

At one level, a reflexive account will be descriptive in terms of providing an account of, for example, how interviews were carried out, what methods of recording data were used and so on. However, at another – and much more important – level a reflexive account should be evaluative in terms of providing some assessment of the likely validity of the conclusions that have been reached. This might, for example, involve a consideration of whether the respondents selected for interview are typical of the group about which conclusions are to be made; whether there is a possibility that responses to questions were the outcome of exaggeration or even downright falsification; and whether the method for recording data resulted in only a partial, or even distorted, account of reality. These are what are known as 'threats to validity'. A researcher may not be able to anticipate and rule these out. However, s/he should be aware of them and provide some assessment of their potential effects on the validity of conclusions. At a minimum, the expectation is that the researcher will provide sufficient detail about the research process – and decisions taken within it – to allow the reader to make some judgement by him/herself.

Ethnographic research on criminal subcultures has produced some classic and colourful reflexive accounts of 'how it was done'. These include William Foote Whyte's account of *Street Corner Society*, Clifford Shaw's life history of *The Jack Roller* and Carl Klockars' interviews with *The Professional Fence*. To take the latter as one example, Klockars describes how he used different data sources – such as letters, newspaper articles, bills, sales receipts and stock certificates – to triangulate his conclusions and thereby improve their validity.

On occasions reflexivity involves not just monitoring and assessing validity (to what extent are the conclusions credible and plausible?) but also questions of ethics (has anyone been harmed by the research?) and questions of politics (whose side am I on, if any?). Validity, ethics and politics can impact on one another. For example, a decision not to publish interview material collected from corrupt policemen, for fear of exposing them, will not result in a full and valid account of the realities of police subcultures. Therefore, reflexivity often involves the researcher in reaching a personal standpoint in relation to trade-offs that often have to be made between validity, politics and ethics.

Evaluation

Reflexivity is concerned with the social production of knowledge. It involves reflecting on the various social roles, interactions and processes that resulted in the kinds of observations and conclusions that emerged. It is possible to consider reflexivity in a sense wider than that of monitoring and assessing the validity of a particular research project. This wider perspective involves viewing critical reflection as a form of research in its own right, and as part of the school of critical thinking and theorizing in the social sciences in general. A critical research agenda could include a consideration of why particular (say, punitive) law and order discourses take the form that they do and come to be accepted as 'truths' when this happens. What is more, it could consider the role of criminological research in the production and dissemination of such 'truths'. This would involve reflecting on the criminological enterprise as a whole and asking such questions as what gets studied, when and by whom, and what gets published, and with what effect?

Victor Jupp

Associated Concepts: appreciative criminology, Chicago School of Sociology, critical research, ethnography, participant observation, research ethics, triangulation

Key Readings

Hughes, G. (2000) 'The politics of criminological research', in V. Jupp, P. Davies and P. Francis (eds), *Doing Criminological Research*. London: Sage.

Jupp, V.R. (1996) *Methods of Criminological Research*. London: Routledge.

Klockars, C.B. (1974) *The Professional Fence*. London: Tavistock.

Shaw, C.R. (1930) *The Jack Roller*. Chicago: University of Chicago Press.

Whyte, W.F. (1943) *Street Corner Society* (2nd edn 1955). Chicago: University of Chicago Press.

REGULATION

See: Governance; Governmentality; Managerialism; Social control

REGULATORY AGENCIES

Definition

The determination of bodies of law and the establishment of some agency, usually a state agency, for enforcing and overseeing compliance with such laws.

Distinctive Features

While the social scientific concern with regulation is long-standing – the first regulatory agency (the British Factory Inspectorate) was documented by Marx in *Capital* – this became prominent in the USA in the so-called Progressive Era of 1900–16, and then again during the New Deal of the 1930s, as part of a general concern with the activities of 'big business'. Bernstein's (1955) path-breaking work on regulation constituted a searing critique of the contemporary state of regulatory enforcement and set out a 'Capture Theory' of regulation, positing that regulatory agencies were not able to maintain themselves as representatives of 'public interest' even if this is why they are formed, because an inevitable life-cycle of enthusiasm, the provocation of a reaction from the regulated, and the demise of original agency zeal will all ensure that the interests of some generalized public will become subsumed to the demands of a regulated industry (Bernstein, 1955). Such a view of regulation continues to have some force. For some (instrumental) Marxists, a regulatory agency is subordinated to a state which is itself simply an instrument of capital or a ruling class; for some neo-liberal thinkers, regulatory agencies are inevitably captured by organized interests to distort 'free' markets. The common feature of these (different) perspectives is that regulatory agencies operate in a biased fashion. Capture Theory has been challenged by other Marxists and some critical criminologists who argue that regulation is the outcome of class conflict and compromise; the role of regulatory agencies is thus to mediate the conflicts between competing class interests as part of the process of maintaining a hegemonic domination.

In the 1970s, studies of the enforcement of new social regulation – for example, around occupational safety and health and environmental legislation – began to emerge in various nation-states, though particularly in the USA. Simultaneously, the new social regulation also prompted (largely neo-liberal) critics to call for the removal of these laws and the bodies designed to enforce them. These latter deregulatory arguments have assumed increasing importance across advanced capitalist economies – albeit variably – in the past quarter of a century. The dominant strand in regulatory concern within and around criminology has contributed to this 'debate' between regulation and deregulation, focusing in particular upon the issue of enforcement; that is, how do and how should regulatory agencies enforce the law?

The distinction between compliance-oriented and punitive modes of enforcement is a key one within the literature on regulatory enforcement. While the aim of the latter is said to be to apply a punishment for breaking a rule and doing harm, the goal of a compliance strategy is to prevent a harm rather than punish an evil. Enforcers advise, educate, bargain, negotiate and compromise with the regulated. While there are, of course, important national differences in enforcement strategies, and in enforcement strategies across different spheres of business activity (for example, financial regulation has generally been stricter than that pertaining to occupational health and safety), it is fair to say that compliance-oriented enforcement techniques do dominate (Pearce and Tombs, 1998: 229–45). There now exist a mass of studies – mostly nationally based, though with some useful cross-national comparative studies also – regarding the practices of a whole range of regulatory bodies. In general, non-enforcement is the most frequently found characteristic. Enforcement activity tends to focus upon the smallest and weakest individuals and organizations, and the sanctions following regulatory activity are light (Snider, 1993: 120–4). Hutter has recently pointed to a body of evidence from Australia, Britain, the Netherlands, Sweden and the USA, indicating that regulators increasingly favour compliance-based methods – an emerging preference which extends to financial regulation and certain areas of 'conventional' policing (Hutter, 1997: 243).

Evaluation

Much work on regulation not only documents a compliance-oriented approach as that which regulators adopt, but also tends to endorse (some version of) this as the most appropriate enforcement approach (Pearce and Tombs, 1998: 223–46). This endorsement is based upon combining a recognition of the power of business *vis-à-vis* regulators – and thus a concern not to provoke counterproductive tendencies through punitive enforcement – and also the claim that business offences call for different forms of regulation from those for other kinds of law breaking – a view reducible to the claim that business crime is not real crime as it differs substantially from 'conventional' crime.

Linked to such claims are arguments around the potential of (enforced) self-regulation, a form of enforcement where the onus for compliance with the law is placed upon the regulated themselves but distinct from deregulation, with the latter term usually referring to the removal of laws designed to regulate the corporation. Increasingly allied to arguments around enforced self-regulation are claims regarding the utility of 'goal-oriented' (reflexive) over prescriptive (command and control) legislation. While the latter is said to specify the means of securing compliance, the former entails an agency negotiating 'the substantive regulatory goal with industry, leaving the industry discretion and responsibility of how to achieve this goal' (Ayres and Braithwaite, 1992: 38).

Regulation raises an enormous range of complex issues which go straight to the core of debates about the nature and role of the law, corporations, contemporary economies and states. Current debates around the need or otherwise for international regulatory structures seem to become more pressing given the increasing momentum of claims regarding the demise of the nation-state, the internationalization of business activity, and the proliferation of social harms associated with these processes.

Steve Tombs and Dave Whyte

Associated Concepts: corporate crime, criminalization, deterrence, extraterritorial law enforcement, governance, self-policing, social harm, the state, transnational policing, white collar crime

Key Readings

Ayres, I. and Braithwaite, J. (1992) *Responsive Regulation: Transcending the Deregulation Debate.* Oxford: Oxford University Press.
Baldwin, R., Scott, C. and Hood, R. (eds) (1998) *A Reader on Regulation.* Oxford: Oxford University Press.
Bernstein, B.H. (1955) *Regulating Business by Independent Commission.* Princeton, NJ: Princeton University Press.
Hutter, B. (1997) *Compliance: Regulation and the Environment.* Oxford: The Clarendon Press.
Pearce, F. and Tombs, S. (1998) *Toxic Capitalism: Corporate Crime and the Chemical Industry.* Aldershot: Dartmouth.
Snider, L. (1993) *Bad Business: Corporate Crime in Canada.* Toronto: University of Toronto Press.

REHABILITATION

Definition

The rehabilitation model takes the stance that crime is best prevented by directly addressing the factors – economic, social or personal – believed to be the cause of crime. The treatment model is a special case of the rehabilitation model in that it seeks to work directly with the individual offender in order to bring about a reduction in offending.

Distinctive Features

The basis of the rehabilitation model is that if the factors that bring about crime can be addressed then it is possible to reduce crime. For example, it is clear from the research literature that there is an association between unemployment and crime. A rehabilitative solution would therefore attempt to enhance the prospects of offenders gaining employment. This aim might be achieved through legislation, or through working with employers, or through working with offenders to give them skills suited to the job market. Similarly, poor educational achievement is another factor associated with crime. A rehabilitative solution might be to improve school conditions and so raise educational standards, or to have educational schemes specifically aimed at offenders. As Cullen and Gilbert (1982) note, the rehabilitative ideal stands directly opposed to ever-escalating levels of punishment as a response to crime. The ethos of rehabilitation holds that not all members of society are equal and that when crime arises from that inequality the constructive response is to redress that inequality. Some agencies within the criminal justice system, such as the probation service, have historically had the rehabilitative ideal as their driving force. In other cases it is voluntary agencies, such as the National Association for the Care and Resettlement of Offenders (NACRO), that seek to put rehabilitation into effect.

The *treatment model* is a special case of the rehabilitative model in that is has as its focus the individual offender. Historically, the development of psychological theories of criminal behaviour led to attempts to turn theory into practice. As new treatment methods followed theoretical advances, so a range of therapeutic approaches began to be applied to work with offenders. The earliest treatments aimed at offenders worked within a psychoanalytic tradition. For example, August Aichhorn (1925/1955) articulated a psychoanalytic formulation within which delinquent behaviour was seen as the product of a failure in psychological development; from this position Aichhorn developed therapeutic methods to work with young offenders. From the 1930s through to the 1970s, treatment with offenders was dominated by psychodynamic theory and practice, with counselling and group therapy being particularly popular. Educational programmes were also widespread during that period: a trend that is still evident today. While treatment within a psychodynamic tradition continues, the decades since the 1970s have seen a rise in treatment programmes based on behavioural and cognitive-behavioural theory.

Jeffery (1960) notes that there are three assumptions inherent within a rehabilitation, and particularly a treatment, philosophy: *determinism, differentiation* and *pathology*. Each of these assumptions sets advocates of rehabilitation in potential conflict with a criminal justice system that is built on principles of individual responsibility.

First, determinism maintains that factors outside of the individual's control – biological, psychological, social, or a combination of all three – bring about the individual's behaviour. Second, the logical conclusion from a deterministic position is that criminals must, in some way, be different from non-criminals. The origin of this differentiation may be biological, psychological or social, but it remains the case that criminals are different from those who are not criminals. Third, the notion of pathology, the logical step from differentiation, is that the difference between criminals and non-criminals is one of abnormality. The cause of the abnormality may be individual to the offender (biological or psychological) or social through learning from an abnormal environment.

As a net result, we arrive at a position in which the offender is portrayed as a victim of circumstance, with some level of individual or social 'wrongness' or abnormality as the root cause of their behaviour. There are cases where the legal system makes due allowances, as for example with mentally disordered offenders, but in the main, determinism, differentiation and pathology stand in direct conflict with a justice system based on the notions of free will and individual agency in making choices. A deterministic position, in which the individual is compelled to offend by forces beyond their control, is not in accord with the classical concept of rational hedonism as the basis for dispensing justice.

During the 1970s and 1980s the rehabilitative ideal fell heavily from favour as the notion that 'nothing works' gathered momentum. However, the 1990s saw a remarkable resurrection of rehabilitation, certainly in Canada and Britain and also in parts of the USA. Its return to grace within the criminal justice system can be directly traced to the impact of a string of meta-analytic studies of the effects of offender treatment (see for example Redondo et al., 1999). The message that emerged from these studies was that treatment with offenders can have a small but significant effect in terms of reducing re-offending. Further, when certain treatment factors are combined, the meta-analyses suggest that this small effect can be amplified. This research gave rise to the movement known as 'What Works?' (McGuire, 1995). The current concern lies with the design, implementation and evaluation of 'high impact' treatment characteristics of programmes for offenders. While practical success might be achievable, there remains the issue of rethinking the conceptual assumptions of determinism, differentiation and pathology (Hollin, 1999).

Clive Hollin

Associated Concepts: behaviour modification, conditioning, determinism, pathology, positivism, probation, social learning theory, 'what works'

Key Readings

Aichhorn, A. (1955) *Wayward Youth* (trans.). New York: Meridian Books. (Originally published 1925.)

Cullen, F. and Gilbert, K. (1982) *Reaffirming Rehabilitation.* Cincinnati, OH: Anderson Publishing.
Hollin, C.R. (1999) 'Treatment programmes for offenders: meta-analysis, "what works", and beyond', *International Journal of Psychiatry and Law,* 22: 361–72.
Jeffery, C.R. (1960) 'The historical development of criminology', in H. Mannheim (ed.), *Pioneers in Criminology.* London: Stevens.
McGuire, J. (ed.) (1995) *What Works? Reducing Reoffending.* Chichester: Wiley.
Redondo, S., Sanchez-Meca, J. and Garrido, V. (1999) 'The influence of treatment programmes on the recidivism of juvenile and adult offenders: a European meta-analytic review', *Psychology, Crime and Law,* 5: 251–78.

REINTEGRATIVE SHAMING

See: Desistance; Shaming

RELATIVE DEPRIVATION

Definition

A concept, latterly most associated with left realism, by which it is maintained that it is not necessarily absolute deprivation or poverty that causes crime but discontent arising from perceptions of disadvantage and injustice.

Distinctive Features

First coined by Sam Stouffer and his associates in their wartime study *The American Soldier* (1949), relative deprivation was rigorously formulated by W.G. Runciman in 1966. Its use in criminology was not until the 1980s, by theorists such as S. Stack, John Braithwaite and particularly the left realists, for whom it is a key concept. Its attraction as an explanatory variable in the postwar period lies in the rise of crime in the majority of industrial societies despite the increase in living standards, that is, where material deprivation in an absolute sense declined and the old equation of 'the more poverty the more crime' was clearly falsified.

Relative deprivation occurs where individuals or groups subjectively view themselves as unfairly disadvantaged over others perceived as having similar attributes and deserving similar rewards (their reference groups). It is in contrast with absolute deprivation, where biological health is impaired or where relative levels of wealth are compared based on objective differences – although it is often confused with the latter. Subjective experiences of deprivation are essential and, indeed, relative deprivation is more likely when the differences between two groups narrow so that comparisons can more easily be made, than where there are caste-like differences. The discontent arising from relative deprivation has been used to explain radical politics (whether of the left or the right), messianic religions, the rise of social movements, industrial disputes and the whole plethora of crime and deviance.

The usual distinction made is that religious fervour or the demand for political change is a collective response to relative deprivation whereas crime is an individualistic response. But this is certainly not true of many crimes – for example, smuggling, poaching or terrorism – which have a collective nature and a communal base, and it does not even allow for gang delinquency, which is clearly a collective response. The connection, therefore, is largely under-theorized – a reflection of the separate development of the concept within the seemingly discrete disciplines of sociology of religion, political sociology and criminology.

The use of relative deprivation in criminology is often conflated with Merton's anomie theory of crime and deviance and its development in subcultural theory by Cloward and Ohlin. There are discernible, although largely unexplored, parallels. Anomie theory involves a disparity between culturally induced aspirations (for example, success in terms of the American Dream) and the opportunities to realize them. The parallel is clear: this is a subjective process wherein discontent is transmuted into crime. Furthermore, Merton, in his classic 1938 article 'Social Structure and Anomie', clearly understands the relative nature of discontent by explicitly criticizing theories that link absolute deprivation to crime by pointing to poor countries with low crime rates in contrast to the wealthy USA with a comparatively high rate. But there are clear differences. In particular, Mertonian anomie involves an inability to realize culturally induced notions of success. It does not involve comparisons between groups but individuals measuring themselves against a general goal. The fact that Merton, the major theorist of reference groups, did not fuse this with his theory of anomie is, as Runciman notes, very strange, but probably reflects the particular American concern with 'winners' and 'losers' and the individualism of that culture. The empirical implications of this difference in emphasis are, however, significant: anomie theory would naturally predict the vast majority of crime to occur at the bottom of society amongst the 'losers', but relative deprivation theory does not necessarily have this overwhelming class focus. Discontent can be felt anywhere in the class structure where people perceive their rewards as unfair compared to those with similar attributes. Thus crime would be more widespread, although it would be conceded that discontent would be greatest amongst the socially excluded.

Evaluation

The future integration of anomie and relative deprivation theory offers great promise in that relative deprivation offers a much more widespread notion of discontent. Its emphasis on subjectivity ensures against the tendency within anomie theory of merely measuring objective differences in equality (so called 'strain' theory). Anomie theory, on its part, offers a wider structural perspective in terms of the crucial role of differential opportunity structures, and firmly locates the dynamic of deprivation within capitalist society as a whole.

Jock Young

375

Associated Concepts: anomie, left realism, strain theory, subculture

Key Readings

Box, S. (1987) *Recession, Crime and Punishment.* London: Macmillan.

Lea, J. and Young, J. (1993) *What is to be Done About Law and Order?* London: Pluto.

Merton, R. (1938) 'Social structure and anomie', American Sociological Review, 3 (5), 672–682.

Runciman, W.G. (1966) *Relative Deprivation and Social Justice.* London: Routledge.

Stouffer, S.A. (1949) *The American Soldier.* Princeton: Princeton University Press.

Young, J. (1999) *The Exclusive Society.* London: Sage.

REPARATION

Definition

Actions that aim to repair the damage caused by crime. These can include restitution for the victim.

Distinctive Features

Although the terms 'reparation' and 'restitution' are often used interchangeably, a distinction can be drawn between them. Restitution implies the restoration of goods or monetary compensation for loss or injury to the victim. Reparation has the wider aims of recognition of the social rights of victims and repairing the social damage caused by crime, in which restitution may play a part.

Principles of reparation and restitution emphasize the right of victims to obtain some redress for the loss or harm they have suffered. Modern Western criminal justice systems, by contrast, give primacy to the punishment of offenders in the general interest, reflecting principles of retribution (the offender should pay a debt to society) or the prevention of future crime. The rights of victims to seek redress have become, at best, marginal in the course of what Christie (1977) famously described as the 'theft' by the state of conflicts between victims and offenders.

More recognition of the rights of victims has been a feature of criminal justice systems in recent decades, largely as a result of the growth in social movements to promote victims' interests. One manifestation of this has been a widening of the powers of courts to order offenders to make some form of restitution (compensation orders) to the victim, either in addition to punishment or as an alternative to it. One of several problems with these schemes (Ashworth, 1986) is that compensation of this type is analogous to civil damages and thus lacks penal value: that is, the payment of compensation does not necessarily meet other penal aims (such as the prevention of future crime). Moreover, the use of such orders by the criminal courts means that compensation for individual victims becomes dependent upon the particular offender being caught and convicted and also being willing and able to pay. State compensation schemes, which have been established in several jurisdictions, may give better assurance of compensation for victims (although eligibility and levels of payment are often restricted), but since they require nothing from the offender, they cannot meet either the traditional aims of punishment or the broader aims of restoration. Advocates of the restitution and reparation principle often argue that state compensation provision is necessary as a back-up, but that restitution should come from the offender wherever possible.

The idea of reparation (and restitution in its wider sense) implies more than the provision of compensation for victims. Repairing the social damage of crime requires that offenders should acknowledge the wrongfulness of their actions. Part of this involves making amends to the victim (through monetary compensation or, especially in the case of poor offenders, the performance of some service) and/or the community (for example, through community service, especially when there is no identifiable victim). It also entails the active participation of both victim and offender in the process, giving both the chance to explain their position and to resolve their own conflict. Since formal court procedures do not allow these voices full expression, particularly that of the victim, informal justice procedures, especially that of mediation, are seen as appropriate. The purpose is to address the full impact of the crime on the victim (for example, increased fear) and to identify a way whereby the offender can do something positive for them. Realization of the harm caused and the making of positive amends may also facilitate the social reintegration of the offender.

Evaluation

Principles of reparation and restitution have assumed greater importance in recent years, as shown by the growth in state-sponsored compensation, in compensation ordered by criminal courts, and in victim–offender mediation schemes at the pre-prosecution, pre-sentence and post-sentence stages of the criminal justice process. However, the traditional principles of punishment have remained dominant. From some critical penological perspectives (notably abolitionism but also other communitarian theories such as 'reintegrative shaming'), it is held to be desirable that reparation, rather than punishment, should become the organizing principle of justice: reparative or restorative justice. Other commentators, while recognizing the importance of addressing the rights and needs of victims, have noted various problems with reparative justice. These focus upon the issue of whether reparation involves an adequate recognition of the harms done to the wider community and whether it has sufficient 'penal value' to control crime.

Maggie Sumner

Associated Concepts: abolitionism, communitarianism, informal justice, redress, restorative justice, shaming, victimology

Key Readings

Ashworth, A. (1986) 'Punishment and compensation: victims, offenders and the state', *Oxford Journal of Legal Studies*, 6: 86–122.

Barnett, R.E. (1977) 'Restitution: a new paradigm in crime control', *Ethics*, 87: 279–301.

Christie, N. (1977) 'Conflicts as property', *British Journal of Criminology*, 17 (1): 1–15.

Hudson, J. and Galaway, B. (1980) *Victims, Offenders and Alternative Sanctions*. Lexington, MA: Lexington Books.

Wright, M. (1991) *Justice for Victims and Offenders*. Buckingham: Open University Press.

Zedner, L. (1992) 'Reparation and retribution: are they reconcilable?', *Modern Law Review*, 37: 228–50.

REPEAT VICTIMIZATION

Definition

Repeat victimization occurs when the same location, person, business, vehicle or household suffers more than one crime event over a specified time period. The offence may be of the same or a contrasting type.

Distinctive Features

Crime is preventable insofar as it is predictable in time and place. 'Sting' operations by the police engineer such predictability, for example by setting up a shop and letting it be known that it will deal in stolen goods, or by leaving a frequently stolen vehicle type in a high crime area, having suitably modified it in order to trap a would-be thief inside. Such operations are liable to the charge of entrapment (literally, in the latter case). A less contentious approach involves targeting people and places that are at a high risk of crime occurring. Recent crime victimization is a good predictor of future victimization – almost certainly the best such predictor available without any additional analysis being necessary (Pease, 1998). An officer attending a crime scene needs no extra information to alert him or her to the elevated risk of future victimization. Targeting prior victims for crime prevention help is an attractive option, for several reasons:

- It requires no analysis; it is light on resources.
- It combines crime prevention help and victim support, since both are required by the same people at the same time.
- The deployment of help can be time-limited, since a repeat crime against the same target *tends* to happen quickly.
- There is emerging evidence that prolific offenders are disproportionately responsible for repeat offending against the same target, so the incapacitation of those inflicting such repeat victimization may be especially productive in crime reduction.

There are two basic reasons for the repetition of a crime against the same target. These are known formally as risk heterogeneity and event dependence, and colloquially as flag and boost accounts. Examples will be taken from the offence of burglary. *Risk heterogeneity* occurs because the same attributes *that flag* a place or person as a good target at time 1, continue to do so at time 2. Thus lace curtains and porcelain ladies in crinolines as window ornaments will alert the passer-by to the likely age of the householder and her possible vulnerability to burglary by deception. They will flag the same message to every passer-by. *Event dependence* occurs when the experience during the first offence *boosts* the attraction of coming back and doing it again. This may be because much cash is found and thus may well be found again. It might also be because any electronic goods will likely be replaced by insurers and therefore the replacement goods could be stolen as well. Being new, these will fetch a higher price. Research evidence, notably offender accounts, suggest that both flag and boost accounts are relevant to repeat victimization (Ashton et al., 1998; Lauritsen and Davis Quinet, 1995).

An important virtue of the concept and associated research programme is that it picks apart the crude notion of crime incidence, defined as the number of crime events per population at risk. Incidence can be seen to be a function of crime prevalence (the number of those victimized within a population at risk) and crime concentration (the number of victimizations per victim). Thus, in a population of 100 homes, a total of 20 burglaries may be suffered. Therefore 0.20 is the burglary incidence. This may be a result of 20 homes being burgled once (i.e., a prevalence of 0.20 and a concentration of 1), or of one home being burgled 20 times (i.e., a prevalence of 0.01 and a concentration of 20), or any intermediate pattern. Research carried out within a repeat victimization framework showed that the extent to which areas differed in crime rate was to a surprisingly large extent a function of area differences in crime concentration (Trickett et al., 1992). It is only when the contribution of prevalence and concentration to an area's crime problem is unpicked that a solution can be intelligently formulated.

The prevention of repeat victimization has been the means whereby some successful crime reduction programmes have achieved their effect (Chenery et al., 1997; Forrester et al., 1988). No doubt the mechanisms involved are complex and varied, but repeat victimization does have the central advantage of directing crime prevention efforts towards individuals at a high risk of crime in areas with high rates of crime. The first part of the advantage is something which hot-spot analysis lacks. The emerging link between prolific offenders and repeat victimization affords a means for targeting prolific offenders through the kinds of crime which they are likely to commit and for avoiding personal surveillance with all its civil rights ambiguities.

Evaluation

Recent work is now developing a more subtle view, invoking the notion of 'virtual repeats' whereby the repetition is not physically against the same object or person but against functionally identical objects, such as the same model of Ferrari or homes with the same floor plan. In this way, repeat victimization is set to merge with the study of offender targeting practices along the dimension of similarity.

Ken Pease

Associated Concepts: community crime prevention, crime prevention, defensible space, geographies of crime, situational crime prevention, social crime prevention, victim surveys, victimology

Key Readings

Ashton J., Senior, B., Brown, I. and Pease, K. (1998) 'Repeat victimization: offender accounts', *International Journal of Risk, Security and Crime Prevention*, 3: 269–80.

Chenery S., Holt, J. and Pease, K. (1997) *Biting Back II: Reducing Repeat Victimization in Huddersfield*, Crime Detection and Prevention Paper 82. London: Home Office.

Forrester D., Chatterton, M. and Pease, K. (1988) *The Kirkholt Burglary Prevention Project, Rochdale*, Crime Prevention Unit Paper 13. London: Home Office.

Lauritsen, J.L. and Davis Quinet, K.F. (1995) 'Repeat victimization among adolescents and young adults', *Journal of Quantitative Criminology,* 11: 143–66.

Pease, K. (1998) *Repeat Victimization: Taking Stock*, Crime Detection and Prevention Paper 90. London: Home Office.

Trickett, A., Osborn, D., Seymour, J. and Pease, K. (1992) 'What is different about high crime areas?', *British Journal of Criminology*, 32: 81–9.

REPLACEMENT DISCOURSE

See: Constitutive criminology; Social harm

RESEARCH ETHICS

Definition

Ethics are ways of thinking about what is right, moral or good, and involve a process of moral reasoning and justification. Work in research ethics entails developing the practices and judgements necessary to undertake research in an ethical manner. It also includes the development and analysis of bureaucratic systems for regulating the ethics of research.

Distinctive Features

The research ethics literature develops traditions of normative ethics to consider morally appropriate responses to ethical dilemmas in research. Deontological approaches view certain sorts of actions as good in themselves, irrespective of the consequences. Sometimes, notions within research ethics of what is good are based on general principles such as those outlined in the Belmont Report (1979) – respect for persons, beneficence and justice. On the other hand, teleological or consequentialist approaches judge the ethics of researchers' decisions on the basis of the consequences of their acts.

Among social scientists, criminologists are particularly likely to face significant ethical issues because of: the sensitive nature of their subject matter; the vulnerability of research participants; the attitudes of criminal justice institutions; the relatively powerful position of state and corporate bodies; and the insensitivity of institutions responsible for research ethics governance. While ethical issues can arise in many guises, four of the major ethical matters that confront criminologists are confidentiality; informed consent; harms and benefits; and the relationships that researchers have with colleagues, sponsors and institutions.

Other than under exceptional circumstances, the guidelines for ethical research require all participants to agree to the research before it can be started. The consent granted by them should be both informed and voluntary. In most cases, researchers need to provide potential participants with information about the purpose, methods, demands, risks, inconveniences, discomforts and possible outcomes of the research. Researchers often document consent in writing at the start of research, though verbal and/or dynamic and continuous forms of consent may be preferable in many forms of criminological research. Criminologists might find it difficult to assess whether potential participants have freedom of action particularly in the context of research on or in institutions. There is a sad history of non-consensual research – mostly not by social scientists – on prisoners.

In some cases, such as passive observational studies carried out in public spaces, researchers have argued that the need for consent has damaged the research and has not been in the best interests of research participants. One area of heated debate among social scientists is the degree to which a deliberate manipulation of the information – deception by lying, withholding information or making a misleading exaggeration – might be warranted. Some sociologists have defended the use of covert methods on the basis that these reduce the disturbance to research subjects and potential risks to researchers in work on illegal activities. Many psychologists have claimed that the integrity of their research design would be compromised if participants were not misled in some way.

While not every research participant may want to be offered or would even warrant receiving assurances of confidentiality, most do. Criminologists have developed a range of methodological precautions in relation to collecting, analysing and storing data as well as strategies to respond to challenges about the confidentiality of their data (Israel, 2004a). These include: not recording names and other data at all, or removing names and identifying details of sources from confidential data at the earliest possible stage; disguising the name of the community where the research took place; masking or altering data; sending files outside of the jurisdiction; and avoiding using the mail or telephone system so that data could not be intercepted or seized by police or intelligence agencies. Some Canadian, Australian and American researchers may receive statutory protection for their data. Recognizing that full confidentiality might not be assured, some

Canadian and Australian research ethics committees have required researchers to offer only limited assurances of confidentiality by indicating to participants that they could be forced to hand data over to courts. This practice has been criticized as undermining the relationship of trust between researcher and participant. Nevertheless, several criminologists have indicated that they would breach confidentiality to protect vulnerable groups such as children or to protect the security of correctional institutions.

Researchers are normally expected to minimize the risks of harm or discomfort to participants in research projects (the principle of nonmaleficence). Criminologists might adopt risk minimization strategies that could involve monitoring participants; maintaining a safety net of professionals who can provide support in emergencies; excluding vulnerable individuals or groups from participation where this is justifiable; considering whether lower risk alternatives might be available; and anticipating and counteracting any distortion of the research results that might be to the detriment of the research participants. In some circumstances, researchers may also be expected to promote the well-being of participants or maximize the benefits to society as a whole (the principle of beneficence).

Criminologists owe a professional obligation to their colleagues to handle themselves honestly and with integrity. Academic misconduct – apparently relatively uncommon in criminology – encompasses the fabrication and falsification of data, the misleading attribution of authorship, and plagiarism. Threats to the research integrity can also stem from the relationships that researchers maintain with corporations and governments. Conflicts of interests occur when various personal, financial, political and academic concerns coexist and the potential is there for one interest to be illegitimately favoured over another interest that has equal or greater legitimacy in a way that might make other reasonable people feel they have been misled or deceived.

Patterns and forms of regulations of research ethics vary between institutions, disciplines and countries. Mostly, these involve national or local policy-making bodies and separate local review structures. Publicly-funded researchers in the USA, Australia, Canada and several Western European countries are answerable to national codes for research ethics (the Common Rule, administered by the Federal Office for Human Research Protections in the USA; the National Health and Medical Research Council, Australia, 1999; the Tri-Council Policy Statement, Canada, 2003). Some codes and guidelines, such as the European Union's RESPECT Code of Practice for Socio-Economic Research, and the World Medical Association's Declaration of Helsinki, exist at international levels. In many countries, codes have also been developed by professional associations (for example, the American Sociological Association, 1997; the Australian and New Zealand Society of Criminology, 2000; the British Society of Criminology, 2003), research institutions and funding bodies, or by groups or organizations that can be accessed by researchers. Several countries have or are in the process of developing local research ethics committees that review individual research proposals. Where a national code exists, these committees' composition, responsibilities and policies may be more or less centrally determined and the committees themselves may be held accountable by an external body. In other countries such as the UK, researchers must currently deal with an uncoordinated patchwork of professional codes, institutional requirements and governance frameworks. In either case, it is becoming increasingly complex to negotiate the ethical approval for multi-centred or transnational research projects.

Evaluation

Many professional associations for criminologists explicitly recognize the importance of ensuring that research is conducted ethically. There is no doubt that many individual researchers also find the process of ethical review to be constructive. However, many of the codes which govern criminological research have been heavily influenced by problems and preferred responses that first emerged in bioethics. In several countries, social scientists have expressed serious concerns about the

impact of research ethics governance on the future of their work (Israel, 2004b; Social Sciences and Humanities Research Ethics Special Working Committee, 2004). At times, researchers have criticized policies that failed to consider the conditions under which criminologists operated. They have also been critical of the increasing interference by local research ethics committees (Haggerty, 2004) that have regulated criminological research on the basis of limited expertise; acting slowly, secretly and arbitrarily; and exercising unfettered discretion according to their own interpretations of amorphously expressed standards or the dictates of institutional risk-management.

Mark Israel

Associated Concepts: appreciative criminology, critical research, reflexivity

Key Readings

Haggerty, K. (2004) 'Ethics creep: governing social science research in the name of ethics', *Qualitative Sociology*, 27 (4): 391–414.

Israel, M. (2004a) 'Strictly confidential? Integrity and the disclosure of criminological and socio-legal research', *British Journal of Criminology*, 44 (5): 715–40.

Israel, M. (2004b) *Ethics and the Governance of Criminological Research in Australia: A Report for the New South Wales Bureau of Crime Statistics and Research*, available at http://www.boscar.nsw.gov.au/lawlink/boscar/11_boscar.nsf/vwFiles/R55.pdf/$File/R55.pdf

National Commission for the Protection of Human Subjects of Biomedical and Behavioral Research (1979) *The Belmont Report: Ethical Principles and Guidelines for the Protection of Human Subjects of Research*. Washington, DC: Department of Health, Education, and Welfare.

Social Sciences and Humanities Research Ethics Special Working Committee (2004) *Giving Voice to the Spectrum*. Ottawa: Interagency Advisory Panel on Research Ethics. Available at http://www.pre.ethics.gc.ca/english/work-groups/sshwc/SSHWCVoiceReportJune 2004.pdf

RESPONSIBILIZATION

Definition

Strategies of crime control which aim to shift primary responsibility for crime prevention and public security away from the state and towards businesses, organizations, civil society, individuals, families and communities. Such a shift has been increasingly expressed in the practical and discursive terms of 'crime reduction partnerships', 'interagency co-operation', 'joined-up government', 'active citizenship' and 'self-help' initiatives that are now common in such countries as the USA, the UK, Australia and Canada.

Distinctive Features

At its most basic the concept of responsibilization appears to simply draw attention to any crime control strategy which aims to make offenders face up to their own responsibilities or which encourages the private sector and communities to take a more active interest in reducing criminal opportunities. Developing the latter, Garland (2001) refers to a community responsibilization strategy involving central government seeking to act upon crime not only in a direct fashion through the established state agencies of police, courts, prisons and social work, but also to directly involve non-state agencies and organizations and the forces of civil society. For example, he notes how from the mid-1980s onwards numerous campaigns (such as Neighbourhood Watch), organizations (such as Crime Concern) and projects (such as Safer Cities) were established in the UK to encourage inter-agency co-operation and local initiative. The key message was (and remains) that property owners and manufacturers as well as school authorities, families and individuals all have a responsibility to reduce criminal opportunities and increase informal social controls. No longer can the sovereign state be expected to control crime on its own.

The concept also has a rather more complex and theoretical legacy. It has been claimed to be at the centre of a new mode of

governance that is characteristic of the neo-liberal, or advanced liberal, state. It has helped to open up a series of important debates about the relationship between the public and the private spheres and the extent to which the state is now prepared, or is preparing, to 'govern at a distance'. This theoretical grounding can be traced to the work of Foucault (1991) on the diffusion of power; to Stanley Cohen's (1985) work on the dispersal of discipline; and to Rose and Miller's (1992) work on the problematics of government within the neo-liberal state.

From Foucault has come the central notion of 'governmentality': that power cannot be simply reduced to the state or a particular mode of production. From Cohen has come a range of insights into how communities have been mobilized to act as voluntary control agents in their own right. From Rose and Miller there has evolved a series of insights into the 'mobile mechanisms' of neo-liberal or 'advanced' governance in which governance is achieved 'at a distance'. This allows the state to give less emphasis to the social contexts of crime and to withdraw from measures of state protection and welfare support. 'Responsibilization' coalesces with a number of related developments whereby criminal justice comes to reflect market-like conditions and processes; its welfarist core is eroded; elements of the state sector are privatized; crime control is commodified; and active entrepreneurship replaces passivity and state dependency.

For O'Malley (1992) responsibilization is but one element within a series of risk reduction or insurance-based strategies in which the burden of managing risk is held by individuals themselves. In other words, crime prevention becomes the responsibility of private individuals who through self-interest and 'liberation' from an over-protective state will now take active steps to ensure themselves against personal harm or property loss and damage. The responsible citizen will take rational measures to guard against injury or loss in order not to be a burden on the state. Investing in security measures becomes an essential action within this newly constituted citizenship (Rose, 2000). Such an approach, of course, inevitably supports the rationalities and technologies of situational crime prevention over and above those strategies which are more avowedly 'social' in character.

Evaluation

Garland (2001) is clear that responsibilization does not simply mean the state is off-loading or intent on privatizing all aspects of crime control. Rather the state retains its sovereign power while also taking on new roles of co-ordination and community activation. On the other hand, there are clear signs that old command and control structures are being reconfigured such that all of us must share some responsibility for the success or failure of law and order: that burden cannot now be simply borne by the state. Within such processes also lies the possibility not only of a greater involvement, but also of a greater participation and empowerment of communities (Garland, 2001: 124). Certainly the notion of responsibilization captures much of the essence of these aspects of contemporary neo-liberal crime control. But responsibilization appears as only one among a number of simultaneous strategies employed by the state. For example, techniques of *remoralization* will typically involve a strengthening and deepening of state interventionist programmes. When the 'problem of crime' is perceived to be greater than offending *per se* but more a break-up of moral fabric and cohesion, then a targeting of the non-criminal or the anti-social is also legitimized. Rather than implying a state withdrawal, remoralization – as a mode of governing – is based on the overt regulation, surveillance and monitoring of entire families and communities. It crucially rests on the identification of a feckless 'at risk' underclass who, through a combination of the refusal to work, teenage parenthood and single parenting, are believed to threaten the entire moral fabric of society. Similarly, strategies of responsibilization typically exist alongside neo-conservative and authoritarian modes of governance. For all the state's tendencies to govern at a distance, it routinely reasserts its sovereign power as expressed most obviously through the institution of the prison. Far from responsibilizing or managing, a neo-conservative mode of governance can be concerned simply to demonize, promote hostility and pursue a politics of fear and vengeance. The key task facing researchers of 'responsibilization' is to understand its co-existence with a number of diverse and contradictory crime control strategies, including those of risk management and community participation as well as of 'privatized prudentialism' and the recurrent 'punitive sovereignty' of individual nation states (O'Malley, 1992: 261).

John Muncie

Associated Concepts: actuarialism, community crime prevention, community safety, crime prevention, governance, governmentality, managerialism, risk, situational crime prevention, social control

Key Readings

Cohen, S. (1985) *Visions of Social Control.* Cambridge: Polity.

Foucault, M. (1991) 'Governmentality', in G. Burchell, C. Gordon and P. Miller (eds), *The Foucault Effect: Studies in Governmentality.* Hemel Hempstead: Harvester.

Garland, D. (2001) *The Culture of Control.* Oxford: Oxford University Press.

O'Malley, P. (1992) 'Risk, power and crime prevention', *Economy and Society*, 21 (3): 252–75.

Rose, N. (2000) 'Government and control', *British Journal of Criminology*, 40: 321–39.

Rose, N. and Miller, P. (1992) 'Political power beyond the state: problematics of government', *British Journal of Sociology*, 43 (2): 173–205.

Stenson, K. and Edwards, A. (2003) 'Crime control and local governance: the struggle for sovereignty in advanced liberal polities', *Contemporary Politics*, 9 (2): 203–18.

RESTITUTION

See: Reparation

RESTORATIVE JUSTICE

Definition

A broad-based international movement with a strong focus on changing existing criminal justice systems. There has been much debate about what the term means.

An oft-quoted definition is by Marshall: 'Restorative justice is a process whereby parties with a stake in a specific offence collectively resolve how to deal with the aftermath of the offence and its implications for the future' (1999: 5). This definition emphasizes the basic *process* requirement for restorative justice: that all parties have the opportunity to be heard about the consequences of the crime and what needs to be done to restore victims, offenders and communities.

Other definitions of restorative justice emphasize *values* and *goals* rather than process. The core values and goals of restorative justice are said to be healing relationships between all parties involved, community deliberation over the problem rather than placing the criminal justice system at the centre of decision making, and non-domination to allow all voices to be heard with respect (Braithwaite, cited in McLaughlin et al., 2003: 157).

Distinctive Features

The primary objectives of restorative justice are (Marshall, 1999: 6):

- to attend fully to victims' needs;
- to prevent reoffending by reintegrating offenders;
- to enable offenders to assume active responsibility for their actions;
- to create a working community that supports the rehabilitation of offenders;
- to provide a means of avoiding the escalation of criminal justice measures.

It has been acknowledged that restorative justice practices will vary significantly in the degree to which they meet restorative justice values: thus we can think of practices that are 'fully' restorative, 'mostly' restorative, and 'partly' restorative. There has also been a debate between those who would opt for a 'purist' definition of restorative justice which is holistic and seeks to meet the needs equally of victims, offenders and communities, and those who would argue for a maximalist definition which recognizes that not all the circumstances in which restorative justice processes occur will be ideal. A maximalist definition is that restorative justice is 'every action that is primarily oriented towards doing justice by repairing the harm that has been caused by crime' (Bazemore and Walgrave, 1999: 48).

Much of the restorative justice literature is concerned with distinguishing its approach from retributive justice. Retributive justice is said to be defined by the negative and hostile relationship between offender and victim and the desire for vengeance against the former. Retributive justice is seen as an approach which determines a punishment based on the offence, one that is state-centred and dominated by legal professionals.

By way of contrast, restorative justice is presented as emphasizing healing and reconciliation between victim and offender.

Restorative justice emerged at a particular historical juncture that displayed a disillusionment with mainstream crime control processes. Mainstream approaches with ever increasing imprisonment levels are seen as expensive and as making little in the way of a verifiable and positive impact on offenders. By contrast, restorative justice is viewed as a distinctive and clearly articulated alternative that can bring together a respect for victims and their needs, a desire to hold offenders responsible for their actions, and the possibility of greater community input into the punishment process. There is also acknowledgment of the emotional need to bring closure to the harm caused by crime, to reintegrate offenders, and to bring about effective reconciliation.

The roots of restorative justice can be found in a range of different approaches in criminology and law emerging during the 1960s and 1970s, including 'informal justice' and mediation, as well as approaches based on different religious traditions, communitarianism, feminism and abolitionism. Early developments in Australia, New Zealand and Canada based restorative justice approaches on connections to Indigenous cultures, and American 'peacemaking' criminology also drew inspiration from Native American traditions. Those who promoted religious underpinnings to restorative justice stressed values of reconciliation, restoration and healing. Communitarians focused on the need to revitalize community associations and attachments in opposition to the individualism they saw as underpinning market economies. The European critical tradition of abolitionism also found some resonance in restorative justice demands as a way of challenging the discourses of criminalization and penality.

Restorative justice provides a critique for some of the key conceptualizations and institutions of the criminal justice system. The state and its role in defining and responding to crime are problematized by restorative justice. The category of 'crime' is decentred to the extent that many proponents prefer to speak of 'harm', 'conflict' or 'dispute' – that is, behaviour beyond the state's definition of crime; the criminal justice system is seen as being incapable of dealing with harm or securing just outcomes for either the victim, the offender or the community more generally. It is the exclusion of these stakeholders from the justice process that unites restorative justice critiques and provides the wellspring for the inclusionary and holistic vision of restorative justice.

These common themes also provide the principles and goals which bring together diverse social and political groups from victims' groups, prisoner action groups, those interested in diverting young people away from formal justice processes, and those with an interest in Indigenous and alternative dispute resolutions.

Restorative justice covers a range of practices that might occur at various points within the criminal justice process, including the pre-court diversion, in processes working in conjunction with the court even up to the point of sentencing, and in the post-sentencing (as well as with prisoners). Four of the major processes of restorative justice are:

- *Victim–Offender Mediation* – These are schemes that bring together victims and offenders with a mediator. The mediation may occur prior to, during or after a court hearing.
- *Family Group Conferences* – Conferencing has been primarily used for juveniles and as a diversionary option to court proceedings, particularly in Australia and New Zealand. A conference convenor brings together the parties to work towards an apology and some form of reparation.
- *Restorative Cautioning* – This is based on the traditional police power of cautioning juveniles for offences. Restorative cautioning is an adoption of this process to cover police-run conferences involving the offender and victim.
- *Sentencing Circles* – These began in Canada in the 1980s and were developed in response to Indigenous demands for more effective sentencing. There is more community input into the 'circles' than in the case for conferences. However, sentencing circles are also more directly captured within the traditional justice system – they are presided over by a judge who is ultimately required to impose a sentence within broadly accepted sentencing principles.
- *Other Settings* – Restorative justice is not only used in relation to criminal matters but also in regard to a range of civil matters, including regulatory settings relating to corporations and consumers; in schools for behavioural problems; in workplaces for resolving disputes; and with families for child welfare and protection matters. In addition, restorative justice has been used as a principle for reconciliation in post-conflict

settings, such as that of the South African Truth and Reconciliation Commission.

Evaluation

Based on a range of evaluations of restorative justice conferences, we can summarize the following findings:

- Victims tend to be more satisfied with the conference outcome than those who go through the court system, and most victims and offenders find the conference process fair.
- Around half of all conferences succeed to some extent in repairing the harm caused to the victim.
- There is a lower level of recidivism among offenders after the conferencing process compared to those who go through court.

These findings are of course highly dependent on context: there is a wide variety of conferencing processes used internationally and various results can be expected.

Restorative justice has generated much controversy and a significant body of literature over the last decade. Its main criticisms have been both procedural and theoretical. At a procedural level there is concern over the loss of due process and other rights (such as an independent and impartial forum, the principle of proportionality in sentencing, and the separation of the police role from sentencing offenders).

At a theoretical level the main criticisms relate to the following:

- A naïve dichotomy between retribution and restorative justice (typically justice processes involve multiple aims and goals).
- A lack of appreciation of the power variables in restorative justice which are likely to work against less powerful and marginalized groups such as women and racial minorities.
- An unrealistic expectation that a restorative justice conference can produce major changes in people (Daly, cited in McLaughlin et al., 2003: 195–214).

Chris Cunneen

Associated Concepts: abolitionism, communitarianism, community justice, informal justice, peacemaking criminology, redress, reparation, shaming

Key Readings

Bazemore, G. and Walgrave, L. (eds) (1999) *Restorative Juvenile Justice: Repairing the Harm of Youth Crime*. New York: Criminal Justice Press.
Johnstone, G. (2002) *Restorative Justice: Ideas, Values, Debates*. Cullompton: Willan.
Marshall, T. (1999) *Restorative Justice: An Overview*. London: Home Office.
McLaughlin, E., Fergusson, R., Hughes, G. and Westmarland, L. (eds) (2003) *Restorative Justice: Critical Issues*. London: Sage.
Weitekamp, E. and Kerner, H.-J. (eds) (2002) *Restorative Justice: Theoretical Foundations*. Cullompton: Willan.
Zehr, H. and Toews, B. (eds) (2004) *Critical Issues in Restorative Justice*. New York: Criminal Justice Press/Cullompton: Willan.

RETRIBUTION

Definition

Punishment inflicted upon offenders in consequence of their wrong-doing. Retributivism is the view that the moral justification for punishment is that the offender deserves it.

Distinctive Features

The term 'retribution' originally referred to the repayment of a debt (Walker, 1991), an idea that can be easily seen in the very old notion of 'An eye for an eye, a tooth for a tooth', or *lex talionis* (the law of the scale). The principle is that it is morally right and good that offenders should suffer: the punishment is deserved and should also be proportionate to the amount of harm done. The offender 'owes a debt', not just to the victim (where restitution might be appropriate) but also to the wider society.

Strict retributivists hold that society has a moral *obligation* to punish wrong-doers. By choosing to break the law individuals are deemed to have disturbed a moral equilibrium which must then be restored through a legal denunciation and/or punishment. Individuals must be treated as rational moral agents and so held responsible for their actions (as in classicism). According to the philosopher Immanuel Kant, offenders therefore have a *right* to punishment as a mark of respect for their human autonomy and membership of society. It follows that (i) only offenders *can* be punished and (ii) all offenders *must* be punished.

The punishment should 'fit the crime', being proportionate to the harm done rather than being tailored to the individual offender, for example to the likelihood of reoffending. In sentencing practice, retribution appears as a 'tariff system', namely a more or less fixed scale of penalties for particular offences.

Punishment is therefore justified by a reference to past action and, for the strict retributivist, it is a natural consequence of human law-breaking (hence retributivism is referred to as a *deontological* theory: the punishment follows on from the nature of the human action to which it is related). The punishment is seen as morally right in itself, regardless of any other effects it may or may not have. Retributivism thus stands in contrast to consequentialist justifications for punishment (rehabilitation, deterrence, incapacitation) which focus upon the future effects that might be achieved (being concerned with outcomes, such theories are described as *teleological*).

Evaluation

Retribution remains an important principle in contemporary penal practice. However, there are a number of problems associated with it. To begin with, the moral philosophical basis for the claim that offenders deserve punishment (rather than, for example, mercy or forgiveness) has been found wanting (e.g., Honderich, 1989; Walker, 1991). Retributivism can appear as no more than a primitive demand for vengeance. A related criticism is that retributivism requires that punishment be inflicted even where no positive good will be achieved, for example, in the case of a remorseful offender who is unlikely to commit further crime. The infliction of punishment on grounds of the harm done, regardless of the circumstances of the individual offender, might not only be pointless: it may also lead to social injustice. It is also difficult to translate the principle of proportionality, the idea that punishment should reflect the degree of harm done, into practice. Two problems arise here. The first is how to determine in absolute terms what *quantum* or amount of punishment is proportionate to a particular offence (the problem of *cardinal proportionality*): there is a vast range of offences to which the 'eye for an eye' principle is not very easily applied. A second problem, that of *ordinal proportionality*, is how different offences and the penalties attached to them are to be ranked (whether, for example, a rape merits more or less punishment than a muti-million pound fraud).

Although strict retributivism is largely discredited on these grounds, the 1970s saw a resurgence in the form of 'just deserts' theory. This was in response to the alleged failings of the then dominant principle of rehabilitation. Right-wing critics of rehabilitation viewed it as a 'soft option' and called for more traditional punitive responses. Liberal and more radical critics saw it as leading to injustice in the form of disparities in sentencing, as well as the use of long and indeterminate sentences, in the name of preventing future crime. They advocated a 'justice model' (as opposed to a treatment model) of sentencing, one that drew on retributivism.

In contrast to pure retributivists, 'just deserts' theorists argued that there was no moral *obligation* to punish offenders: whether the power to punish was exercised in a particular case could be decided on consequentialist grounds. However, punishment could be given *only* when it was deserved: people should be punished for what they had done and not for what they might do, i.e., for past rather than future crimes (von Hirsch, 1985). The desert principle acts as a limit on the distribution of punishment.

Similarly, the principle of proportionality provides a ceiling for the amount of punishment. The severity of the punishment does not always have to match the gravity of the offence: something less (though nothing more) is therefore permissible. Arguments in which just deserts and proportionality are employed as limiting principles are sometimes referred to as 'negative retributivism'.

A number of jurisdictions, influenced by the just deserts movement, have introduced systems of mandatory or presumptive sentences either through legislation or in the form of guidelines for sentencers. While these may have resulted in increased consistency, the difficulties of determining levels of proportionality have often led to greater severity of punishment, contrary to the implicit aims of the neo-retributivist 'just deserts' advocates (Hudson, 1987).

More fundamental criticisms of retributivism, even in its modified form, concern the continued focus on the punishment of the individual offender, without questioning the nature of criminal justice and its relationship to social justice (e.g., Braithwaite and Pettit, 1990; Hudson, 1987).

Maggie Sumner

Associated Concepts: classicism, deterrence, incapacitation, just deserts, proportionality, punitiveness, rehabilitation

Key Readings

Braithwaite, J. and Pettit, P. (1990) *Not Just Deserts: A Republican Theory of Criminal Justice.* Oxford: The Clarendon Press.
von Hirsch, A. (1985) *Past and Future Crimes.* Manchester: Manchester University Press.
Honderich, T. (1989) *Punishment: The Supposed Justifications.* Cambridge: Polity Press.
Hudson, B. (1987) *Justice through Punishment: A Critique of the Justice Model of Corrections.* London: Macmillan.
Walker, N. (1991) *Why Punish? Theories of Punishment Reassessed.* London: Opus.

RIGHT REALISM

See: Administrative criminology; Neo-conservative criminology; Rational choice theory

RISK

Definition

In criminology, risk refers to the probability of harm, the role of its calculation or assessment in making decisions about whether to perform criminal actions, and its role in criminal justice decision making.

Distinctive Features

Risk has a foundational role in modern criminology, in classical criminology's focus on the calculation of probable gains and losses in projected offending, and – as well – much of the current research focusing on crime as risk taking, especially where doing so is a source of excitement that brings people into contact with criminal justice. Today, risk increasingly refers to governing crime through official discourses and techniques of risk management, especially 'actuarial justice' (Feeley and Simon, 1994), a term that refers to the displacement of individually based justice by decision making based on the statistical probability of reoffending.

However, actuarial justice is only one risk managerial response to crime. For example, English 'Sex Offender Orders', under the Crime and Disorder Act 1998, allow for restraints on former offenders on the basis of 'reasonable' fears that they represent risks to the community. Such judgements are made by the police, using traditional means of discretionary assessment rather than statistical data or processes. Similarly, requiring a community notification about resident former sex offenders is the focus of 'Megan's Laws' in the USA, even though it is not clear whether this is resulting in risk reduction (Simon, 1998). As these examples also suggest, risk refers not only to statistical probabilities of harm but also to other forms of estimating probability, as well as to harm's moral magnitude: a 'high risk' may refer to an intolerable risk of incalculable or uncalculated probability (Beck, 1992). Thus much 'risk' legislation of this sort arises out of a community pressure rather than having sound foundations in actuarial evidence. 'Risk talk' has also entered other areas of criminal justice without necessarily implying a statistical risk assessment. Decision making about risk in areas such as inmate security, pre-sentencing reports and prison parole decisions usually reflects an expert evaluation of individual cases rather than an actuarial classification. In all these instances, the spread of risk appears as a matter of governmental fashion and popular consciousness that extends well beyond actuarialism's power to predict (Beck, 1992). But this also indicates that discourses and practices of risk are multiple, not just statistical, and are mobilized in different ways in different parts of criminal justice (O'Malley, 1998).

Crime risk thinking extends far beyond criminal justice. Under the banner of governing crime risks, streetscapes, the design of people's homes, 'gated communities' and the planning and operation of shopping centres are being organized around crime prevention. In governing illicit drug use, criminal justice may be deliberately marginalized in favour of preventative, risk-reducing programmes such as needle exchanges and safe injecting facilities, and police officers might be instructed not to enforce the law against drug users. Indeed for some writers the development of a 'risk society' implies a new governmental principle in which the place of criminal justice, and not merely its organization, changes dramatically (Simon, 1987).

Numerous fears have been raised about the spread of risk frameworks in criminal justice. First is the potential for net-widening as 'unacceptable risks' become subjects for justice. Second are fears concerning the marginalization of individualized justice, the abandonment of the proportionality of offence and punishment, and the diminishment of judicial discretion. Such concerns generate considerable resistance to risk-based justice, particularly on the part of the judiciary. More generally, however, the development of risk technologies and practices might produce a society that is increasingly insecure: the fear of crime may be exaggerated by high profile crime prevention initiatives; social isolation and divisiveness may spread with the rise of 'gated communities'; and fears of 'Big Brother' surveillance are increased as invasive technologies preventatively govern crime 'in the community' (Ericson and Haggerty, 1997).

These observations raise the issue of a politics of risk. Some argue that the emergence of risk in government reflects the rise of neo-liberalism (see O'Malley, 1992). Such politics have shaped the character of risk, making citizens and communities (neighbourhoods, women, home-owners, etc.) more 'responsible' for managing their own crime exposure – for example, by forming 'partnerships' with the police and avoiding high risk situations. Likewise, they foster a rational-choice 'risk-taking' image of offenders, who calculate the risks and benefits of their offending and thereby become more criminally 'responsible' than would be the case under therapeutic regimes of rehabilitation. Risk, in this view, is being politically reshaped rather than actuarialized in the current politics of crime risks.

Evaluation

There is no doubt that crime-risk discourses are becoming more prevalent. The theoretical and political implications of these changes are considerable. As with all models, however, these are prone to exaggeration. While many illustrations are provided, there is no systematic evidence of risk's relative increase or dominance. Certainly, outside certain US jurisdictions, actuarial sentencing has remained marginal. Minimal research has been carried out on the variety of risk discourses and techniques, leading to some misleading characterizations of risk-oriented justice as 'actuarial'. There is also a tendency to ignore the continuity of long-established risk techniques (e.g., in parole decisions), perhaps giving exaggerated impressions of risk's 'rise'. Explanations of this ascendancy are also impressionistic rather than solidly grounded. Most rely on largely speculative and poorly evidenced accounts that link risk-based justice with mega-crises of modernity (see Ericson and Haggerty, 1997) or the rise of postmodernity (Feeley and Simon, 1994), or simplistically reduce a wide diversity of changes to a single effect of neo-liberalism (O'Malley, 1992). At present, despite the apparent importance of justice through risk, we have no more than descriptive accounts – possibly selective, conceptually varied, and of debatable generality.

Pat O'Malley

Associated Concepts: actuarialism, defensible space, fear of crime, governance, governmentality, hedonism, managerialism, net widening, opportunity theory, rational choice theory, situational crime prevention, surveillance

Key Readings

Beck, U. (1992) *Risk Society.* London: Sage.
Ericson, R. and Haggerty, K. (1997) *Policing the Risk Society.* Toronto: Toronto University Press.
Feeley, M. and Simon, J. (1994) 'Actuarial justice: the emerging new criminal law', in D. Nelken (ed.), *The Futures of Criminology.* London: Sage.
O'Malley, P. (1992) 'Risk, power and crime prevention', *Economy and Society,* 21: 252–75.
O'Malley, P. (ed.) (1998) *Crime and the Risk Society.* Aldershot: Dartmouth.
Simon, J. (1987) 'The emergence of the risk society', *Socialist Register,* 95: 61–89.
Simon, J. (1998) 'Managing the monstrous: sex offenders and the new penology', *Psychology, Public Policy and the Law,* 4: 452–67.

RISK FACTOR RESEARCH

Definition

Risk factor research (RFR) is an empirical paradigm that attempts to identify the factors, circumstances and experiences in an individual's life that increase their risk of offending/reoffending and committing offending-related behaviours (e.g., substance use, anti-social behaviour). RFR also attempts to identify the 'protective' factors and influences that purportedly mitigate, moderate and insulate against the effects of an exposure to risk. The findings from RFR are typically employed to inform offence- and offender-focused interventions that are targeted on reducing risk and increasing protection – an intervention model known as the 'Risk Factor Prevention Paradigm'.

Distinctive Features

Criminological RFR has its origins in the medical 'public health model' of identifying and treating the risk factors for physical illness. Building on the early twentieth century RFR research of William Healy in the area of psychiatry and Richard Clarke Cabot in the clinical field of cardiac disease prediction, Sheldon and Eleanor Glueck initiated criminological RFR in the USA with three longitudinal studies – '500 Criminal Careers' (1930), 'One Thousand Juvenile Delinquents' (1934), and 'Unravelling Juvenile Delinquency' (1950). The Gluecks were motivated by a desire to understand the elements of a life history that predisposed juveniles (typically males in the early studies) towards officially-recorded offending and recidivism, in order to inform more effective criminal justice responses (e.g., court sentences, rehabilitation in the community and custodial institutions). Combining detailed analysis of official records with offender and key stakeholder interviews, the Gluecks identified a group of family-, school-, neighbourhood-, lifestyle- and personal/emotional-based problems that were relatively common in the life histories (during childhood and adolescence) of convicted and reconvicted juvenile male offenders, particularly when compared to a sample of non-offenders. They then converted these 'psychosocial' issues (located in the psychological and immediate social domains of life) into 'factors' by measuring the exposure to them along a specially-constructed quantified ratings scale. These numerical ratings were in turn statistically linked to quantified measures of offending behaviour to produce so-called predictors of the likelihood of juvenile offending – predictors that subsequently became known as 'risk factors'.

In the early 1960s in the UK, Donald West and (later) David Farrington built upon the Gluecks' longitudinal RFR model with their 'Cambridge Study in Delinquent Development', which set out 'to investigate the development of juvenile delinquency in a normal population of boys' (West and Farrington, 1973: xiii). The 'Cambridge Study' elaborated on the Gluecks' research in a number of key areas:

- by introducing a *prospective longitudinal* element to a previously-retrospective RFR;
- by focusing on a *non-convicted* group of males rather than identified offenders;
- by expanding the *multi-method* nature of RFR by supplementing official records analysis and interviews with questionnaires and psychometric testing;
- by measuring the statistical relationships between risk factors and *self-reported offending*, rather than limiting the focus to identified and officially-recorded offenders;
- by investigating the potential for *protective factors* to mitigate and moderate the influence of risk factors.

The Cambridge Study has tracked the influence of risk and protective factors in the lives of its original sample of just over 400 young white boys from its inception in 1961 to the present day and has subsequently expanded its foci to track female relatives of the boys and examine a broader range of risk factors (e.g., certain situational and socio-structural influences).

An international movement of RFR has proliferated since the early Glueck studies in the USA and their expansion by the Cambridge Study in the UK. The developmental RFR model has been widely replicated, and other strands of RFR have emerged to complement and expand on this, including:

- *Life-course* RFR – this traces the trajectories and influences of risk/protective factors and life events throughout childhood, adolescence and into adulthood.
- *Social Development Model* RFR – this examines how risk/protective factors (involvement, interactions, skills, perceived reinforcements) interact with socio-structural status, cognitive ability and external constraints to produce anti-social and prosocial behaviours at different developmental stages.
- *Ecological* RFR – this identifies the community and neighbourhood influences that interact with psychosocial risk/protective factors to precipitate offending and desistance.

RFR has been typically *artefactual* (founded on the 'factorization' of risk into numerical quantities) and *positivist* in orientation, seeking to identify and quantify/factorize risk in *psychosocial* domains and present these 'risk factors' as reliable statistical *predictors and causes* of future offending. Artefactual RFR (see Kemshall et al., 2006) has tended to be *longitudinal* in design (although a growing body of cross-sectional RFR has emerged) and *developmental* in nature, using survey methods to identify risk factors in childhood/adolescence and linking these in a *deterministic* way to offending in late adolescence and adulthood.

In the early 1990s, the 'Risk Factor Prevention Paradigm' began to gain popularity as a way of understanding and applying the findings of RFR to meet the practical goals of crime prevention. It has now become the hegemonic model of how to respond to youth offending in the Western world and has influenced a series of risk-based policy and practice developments, including the mainstream acceptance of risk assessment and risk-focused intervention within the Youth Justice

System of England and Wales (see Case and Haines, 2009).

In the early twenty-first century, a 'constructivist' RFR movement (Kemshall et al., 2006) gained momentum as a model for addressing the perceived weaknesses of artefactual RFR, most notably the 'Pathways Into and Out of Offending' partnership (France and Homel, 2007) and the 'Teeside Studies'. Constructivist RFR retains a focus on risk, but as a more dynamic and constructed process than a static and irresistible factor in the lives of young people (see France and Homel, 2007). This interpretivist model has utilized qualitative research methods to access the biographies, narratives and voices of young people in order to better understand how they understand, make sense of and negotiate their exposure to risk in their own specific localized, historical and socio-structural contexts (e.g., in relation to gender, age, ethnicity and socio-economic status). Consequently, constructivist RFR has challenged artefactual RFR for its representations of risk as a static factor and young people as the passive recipients of its effects, its deterministic explanatory bases and its perceived psychosocial biases.

Evaluation

RFR – in its artefactual and developmental form – has proliferated across the Western world since the 1990s. It has been heralded as an evidence-based, reliable, methodologically-robust and practical branch of criminological research that 'links explanation and prevention, fundamental and applied research, and scholars and practitioners ... is easy to understand and to communicate, and it is readily accepted by policy makers, practitioners, and the general public' (Farrington, 2007: 7). A series of psychosocial risk factors have been consistently replicated as predictors of (youth) offending and reoffending for both genders across a broad range of countries, ethnicities and age groups, as well as identified as promising targets for ameliorative interventions. Situating aetiologies within an examination of risk factors has become

the hegemonic means of understanding and responding to youth offending in the Western world (Laub and Sampson, 2003).

Notwithstanding its dominance within the academic, policy and practice arenas, RFR has been subjected to sustained critique in recent years (see Case and Haines, 2009; also Armstrong, 2004). RFR has come under particularly intense scrutiny for its perceived methodological weaknesses and consequent invalid conclusions based on:

- *Reductionism* – the reduction of risk to quantifiable factors has been criticized for over-simplifying a potentially complex set of processes and contextualized experiences into crude and unrepresentative numerical figures/statistics. The subsequent aggregation of numerical risk measures to general populations (to facilitate more straightforward, group-based statistical analyses) further over-simplifies RFR, as the aggregated group risk profile (used to inform interventions) does not necessarily represent, apply to or respond to the risk experienced by individual members of that group.

- *Ambiguities* – RFR has been beset by ambiguities throughout its development, which threaten the validity of any conclusions drawn from the empirical research. The exact nature of a 'risk factor' has yet to be consistently defined within RFR, and the precise relationship between risk and offending remains ambiguous, with different studies identifying risk factors as causal (deterministic), predictive (probabilistic), correlated with offending (with the direction of the relationship undefined), or symptomatic of it. Furthermore, the nature of the outcome measure/behaviour has been inconsistent, with risk factors linked to offending behaviour that has been variously defined as officially recorded, self-reported, first-time, reoffending, reconviction, property, violent, serious, etc. Therefore, RFR has not constituted a homogeneous and replicable set of methods and findings, but rather a heterogeneous research movement with disparate studies with differing under-standings of risk factors, offending behav-iours and the nature of the relationship between the two – thereby raising serious doubts as to the validity and replicability of the findings and conclusions made.

- *Restricted foci* – RFR has been accused of evolving as a narrow exercise grounded in restricted theoretical understandings of youth offending (largely developmental) and the self-fulfilling replication of a restricted body of (largely psychosocial) risk factors (see Case and Haines (2009) for a more detailed critique). Although constructivist RFR has emerged to chal-lenge more deterministic developmental explanations and to expand the foci of RFR into a greater consideration of the agentic, contextual and socio-structural influences, it has remained (in part) wed-ded to the traditional developmental, fac-torized and psychosocial foundations of artefactual RFR. Furthermore, RFR has privileged risk- and deficit-based explora-tions and understandings of offending, even to the point of exploring protective factors in a risk-dependent manner (e.g., as dichotomies of risk factors that protect against risk) rather than as potentially pro-social influences that could promote posi-tive behaviours and outcomes.

Despite the hegemony of RFR in dominating political, official and practice-based under-standings of, and responses to, young people who offend, it remains contentious. RFR has been heavily criticized for its narrow focus on individualized factors and neglect of socio-structural interpretations of youth behaviour, for the way it has been used to neglect the wel-fare and/or rights of young people, and for the way in which it privileges offence- and offender-focused interventions (Armstrong, 2004).

Stephen Case and Kevin Haines

Associated Concepts: determinism, develop-mental criminology, evaluation research, experimental criminology, life course theories of crime, longitudinal study, prediction stud-ies, 'what works'

Key Readings

Armstrong, D. (2004) 'A risky business? Research, policy, governmentality and youth offending', *Youth Justice*, 4 (2): 100–116.

Case, S.P. and Haines, K.R. (2009) *Understanding Youth Offending: Risk Factor Research – Policy and Practice.* Cullompton: Willan.

Farrington, D.P. (2007) 'Childhood risk fac-tors and risk-focused prevention', in M. Maguire, R. Morgan and R. Reiner (eds), *The Oxford Handbook of Criminology*, 4th edn. Oxford: Oxford University Press.

France, A. and Homel, R. (2007) *Pathways and Crime Prevention: Theory, Policy and Practice.* Cullompton: Willan.

Kemshall, H., Marsland, L., Boeck, T. and Dunkerton, L. (2006) 'Young people, path-ways and crime: beyond risk factors', *Australian and New Zealand Journal of Criminology*, 39 (3): 354–70.

Laub, J. and Sampson, R. (2003) *Shared Beginnings, Delinquent Lives: Delinquent Boys to Age 70.* London: Harvard Univer-sity Press.

West, D. J. and Farrington, D. P. (1973) *Who becomes delinquent?* London: Heinemann.

ROUTINE ACTIVITY THEORY

Definition

According to Marcus Felson, mainstream criminology has devoted the majority of its attention to 'the criminal', investigating why certain individuals are more criminally inclined than others. As a consequence of this fixation, criminology has given very little thought to either the context or nature of criminal acts or the role of victims as active participants in crime production and preven-tion. His writings represent one of the most significant attempts to redress this imbalance and he does so from a rational choice perspective. Crime, for Felson, is first and foremost a physical act and a product of the recurrent, routine activities and structuring of everyday life. This means that the potential for crime is inevitable and constant. A utilitarian motivation to commit crime is taken as given. This also means that criminologists can contribute in a practical manner to criminal justice policy debates by shifting the focus from the detection and punishment of the criminal to the reduction and prevention of a criminal event.

Distinctive Features

The original formulation of routine activities postulated that the volume and distribution of 'predatory crime', that is, those direct contact crimes in which one or more individuals attacks the person or property of another, are closely related to three variables. First, motivated offenders, usually young males, must be in attendance. Second, 'suitable targets', in the form of person or property, must be available. Routine activity theory prefers to use the term 'target' instead of 'victim' because it emphasizes that most criminality is geared towards the acquisition of property. Suitability is characterized by four attributes (VIVA):

- **Value**, which is calculated from the offender's perspective.
- **Inertia**, which concerns the physical aspects of the person or property that will hinder or interrupt target suitability.
- **Visibility**, which marks out the person or property for attack.
- **Accessibility**, which increases the risk of attack.

The third variable is the absence of 'capable guardians' against crime. According to Felson, individuals looking after a household, family members, colleagues in the workplace, friends, or indeed strangers on the street are more likely to act as 'capable guardians' than police officers.

It is the physical coming together of these three variables that produces the opportunity for a predatory crime to occur. To put it succinctly, a predatory crime is most likely to occur when an offender meets in time and space with a viable target in the absence of a capable guardian. Crucially, the convergence transpires because of the routine practices of everyday life. Hence, criminal acts are intimately related to and feed off normal behaviours associated with work, school, transportation, recreation, shopping, the production of consumer goods, and so on. Changes in routine activities and the rhythms of life have placed more people in particular places at specific moments, and this increases their accessibility as realistic targets of crime. People are also more likely to be away from their homes, thus reducing their ability to act as capable guardians of their property and opening up new opportunities for crime through the ever increasing number of portable possessions. For Felson, contemporary society invites high crime rates by generating a huge number of illegal opportunities.

Routine activity theory was subsequently developed by Felson and applied to four other types of crime: exploitative (robbery, rape); mutualistic (gambling, prostitution, selling and buying illegal drugs); competitive (fighting); and individualistic (individual drug use, suicide). In so doing he identified a fourth element that would allow a criminal event to happen – the absence of an 'intimate handler', namely a significant other who can impose informal social control on the offender. A potential offender must break free of the 'intimate handler' and then find a target for crime, unmonitored by a 'capable guardian'.

More recently Felson, in conjunction with Ron Clarke, has claimed that the principles underpinning routine activity can provide criminology with a new general opportunity-based theory of crime that would force criminologists to move away from using vague criminological concepts and formulate precise research questions.

Evaluation

Routine activity theorizing has opened up an important debate about the context within which crime takes place. The crime prevention implications focus on changing routine activities and practices to frustrate potential offenders and prevent easy victimization. As a result it underpins situational crime prevention and personal risk assessment strategies such as defensible space and target hardening and arguments for increasing the presence of 'capable guardians' and 'eyes on the street'. Critics argue that it overlooks the offender and cannot answer the question why some individuals are more motivated to commit criminal acts than others. It also carries with it a tendency to blame the victim. In addition, in its original focus on 'predatory crime', it reproduced stereotypical representation of the problem of crime. Although it makes increasing claims to be enriching criminological theory, its primary concern remains the production of practices that will help policy makers.

Eugene McLaughlin

Associated Concepts: crime science, defensible space, opportunity theory, rational choice theory, situational crime prevention, surveillance

Key Readings

Birkbeck, C. and La Free, G. (1993) 'The situational analysis of crime and deviance', *Annual Review of Criminology*, 19: 113–37.

Cohen, L.E. and Felson, M. (1979) 'Social change and crime rate trends: a routine activity approach', *American Sociological Review*, 44: 588–608.

Felson, M. (1986) 'Routine activities, social controls, rational decisions and criminal outcomes', in D. Cornish and R.V. Clarke (eds), *The Reasoning Criminal*. New York: Springer-Verlag.

Felson, M. (1987) 'Routine activities and crime prevention in the developing metropolis', *Criminology*, 25: 911–31.

Felson, M. (1998) *Crime and Everyday Life*, 2nd edn. Thousand Oaks, CA: Pine Forge Press.

Felson, M. (2000) 'The routine activity approach as a general social theory', in S.S. Simpson (ed.), *Of Crime and Criminality: The Use of Theory in Everyday Life*. Thousand Oaks, CA: Pine Forge Press.

SAMPLING

Definition

The process of selecting a sub-set of cases from a wider population with a view to making inferences from the sample to the wider population.

Distinctive Features

The cases sampled from a population are largely determined by the focus of the research and can include documents, interactions, institutions, communities and societies. However, in social surveys the basic sampling unit is usually the individual (for example, offender, victim, police officer, magistrate). The term 'population' is used in the statistical rather than the geographical sense and refers to the total category or group of cases about which the researcher wishes to reach conclusions. However, the statistical population in which the researcher is interested may correspond with a geographical area, for example, 'all victims of house burglary living in London, 1990–2000', but that is not a requirement.

The basis for making inferences from samples to populations is sampling theory, which is a set of assumptions and mathematical deductions. One key assumption is that samples are selected from the population at random. This means that every case in the population must have an equal and non-zero chance of being selected as part of the sample. In order to carry out random sampling it is necessary to have a sampling frame, which

is a listing of all cases in the population (for example, a list provided by the police of all victims of house burglary in London, 1990–2000). It is rarely, if ever, possible to produce completely accurate estimates of population values, perhaps due to errors in the process of sampling. Fortunately, provided the sample has been selected using random techniques, it is possible to estimate the sampling error (which provides a calculable margin of error).

In many instances it is not desirable or feasible to collect findings from random samples. For example, tracing each member of a sample can be a costly and time-consuming business. Therefore – where results are required quickly and cheaply – researchers often use quota sampling whereby the population to be studied is divided into categories that are relevant to the topic of investigation (for example, categorized by gender, age and ethnicity). Interviewers are given quotas for the types of people to interview. These quotas are often proportionate to the significance of the categories in the population as a whole, and the interviews usually take place after stopping people in public areas. Quota sampling is typically used to obtain a cheap and quick estimate of public opinion on a recent issue or event (for example, the introduction of a new policing strategy).

For some topics of study a sampling frame is not available and therefore random sampling is not feasible. In such instances researchers may turn to 'volunteer sampling' – whereby respondents volunteer to be part of a study – or 'snowball sampling' – whereby the researcher makes an initial contact with one person and then is introduced to others in a 'chain-letter' style. Both types of sample have been used in research involving drug-takers.

Quota, volunteer and snowball samples share the feature of not having been selected by random procedures. This means that, in contrast with random samples, it is not possible to estimate sampling errors.

Evaluation

Where researchers are interested in reaching conclusions about reasonably sized populations it is fairly rare to investigate every case in that population (which is known as a census). The advantages of sampling over a census are that it is cheaper, quicker and there is the potential for greater efficiency per unit of analysis. However, such advantages need to be balanced against the desirability of deriving accurate estimates of population values from samples. A key factor in this is the degree to which samples are representative of the populations from which they are drawn, especially in relation to the central topic of the research.

Although sampling is typically associated with quantitative and in particular social survey approaches to criminological research, some qualitative approaches employ what is often termed 'theoretical sampling'. Theoretical sampling is much less technical and much more flexible than statistical sampling. It involves selecting groups or cases as the research develops in order to discover meaningful categories and develop theory. For this reason, theoretical sampling is often closely associated with the development of grounded theory. Groups or cases may be selected so as to maximize or minimize their differences on some features while seeking to make comparisons between them on other features. For example, 'rookie' and 'old stager' police officers may be selected and compared with regard to their attitudes towards young offenders. The research may then progress by making further selections in terms of male rookie police officers. When new ideas and theoretical revisions stop emerging, the point of theoretical saturation will have been reached and the process of theoretical sampling will be terminated.

Victor Jupp

Associated Concepts: comparative method, ethnography, longitudinal study, social survey, victim surveys

Key Readings

Arber, S. (1993) 'Designing samples', in N. Gilbert (ed.), *Researching Social Life*. London: Sage.
Sapsford, R. (1999) *Survey Research*. London: Sage.
Schofield, W. (1996) 'Survey sampling', in R. Sapsford and V. Jupp (eds), *Data Collection and Analysis*. London: Sage.

SCAPEGOATING

Definition

To cast blame or guilt on an innocent person, group or object.

Distinctive Features

The biblical scapegoat was an animal onto which the sins of the people were transferred and erased through the expulsion of the goat. In anthropology the role of the scapegoat has usually been analysed as a purification ritual or ceremonial process by which evil is dealt with. In racial and ethnic studies, particular groups – such as blacks and Jews – have commonly been seen to be scapegoated for wider social and economic problems such as unemployment. These examples indicate that blame or guilt for social problems is attached to groups that may have little or no responsibility for an event; in fact, a strict definition of scapegoating would require that those who are scapegoated should be innocent of any responsibility for events. This is similar to the process of 'victim blaming'. Scapegoating processes include the identification of relatively powerless individuals or groups who can easily be blamed for a condition and amplification by the media through representing particular groups as a threat, probably in a stereotypical way. The objects or victims of scapegoating are thought to be chosen because they are identifiably 'different', for example due to external markers such as their skin colour or some other bodily sign, which therefore connects scapegoating to both racialization and stigmatization. However, not all instances of scapegoating involve visibly different individuals or groups or the powerless. The powerful can also be scapegoated, for instance when army commanders and politicians are held responsible for particular defeats or, more generally, for national decline.

Scapegoating is said to be a product of a universal societal requirement for some 'other' or 'out group' that serves a need to foster and maintain integration. Scapegoating is a social process that can be observed historically and cross-culturally, which has been taken to indicate that it is an expression of a deep human need to transgress and to reaffirm boundaries in order to maintain group solidarity. Indeed for Erikson (1966) deviants have a maintenance function, so groups need to induce and sustain deviant behaviour in order to help them maintain and restore the social equilibrium. Strategic scapegoating describes the use of tactics to deflect blame by an individual or group fearing exposure. Scapegoating is therefore a diversionary process that serves to demonize particular groups and as such this may result in moral panics. In this view, scapegoating is a form of mystification that obscures the real or essential problem. Nevertheless, no uniform motivations for scapegoaters have been identified. Their actions can be seen as rational or irrational. Some explanations suggested are that scapegoaters act out of frustration, aggression, or a desire to displace certain feelings (the frustration–aggression hypothesis); or because of projection and psychic discomfort (a reaction to, or denial of, tension), or as the result of a general hostility to others. The latter has been associated with the idea of the authoritarian personality (Douglas, 1995).

Scapegoating entails the drawing of a boundary between good and evil. It is something that is usually seen as pre-criminological superstition. However, Tannenbaum (1938) argued that criminological theories persistently reproduced this distinction, so that terms such as 'normal' and 'abnormal' stand in exactly the same relation as good and evil: instead of 'demonic possession' classical criminology employed the idea of rationally choosing to do evil; positivism differentiated the abnormal through various bodily manifestations as predictors or determinants of criminality; and functionalists choose to see the criminal as socially maladjusted. Each involves the dramatization and symbolization of difference and, in the process, the deviant is tagged or stigmatized.

Evaluation

The idea that a group or individual is a scapegoat for some wider ill is in common use. The term is frequently and loosely adopted, and because of this its many applications defy an overall definition of its usages. This wide utilization makes it difficult to evaluate or assess its veracity, particularly since there is room for debate on how far the scapegoated are 'innocent' or totally blameless, whether scapegoating can be explained in functionalist terms of serving group needs, and whether expurgation or purification actually occurs. Individuals, groups and both animate and inanimate objects (animals, financial markets) as well as nation-states have been regarded, and have sometimes defined themselves, as scapegoats. For instance, in the Balkans war the Bosnian government asserted that it was made a scapegoat to justify US military action. Similar claims were made by Iraq following the Gulf War. At another level, the blaming of individuals and/or paediatricians and social workers for being the perpetrators of or uncovering child abuse has been seen as a mode of scapegoating for a society that could not accept such transgressions of family norms or that there might be widespread abuse in society.

The idea of scapegoating as a mode of boundary maintenance is basically functionalist. This is problematic when boundaries have been transgressed or at least have become blurred. The objects of scapegoating may also be much more able to challenge images and representations and this too indicates that understanding and accounting for scapegoating is far from being a straightforward process.

Karim Murji

Associated Concepts: demonization, folk devil, labelling, moral panic, social censure, stereotyping, stigma

Key Readings

Douglas, T. (1995) *Scapegoat*. London: Routledge.

Erikson, K.T. (1966) *Wayward Puritans*. New York: Wiley.

Jenkins, P. (1992) *Intimate Enemies*. New York: Aldine de Gruyter.

Tannenbaum, F. (1938) *Crime and the Community*. New York: Colombia University Press.

SECONDARY DEVIATION

See: Labelling; Social reaction

SECURITY

Definition

The state of being secure, specifically being free from fear, danger, risk, care, poverty or anxiety. Security also implies certainty. The roots of the term are in the Latin *securitas/securus*, derived from *sine* (meaning without)

cura (care, anxiety, pains, worry). Safety is closely related to security. Safety also means being freed from danger or risk. However, it also has additional connotations which have more to do with physical conditions, e.g., freedom from injury, the safety of the body and of property. In this context certainty refers to certainty of order, assurance and predictability.

Distinctive Features

Security has often been defined through its juxtaposition and contrast with insecurity. The source of personal insecurity is thus the threat – imminent or remote, direct or indirect, imaginary or real – posed for individuals by other people, identifiable groups, larger and impersonal entities like the system, the market, the establishment, or even society in the abstract (Berki, 1986).

Originally the term 'security' was thought of as a negative state (i.e., carelessness, described for instance in Shakespeare's *Macbeth*: 'security is mortal's chiefest enemy'). Alternatively, eighteenth-century liberals treated security and liberty as synonymous. Later on security and freedom came to be viewed as mutually exclusive.

The crucial aspect of the term 'security' is personal security (individual well-being), but another equally significant aspect is security as a political construct (e.g., national security, social security, human security). The term 'human security', recently adopted in EU security politics, has emerged as a broad category of research giving privilege to non-military and non-state threats. Under the rubric of concepts like human security, and in the context of the collapse of the Iron Curtain and postmodernism, security has moved towards a more holistic view of security.

In criminology the concept of security has lately benefited from 'governmentality studies'. For Foucault, security was a specific principle of political method and practice and the dominant component of modern governmental rationality. The principles of security address themselves to a series of possible and probable events, and the rationality of security is an inherently open-ended one: it deals in calculations of the possible and the probable. 'Risk assessment' is a familiar illustration of these calculations.

The fundamental paradoxical quality of security, both as a concept and as a value, has been presented by R.N. Berki (1986) in terms of four distinct qualities: the social; the moral; the political; and the existential paradox of security. The social paradox of security refers to the threat of 'strangers', the threat to one's life and freedom caused by the action of others, and our vulnerability to others in the society we all inhabit and share. The question 'who are the strangers?' is also closely related to the moral paradox. Seeking security for oneself and being a cause of insecurity for others – as a stranger to them – might contradict the principles of universal humanity.

The political paradox derives from the view that politics is predicated on the process of differentiation or particularization within society, the division of people into actual or potential allies and enemies. On the collective level, as distinguished from the more abstract and fundamental level of strange individuals, security manifests itself as a scarce good that is distributed differentially. Consequently, fully impartial action is highly problematic in a situation which itself is partial, in a social world which is made up of differing and conflicting parts. The final and most fundamental issue is the existential paradox of security; life itself – its continuation – has the character of basic unknowability and unpredictability.

Evaluation

Concepts are said to be more important for what they do than for what they mean (Rose, 1999). The private commercial security industry has grown swiftly, and contemporaneously an increasing fragmentation has emerged in public security provision, mainly in terms of 'security networks' and partnerships. A community safety partnership is the main contemporary framework and strategy for local crime prevention, welfare and security management initiatives.

In the recent processes of building safety, security has become to be understood as a commodity. Rose (1999) discusses the new individualization of security and the 'securitization' of identity and habitat via multiple technological means. Within security markets, and also within varieties of community safety partnerships, the securitization of social life is a condition in which issues are depoliticized and alternative ways of framing and responding to the problems are easily lost. The discourse of security tends to be so powerful that objections, or arguments against security, are out of place.

In the context of local safety planning, and within community safety partnerships and policy making in general, claiming security status for an issue (e.g., for deprivation, social exclusion, anti-social behaviour) is said to render it somehow more important (and the need to deal with it more urgent) than simply designating it a problem. The outcome is usually a demand for more security and control. Instead of dealing with political, social, environmental and welfare issues in general in the name of security, we should be looking for ways to treat these in non-security ways (the dissolution of securitization) – for instance, to tackle exclusion from schools instead of building more CCTV systems.

The security frame has also expanded in international relations. External threats to states are treated as part of a larger security ecology which includes the claims of nations, groups, individuals, ecosystems and biodiversity. However, it has been suggested (de Lint and Virta, 2004) that instead of the discovery and production of security gaps (i.e., security knowledge deficits) and the endless expansion of security frameworks, this should be narrowed according to political necessity rather than that of the state and control. This claim also includes the necessity for democratic accountability, openness and public deliberations about the means and ends for personal as well as national and human security, and therefore, security for democracy. Despite the different views about the means by which we may achieve security, it can well claim to be the chief human value.

Sirpa Virta

Associated Concepts: community safety, governmentality, private policing, risk, social harm

Key Readings

Berki, R.N. (1986) *Security and Society: Reflections on Law, Order and Politics.* London: Dent.

de Lint, W. and Virta, S. (2004) 'Security in ambiguity: towards a radical security politics', *Theoretical Criminology*, 8 (4): 465–89.

Gordon, C. (1991) 'Governmental rationality: an introduction', in G. Burchell, C. Gordon and P. Miller (eds), *The Foucault Effect: Studies in Governmentality.* Hemel Hempstead: Harvester.

Neocleous, M. (2000) 'Against security', *Radical Philosophy*, March–April: 7–15.

Rose, N. (1999) *Powers of Freedom: Reframing Political Thought.* Cambridge: Cambridge University Press.

SELF-POLICING

Definition

A criminal justice concept that draws attention to the capacity of members of the community to make decisions about the appropriate level and means of control response without necessarily invoking criminal law agents.

Distinctive Features

There is a real sense in which society is self-policing. Formal policing measures are most often the result of calls for action from members of the public. Crime surveys tend to show that about one-half of the most common types of crime are not reported to the police. This suggests members of the public will judge that a formal invocation of the law enforcement machinery is not necessary, even when the instance in question is understood to be a crime or otherwise somehow answerable to police action. Even quite serious issues can be negotiated without recourse to the criminal law. Extended family, religious organizations, friendship and neighbourhood networks can all be drafted in to control forms of rule-breaking, disorder and conflict that otherwise might become the object of the criminal justice process.

Evaluation

There are several limitations to the notion of society as self-policing that are worth noting. First, although crime surveys do indicate that a large proportion of scenarios that people would regard as in some sense criminal are not reported to the police, an unquantified proportion of them may be due to pessimism about the effectiveness of formal criminal justice responses. In such instances it is not so much self-policing as it is non-policing. Second, perhaps one-quarter of indictable crimes are discovered by the police themselves; proactive policing – particularly in such areas as drink driving, illicit drug markets and other forms of vice – shows that a significant proportion of policing activity comes about as a result of priorities set by control agencies. This raises knotty questions about the relationship between policing and society that the notion of self-policing cannot wholly clarify. This in turn leads to a third difficulty with the idea of society as self-policing: some police and/or control functions are tangential to the awareness of most citizens. The activities of the Serious Fraud Office might be an example here, but policing (in the sense of maintaining peace, order and good government) also extends to the activities of inspectorates for pollution, fire, and health and safety, as well as many of the tasks undertaken by the uniformed public police. Of course, the public may make reactive demands of such governmental services in some fraught circumstances, but the routine activity of such agencies largely lies outside of common perceptions of policing (as simply crime control) and yet it has become an indispensable aspect of social ordering and the maintenance of the 'health of the social body'. Finally, the idea of society as self-policing may lend legitimacy in some instances of the social reaction to alleged criminal wrong-doing – which would be better characterized as vigilantism.

James Sheptycki

Associated Concepts: community policing, criminal justice, governance, informal justice, redress, social control, social justice

Key Readings

Ashworth, A. (1994) *The Criminal Process: An Evaluative Study.* Oxford: The Clarendon Press.
Brown, R.M. (1969) 'The American vigilante tradition', in H.G. Graham and T.R. Gurr (eds), *The History of Violence in America.* New York: Bantam Books.

SELF-REPORTS

Definition

The self-report method is a means of collecting information about aspects of an individual's personal experience – such as their involvement in offending – using a structured interview. The method can generate both statistical and qualitative data, but has most commonly been used to quantify rates of self-reported crime and drug use.

Distinctive Features

Self-report methods have been used to investigate forms of behaviour as varied as alcohol and drug use (both legal and illegal), tobacco smoking, sexual experiences, diet and other aspects of physical health. Respondents are asked to describe an aspect of their behaviour or life experience, and often to give views and opinions about a particular topic, either in a face-to-face interview, by completing a questionnaire or, increasingly, by using a computer. Of most relevance to criminology are the self-report *offending* surveys that have a history in criminology dating back to the 1940s (Coleman

and Moynihan, 1996). The method has been used to estimate rates of offending in the general population, among university students, 'persistent offenders' and those in prison or on probation orders. Recently, in the UK, self-report offending surveys have been suggested for evaluating crime reduction strategies, as an alternative to reconviction studies. The method has also been used for the comparative analysis of crime and deviance.

Surveys using this method have contributed to knowledge about deviance, often producing a picture that contradicts 'conventional wisdom'. For example, self-report studies indicate that drug use and crimes including theft, violence and fraud are much more widespread among the general population than commonly imagined, most of which goes undetected. Self-report offending survey rates among males in one cohort study exceeded 95 per cent by the time they reached early middle age, many more than the one in three who were convicted in court of a non-motoring offence (Farrington, 1997). Self-report offending surveys conducted in the USA, the UK and continental Europe also suggest that gender, ethnic and class differences in offending are much smaller than those in the picture painted by arrest and imprisonment statistics. Despite methodological weaknesses (see below), this finding lends weight to evidence which suggests that selective enforcement and discrimination in criminal justice processing can explain the disproportionate rates of imprisonment among particular ethnic groups.

The self-report method offers the possibility of attempting to explain offending from the offender's perspective and to discover the personal and social factors that can be identified as the 'correlates' of offending. This lends itself to 'control theories' of offending, focusing on aspects of the life of the 'admitted offender', their social bonds to family and friends, school and work experiences, and attitudes towards life in general. The statistical correlations that emerge from self-report studies cannot be taken as causative, however, because so little light is shed on the mechanisms and processes required to explain deviance and the process by which labels are attributed and acquired.

A method that relies on the honesty of interviewees to disclose dishonest and violent acts is obviously vulnerable to challenges to its validity. How can we be sure that respondents are not lying, or (more charitably) saying what they think the interviewer wants to hear? Attempts to test the extent to which self-report studies will generate valid and meaningful information about crime and deviance have included the use of polygraph ('lie detector') tests, the use of questions designed to identify exaggeration or embellishment (such as questions about fictitious drugs), and back-checking what interviewees have said against police records. (In some studies, this back-checking has been done without the interviewee's consent, thereby raising ethical concerns.) In general, surveys have tended to show greater levels of concealment than exaggeration, and given that the extent of self-reported offending is often much higher than many people assume, it seems reasonable to accept that they are indeed a useful alternative measure of people's unrecorded delinquent behaviour. The method has been shown to be reliable using various tools such as 'test-retest' and through the application of repeated measurement.

Self-report offending and drug surveys uncover a very large number of people who have committed unlawful acts, some of which would result in harsh penalties in the event that they were caught, prosecuted and convicted. However, self-report surveys also capture a great deal of less serious offences, laying the method open to the charge that it places excessive emphasis on trivial offences. Care has to be taken to identify the minority of more serious offenders among the huge numbers of people (the majority of the population) who admit to committing minor offences.

Self-report studies have been limited by a more or less exclusive focus on the descriptive quantification of offending rates. They can also be criticized for seeking to explain patterns at the population level, rather than shedding much light on what happens in individual lives or on the dynamics of communities. To overcome these limitations, some surveys have combined self-report offending and victimization into one questionnaire (Anderson et al., 1994). Others have conducted follow-up qualitative interviews to illustrate the dynamics of offending and desistance (Graham and Bowling, 1995).

Evaluation

In sum, the self-report method can provide a helpful, but limited, alternative to recorded crime statistics and victimization surveys. It is, arguably, the only way to estimate the extent of 'primary deviance' in the general population (Box, 1981). Certainly, self-report studies do uncover forms of behaviour that could not be quantified using other means – including 'victimless' deviant acts (such as drug use), those that have a low likelihood of detection (such as handling stolen goods and fraud), and undetected offences in general. The method has tended to focus on the crimes of the powerless, though a wider application might be estimating the extent of corporate and white collar crime.

Ben Bowling

Associated Concepts: hidden crime, labelling, official criminal statistics, social reaction, social survey, victim surveys, victimology

Key Readings

Anderson, S., Kinsey, R., Loader, I. and Smith, C. (1994) *Cautionary Tales: Young People, Crime and Policing in Edinburgh.* Aldershot: Avebury.

Box, S. (1981) *Deviance, Reality and Society,* 2nd edn. London: Holt Rinehart and Winston.

Coleman, C. and Moynihan, J. (1996) *Understanding Crime Data.* Buckingham: Open University Press.

Farrington, D. (1997) 'Human development and criminal careers', in M. Maguire, R. Morgan and R. Reiner (eds), *The Oxford Handbook of Criminology.* Oxford: The Clarendon Press.

Graham, J. and Bowling, B. (1995) *Young People and Crime,* Home Office Research Study No. 145. London: HMSO.

Ramsay, M. and Spiller, J. (1997) *Drug Misuse Declared in 1996: Key Results from the British Crime Survey,* Home Office Research Findings No. 56. London: HMSO.

SERIAL KILLING

Definition

Stranger-perpetrated murders – usually by men – which often appear motiveless and are characterized by gratuitous violence. Though rare, serial killing stands at the apogee of a popular fascination with crime, fuelling both a robust mythology and demands for retribution to be at the heart of criminal justice, in particular in the USA – the 'natural' habitat of such criminals.

Distinctive Features

Criminologists are in broad agreement that the serial killer is different from the 'normal' single incident murderer and other types of multiple killer, for example the *'mass murderer'* and the *'spree murderer'*. The serial killer is said to exhibit some or all of the following definitional characteristics. First, the killings are repetitive or 'serial' and, because the murder is in itself the motive, these will continue until the serial killer is caught. Second, the majority of serial killers like to work on their own and this is why they are so difficult to track down. There are, of course, well-known 'killer couples', 'partnerships' and 'groupings', but these run a greater risk of detection. Third, there is little personal connection between the perpetrator and the victim. These are classic stranger-perpetrated murders and a significant number will be 'motiveless'. There is nothing personal in the choice of victim, other than that person may belong to a particular cultural/social grouping. Fourth, very few will display a clearly defined or rational motive. It may not become apparent until a killer is arrested that a series of unsolved murders/attempted murders may be related. Fifth, increased spatial mobility and social fragmentation will enable a serial killer to extend and intensify their killing capacity. And because the communication flows between different police forces are haphazard and uncoordinated, serial killers can escape detection. Sixth, there is often a high degree of gratuitous violence. Experts argue that this is because of the motivation for the crime. The killing is not the means to another end but an end in itself. Finally, because the majority of serial killers are men, we need to consider the complex relationship between particular forms of *masculinity* and violent criminality.

Studies suggest that there are four main motivational typologies:

- *Visionaries:* Included in this typology would be those killers who claim to be reacting to or directed by 'voices' and alter egos, where the 'instructions' received will justify and legitimize the murders.
- *Missionaries:* Included in this category are 'clean-up' killers, who are quite willing to accept responsibility for 'cleansing' society of its 'undesirable' or 'unfit' elements. Any 'group' could become a target for the 'missionary' killer. However, the majority of targets are chosen from 'deviant' groupings such as prostitutes, homosexuals or drug addicts. The killer can justify their actions on the grounds that they are acting on behalf of decent people. In doing so, they can utilize a classic 'technique of neutralization'.
- *Hedonists:* A broad category which includes the types of killer for whom 'pleasure' is the 'reward' of murder. This category includes lust killers, fantasy killers and thrill killers.
- *Power seekers:* Domination is the strong motive force but these killers are aware of their behaviour and can describe their motivational state.

In response to the inadequacy of traditional techniques of murder investigation, the FBI began to develop a system of analysing evidence, both tangible and intuitive, collected by law enforcement officers from scenes of crime. A 'psychological profile' was then constructed using a contextual analysis of (a) victim traits, (b) witness reports and (c) the method of killing. A detailed list of physical and psychological characteristics was built up until a portrait of the killer and their behavioural patterns appeared. Included on the list would be: age, sex, marital status, occupation, race, criminal record, class, sexual preferences, etc. A considerable amount of intuitive guesswork would be involved here, but this does not seem to damage the investigative procedure because, as David Canter (1992) argues, a criminal will leave evidence of their personality through their criminal actions. An individual's behaviour, according to Canter, will exhibit characteristics unique to that person, as well as patterns that are typical of the subgroup to which they belong. Law enforcement agencies throughout the world have realized that they also need to develop sophisticated information collection systems which can coordinate, analyse and review reports from different agencies and identify early serial killing patterns. These developments have allowed them to compile personality profiles which can enhance the early identification of a potential or 'emergent' serial killer. Psychologists and psychiatrists working in this field argue that there are significant levels of childhood violence, abuse and neglect present in the backgrounds of some of the most notorious serial killers that may provide a clue to their subsequent actions. Such connections lend weight to their arguments that efforts and resources should be focused on the early identification of violent behaviour that could escalate into murderous thoughts and deeds. This will necessitate monitoring the child-rearing practices of families for signs of maladjusted relationships and pathological dynamics.

Others argue that there are very clear links between alcohol dependency and violence, and pornography and violence, and that their availability should be proscribed and policed more rigorously. Yet others point to testimony from serial killers that it was fictional representations of violence which 'triggered' their actions. Psychologists argue that in order to kill, a person must dehumanize their victim, reducing that person to the status of an object. Constant exposure to graphic, highly glamorized violence desensitizes viewers and readers to human pain and suffering and paves the way for certain individuals to view murder as a 'normal' course of action. For certain serial killers it is clear that they view themselves as 'actors' in a Hollywood film scripted by Quentin Tarantino or Oliver Stone. Again, such connections have brought forth a chorus of demands for tighter regulation and control of the entertainment industry.

Evaluation

The mythological status of the threat posed by the serial killer to American society has led to civil liberties objections being neutralized. In the twenty-first century, it seems as if there will be only one answer to the following question. Which are more important, the civil liberties of law-abiding innocent citizens or those of a potential killer?

Eugene McLaughlin

Associated Concepts: masculinities, neutralization (techniques of), personality theory, victimology

Key Readings

Canter, D. (1992) *Criminal Psychology.* London: Routledge.
Egger, S.A. (1998) *The Killers Among Us.* New York: Prentice-Hall.
Fox, J.A. and Levin, J. (1994) *Overkill: Mass Murder and Serial Killing Exposed.* New York: Plenum Press.
Holmes, R.M. (1987) *Serial Murder.* Beverly Hills, CA: Sage.
Leyton, E. (1988) *Hunting Humans.* New York: Pocket Books.
Seltzer, M. (1998) *Serial Killers: Death and Life in American Wound Culture.* New York: Routledge.

SEX CRIME

Definition

Sexual acts and behaviours proscribed by the legal statutes of the jurisdiction within which they are enacted.

Distinctive Features

The term 'sex crime', like 'crime' more generally, is neither fixed nor immutable, but constantly changing and highly contested. It refers to an enormous diversity of behaviours, from unsolicited sexual comments in the workplace to serial rape and sex murder. What is defined and labelled as sex crime may vary considerably across time and place. For example, many homosexual activities were legalized in the 1960s as a reflection of changing social attitudes, and it was not until 1992 in the UK that a man could be convicted of raping his wife. Meanwhile, a serious sexual offence in one country (e.g., consensual sex between an adult and a 13-year-old in the UK) may be legal in another (in Spain the age of consent is 13).

A key concept in defining sex crime is 'consent'. For cases involving adults, the legal process frequently hinges on the prosecution's ability to prove beyond reasonable doubt that consent was absent or given on the basis of force, fear or fraud. When children and young persons are involved, consent ceases to be an issue, since it is widely accepted that children below the legal age of consent are not capable of making 'competent' decisions about their sexual activities. Thus sex with a child is, in all circumstances, unlawful. Consensual sex acts between adults may also be unlawful. Certain homosexual activities in a public place, for example, though 'victimless', are criminalized because these are deemed to offend against public decency.

Assessing the nature and extent of sex crime is rife with complications, and official statistics are woefully inadequate as indicators of the actual levels of offending. Due to the highly sensitive nature of sexual victimization, and in England and Wales an adversarial justice system which – despite significant improvements over recent decades – may still involve aggressive cross-examination in an open courtroom, only a fraction of victims report their abuse to the police, and still fewer pursue legal action. Of those offences reported, there is frequently insufficient evidence – particularly forensic

evidence – to proceed with a case, leading to significant levels of 'no-criming' by the police and many reported incidents going unrecorded. Changing definitions for sex crime further complicate the monitoring of offending rates. The lowering of the age of homosexual consent from 18 to 16 in England, Wales and Scotland in 2000 reduced substantially the total volume of recordable sex offences, while the creation of a new offence in 2003 of meeting a child following sexual grooming constituted a brand new category of sex crime and, as such, a new source of statistical inflation.

Victim surveys, which generally offer a more accurate if still flawed picture of 'the crime problem', have had limited success in uncovering the 'dark figure' of sex crime. The national British Crime Survey, for example, excludes estimates of sexual offending from its main sweeps because the response rates are so low. In local surveys, by contrast, the proportion of respondents disclosing some form of sexual victimization has exceeded two-thirds (Maguire, 2002). Due to these variations and constraints as well as others, it is impossible to know how much sex crime there is in any given society at any one time.

Evaluation

Sex crime is, in large part, a problem of men offending against women and children. Due to its highly gendered nature, some of the most important contributions to understanding sexual offending have come from feminists. Indeed, it was only with the growing influence of the women's movement in the 1970s that the previously 'hidden' problem of violence – including sexual violence – against women and children was recognized as a serious problem that demands sustained political, academic and public attention.

Though feminist perspectives are diverse, a powerful theme has been the conceptualization of sexual violence as the extension of a patriarchal order in which women are systematically subjugated by men to positions of dependency and subordination. Male behaviour towards women, including sexual victimization, has been viewed as existing along a 'continuum', with rape and sexual assault at one end and, for example, limited career opportunities near the other. These behaviours differ only by degree, rather than in kind, and all are seen as serving the same ultimate purpose of controlling women (Kelly, 1988).

Some feminist approaches advocate working with victims – or, as radical feminists prefer, 'survivors' – of sex crime and criminal justice practitioners. Others retain a deep suspicion, particularly of police attitudes, and avoid interacting with official agencies. Some feminists seek to achieve a balance between victims' and offenders' rights, while others see the latter as relatively unimportant. Whatever the differences between approaches, their collective impact has been enormous. Feminism has been central in securing improvements in the treatment of sex crime victims in the criminal justice system, increasing the quality and availability of advice and support, and raising social awareness about the 'normality' of much male (sexual) violence against women and children.

Diverse attempts to explain sex crime have also come from within the medical profession, focusing variously on psychiatric and psychoanalytic theories, biochemical imbalances and genetic abnormalities. For many, the most promising outcomes, particularly with child abusers, are offered by 'cognitive-behavioural' interventions, which maintain that individuals choose to perpetrate sex crimes, but due to various cognitive distortions may not believe their actions are wrong or may be in denial about the harm caused. The aim is to address these distortions through developing 'avoidance' and 'coping' mechanisms, increasing social competence and encouraging empathy with the victim. Evaluations appear to indicate that, while the urge to reoffend cannot be removed, it can be managed (Beckett, 1994).

The assessment and management of 'risk' has become a central theme in dealing with sex offenders both in custody and in the community. Risk assessment combines a consideration of individual characteristics – such as offending history – with the environmental influences on recidivism – for example, family support – in order to evaluate an offender's 'dangerousness'. Once assessed, risk management strategies can follow. Risk assessment involves making predictions about future behaviour; some critics have challenged the ethics of incarcerating individuals on the basis of what they might do rather than what they have already done. Advocates maintain, however, that increasingly sophisticated assessment tools and the growth in multi-agency partnership working can support informed decision making about such future behaviour, albeit within a range of probabilities (Thomas, 2000). Risk assessment is ongoing and takes place during trial and sentencing, throughout a person's incarceration (notably in sex offender treatment programmes) and, crucially, on their release back into the community.

The 1990s witnessed the introduction of Sex Offender Registers across Europe and America. Registration – lasting from five years to life in the UK – requires offenders to notify the police of, among other things, any change of address. The aim is to keep track of offenders, manage risk and protect the public. Public confidence in official agencies' ability to achieve these objectives has been shaken by high profile cases of convicted offenders killing, post-release. Such cases, though extremely rare, have received enormous levels of media attention which, in turn, has fuelled the ongoing debate around 'public notification' – granting limited public access to information about sex offenders in the community (Matravers, 2003). Supporters stress the right to access information which will enable people to better protect their children and themselves. Critics claim that such access encourages vigilantism and forces sex offenders underground, where, deprived of family support and professional help, the risks of reoffending may increase considerably.

The mass media's insatiable appetite for sex crime has generated both positive and negative outcomes. On the one hand, media attention has helped bring certain forms of offending from the private to the public domain, and in so doing has contributed to reducing the stigma of being a victim. On the other, the selective, sensational and misleading nature of much media coverage perpetuates the myth of 'stranger-danger', when adults and children are most often victimized by someone they know, and reinforces stereotypes of who may legitimately claim victim status (Greer, 2003). The undifferentiated fear and loathing of sex offenders throughout society, actively encouraged in sections of the media, arguably does more to hinder than help the development of measured debate about how best to deal with the problem of sex crime – in all its myriad forms – and reduce the risk of victimization for adults and children alike.

Chris Greer

Associated Concepts: crime, crime news, family crime, newsmaking criminology, personal safety, victimization, violence

Key Readings

Beckett, R. (1994) 'Cognitive-behavioural treatment of sex offenders', in T. Morrison, M. Erooga and R.C. Beckett (eds), *Sexual Offending Against Children: Assessment and Treatment of Male Abusers*. London: Routledge.
Greer, C. (2003) *Sex Crime and the Media: Sex Offending and the Press in a Divided Society*. Cullompton: Willan.
Kelly, L. (1988) *Surviving Sexual Violence*. Cambridge: Polity Press.
Maguire, M. (2002) 'Crime statistics: the "data explosion" and its implications', in M. Maguire, R. Morgan and R. Reiner (eds), *The Oxford Handbook of Criminology*, 3rd edn. Oxford: Oxford University Press.
Matravers, A. (ed.) (2003) *Sex Offenders in the Community: Managing and Reducing the Risks*. Cullompton: Willan.
Thomas, T. (2000) *Sex Crime: Sex Offending and Society*. Cullompton: Willan.

SEXUALITY

Definition

Literally being sexual, possessing the capacity for sex or sexual feelings. However, within lesbian and gay movements, sexuality has become a cornerstone of identity and political campaigning around it. Some gay activists welcome 'gay gene' research as affirming the 'normality' of all sexualities; for most, sexuality has been seen as defining one's identity and self-hood. That is, gay liberation could be achieved by gay identification. 'Coming out' came to be seen as revealing a 'true' self to oneself, family, friends and wider society. Both identity politics and popular prejudice might concentrate on homosexuality and bisexuality – in often opposing ways – but heterosexuality needs to be considered too. Katz (1995) argues for the invention of 'heterosexuality' by the discipline of sexology, which also discursively produced 'homosexuality'. Smart (1996) suggests that probably only the male heterosexual was conceived as possessing a sexuality. In criminology in general sexuality is normatively and implicitly heterosexual and often only explicitly possessed by the young or black. Sexuality is also often seen as pathological.

Distinctive Features

Typically, sociology has ignored sex and sexuality, leaving the debate and discourse to a variety of sexologies which derive their methods and concerns primarily from medicine and psychoanalysis. Early criminology shared practitioners with medicine so some mention of sexuality as pathology can be found in early works. For instance, Lombroso favoured light punishments for those deprived of heterosexual outlets, but long-term incarceration for the congenital homosexual. The effect of this would be to deprive the offender of 'homosexual outlets'. Moreover much homosexual – and some heterosexual – activity is illegal and therefore falls within the ambit of criminology. The conflation is evident in the UK Wolfenden Committee's remit to study both homosexuality and prostitution.

The 1970s onward have shown small but steady advances by feminism into sociology and eventually criminology. This has raised the interest in and knowledge of gender as an issue in studies of crime and criminal justice. With that recognition has grown an interest in masculinities – the acceptance that whilst the problem may still be men, men still have problems. However, this emphasis on gender has continued to obscure the cross-cutting issues raised by sexuality. There are sexist gay men but the main complaint of women and of feminism has been against heterosexual men – their sexual, domestic and economic violence. However, much of that feminism had assumed a unified 'sisterhood' which simply aggregated the problems faced by educated, middle-class white wives with those of lesbians, women of colour and so forth.

Apart from early criminology's assumption of the pathology of homosexuality (maintained by psychology until the 1970s), issues of sexuality have been downplayed as purely personal or left to other disciplines. However, under the banner of the sociology of deviance a number of sensitive studies have been carried out. Humphreys' (1970) study of men who had sex with men in public toilets found that many lived ostensibly heterosexual lives, while Reiss (1961/1968) explored the extent to which young 'delinquents' were prepared to receive oral sex from gay men without peer group damage to their heterosexual identity.

Evaluation

In as much as criminology is concerned about order it should be concerned with issues of sexuality. Plummer argues that a 'central problem for sociologists is that of order and control, and sexuality is sometimes seen as playing an important part in this order. Either it is argued that through sexuality our social order is channelled, or it is argued that through social order our sexuality is channelled' (1975/1980). Yet, other than the 'commonsense' criminology that sees homosexuality as 'symptomatic of treason and political deviancy' (Collier, 1995: 97–8), sexuality has been treated poorly in criminology.

However, just as gender has begun to make an impression within criminology, it is argued that sexuality must do this also. Empirically it has already begun (and largely remained) outside the discipline with activists contesting homophobic violence and policing priorities. Left realist victimology should be able to take this on board without adopting a specifically gay standpoint or perspective. It remains to be seen whether a full blown – possibly queer – consideration of sexuality is possible within criminology. Much of the work on male heterosexuality has been undertaken by feminists – as a problem to be explained – and is now carried forward under the banner of the 'masculinities' literature. Much of that literature fails to acknowledge the work of lesbian feminists or gay men's attempts to explain heterosexuality.

Nic Groombridge

Associated Concepts: feminist criminologies, hegemonic masculinity, masculinities, pathology, queer theory, victimology

Key Readings

Collier, R. (1995) *Masculinity, Law and the Family.* London: Routledge.

Humphreys, L. (1970) *Tearoom Trade: Impersonal Sex in Public Places.* London: Duckworth.

Katz, J.N. (1995) *The Invention of Heterosexuality.* New York: Dutton.

Plummer, K. (1975/1980) 'Sexual stigma: an interactionist account', in R. Bocock, P. Hamilton, K. Thompson and A. Walton (eds), *An Introduction to Sociology.* London: Fontana.

Reiss, A.J. Jr (1961/1968) 'The social integration of queers and peers', in E. Rubington and M.S. Weinburg (eds), *Deviance: The Interactionist Perspective.* London: Macmillan.

Smart, C. (1996) 'Collusion, collaboration and confession: on moving beyond the heterosexuality debate', in D. Richardson (ed.), *Theorizing Heterosexuality.* Buckingham: Open University Press.

SHAMING

Definition

The mode of punishment stigmatizing deviant individuals or groups which turns them into identifiable outcasts, either on a temporary or permanent basis. Shaming may take disintegrative as well as reintegrative forms.

Distinctive Features

There is a long tradition of the use of shaming as one component of stigmatizing punishments in pre-industrial and traditional communities. However, processes of shaming also continue into modern times. Doubtless everyone has encountered some form of shaming at some point in their lives, especially in the micro-interactions between people in both formal and non-formal settings, such as in school or within the family. But shaming has not been generally recognized as a legitimate and explicit criminal justice strategy in most modern systems of justice and punishment. There are, of course, some notable exceptions to this tendency. In particular we may note the cultural embeddedness and acceptance of the legitimacy of shaming in Japan, where there is widespread use of shaming techniques for offenders in the country's system of criminal justice. Furthermore, shaming was crucial to punishment by public disgrace in the 'community courts' of the Soviet Union and Maoist China. And, of course, there has also been a recent growth and rebirth of the appeal to public shaming in the contemporary campaigns and movements to 'name and shame' offenders in many contemporary Western countries. In the USA, for example, current shaming techniques include the forced carrying of sandwich boards announcing 'I am a criminal': a throwback to the kinds of public shaming that were standard practice in the North American English colonies of the seventeenth century. We should note here the danger of shaming in practice degenerating into vindictiveness. The latter development appears in part to be influenced by the conservative communitarian impulse over 'community' justice and punishment and the emotive politics of popular punitiveness, as well as being indicative of the lack of trust in the workings of the formal criminal justice system.

The recognition of the importance of shaming to modern criminological thinking and its potentially positive role in the workings of social control has largely been the result of John Braithwaite's (1989, 1993) important work. He has noted that shaming may take both disintegrative and reintegrative forms. The former stigmatizes people and turns them into outcasts (as in the examples of punitive exclusion through imprisonment and the use of banishment in pre-modern societies). Disintegrative shaming is the norm in modern Western states, as a result of which there is labelling and stigma and the creation of a class of outcasts. By way of contrast, reintegrative shaming offers gestures of reacceptance.

According to Braithwaite, reintegrative shaming is a form of disapproval dispensed within an ongoing relationship with the offender based on respect. It focuses on the evil of the deed rather than on the offender as an irredeemably evil person. In turn, degradation ceremonies are followed by ceremonies to decertify deviance, where forgiveness, apology and repentance are culturally important (Braithwaite, 1993: 1). Reintegrative shaming also expresses society's disapproval of the act by bringing the wrongdoer, the victim and close associates of each party together in a group setting. It has been argued that much of its preventive success lies in work on the offender's conscience. However, such preventive processes will only be effective in situations where the loss of respect counts heavily. Braithwaite thus acknowledges that it is 'communitarianism that makes shaming possible' (1993: 2). Unlike modern Western systems of justice and punishment, which isolate and stigmatize the guilty through exclusionary disposal (such as custody), reintegrative shaming therefore aims to accept the guilty back into the community and so help prevent future offending through a process of active reintegration.

There are obvious risks to using this strategy, of which Braithwaite is well aware. As he notes, shaming can become the principal weapon for the tyranny of the majority over vulnerable minorities (1989: 158). This concern has led him to argue that the securing of liberty must lie at the centre of what he terms 'civic republican justice'. Despite claims that shaming is unlikely to work in the complex, anonymous societies of the modern era, Braithwaite has made a strong argument for its continuing salience as a crime prevention approach today. Indeed, it may be argued that the current proliferation of roles makes us all more vulnerable to shame in a way that is peculiar and specific to a world with this proliferation. According to proponents of reintegrative shaming, this mode of restorative justice is far from being reactionary and targeted at the most vulnerable minorities. Instead, it is viewed as a crucial communitarian resource in mobilizing against those offenders who brutalize (such as abusers) and exploit (such as corporations) as well as restraining those who would wish to trample on the rights of citizens who wish to be (harmlessly) deviant. However, the extent to which reintegrative shaming is employed routinely against powerful individuals and agencies, not least when shaming intolerable criminal justice practices, needs to be given critical attention.

Evaluation

Significant and worrying questions remain regarding the theory and practice of shaming, whether this is disintegrative or reintegrative. It has as yet to be proven that shaming will not be used and mobilized against the most vulnerable, deviant sections of the population with scant concern for their legal and human rights. Given the previous history of other community justice-based initiatives, it is also quite possible that (reintegrative) shaming will be used chiefly for trivial offences and young offenders without any reduction in the use of traditional, disintegrative custodial sentences. Indeed, critical authors, such as Blagg (1997), have noted that the 'product' of reintegrative shaming being franchized in Australia is being targeted at Aboriginal people and may intensify rather than reduce police controls over this already victimized population. More general criticisms may be made of the notion that shaming is a universal trait in all human cultures. If shaming is a forced and ingenuine process imposed on the offender, its reintegrative efficacy may be open to question and instead result in the more traditional consequence of stigmatizing criminalization.

Gordon Hughes

Associated Concepts: communitarianism, community justice, restorative justice, stigma

Key Readings

Blagg, H. (1997) 'A just measure of shame: Aboriginal youth and conferencing in Australia', *British Journal of Criminology*, 37 (4): 481–501.

Braithwaite, J. (1989) *Crime, Shame and Reintegration*. Oxford: Oxford University Press.

Braithwaite, J. (1993) 'Shame and modernity', *British Journal of Criminology*, 33 (1): 1–18.

SIGNAL CRIME

See: 'Broken windows'; Zero tolerance

SITUATIONAL CRIME PREVENTION

Definition

Crime prevention as a whole can be defined as reducing the risk of occurrence and the potential seriousness of criminal events by intervening in their causes. Situational crime prevention (SCP) intervenes in those causes which the offender encounters, or seeks out, in the immediate circumstances of the criminal event.

Distinctive Features

SCP methods aim to reduce a wide range of crimes. They commonly involve the design of products, services, environments or systems to make them crime-resistant – a strategy implemented alone or in combination with certain social activities, such as surveillance and the response to crimes by people in various roles: householder, passer-by, employee or security personnel, and the more strategic managers of places. Methods range from supplying toughened drinking glasses to reduce injury from fights in bars, to establishing rules for acceptable behaviour in shopping centres and football matches; from traffic enforcement cameras to anti-climb paint; from the encryption of financial data to CCTV in banks; from better laid-out housing estates to hard-to-forge holographic labels to discourage counterfeit vodka; from airport metal detectors and security guards to Farm Watch and similar community-based schemes.

SCP does not rely on past improvements in society, treatment regimes for offenders or early interventions in children's socialization to reduce current criminality; nor on the sheer aversive intensity of sanctions anticipated at some remote point in the future to deter or incapacitate present offending. It does not directly aim to change *offenders'* propensities or motives for crime at all. It takes these as given and, proceeding from an analysis of the circumstances engendering particular crimes, it introduces specific changes to influence the offender's *decision* or *ability* to commit these crimes at given places and times. These interventions usually act on the here-and-now of the immediate crime situation, removing or altering some of its components or preventing them from coming together. The generic components of the crime situation include a human, material or informational target of crime; a target enclosure, such as a safe or a building; a wider environment, such as a housing estate or town centre; and people or institutions playing two opposing roles – preventers, who will make crime less likely, and promoters, who will carelessly or deliberately make it more likely. Interventions may sometimes act on prior *'scenes'* (Cornish, 1994), in which offenders prepare, or become primed for, crime (such as acquiring weapons, getting drunk or engaging in disputes over parking). Interventions may be implemented indirectly – for example, by helping people protect their own homes, or by naming and shaming manufacturers of insecure vehicles so *they* are motivated to make these harder to steal.

SCP methods are widely adopted in society, shading into common-sense 'routine precautions' (Clarke, 1997). But it is only in the past twenty years that the 'official' world of government and police has taken them seriously. In the USA, the approach developed through the Crime Prevention through Environmental Design movement (National Crime Prevention Council, 1997). In the UK, a programme of practical research directed by Ron Clarke at the Home Office inspired the search for a more theoretical foundation built around the concept of crime as opportunity. This was based (at a time of 'nothing works') on dissatisfaction with the limited effectiveness of crime prevention through conventional means, particularly attempts to change the disposition of the offender, and growing academic awareness of the general limits of 'personality' in explaining behaviour. Two main theoretical approaches now underlie SCP. Both take offender characteristics, including motivation, as given.

The *rational choice* perspective sees the fundamental causal mechanism of SCP as making the commission of specific sets of crimes more risky (deterrence), requiring of more effort and less rewarding (discouragement), or less comfortable (removing excuses) (adapted from Clarke, 1997). For SCP to work – at least in the short term – deterrence and discouragement need only be *perceived* barriers.

Routine activity theory (Felson, 1983) takes a wider causal view. Here, criminal events stem from the conjunction of a likely (motivated) offender, a suitable target and the absence of capable guardians. SCP is about changing the last two. A related approach, which attempts to understand and predict what brings these ingredients together in terms of spatial arrangements, patterns of travel and so on is *environmental criminology* (Brantingham and Brantingham, 1995).

Evaluation

The main practical criticism of SCP centres on *displacement,* that is, where an offender, blocked by an SCP measure, seeks a similar target at another time or place and changes methods or changes the target altogether. Clarke (1997) has, however, shown displacement to be limited in effect and sometimes even reversed (*diffusion of benefit*, where cautious offenders avoid more than just the officially protected site); but the possibility of displacement can never be ruled out in any specific circumstances.

Aesthetic criticisms centre on fears about a 'fortress society' and ethical ones on a loss of privacy or freedom. According to advocates of SCP, both can be minimized through the good design of products, environments and procedures to reconcile security with these potentially conflicting requirements. Some practitioners – and criminologists – whose primary interest is in offenders and their motives find SCP trivial; some situationalists in their turn regard offender-oriented approaches as over-optimistic or misguided. Having 'two cultures of prevention' blocks practical and theoretical progress.

Theoretical criticisms highlight the limits to offenders' rationality – but these are neither fatal to SCP nor contested by its protagonists. More recently (e.g., Ekblom, 2000) there have been attempts to integrate SCP with a wider understanding of offenders – their criminal predispositions, immediate motives to offend and resources for offending (tools, weapons, knowledge and skill). From this perspective, the concept of *opportunity* for crime is not simply a property of the crime situation, but is conjointly dependent on the offender's resources to exploit it and cope with the risks (an open window three floors up is only an opportunity to someone with agility, courage and perhaps a ladder).

Paul Ekblom

Associated Concepts: carceral society, community safety, crime prevention, crime science, defensible space, geographies of crime, opportunity theory, rational choice theory, routine activity theory, surveillance

Key Readings

Brantingham, P. and Brantingham, P. (1995) 'Criminality of place: crime generators and crime attractors', *European Journal on Criminal Policy and Research*, 3 (3): 5–26.

Clarke, R.V.G. (1997) *Situational Crime Prevention: Successful Case Studies,* 2nd edn. Albany, NY: Harrow and Heston.

Cornish, D. (1994) 'The procedural analysis of offending and its relevance for situational prevention', in R. Clarke (ed.), *Crime Prevention Studies*, 3. Monsey, NY: Criminal Justice Press. pp. 151–96.

Ekblom, P. (2000) 'The conjunction of criminal opportunity – a tool for clear, "joinedup" thinking about community safety and crime reduction', in K. Pease, S. Ballintyne and V. McLaren (eds), *Key Issues in Crime Prevention, Crime Reduction and Community Safety.* London: Institute for Public Policy Research.

Felson, M. (1983) 'Linking criminal choices, routine activities, informal control, and criminal outcomes', in D. Cornish and R. Clarke (eds), *The Reasoning Criminal.* New York: Springer-Verlag.

National Crime Prevention Council (1997) *Designing Safer Communities: A Crime Prevention through Environmental Design Handbook.* Washington, DC: NCPC.

SOCIAL CAPITAL

Definition

Reflecting its increasingly wide usage and application, and its travels across both North American and European academic and policy-making communities, it is not surprising that social capital is a highly contested and controversial idea characterized by different definitions. Broadly speaking, social capital relates to the values that individuals and groups possess and the resources that they have access to which can promote, or result from, diverse social relationships and ties.

Social capital is therefore primarily concerned with social networks, norms of reciprocity, forms of socialization, social bonds, trust and resources, and the multiple and changing relationships between them.

Distinctive Features

Social capital is one of those relatively rare concepts originating in the social sciences that transcends academic boundaries and enters the world of policy making at multiple and diverse levels, from local level discussions of crime prevention and community participation for example, through to the policy agendas of the World Bank in relation to poverty reduction and social development. If the explosion and popularizing of use of the term 'social capital' since the 1990s has been largely due to the work of American political scientist Robert Putnam (2000), it is important to acknowledge that the concept has a much longer historical pedigree. French Marxist social theorist Pierre Bourdieu is generally (if decreasingly) recognized as the first major thinker associated with social capital. For Bourdieu (1986), social capital represents but one of the different forms of capital which emerge in capitalist society, here taken to refer to the networks of connections that an individual possesses or can access. Reflecting his Marxist leanings, social capital is always seen as secondary to and associated with economic capital. It is primarily a product of an individual's class position and is part and parcel of the reproduction of social inequalities that characterize class society.

This emphasis on social capital as reflective of class inequalities has largely been expunged in the accounts and explanations of social capital that have come to dominate both academic and policy-making debates in recent years. This is largely due to the work of the aforementioned Putnam and also the American sociologist Coleman (1988–89). Thanks in the main to their work, social capital has come to be interpreted largely as a 'social' or 'public' 'good', often depicted as the 'glue' that binds society together or, in a Durkheimian sense, as a form of social solidarity. In Coleman's approach social capital is understood as something that enables or facilitates the attainment of collective goals. He highlights social capital as a particular resource within families that promotes intergenerational relationships between parents and children and which in turn can enhance not only socialization but also educational attainment.

For Coleman social capital allows individuals and collectives to achieve specific ends without which these could not be attained. Putnam extends this approach by arguing that society benefits economically, socially and politically by the acquisition and generation of social capital. Networks, and their norms of trustworthiness and reciprocity, are socially productive and positive in their own right. Associational life through voluntary associations helps to promote wider civic and political engagement. Thus, for Putnam, a decline in democratic and political engagement can be explained by exploring the quality of social capital that underpins it. In not inconsiderable part, it is his concerns with an apparent decline in participation that help to explain the popularity of both his ideas and the notion of social capital itself. Putnam sees in the decline of social capital in the United States (and in comparable societies) the source of a wide range of social problems, notably in relation to educational underachievement and public safety. He makes a distinction between what he terms *bridging* and *bonding* social capital. Bridging or 'inclusive' social capital helps to bring people together from across different social divisions and positions, whereas bonding or 'exclusive' forms of social capital tends to reinforce exclusive identities and maintain homogeneity. This allows him to acknowledge, in his response to criticisms of his earlier work, that social capital can have what is termed a 'dark side', namely that strong communities can be both oppressive in terms of their social controls as well as encourage conformity while promoting damaging behaviour.

It is through the notion of social capital as constructed by both Coleman and especially Putnam that we can begin to understand the attractiveness of the concept for criminologists and policy makers who are concerned with crime prevention and community safety. Social capital is increasingly interpreted as a form of community resource that is linked with 'better' socialization and the promotion and reinforcement of pro-social norms that will allow transgressors to be more readily identified and sanctioned. Communities with 'healthy' amounts of social capital are viewed as more socially stable and more self-sustaining and it is within these that educational attainment, better health programmes and crime reduction among other collective goods can be promoted. Put simply, the thesis is that neighbourhoods with strong levels of social cohesion and institutional leadership, and a determination not to tolerate anti-social behaviour and disorder, have significantly lower crime levels and rates of victimization. Hence effective neighbourhood crime prevention is related to residents' sense of security, control and responsibility and the presence of pro-social communal bonds.

Evaluation

The popularity of the social capital idea should not blind us to the obvious problems that tend to characterize its analysis. Indeed it is in part through the popularity of the term that we can begin to understand some of these limitations. It is a highly flexible notion, one that is used in a wide range of social situations to explain diverse social, economic, cultural and political processes. However, producing a definition that is both internally coherent and allows for measurement has as yet escaped those of us who find it a useful analytical tool. At its simplest, problems of measurement result from the methodological individualism that lies at the core of the more popular (and populist) accounts of social capital where social and collective goods are defined in and through individual measures.

Taking the critique of social capital further, a number of opponents argue that it does not work at the level of description, let alone provide any analysis or allow for an explanation of the phenomena it purports to understand. Beyond these conceptual, definitional and methodological problems, however, critics have also focused on the ideological underpinnings of social capital, frequently interpreting this as part and parcel of a neoliberal world view that operates to marginalize issues of historical and material inequality. In the work of Coleman, Putnam and others, it both reflects and encourages a rather conservative understanding of social relations and structures. In this we are presented with a vision of an 'ordered' and 'stable' 'family' life, and ordered communities in which the norm is one of trust, belongingness/togetherness and participation, all the while counterposed by a dystopic view of other locales and communities as places of social disorganization and crime in which, in the approach of Coleman for example, family 'breakdown' is cited as one of the main factors contributing to a decline in social capital.

In other ways, opponents of social capital have argued that it is a deeply depoliticizing – though itself highly political – discourse. Power, conflict and class, notwithstanding the (largely marginalized) work of Bourdieu, are missing. Putnam in particular is seen as being guilty of neglecting class as a highly constraining factor in relation to social capital; that accessing material resources is a central factor which underpins his largely middle-class America view of associational life.

Despite the many criticisms that have been advanced, social capital is increasingly entering public and policy-making discourse on both sides of the Atlantic, albeit in different though equally contested ways. In the emerging and spreading industry of crime prevention and community safety it is sure to take on a renewed vigour in the years to come.

Gerry Mooney

Associated Concepts: anti-social behaviour, 'broken windows', community crime prevention, community justice, governance, social control, social ecology

Key Readings

Bourdieu, P. (1986) 'The forms of Capital', in J.G. Richardson (ed.), *Handbook of Theory and Research for the Sociology of Education*. New York: Greenwood Press.

Bursik, R.J. and Grasmick, H.G. (1993) *Neighbourhoods and Crime*. Lexington, KY: Lexington Books.

Coleman, J. (1988–89) 'Social capital in the creation of human capital', *American Journal of Sociology*, 94: 95–120.

Fine, B. (2001) *Social Capital versus Social Theory*. London: Routledge.

Putnam, R.D. (2000) *Bowling Alone: The Collapse and Revival of American Community*. New York: Simon & Schuster.

Sampson, R.J. (2001) 'Crime and public safety: insights from community level perspectives on social capital', in S. Saegert, P. Thompson and M. Warren (eds), *Social Capital and Poor Communities: Building and Using Assets to Combat Poverty*. New York: Russell Sage Foundation.

World Bank, www.worldbank.org.social-capital (last accessed 20 November 2004).

SOCIAL CENSURE

Definition

To censure is to blame, criticize, express disapproval or condemn. A social censure is a category expressing cultural disapproval, or a sign of blame.

Distinctive Features

The process of blaming and stigmatizing others in general is of core interest to criminology, but the social patterns of censure are of particular concern to sociologists. Psychologists are interested in the censorious personality or the roots of individual prejudice; sociologists in the political uses and social functions of scapegoating.

The concept of social censure refers to those censures which are common within a culture and which reflect the dominant or key relationships or structures of the society.

Censures mostly reinforce the established order and its institutions – for example, the social censure of bastardy reinforces the normative reverence for procreation within marriage. Some can be seen as master-censures in that they are so deep-rooted within the culture and its forms of thought that they permeate many other forms of censure. However, some are counter-censures, expressing the opposition or criticism of subordinate social groups to the social system or its institutions.

The concept of social censure differs from that of the label because the latter belongs to a theoretical standpoint which emphasizes conscious blaming practices using ideas as a kind of stick to beat people with. This is a liberal 'voluntarist' approach which supposes all is rational choice – and that categories of blame are not generated by the social structure nor creep quietly into our unconscious minds loaded with ideological or cultural baggage. Censure theory, as developed by Sumner (1990a, 1990b, 1994, 1997), is lodged within a theoretical analysis which emphasizes that feelings of disapproval are as much unconscious and emotional as they are conscious and rational, that social structures by their very nature imply, and predispose us to, certain categories of blame, and that social censures come to us already steeped and rooted within the structures and events of social history and thus coated with acquired meanings and implications.

The concept draws upon the idea of a vote of censure in Parliament or Congress to imply that even everyday social censures have a political, organized dimension – something which reflects the fact that most practices and institutions in modern 'disciplinary' societies are deeply permeated, and even structured, by normative judgements and judgemental or inspectorial practices, and that the interests of the state have been inserted into most dimensions of private morality (Foucault, 1967, 1975). Governance cannot evade moral propriety, and custom has long lost its virginity to state interference. Public and private worlds were linked up by the seventeenth-century European city-states concerned with the conservation of healthy populations (see Shakespeare's *Measure for Measure*), but they were fully merged in the formation of the welfare state and have never been de-coupled. This linkage was a vital part of the imperialist expansion into and creation of the 'Third World', leading later critics to observe that the cultural colonization of the mind was the most debilitating aspect of being colonized.

In European and New World societies of the twentieth century the dominant social censures were probably those of property crime and communism, both censures of activities directed at the fundamental structures of private property. These were, arguably, closely followed by the social censures of women, homosexuals and immigrants, groups whose existence and self-expression constantly challenged the established order of white, patriarchal power in the home and the local community.

Designed as a replacement for the concept of social deviance, which is itself a social censure favoured by sociologists in the twentieth century, the concept of social censure signifies the way that notions of the disapproved or immoral have over time acquired surplus associated meanings, such as stereotypes, which specify likely offenders, appropriate emotional responses to the act, contexts of commission and possible consequences. It thus designates cultural packages of blame which, insofar as they reflect social-structural needs, partisan interests, belief-systems and traditional assumptions, amount to ideological formations that target groups or acts or styles perceived by the dominant culture to be its enemies. As such, their function is usually to denounce and regulate rather than to explain or understand. They demarcate the regulator from the offender, the normal from the abnormal, the healthy from the unhealthy, and the good from the bad.

Since social censures are cultural, or even ideological formations tied to a will to punish or to social control, they are not good foundations for open-minded or scientific analysis.

Social scientists do not begin with the idea that, for example, terrorism is a neutral, descriptive category; they take it as an object whose significance needs to be explored for its variety of meanings, functions and roles for different groups at different historical moments. Censures are objects of study not tools of enquiry. Social research using the concept of social censure has found it valuable in analysing culturally and politically loaded data and attempting to distinguish social attributions from ontological realities.

Colin Sumner

Associated Concepts: deviance, labelling, racialization, scapegoating, stereotyping

Key Readings

Foucault, M. (1967) *Madness and Civilization: A History of Insanity in the Age of Reason.* London: Tavistock.

Foucault, M. (1975) *Discipline and Punish: The Birth of the Prison.* London: Allen Lane.

Sumner, C.S. (ed.) (1990a) *Censure, Politics and Criminal Justice.* Milton Keynes: Open University Press.

Sumner, C.S. (1990b) 'Foucault, gender and the censure of deviance', in L. Gelsthorpe and A. Morris (eds), *Feminist Perspectives in Criminology.* Milton Keynes: Open University Press.

Sumner, C.S. (1994) *The Sociology of Deviance: An Obituary.* Buckingham: Open University Press.

Sumner, C.S. (ed.) (1997) *Violence, Censure and Culture.* London: Taylor and Francis.

SOCIAL CONSTRUCTIONISM

Definition

A perspective that explores the assumptions embedded in the labelling of people and places and emphasizes the importance of social expectations in the analysis of taken-for-granted or apparently natural social processes.

Distinctive Features

A naturalistic or realist perspective in the social sciences treats social problems as though they are given: namely phenomena about whose existence we can all agree. The social constructionist perspective insists on the necessity of taking a step back from this view and asks instead: who says this is a social problem – and what sort of social problem do they think it is? This perspective draws on a very different sociological inheritance, one that treats society as a matrix of meaning. It accords a central role to processes of constructing, producing and circulating meanings. Within this perspective, we cannot grasp reality (or empirical phenomena) in a direct and unmediated way. Reality is always mediated by meaning. Indeed, some of its proponents argue that what we experience is 'the social construction of reality' (Berger and Luckmann, 1966). How something (or someone) is named, identified and placed within a 'map' of the social order has profound consequences for how we act towards it (or them). There cannot be 'social problems' that are not the products of processes of social construction – naming, labelling, defining and mapping them into a place – through which we can 'make sense' of them.

The crux of this argument was established by Howard Becker (1963) in relation to deviant behaviour. Realist explanations attempt to account for deviance by identifying differences between those who behave 'normally' and those who behave in an 'abnormal' way. Becker pointed to a number of problems with this approach. First, it assumed the accurate and unproblematic knowledge of who was normal and who was deviant. But, said Becker, the distinction is socially constructed. It involves the exercise of judgement by social actors, located in social institutions, applying social norms. Second, deviance is context-specific rather than universal. Behaviour that is viewed or classified as deviant varies between and even within societies and

shifts over time. As a result, Becker argued, it is analytically and methodologically incorrect to pursue the explanation of deviance in terms of discovering the 'deviant characteristics' of the 'deviant' person, when deviance is a product of a process of labelling some behaviours as deviant and others not. In short, deviance is socially constructed.

This basic social constructionist view has been subjected to a wide range of criticisms, some of which have attempted to refute its claims while others have tried to develop and enhance the approach. Many of these developments centre on three key issues: the social context of social constructions; the conflictual or contested character of social constructions; and the unstable or changeable character of social constructions. In particular, attempts at developing social constructionism have hinged around issues of power (Bacchi, 1999: 50–64). This interest in social constructionism and its potential development is part of wider shifts in the social sciences in which a cluster of concerns with culture/meaning/language have come to occupy a more central place (Clarke, 1999). Social constructionism is one tributary that flows into this wider movement, intersecting with questions of ideology, discourse and the articulation of power in a range of ways (Burr, 1996; Saraga, 1998).

Evaluation

The social constructionist perspective has been subject to criticisms that challenge its value for the study of crime in particular and social problems in general. Social constructionism is sometimes seen as trivializing the reality of social problems – implying that such issues are *merely* social constructions. It may be that the emphasis on language, meaning, imagery and so on involved in social constructionist analyses foregrounds what we are used to seeing as peripheral or epiphenomenal matters (compared with the gritty stuff of 'real life'). But if we can only apprehend and act on 'real life' through language, then social constructions matter profoundly. Constructions, ideologies and discourses become institutionalized. They become the 'taken-for-granted' wisdom about the way of the world and what can be done in it. They define the thinkable (and attempt to dismiss alternatives as unthinkable, utopian, politically motivated and the like). In the process, dominant constructions become 'solidified' – apparently immovable and irresistible ways of thinking and acting that sustain existing patterns of social arrangements. They are supported by knowledges and become embedded in institutional arrangements and embodied in social practices that attempt to realize their 'truth claims' in practice. These solidifications – patterns of institutionalized habit and repetition – are not insubstantial and nor are they 'just words'. A social constructionist perspective, however, insists that such solidity is still a social accomplishment – it is not natural, it is not universal, and it is not eternal. Social constructionism insists, abstractly, that all social practices have the potential to be deconstructed and reconstructed, however inert and immovable they may appear. What the perspective reveals is how the density and solidity of social reality have been constructed and how many layers of habit, everyday wisdom, institutionalized norms, and forms of social power have been built up to keep things that way. But such conditions are always in need of being reproduced – they do not carry on without the expenditure of social energy. They may, then, be reproduced differently through conflict, contestations and challenge.

John Clarke

Associated Concepts: crime, deconstruction, deviance, discourse analysis, interactionism, labelling, left realism, social harm, social reaction

Key Readings

Bacchi, C. (1999) *Women, Policy and Politics: The Construction of Policy Problems.* London: Sage.
Becker, H. (1963) *Outsiders: Studies in the Sociology of Deviance.* New York: The Free Press.

Berger, P. and Luckmann, T. (1966) *The Social Construction of Reality.* New York: Doubleday.
Burr, V. (1996) *An Introduction to Social Constructionism.* London: Routledge.
Clarke, J. (1999) 'Coming to terms with culture', in H. Dean and R. Woods (eds), *Social Policy Review 10.* London: Social Policy Association.
Saraga, E. (ed.) (1998) *Embodying the Social: Constructions of Difference.* London: Routledge/Open University.

SOCIAL CONTROL

Definition

A poorly defined concept which has been used to describe all means through which conformity might be achieved – from infant socialization to incarceration. It has been employed in various guises within interactionism, labelling, control theory, feminism, critical criminology and post-structuralism.

Distinctive Features

The precise parameters of 'social control' escape any straightforward demarcation. The standard definition simply describes all the means and processes through which social conformity is achieved, ranging from primary socialization, through informal mechanisms (such as peer group pressure), to formal methods associated with the police and the legal system. Within interactionism the key concern is with how co-operation and social integration are achieved, usually without recourse to a coercive and authoritarian discipline. Interactionists broadly conclude that the key to the maintenance of social order lies in the realm of informal and primary socialization processes through which core social values are transmitted and internalized. This benign reading of 'social control' as a functional and political necessity was mirrored in traditional positivist criminology. Within such readings it is widely assumed that a consensus exists in society, that primary socialization is largely successful in achieving a widespread and uncontested conformity, and that external agencies are only called upon to 'mop up' those deviants who have suffered a failure or lack of adequate socialization.

In the late 1960s an alternative view of social control came to the fore. Generated by the protest movements in America (civil rights, Vietnam, the Counterculture) and the emerging utopian and personal politics of the New Left in Britain, arguments concerning the essential consensual nature of society became harder to sustain, and social control came to be seen as organized repression. In particular, the labelling perspective argued that social control was not simply a reactive and reparative exercise, but an active force in the identification and creation of the deviant. In effect, labelling challenged notions of 'social control' as 'doing good' and replaced them with notions of 'doing bad'.

Such a premise became particularly influential in critical readings of a wide range of purportedly reformist and welfare-related practices. The coercive – but often hidden – aspects of control entailed in the professional practices of youth training, social work, law, probation, medicine, schooling and psychiatry were highlighted and analysed as part of a burgeoning social control culture. An image of society as moving incessantly towards more sophisticated means of repressive control was created. The intrusion of the state into the private and familiar, the capacity for behaviour to be continually subjected to surveillance, monitoring and regulation, and the spectre of mind control constructed a powerful portrayal of a one-dimensional society in which 'social control has become Kafka-land' (Cohen, 1985: 6).

While moving the concept of social control away from its benign underpinnings, this new interpretation maintained that social control, whether weak or strong, informal or formal, remained all-pervasive. But the key neglected issues remained of how and why such control operated differently in different social contexts. It was also often in danger of caricaturing all

police, social workers and teachers as agents of repression. Lacking any precise definition and consistent use, the concept was aptly described by Cohen (1985: 2) as 'Mickey Mouse' and by Lowman et al. (1987: 4) as 'a skeleton key opening so many doors that its analytic power has been drained ... a spectral category which becomes all things to all theorists'.

It was only following the work of Foucault that the term 'social control' was resurrected in the 1980s as a means through which analytical justice could be done to the complex and contradictory means by which order was achieved in democratic societies. Foucault's recognition of processes of diffuse societal power (or the 'microphysics of power') significantly broadened the concept of social control to include not only institutional practices, but also the realms of discursive construction, ideology and the production of meaning. For example, Foucault refers to a continuous disciplinary discourse, in which no one source is given privileged attention, that informed and was intertwined with all forms of social control in the late eighteenth century. Thus the reform of prisoners, confinement of the insane and supervision of industrial workers, as well as the training and education of children, all formed part of an emerging carceral society, in which it was not only deviance or crime that was controlled, but also every irregularity or the smallest departure from the norm. This power emanated not simply from the state or a mode of production but, for Foucault, from forms of knowledge that informed all social relations. It is because of this broad canvas that Foucault's work has remained influential in historical and contemporary readings of social control. It allows for greater sensitivity towards the interrelations of social structure with processes of power, knowledge and governance. It is more attuned to processes of domination and enablement, of constraint and resistance. As a result terms such as 'regulation', 'knowledge', 'normalization', 'governmentality' and 'discipline' have come to hold a central place in a 'revisionist' literature of social control.

Of note here is Cohen's (1979, 1985) 'dispersal of discipline' thesis, as this contends that as control mechanisms are dispersed from custody into the community they penetrate deeper into the social fabric. A blurring of boundaries between the deviant and non-deviant, the public and the private, occurs. A 'punitive archipelago' is expanded as new resources, technology and professional interests are applied to an increasing number of 'clients' and 'customers'. Entrepreneurs are drawn into the control enterprise in search of profits. Communities are mobilized to act as voluntary control agents in their own right. But throughout, the growing invisibility and diversification of the state's role do not mean it has withered away. The prison remains at the core of the system.

Lowman et al. (1987: 9) argue that these developments can best be captured in the concept of transcarceration. They point out that as the old institutions of control remain and new ones are created, we are now being confronted with a 'peno-judicial, mental health, welfare and tutelage complex ... for delinquents, deviants and dependants this means that their careers are likely to be characterized by institutional mobility as they are pushed from one section of the help–control complex to another. For control agents, this means that control will essentially have no locus and the control mandate will increasingly entail the "fitting together" of subsystems'. This formulation of control continues to acknowledge its versatility, by infiltrating many levels of discourse and 'arenas of action' and serving and constituting a diversity of interests. Of particular note is how, by the 1990s, much of this control had become privatized – that is, removed from direct state control and activated by communities, voluntary agencies and private security companies. It was in this context that Cohen (1994: 74) began talking of social control as a commodity: as something to be purchased and sold.

David Wilson

Associated Concepts: carceral society, control balance theory, desistance, governmentality, labelling, net widening, policing, social control theory, social reaction, the state, transcarceration

Key Readings

Cohen, S. (1979) 'The punitive city: notes on the dispersal of social control', *Contemporary Crises*, 3 (4): 341–63.

Cohen, S. (1985) *Visions of Social Control*. Cambridge: Polity Press.

Cohen, S. (1989) 'The critical discourse on "social control": notes on the concept as a hammer', *International Journal of the Sociology of Law*, 17: 347–57.

Cohen, S. (1994) 'Social control and the politics of reconstruction', in D. Nelken (ed.), *The Futures of Criminology*. London: Sage.

Cohen, S. and Scull, A. (eds) (1983) *Social Control and the State: Historical and Comparative Essays*. Oxford: Martin Robertson.

Lowman, J., Menzies, R.J. and Palys, T.S. (eds) (1987) *Transcarceration: Essays in the Sociology of Social Control*. Aldershot: Gower.

SOCIAL CONTROL THEORY

Definition

A sociological approach to understanding the causes of conformity that focuses on the ability of society and its institutions (parents, peers, schools, spouses and jobs) to restrain human behaviour. From this theoretical perspective, human nature is assumed to be essentially anti-social – a view borrowed directly from Thomas Hobbes's (1985 [1651]: 188) description of life in a world without externally imposed control as a 'war of every man against every man'. Thus the central question is, 'What is it about society that restrains individuals from deviance?' The basic premise is that conformity results when societal ties are strong.

Distinctive Features

Social control theory includes a number of related sociological explanations that variously explain how social institutions restrain individuals to societal norms. While human behaviour is the result of both motivations and restraints, social control theorists find it more fruitful to focus on variations in restraints to explain orderly behaviour. As a result, various approaches to social control theory all explain why individuals conform to societal norms rather than why they deviate.

Early social control theorists speculated that juvenile delinquency (the primary area of study) was mainly caused by a weak ego or poor self-concept. Reiss's (1951) theory of personal and social controls described how weak egos of juvenile delinquents lacked the requisite personal controls to produce conforming behaviour. Similarly, Briar and Piliavin (1965) believed that adolescents who feared getting caught for delinquent activities were the most likely to conform to society's rules because it could damage their self-image. A positive attitude purportedly helped the adolescent to resist negative influences, especially delinquent peers. Similarly, Reckless (1967) argued that a good self-concept assisted boys with insulating themselves from negative influences while growing up in criminogenic areas. Certain internal (e.g., positive self-concept) and external (e.g., positive peer support) factors or 'containments' helped to insulate youths from delinquency-promoting situations.

Other control perspectives explain conformity by variations in basic 'ties' or 'commitments' to the conventional social order. Nye (1958) identified four types of social control: (1) direct control, based on the threat of punishments and rewards to gain compliance to societal norms; (2) indirect control, based on affectional attachments to conventional persons; (3) internalized control, based on the development of the individual personality, self-concept or conscience; and (4) control over opportunities for deviant and conventional activities.

Among the various social control perspectives, however, Hirschi's (1969) 'social bond' version is probably the most widely known and cited. It is relatively explicit, well developed and amenable to empirical tests. The social bonds have four components (attachment, involvement, belief and commitment) which are positively related to conformity (and to each other) and are thought to have independent effects on delinquency.

'Attachment' refers to the affective ties that adolescents form with significant others – especially their parents, peers and school. The central principle is that adolescents who are only weakly attached to others are also insensitive to their opinions, thereby 'freeing' the child to deviate in response to situational demands and peer pressures. Thus attachment is essentially a social-psychological concept, involving the motivational value of social approval. 'Involvement' refers to the idea that juveniles may get so caught up in conventional activities that they do not have the time for delinquent behaviours. 'Commitment' is synonymous to the idea of 'stakes in conformity' in that deviation jeopardizes the chances for success. For example, those adolescents committed to a college education are less likely to commit delinquency because such behaviours (if caught and punished) can jeopardize their chances for future success and accomplishments. 'Belief' refers to respect for society's laws. If children have been socialized to respect the law, they should be less inclined to commit legal violations of the law.

Hirschi's (1969) concepts of attachment and belief correspond conceptually to Nye's concepts of indirect and internalized controls, except that Hirschi locates the conscience in the social bond to others rather than making it part of the individual personality. In addition, Nye's concept of direct control and Hirschi's concept of involvement have some conceptual overlap but they are clearly not identical. The premise behind involvement is time ('Idle hands are the devil's workshop'), while direct controls are more indicative of physical restriction, surveillance, monitoring and the punishment of behaviours. Both Nye and Hirschi argued that the utility of direct monitoring and supervision by parents is probably limited, since adolescents are relatively autonomous from their parents. The inference is that the major controlling mechanisms will be through attachments or indirect controls.

Evaluation

On the one hand, much of Hirschi's theory has been corroborated by empirical research, indicating that delinquents often feel detached from typical societal bonds. Indeed, research generally supports Hirschi's basic proposition that weak school and parental attachments increase the probability of delinquency. On the other hand, various measures of belief and especially involvement (e.g., sports activities, hobbies, extracurricular school activities) have revealed few statistically reliable associations with delinquency. In addition, evidence suggests that strong attachments to *delinquent* peers actually increase deviance rather than having a beneficial effect, as suggested by Hirschi. Research also has indicated that direct parental controls should not be dismissed as theoretically and empirically irrelevant, as suggested by both Nye and Hirschi. Empirical evidence indicates that direct parental controls (such as monitoring, rewards, punishments) are just as effective as indirect controls or attachments in controlling delinquency.

Furthermore, Agnew (1985) suggests that the temporal ordering of the variables in Hirschi's model should be reversed. Rather than weak social bonds being a cause of delinquency – as suggested by Hirschi – Agnew's research indicates that delinquent behaviour may actually result in weakened social bonds. While plausible, this criticism can be levelled against virtually all theories tested by means of empirical research that is cross-sectional – rather than longitudinal – in design.

Generally, however, social control theory is probably more incomplete than it is incorrect; because of this researchers have sought to extend, clarify and refine its basic tenets. Most of this research has led to modifications in the operational measures and conceptual qualifications in the empirical interpretation of the perspective rather than to an outright rejection or overhaul of the entire theory. For example, researchers have interpreted the actual measurement of parental attachments in a variety of ways, including indicators of affection and love, interest and concern, support, encouragement, the desire for physical closeness, and positive communication. Although all are correlated with delinquency to about the same degree, they may reflect different dimensions of parental attachment.

Furthermore, there is a lack of conceptual development by social control theorists about the interactive effects of various variables. Indeed, there is a tendency to predict the impact of one measure of social control quite independently from other variables, implying a simple additive model. For example, what is the probability of delinquency under the condition that the attachment to both parents is strong, while simultaneously the adolescent is strongly attached to delinquent peers? Similarly, what is the conjunctive impact of both direct (monitoring) and indirect (attachment) parental controls on delinquency? A child may place little value on parental approval but conform to parental expectations out of a belief that they are monitoring his or her behaviours closely and will punish any deviation. On the other hand, some children may behave solely because they desire parental acceptance. Generally, explications of social control theory have failed to predict behavioural outcomes beyond the bivariate level. Because scant theoretical and empirical attention has been directed toward the examination of such effects, many questions remain unresolved.

In sum, empirical research has generally supported the core concepts of Hirschi's version of social control theory. While some critics question its validity, few would dispute that it has been the most influential theory of delinquency over the past thirty years.

Joseph Rankin and Roger Kern

Associated Concepts: conditioning, containment theory, cross-sectional design, delinquency, developmental criminology, longitudinal study, neutralization (techniques of), risk factor research

Key Readings

Agnew, R. (1985) 'Social control theory and delinquency: a longitudinal test', *Criminology*, 23: 47–61.

Briar, S. and Piliavin, I. (1965) 'Delinquency: situational inducements and commitment to conformity', *Social Problems,* 13: 35–45.

Hirschi, T. (1969) *Causes of Delinquency.* Berkeley, CA: University of California Press.

Hobbes, T. (1985 [1651]) *Leviathan.* New York: Viking Penguin.

Nye, F.I. (1958) *Family Relationships and Delinquent Behavior.* New York: John Wiley.

Reckless, W. (1967) *The Crime Problem.* New York: Appleton-Century-Crofts.

Reiss, A.J. (1951) 'Delinquency as the failure of personal and social controls', *American Sociological Review,* 16: 196–207.

SOCIAL CRIME PREVENTION

Definition

Measures to prevent crime which are aimed at the social causes of crime rather than those concerned with the mechanical reduction of opportunities (situational crime prevention) or with deterrence (the criminal justice system).

Distinctive Features

The distinction between social and situational revolves around the focus on causes (Crawford, 1998). Both situational crime prevention and deterrence explicitly disavow causality (hence their designation as administrative criminology). The difference does not hinge on the social – for situational crime prevention can have social aspects, for example, the increase in the facilitation of surveillance in neighbourhood watch and in the environmental design of housing estates. The emphasis on social causes, therefore, relates social crime prevention to any causal theory of crime (for example, whether strain, relative deprivation, control, labelling or criminal careers are highlighted as causative factors). In common with crime prevention strategies in general, it is aimed at intervention before the offence has occurred rather than after (for example, in the arrest and punishment of offenders and victim support).

Interest in both situational and social crime prevention has risen concomitantly with the postwar rise in crime in industrial societies and the recognition of the strained resources and limits of efficacy of the criminal justice system. In general, situational crime prevention has been predominant in neo-liberal political contexts, and social crime prevention in those that have a stronger social democratic setting (see Hughes, 1998). Social crime prevention is seen as being expedited by multi-agency initiatives outside of the criminal justice system – the precise forms of intervention and the major institutions involved depending on whether causality is located primarily in employment, the family, education or community. Both situational and social crime prevention form part of most community safety programmes, although Elliott Currie (1988) makes the useful distinction between those projects that view crime as an outside threat to the community (in which situational crime prevention is paramount) and those where crime is seen as a product of the institutions and structure of the community (in which social crime prevention is seen as appropriate).

Social crime prevention is viewed by left realists as the key platform for tackling crime (Currie, 1998; Young, 1991), although both situational crime prevention and the criminal justice system are accorded supporting roles.

Jock Young

Associated Concepts: communitarianism, community crime prevention, community safety, crime prevention, left realism, situational crime prevention

Key Readings

Crawford, A. (1998) *Crime Prevention and Community Safety.* London: Longman.

Currie, E. (1988) 'Two visions of community crime prevention', in T. Hope and M. Shaw (eds), *Communities and Crime Reduction.* London: HMSO.

Currie, E. (1998) *Crime and Punishment in America.* New York: Metropolitan Books.

Hughes, G. (1998) *Understanding Crime Prevention*. Buckingham: Open University Press.

Walklate, S. (1996) 'Community and crime prevention', in E. McLaughlin and J. Muncie (eds), *Controlling Crime*. London: Sage.

Young, J. (1991) 'Left realism and the priorities of crime control', in K. Stenson and D. Cowell (eds), *The Politics of Crime Control*. London: Sage.

SOCIAL DEFENCE THEORY

Definition

A penal philosophy developed in the early twentieth century that adhered to the 'protection of society' by the neutralization and resocialization of the offender, whereby fixed penalties were set aside for individualized punishment.

Distinctive Features

The development of a 'social defence theory' has been accredited to the Belgian jurist Adolphe Prins following the publication of his book *La Défense Sociale* in 1910 (see Ancel, 1965). As a penological concept, however, its origins are to be found in the early nineteenth century. In 1831, the Italian jurist Carmignani argued that the rigid administration of crimes and punishments should be replaced with a new penal theory based on the concepts of 'social offence' and 'social defence' (see Pasquino, 1980). Its origins are clearly European, notably Italian, German, French and Belgian. Carmignani's vision of a social defence doctrine gathered momentum and acceptance during the positivist revolt of the late nineteenth century. Radzinowicz describes the place of social defence within positivist ideology:

It was not the business of the criminal justice system to assess and to measure the moral guilt of an offender but only to determine whether he was not the perpetrator of an act defined as an offence and then to apply to him one of the measures of 'social defence' so as to restrain him from committing further crimes. (Radzinowicz, 1961: 17)

Social defence is a phrase that has been subject to widespread interpretation and distortion (Ancel, 1962). During the late nineteenth and early twentieth centuries some social theorists and penal philosophers in Europe, such as Tarde and Signorel, argued that it was the repression of crime by the criminal law and the administration of 'stern' punishment, thus reflecting the classicist doctrine or principles of the *ancien régime*. However, the positivists of this era adopted an alternative interpretation that was more widely accepted into criminal science rhetoric. For them, social defence centred on the protection of society from dangerous and habitual criminals (see Ancel, 1965). Enrico Ferri used the term 'social defence' to describe the purpose and justification of punishment as an indeterminate treatment reflecting the needs of the individual rather than moral culpability and retribution.

The Italian positivist school at the end of the nineteenth century referred to the failures of social defence, as expressed by the repressive criminal law and deterrent-based punishments of the nineteenth century. In its place, they argued that a doctrine of social defence should no longer focus on individual and moral responsibility but be replaced with preventative measures that would address the criminal's 'dangerous condition' (Ancel, 1962: 498). Pratt (1997) states that a 'new penality' emerged in Europe in the late nineteenth and early twentieth centuries, one that classified criminals into categories (insane, habitual, degenerate, weak-minded, etc.) and subsequently tailored punishment on an individual basis. For Pratt 'the individualization of punishment' serves a broader social purpose. He argues, '[the penal process] would now be a form of social defence, providing insurance against the risks that the habitual criminals presented, alongside the other strategies that the emerging welfare state had introduced to protect its citizens from risk and ensure their security' (1997: 47).

As a concept, social defence in the first half of the twentieth century received much criticism because of its suppression of the individual in favour of social protection, or as Radzinowicz (1999: 38) has argued 'social defence [sliding] into social aggression'. Individual freedoms were viewed as subsidiary to those justified measures that aimed to protect the moral and legal fabric of society. Social defence has also been interpreted as a form of social hygiene. The International Union of Penal Law founded in 1889 was composed of an alliance of European penal reformists. It adopted an interventionist approach to penology, and interpreted social defence to mean 'social hygiene', involving the 'mopping-up of the social breeding grounds of crime' (Pasquino, 1980).

Marc Ancel (1965) describes the more extreme applications of social defence expressed through repressive governmental regimes such as those of Communist Russia, Nazi Germany and Fascist Italy, where social defence was viewed as a form of 'community protection' but completely eroded human rights and civil liberties.

Evaluation

The earliest usage of social defence is, therefore, founded on broad and changing interpretations. Its 'modern' definition and application are, however, applied with greater consistency. The United Nations resurrected the term in 1948 as 'the prevention of crime and the treatment of offenders'. This definition has focused on positivist explanations of criminality and penal solutions that serve to protect society while addressing the criminogenic characteristics of the offender.

Nowadays, social defence theory is rarely used within criminal justice rhetoric. However, its underlying principles of protecting society through individualized punishment; for example, indeterminate sentences, preventative detention and dangerousness legislation have re-emerged in late modernity as important facets of penal and criminal justice policy and realist criminological thinking.

Reece Walters

Associated Concepts: crime control model, crime prevention, deterrence, positivism, risk

Key Readings

Ancel, M. (1962) 'Social defence', *The Law Quarterly Review*, 78: 497–503.
Ancel, M. (1965) 'Social defence', in *A Modern Approach to Criminal Problems*. London: Routledge and Kegan Paul.
Pasquino, P. (1980) 'Criminology: the birth of a special saviour: transformations in penal theory and new sources of right in the late nineteenth century', *Ideology and Consciousness*, 7: 1–17.
Pratt, J. (1997) *Governing the Dangerous: Dangerousness, Law and Social Change*. Sydney: The Federation Press.
Radzinowicz, L. (1961) *In Search of Criminology*. London: Heinemann.
Radzinowicz, L. (1999) *Adventures in Criminology*. London: Routledge.

SOCIAL DISORGANIZATION

See: Chicago School of Sociology; Geographies of crime; Social ecology

SOCIAL ECOLOGY

Definition

Social ecology explanations of crime are a variant of sociological positivism. They imply that crime is not caused by aberrant individuals but by the 'pathological' conditions of particular areas or communities. They draw upon modes of analysis developed within human geography and biology to argue that one outcome of the structuring of space is a patterned distribution of crime.

Distinctive Features

Crime is always subject to uneven geographical distribution. Urban areas appear to have higher recorded crime rates than rural areas, and within cities there are presumed to be 'criminal areas' or 'hotspots' of crime. To explain these patterns of crime distribution, analogies have been made between the ecology of plant life and human organization. Cities are viewed as akin to living and growing organisms, with individuals growing together over time and declining when superseded by other individuals with different forms of social organization. In the 1920s and 1930s sociologists at the University of Chicago embarked on a systematic study of all aspects of their local urban environment. Park, a newspaper reporter turned sociologist, and Burgess, his collaborator, were particularly influential. They noted that, as with any ecological system, the development and organization of the city of Chicago was not random but patterned, and could be understood in terms of such social processes as invasion, conflict, accommodation and assimilation. They likened the city to a living and growing organism and viewed the functions of various areas of the city as fundamental to the survival of the whole. The city's characteristics, social change and distribution of people were studied by use of Burgess's concentric zone theory. The city was divided into five areas: zone 1, the central business district; zone 2, a transition from business to residences; zone 3, working-class homes; zone 4, middle-class homes; zone 5, commuter suburbs. Zone 2 – the zone in transition – was a particular focus for study. Here the expansion of the business sector continually meant that residents were displaced. It became the least desirable living area. It was characterized by deteriorating housing stock, poverty, pawn shops, cheap theatres, restaurants, casual workers, new immigrants and a breakdown in the usual methods of social control. It was hypothesized that it was in this zone that crime and vice would flourish. Shaw (1929) and Shaw and McKay (1942) set out to test this hypothesis by using juvenile and adult court and prison statistics to map the spatial distribution of the residences of delinquent youths and criminals throughout the city. They were eventually to conclude that as this particular

zone maintained a regular crime rate even when its populations completely changed, then there must be something about particular places that would sustain crime.

Evaluation

Such early social ecology theory has subsequently been critiqued for its denial of human choice; its reliance on official definitions and statistics as 'true' indices of crime; and its inability to account for contra evidence, such as high rates of crime in stable communities or low rates in areas of high social disorganization. Nevertheless, the approach experienced something of a revival in England in the 1970s and in the USA in the 1980s. These have added spatial analysis, victimization data and accounts of political economy to the original formulation. For example, Morris (1957) found that the areas showing peak crime rates in Croydon, South London, were two of the inter-war council housing estates and two older residential areas noted for their slum housing and physical deterioration. From this he argued that the political decision by local authorities to concentrate certain of their tenants in less desirable housing was central to the creation of distinct 'criminal areas'.

Later studies widened the focus further to include the study not only of differential access to housing space and of the effects on people compelled to live in low-grade housing in 'rough' areas, but also of the relevance of social *class* and differential access to *power* for understanding the continuing 'competitive struggle for space'. New versions of spatial analysis (Bottoms and Wiles, 1992; Brantingham and Brantingham, 1984) have succeeded in substantiating that crime is not only spatially as well as socially defined, but also that it is a natural and normal expression of social interaction given the organization of specific localized communities. In particular, it is how individuals recognize the role of space in their own biographies and how space mediates the relationship between individual and environment that will create different *opportunities* for crime.

John Muncie

Associated Concepts: 'broken windows', Chicago School of Sociology, community policing, defensible space, geographies of crime, situational crime prevention, sociological positivism

Key Readings

Bottoms, A. and Wiles, P. (1992) 'Explanations of crime and place', in D.J. Evans, N.R. Fyle and D.T. Herbert (eds), *Crime, Policing and Place*. London: Routledge.

Brantingham, P.J. and Brantingham, P.L. (1984) *Patterns of Crime*. New York: Macmillan.

Morris, T. (1957) *The Criminal Area: A Study in Social Ecology*. London: Routledge.

Park, R.E. (1936) 'Human ecology', *American Journal of Sociology*, 42 (1): 15.

Shaw, C.R. (1929) *Delinquency Areas*. Chicago: University of Chicago Press.

Shaw, C.R. and McKay, H.D. (1942) *Juvenile Delinquency and Urban Areas*. Chicago: University of Chicago Press.

SOCIAL EXCLUSION

Definition

Refers to the dynamic, multidimensional process of being shut out, fully or partially, from the various social, economic, political or cultural systems that serve to assist the integration of a person in society. When combined, acute forms of exclusion are created that will find a spatial and concentrated expression in particular localities and communities.

Distinctive Features

Social exclusion can be best thought of as a dynamic and fluid process rather than as a static and clearly defined condition. It refers to marginalization, social isolation and dislocation, disaffiliation and vulnerability. More than simply the circumstances of the poorest individuals, social exclusion describes a pattern of profound changes in social arrangements and the ever-increasing growth in inequalities and insecurities produced by those changes. Thus the concept of social exclusion has to be understood within the context of the transition from modernity to late modernity. It covers not only the unemployed and economically inactive but also the 'working poor' and those sections of the economically active increasingly affected by the 'structural insecurity' generated by the new 'flexible' labour market. It is an extended concept that includes situations of distress, discrimination and disadvantage that are largely, although not exclusively, socioeconomic in nature. Social exclusion occurs primarily on three levels: the economic and material exclusion of individuals denied access to paid, full-time employment; the isolation from relationships produced by social and spatial segregation; and the ever-increasing exclusionary policies and practices of the criminal justice system.

During the 1960s and 1970s the cultural revolution of individualism and the economic crisis and subsequent restructuring of the labour market signalled the beginning of the transition from modernity to late modernity. Three discernible and interrelated trends indicative of this shift are of particular relevance here. First is the economic crisis of the 1970s and the 'hollowing out' and 'rolling back' of the state. The more important aspects of this transformation have involved the abandonment of attempts to provide the social 'rights' of citizenship, including full employment, and a significant reduction in 'welfare' assistance. Thus the influence of neo-liberalism and its conception of freedom as the absence of state control and intervention has changed the relationship between citizens and the state. Subsequently a deconstruction of the previous consensus on social and political values has taken place.

Second, the transition to late modernity has also led to radical changes both in the mode of production and in the organization of the workforce. The full employment of modernity has been replaced by structural unemployment, casual/part-time (under-) employment and the insecure employment of late modernity. The most significant products of these changes are unpredictability, uncertainty, precariousness and insecurity. What we have witnessed is a tripartite division of society made up of a securely employed or wealthy minority, an increasingly squeezed middle of insecurely employed, and the part-time/casually employed and unemployed poor. Thus work is a much-decreased means by which risk is managed, identities are formed and maintained, and citizenship and participation achieved.

Third, profound changes in the meanings of inclusion and citizenship have occurred. Social citizenship and identity are increasingly constructed around levels of consumption and lifestyle choice as opposed to work and each person's relationship with the state. The state now argues that the inclusion of individuals is not its proper role and instead it is our individual responsibility to gain inclusion via choices made in the marketplace. However, given structural unemployment and job insecurity, a section of the population will constantly remain surplus to the requirements of advanced capitalism. The resulting lack of access to material resources via paid work combined with the reduction in state welfare means that the market and lifestyle choices of an increasing number of individuals and families will be severely constrained.

In relation to crime, social exclusion is an inevitable by-product of the activities and operations of an increasingly punitive criminal justice system. Prison is the definitive form of exclusion and the imprisoned are a distinctly excluded population. Fear of crime has produced perceptions of the late modern city as an uneven patchwork of safe and unsafe, high- and low-risk areas, and has resulted in social and spatial segregation. In public places a whole series of exclusionary technologies and practices have been generated and designed to provide consumer security and crime prevention. In the interests of increasing consumption levels, business is increasingly excluding non-consumers, particularly young people who are perceived as a threat to the efficient flow and activity of legitimate consumers. The privatization of public space and the creation of 'mass private property' are set to continue and, with these, the exclusion of youth and other marginalized groups from the very locations in which their market and lifestyle choices are made.

Finally, the new 'social' crime prevention policies of government are themselves exclusionary in that they entail a process of categorization, a separating out of the population according to actuarially-based calculations of risk.

Evaluation

Social exclusion is increasingly coming to replace the more pejorative concept of 'underclass' in debates about the poor. 'Social exclusion', unlike 'underclass', implies that the process of exclusion is the result of society-wide forces beyond the control of the individual who is in some way responsible for his/her own exclusion.

Critics of the concept argue that it glosses over inherent divisions within capitalist societies. In referring to the shift from modernity to late modernity, critics claim that the concept implies some sort of 'golden age' where social consensus and growing equality were achieved and, therefore, the term fails to acknowledge the ongoing poverty- and class-based divisions in society. Finally, social exclusion may have become the preferred term in political debate because it can depoliticize poverty in relation to income distribution. Political leaders are able to speak of social exclusion while also denying the existence of poverty. Thus social exclusion can have two forms, one weak and one strong. 'Weaker' versions look for solutions in altering the characteristics of the excluded. 'Stronger' versions emphasize the uneven patterns of resource and income distribution and the role of the excluders, then aim to address these patterns and thereby reduce the power of the excluders.

Trevor Bradley

Associated Concepts: left realism, risk, social capital, social crime prevention, underclass

Key Readings

Byrne, D. (1999) *Social Exclusion.* Buckingham: Open University Press.
Donnison, D. (1998) *Policies for a Just Society.* London: Macmillan.
Finer, C. and Nellis, M. (eds) (1997) Special Edition: 'Broadening perspectives on social policy: crime and social exclusion', *Social Policy and Administration,* 31 (5).
Jordan, B. (1996) *A Theory of Poverty and Social Exclusion.* Cambridge: Polity Press.
Madanipour, A., Cars, G. and Allen, J. (eds) (1998) *Social Exclusion in European Cities.* London: Jessica Kingsley.
Young, J. (1999) *The Exclusive Society.* London: Sage.

SOCIAL HARM

Definition

A social harm perspective is based on the premise that notions of 'crime' offer a particularly narrow version of the range of misfortunes, dangers, harms, risks and injuries that are a part of everyday life. A concept of social harm enables criminology to move beyond legal definitions of 'crime' and acknowledge a wide range of immoral, wrongful and injurious acts that may or may not be deemed illegal, but are arguably more profoundly damaging. In doing so, a social harm perspective may require an abandonment of criminology (as it has thus been conceived).

Distinctive Features

The intrinsic limitations of 'crime' as a signifier of harm have a long history, dating back at least to the 1940s and Sutherland's pathbreaking work on white collar crime. He reformulated 'crime' through such concepts as *'injury* to the state' and by designating certain behaviours and events as 'socially *harmful'.*

In the 1970s some radical criminologists advocated a further deepening of the criminological agenda to include racism, sexism and economic exploitation as core concerns (Schwendinger and Schwendinger, 1970). By the mid-1990s critical theorists in the USA (e.g., Henry and Milovanovic, 1994) had developed a *constitutive criminology* in which crime was defined as the 'power to deny others'. Crime was characterized as taking two major forms: *harms* of reduction and *harms* of repression. Harms of reduction referred to situations when an offended party experienced some *immediate* loss/injury because of the actions of others. Harms of repression referred to situations when power was used to restrict *future* potential human aspirations and development. These concepts of harm were primarily designed to allow a wide range of 'hidden crimes' to be brought to criminological attention and to reveal how some harms, far from being condemned, are legitimized through the activities of various legal and social institutions. For example, certain 'crimes' – sexual harassment, racial violence, hate crime and so on, which threaten human dignity (Tifft, 1995) – often seem to be lacking in legal status or traditionally have been given scant attention by law enforcement agencies.

Latterly, Hillyard and Tombs (2004; 2007) have been influential in extending the boundaries for how critical criminologists might think about and define the concepts of 'crime' and 'harm'. Initially this entailed the formulation of a new disciplinary basis grounded in 'zemiology' (from the Greek *zemia,* meaning harm), and ultimately it explored how we might move 'beyond' criminology itself. This project rested on nine key propositions:

- *Crime has no ontological reality:* There is little or nothing intrinsic to any particular event or behaviour that defines it as 'crime'.
- *Criminology perpetuates the myth of crime:* In general the discipline is marked by a failure to be self-reflective about dominant, state-defined notions of crime. The power to render certain harmful acts visible and define them as 'crime', whilst maintaining

the invisibility of others (or defining them as beyond criminal sanction), lies at the heart of the problem of allowing the state and legal definitions to pre-determine the subject matter of criminology.

- *Crime consists of many petty events:* Much of what is defined and processed as 'crime', such as petty theft, shoplifting, recreational drug use, vandalism, brawls and anti-social behaviour, would not seem to score particularly high on a scale of serious social harm. Despite this it is often these 'minor' events that take up much of the time and preoccupation of law enforcement agencies as well as the criminal justice system.
- *Crime excludes many serious harms:* Poverty, malnutrition, environmental pollution and degradation, medical negligence, breaches of workplace health and safety laws, corporate corruption, state violence, genocide, human rights violations, and so on, all carry with them more widespread and damaging social and economic consequences than most of the behaviours and incidents that are typically assumed to make up the 'problem of crime'.
- *Particular constructions:* The law has an individualizing ethos such that the liability for 'crime' is more readily accorded to culpable individuals rather than to corporations, states or organizations.
- *Criminalization and punishment inflict pain:* Criminal justice is self-defeating. It tends to reproduce or exacerbate harm rather than alleviate it.
- *Crime control is ineffective:* Criminal justice does not work according to its own aims, whether these are deterrence, rehabilitation, prevention and so on.
- *Crime gives legitimacy to the expansion of crime control:* Discourses of crime and the fear of crime create a vicious circle of investment and expansion of crime control measures which in turn only help to discover more 'crime'.
- *Crime serves to maintain power relations:* Relations of social, political and economic power embedded in social orders generate a whole series of social problems for their populations, particularly marginalized and

powerless populations, but only a selected few are considered worthy of criminal sanctions.

By the 1990s the notion of harm had indeed begun to circulate on the margins of some criminological enquiry. Questions of human rights denial entered the agenda, not simply through extending conceptions of 'what is crime?' but by recognizing the legal transgressions routinely employed by those wielding political and economic power and their ability to deny or conceal the harms they unleashed under the protection of the law. State crime in the form of illegal arms dealing, genocide and torture has been consistent front page news following successive wars in the Balkans, Iraq and Afghanistan. Numerous aspects of social policy (in particular housing policy and youth homelessness), environmental policy (in particular road building and pollution) and economic policy (in particular Third World debt, the arms trade and corporate greed) have all begun to be described (by some) within a crime discourse.

This deepening of the criminological agenda inevitably forces a re-conceptualization of the constitution of 'crime', a querying of the purpose and function of criminal justice, and thereby a radical reassessment of the proper domain of criminology.

Evaluation

A concept of 'harm' clearly offers a fresh perspective from which to consider issues of social and global concern. The casting off of the constraints of a strictly legal – and nation-state specific – definition of crime removes some of its geographical, historical and cultural contingencies. The notion of 'social harm' allows for a broadening of the criminological gaze to include considerations of human activities that cause serious damage to human and social life but may also fall outside the narrow confines of national or international 'criminal justice' (Muncie et al., 2010).

What has remained unclear, however, is how far the recoding of crime as harm is capable of challenging and overthrowing legal definitions. Campaigns to extend the criminal label so that it includes new forms of injury continually run the risk of reinforcing the concept of crime even when it is seemingly being attacked. Harm is also far from a unitary and uncontested concept. Harm can signify a host of material and emotive negativities – from notions of pain to fear, insecurity, violation, grief, powerlessness, dispute and transgression – which may also be culturally defined rather than universally acknowledged (Muncie, 2000).

The abandonment of 'crime' in favour of 'harm' is ultimately, however, a political project. Whenever we read the latest crime news or are bombarded with remonstrations against the 'anti-social', a social harm perspective reminds us that the systematic production of inequalities, poverty, destitution and exploitation (and governmental denials of any complicity in their production) introduces far more violence, suffering and death into this world than anything currently subject to criminal law sanctions.

John Muncie

Associated Concepts: abolition, constitutive criminology, crime, redress, state crime

Key Readings

Henry, S. and Milovanovic, D. (1994) 'The constitution of constitutive criminology', in D. Nelken (ed.), *The Futures of Criminology*. London: Sage.

Hillyard, P., Pantazis, C., Tombs, S. and Gordon, D. (eds) (2004) *Beyond Criminology: Taking Harm Seriously*. London: Pluto.

Hillyard, P. and Tombs, S. (2007) 'From crime to social harm', *Crime Law Social Change*, 48: 9–25.

Muncie, J. (2000) 'Decriminalizing criminology', in G. Lewis, S. Gewirtz and J. Clarke (eds), *Rethinking Social Policy*. London: Sage. pp. 217–28.

Muncie, J., Talbot, D. and Walters, R. (eds) (2010) *Crime: Local and Global*. Cullompton: Willan/Open University.

Schwendinger, H. and Schwendinger, J. (1970) 'Defenders of order or guardians of human rights?', *Issues in Criminology*, 5: 123–57.

Tifft, L. (1995) 'Social harm definitions of crime', *The Critical Criminologist*, 7 (1): 9–13.

SOCIAL JUSTICE

Definition

The fair distribution of opportunities, rewards and responsibilities in society, as well as principles and institutions for the distribution of meaningful social goods – income, shelter, food, health, education, the freedom to pursue individual goals.

Distinctive Features

Theories of social justice focus on two main questions. First, how the rules for a fair distribution of meaningful social goods can be determined; second, how much or how little inequality is permissible in a socially just society.

Over the past few decades, the most influential theory of social justice has been John Rawls' (1972) notion of *justice as fairness.* He draws upon social contract theory and the Kantian philosophical tradition of justice as impartiality, stating that in order for people to devise rules that are fair to all they must be unaware of their own position in society. A rich person, or someone who confidently expects to become rich, for example, would favour rules that advantage the rich, such as low taxation and low public spending, whereas someone who is poor or expects to be poor would probably favour high taxation and high public expenditure. Only someone unaware of their own position or expectations would come up with levels of taxation and spending that were fair to all. Rawls therefore says that the rules and institutions of a just society can only be arrived at by people acting in an 'original' (pre-social) position, or from behind a 'veil of ignorance' in which they are unaware of their own actual or potential social position. He realizes, of course, that the people deciding actual rules for actual societies are not in this position; he is suggesting that such fair distribution can only be arrived at by adopting procedures that have been designed to secure impartiality as far as possible.

Rawls' answer to the question of degrees of inequality is his *difference* principle: social and economic inequalities are just to the extent that they benefit everyone. This principle allows some inequality, but also protects the least well-off, and because of this protection his theory is often classified as welfare-liberalism.

Rawls tries to strike a balance between equality and freedom; alternative theories prioritize one or the other. Marxist theories prioritize equality, whereas libertarian and neo-liberal theories prioritize freedom. Libertarians argue that governments should not involve themselves in the distribution of social goods. A just distribution, for libertarians and neo-liberals, arises from individual decisions to give or exchange goods which they legally hold. Any state interference with distribution, beyond establishing property laws, represents an unwarranted interference with individual freedom.

A variant of welfare-liberalism has been put forward by Michael Walzer (1983). He argues that Rawls was mistaken in trying to suggest one principle of distribution for all social goods. For Walzer, the principle of distribution and the amount of inequality in its distribution that is socially just must arise from the nature of the good in question. With medical care, for example, distribution should be on the basis of need and there should be no inequality of access; for education, the principle should be that each should have as much education as s/he desires and can derive benefit from. In Walzer's opinion, the key issue is *domination*: the distribution of no one good should dominate the distribution of others. In a capitalist society, the distribution of money can dominate the distribution of other goods; in communist societies the dominant good may be political influence.

Evaluation

Social justice is relevant to criminology in several ways. Rawls' justice as fairness is reflected in contemporary just desert theories of punishment, and a major point of contention between desert theorists and their critics has been the extent to which criminal justice should take account of social injustice. It is also suggested that high levels of social injustice bring into doubt the legitimacy of law and criminal justice.

High rates of social inequality are associated with high crime rates and high imprisonment rates, and criminologists have criticized the reliance on penal policy rather than social policy to combat crime in the UK and the USA (Young, 1999). Some criminologists explicitly advocate social justice as a value-base for criminology and have argued that penal crime prevention and community safety policies need to be mindful of the rights and opportunities of those at whom they are targeted (Arrigo, 1999; van Swaaningen, 1997).

Barbara Hudson

Associated Concepts: criminal justice, human rights, just deserts, natural justice, social exclusion

Key Readings

Arrigo, B. (ed.) (1999) *Social Justice/Criminal Justice.* Belmont, CA: Wadsworth.

Bouchier, D. and Kelly, P. (eds) (1998) *Social Justice: From Hume to Walzer.* London: Routledge.

Rawls, J. (1972) *A Theory of Justice.* Oxford: Oxford University Press.

van Swaaningen, R. (1997) *Critical Criminology: Visions from Europe.* London: Sage.

Walzer, M. (1983) *Spheres of Justice: A Defense of Pluralism and Equality.* New York: Basic Books.

Young, J. (1999) *The Exclusive Society.* London: Sage.

SOCIAL LEARNING THEORY

Definition

A theory of learning which maintains that in order to understand behaviour it is necessary to account for the reciprocal relationship between a person and their environment. Its defining characteristic as a learning theory is the role it gives to cognitive variables.

Distinctive Features

As originally formulated, behavioural theory concentrated on the relationship between the environment and observable behaviour. The contribution of social learning theorists was to attempt to incorporate more explicitly the role of cognition into an account of human behaviour (Bandura, 1977, 1986). The beginnings of the departure from mainstream behavioural thinking came with research that focused on the phenomenon of learning by observation. Traditionally, the accepted position within learning theory was that behaviour developed through the individual's experience of the rewarding or punishing consequences, contingent on their actions, that were delivered by the environment. Social learning theorists departed from this position in that, while continuing to acknowledge the role of external reinforcement, they suggested that learning could also take place purely at a cognitive level. Thus, behaviour could be acquired simply through observing models in the social world. Bandura suggested that there were three potent sources of modelled behaviour: family members, members of one's peer group, and symbolic models, as for example in the popular media.

Further, Bandura advanced the concept of 'motivation' to supersede reinforcement. In social learning theory terms motivation is held to take three forms: *external reinforcement,* in the traditional sense that the term is used in behavioural theory; *vicarious reinforcement,* where actions are based on observing what happens to other people who behave in a particular way; and actions that produce *self-reinforcement,* as in a sense of personal pride or achievement. As social learning theory stimulated interest in the role of cognition within an overarching behavioural framework, the term *cognitive-behavioural* became more widely used.

One of the consequences of the rise of social learning theory was an upsurge in interest in cognition and cognitive processes. The notion of *social information processing* seeks to develop an understanding of the cognitive processes when we interact with other people. The basis of this approach is that when we interact socially, there is a flow of verbal and nonverbal information between those involved. This flow of information communicates details of emotional state, level of

interest in the other person, and so on. The social tasks facing those engaged in an interaction are first to be sensitive to this social information, then to decode or understand the information, and finally to use this information to inform their own behaviour. It is argued that biases at any of these cognitive stages can result in socially dysfunctional behaviour and in particular aggressive behaviour (Akhtar and Bradley, 1991).

Social learning theory has been applied to the study of criminal behaviour by psychologists (e.g., Nietzel, 1979), and interventions based on the principles of social learning have also been developed for use with offenders (e.g., Hollin, 1990). These interventions might include working with offenders to help improve levels of social ability, as with social skills training and social problem-solving skills training; or to challenge offenders' thinking, for example, by increasing their awareness of the effects of victimization or beliefs about, say, sexual acts with young children.

Criminologists have also attempted to develop a mainstream theory of crime using differential association theory, reinforcement theory and social learning theory (e.g., Akers, 1990). In a social learning theory account, the acquisition of criminal behaviour (that is, attitudes and skills as proposed by differential association theory) is via direct reinforcement from the environment, as in operant terms, or through modelling and imitation. The models for all behaviour, including criminal behaviour, are to be found directly in the behaviour of friends and family and more abstractly in cultural forces such as visual images and the written word. (This is close to Sutherland's differential association theory articulated before the theoretical advances of social learning theory.) In terms of its maintenance and in line with traditional learning theory, criminal behaviour is reinforced by the external rewards that it produces: these include tangible, often financial, gains along with social rewards such as peer group status. However, social learning theory would add personal, internal rewards as factors that maintained criminal behaviour: these might include the excitement of stealing a car and joyriding, or a sense of personal pride in avoiding detection for a theft.

Further, the meaning (or definitions in differential association terms) of criminal behaviour for the offender should be taken into account as this gives some level of understanding of that behaviour for the individual concerned. Thus, the offender's definition of their actions may be positive, so that offending is seen as desirable: for example, those who commit sexual offences against children may say that their actions are desirable because in reality children enjoy sex and such early sexual encounters act for the child's benefit in later life. Alternatively, the offender's definition of their actions may be neutralizing, negating the impact of what society sees as intolerable behaviours: for example, burglars may say that stealing from people's homes is defensible because their victims are insured and therefore no real loss is caused.

Evaluation

The criticism of social learning theory, or more accurately the *application* of social learning theory, is that it focuses on the individual and their close social world, but fails to take into account large-scale sociological factors. The development of a theoretical model to take such broad factors into account is a project waiting to happen.

Clive Hollin

Associated Concepts: behaviour modification, conditioning, differential association, differential reinforcement

Key Readings

Akers, R.L. (1990) 'Rational choice, deterrence, and social learning theory in criminology: the path not taken', *Journal of Criminal Law and Criminology*, 81: 653–76.
Akhtar, N. and Bradley, E.J. (1991) 'Social information processing deficits of aggressive children: present findings and implication for social skills training', *Clinical Psychology Review*, 11: 621–44.

Bandura, A. (1977) *Social Learning Theory.* Englewood Cliffs, NJ: Prentice-Hall.
Bandura, A. (1986) *Social Foundations of Thought and Action: A Social Cognitive Theory.* Englewood Cliffs, NJ: Prentice-Hall.
Hollin, C.R. (1990) *Cognitive-Behavioral Interventions with Young Offenders.* Elmsford, NY: Pergamon Press.
Nietzel, M.T. (1979) *Crime and its Modification: A Social Learning Perspective.* Oxford: Pergamon Press.

SOCIAL REACTION

Definition

The social process characterizing media, public, political and criminal justice responses to crime and deviancy. These responses often stereotype, stigmatize, label, criminalize, scapegoat and/or amplify the behaviours of certain individuals and groups.

Distinctive Features

Historically, some authors referred to social reaction (or societal reaction) as a theoretical perspective, using it interchangeably with interactionist, labelling and transactional perspectives. However, social reaction is more usefully viewed as a theoretical concept central to these perspectives, and to a broader understanding of the nature and impact of societal responses to crime and deviance.

The theoretical legacy of social reaction and the labelling perspective derived from it lie in the work of symbolic interactionists, notably Charles Horton Cooley and George Herbert Mead. In the tradition of Mead, Tannenbaum (1938) acknowledged that crime and deviance were created through processes of social interaction, especially through societal responses like tagging, definition, identification and segregation. This culminated in a person becoming what they were described as, separating the 'criminal' from the group in a process that Tannenbaum called the 'dramatization of evil'. However, it was Lemert's

(1951) theory of sociopathic behaviour which undertook a systematic analysis of societal responses to deviation. His basic premise was that social control created deviance. Distinguishing between original causes and effective causes, he argued that there were many original causes of initial or 'primary' deviance, but that importantly this deviance was of little consequence to one's self-concept. The societal reaction, however, was seen as the effective cause of 'secondary' deviance, whereby an individual used their deviant behaviour or status to defend, attack or adjust to the problems created by societal responses to primary deviance. Lemert suggested that responses to deviation ranged from strong approval to indifference to strong disapproval, but sociopathic behaviour was that which was effectively disapproved. Furthermore, one's deviant identity was shaped by the level of deviation engaged in, its social visibility, and the exposure, nature and strength of the societal reaction. Recognizing both formal and informal responses to crime and deviance, he argued that formal agents of social control extended and formalized informal responses.

The 1960s witnessed a further development of these ideas by Kitsuse (1962), Becker (1963) and Erikson (1966). In what came to be known as the labelling perspective, the concept of social reaction was pivotal. Following their theoretical predecessors, proponents of this perspective focused on the social processes by which persons and behaviour come to be defined as deviant, as well as who had the power to confer such a label. As the most famous advocate of labelling suggested, 'social groups create deviance by making the rules whose infraction constitutes deviance, and by applying those rules to particular people and labelling them as outsiders. From this point of view, deviance is not a quality of the act the person commits, but rather a consequence of the application by others of rules and sanctions to an "offender"' (Becker, 1963: 9). Thus, nothing was inherently criminal and it was the social reaction that created deviance.

While interactionism and labelling are the key theoretical perspectives associated with social reaction, there are also a number of interrelated theoretical concepts crucial to illustrating the nature and impact of societal responses to crime and deviance. As Lemert suggested '[m]ythologies, stigma, stereotypes, patterns of exploitation, accommodation, segregation, and methods of control spring up and crystallize in the interaction between the deviants and the rest of society' (1951: 55). Indeed, the crux of social reaction is that behaviour that is subjectively stigmatized, stereotyped, labelled and criminalized may create moral panics and 'folk devils' (Cohen, 1972) and facilitate 'criminal careers' and self-fulfilling prophecies of deviance amplification and scapegoating.

Up until this point, social reaction has been examined as an 'active' concept. However, in some instances this may also be 'inactive' or lacking, for example, in terms of the lack of negative societal responses to white collar and corporate crime as compared to 'conventional' crime.

Evaluation

Together with interactionist and labelling perspectives, and related theoretical concepts, social reaction shifted the focus of sociological enquiry from causes and explanations of crime and deviance to societal responses. In doing so it presented crime and deviance as social constructs. Furthermore, it examined the unintended consequences of media, public, political and criminal justice responses to crime and deviance, providing the impetus for non-interventionist criminal justice strategies.

Overall, social reaction has proved a valuable theoretical concept for explaining processes of marginalization, especially where gender, ethnicity, mental illness and youth are concerned. Indeed, in the case of young people, social reaction has highlighted the continued association between 'youth' and 'crime', which has contributed to the criminalization of youth and non-criminal behaviour and perceptions of young people as 'other'.

Many criticisms of labelling also apply to social reaction, including that it does not explain the causes of primary deviance (although advocates would argue they did not seek to explain these). Furthermore, the extent to which the social reaction to crime and deviance is wholly subjective is questionable, for example, in the case of societal responses to murder. Finally, the extent to which social reaction causes deviance is surely unmeasurable and therefore unknowable.

Anna Duncan

Associated Concepts: crime news, criminal careers, criminalization, deviancy amplification, folk devil, interactionism, labelling, moral panic, scapegoating, social constructionism, stereotyping, stigma

Key Readings

Becker, H. (1963) *Outsiders: Studies in the Sociology of Deviance.* New York: The Free Press.
Cohen, S. (1972) *Folk Devils and Moral Panics.* New York: St Martin's Press.
Erikson, K. (1966) *Wayward Puritans: A Study in the Sociology of Deviance.* New York: Macmillan.
Kitsuse, J. (1962) 'Societal reaction to deviant behaviour', *Social Problems,* 9: 247–56.
Lemert, E. (1951) *Social Pathology: A Systematic Approach to the Theory of Sociopathic Behavior.* New York: McGraw-Hill.
Tannenbaum, F. (1938) *Crime and the Community.* New York: Columbia University Press.

SOCIAL SURVEY

Definition

A research design that firstly collects and assembles a structured set of data about a large number of cases (or units of analysis) and secondly involves a form of statistical analysis that seeks to describe the characteristics of the set of cases and sometimes also attempts to provide explanations of such characteristics.

Distinctive Features

Surveys can embrace a wide range of activities involving a wide range of types of cases. However, the case or unit analysis about which data are collected is often the individual, although that is not an essential requirement. For example, it is possible to survey police–public interactions to describe them in terms of, say, 'friendliness' or 'hostility'; incidents may be surveyed in order to count how many of them are recorded as crimes; and newspaper articles might be analysed to find out how many argued for 'justice through punishment'.

All of the cases in a given population may be surveyed, in which instance it is usual to use the term 'census'. For example, the British Census has taken place every ten years since 1801 to provide a count of the population of England and Wales on one particular day as well as describe the population in terms of basic characteristics. Most developed countries will carry out a census. For example, the Census of the Population of the United States has been held every ten years since 1790. However it is much more common to study only a sample of the population. This is done on the grounds of cost and time and also because the principles of statistical inference can permit accurate estimates of the population to be obtained (with calculable margins of error) from relatively small samples. It is because most surveys will involve some form of selection that the term 'social survey' is often taken as being synonymous with a sample survey rather than a census. What is more, as indicated above, although a wide range of units may be surveyed the most common of these is the individual.

As a result, in the narrow sense, social surveys are often taken to refer to the selection of individuals drawn from some wider population with the aim of making inferences from the sample to that population. In such instances data will be collected either by conducting interviews, usually structured interviews, or by respondents completing a questionnaire by themselves.

There are two broad strategies for selecting individuals to be members of samples. The first is known as random or probability sampling, whereby everyone in the designated population is given an equal chance of selection. The other is known as purposive or non-probability sampling, whereby individuals are deliberately selected for inclusion in a sample because they have certain distinctive features that are relevant to the research (for example, some specialist knowledge, particular background attributes or a willingness to participate). Both random and purposive samples can have variations in terms of design, for example to make them more or less representative of the wider population. In order to make reasonably precise and calculable estimates about the characteristics of a population it is advisable to select random, but more importantly, representative samples.

Data may be collected from samples of individuals at a key point in time, in which case it is common to refer to *one-shot* or *cross-sectional designs*. For example, a crime survey that involves interviewing a sample of the population of a town during, say, the month of January in order to estimate the total amount of victimization during that month is a cross-sectional survey. Sometimes researchers will be interested in investigating trends and patterns over time and will then interview an equivalent but different selection of people each January over a 10-year period. This is known as a *time series design*. The British Crime Survey is one example of a time series survey (Mayhew, 2000). Where the same group of people are interviewed at different periods of time, perhaps to study their personal development, it is common to refer to them as *longitudinal studies* or *cohort studies*. Longitudinal studies have been used to follow up a cohort of individuals into early adulthood so as to see which ones engage in criminal careers and why this happens. An example of this

is the Cambridge Study of Delinquency Development (West, 1982).

Evaluation

Social surveys are valuable instruments of criminological research because they provide means of collecting a good deal of information about a lot of cases over a relatively short period of time (with the exception of longitudinal surveys) and at a reasonable cost per unit of analysis. They are means by which the main features of populations can be described, usually statistically, by studying relatively small samples. What is more, forms of statistical analysis – especially those based on correlations – allow the researcher to look for patterns in the populations and then seek to explain one set of characteristics in terms of another set. For example, a researcher may move beyond estimating the number of victims of crime towards explaining victimization in terms such as age, gender, ethnicity and lifestyle.

It is, however, also necessary to recognize the limitations of social surveying. There are many potential sources of bias, for example, in the ways interviewers ask questions and the ways respondents interpret and answer these. The questionnaires or interview schedules may force answers that do not truly reflect how individuals wish to respond, and samples may be so unrepresentative as to make inferences drawn from them worthless. Such matters can be addressed via careful planning and research design. However, more fundamental issues have been levelled at surveys. One is that by their very nature (for example, collecting data from large numbers of cases) they are shallow and superficial and do not allow researchers to capture the depth of meaning which criminological understanding requires. Typically, such an argument will come from those who advocate an appreciative criminology. Other viewpoints are that social surveys have certain in-built quantitative and positivist assumptions and also tend to be favoured research instruments of the 'official' criminology of government departments and other state institutions such as the police and prison services. Because of this, they do not address fundamental issues of criminal justice such as inequality, power and oppression. Typically, such an argument would come from those who advocate a critical criminology.

Victor Jupp

Associated Concepts: appreciative criminology, cross-sectional design, longitudinal study, sampling, structured interviews, time series design, victim surveys

Key Readings

Jupp, V., Davies, P. and Francis, P. (eds) (2000) *Doing Criminological Research.* London: Sage.

Mayhew, P. (2000) 'Researching crime and victimization: the BCS', in P. Davies, P. Francis and V. Jupp (eds), *Victimization: Theory, Research and Policy.* London: Macmillan.

Sapsford, R. (1999) *Survey Research.* London: Sage.

de Vaus, D.A. (1995) *Surveys in Social Research,* 4th edn. London: UCL Press/ Sydney: Allen and Unwin.

West, D.J. (1982) *Delinquency: Its Roots, Careers and Prospects.* London: Heinemann.

SOCIO-BIOLOGY

See: Biological criminology

SOCIOLOGICAL POSITIVISM

Definition

Sociological positivism stresses the importance of social factors – such as anomie, social disorganization and economic recession – as causes of crime. The broad aim is to account for the *distribution* of varying amounts of crime within given populations.

Distinctive Features

A sociological form of positivism was first developed by philosophers such as Comte and Saint-Simon in the early nineteenth century. Comte's insistence that society both predates and shapes the individual psychologically provided the foundation for sociological criminology. This mode of analysis can be traced back to the work of the French statistician Guerry and the Belgian mathematician Quetelet in the 1830s. They analysed official statistics on variables such as suicides, educational levels, crime rates and the age and sex of offenders, within given geographic areas for specific time periods. Two general patterns emerged: types and the amount of crime varied from region to region, but within specific areas there was little variation from year to year. Because of this regularity it was proposed that criminal behaviour must be generated by something other than individual motivation. Quetelet (1842) found that the factors most strongly tied to criminal propensity were gender, age, occupation and religion. Fluctuations in crime rates were explained with reference to changes in the social, political and economic structures of particular societies, while crime itself was viewed as a constant and inevitable feature of social organization.

At the turn of the century its most influential advocate was Emile Durkheim (1964 [1895]). He argued that in any given social context the predictability of crime rates must mean these are social facts and thus a normal phenomenon. Crime is rarely abnormal – it occurs in all societies, it is tied in with the facts of collective life, and its volume tends to increase as societies evolve from mechanical to more complex organic forms of organization. Above all, crime and punishment perform a useful function for society because they maintain social solidarity by establishing moral boundaries and strengthening the shared consensus of a community's beliefs and values. Crime, then, is positive – an integrative element in any healthy society. In other words, Durkheim reasoned that societies without crime must be extremely repressive and incapable of adapting to social change.

One of the most influential forms of sociological positivism was developed by the Chicago School in the 1920s. Their early work argued that crime rates were determined by certain economic, environmental and spatial conditions. They noted that rates of truancy, delinquency and adult crime tended to vary inversely in proportion to their distance from the city centre. The closer to the city, the higher the rate of crime. These rates reflected differences in the physical make-up of different communities. High crime rates occurred in areas characterized by deterioration and declining populations. Moreover, relatively high rates of crime persisted in certain areas even when the composition of their population had changed significantly.

These observations suggested that it was the nature of neighbourhoods, and *not* the nature of the individuals who lived there, that determined levels of criminality. As a result, this line of reasoning has also been termed 'environmental determinism'. The concentration of crime and delinquency in particular areas was also viewed as indicative of processes of *social disorganization*. As industry and commerce invaded, and transient populations entered such areas, community ties were destroyed and resistance to deviance lowered.

Evaluation

Sociological positivism views the individual as a body that is acted upon and whose behaviour is determined by external forces. Little or no role is given to the processes of choice, voluntarism or self-volition. While Durkheim argued that crime was a normal social fact, he also acknowledged that in given contexts its rate might be abnormal. Thus crime is also regarded in terms of some form of pathology: if not the abnormality of individuals, then the dysfunctions in social systems. The study of crime remains in the tradition of scientism, essentialism and positivistic method: that is, it can be measured and evaluated by means of statistical methods and empirical data. It also assumes that there must be something distinguishable about crime that differentiates it from normal behaviour. A consensus, or in Durkheim's terms, a 'collective conscience', exists which marks out the criminal from the non-criminal. The role of social conflict between individuals and among competing groups is downplayed. Compared to individual positivism, sociological theories appear less interested in crime as a particular pattern of behaviour and more in *probabilistic* accounts of variations in crime rates given particular social, geographical and economic circumstances. They focus on general patterns of criminality rather than on individual motivations. Nevertheless, the concern remains to isolate key causal variables, such as social disorganization and criminal area, and to infer that such conditions *determine* rates of criminality. Crime remains a violation of a social order that is considered to be based on a consensus of legal and moral codes. Little room is given for the contrary positions that crime may be a freely chosen course of action and that it may be due to *different* forms of socialization, rather than a lack of socialization.

John Muncie

Associated Concepts: anomie, Chicago School of Sociology, geographies of crime, positivism, social ecology

Key Readings

Durkheim, E. (1964 [1895]) *Rules of Sociological Method.* New York: The Free Press.
Quetelet, A. (1842) *A Treatise on Man.* Edinburgh: Chambers.
Shaw, C.R. (1929) *Delinquency Areas.* Chicago: University of Chicago Press.

SOMATOTYPING

Definition

A means of measuring variations in body types through which certain physiological features have been claimed to be causative of crime and delinquency.

Distinctive Features

The classifying of criminal types by physiological characteristics was the hallmark of early biological criminology, in particular the work of Lombroso, Goring and Hooton. The Harvard anthropologist Earnest Hooton, for example, studied over 17,000 criminals and non-criminals and reported that the former tended, amongst many other characteristics, to have sloping foreheads, thin lips, long necks and sloping shoulders (Hooton, 1939). He maintained that tall thin men tended to commit fraud, short heavy men to carry out sex crimes, and men of moderate physique to have no crime speciality.

Despite the obvious over-generalized nature of the conclusions to such research, work into body types continued in the mid-twentieth century. The German psychiatrist Ernst Kretschmer (1925) identified three major types: thin (asthenic), heavy (pyknic), and muscular (athletic). The American psychologist William Sheldon (1949) then expanded on this model by correlating body build with behavioural tendencies. His analysis of somatotyping suggested that the shape of the body correlated with individual temperament and mental well-being. A person's somatotype is made up of three components: mesomorphy, ectomorphy and endomorphy.

- *Mesomorphs* have well-developed muscles and an athletic appearance. The body shape is hard and round. The personality is strong, active, aggressive and sometimes violent.
- *Ectomorphs* have small skeletons and weak muscles. The body shape is fragile and thin. The personality is introverted, hypersensitive and intellectual.
- *Endomorphs* have heavy builds and are slow moving. The body shape is soft and round. The personality is extrovert, friendly and sociable.

Analysing and comparing 200 boys in a reformatory in Boston with 4,000 students, Sheldon concluded that most delinquents tended towards mesomorphy. Ectomorphs had the lowest criminal tendencies. Glueck and Glueck (1950), using large samples of delinquent and non-delinquent boys, similarly found that there were twice as many mesomorphs among delinquents than could have occurred by chance. Sixty per cent of delinquents were mesomorphic, while only 14 per cent were ectomorphic, compared with 40 per cent of non-delinquents. The Gluecks contended that strength and agility might enable boys to fill a delinquent role. Endomorphs were too clumsy, and ectomorphs too fragile, to be successful delinquents. On reviewing a number of such studies, Wilson and Herrnstein (1985: 89) felt confident enough to conclude that criminals did differ in physique from the population at large. Physique, however, does not cause crime; it correlates with temperaments that are impulsive and given to uninhibited self-gratification.

As is common with such studies, it is not *causes* that are revealed but *correlations*. Being athletic in stature may be correlated with delinquency, but this does not mean that either is the cause of the other. Both are probably influenced by other factors, including the adequacy of nutrition, extent of manual labour and social class position. Similarly, what Hooton and Sheldon were measuring were not the characteristics of the criminal *per se* but of the identified and processed criminal, who is most likely to be of working-class origin. Above all, any association between body type and crime remains in need of an explanation. Are mesomorphs biologically predisposed towards crime or is their criminality simply more socially visible? Such questions continue to plague physiological research, but it is clear that its assumptions continue to impact on popular conceptions of crime. Research undertaken in the 1970s showed that members of the public and the police would readily and consistently put the same faces together with particular crimes even when the individuals involved had not been convicted of any crime at all.

John Muncie

Associated Concepts: biological criminology, causation, correlational analysis, determinism, genetics, individual positivism

Key Readings

Glueck, S. and Glueck, E. (1950) *Unravelling Juvenile Delinquency.* New York: Harper & Row.
Hooton, E. (1939) *Crime and the Man.* Cambridge, MA: Harvard University Press.
Kretschmer, E. (1925) *Physique and Character.* New York: Harcourt Brace.
Sheldon, W. (1949) *Varieties of Delinquent Youth.* New York: Harper.
Wilson, J.Q. and Herrnstein, R.J. (1985) *Crime and Human Nature.* New York: Simon and Schuster.

THE STATE

Definition

A set of historically variable, macro institutions and organizations charged with the maintenance of order over a given terrain. This heterogeneity within the state form – its traversing of public/private boundaries – implies disunity as well as unity, conflict and consensus within and between state organs. States display a balance between the use of coercive and consensual means to maintain social order. In that states attempt to provide a focus for leadership in society, they are always implicated in articulating the parameters of the general social interest. Thus state institutions are involved in constructing and maintaining, not always successfully, a popular legitimacy for the state form itself.

Distinctive Features

The relationship between state institutions, crime, deviance and social order has been the subject of fierce dispute within criminology. Whether the state merely responds to problems of crime and disorder or is active in their precipitation is one such contention. Furthermore, in its dealings with 'the problem of crime' the state has been conceived of in relatively neutral terms in that institutions will intervene to preserve a notion of order based on a given social consensus. On the other hand, the state has been drawn in more partial terms in that its actions, interventions and legal prescriptions can only be understood as serving to promote particular interests within societies based on division, inequality and conflict.

Early attempts at establishing a scientific positivistic criminology in the late nineteenth century framed its terms of reference and objects of enquiry in such a way as to make it compatible with penal administration, structures of law and political ideology. In order to make itself a policy-relevant discipline, criminology for much of its growth and development did not problematize state processes and instead searched for the causes of criminality as located within individual and environmental processes.

It was with the turbulent changes associated with developments in industrialism, urbanization and technological advances that the state began to emerge as an object of social scientific analysis. Writing at the end of the nineteenth century, Emile Durkheim was concerned with the seemingly fragmentary, amoral and uncivilizing effects of these rapid social and economic changes that undermined the traditional sources of control and social bonding found within families and community structures. He saw the increases in crime and conflict as inevitable features of a fragmenting social order. The decline of traditional forms of solidarity had encouraged normlessness, which for Durkheim would be best countered by a state that operated on and through the 'public interest' to foster unity and consensus via a combination of the law, punishment and community organizations. The modern state according to Durkheim, through law and punishment based on restitution, reflected popular sentiment and morality, which dictated what was to be punished, and at what level of severity.

This view of the state as standing above social antagonisms and reflecting the greater 'social good' was developed in the writings of the 'Chicago School' in the 1920s and by Parsons' structural functionalism which dominated social science in the 1950s. Essentially, the state was depicted in conservative and/or pluralist terms: a preserver of an already existing moral order, divorced from particular powerful social interests. State institutions were seen as disinterested referees in times of social conflict whose policies reflected the 'general interest'. Thus laws and policies were enacted on this basis. Max Weber's conception of the state extended these formulations, depicting it as imbued with a rational, bureaucratic set of procedures while exerting its monopoly of the legitimate use of physical force.

These liberal – essentially benevolent – views of the state were challenged in the 1960s with the new control culture theories emerging out of the labelling perspective. Although writers within this perspective such as Becker did not provide a clear conceptualization of the state they did focus attention on the agents of social control whose actions, through the application of labels, constructed 'crime' and 'deviance' in the interests of the control culture. Thus the notion of agents of social control acting in the 'public interest' was challenged. Questions remained, however: in whose *specific* interests were deviant labels applied and *why* were they applied to particular groups at particular times? These questions led to a shift towards a more radical analysis – a Marxist account – which linked crime and the state to the dynamics of the political economy of capitalism.

Marxist accounts sought to conceptualize the state in more substantive and specific terms. Quinney straightforwardly argued that the state and rule of law served to secure the interests of the dominant class. This instrumentalist view developed out of the writings of Marx and Engels who depicted the state as an arena for the material and ideological organization and continued dominance of the ruling class. Ralph Miliband continued this perspective through his examination of the formal and informal connections between those in positions of power within the state and ruling class fractions. For others in the Marxist tradition this was a crude model of state processes tainted with a 'functionalist' gloss. Poulantzas was particularly critical of Miliband's functionalism and pointed to the shift towards a more authoritarian state form that was emerging in Western Europe in the 1970s. This he termed 'authoritarian statism'. Althusser, another structural Marxist, also expanded the analysis by focusing on the different sites where the authority of capitalist social relations was maintained and reproduced. These he termed 'ideological state apparatuses' (family, school and media) and 'repressive state apparatuses' (police, courts, prisons and army).

Other neo-Marxist studies then followed. Thompson, Hay and Linebaugh's work on the eighteenth-century state as a social relationship pointed to its position both as a site for class struggle and its role in the formation and reproduction of the new bourgeois social order. Hall et al. (1978) developed a model of the capitalist state derived from the work of the Italian Marxist Antonio Gramsci. Here the state is conceived of as a historically specific set of institutional arrangements whose 'independent' stance becomes untenable in times of crisis and whose leadership or hegemony is a matter of struggle within and outside of state institutions. The work focuses on the structural economic crisis of British capitalism which underpinned the social, political, cultural and moral crisis of authority signalled by youth rebellion, industrial militancy, anti-racist and anti-sexist movements, student protests and the rise of permissiveness in the 1960s and 1970s. In times of crisis the 'spontaneous consent' for state rule becomes exhausted and the more coercive character of state rule becomes visible. In this context, the state 'is progressively drawn ... down into the arena of struggle and direction, and exhibits more plainly than it does in its routine manifestations what it is and what it must do to provide the cement which holds a ruptured social formation together' (Hall et al., 1978: 217).

This line of thinking led to an analysis of the ideological aspects of state power: how popular consent for state coercion was produced and struggled over; how the hegemony of ruling economic and political alliances was established through negotiation and compromise; and how, ultimately, in times of economic crisis, the popular masses come to support processes of criminalization in the construction of social consensus. Hall termed this 'authoritarian populism'. Thus state institutions are very much at the centre of social struggles, and through the process of criminalization, construct discourses of censure and moral culpability – particularly aimed at the powerless – in an attempt to order and lead the society in a particular direction. This process reinforces the interests of the powerful, the majority of whose own crimes and illegal activities are not subject to scrutiny, sanctioning or punishment. Importantly, when the consensus fragments, coercion will be mobilized to restore order. However, unlike earlier Marxist formulations the state does not always 'win' this struggle in every instance. Instead, the state was itself characterized as an arena of struggle where definitions prescribing what was criminal and the responses to crime could be challenged, resisted and occasionally overturned, as in the case of feminist struggles around the law on rape and marriage.

Feminist perspectives that emerged in the 1970s and 1980s questioned the view that depicted state institutions in class terms and as always repressive in their actions. Feminist writers pointed to what the state omitted to do as much as what it did. Thus it was not so much a case of *over-regulation* but the *under-regulation* of crimes against women – for example, in areas of domestic and sexual violence.

The state was reconceptualized as a gendered set of apparatuses, serving the aims of a patriarchal order. It is not only that state institutions are overwhelmingly staffed by men but also that masculinist ideologies inform the policy and decision-making process. This analysis has focused on the differential treatment of women within state criminal procedures and how regimes of control are as much about the penalization of behaviours that step outside of ascribed feminine boundaries as about the control of crime (Hester et al., 1996). This work also emphasized engaging with the state in order to generate social change for women. This perspective was particularly evident in the work of a number of Australian feminists, such as Sophie Watson.

More recently, under the impact of privatization and managerialist discourses, some writers have identified a fragmentation of the state both in practical and theoretical terms. Thus policies of decentralization, partnership and the growth of private policing in theme parks and retail centres has led some to argue that the state monopoly on policing and justice is being eroded. Corporations and other private interests are increasingly defining and responding to problems of order without any recourse to the public interest. Following the work of Michel Foucault, this has led to a move away from the state as a privileged centre of power relations. This perspective is particularly critical of Marxist theorists and what is regarded as their homogeneous and economically reductionist views of state institutions. Much of this work has focused on 'neo-liberalism' as a form of rule that traverses and empowers a range of non-state agencies that 'seek to employ forms of expertise in order to govern society at a distance, without recourse to any forms of direct repression or intervention' (Barry et al., 1996: 14). Thus a range of expertise is at work in the assessment and containment of risks from crime, which moves beyond so-called modernist views of the state as a clearly defined set of institutional mechanisms with precise boundaries. The state's decline in power and influence has been depicted in terms such as the 'lean' state, the 'hollowed out' state and the 'stretched' state.

Other writers, particularly in the Marxist and neo-Marxist traditions, continue to develop and refine a concept of the state that does not presuppose fragmentation, ideological coherence, institutional unity or functionality. These writers include: Jessop (1990), with his emphasis on the contingency and contradiction inherent in state practices; Clarke and Newman (1997), who highlight the state as a managerial set of institutions; and Coleman and Sim (1998), with their analysis of the dialectical inter-relationship between 'old' forms of state power (e.g., the police) and 'new' forms of state control (e.g., CCTV cameras). Writers working around the human rights group *Statewatch* have argued that the state is becoming both increasingly authoritarian and increasingly internationalized through the interpersonal and ideological connections of those working within different nation-states. Consequently, Europe is witnessing the emergence of a pan-European, minimally accountable state that has been designed to manage an increasingly unmanageable detritus comprising conventional criminals, asylum seekers, drug users, single parents (particularly women) and the homeless. At the same time, crimes committed by the powerful including the state's own servants effectively remain beyond scrutiny and punishment. In different ways such writers have helped maintain a critical focus on the processes of state formation (its shifting boundaries, central–local relations) and the exercise of state power in the arena of crime control (its targets, legitimating discourses and impact on social divisions and inequality).

Roy Coleman and Joe Sim

Associated Concepts: authoritarian populism, Birmingham 'school', critical criminology, hegemony, radical criminologies, radical feminism, social control, state crime

Key Readings

Barry, A., Osborne, T. and Rose, N. (eds) (1996) *Foucault and Political Reason.* London: UCL Press.

Clarke, J. and Newman, J. (1997) *The Managerial State.* London: Sage.

Coleman, R. and Sim, J. (1998) 'From the dockyards to the Disney store: surveillance, risk and security in Liverpool city centre', *International Review of Law, Computers and Technology,* 12 (1): 27–45.

Hall, S., Critcher, C., Jefferson, T., Clarke, J. and Roberts, B. (1978) *Policing the Crisis.* London: Macmillan.

Hester, M., Kelly, L. and Radford, J. (1996) 'Introduction', in M. Hester, L. Kelly and J. Radford (eds), *Women, Violence and Male Power.* Buckingham: Open University Press.

Jessop, B. (1990) *State Theory.* Cambridge: Polity Press.

STATE CRIME

Definition

Covers forms of criminality that are committed by states and governments in order to further a variety of domestic and foreign policies.

Distinctive Features

State crime is one of the most serious forms of criminality for the following reasons. First, the monopoly of violence enjoyed by the state means that it has the potential to inflict massive violations of human rights on its own citizens and foreign nationals. Second, the state is the primary source of laws, and this provides it with the ability to define what is criminal. Third, the state's control of the institutions and personnel of the criminal justice system enables it to target and neutralize its economic, social or political enemies. Finally, the state is in the strategic position to conceal its criminality. To date, state crime has been broken down into four categories:

1 Acts of political criminality, for example, corruption, intimidation, manipulating the electoral process, censorship.
2 Criminality associated with the security and police forces, for example, war-making, genocide, ethnic cleansing, torture, disappearance, terrorism, assassination.
3 Criminality associated with economic activities, monopolization practices, violations of health and safety regulations, illegal collaboration with multi-national corporations.
4 Criminality at the social and cultural levels, which includes the material immiseration of sections of the community, institutional racism, cultural vandalism.

Although there are national and international laws and conventions which regulate the state and protect citizens, the principle of national sovereignty makes it extremely difficult for these protections to be accessed.

Eugene McLaughlin

Associated Concepts: capital punishment, crimes against humanity, eco crime, ethnic cleansing, genocide, human rights, institutional racism, obedience (crimes of), terrorism, torture, war crimes

Key Readings

Cohen, S. (2002) *States of Denial*. Cambridge: Polity.
Fredrichs, D.O. (ed.) (1998) *State Crime*, vols 1 and 2. Aldershot: Gower.
Green, P. and Ward, T. (2004) *State Crime*. London: Pluto.
McLaughlin, E. (2001) 'States of fear', in J. Muncie and E. McLaughlin (eds), *The Problem of Crime*. London: Sage.
Strasser, S. (2004) *The Abu Ghraib Investigations*. New York: Perseus Books.

STATUS FRUSTRATION

Definition

The concept of status frustration is used to explain crime and delinquency by strain theorists. Individuals who cannot achieve their status goals through legitimate channels become frustrated and they may (a) try to achieve their status goals through illegitimate or criminal channels; (b) vent their frustration on others; (c) make themselves feel better through illicit drug use; or (d) focus on alternative status goals that they can achieve, with these goals sometimes involving crime.

Distinctive Features

Some strain theorists, such as Robert Merton (1938) and Richard Cloward and Lloyd Ohlin (1960), have argued that people in the USA are most concerned with their monetary status. That is, they desire a lot of money. They are encouraged to do so by the people around them and the larger culture and they are regularly exposed to all the wonderful things that money can buy. Many people, however, are unable to achieve monetary success through legitimate channels – like getting a good education and then a good job. This is especially true of lower-class individuals, although many higher-class individuals may also have trouble achieving their monetary goals. Such people become frustrated and may turn to crimes such as theft, prostitution and drug dealing in order to achieve their monetary goals.

Other theorists, such as Albert Cohen (1955), argue that individuals have a more general desire for middle-class status. They not only want to have money, they also want to be viewed and treated with respect by others. Once again, lower-class individuals can often have difficulty achieving this goal through legitimate channels. Unlike money, middle-class status is not something that one can easily obtain through crime. Some lower-class individuals, however, respond to their status frustration by setting up an alternative status system in which they can successfully compete. Their hostility toward the middle class, among other things, might lead them to set up a status system that values behaviours like fighting and theft in certain conditions.

Still other theorists, such as James Messerschmidt (1993), focus on males' desire for a 'masculine status'. While there are different views of what it means to 'be a man', most such views emphasize traits like independence, dominance, toughness, competitiveness and heterosexuality. Certain people – especially juveniles, lower-class individuals and members of minority groups – may have trouble exhibiting these traits through legitimate channels. They might engage in crime in order to demonstrate their dominance and toughness and coerce others into giving them the respect they feel they deserve as real men.

Finally, several theorists argue that many adolescents desire adult status – particularly the autonomy or freedom associated with being an adult. Delinquency may be a means to assert or achieve autonomy (for example, via sexual intercourse, under-age drinking, stealing to gain financial independence from parents) or to vent their frustration against those who would deny such autonomy.

Evaluation

The effect of status frustration on crime and delinquency has not been well tested, although several observational studies suggest that the above types of status frustration do contribute to crime. And limited survey data suggest that individuals high in status frustration may be more likely to engage in crime, although status frustration does not lead to crime in most cases.

Robert Agnew

Associated Concepts: anomie, masculinities, strain theory, subculture

Key Readings

Agnew, R. (1992) 'Foundation for a general strain theory of crime and delinquency', *Criminology*, 30: 47–87.

Cloward, R.A. and Ohlin, L. (1960) *Delinquency and Opportunity*. New York: The Free Press.
Cohen, A.K. (1955) *Delinquent Boys*. New York: The Free Press.
Merton, R.K. (1938) 'Social structure and anomie', *American Sociological Review*, 3: 672–82.
Messerschmidt, J.W. (1993) *Masculinities and Crime*. Lanham, MD: Rowman and Littlefield.

STEREOTYPING

Definition

The process of applying condensed images to a group or category of people. These images represent over-simplified and over-generalized abstractions regarding such people, their values, behaviour and lifestyle. Stereotyping involves not only categorizing and classifying people but also acting towards them in particular ways.

Distinctive Features

As a theoretical concept stereotyping has a disciplinary base in both social psychology and sociology. Social psychologists focus on stereotyping as part of unconscious and conscious thought processes and explore its link with perception (how individuals give coherence and unity to sensory inputs, such as observing the actions of others) as well as with prejudice (negative attitudes towards a group of persons based not on individual qualities but on traits assumed to be uniformly shared by all members of the group). In addition to exploring the negative aspects of stereotyping, especially in its connection with prejudice, they also examine its positive functions as a means by which individuals can bring order to a potentially complex – even chaotic – social environment, thereby facilitating ease of communication and interaction.

Sociologists have located stereotyping within interactionist, labelling and new deviancy approaches. All of these share a concern with examining the ways in which rounded images are applied so as to define some people as 'deviant' or 'other' and others as 'normal'.

They emphasize the tendency for stereotypes to be structural – namely, embedded in key criminal justice agencies and also in the everyday practices of their personnel. Although stereotypes are expressed in interactions between individuals, they are not idiosyncratic and nor are they applied randomly: rather they exhibit patterns and regularity in the ways in which they are generated and applied. A sociological approach seeks to explore the relationship between such patterns and the exercise of power by one group of people over another. In this respect, sociologists tend to focus on the process of negative stereotyping by one group and its effect on another group.

The concept 'stereotype' is relatively imprecise and there can be variations in the ways in which it is applied. In some cases it is restricted to negative unfavourable imagery, whereas for others it can embrace positive portrayals of categories of people. Stereotypes may be viewed as relatively fixed, rigid and enduring, or subject to manipulation and change. There are also differences as to whether stereotypes necessarily involve biased and inaccurate as opposed to valid – although simplified – portrayals. Finally, stereotypes are sometimes conceptualized as representing a universally shared set of beliefs: alternatively they are viewed as means by which one group characterizes and acts towards another group with adverse consequences for the latter. This formulation links the process of stereotyping to the exercise of power.

There are overlaps between the concept 'stereotype' and others used within an interactionist perspective such as 'label', 'symbolic representation' and 'folk devil'. The notion of the folk devil was central to Cohen's (1973) analysis of violence at an English seaside resort and the creation of rounded images of 'Mods' and 'Rockers'. This analysis generated a wider thesis that society will go through periodic moral panics during which 'folk devils' are constructed and portrayed as the essence of 'what is wrong with society'.

The media play an important role in the formation and transmission of stereotypes. In doing so they are often influenced by primary definers such as the police, who give information to the press and provide initial stereotypes. Such stereotypes are fed into the public domain and also back into a formal and informal police culture.

The use of stereotypes by police in their interactions with others can generate actions that fit the stereotype. In this way they can become amplified and self-fulfilling. Sometimes this is known as deviancy amplification.

Evaluation

Along with other concepts deriving from an interactionist perspective, stereotyping has contributed to criminology in terms of highlighting the social construction of crime and the process of criminalization as opposed to explanations cast in causal terms. However, it runs the risk of contributing to explanations that suggest crime and criminality are the outcome of stereotyping by the media and police, rather than a reality for those who are victims.

Victor Jupp

Associated Concepts: deviance, deviancy amplification, folk devil, interactionism, labelling, moral panic, racialization, scapegoating, social constructionism, social reaction, stigma

Key Reading

Cohen, S. (1973) *Folk Devils and Moral Panics.* London: Paladin.

STIGMA

Definition

A sign of disgrace imposed upon certain identified individuals as a means of marking them out as different, deviant or criminal.

Distinctive Features

The term 'stigma' derives from the practice in ancient Greece of marking the bodies of individuals with cuts or brands to signify them as morally inferior, blemished or polluted and to be avoided, especially in public places. Goffman (1963) distinguishes between three types of stigma: physical deformity, blemishes of character (dishonesty, criminality, radical politics, unemployment, mental disability and so on), and the 'tribal' stigma of race, nation and religion. In his sociological and interactionist analysis, stigma is derived less from a particular attribute (stigmata) and more through a social process in which particular attributes are discredited at particular times and in particular places. It is described as a discrepancy between one's virtual and actual social identity. The normal and the stigmatized are not persons, rather they are perspectives. Stigma is a relational phenomenon. For example, having a university degree may be a sign of success in one social context but a sign of oddity in others. And in some contexts killing will be an act of heroism, while in others it will be viewed as murder. The meaning of stigma also varies across gender and class. Sexual promiscuity may be condemned for women (sluts) but may be a source of esteem for men (studs). Goffman observed that there is no possibility of objectively defining stigma. There is no clear and universal distinction between the normal and the deviant. In pluralistic and heterogeneous societies we continually move from one to the other. Stigma is a 'two-role social process in which every individual participates in both roles, at least in some connections and in some phases of life' (Goffman, 1963: 138).

However, he also noted that certain people – such as in-group deviants, those engaged in a collective denial of the social order, minorities and the lower classes – are all likely to find themselves functioning as stigmatized individuals at some time or other. This is because the actual identity of such groups is more likely to confront a virtual middle-class ideal. Difference is translated into undesirability or inferiority. The stigmatized are cast as not quite human. Reactions against such castings are likely to

be viewed as confirming the original defect. The stigmatized individual may attempt to correct the condition, but this can also affect their self-esteem, self-concept and future behaviour. The stigmatized may come to resist their classifiers as unjustly exercising the power to deny them their full humanity.

It is in all these senses that the concept has been most widely employed in criminology. In Becker's (1963) and Lemert's (1967) labelling analysis the stigma process cements rather than prevents the onset of deviant careers. Applied to prisoners and the inmates of mental hospitals, the stereotyping of them as 'spoiled' precludes their ability to return to a mainstream life. Further deviance is entertained when opportunities are foreclosed by persistent readings of character as negative and by related feelings of estrangement, self-doubt or resistance. Schwartz and Skolnick's (1964) study of legal stigma found consistent discrimination by employers when considering job applications from unskilled workers with a criminal record. However, stigma also varies according to social status. Examining the subsequent careers of doctors who had been accused of malpractice, this research found almost no subsequent negative effect. As a result, only a partial and distinct population of deviants will emerge: a direct result of the stigma of imprisonment and of a collective intolerance towards the relatively powerless. Stigma, too, can also be used for wider political purposes through which moral entrepreneurs will choose to engage in moral crusades (or 'stigma contests') to manipulate public opinion against specific groups, such as youth subcultures, asylum seekers, working mothers, teenage mothers, drug users and so on (Schur, 1980).

John Muncie

Associated Concepts: deviance, deviancy amplification, folk devil, labelling, moral panic, radical non-intervention, recidivism, scapegoating, stereotyping, social censure

Key Readings

Becker, H. (1963) *Outsiders*. New York: The Free Press.

Goffman, E. (1963) *Stigma*. Englewood Cliffs, NJ: Prentice-Hall.

Lemert, E. (1967) *Human Deviance, Social Problems and Social Control*. Englewood Cliffs, NJ: Prentice-Hall.

Schur, E. (1980) *The Politics of Deviance: Stigma Contests and the Uses of Power*. Englewood Cliffs, NJ: Prentice-Hall.

Schwartz, R. and Skolnick, J. (1964) 'Two studies of legal stigma', in H. Becker (ed.), *The Other Side*. New York: The Free Press.

STRAIN THEORY

Definition

Strain theory argues that people are more likely to engage in crime when they cannot get what they desire through legitimate channels. They become frustrated or angry, and they may (a) try to obtain what they want through illegitimate or criminal channels; (b) strike out at others in anger; or (c) make themselves feel better through illicit drug use. Strain theories describe the types of strain that contribute to crime and the factors that influence whether one responds to strain with crime.

Distinctive Features

Robert Merton (1938) developed the first major strain theory of crime. He argued that people in the USA were encouraged to pursue the goal of monetary success, but that lower-class individuals were often prevented from achieving such success through legitimate channels – like getting a good education and then a good job. The inability to achieve economic success would then create huge frustration, and individuals would sometimes respond to this by engaging in crime. Most notably, they might try to achieve economic success through illegitimate channels, like theft, prostitution and drug dealing. Some

individuals might also deal with their frustration through drug use.

Albert Cohen (1955) and Richard Cloward and Lloyd Ohlin (1960) drew on Merton's strain theory in order to explain the origin of juvenile gangs in the lower class. Cohen argued that lower-class boys desired middle-class status, which included both money and respect from others. Many lower-class boys, however, would be unable to achieve such status through legitimate channels. For example, they would not have been taught the skills and attitudes necessary to perform well in school. As a consequence, they could not live up to the expectations of their middle-class teachers or compete effectively against middle-class students. If these strained boys were then in contact with one another, they might cope with their frustration by setting up an alternative status system in which they could successfully compete. Their hostility toward the middle class, among other things, would result in them setting up a status system that valued criminal acts like fighting and theft. Thus, the gang would be born.

Cloward and Ohlin, like Merton, argued that most lower-class boys wanted to achieve monetary success. They realized that they would not be able to achieve such success through legitimate channels and so would be ripe for delinquency. But like Cohen, Cloward and Ohlin argued that juveniles were unlikely to violate the law unless they received support from others. They then discussed the conditions that would influence whether strained individuals would form delinquent gangs. Among other things, strained individuals would have to blame their strain on the larger social system and be in contact with one another. The gangs that arose would support and help justify juveniles' crimes.

The strain theorists mentioned above focused on the inability to achieve the goal of monetary success or middle-class status. More recent strain theorists, such as David Greenberg (1977) and Delbert Elliott and associates (1979), have expanded the theory by arguing that juveniles could pursue a variety of goals in addition to money. Such goals include autonomy from adults, positive relations with family members and popularity with peers. Further, they note that middle-class as well as lower-class juveniles may have trouble achieving certain of these goals. They thus provide an explanation for middle-class delinquency.

Most recently, Robert Agnew (1992) has further expanded strain theory. Like his predecessors, Agnew has argued that strain may result from the failure to achieve a range of goals, including financial goals, autonomy and status goals – and especially the desire held by certain males to be viewed and treated like 'real men'. Agnew, however, goes on to say that failing to achieve positively valued goals is only one type of strain. Strain may also result from the loss of positive stimuli (for example, the death of a relative or friend, a break-up with a romantic partner, moving to a new community) and from the presentation of negative stimuli (for example, physical assaults, verbal insults, unreasonable demands). Agnew also discusses the factors that will influence whether people respond to strain with crime. A criminal response is said to be more likely when individuals blame their strain on the deliberate actions of others; have poor coping skills and resources; have little social support from conventional others; are in situations where the costs of crime are low and the rewards are high; and are disposed towards crime. This disposition towards crime is influenced by individuals' traits (such as impulsivity, irritability), their level of social control, and the extent to which they have been taught to engage in crime.

Evaluation

The effect of goal blockage on strain has not been well examined. Researchers typically look at whether juveniles expect to achieve their educational and occupational aspirations (or ideal goals). They will ignore the monetary and other goals emphasized by strain theorists. And the inability to achieve one's aspirations or ideal goals is unlikely to result in much strain, since such goals have something of the utopian in them and are probably not taken seriously in most cases. It is not surprising, then, that studies indicate that the failure to achieve one's ideal educational or occupational goals is not related to delinquency. Limited data, however, suggest that crime is more common among people who are dissatisfied with their monetary situation – with such dissatisfaction being higher among people who are lower class and who state that they want 'a lot of money'. There are also some data to suggest that the failure to achieve autonomy and 'masculinity' goals may contribute to crime.

Data indicate as well that the other two types of strain – the loss of positive stimuli and the presentation of negative stimuli – may contribute to crime. In particular, crime and delinquency are associated with child abuse and neglect; criminal victimization; physical punishment by parents; negative relations with peers; neighbourhood problems; homelessness; and a wide range of stressful life events (like the divorce/separation of a parent, parental unemployment and changing schools). Further, there is some, albeit limited, evidence that at least certain of these types of strain will affect crime, partly through their effect on the individual's level of anger/frustration.

At the same time, strain theory does suffer from certain problems. While some types of strain are related to crime, other types are not. The theory does not currently offer a good explanation as to why only some types of strain contribute to crime. In addition, studies examining the factors that influence the effect of strain on crime have produced mixed results. As a result we do not as yet have a good idea of why some people are more likely to respond to strain by committing crimes than others. Strain theory therefore may be described as promising but in need of further work.

Robert Agnew

Associated Concepts: anomie, gangs, status frustration, subculture

Key Readings

Agnew, R. (1992) 'Foundation for a general strain theory of crime and delinquency', *Criminology*, 30: 47–87.

Cloward, R.A. and Ohlin, L. (1960) *Delinquency and Opportunity*. New York: The Free Press.

Cohen, A.K. (1955) *Delinquent Boys*. New York: The Free Press.

Elliott, D.S., Ageton, S.S. and Canter, R. (1979) 'An integrated theoretical perspective on delinquent behavior', *Journal of Research in Crime and Delinquency*, 16: 3–27.

Greenberg, D.F. (1977) 'Delinquency and the age structure of society', *Contemporary Crises*, 1: 189–223.

Merton, R.K. (1938) 'Social structure and anomie', *American Sociological Review*, 3: 672–82.

STRUCTURATION

Definition

A term coined by the English sociologist Anthony Giddens in the 1970s to refer to the processes by which social structures come into being and persist. In the following decade Giddens (1984) developed an ambitious theory to explain how social structures, such as class relations, will combine with human agency, in a mutually constitutive fashion, to reproduce themselves. Structuration theory promises to balance the objective and subjective features of social life – a feature that it shares with Pierre Bourdieu's (1977) theory of *habitus*.

Distinctive Features

Structuration theory arose out of debates in the 1950s and 1960s about how social order was possible. An impasse had been reached between theories that stressed the generative powers of social structures and others that believed in the primacy of human agency. Giddens has insisted that social order emerges from the intermingling of both institutional conditions and the daily interaction of people. For example, the persistence in, or desistence from, a 'criminal career' is neither the sole product of individual decision making, nor the simple reflection of the social background of the individual concerned. Instead these should be seen as a product of both: what Bourdieu would call a habitus predisposed to certain actions. According to this account, offenders are neither super-agents – able turn their lives around at will – nor super-dopes –who are helpless before social circumstances (Vaughan, 2001).

Giddens insists that structural forces and agency are not separated but are joined through social practice, what he calls the 'duality of structure'. Structure is implicated in action through agents drawing upon structural properties – rules and resources – so reproducing structures. Neither structure nor agency has a separate existence. Structures exist only 'virtually' until called upon by agents, but agents are structured by the past which sediments into a practical consciousness (akin to Bourdieu's habitus) directing the agent towards routines. Large-scale systems are the 'unintended consequence' of various agents invoking such rules and resources. Giddens insists that this does not entail that the future is destined to be a repetition of the past. Agents always have the freedom to reject structural conditioning and break with the past. This is exemplified by what he calls the 'dialectic of control': even the most subjugated have the power to weigh up their situation and do otherwise.

Structuration theory has been utilized by a number of criminologists in a variety of research settings since the 1990s (see Vaughan, 2001, for a comprehensive account). It is not surprising that structuration theory should prove attractive since criminologists have always grappled with balancing the subjective and objective features of social life which feature in any explanation of criminal conduct. Structuration theory has been used in environmental criminology, in analyses of the sentencing process and of criminal desistance, and perhaps most ambitiously in a study of prisons (Sparks et al., 1996). In the latter study, structuration theory is deployed due to its emphasis on routine – so evident in any prison – and on the importance of human agency – which indicates that the reproduction of order in a prison is a skilled accomplishment rather than a *fait accompli*.

As noted, Giddens's structuration theory has many affinities with Pierre Bourdieu's work, especially his notion of habitus (Parker, 2000). Bourdieu rails against the same sorts of dualisms that had worried Giddens, particularly the opposition between subjectivism and objectivism and the individual and the social. For Bourdieu, people will respond to given situations (the 'urgency of practice') neither in a solipsistic, self-seeking way nor in a wholly mechanical manner dictated by circumstances. They are neither free from history nor are they subordinate to it. Instead, they are equipped with a habitus, the 'concrete, embodied, interest-laden disposition which flows from being formed' (Parker, 2000: 44) in a socio-historical field in which groups must strive to maintain their primacy. The habitus inclines a person to maintain the political, economic, social and cultural capital of their collectivity, indicating its dependence upon the field in which it is embedded (Bourdieu, 1977). Past struggles seep into it thereby endowing it with a degree of inertia.

The usefulness of the concept of a habitus has been explored in relation to efforts to combat police racism (Chan, 1997). Two options for changing the practice of police racism are usually posited: either alter the institutional conditions in which policing occurs or else change the actual culture of policing through, for example, improved training. In other words, adjust the field or the habitus. From the perspective of structuration theory both approaches are flawed since they accentuate only one aspect of the duality of structure. Agency (or habitus) cannot be considered apart from the structures (or fields) in which it is embedded. To the practical reformer, it may seem like they are confronting a chicken-and-egg scenario. They are being told that it is necessary to alter both the social environment and the inclinations of agents within it, but where does one start?

Does structuration theory clasp structure and agency together so tightly that it is difficult to seize a vantage point for change?

Evaluation

The promise of structuration theory lies in its claim to reconcile subjective agency and objective structural influences in a causal explanation of action. These were joined together, by both Bourdieu and Giddens, in the moment of practice in which structure (or field) is both the precondition and outcome of agency (or habitus). Structure relies on agency being habituated for it to be reproduced.

It is a legitimate question whether structuration theory grants sufficient weight to the respective influence of both structure and agency in its explanatory schema. It is one thing to assert that this can be done by insisting on maintaining a duality of structure, but quite another to show that this is actually the case. In fact, there are grounds for suggesting that both Giddens and Bourdieu give undue weight to one aspect of the duality they delineated. It could be said that Giddens reduces structure to a moment of agency and Bourdieu makes agency an appendage of structure.

Critics of Giddens argue that his formulation of structure as the instantiation of rules and resources fails to capture the fundamental levels of constraint that underlie a great deal of social life. They suggest that agents need to be construed as being embedded in a set of social relations before they invoke any rules. The unequal access of agents to power and resources cannot be explained by referring to a rule, rather it must be considered as being the outcome of a previous social struggle. On this account, we would neither explain racism within criminal justice systems as the result of invoking rules – this is too determinate – and nor would we explain it as the outcome of unintended consequences – this is too arbitrary. Instead, it might best be explained as a product of the differential access various groups have to sources of social power, which is an institutional heritage that has not been produced by anyone in the present.

Bourdieu is well aware of this pitfall and adamant about defining a social field as the product of a struggle between groups to maintain primacy. The inclinations or habitus of present-day groups originate from the social conflict that they have been engaged in previously. But if this is the case, where does change come from? If groups have been browbeaten in the past (like ethnic minorities in their dealings with criminal justice systems), how do they cast this heritage off and demand more equal treatment? Could it be that people are able to reflect on their plight and recognize the difference between their present status and intrinsic worth? This could be read as a rationalization of a power struggle – victimhood is a means of gaining status – but this collapses morality into Machiavellian politics. If we wish to avoid this conclusion, then how do we theorize the existence of this moral habitus? Such a standpoint is vital because to reduce everything to power is also to admit that change can only come from altering conditions on the field or the structural conditions (Chan, 1997), which, of course, is to underplay agency.

The problems that structuration addresses may seem like unnecessary luxuries to the empirical social scientist, and considering them can look like a vain pursuit of cultural capital. But the questions that structuration addresses are implicit in most research projects and so its agenda is worthy of attention.

Barry Vaughan

Associated Concepts: classicism, determinism, free will, interactionism, positivism

Key Readings

Bourdieu, P. (1977) *Outline of a Theory of Practice*. Cambridge: Cambridge University Press.
Chan, J. (1997) *Changing Police Culture*. Cambridge: Cambridge University Press.
Giddens, A. (1984) *The Constitution of Society*. Cambridge: Polity Press.
Parker, J. (2000) *Structuration*. Buckingham: Open University Press.

Sparks, R., Bottoms, A.E. and Hay, W. (1996) *Prisons and the Problem of Order*. Oxford: Clarendon Press.
Vaughan, B. (2001) 'Handle with care: on the use of structuration theory within criminology', *British Journal of Criminology*, 41 (1): 185–200.

STRUCTURED INTERVIEWS

Definition

Research interviews in which questions are asked in accordance with precisely defined instructions and the answers are recorded in pre-determined categories. Such interviews are usually facilitated by a formal interview schedule for the collection and analysis of data. Structured interviews are in contrast to other forms of interviewing which grant much greater freedom to the respondent to answer in his or her own terms, such as life histories, oral histories and conversational analysis.

Distinctive Features

Structured interviews are used to collect observations from respondents in – usually large-scale – social surveys. The same questions are asked of every respondent in the same way. The range of answers is usually pre-set and may even be pre-coded. The interviewer should be able to categorize the responses to any questions into a set of mutually exclusive and exhaustive categories. As far as possible, the context in which the interview is carried out, and the procedures which are followed, should be standardized. In some cases the role of the interviewer will be reduced to a minimum by respondents interacting with a laptop computer. One example of a structured interview is a battery of questions that will collectively measure or 'scale' respondents' attitudes, such as attitudes towards the police or attitudes towards rehabilitation as opposed to punishment. A number of established techniques exist to measure attitudes, such as the Thurstone scale, the Likert scale and the Guttman scale.

The principle underlying structured interviews is that different individuals should be presented with an 'equivalence of stimulus', thereby facilitating a comparability of responses across the sample in the belief that the research procedures have not affected the responses. The aim is to keep what is known as procedural reactivity to a minimum. In addition, structured interviews seek to reduce personal reactivity in the form of interview bias. The latter can occur when responses are affected by the attitude or behaviour of the interviewer as expressed in the ways he or she asks questions, probes or interprets answers.

Evaluation

Despite these advantages, structured interviews can have weaknesses. For example, they can be too shallow, especially where the researcher is seeking to examine the variety and depth of meanings or attitudes which respondents hold. For this reason some would argue that structured interviews are only appropriate when collecting responses that cover factual matters. A further problem is that structured interviews can result in data degradation (that is, the irretrievable loss of data as a result of reducing the breadth of responses to a few categories). What is more, the imposition of structure may produce a distortion of the ways in which respondents would want to respond, for example because the range of categories offered is inappropriate or not sufficiently exhaustive. One way to overcome this is by undertaking exploratory in-depth research, for example by using in-depth interviews or focus groups to uncover a range of issues and responses that are valid in so far as they are grounded in the frames of reference of the subjects themselves rather than those of the researchers. Such exploratory research with small but representative groups can provide a basis for the design of valid and meaningful questions for use in structured interviews with large samples. Even after this has been done, structured

questionnaires or interview schedules should be 'tested' for their appropriateness in pilot surveys.

Victor Jupp

Associated Concepts: conversational analysis, focus groups, self-reports, social survey

Key Readings

May, T. (1997) *Social Research: Issues, Method and Process*. Buckingham: Open University Press.
Oppenheim, A.N. (1973) *Questionnaire Design and Attitude Measurement*. London: Heinemann.
Wilson, M. (1996) 'Asking questions', in R. Sapsford and V. Jupp (eds), *Data Collection and Analysis*. London: Sage.

SUBCULTURE

Definition

First used by anthropologists, the concept of subculture was applied to the study of delinquency in the mid-1950s. It was used to understand social deviance, and delinquency in particular, by referring to distinctive sets of values that set the delinquent apart from mainstream or dominant culture. It made sense of the apparently senseless by arguing that delinquency was a solution to the structural and cultural problems facing marginalized groups.

Distinctive Features

American in origin, a theory of *youth subculture* gained criminological prominence through Albert Cohen's (1955) research into the culture of gangs in Chicago. Cohen viewed these gangs as a subculture, with a value system different from that of mainstream American culture and distinguishable through a special vocabulary, shared internal beliefs and specialized ways of dressing and acting. He attempted to account for the working-class gang in terms of a lower-class adaptation to a dominant and discriminatory middle-class society. According to Cohen, subcultures of delinquency could be characterized by a working-class membership, masculinity, group loyalty, short-term hedonism, non-utilitarianism and a lack of specialism in delinquent acts. He developed the notion of *status frustration* to explain how the subculture would act as a means for working-class boys to find a solution to the lack of status in middle-class life. The development of a specialized vocabulary, internal beliefs and innovative ways of dressing and acting, he argued, represented an inversion of the dominant values. Status frustration would become visible in negative forms of behaviour whereby the dominant goals of ambition and achievement, deferred gratification and a respect for property were rejected and reversed. By a process of *reaction formation,* dominant values would be inverted to offer a collective solution to restricted opportunity in which 'the delinquent conduct is right by the standards of his subculture precisely because it is wrong by the norms of the larger culture' (Cohen, 1955: 28).

Similarly, Cloward and Ohlin (1961) explained working-class deviancy as a collective rather than an individual solution. In this version, however, the problem for the delinquent is achieving a high status position in terms of lower-class rather than middle-class criteria. They distinguished between three types of delinquent subculture relative to the differential availability of legitimate and illegitimate means to gain material and status success. A *criminal subculture* would develop mainly in lower-class neighbourhoods where the successful criminal not only would be visible to young people, but would also be willing to associate with them. Denied access to conventional role models of success, these youths would access criminal success models instead. However, in more disorganized neighbourhoods when access to a criminal subculture was denied, a *conflict subculture* was more likely to arise in which the lack of legitimate

and illegitimate opportunities for material success would be solved by achieving status through fighting and violence. A *retreatist subculture* would arise where neither of these options was available and the gang resorted to hustling and drug usage.

Evaluation

These formative subcultural theories were influential because they showed that delinquency resulted not from psychologically damaged individuals but through a series of collective, local and cultural solutions to the blocked opportunities and inequalities of the American class structure. Such theory underpinned a variety of crime prevention programmes in the USA in the 1960s. The most famous was *Mobilization for Youth,* which was designed to open up new opportunities for working-class youth through educational and employment support. However, subcultural theory in general came to be critiqued because of its almost sole concern to explain high rates of delinquency within the male lower classes. Criminal law and statistical representations of offending rates were taken as givens. Subsequent studies, based in particular on self-reports, found that most people, irrespective of their gender and class position, would commit acts for which they could be adjudicated criminal or delinquent. In ignoring both the ubiquity of crime, and its white collar variants, it conveys the impression that lawlessness is exclusively both a lower-class and a male phenomenon. The degree to which behaviour is determined by structure and class position and the sharp separation of delinquent and non-delinquent values on which these studies were based has also been heavily criticized.

For example, David Matza's (1964) research found that individual members of a gang were only partially committed to subcultural norms. Rather than forming a subculture that would stand as the antithesis of the dominant order, he argued that the delinquent *drifted* in and out of deviant activity. This was made possible because there was no consensus in society – no set of basic and core values – and instead there existed a plurality in which the conventional and the delinquent would continually overlap and interrelate. Instead of delinquent acts being conceived as a direct expression of delinquent norms and thus system-determined, Matza was more concerned to illustrate how their diversity was dependent on particular individuals and situations. He insisted that *pluralism* rather than consensus, and *interaction* rather than determinism, provided more adequate means for studying deviant behaviour.

Downes's (1966) research in Britain also found scant evidence for Cohen's 'status frustration' among the working-class boys of East London, either in school or work. Rather they *dissociated* themselves from the labour market and deflected their interests, achievements and aspirations into leisure pursuits. As such, leisure, rather than delinquency, provided them with a collective solution to their problems. The connection between leisure and delinquency only becomes apparent if leisure aspirations also remain unfulfilled. Some working-class youths reached a 'delinquent solution' by 'pushing the legitimate values of teenage culture to their logical conclusion' (Downes, 1966: 134). Nor did this research find any evidence of structured gangs in Britain. While definitions of the 'gang' are often loose and variable, the term implies some form of identifiable leadership, membership criteria and organizational structure. Contemporary and classic subcultural studies of white, black, Chinese and Puerto Rican gangs in America paint a picture of neighbourhood groups organized largely along racial lines, with a strong sense of local territory, mutual obligation and, latterly, their direct involvement in extortion, trafficking and the drugs trade. However, in the British version of subcultural theory criminal activity is not a key concern. Instead it is argued that leisure and delinquency combine to provide the conditions in which aspects of subcultural behaviour can become *criminalized*. Indeed, in Britain, Downes's study was influential in various respects. Not only did it shift the debate away from discourses of crime and

delinquency and towards discourses of leisure and entertainment as a means of securing 'cultural space', it also recognized how subcultural experiences and opportunities were structured by class-based material and economic conditions.

These twin concerns were elaborated on by various subcultural studies published by 'the Birmingham School' at the Centre for Contemporary Cultural Studies in the UK during the 1970s. On the one hand, the meaning of subcultural style was examined through various ethnographic and semiological analyses; on the other, the political implications of deviancy were explored by undertaking investigations of the structural and class position of various subcultures and their propensity to create 'moral panics' (Hall and Jefferson, 1976). By drawing on the work of the Marxist author Gramsci, these subcultures were located not just in relation to their parent cultures but also in relation to the structures of class conflict. The British working class, it was argued, had developed their own historical cultures, and the relations between these and the dominant culture were always negotiable. Working-class culture was always in a position to win 'space', because the hegemony of the dominant culture was never completed. It was always in the process of being contested and fought for. Subcultures would contest this space through their 'focal concerns' and in the moments of originality created by the formation of deviant subcultural styles. Above all, subcultures were viewed as symbolic representations of social contradictions and as offering a symbolic critique of the established order: they were seen as *oppositional* rather than simply deviant formations.

John Muncie

Associated Concepts: anomie, Birmingham 'school', delinquency, differential association, gangs, hegemony, neutralization (techniques of), new deviancy theory, status frustration, strain theory

Key Readings

Campbell, A. and Muncer, S. (1989) 'Them and Us: a comparison of the cultural context of American gangs and British subcultures', *Deviant Behaviour*, 10: 271–88.

Cloward, R. and Ohlin, L. (1961) *Delinquency and Opportunity: A Theory of Delinquent Gangs*. London: Routledge.

Cohen, A. (1955) *Delinquent Boys: The Culture of the Gang*. New York: The Free Press.

Downes, D. (1966) *The Delinquent Solution*. London: Routledge.

Hall, S. and Jefferson, T. (eds) (1976) *Resistance through Rituals*. London: Hutchinson.

Matza, D. (1964) *Delinquency and Drift*. New York: Wiley.

SURVEILLANCE

Definition

The ability to monitor public behaviour for the purposes of crime and population control. Associated, in the main, with measures to reduce the opportunities for crime within the rubric of situational crime prevention.

Distinctive Features

In 1778 Jeremy Bentham coined the term 'Panopticon' to describe a prison design which allowed for the uninterrupted inspection, observation and surveillance of prisoners. He envisaged replacing old dark and dank prisons with a light, visible architectural form in which inmates would be separated off from each other and placed permanently in full view of a central but unseen observer. Prisoners would never know when they were being observed but would be forced to behave at all times as if this was happening. A state of conscious and permanent visibility would assure the automatic functioning of self-control and self-discipline. In this way, Bentham was first and foremost championing a new conception of surveillance. He dreamed of entire cities being reorganized along panoptic lines. He believed that the principle of continual surveillance would be applicable to any establishment where a number of persons were meant to be kept under restriction, no matter how different or how opposite their purpose. In other words, the notion of perpetual surveillance could be applied not just to prisons but also to workhouses, factories, asylums, hospitals and schools. Although the panoptic prison was never built, as Foucault (1977) pointed out, many of the emergent urban institutional arrangements of the early nineteenth century began to work on the principle that populations could be ordered through surveillance.

By the late twentieth century a range of surveillance techniques, such as CCTV and biometric scanning devices (smart cards, fingerprinting, iris scans, hand geometry scans, voice recognition, DNA testing and digitized facial recognition), was rapidly being removed from the realm of science fiction. The potential for national and international systems of intimate monitoring to classify individuals into appropriate spaces and times where they would 'belong' was rapidly being realized. The retinal scanning of prison inmates is now in operation in Cook County, Illinois; frequent travellers between Canada and Montana can use automated voice recognition to enable their speedier clearance through border controls; and a national DNA database operates in the UK for tracking criminals. Commercial DNA databases are also raising the prospect of gene tests to underpin surveillance systems in the health insurance industry, excluding those who are recorded as 'abnormal' or 'high-risk'. By the mid-1990s the UK had the highest penetration of CCTV cameras in the world. Pictorial databases of such groups as hooligans, political demonstrators, bank robbers, suspected illegal immigrants and environmental campaigners have been established as a result.

All these developments have potentially enormous consequences for population control and urban regulation in the twenty-first century. Bentham's original conception of the

Panopticon was of the use of architecture to control prison populations. Modern forms of social panopticism extrapolate from the 'unseen eye' of the penal realm and apply its logic to entire populations. Control is accomplished by unobtrusive but pervasive means through which notions of public or private space become increasingly blurred. The information collected by the new technologies of surveillance allows for the systematic categorization of whole populations. Gandy (1993) refers to this as a 'panoptic sort': a process whereby individuals in their daily lives as citizens, employees and consumers are continually identified, classified and assessed, and the information is then used to co-ordinate and control their access to goods and services. In an age of electronic networks, virtual memory and remote access to information and data, the disciplinary surveillance of the Panopticon identified by Bentham and Foucault is increasingly being dispersed beyond architectural boundaries and walls. Observation is no longer limited to what the eye can see. As Gandy (1993: 15) argues, this is not just a vision of the future. Rather the 'panoptic sort' has been institutionalized: 'It is standard operating procedure. It is expected. It has its place. Its operation is required by law. And where it is not, people call out for its installation. Its work is never done. Each use generates new uses. Each application justifies another.' It has become a system of power on which the survival of corporate capital exists. It endlessly searches for the norm and disregards those who are classified as 'abnormal'. It selectively allocates privilege on the basis of information stored, perpetuating inequality and a mistrust which will then result in further surveillance: 'each cycle pushes us further from the democratic ideal' (Gandy, 1993: 230).

A similar vision is offered by Bogard's (1996) notion of a 'telematic society'. For Bogard the surveillance capacities of late modern societies are characterized by:

- the application of military-initiated simulation technologies and command and control communications;

- the commodification of spaces of cities and spaces of information;
- globalization, whereby corporate state interests depend on the global words of digitally interconnected control systems.

Surveillance and simulation have become increasingly interwoven. Telematic technologies, such as virtual reality and image databases, continually produce electronic data which are then taken to be 'reality' by dominant institutions. The key to understanding modern social control, Bogard argues, lies not simply in the extension of surveillance but also in the generation of *simulated* notions of order/disorder. Social relations are reduced to a 'space between the keyboard and the screen'. People are known and situated only as they are reproduced in the hyper-real space generated by electronic data banks, electronic communities or genetic algorithms. It is surveillance without any limits.

These visions of a dystopian future (and present) rely on a reading of Foucault which promises the 'disciplinary society'. But his work can also be read as allowing for resistance. Strategies of power and knowledge are never pre-determined but always contested and contingent, and may enable as well as constrain. Lyon (1994), for example, considers that modern surveillance brings with it real benefits as well as real harms. By linking the expansion of surveillance to a simultaneous growth in citizenship, he argues that it is the very improvements in civic and political entitlement which have generated demand for a greater documentary identification, which in turn depends on a growing sophistication in methods of recording and surveillance. As a result he identifies not one omnipotent Big Brother, but a variety of dispersed 'little brothers'. Panoptic power is partial, contingent and unevenly developed. The sheer volume of new data becoming available is always likely to create contradictory and contingent simulations of people and places. Its meaning becomes ever less verifiable and forever open to contestation.

These macro political economic visions also need to be balanced with finer-grained analyses of how surveillance impacts differently on different populations, at different times and in different places. *Selective* surveillance has clearly played a role in furthering processes of spatial segregation and social polarization. There are obviously various risks involved in the entrenchment of 'suspect populations' in outcast, under-protected ghettos and of 'innocent populations' in over-protected consumerist citadels and residential enclaves. A measured response to modern regulation and surveillance probably requires neither outright acceptance nor paranoia. Subtle distinctions need to be made in order to unravel the complexities involved in addressing whether the future holds a nightmare vision of zones of exclusion and zones of safety or whether surveillance can allow us to re-imagine the urban as rejuvenated, repopulated and more secure.

John Muncie

Associated Concepts: defensible space, globalization, governmentality, panopticism, policing, risk, situational crime prevention, social control

Key Readings

Bogard, W. (1996) *The Simulation of Surveillance: Control in Telematic Societies.* Cambridge: Cambridge University Press.

Foucault, M. (1977) *Discipline and Punish.* London: Allen Lane.

Gandy, O. (1993) *The Panoptic Sort.* Boulder, CO: Westview Press.

Lyon, D. (1994) *The Electronic Eye: The Rise of Surveillance Society.* Cambridge: Polity Press.

Norris, C., Moran, J. and Armstrong, G. (eds) (1999) *Surveillance, Closed Circuit Television and Social Control.* Aldershot: Ashgate.

SYMBOLIC INTERACTIONISM

See: Interactionism

T

TARGET HARDENING

See: *Crime science; Defensible space; Opportunity theory; Repeat victimization; Situational crime prevention; Surveillance*

TERRORISM

Definition

Producing an adequate definition of 'terrorism' is extremely difficult. The League of Nations made the first attempt to create an internationally acceptable designation in 1937. However, the convention of which it was part was never enacted. There have been numerous subsequent attempts to pin down the phenomenon conceptually, particularly in the aftermath of the 9/11 attacks. For the purposes of this discussion, terrorism is defined as an essentially premeditated political act. The intention is to inflict serious injury on the civilian population and to influence government policy by creating an atmosphere of fear and threat, generally for a political, religious or ideological cause. Hence, it also has far-reaching psycho-political implications. In addition, terrorism is recognized as a criminal act by most legal codes, and those groups who are defined by the state as 'terrorists' will have to negotiate an extreme form of criminalization.

Distinctive Features

From the late 1960s onwards, terrorism was elevated to the status of the ultimate criminal threat to world order because it had the capacity to disrupt and paralyse, on a national and transnational scale, virtually every aspect of life. During the 1980s and 1990s the news media were saturated with reports of national and global 'terrorist' incidents, ringing condemnations of atrocities that were said to plumb new depths of savagery, and new governmental agreements for the prevention and punishment of such inhumanity. Very soon it was possible to provide seemingly definitive answers to the questions, 'What is terrorism?' and 'Who are the terrorists?' First, terrorism is defined as violence that is intended to spread fear and insecurity by deliberately targeting civilians who have no chance of defending themselves. The rationale underpinning acts of indiscriminate violence is that if no-one in particular is the target no-one can feel safe. Thus the terrorist act is a form of 'symbolic communication' designed by its perpetrator(s) to cause fear and terror in an audience much broader than the immediate victim (the so-called 'amplifying effect'). Acts of terrorism are the most visible manifestation to a citizenry that the state has lost control of one of its main marks of sovereignty – its monopoly and governance of violence. This is what marks terrorism out as being manifestly different from conventional warfare and, indeed, from the actions of freedom-fighters. And we can all, for example, recall the carnage and devastation caused by spectacular no-warning bomb and gun attacks in various parts of the world during the past twenty years. Second, terrorism is conducted by sub-state groups and is revolutionary in nature. Third, terrorists are routinely portrayed as psychologically deranged, fanatical individuals who operate in a clandestine manner with the support of a minority of 'rogue' states who use them to advance their own geopolitical interests. The most recent and disturbing manifestation of this fanatical mindset has been the suicide martyr bomber.

Examinations of these defining features illustrate that it is a highly problematic endeavour to attempt to draw clear boundaries around who the 'terrorists' are and to distinguish between 'terrorism' and orthodox forms of warfare. To begin with, officially designated terrorists repeatedly deny that they primarily target civilians, and in certain instances have publicly apologized for what they define as 'military actions' that have gone disastrously wrong. They also argue, in the classic 'just war' tradition, that physical force is used only in so far as no other political methods are available or effective. The violence has a specific and identifiable purpose and is measured by its likely outcome. It is also probably fair to conclude that the targeting of unsuspecting civilian populations is not the sole preserve of officially defined terrorist campaigns. Indeed, some would argue that, by comparison with the degree of violence used by conventional armies, these groupings have been remarkably restrained. The totalizing nature of contemporary wars, in conjunction with the lethal nature of the weaponry available, means that there is the distinct possibility that 'collateral damage' – that is, mass civilian casualties – will continue to be excessive.

The problem of terrorism becomes more complicated when we evaluate the assertion that terrorism is practised by extremist revolutionary groups and individuals committed to seizing political power. This representation of terrorism conflates very different political struggles and thereby runs the risk of draining them of their political meaning and specificity. For example, many of the most notorious terrorist groups such as ETA, the IRA and the PLO were or are still demanding some form of national self-determination or autonomy from or within existing nation-states. In addition, we need to recognize the historic links that exist between extremist right-wing political groups and acts of terrorism premised upon the hatred of racial, ethnic or religious minority groupings or in support of the political status quo or as part of a *coup d'état*.

Orthodox conceptualizations also fail to recognize the degree to which nation-states, because of their monopolization of violence, have the potential to become epicentres of terrorism. States have, for example, displayed a remarkable similarity in their attempts to pursue a 'war on terrorism' – namely, a mixture of surreptitious negotiations and repressive emergency legislation strategies. They can upgrade the coercive and intelligence capacity of the national security agencies and/or establish covert military/paramilitary counterinsurgency units to terrorize or eradicate the 'terrorists'. The advantage of 'non-sanctioned' terrorist actions by shadowy freelance groups is that these furnish the state with the ability to distance itself from and also condemn the violence. Torture is also practised by various states and is regarded as the ultimate form of individualized terror. In parts of the world where states are waging a 'war on terrorism' or are in conflict with sections of their own citizenry, national security agencies have been transformed into bureaucratic instruments of terror, complete with networks of clandestine torture and death centres. Disappearance – that is, the extra-judicial arrest or abduction of alleged critics and opponents, usually followed by their torture, secret execution and burial – is another form of state terrorism. Ethnic cleansing and genocide could also be included in this expansive definition of terrorism.

Many of the most influential texts on terrorism assert that the 'terrorist' is the pathological 'other' who glories in remorseless, senseless violence (see for example Hoffman, 2002). 'The terrorist' is either criminally insane or a cold-blooded psychopath addicted to violence and mayhem. In this narrative, such individuals cynically use politics as an excuse for their barbaric actions. It may well be the case that individuals can be cited who fit the stereotype. However, the 'terrorist psychology' concept is an opportune way of evading the political complexities. Most 'terrorist' groupings are allied to political parties and go to great lengths to reject the terrorist-criminal label and assert that they have been forced to resort to violence because of the impossibility of achieving meaningful political change through peaceful means. We also need to pose a question here: are those who are officially labelled 'terrorists' any more 'psychopathological', for example, than soldiers in conventional armies? It is argued that, in order to justify their murderous deeds, 'terrorists' depersonalize and dehumanize their victims, but this dehumanization, desensitization, 'conscience narrowing', 'dissociation', indifference and demonization are also inescapable parts of military socialization generally and one of the reasons why 'guilt-free' atrocities are able to occur.

Evaluation

So what can we conclude from our brief survey of the supposedly unproblematic defining features of terrorism? Overall, it can be argued that terrorism should be defined, first and foremost, as an ideological censure which, if successfully applied, can play a decisive role in forming and inflecting the public understanding of complicated geo-political conflicts – and that it has been deployed in a highly selective manner. There are numerous examples to suggest that there is more likelihood that the violence of the powerless will be defined as 'terrorism' than will the violence of the powerful nation-state.

This raises the central question of whether social scientists should continue to use the terms 'terrorism' and 'terrorist'. There is a strong argument that we should not. Both terms are polemical and a pathologizing device which makes a rational discussion of the causes of political conflict impossible. From this perspective, it is more fruitful to recognize that there is a continuum of politically motivated and enacted violence. To bolster the argument that the term 'terrorist' is an 'explanatory fiction', we could cite the many historical examples of officially labelled

'terrorists' becoming rehabilitated as 'freedom fighters' and – eventually – respected leaders of nation-states, and of successful 'terrorist' campaigns being redefined as national wars of liberation or independence.

Other writers such as Honderich (2002) argue that we should retain these terms but deploy them in a much more judicious manner. Essentially the argument is that we need to acknowledge that not all politically inspired acts of anti-state violence are legitimate. Detonating no-warning car bombs in busy shopping areas, machine-gunning a packed marketplace, and kidnapping, torturing and beheading hostages are all acts of unacceptable savagery. But in pursuit of analytical precision we need a *co-extensive* definition of terrorism to recognize on the one hand that terrorism is a regular feature of most modern conflicts. Reduced to its essentials, the uncomfortable reality is that terror can be used by a variety of political, military and law enforcement actors in order to effect, deter or undermine political change. Consequently, states, governments and sub-state groupings, of all ideological configurations, are capable of resorting to terror in the pursuit of socio-political and military objectives.

A radical perspective argues that a full analytical grasp of what true terrorism is and who the real terrorists are can only be achieved through reconstructing and reversing the official gaze. In this 'state-terrorist' perspective, only nation-states can be truly terrorist because only they have the 'wholesale' capacity to deploy 'terror' as a mode of domination and institutional governance. Restricting the use of the term in this way would allow for a recognition that nation-states can have criminogenic and homicidal tendencies (see Chomsky, 2002).

Even before the 9/11 attacks terrorologists were expressing concern about what the twenty-first-century face of terrorism would look like. There were discussions surrounding the implications of the emergence of nuclear, radiological, biological and chemical terrorism and of cyber or virtual terrorism; the appearance of a new generation of terrorists made up of 'unabombers' with a grudge against society, extremist religious communities, ethnonationalist groups and organized crime networks; and the diversification of funding and resourcing for spectacular terrorist acts. The 9/11 attacks (as well as the Madrid bombings) radically altered the nature of the terrorism debate by forcing the West to recognize that a mass transport system could be transformed by its ideological enemies into a cost-effective weapon of mass destruction. This debate foregrounded the possibility that the West could be fighting 'asymmetric' or '4th generation' warfare.

Anthony Giddens (2005) has distinguished between what he defines as 'old type' and 'new type' terrorism. 'Old type' terrorism as practised by the Red Brigades, Baader-Meinhoff, ETA and the IRA was defined by specified local political objectives – relatively low levels of violence and restraint shown in terms of tactics. For Giddens, globalization has given rise to the 'new style' terrorism as epitomized by Al Qaeda. This is characterized by loose, disparate multi-national networks and cells held together by a sense of vocation, and the use of hi-tech communication systems to co-ordinate actions and promote the cause. The home bases for these 'new terrorists' are failed or failing states that they can effectively take over. These terrorists are more ruthless in that they are willing to contemplate using weapons of mass destruction. For Giddens, the 'new terrorism' is an unprecedented threat not just to the strategic interests of the West but also to any notion of a cosmopolitan global civil society.

There has also been an extensive debate about the need for a radical shift in balance between civil liberties and human rights and national security. This discussion has focused on whether the West should contemplate counter-terrorism measures that would legalize the coercive interrogation ('torture-lite') of terrorist suspects and introduce targeted assassinations; the pre-emptive bombing of terrorist bases; the preventive detention of terrorist suspects; and the 'threat profiling' and covert tracking of suspect populations (see Dershowitz, 2002). Critics argue that

Western governments are cynically using a 'politics of fear' and the 'war on terrorism' to justify the move towards a 'national security state' or 'surveillance state' which is intent on blurring the distinction between war and peace in order to implement an unwarranted radical curtailment of civil liberties and human rights (see BBC, 2004).

Eugene McLaughlin

Associated Concepts: criminalization, emergency legislation, genocide, globalization, hate crime, human rights, political crime, state crime, torture

Key Readings

BBC (2004) *The Power of Nightmares*. BBC2, 20/27 October and 3 November.
Burke, J. (2003) *Al-Qaeda: Casting a Shadow of Terror*. London: I.B. Tauris.
Chomsky, N. (2002) 'Who are the global terrorists?', in K. Booth and T. Dunne (eds), *Worlds in Collision: Terror and the Future of the Global Order*. Basingstoke: Palgrave.
Dershowitz, A.M. (2002) *Why Terrorism Works: Understanding the Threat, Responding to the Challenge*. New Haven, CT: Yale University Press.
Giddens, A. (2005) 'Scaring people may be the only way to avoid the risks of new-style terrorism', *New Statesman*, 18 (840): 29–31.
Hoffman, B. (2002) 'Rethinking terrorism and counter-terrorism since 9/11', *Studies in Conflict and Terrorism*, 25: 303–16.
Honderich, T. (2002) *After the Terror*. Edinburgh: Edinburgh University Press.

TIME SERIES DESIGN

Definition

A research design in which measurements of the same variables are taken at different points in time, often with a view to studying social trends. For this reason such designs are sometimes also known as trend designs and are distinguishable from 'one shot' cross-sectional designs in which measurements are taken only once.

Distinctive Features

Time series designs can be used in conjunction with official data, for example by plotting crime rates for the same area but at different points in time (monthly, quarterly, annually). This acts as a basis for making statements about trends in levels of crime. When this is done it is known as univariate time series analysis. It is possible to plot the trends for different variables at one and the same time with a view to making inferences about their relationship. This is known as multivariate analysis and involves comparing one variable with another or others within the context of believing that there are strong theoretical reasons for the variables concerned being causally connected. It is possible, for example, to map unemployment rates against crime rates for England and Wales, 1990–2000, in order to consider whether changes in one rate coincide with changes in the other. Although such analysis may provide evidence of an association – that is, that changes in the crime rates are correlated with changes in the unemployment rates – this does not by itself provide sufficient basis for making inferences about causality (namely, that changes in the crime rates are *caused* by changes in the unemployment rates). It would be necessary, for example, to have evidence that changes in one variable consistently preceded change(s) in the others.

The term 'time series' is sometimes also used to refer to a form of survey design in which equivalent samples of the population are taken at different points in time and data are collected about them, usually by interviewing sample members. The samples are equivalent because they are collected by the same principles and using the same criteria, but that does not mean that the same individuals are selected (although in statistical terms that is a theoretical possibility). The British Crime Survey (BCS), carried out under the auspices of the Home Office, is an example of a time series sample survey. The first BCS was carried out in 1982 and has since been repeated at regular (usually four-year) intervals. Although there are some variations, at each point in time, sample members will be asked if they have recently been a victim of crime, and if so, to specify the type of crime; they will also be asked to indicate whether the crime was reported to the police. Adjustments are then made to the number of crimes reported by sample members to facilitate comparisons with crimes officially recorded in the publication *Criminal Statistics*. In this way an estimate of the 'dark figure' of unrecorded crime is obtained.

The BCS also provides evidence of trends in crime levels, and because of recognized deficiencies in official recorded data, this is usually viewed as a more reliable indicator.

Evaluation

Time series designs are predominantly descriptive rather than explanatory. For example, victim surveys such as the BCS are descriptive studies which measure crime at particular points in time and look for trends, but make no great claims to provide explanations. There is the potential, as with all trend designs, to theorize about why such changes in trends have occurred, but surveys do not by themselves provide sufficient evidence as to causality.

The value of time series surveys is that they can be used to map changes and trends in society (or a sub-section of it). However, as indicated earlier these are based on equivalent and not identical samples in terms of including the same individuals. Therefore they should not be used as a basis for making inferences about individual development (for example, the development of criminal careers). For this, some variant of a longitudinal cohort survey will be required.

Victor Jupp

Associated Concepts: causation, cohort studies, cross-sectional design, longitudinal study, multivariate analysis, official criminal statistics, victim surveys

Key Readings

Jupp, V.R. (1996) *Methods of Criminological Research*. London: Routledge.
Magnusson, D. and Bergman, L.R. (1990) *Data Quality in Longitudinal Research*. Cambridge: Cambridge University Press.

TOLERANCE

Definition

As a criminal justice concept, tolerance is a form of partial non-intervention. It is based on the acknowledgement that (1) a dominantly moralistic approach is unsuited to actually solve social problems; (2) not all (legal) norms can be upheld and enforced; and (3) in many cases subtle problem-management or nonintervention is socially less damaging than repression.

Distinctive Features

Four centuries before the emergence of the labelling approach in criminology, the ideas that deviance is partly created by the social reactions to it and that a tolerant attitude is a more pragmatic way to control deviance were already in existence (Gijswijt-Hofstra, 1989). The cradle for this idea of tolerance is often sought in the Reformation and the Dutch revolt against the Spanish occupation and the Inquisition in the sixteenth century. In this era, tolerance was a philosophical argument within the plea for freedom of religion and a political argument against the intolerant Spanish ruler. Already in 1525, when Erasmus was asked to advise on how the religious peace could be best guaranteed, he had argued that both Protestant and Roman Catholic services should be allowed because tolerance would be the best ruler. Spinoza has contributed largely to the theoretical development of tolerance, in his book *Tractatus theologico-politicus* of 1670, by separating philosophy from religion. In Britain, John Locke defended a political concept of 'tolerance'. In his *Epistola de tolerantia* of 1689, he calls 'tolerance' the starting-point for every reasonable morality.

David Downes (1988) has used the term 'tolerance' to describe the cultural phenomena that accompanied a period of decarceration in the Netherlands from 1950 to 1975. He focuses in this respect on tolerant outcomes, rather than on an inherent, principled tolerance. Tolerance in social control is rooted in the Eliasian civilization process. If the citizen is expected to control himself, any external control becomes less necessary. Tolerance implies both a moral appeal for self-control and a pragmatic *modus vivendi* to keep things as quiet as possible by not provoking unnecessary unrest in society. In line with Herbert Marcuse's model of repressive tolerance – whereby people are given a wide range of 'innocent' freedoms in order to avoid protest against more structural confinements – Nils Christie (1993: 41–6) has described the Dutch mode of social control as *tolerance from above* (that is, a tolerance that depends on the definitory power of a changing group of dominant professionals). In this sense tolerance does not imply a real acceptance of difference on an equal basis; it implies a kind of moral superiority of those who can tolerate deviations from their own normal standard. It is quite nice to be tolerant, but it is much less enviable to be tolerated.

A policy of tolerance does not imply that authorities think of certain practices as being without problems. It shows a realist appraisal of the modest possibilities of social engineering through penal means, as well as an awareness of the counter-effects of penal intervention as an effective form of control. A tolerant penal approach is, first, a product of pragmatic considerations of control – often combined with an ideology of benevolence and humanism – and second, it goes together with a tight net of other forms of social control – like health care, social work and so on. An example of how tolerance functions as a criminal justice concept is the decriminalization of so-called victimless offences without actually taking these formally out of the criminal code. Law and morality are treated as separate fields. In Dutch legal practice, limited penal intervention is pursued in cases where no individual victim makes a claim for state intervention – such as (soft) drug-taking, abortion, euthanasia, pornography, prostitution and so on. These morally loaded issues are subject to an eternal public debate which ensures that the policy of tolerance (*gedoogbeleid* in Dutch) adopted in these fields is carried by a rather wide consensus in society (Blankenburg and Bruinsma, 1991). The major advantage of a policy of tolerance is the practicability by which law and practice can be attuned. The dangers are, first, that the law derails into an opaque political instrument ruled by administrative opportunism, and second, that it becomes a synonym for indifference.

René van Swaaningen

Associated Concepts: decriminalization, labelling, radical non-intervention, restorative justice, shaming

Key Readings

Blankenburg, E. and Bruinsma, F. (1991) *Dutch Legal Culture*. Deventer: Kluwer.

Christie, N. (1993) *Crime Control as Industry: Towards Gulags Western Style?* London: Routledge.

Downes, D. (1988) *Contrasts in Tolerance: Post-War Penal Policy in the Netherlands and England and Wales*. Oxford: The Clarendon Press.

Gijswijt-Hofstra, M. (ed.) (1989) *Een Schijn van Verdraagzaamheid: Afwijking en tolerantie in Nederland van de zestiende eeuw tot heden*. Hilversum: Verloren.

Marcuse, H. (1971) 'Repressive tolerance', in R.P. Wolff, B. Moore and H. Marcuse (eds), *A Critique of Pure Tolerance*. Boston, MA: Beacon.

Schur, E. (1965) *Radical Non-Intervention: Rethinking the Delinquency Problem*. Englewood Cliffs, NJ: Prentice-Hall.

TORTURE

Definition

Torture (from the Latin *torquere* meaning to twist, rack, intimidate) is the infliction of severe physical and/or mental pain or suffering as punishment and/or as a means of persuasion and confession. It is the ultimate form of individualized terror and is universally prohibited by the UN Convention Against Torture and Other Cruel, Inhuman or Degrading Treatment or Punishment, and other human rights conventions. However, despite being defined as a 'crime against humanity' its use remains commonplace in totalitarian regimes and, as a consequence of the lucrative global market in 'internal security' and 'law enforcement' technologies, is undergoing constant refinement.

Distinctive Features

Torture was a legally-based practice in many countries until the seventeenth century and was not completely forbidden in any country until the nineteenth century. The 1948 United Nations Declaration on Human Rights proclaimed unambiguously that no-one should be subject to torture. It is one of the few human rights which may not be derogated – there can be no excuse for torture nor mitigating circumstances which can be cited. US military intelligence guidelines are remarkably precise on the issue, declaring that soldiers 'cannot use any form of physical torture, including food deprivation, beatings, infliction of pain through chemicals, or bondage or electric shock'. Soldiers are also not allowed to use 'mental torture, such as mock executions, abnormal sleep deprivation or chemically induced psychosis'. Despite the fact that a variety of United Nations, regional and national conventions and statutes and military guidelines have reiterated that torture is illegal, human rights groups report that it is used across every continent. This is all the more remarkable when one considers that there is a widespread consensus that the information elicited under torture is likely to be of questionable quality because it fundamentally distorts the behaviour of those being tortured.

Research suggests that torture is practised by state security and policing institutions for a variety of logistical reasons: to elicit information; to prepare enemies for public trials; to terminate the political effectiveness of the victim; and to create a 'culture of terror' permeating every milieu of society. In this last scenario, torture is utilized intentionally as a mode of social control and governance. And because it is being used to intimidate and silence the general population and deter opposition, innocent surrogate victims are just as effective as political activists. In parts of the world where states are at war or in conflict with sections of their own citizenry, criminal justice and military agencies have been transformed into bureaucratic instruments of terror, complete with networks of clandestine torture and death centres with routine operating procedures and professionals whose specialist knowledge and methods are employed to keep people alive for as long as is deemed either useful or necessary.

Although popularly depicted as psychopaths, research into the 'world of the torturer' indicates that, more often than not, torturers are state employees who have undergone specialist training and group socialization and also, by and large, regard their work with a degree of professional detachment. In essence, torture becomes a form of state-sanctioned routine activity. The 'making of a torturer' would appear to have less to do with 'individual psychology' and more to do with the social and political order in which the torture is licensed to take place. A number of studies have made it clear there is no one 'type of person' who is more likely to become a torturer. If the appropriate learning procedures are applied in the right context, a significant number of individuals will have the potential to be torturers. Kelman and Hamilton (1989) have argued that the three contextual traits necessary for torture are:

- authorization from superior officers and commanders;
- a routinization of the torture practices;

- a dehumanization which allows security and police personnel to sever any empathetic human connection with the person being tortured.

Because of the existence of various human rights conventions, torture is constantly being 'modernized' and sanitized by certain nation-states. In the 1980s Israel tried to codify a distinction between torture, which was banned under international law, and 'moderate physical pressure', which was permitted in exceptional cases. There is of course a very thin dividing line between psychological modes of torture and sophisticated 'interrogation' techniques which have, as their intention, the mental breaking of a detainee. The 'torture lite' practices of a new generation of 'intelligence professionals' posed a problem for human rights campaigners because the stereotypical representations of physical torture that they had been working with could no longer apply.

Evaluation

What took human rights groups by surprise was the heated debate that erupted in the aftermath of the attacks of 9/11 and the bombs in Bali, Kenya, Madrid and Istanbul, as to whether Western democracies are now justified in employing torture techniques to prevent further mass casualty terrorist attacks orchestrated by Al Qaeda and allied Islamic fundamentalist groupings. Alan Dershowitz (2002), one of America's best-known authorities on civil liberties, argued that there was an urgent need to conduct a review of the law on the issue of torture. He noted that although the USA had signed and ratified the UN Convention on Torture, judicial torture was not actually prohibited by the US constitution. The Fifth Amendment, which prohibits self-incrimination, only means that statements extracted by torture could not be introduced as evidence against the tortured defendant.

And the Eighth Amendment prohibition of 'cruel and unusual punishment' is not violated by torture either, as it applies only to punishment after an individual has been convicted.

Members of the US military intelligence community began to talk about the viability of introducing 'torture warrants' to combat the 'ticking bomb' scenario and argued that corner-cutting on human rights was justified because Al Qaeda and the Taliban operated outside the laws of war. It also transpired that the USA had been using other countries who were not so concerned about the human rights implications of using torture to undertake the breaking of terrorist suspects thought to be in possession of important information.

The torture debate shifted dramatically in the opposite direction when in April 2004 CBS's *60 Minutes II* broadcast lurid digital photographs recording the physical torment and sexual humiliation of Iraqi prisoners by a group of smiling US soldiers in Abu Ghraib, the same prison Saddam Hussein had used to torture and murder his political enemies. In one infamous photograph a female soldier holds a dog leash attached to a naked Iraqi prisoner lying on the floor. In another we see soldiers with a pyramid of naked, bound prisoners and still another a hooded prisoner standing on a box being threatened with electrical shocks. There were also photographs of naked male prisoners simulating having sex. In answer to the question 'why did they do it?', US government representatives argued that the Abu Ghraib abuses were the sadistic actions of ill-trained, unsupervised 'rogue' soldiers who had been involved in a bizarre subcultural form of hazing and horseplay. Their actions had nothing to do with counterterrorism and did not reflect the value system of the US military forces deployed in Iraq. Critics insisted that these practices had to have been sanctioned by military intelligence specialists as part of a concerted programme for 'softening up' prisoners before their real interrogation began (Strasser, 2004). In the aftermath of Abu Ghraib, renewed concerns were expressed about the 'stress and duress' techniques that were being used by US interrogators on 'enemy combatants' held for interrogation in other Iraqi prisons as well as in Afghanistan, Camp X-Ray (Guantanamo Bay, Cuba) and other undisclosed locations. Of particular significance is the claim that the USA, whilst apologizing

for the Abu Ghraib abuses and reiterating its public support for international conventions outlawing torture, is in practice using the global war on terrorism to redefine torture and permit its interrogators to employ whatever coercive measures they deem appropriate.

Eugene McLaughlin

Associated Concepts: crimes against humanity, neutralization (techniques of), obedience (crimes of), state crime, terrorism

Key Readings

Basoglu, M. (ed.) (1999) *Torture and its Consequences*. Cambridge: Cambridge University Press.

Cohen, S. (2001) *States of Denial*. Cambridge: Polity Press.

Conroy, J. (2000) *Unspeakable Acts, Ordinary People: The Dynamics of Torture*. New York: Alfred A. Knopf.

Crelinsten, R.D. (2003) 'A world of torture: a constructed reality', *Theoretical Criminology*, 7 (3): 293–318.

Dershowitz, A. (2002) *Why Terrorism Works: Understanding the Threat, Responding to the Challenge*. New Haven, CT: Yale University Press.

Kelman, H.C. and Hamilton, V.L. (1989) *Crimes of Obedience*. New Haven, CT: Yale University Press.

Strasser, S. (2004) *The Abu Ghraib Investigations*. New York: Public Affairs Books.

TRANSCARCERATION

Definition

The movement of offenders between different institutional sites, state agencies and correctional programmes, so that the network of social control is expanded rather than reduced.

Distinctive Features

The concept of transcarceration provides an important reworking of the decarceration thesis, as it argues that the 'clients' of institutions are not returning to the community, rather they are experiencing an institutionally mobile career (Lowman et al., 1987). For instance, offenders can move between local prisons, half-way houses, sheltered accommodation, or in some cases to high security prisons or large mental hospitals. Their institutional location depends not so much on their actual behaviour but on whether this is defined as an illness or criminal. The move from understanding drug addiction as a sickness to viewing it as a crime provides a good example of how constructions of deviant behaviour can shift from medical to penal responses, and the 'War on Drugs' is one of the main reasons for the recent increases in US prison populations.

The intellectual origins of transcarceration lie in Cohen's (1985) application to the community corrections movement of Foucault's (1977) account of incarceration. He argues that the movement represents an extension of the disciplinary project identified by Foucault. While social control had initially focused on the concentration and segregation of deviant populations into specially designed institutions, such as prisons and asylums in the nineteenth century, the community corrections movement represents the dispersal of discipline and surveillance at a deeper level within civil society. The overall effect is that more people are caught up in the web of control and the boundaries between liberty and confinement become so blurred that it is difficult to identify the differences between prisons and the community.

The concept of transcarceration builds on these insights to account for the expansion rather than the decline of prison populations as community sanctions have proliferated. It also intimates that deviant destinations are not just restricted to the realm of criminal justice but can also encompass mental health and social welfare systems. For instance, the criminalization of homelessness and mental illness is an example of how social policy has been replaced by penal regulation in recent years. Yet in order to account for these processes, the dispersal of discipline thesis needs

to be complemented by an analysis that directs attention towards the ways in which particular groups become ideologically vilified and the targets of repression. It is no coincidence that transcarceration, as a theoretical concept, rose to prominence in the 1980s, when the New Right came to power and mounted attacks on health, education and welfare spending while also instigating authoritarian, punitive campaigns against populations that were marginalized from economic well-being. The important point here is that the prison remains the focal point and organizing principle for this project.

Eamonn Carrabine

Associated Concepts: carceral society, community corrections, decarceration, incarceration, social control

Key Readings

Cohen, S. (1985) *Visions of Social Control.* Cambridge: Polity Press.
Foucault, M. (1977) *Discipline and Punish: The Birth of the Prison.* Harmondsworth: Penguin.
Lowman, J., Menzies, R. and Palys, T. (eds) (1987) *Transcarceration: Essays in the Sociology of Social Control.* Aldershot: Gower.

TRANSNATIONAL ORGANIZED CRIME

Definition

Transnational organized crime (TOC) refers to certain types of criminal activity that transgress national boundaries. It is usually associated with illicit markets, for example in weapons, drugs, products made from endangered species, and so forth. The smuggling of licit goods so as to avoid import duties may also come under the concept. This can include the smuggling of tobacco, alcohol and luxury goods such as jewellery, coins, art, antiques and other high-value items, whether stolen or legally acquired. Fraud may be perpetrated transnationally, but corruption and white collar-type crimes are seldom presented under this rubric. Immigration controls create market opportunities for criminal entrepreneurs; the sex industry and other low paid and low-skill occupations which provide employment opportunities in the 'developed world' for workers from less developed countries are exploited in this manner. Moral campaigners have also tried to raise the profile of a transnational trade in human organs, as well as children and babies sold for adoption, as issues related to TOC.

Distinctive Features

Transnational organized crime is often said to be the product of criminal networks or criminal organizations that will consciously employ national jurisdictional boundaries so as to avoid criminal law enforcement efforts. It is uncertain to what extent these criminal enterprises will arise because of the presumed weakened ability of criminal justice agents to act transnationally, and to what extent they will arise simply because illicit transnational trade is profitable in its own right. It seems likely that profitability provides the basis for criminal markets in the first instance and that some criminal entrepreneurs will then use the potential of jurisdictional fragmentation to insulate themselves from arrest and protect their accumulated capital from asset forfeiture (via the process of money laundering).

Evaluation

There is no accurate or independent measure of the extent of TOC. Pronouncements about the 'threat' posed by its manifestations are based on control agency estimates, which imply the same caveats (with a due alteration of the details) that are placed on police statistics relating to more conventional types of crime. The concept undoubtedly refers to negative features of the global free-market economy, which may in fact be more amenable to control through economic regulation than by criminal law enforcement. However, there are some additional issues which complicate our criminological understanding of TOC. The TOC concept came into use after the end of the Cold War. According to some, the 'threats to international security in the 1990s are less direct and apocalyptic than they were during the Cold War ... one of the most serious of these threats is that posed by transnational organized crime' (Williams and Savona, 1995: vii). The control of TOC by police agencies (the FBI in America, the RCMP in Canada, the NCIS in the United Kingdom, Europol in Europe, etc.) has become entwined with the control efforts of Secret Service-type institutions (the CIA and NSA in America, MI5 and MI6 in the UK, the DST and RG in France, etc.). The CIA has been implicated in drug and weapons smuggling that was uncovered as a result of the investigations that followed the Iran-Contra scandal, and in 1985 the French Secret Service planted a bomb on the Greenpeace ship *Rainbow Warrior*, sinking the vessel in Auckland Harbour and causing the death of one person. There are also documented cases of transnational actions by ordinary police agencies that involve illegalities.

While the TOC concept draws attention to criminal activity that is difficult for traditional police agencies to address, by virtue of their embeddedness in nation-states (which raises questions about extraterritorial law enforcement), it also tends to elide the possibility of state agents themselves committing criminal acts. TOC discourse has also largely been framed in such a way that crimes perpetrated by multi-national corporations (for example, despoliation of the environment) are left out of the picture. Some criminologists argue that 'state crimes' and other 'crimes of the powerful' require a degree of organization that makes the TOC label an apt one, but these concerns have largely been put to one side by law enforcement practitioners.

Despite the conceptual difficulties posed for academic criminology, transnational organized crime, and the illicit markets associated with it, have been placed high on the agenda of the United Nations. It is evident that the international community will, over the foreseeable future, continue to build up systems of transnational police co-operation in response to it.

James Sheptycki

Associated Concepts: extraterritorial law enforcement, globalization, governmentality, human trafficking, organized crime, state crime, transnational policing

Key Readings

Beare, M.E. and Naylor, T. (1999) *Major Issues Relating to Organized Crime within the Context of Economic Relationships*. York, ON: Nathanson Centre for the Study of Organized Crime and Corruption (presented to the Law Commission of Canada).

Block, A. (1994) *Space, Time and Organized Crime*, 2nd edn. New Brunswick, NJ: Transaction.

Naylor, T. (1999) *Patriots and Profiteers: On Economic Warfare, Embargo Busting and State-Sponsored Crime*. Toronto: University of Toronto Press.

Pearce, F. and Woodiwiss, M. (1993) *Global Crime Connections: Dynamics and Control*. London: Macmillan.

Williams, P. and Savona, E.U. (1995) 'The United Nations and transnational organized crime', *Transnational Organized Crime Special Issue*, 1 (3).

TRANSNATIONAL POLICING

Definition

Policing activity involving systems of co-operation that cross national boundaries. Such activity need not be restricted to law enforcement, but may be extended to take in the whole range of police functions including crime prevention activity, social service provision, training, risk assessment and management, and state security.

Distinctive Features

Policing is a modern institution which grew up during the period of state-building that occurred first in Europe and then, through the processes of colonialism, elsewhere. As such, policing is an expression of sovereignty understood as a governmental activity intended to secure the peace, prosperity and good order of territorially-bounded states. Since policing has been conceived of as an activity that is geographically circumscribed, difficulties arise when such action extends across national borders. The transnationalization of policing is profoundly effected by the doctrine of sovereignty which suggests that the jurisdiction for criminal law enforcement is strictly territorial. Transnational policing therefore involves and requires reciprocal arrangements for the exchange of criminal intelligence, police expertise, evidence and so on, so that jurisdictional boundaries are not an impediment to the policing function. Jurisdictional fragmentation characterizes the legal landscape for transnational policing, and concomitant worries about jurisdiction shopping raise questions about 'due process' constraints on transnational policing activity.

Interpol is the most famous instance of institutionalized reciprocity between police organizations across national boundaries. The Interpol system provides a channel of communication between police forces, but strictly speaking it is not 'operational': the 'man from Interpol' never arrests anyone. Its primary role is the exchange of messages between police forces and the judicial authorities of its member countries. This is facilitated by its system of 'coloured notices': red notices are in effect international arrest warrants, blue notices are requests for information on a specific individual, green notices contain information on suspected criminals that is intended for circulation, yellow notices contain the details of missing persons, and black notices concern the finding of unidentified bodies. Additionally, there is the circulation of information about stolen goods and notifications regarding the *modus operandi* of criminals and criminal groups. Interpol has developed databanks relating to drugs importation and manufacture and has also developed systems of crime analysis to mine these data, which signal the priorities for international law enforcement. The organization also holds conferences on a range of matters such as counterfeiting, fraud, drug smuggling and money laundering. It is thus through the circulation of information, and by shaping the interpretation of that information, that Interpol influences the nature of transnational policing.

At first sight it seems that this organization would be an obvious choice to develop as *the* institution for co-ordinating transnational policing in Europe as well as more globally. It provides an established international infrastructure and communication network and has accumulated the relevant expertise. Yet it has been displaced as the transnational policing institution in Europe by the development of Europol. One reason for this has been the uncertainties caused by the unusual legal position of the organization. Importantly, Interpol was not established by any international treaty but was instead developed by police agencies themselves. At present there is no method for making it democratically accountable, as the organization publishes no financial records (despite, ultimately, being funded by taxpayers' money) and there is only limited provision in respect of data protection (despite its accumulation of large amounts of data). There are also lingering doubts about the organization's efficiency and concerns about its lack of security.

The idea of Europol was first put forward by Helmut Kohl in 1991. Then Chancellor of West Germany, Kohl envisaged an agency akin to the Federal Bureau of Investigation in the USA. However, while the FBI could be fostered in the context of the US federal system (in order to overcome the logistical problems of policing inter-state crimes), in the European context the lack of harmony between national criminal justice systems and the concurrent effects of the doctrine of sovereignty have, thus far, limited the development of this new institution. The consequence is that Europol has evolved to be primarily concerned with the acquisition, analysis and dissemination of criminal intelligence pertaining to transnational crimes. The agency was first established in January 1994, with a brief to support the member states of the European Union in their drug-related law enforcement, including money laundering. In July 1999 it began its activities under the Europol Convention with the specific competence for a range of criminal activities. These included illegal immigration and 'human smuggling' (special mention is made of child pornography and the sex industry in this regard); the trafficking of stolen vehicles and nuclear materials; the counterfeiting of currency (especially the new Euro); money laundering; and terrorism. As is the case with Interpol, Europol officers have no powers of arrest: they instead depend on domestic police acting within their respective national jurisdictions to undertake this aspect of police operations. The difference between Europol and Interpol is not so much in the way that the agencies are organized (both are essentially institutions that process knowledge about criminals and criminal activity) but more in their legal constitution. Europol has recognition under the Treaty of the European Union. Further, under the terms of the Europol Convention, the Council of Ministers is accorded executive, but not legislative, authority while two other institutions, the European Commission and the European Parliament, are also accorded formal, although limited, oversight. While the mechanisms of accountability for Europol can be characterized as meagre (Anderson et al., 1995: 253), there is not the degree of ambiguity that surrounds Interpol.

The role of the 'liaison officer', an officer seconded to another force in something akin to a 'diplomatic capacity', has been developed internationally since the 1970s. These officers also facilitate the smooth transnational flow of police information, but, in comparison with the Europol and Interpol frameworks, this information exchange is much less formal and, hence, it is also much less visible. The development of training schools and the exporting of policing expertise should also be considered a transnational activity, but very little systematic attention has been given to these programmes to date. Increasing attention is being paid to the transnational activities of private security providers.

Evaluation

Overall, outside of academic circles, debates about the accountability of transnational policing enterprises have been muted. While academic criminology has maintained an interest in comparative police systems for many years, the study of transnational police activity is quite new. As such, evaluation studies have not yet produced a measure of efficacy or effectiveness, and the doubts that have been raised about the accountability of the transnational police enterprise have yet to be comprehensively articulated.

James Sheptycki

Associated Concepts: comparative criminology and criminal justice, extraterritorial law enforcement, globalization, policing, transnational organized crime

Key Readings

Anderson, M., de Boer, M., Cullen, P., Gilmore, W.C., Raab, C. and Walker, N. (1995) *Policing the European Union*. Oxford: The Clarendon Press.

Sheptycki, J.W.E. (1995) 'Transnational policing and the makings of a postmodern state', *British Journal of Criminology*, 35 (4): 613–35.

Sheptycki, J.W.E. (1997) 'Transnationalism, crime control and the European state system: a review of the scholarly literature', *International Criminal Justice Review*, 7: 130–40.

Sheptycki, J.W.E. (1998a) 'The global cops cometh', *British Journal of Sociology*, 49 (1): 57–74.

Sheptycki, J.W.E. (1998b) 'Policing, postmodernism and transnationalization', *British Journal of Criminology*, 38 (3): 485–503.

TREATMENT MODEL

See: Rehabilitation

TRIANGULATION

Definition

The use of different methods of research, sources of data or types of data to address the same research question.

Distinctive Features

The term 'triangulation' was first propounded in the context of social research by Campbell and Fiske in 1959, but became much more widely known after the publication of *Unobtrusive Measures: Non-Reactive Research in the Social Sciences* in 1966 by Eugene Webb and others. The concept emanates from an analogy with navigation and with surveying, whereby one 'fixes' a position in relation to two or more landmarks or objects. The rationale is that the position will be more accurate and precise than it would be if located in relation to only one landmark or object. When transferred to the context of social research, the argument is that if the same conclusions can be reached by using different methods of research there can be a stronger belief in the validity of these conclusions than if they were founded on the use of only one method. There is, therefore, a strong link between triangulation and validity, which is the extent to which conclusions are believed to be plausible and credible. At the heart of this argument is the viewpoint that various research methods have different strengths and weaknesses and that triangulation – in theory at least – can serve to 'trade off' the weaknesses of one method against the strengths of another. In this way the convergence of methods or data produces 'value added' in terms of validity.

There is a much less bold and precise claim for triangulation, namely that the use of different methods can assist in examining different aspects or dimensions of the same problem. For example, victim surveys that use structured questionnaires are able to measure the extent of victimization in a community but these would need to be supplemented with in-depth semi-structured interviews with individuals (such as narrative interviews) in order to gain some appreciative understanding of the experience of victimization for those individuals. Similarly, quasi-experimental methods can be used to assess the efficiency of criminal justice policies but would need to be combined with qualitative methods such as observation or interviews to understand the social processes by which policies do or do not work.

It is common to distinguish different types of triangulation. Data triangulation refers to the collection of different types of data on the same topic, for example statistical indicators of fear of crime complemented with appreciative, qualitative accounts collected from individuals. These various types of data may be collected during different phases of the fieldwork; for instance, qualitative data collected in focus groups or by in-depth interviews may be used to uncover the dimensions of the concept 'fear of crime' (such as psychological dimensions and social dimensions or the fear of different types of crime such as personal crimes and property crimes). This is known as the process of elaborating a concept into dimensions. Such qualitative work can act as a precursor to the development of formal questions structured around such dimensions which, when combined together, will produce a statistical scale or index of 'fear of crime'.

Investigator triangulation refers to the collection of data by more than one researcher. This is especially useful when ethnographic studies of institutions, communities or social groupings are fragmented and entry into one part of the social field precludes the entry to another (for example in prison research, which requires participation in both inmate and prison officer subcultures).

Method triangulation involves the collection of data by different methods so as to counterbalance the different threats to validity which each entails. For example, official statistics on crimes recorded by the police play an important part in criminological research. They are detailed, readily available, and there are no fieldwork costs incurred in collecting them. However, other deficiencies are well known. In order to counteract some of these deficiencies, especially those relating to under-reporting, victim surveys are used. A sample of the general population is selected and individuals are asked whether they have recently been a victim of crime and whether they reported that crime to the police. The results of such surveys can give some measure of the extent of unreported crimes (and of crimes of different kinds).

Evaluation

The previous example illustrates one way in which a convergence of methods can make a contribution to the validity of measurements of crime. However, not all combinations of methods will work in this way. Different methods of research, for example qualitative ethnographic methods in contrast to highly statistical social surveys, are often founded on a variety of assumptions about the nature of the social world and the nature of explanation. In such cases it is not possible to think in terms of contrasting methods being combined in a simple additive way which provides 'value added' in terms of validity.

The notion of triangulation is very plausible in principle but in practice it is necessary to be explicit about the ways in which different data and methods can support each other, especially in relation to improvements in validity.

Victor Jupp

Associated Concepts: appreciative criminology, self-reports, structured interviews, victim surveys

Key Readings

Campbell, D.T. and Fiske, D.W. (1959) 'Convergent and discriminant validation by the multitrait-multimethod matrix', *Psychological Bulletin*, 56: 81–105.

Denzin, N. (1970) *The Research Act*. London: Butterworths.

Jupp, V.R., Davies, P. and Francis, P. (2000) *Doing Criminological Research*. London: Sage.

Webb, E.J., Campbell, D.T., Schwarz, R.D. and Sechrest, L. (1966) *Unobtrusive Measures: Non-Reactive Research in the Social Sciences*. Chicago, IL: Rand McNally.

U

UNDERCLASS

Definition

In its contemporary guise, underclass refers not to the especially poor but to the cluster of pathological and destabilizing cultural attitudes and lack of moral values associated with a particular section of the poor – the 'feckless', 'the undeserving', 'the disreputable', 'the depraved' and 'the criminal'.

Distinctive Features

The idea of an 'underclass' has been around in various popular discursive forms, for example, the dangerous classes, since the late eighteenth century. However, during the 1980s and 1990s in the USA and the UK the term was 'rediscovered' and popularized by neo-conservative commentators such as Charles Murray. His central argument was that postwar liberal and social democratic social and criminal justice policies had produced a growing population of work-age, healthy people who inhabited a 'different world' from that of decent, respectable citizens. The pathological core values and attitudes of this emergent underclass were contaminating not only their own children but also spreading throughout neighbourhoods. For Murray the three interconnected defining features of the underclass were illegitimacy, criminality and a refusal to participate in the formal labour market. The massive increase in illegitimacy, which was concentrated in the poorest neighbourhoods, was having a devastating impact on child-rearing practices and social controls, especially those for male children. Crime was also disproportionately located in underclass neighbourhoods because, at a very early age, young males were being socialized to view criminal activity as normal. The presence of high levels of criminal victimization also had a demoralizing impact on these neighbourhoods. Equally alarming, as far as Murray was concerned, was the drop-out rate in underclass neighbourhoods of a large number of young males from the labour market. In his view, young males were 'essentially barbarians' who needed the disciplines and routines associated with the work ethic in order to make the transition to responsible adulthood. In the absence of this they would find other ways of proving their masculinity, impressing young women and surviving economically, for example, by violence and criminality. These three defining features produced pathological neighbourhoods in which children were encultured into an antisocial set of norms and having young single mothers and violence-obsessed young males as their role models. In a subsequent elaboration of his thesis, Murray re-named this underclass 'the new rabble', arguing that we could identify them through high levels of illegitimacy, child neglect and abuse, drug use, and crime and welfare fraud.

In terms of solutions to this predicament, Murray has argued that a radical departure from the status quo is needed if we are to reverse the drift into the 'underclassization' of significant sections of the lower class. Not surprisingly, he blames postwar welfare policies for creating and perpetuating this underclass and advocates policy initiatives that will change the incentives. Policy needs to distinguish between the respectable and the disreputable, and he supports a punitive approach to single mothers, Draconian cuts in welfare support and the stigmatization of illegitimacy. Murray has also allied himself with right realist prison-centred law and order policies to restore lawfulness and take young criminal males off the streets. As far as he is concerned, crime levels are low when criminals realize that crime does not pay.

Evaluation

Murray has been heavily criticized for individualizing and racializing the problem of poverty, pathologizing the poor, absolving the state of its welfare responsibilities, and demonizing young single mothers. However, despite the intensity of the criticism it is important to note that many of his core ideas have found a 'softer' moral expression in 'workfare' policies in the USA and 'social exclusion' policies in the UK. They also continued to echo within the UK via New Labour's highly moralistic 'tough on crime' discourses on anti-social behaviour, incivility and public disorder.

Eugene McLaughlin

Associated Concepts: anti-social behaviour, 'broken windows', demonization, moral panic, neo-conservative criminology, racialization, right realism, social capital, social ecology, social exclusion

Key Readings

Levitas, R. (1998) *The Inclusive Society? Social Exclusion and New Labour.* London: Macmillan.
Murray, C. (1989) 'Underclass; a disaster in the making', *Sunday Times*, 26 November, pp. 26–45.
Murray, C. (1994) 'Underclass: the crisis deepens', *Sunday Times*, 22 May, pp. 10–11.
Murray, C. (ed.) (1997) *Does Prison Work?* London: Institute of Economic Affairs.
Murray, C. (2000) 'The British underclass', *Sunday Times*, 13 February, News Review section, pp. 1–2.
Young, J. (1999) *The Exclusive Society.* London: Sage.

UTILITARIANISM

See: Classicism; Deterrence; Rational choice theory

V

VICTIM SURVEYS

Definition

In differing ways, victim surveys are concerned with crime measurement and reasons for the under-reporting of crime; the correlates of victimization; the risk of victimization; the fear of crime and its relationship to the probability of victimization; the experience of crime from the viewpoint of victims; and the treatment of victims in the criminal justice system.

Distinctive Features

In part, victim surveys developed as a result of the recognized deficiencies of official crime statistics as valid measures of the extent of crime in society. For example, crimes recorded by the police must rely to a great extent on members of the public reporting such crimes. There are several reasons for not reporting crime, for example the sensitivity of the criminal act, the triviality of the offence, or distrust of the police. Victim surveys collect data on the occurrence of criminal acts irrespective of whether these have been reported to the police or not and thereby gain some measure of the extent of the 'dark figure' of unreported crime. Further impetus has come from a direct concern for the victim within criminology and also within criminal justice policy. This coincided with the formation of victim support schemes and the publication of victims' charters.

Four broad patterns in victim surveys are discernible. These are local cross-sectional sample surveys; 'appreciative' surveys; national trend sample surveys; and cross-national surveys. In local cross-sectional studies a representative sample of the population of a particular area or district is selected and sample members are asked if they have been the victim of a crime within a specified period of time and also whether they reported that crime to the police. Sometimes they will also be asked about their experiences of, and relationships with, the police in that particular area. In the United Kingdom such surveys are exemplified by research associated with left realist criminology (which, in general terms, is concerned with facing up to the reality of crime from a social democratic standpoint). Realist surveys pay particular attention to the experiences of vulnerable groups within a particular locality. There is the opportunity for such cross-sectional surveys to be repeated, as with the first and the second Islington Crime Survey in London, thereby facilitating a certain amount of comparison over time (see for example Crawford et al., 1990; Jones et al., 1986).

Typically, appreciative studies are less concerned with seeking precision in estimates of victimization in the community and more with the qualitative descriptions of the experience of crime from a victim's point of view. They may also seek to examine victims' experiences of being processed within the criminal justice system, for example by the police and courts. The research design is typically based on purposive rather than random sampling. Appreciative victim studies are likely to be associated with victim support groups and feminist approaches within criminology (especially in relation to women as the victims of sexual crimes). In some cases such studies are closely related to social and political action to reduce victimization of vulnerable groups and to improve the treatment of victims in the criminal justice system.

Large-scale national trend victim surveys were given impetus by their use in the United States in the 1960s, specifically in relation to President Johnson's war against crime as expressed in the Commission on Law Enforcement and Administration of Justice that was established in 1965. There was recognition of the need to supplement official crime statistics with data that had been collected first-hand from victims. After a number of pilot studies the National Crime Survey was carried out in 1972. It was composed of three parts: commercial surveys, city surveys and a large-scale National Crime Panel survey. The latter is the only part of the US National Crime Survey that has remained.

In the UK national trend studies have been typified by the British Crime Survey (BCS) which is sponsored by the Home Office. The BCS is an example of what is known as administrative criminology because of its close association with government and official policy making. The first survey was conducted in 1982 and subsequent surveys have been carried out at regular intervals. Various independent samples are selected with each sweep and therefore a panel element is missing. For example, in 1994 a sample for England and Wales of 15,000 adults over 16 years of age was chosen. Respondents were interviewed and asked about their experience of crimes committed against them as individuals and against their household since the beginning of the previous year (Mayhew et al., 1994). The BCS facilitates an examination of trends in the extent of crime, the risk of crime and the fear of crime (Mayhew and Hough, 1991). This examination is for the country as a whole or for subcategories and local areas. The lack of a panel element does not permit such analysis for particular individuals. A major flaw with the BCS is that it is believed that it does not

capture sufficiently the extent of sensitive crimes, especially sexual crimes and domestic violence. A Computer Assisted Personal Interviewing (CAPI) system of self-completion was introduced in 1998 in order to alleviate this.

A fourth type of study is concerned with cross-national comparisons of victimization rates. For example, the International Crime Survey (ICS) is a large-scale survey of experiences of crime in 17 countries. A standardized interview schedule, translated into different languages, is administered to respondents by telephone using a method that allows for the random dialling of private phone numbers (van Dijk et al., 1990). The survey provides a valuable source of data in victimization among different groups and areas within countries and between countries. It does not, however, consider victims' experiences in relation to the economic and social conditions of each country nor in regard to the various institutional arrangements that exist for dealing with crime and with victims in particular.

Evaluation

Victim surveys have played an important role in criminology, and in policy-making especially, in providing better estimates of the extent of crime than those provided by official criminal statistics and in giving insights into victims' experiences of crime and of the criminal justice system. However, these do have some deficiencies, for example in not being able to provide estimates of 'victimless' crimes such as drug-taking; in not addressing crimes affecting large populations, such as mass pollution; and in not providing measures of crimes, for example fraud, of which individuals are not aware.

Victor Jupp

Associated Concepts: appreciative criminology, cross-sectional design, hidden crime, left realism, official criminal statistics, public opinion, self-reports, victimology

Key Readings

Crawford, A., Jones, T., Woodhouse, T. and Young, J. (1990) *Second Islington Crime Survey*. London: Centre for Criminology, Middlesex Polytechnic.

Jones, J., Maclean, B. and Young, J. (1986) *The Islington Crime Survey*. Aldershot: Gower.

Mayhew, P. and Hough, M. (1991) 'The British Crime Survey: the first ten years', in G. Kaiser, H. Kury and H.-J. Albrecht (eds), *Victims and Criminal Justice*. Freiburg: Max-Planck Institute for Foreign and Penal Law.

Mayhew, P., Mirrlees-Black, C. and Aye Maung, N. (1994) *Trends in Crime: Findings from the 1994 British Crime Survey*, Home Office Research and Statistics Department, Research Findings No. 14. London: HMSO.

O'Brien, R. (1985) *Crime and Victimization Data*. London: Sage.

van Dijk, J.J.M., Mayhew, P. and Killias, M. (1990) *Experiences of Crime Across the World: Key Findings of the 1989 International Crime Survey*. Deventer: Gower.

VICTIMIZATION

See: Repeat victimization; Sex crimes; Victim surveys; Victimless crime; Victimology; Violence

VICTIMLESS CRIME

Definition

A form of behaviour that is illegal but also consensual in nature and lacks a complaining participant.

Distinctive Features

In conventional forms of crime it is possible for the police and courts to establish the harm that has been done and the respective status, identity and roles of perpetrator, victim and complainant. However, victimless crimes or 'crimes without victims' or 'public morality crimes' normally involve participants in illegal but consensual activities. Because no criminal victimization is occurring the participants have no reason to complain to the police. Classic victimless crimes include the use of illegal drugs, gambling, homosexuality and prostitution. The notion that these activities are victimless is used to further campaigns for legalization and decriminalization.

This concept has been criticized on the grounds that it works with simplistic notions of 'consensus', 'harm' and 'victimization'. Many feminist criminologists, for example, argue that prostitution is not a victimless crime for the majority of women involved. They are forced to engage in prostitution because of their economic circumstances or as a result of coercion by individual men or criminal gangs. Women run the risk of physical and sexual violence at the hands of clients and are open to blackmail by police officers. There is also the distinct possibility that if they do report a crime to the police they will not be taken seriously. Society is also affected by the crime because it reinforces stereotypical representations of women. Similar criticisms have also been made of those who argue that illegal drug-taking is a victimless crime. All drugs are addictive and drug addiction affects the health of individuals and their families. At a macro level, the production of illicit drugs diverts scarce resources from more productive activities and fuels organized criminal activity. Thus many criminologists would argue that a closer inspection indicates there is no such thing as a victimless crime and that the very use of the term constitutes a process of denial and revictimization.

Eugene McLaughlin

Associated Concepts: decriminalization, denial, interactionism, tolerance, victimology

Key Readings

Gusfield, J. (1986) *Symbolic Crusade: Status Politics and the American Temperance Movement*, 2nd edn. Urbana, IL: University of Illinois Press.

Schur, E.M. (1965) *Crimes Without Victims: Deviant Behavior and Public Policy*. Englewood Cliffs, NJ: Prentice-Hall.

Schur, E.M. and Bedau, H.A. (1974) *Victimless Crimes: Two Sides of a Controversy*. Englewood Cliffs, NJ: Prentice-Hall.

VICTIMOLOGY

Definition

There is some dispute as to who first coined the term 'victimology' but what is not in dispute is that its usage first appeared in the late 1940s. As a term it was originally used to designate an area of study concerned with addressing the relationship between victim and offender, though since the late 1970s it has been used to delineate a more general concern with victims of crime. Often referred to as a sub-discipline of criminology, it has paralleled the development of its parent discipline by demonstrating an early concern with victim typologies and the victim's responsibility for the creation of a criminal event, as well as a more recent focus on the structural dimensions of criminal victimization.

Distinctive Features

There are various theoretical and conceptual strands within the sub-discipline of victimology reflecting the different definitions of who it is that constitutes the victim of crime (from the victim of a street crime to the victim of a state crime). Understanding the nature and impact of criminal *victimization* has been one of the key concerns of victimology. This concern has manifested itself in different ways. Early victimologists endeavoured to understand victimization through the construction of 'victim typologies', that is, by looking for a

way to identify different types of victims. For example, von Hentig (1948) constructed a typology based on an understanding of 'victim proneness', namely, that some people were more prone to victimization than others, whilst Mendelsohn's (1956) typology was more concerned with 'victim culpability', that is, the extent to which the victim could be held responsible for the events that had occurred. This latter concept has been particularly influential in articulating one way of understanding the process of victimization: the notion of victim precipitation. The use of this concept as a way of explaining cases of rape led those associated with the feminist movement to see victimology as shorthand for victim blaming.

Later victimologists looked towards less individual and more structural understandings of the process of victimization by understanding the impact of patterns of lifestyle on patterns of criminal victimization – the lifestyle exposure model (Hindelang et al., 1978). This concept has underpinned much of the thinking associated with, and has contributed to the development of, the criminal victimization survey. Hence the inclusion of questions concerning routine patterns of behaviour such as use of public transport or drinking habits. This understanding of victimization, however, whilst structural in its approach, remained focused on understanding those patterns of criminal victimization that were largely associated with crime as it is conventionally understood, that is, street crime and household crime. In order to incorporate an understanding of other forms of victimization, for example, those which occurred behind closed doors (child abuse, domestic violence), Mawby and Walklate (1994) articulated a view of victimization as structural powerlessness. This view recognized that the impact of criminal victimization was mediated and rendered more complex by factors such as age, sex and race.

Evaluation

While it can be seen that, at an analytical level, victimization may be understood as an individual or a collective attribute of power-lessness, experientially there are different ways in which individuals might respond to such powerlessness. The uneasy relationship that exists between victimology and femi-nism articulates some of the tensions between analysis and experience. Feminism's prefer-ence for the term 'survivor' rather than 'vic-tim' is not just a matter of semantics, though it is the case that the genealogy of the term 'victim' connotes the sacrificiant, who was more often than not female. Indeed, when the word is itself gendered, as in French, it is denoted as female. Feminists, recognizing the power of linguistics, object to the term 'vic-tim' because of its emphasis on passivity and powerlessness and prefer instead to focus on ways in which women actively resist the oppression of their personal and structural locations. However, while these terms are presented as oppositional, in experiential terms such oppositions are much more diffi-cult to identify. It is possible to think in terms of both active and passive victims and active and passive survivors in relation to experi-ence. This is more than an argument about semantics. Understanding victimization as a process in which individuals express differ-ent feelings at different points, and make choices about what to do or not to do as a consequence, is just as important as under-standing victimization as a structural loca-tion. Both differently inform policy responses and the appropriateness of support services.

Sandra Walklate

Associated Concepts: family crime, fear of crime, left realism, repeat victimization, vic-tim surveys, victimless crime, violence

Key Readings

Davies, P., Francis, P. and Jupp, V. (2000) *Victimization: Theory, Research and Policy*. London: Macmillan.
von Hentig, H. (1948) *The Criminal and his Victim*. New Haven, CT: Yale University Press.

Hindelang, M.J., Gottfredson, M.R. and Garofalo, J. (1978) *Victims of Personal Crime: An Empirical Foundation for a Theory of Personal Victimization*. Cam-bridge, MA: Ballinger.
Karmen, A. (1990) *Crime Victims: An Introduction to Victimology*. Pacific Grove, CA: Brooks Cole.
Mawby, R. and Walklate, S. (1994) *Critical Victimology*. London: Sage.
Mendelsohn, B. (1956) 'Une nouvelle brouche de la science bio-psycho-sociale: victimologie', *Revue Internationale de Criminologie et de police technique*: 10–31.

VIGILANTISM

See: Informal justice; Self-policing

VIOLENCE

Definition

Our thinking about what constitutes 'vio-lence' is distorted by the traditional way this is treated as a phenomenon in law and in criminology. Framed by criminal statute, legal definitions of violence emphasize the outcome – how badly the person was hurt (injury, proof of identity of the particular assailant and so forth) – and the intention, *mens rea,* of the violent act. Its impact and the motivation of the offender are influential in defining its seriousness. When a court of law considers a case of criminal assault, most of us assume that these are the most serious forms of violence. However, crime surveys show quite clearly that most violence is kept outside the purview of the criminal justice system. Research shows that individuals largely manage the violence of others without the aid of so-called expert systems, such as the criminal justice system. Those who are its victims are most likely to seek advice from family and friends first when searching for ways to minimize the impact of violence. Feminist researchers, and those studying other forms of hatred such as racist or sexualized hatreds, also consistently demonstrate that many very serious acts of violence are not reported to the police.

Distinctive Features

Violence is 'rarely' random or without a purposeful target (Stanko, 1998). Violence typically (although not exclusively) takes place between those who are familiar with each other. Harris and Grace's (1999) report on rape found that so-called stranger rapes only constituted 12 per cent of rape complaints in the 1990s, as opposed to 30 per cent in 1985. Whether the very low conviction rate (only 6 per cent in the 1990s) for rape in the criminal justice system in England and Wales is linked to judges' and juries' difficulty in understanding sexual violence between those who are known to each other is difficult to say. However, this study leads one to ask how familiarity and sexual violence might pose difficulties for criminal justice decision makers who may link rape to the actions of strangers. Thus, even if violent acts are reported to the police, considerations other than the seriousness of the act may also influence whether the law mediates an act of violence.

The complexities of the way violence dovetails with social relations continue to show us that the criminal law is a blunt instrument when it comes to intervening into violence and threat. In order to think about minimizing its impact, violence must first be understood as part of the wider social foundations of everyday life. Its use has meaning for victims and offenders in terms of people's grounded social knowledge about the way the social world 'works' to maintain personal and institutional power. This understanding is used by those who threaten and hurt – either as individuals acting alone, or on behalf of a collective group or the state. Violence and its threat can be mobilized on behalf of institutions or the state to keep particular people 'in line'. The brutality of a police officer or a prison officer, for instance, has an additional impact on people's

lives because the individual meting out violence has been authorized to do so. Even if unauthorized, it is up to the victim of the violence to demonstrate that such brutality was 'outside' the official remit of the person who committed the act on behalf of the state. Victims of violence also understand that its use is woven into the basic fabric of social relations. Depending on the circumstances (or lack) of an intervention, together with the meanings individuals give to such threats and acts, violence may be treated as acceptable, unacceptable, lawful or unlawful.

Perhaps a more adequate description of violence would include the following. It involves any form of behaviour by an individual that intentionally threatens or does cause physical, sexual or psychological harm to others or to her/himself. It is not a phenomenon framed only through/by criminal statute. It is framed through and by the perceptions of and actions of those directly involved as well (Cretney and Davis, 1995). It is then re-framed through and by institutionally based decision makers, witnesses and commentators (Harris and Grace, 1999; Hoyle, 1999; Stanko, 1985). How authorities and individuals label acts as *violence* and assess its impact depends on the situational contexts within which violence occurs. The institutional circumstances, which intersect both, affect this process of labelling acts 'as violence'. How the parties involved and institutional decision makers make judgements about violence has consequences. As Stanko (1990) has argued, many of our experiences of threat and physical harm are considered ordinary and routine parts of everyday life.

The way in which people define violence and institutional responses to it remains highly contested ground. Work on bullying, sexual harassment, racist abuse and so forth has specified a whole range of interactions and actions, implicit and explicit verbal abuse, that people interpret as threatening and hurtful. The wide range of types of threatening behaviour may include name calling, stalking, vandalism and other forms of intrusive behaviour that make people feel uncomfortable and unsafe, that is, they feel under intimidation by violence. Such a continuum of harm not only contains elements of physical, sexual and psychological damage. People's wider social contexts also exacerbate or minimize the psychological and social consequences of violence. Such differential damage is evidence that individual violent behaviour has varying impacts on people. People's vulnerability to violence and its effects is rooted in individual and social resources. For instance, sexual abuse and threat, by all research findings, impacts on women's lives more than men's lives. The consistent evidence of higher levels of sexual harassment, abuse and threat that women experience, feminists would argue, underpins gendered discrimination. Similarly, higher levels of racist abuse reported by minority groups demonstrate the way in which inequalities founded on the hierarchies of 'raced' social privilege will impinge on many people's everyday lives. Such abuse that is based on and in a racialized knowledge of the way threats can intimidate different people who have differential social capital (so to speak) holds a unique but often hidden place in the way people understand their social worlds. This is one way to link violence to other structures of social exclusion. One interesting observation from research on violence is that actual physical harm is not necessary in order to demand and receive compliance from people. Threats 'work' because people do not wish to experience physical harm. Debates about how social differences are maintained through violence and intimidation can be found in the scholarly discussions of gender, race, age, religious and ethnic social exclusion, poverty and social assistance, employment discrimination, homelessness and so forth. These are often linked to the naming of violence and fear of violence as a serious problem for many categories of people simply because of who they are.

In this way, debates about forms of violence often challenge institutions to recognize their role in the perpetuation of violence and how it creates and maintains social disadvantage in contemporary society. To a large extent, violence as a phenomenon has been made more visible through these challenges to institutional practices. For example, the debate about the high levels of violence met by Health Service staff is as much about the potential for experiencing physical harm as it is about being expected to work under conditions that are dangerous. In a similar vein, the debate about bullying at school is presented as a problem with the working conditions for teaching staff as well as the education of students. Alongside this impediment to learning that bullying poses are the detrimental consequences of such intimidation for the health and development of children. But what is significant here is how many forms of violence that were once treated as part and parcel of everyday life have now been elevated to social problems. The harassment of women, for instance, was considered a routine part of being female. However, when it was problematized as a condition of being female, the consequences of such harassment for women's feelings of safety become evidence of gender discrimination.

Evaluation

What continues to hamper our understanding about violence is the persistence of a framework that has long outlived its usefulness but not its popularity. Violent offenders are still imagined as people 'out-of-control', psychologically disturbed, distant and different from the rest of us law-abiding folk. An emphasis is placed on people's psychological motivation for committing acts of violence. The result of looking towards biology or psychology to explain any violent act overlooks many of the common features of violence. Because most violent acts are committed by men against other men, such violence is explained as part of men's nature. When violence occurs between women and men, this violence is assumed to flow from men's right to control women. And when women commit violence, they are often treated as if they have stepped beyond the respectable boundaries of non-violent femininity. These common explanations about violence dominate popular culture and media representation.

The use of violence, how victims, offenders and institutions define it, and its public imagery show the complex set of social relations embedded in hierarchies of the distribution of power in society. Its impacts are not only limited to the personal consequences for individuals linked to their own health and well-being; these are also firmly rooted in social structures and the social privileges of individuals and social groups. Those who assess the impact of violence on behalf of institutions and in particular on behalf of the criminal justice apparatus display their knowledge of such social relations when deciding when, how and why intervening in violence is important for the health and well-being of the nation as a whole.

Elizabeth Stanko

Associated Concepts: crime, family crime, hate crime, hegemonic masculinity, masculinities, personal safety, sex crime, social harm, victimization

Key Readings

Cretney, A. and Davis, G. (1995) *Criminalizing Assault*. London: Routledge.
Harris, J. and Grace, S. (1999) *A Question of Evidence: Investigating and Prosecuting Rape in the 1990s*, Home Office Research Study No. 196. London: HMSO.
Hoyle, C. (1999) *Negotiating Domestic Violence*. Oxford: The Clarendon Press.
Stanko, E.A. (1985) *Intimate Intrusions*. London: Routledge.
Stanko, E.A. (1990) *Everyday Violence*. London: Pandora.
Stanko, E.A. (1998) *Taking Stock: What Do We Know about Violence in the UK?* Swindon: ESRC.

VIRTUAL CRIMINOLOGY

Definition

Since the mid-1990s, a range of work that may loosely be called 'virtual criminology' has emerged, concerned with the implications of contemporary 'technocultures' for the ways in which we understand crime, law and control. US lawyer Curtis Karnow (1994: 1) marked the moment when he argued in an important paper that 'we are leaving the physical world behind, and with it the touchstone of physical and natural laws, together with the [legal] notion of irreducible limits'.

Distinctive Features

Although much of this work relates to the study of cybercrime and Internet crime its scope is far wider and has roots in the expansion of cybernetics, studies of cybercommunities, and virtual reality, as well as information theory more generally, social studies of science and technology, and media theory (see for example Brown, 2003; Capeller, 2001; and Williams, 2000). Its tentative coherence stems not from a deliberately constructed 'agenda' but from points of commonality, notably a critique of criminology (or law's) traditional embodied modes of analysis. Historically, criminology has focused on the deviant mind and body as the subject and object of crime and control. It has also often been assumed that technology is a medium, or external appendage, and simply a tool whether in criminal endeavour or social control. In virtual criminology both of these are contested: technology is not reducible to the social, and vice versa; rather it places simulation and disembodied relations centre stage, drawing variously on 'postmodern' theorists such as Jean Baudrillard and Paul Virilio, on theorists of late modernity represented by Anthony Giddens and Ulrich Beck and the media theorist Marshall McLuhan (Brown, 2003; Capeller, 2001).

The late twentieth century saw the transformation of the merely human into the always-computer-mediated human. The definition and nature of virtuality itself are complex; it does not only refer to 'cyberspace' and Internet use but also to any area of human activity where the living organism and software/hardware are fused or networked into one entity. Virtual criminology considers such technocultures in relation to criminological phenomena – crime, justice, law and social control. However, it is also concerned with what might be called the grey areas or quasi-criminological phenomena: that is, areas of behaviour that are not necessarily defined as 'criminal', or areas that have not traditionally been regarded by the criminological establishment as part of its domain, precisely *because* they are 'virtual'. What is at stake theoretically in virtual criminology is the notion of the *interface* between the human and the software/hardware; the human sensorium extends into virtuality and makes the human being and the machine co-constituents.

Amongst the foci of virtual criminology are 'interpersonal' cyber-victimizations – which may or may not be illegal. All sorts of difficult definitional and normative questions are raised by these phenomena. How important is textual or image-based harassment? Can chat-room 'rape' be classified with 'real' or offline sex attacks (Williams, 2000)? What about virtual 'hate crime' practices – racist, misogynist, homophobic, religious hatred? If pornographic or child abuse images are digitally manufactured and not taken 'from life', unlike video footage, realtime vidi-cam or photography, what counts as harmful material, normatively and legally speaking? What is the line to be drawn between 'real' images and 'fantasy' images (as, say, in computer gaming; see Brown, 2003)?

All of this raises the question of disembodiment and deception. Can creating identities which are not those of the 'real' offline computer user cause real harm, and at what point does that become 'criminal', since what would be called 'imposture' in offline settings is part of a 'normal' cyberculture which celebrates alternative personas? A man can win the confidence of young children online by pretending to be thirty years younger than he is; or a 12-year-old can sell sex to adult men by pretending to be fifteen years older than s/he is; or a man who rapes can set up a website to counsel rape survivors and win their trust. Despite this being raised several years ago in the cyberculture literature (Donath, 1998) these areas remain inadequately conceptualized.

A further question is that of cybercultural criminology: modes of deviance, order and control *within* virtual worlds are not necessarily the same as those in the embodied or 'real world'. Cybercultures will display particular complex patterns and rules of interaction. Punishment for their infringement ranges from textual sanctions through to the taking down of websites or information-bombing and counter-cyberterrorism. Ethnographies of deviance and control in virtual communities have been growing in sophistication since the mid-1990s and have an important contribution to make to understanding the continuities and differences between crime and deviance in offline and online worlds (Donath, 1998).

The problematic of continuity and difference becomes clearest in the case of VR (virtual reality) systems, where the human participant is embedded in settings they *experience* as an all-surround sensorium and become effectively a co-constituent of the system. This means that, for example, they can kill, maim or torture 'virtual' victims and experience this in a 'realistic' way. Whether such activity occurs in a setting such as military training or for 'leisure/pleasure', its implications are extremely difficult. Similarly, controversy surrounds advanced virtual prosthetics which allow the creation of cyborgs or part-human, part-computer-controlled hybrids. Think *Terminator* here, but the reality is seen in the kind of cybernetic arrangements that have empowered the physicist Stephen Hawking and in life 'support' systems so advanced that they can replace essential human functioning yet remove control completely from the person linked to them. Even benign applications are ethically controversial, so what of deliberately *malign* ones?

At the furthest end of the spectrum is the 'virtual' or 'itinerized' human, created in and through technology. The science fiction extreme of this is the capturing of human data that is so complete that one need never 'die' because a perfect replica is being stored in a database. 'Real' examples include the Visible Human Project, where an executed convict was bisected by laser technology whilst simultaneously scanning the organic information to a computer to form a simulated human, and the Human Genome database which models genetic information on the basis of which genetic engineering can be facilitated. At the same time we see the digitalization of identity through data capture from unique markers (in DNA, the iris) with implications for the detection of crimes and treatment of suspects and evidence, surveillance and intelligence, prosecution and conviction. If the human being is treated as an information entity in these ways, it can be virtually (re)created and infinitely morphed as well as infinitely policed. Thus the body-in-law becomes surplus to requirements.

Evaluation

The critical question for virtual criminology must be, does it exist? Is there anything 'different' about virtual criminology that cannot be accommodated by traditional criminology? Realists would claim that the 'virtual' is no more than an extension of existing social arrangements and that the kinds of criminological phenomena that occur in virtuality are also no more than 'old wine in new bottles'; off-the-peg criminological analyses from the real world only need some tailoring in order to adapt – after all, is computer fraud through identity deception any more than masked highway robbery by computer, as Grabosky (2001) would have it? However, such 'debunkers' of the call for new forms of analysis tend to focus on crimes which 'translate' easily from the real to the cyber, such as fraud or a simplistic conceptualization of online child pornography. They play down or ignore the merging of the human and the technical through sociotechnical environments such as the dissolution of the body into information, disembodied identities, digitalizing the human, simulated consciousness, and cybernetics.

The questions of interactivity and interface remain, however: virtual practices do not float outside existing (embodied) institutions and sites of power. So where does the human end and the machine begin? And what might the consequences be for questions of trust, risk, anxiety and blame that are so central to the contemporary criminological debate? Traditional criminology and traditional law rest on the assumption that human agency, culpability and motivation are distinguishable from technology and non-human objects. They also assume that the essence of humanity is self-evident. In increasing numbers of instances we are no longer able to say this with any degree of assurance.

Sheila Brown

Associated Concepts: cultural criminology, cybercrime, postmodernism

Key Readings

Brown, S. (2003) '(S)talking in cyberspace: virtuality, crime and law', Chapter 5 in S. Brown, *Crime and Law in Media Culture*. Buckingham:Open University Press.

Capeller, W. (2001) 'Not such a neat net: some comments on virtual criminality', *Social and Legal Studies*, 10: 243–39. (Reprinted in D. Wall (ed.) (2003) *Cyberspace Crime*. Aldershot: Ashgate.)

Donath, J. (1998) 'Identity and deception in the virtual community', in M.A. Smith and P. Kollock (eds), *Communities in Cyberspace*. London: Routledge.

Grabosky, P.N. (2001) 'Virtual criminality: Old wine in new bottles?', *Social and Legal Studies*, 10: 243–9. (Reprinted in D. Wall (ed.) (2003) *Cyberspace Crime*. Aldershot: Ashgate.)

Karnow, C.E.A. (1994) 'Recombinant culture: crime in the digital network'. Paper presented to the DEFCON II Conference, Las Vegas, July. Available at www. defcon. org/html/TEXT/2/KARNOW-2.TXT

Williams, M. (2000) 'Virtually criminal: discourse, deviance and anxiety within virtual communities', *International Review of Law Computers and Technology*, 14: 11–24. (Reprinted in D. Wall (ed.) (2003) *Cyberspace Crime*. Aldershot: Ashgate.)

W

WAR CRIMES

Definition

Acts that retain their essential criminal nature even though they are committed by individuals in time of war and/or under official military orders.

Distinctive Features

By the outbreak of the First World War, European nation-states had accepted that certain breaches of the laws of war were crimes. The International Military Tribunal at Nuremberg (1945–6) opted for a criminal justice, rather than political or military, approach to produce the basic definition of what constituted a war crime. This, according to the Tribunal, was composed of the murder, ill treatment or torture, or deportation to slave labour or for any other purpose, of civilians of or in occupied territory; the murder, ill treatment or torture of prisoners of war; the killing of hostages; the plunder of property; the wanton destruction of human settlements; and devastation not warranted by military necessity. Members of the armed forces and civilians who violated these laws were guilty of committing war crimes and could be individually judged and, where appropriate, punished by international or national courts and military tribunals. This would be the case whether or not such war crimes had been ordered by a political leader or by commanding officers. Individuals accused of war crimes could not absolve themselves of criminal responsibility by citing an official position or that they obeyed superior orders – namely, the crime of obedience. Conversely, commanding officers were responsible for violations carried out by their troops unless they had self-evidently attempted to suppress them. The 1949 Geneva Conventions codified the set of war crimes settled on by the Nuremberg trial, and subsequent protocols have expanded the protection available to combatants and civilians in times of war. For human rights campaigners, the crucial issue is not the existence of a body of laws covering war crimes but the willingness to enforce them. Although nation-states have a legal right to prosecute war criminals, the dominant pattern is either impunity or administrative punishment.

Eugene McLaughlin

Associated Concepts: crimes against humanity, genocide, obedience (crimes of), state crime, torture

Key Readings

Gutman, R. and Reiff, D. (eds) (1999) *Crimes of War: What the Public Should Know*. New York: W.W. Norton.

Neier, A. (1998) *War Crimes: Brutality, Genocide, Terror, and the Struggle for Justice*. New York: Times Books.

Ratner, S.R. and Abrams, J.S. (1997) *Accountability for Human Rights Atrocities in International Law: Beyond the Nuremberg Legacy*. Oxford: Oxford University Press.

Roberts, A. and Guelff, R. (2000) *Documents on the Laws of War*. Oxford: Oxford University Press.

Robertson, G. (2000) *Crimes Against Humanity*. Harmondsworth: Penguin.

'WHAT WORKS'

Definition

The term widely used to describe the processes of targeting 'evidence-based' 'programmes' of structured intervention at offenders' 'criminogenic needs' and 'risk factors' in order to prevent their reoffending.

Distinctive Features

Some thirty years ago, Robert Martinson (1974) published an article in which he analysed 231 evaluations of offender treatment programmes dating from the period 1945–67. He concluded that: 'with few and isolated exceptions, the rehabilitative efforts that have been reported so far have had no appreciable effect on recidivism.' The article was widely read and, before long, it was taken as providing conclusive evidence of the failure of all rehabilitative interventions to prevent reoffending. It then formed the basis for the devastating claim that 'nothing works', and it prompted a collapse of faith in correctionalism. A wave of practitioner and academic demoralization followed and, at least for a period, cast doubt over the efficacy of the entire criminal justice system.

The notion that 'nothing works' was initially applied to prison-based 'treatment programmes' but was subsequently expressed in relation to probation interventions and community corrections. It paved the way for the emergence of new forms of criminal justice, a new crime control agenda, and new technologies of intervention that were developed and popularized through 'What Works' discourses. Influenced in particular by cognitive-behavioural 'programmes' developed in Canada, and validated by evaluative research – especially meta-analytical research – 'What Works' protagonists claim that carefully executed 'treatment' can yield positive 'results' with some offenders under some circumstances. 'What Works', therefore, emerged largely as a reaction to the nihilistic charge that 'nothing works'; it restored correctionalist ideology and, to some extent at least, it

appeared to represent a renewed faith in individualized 'treatment' and 'rehabilitation'.

In 1999, a Joint Prisons and Probation Accreditation Panel (JPPAP) was established in the UK, comprising a range of academics and criminal justice professionals. The JPPAP is responsible for accrediting correctionalist programmes that, on the basis of 'evidence', are thought to reduce reoffending. The defining components of effective interventions, or what have become known as 'What Works' principles (McGuire, 1995), include: an explicit focus on the causes of crime; clear 'risk classification'; effective 'risk management'; a targeted approach to 'criminogenic needs' and 'offending behaviour'; responsive modes of delivery that take account of individual learning styles; cognitive-behavioural techniques; and rigid adherence to 'programme integrity'. According to Peter Raynor (2002), an academic member of the JPPAP, the approach – informed by similar developments in Canada and the USA – is the largest evidence-based corrections initiative to be undertaken anywhere in the world. Moreover, '"What Works" is no longer a minority interest struggling for influence in penal policy, but an orthodoxy and a basis for policy, with all the benefits and costs which that implies' (2002: 167).

'What Works' is derived from a psychological criminology that emphasizes the impact of individually grounded 'risk factors' on the onset of offending behaviour, the persistence of offending over time and the prospect of desistance from crime (Farrington, 1997). 'Risk factors' are represented in two forms: 'static' and 'dynamic'. As static factors are fixed and beyond change (for example, offending history), modes of intervention are targeted at dynamic factors (for example, education and employment status or patterns of substance misuse), with a view to reducing the likelihood of further offending. Given that offenders often have multiple 'criminogenic needs' and are exposed to various 'risk factors', interventions that address a range of problems have been shown to produce a more effective 'treatment effect' (reducing offending) than those that retain a single issue focus (McGuire, 2002).

In the UK – where 'What Works' priorities have made an enormous impact on contemporary criminal justice policy and practice – a sequence of accredited 'Pathfinder' programmes was implemented in 2000 including: 'Think First' (a general group work offending behaviour programme based on cognitive-behavioural principles and designed to address 'cognitive deficits'); 'Reasoning and Rehabilitation' (a programme originally developed in Canada with a similar rationale to 'Think First'); 'Enhanced Thinking Skills' (a shorter version of 'Reasoning and Rehabilitation'); 'Priestley One-to-One' (a general offending behaviour programme designed for delivery with offenders who are considered unsuitable for group work or for use in areas where no group work is available – the emphasis is placed upon teaching and improving 'social skills', 'problem solving', 'self-management', 'victim empathy', 'goal setting' and 'attitudes' and 'personal values' in respect of crime); and, finally, 'Addressing Substance-Related Offending' (another programme based on cognitive-behavioural principles for use with offenders with drug and alcohol-related problems). A distinctive feature of such correctional interventions is that they are all said to be 'evidence-based': their positive impact on the reduction of offending is proven.

Indeed, 'programme evaluation' is a fundamental tenet of 'What Works', and significant effort is invested in refining research methodologies and applying them to increasingly sophisticated evaluation studies, designed to measure the 'treatment effect' of the various 'programmes'. Reconviction rates form the principal evaluation criteria, and studies frequently focus on three discrete groups of offenders: those who are allocated to a programme and complete it; those who are allocated to a programme but fail to complete it (the experimental groups); and a comparable group of offenders who are not allocated to a programme at all (the comparison group). This approach is designed to allow for the measurement of programme impact on recidivism rates and it is said to provide evidence of 'What Works' in addressing 'criminogenic needs' and obviating 'risk factors' and, conversely, what doesn't.

Evaluation

Whatever the achievements of 'What Works' and notwithstanding the significance it attaches to evaluation, much of the available evidence is derived from Canada and the USA whilst elsewhere, including the UK, the evidence base is comparatively scant. This raises the problem of generalizability because it cannot be assumed that 'programmes' are readily transferable, or that positive 'results' may be replicated from one context to another. Furthermore, sub-optimal research design has contributed to the shortcomings of some of the available 'evidence', just as insufficient sample sizes have raised questions in respect of statistical significance. Equally, using reconviction rates as a key evaluation criterion is itself problematic, not least because they often comprise an undercount of actual offending; they are contingent upon the vagaries of police and prosecution practices that operate quite independently of correctional 'programmes'; and they pay little or no regard to variations in the gravity or frequency of offending (Harper and Chitty, 2004).

'What Works' can be more broadly challenged with regard to its intrinsic technicalist, deprofessionalizing, dehumanizing and decontextualizing impulses, however. The slavish adherence to 'programme integrity' closes the spaces within which professional skill and judgement might otherwise be expressed, and human relations developed. Its pragmatic orientation in identifying 'risk factors' and 'curing' offenders with 'treatment' privileges a particular aspect of psychology (cognitive behavioural theory), whilst essentially disregarding social-structural analyses and the theoretical priorities that inform sociology and critical criminology. Just as the 'scientific' and technical imperatives of 'What Works' are profiled, the socio-political and moral debates about aetiology, the purpose of intervention and the wider social justice project are essentially overlooked. In this way, transformative and redistributive agendas are subsumed under the weight of public sector managerialism, and the contradictions and consequences of structural injustice are reformulated in the guise of individual failings.

Indeed, 'What Works' is located within a wider ideological context in which social, economic and political issues are redefined as problems to be *managed* rather than issues to be *resolved*. It follows that 'rehabilitation' is conceptualized primarily with reference to 'risk' rather than 'welfare'; and 'treatment' is legitimized in respect of 'protecting the public' as distinct from providing 'advice, assistance and befriending'. 'What Works' might enable the Probation Services in the UK, and elsewhere, to re-establish credibility with governments that are increasingly keen to be 'tough on crime'. This requires tightening procedures, however, emphasizing the capacity to 'manage' offenders in the community, downplaying social welfare traditions and profiling overtly controlling functions. In this respect 'What Works' can be interpreted as part of a broader and deeper movement in criminal justice, away from rehabilitative and transformative optimism and towards greater control, management and regulation.

Barry Goldson

Associated Concepts: actuarialism, administrative criminology, cognitive behaviourism, desistance, developmental criminology, evaluation research, longitudinal study, managerialism, probation, rehabilitation, risk factor research, situational crime prevention

Key Readings

Farrington, D. (1997) 'Human development and criminal careers', in M. Maguire, R. Morgan and R. Reiner (eds), *Oxford Handbook of Criminology*, 2nd edn. Oxford: Clarendon Press. pp. 361–408.

Harper, G. and Chitty, C. (eds) (2004) *The Impact of Corrections on Re-Offending: A Review of 'What Works'*, Home Office Research Study 291. London: Home Office.

Martinson, R.L. (1974) 'What Works? Questions and answers about prison reform', *The Public Interest*, 35: 22–54.

McGuire, J. (1995) *What Works: Reducing Re-Offending – Guidelines for Research and Practice*. London and New York: John Wiley and Sons.

McGuire, J. (ed.) (2002) *Offender Rehabilitation and Treatment: Effective Programmes and Policies to Reduce Re-offending*. London and New York: John Wiley and Sons.

Raynor, P. (2002) 'What Works: have we moved on?', in D. Ward, J. Scott and M. Lacey (eds), *Probation: Working for Justice*. Oxford: Oxford University Press.

WHITE COLLAR CRIME

Definition

A heterogeneous group of offences committed by people of relatively high status or enjoying relatively high levels of trust, and made possible by their legitimate employment. Such crimes typically include fraud, embezzlement, tax violations and other accounting offences, and various forms of workplace theft and fiddling in which the organization, its customers or other organizations are the victims.

Distinctive Features

In developing the concept of 'white collar crime' – 'a crime committed by a person of respectability and high social status in the course of his [sic] occupation' (Sutherland, 1945, 1949) – Sutherland challenged the stereotypical view of the criminal as typically of a lower class, arguing that the powerful routinely committed crimes. Some individual white collar offenders avoid criminal prosecution because of the class bias of the courts, but more generally they are aided by the power of their class to influence the implementation and administration of the law. Thus the crimes of the upper and lower classes differ mainly in the implementation of the criminal laws that apply to them. Given that 'upper-class' criminals often operate undetected, that if detected they may not be prosecuted, and that if prosecuted they may not be convicted, Sutherland argued that the criminally convicted are far from the closest approximation to the population of violators.

Sutherland produced a more encompassing and abstract version of 'crime', defined through the 'legal description of an act as socially injurious and legal provision of a penalty for the act' (1949: 46). While retaining a reference to law, he sought to encompass acts beyond those proscribed by criminal law; the content of laws and the nature of legal distinctions were social products, and 'crimes' were illegalities which were contingently differentiated from other illegalities by virtue of the specific administrative procedures to which they were subject. Sutherland's arguments regarding the nature and significance of 'white collar' crime were part of a much broader theoretical project which sought to redefine the scope and substance of criminology, organized around the explanatory concept of differential association, through which he sought (highly imperfectly) to provide an explanation for lower- and upper-class crime.

In his article 'Who is the criminal?' (1947), Paul Tappan developed a systematic criticism of Sutherland's work, focusing first on his sociological definition of crime and seeking to provide a 'rigorous' (legalistic) definition, then to organize this around intention, the criminal law and a successful prosecution following due process. In Tappan's view, it would be illegitimate to describe people as criminal when they had not been successfully prosecuted for a crime; this would entail engaging in normative reasoning or moralizing. Ironically, Tappan went on to argue that much of what Sutherland wanted to label as crime constituted 'normal business practice', and in so doing pointed out that those offences typically committed by business people were inherently different from criminal offences, a view still held by many academics who comment upon white collar and corporate crime (Pearce and Tombs, 1998).

Evaluation

These – and other – aspects of the dispute between Sutherland and Tappan have endured and remained pertinent for contemporary attempts to define and understand white collar crime. These disputes encompass disagreements about values, politics, theory, epistemology and methodology.

Among the recent debates around white collar crime, perhaps the most significant has been that which distinguishes between occupational and organizational crimes. Thus one view is that the term 'white collar crime' should be restricted to the study of crimes by the individually rich or powerful that are committed in the furtherance of their own interests, often against corporations or organizations with, for or within which they are working. These occur when individuals or groups of individuals make illegal use of their occupational position for personal advantage and victimize consumers or their own organization, for example, either directly through theft or indirectly by damaging their reputation. Such acts or omissions are distinct from organizational illegalities or corporate crimes that have been designed to further organizational ends.

This indicates that opportunity structures are important when trying to understand the incidence of white collar crime. Some criminologists have begun to shift from a focus upon the status of the offender to the nature of the crime; Shapiro (1990), for example, concentrates on the (differential) levels of opportunity and temptation to commit crime in different social situations, with her central concern being the way that trust is differentially distributed throughout occupational hierarchies.

For others, white collar crime is an illusory concept. Thus, for example, Hirschi and Gottfredson have argued that as with conventional crime, the white collar offender seeks some personal benefit (a short-term gratification) and that the setting for the offence or the status of the offender is simply not relevant to the cause of crime and criminality.

White collar crime, then, is certainly a contested concept. In that the term emphasizes the social characteristics of individual offenders, it invariably leads us into inadequate attempts to characterize certain forms of criminality in terms of respectability, status, trust and so on. Moreover, it subsumes within one category what is a heterogeneous group of phenomena with different rationales, methods, effects, likelihood of detection, and so on. Indeed, while Sutherland 'named' white collar crime, his own fundamental concern was with what is now commonly known as corporate crime. The value of retaining a focus on white collar crime is perhaps that this topic 'illustrates the possibility of divergence between legal, social and political definitions of criminality [and] ... in so doing it reminds us of the artificiality of all definitions of crime' (Nelken, 1994: 84).

Steve Tombs and Dave Whyte

Associated Concepts: anomie, corporate crime, crime, criminalization, critical criminology, deviance, differential association, globalization, governmentality, social control theory, social harm, transnational organized crime

Key Readings

Friedrichs, D. (1996) *Trusted Criminals: White Collar Crime in Contemporary Society.* Belmont, CA: Wadsworth.

Nelken, D. (1994) 'White collar crime', in D. Nelken (ed.), *White Collar Crime.* Aldershot: Dartmouth.

Pearce, F. and Tombs, S. (1998) *Toxic Capitalism.* Aldershot: Dartmouth.

Shapiro, S. (1990) 'Collaring the crime, not the criminal: reconsidering the concept of white collar crime', *American Sociological Review*, 55: 346–65.

Sutherland, E.H. (1945) 'Is "white collar crime" crime?', *American Sociological Review*, 10: 32–9.

Sutherland, E.H. (1949) *White Collar Crime: The Uncut Version.* New Haven, CT: Yale University Press.

Tappan, P. (1947) 'Who is the criminal?', *American Sociological Review*, 12: 96–102.

Y

YOUTH JUSTICE

See: Juvenile justice

Z

ZEMIOLOGY

See: Social harm

ZERO TOLERANCE

Definition

Zero tolerance policing is a high profile, proactive, maximum-enforcement street policing strategy that requires police officers to pursue even the most minor offences with the same vigour as they would adopt with more serious forms of criminality. This policing style is intended to send a 'signal' to criminals and law-abiding citizens that police officers have the capacity and motivation to tackle the spectrum of anti-social and petty criminal behaviours that make a city or neighbourhood feel and look unsafe.

Distinctive Features

During the late 1990s the term 'zero tolerance policing' was the subject of considerable media attention, with proponents of this particular style elevating it to the status of a miracle treatment for crime. It can be defined in a number of ways but it primarily involves a strict, aggressive enforcement of laws irrespective of the circumstances on the grounds that eradicating minor crime can contribute to a notable reduction in serious crime. Zero tolerance policing is most closely associated in the public imagination with the innovative policing strategies developed by William Bratton in the aftermath of his appointment as commissioner of the New York Police Department by Mayor Rudolph Giuliani in 1994. Prior to taking control of the NYPD, Bratton, a strong supporter of 'broken windows' theory as developed by George Kelling and James Q. Wilson, had already tested zero tolerance policing tactics on the New York Transit system and as commissioner of the Boston Police. Bratton promised New Yorkers that the NYPD 'were going to fix broken windows and prevent anyone from breaking them again'. In order to heighten their visibility, New York's police officers were put back on the beat and encouraged to look for the signs of crime and take an interventionist stance. They were directed to focus on low-level infringements of the law, public nuisance violations and incidents of incivility such as pan handling, fare dodging, public drinking, jay walking and the activities of graffiti artists and squeegee merchants, on the grounds that these were the forms of behaviour that would make citizens feel unsafe in public places. Suspects were stopped, frisked and questioned about a range of criminal activities occurring in a given neighbourhood in order to access information about more serious forms of crime and deter offenders. Officers on the beat were also encouraged to arrest suspects and process them through the criminal justice system and to break away from the idea that certain forms of crime were the preserve of specialist squads. Organizational re-engineering of the NYPD also accompanied this zero tolerance policing. William Bratton decentralized the management structure by pushing authority and responsibility onto precinct commanders and introduced new technologies, such as COMPSTAT, to monitor and map crime events and make these commanders focus on the emergent patterns and results. This technology also allowed the NYPD to update their database on the city's population and crime flows across and within neighbourhoods.

Evaluation

This policing strategy scooped up honours both within the USA and internationally because it was represented as being responsible for a dramatic decrease in the crime rate – particularly the murder rate – across New York boroughs and reclaiming the main thoroughfares and parks of 'Gotham City' from criminal and disorderly elements. A central attraction for police chiefs in various parts of the world was that zero tolerance policing provided badly needed proof that order maintenance policing was central to effective crime control and to garnering support amongst both the general public and rank-and-file officers. However, critics of zero tolerance policing insisted that as a result of the relentless PR activities of Bratton and Giuliani zero tolerance policing had been given more credit than it deserved for reductions in serious crime. There was evidence that the crime rate was falling in New York before zero tolerance policing was introduced and that the downward trend in the murder rate across the USA was related to a waning of the crack epidemic of the early 1990s as well as broader demographic shifts. There was also mounting evidence that the strategy was promoting an aggressive attitude amongst police officers; encouraging discriminatory and insensitive policing; resulting in the harassment and criminalization of powerless groups who were already disproportionately represented in the criminal justice system; and enflaming racial divisions. The zero tolerance policing philosophy came into disrepute as a result of a sharp rise in complaints and public protests about the torture of Abner Louima, a Haitian security guard, by officers from the 70th precinct in Brooklyn in August 1997, and the murder of Amadou Diallo, an unarmed West African street vendor, in February 1999, by the NYPD's renowned Street Crimes Unit. The police brutality associated with these incidents provided evidence that 'letting the cops off the leash' had given licence to certain officers to override civil liberties and human rights. In the aftermath of these cases, William Bratton and senior police officers in other countries who were converts to his aggressive policing philosophy became considerably more cautious in their use of the term 'zero tolerance policing', preferring instead to emphasize the value of community and problem oriented policing strategies and policing by consent.

Eugene McLaughlin

Associated Concepts: 'broken windows', community policing, COMPSTAT, policing, policy transfer, problem oriented policing, punitiveness

Key Readings

Bratton, W.J. and Dennis, N. (eds) (1997) *Zero Tolerance: Policing a Free Society.* London: IEA Publications.

Bratton, W.J. and Knoblach, P. (1998) *Turnaround: How America's Top Cop Reversed the Crime Epidemic.* New York: Random Books.

Chua-Eoan, H. (2000) 'Black and blue: cops, brutality and race', *Time*, 6 March, pp. 24–8.

Human Rights Watch (1998) *Shielded from Justice: Police Brutality and Accountability in the United States.* New York: Human Rights Watch.

Kelling, G. and Coles, C. (1996) *Fixing Broken Windows.* New York: The Free Press.

Silverman, E.B. (1999) *NYPD Battles Crime.* Boston, MA: Northeastern University Press.

ZONAL THEORY

See: Chicago School of Sociology; Social ecology

Name Index

Subject Index

Research Methods
Books from SAGE

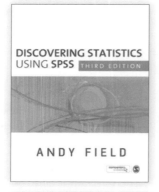

DISCOVERING STATISTICS USING SPSS THIRD EDITION

ANDY FIELD

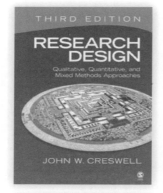

THIRD EDITION

RESEARCH DESIGN

Qualitative, Quantitative, and Mixed Methods Approaches

JOHN W. CRESWELL

Robert K. Yin

Case Study Research

Design and Methods

Fourth Edition

APPLIED SOCIAL RESEARCH METHODS SERIES

Second Edition

QUALITATIVE INQUIRY & RESEARCH DESIGN

Choosing Among Five Approaches

John W. Creswell

Doing a Literature Review

Chris Hart

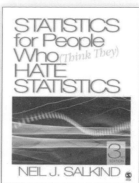

STATISTICS for People Who (Think They) HATE STATISTICS

NEIL J. SALKIND

SECOND EDITION

INTERVIEWS

Learning the Craft of Qualitative Research Interviewing

Steinar Kvale
Svend Brinkmann

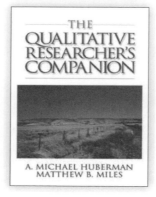

THE **QUALITATIVE RESEARCHER'S COMPANION**

A. MICHAEL HUBERMAN
MATTHEW B. MILES

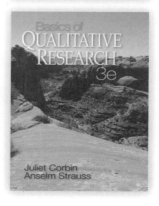

Basics of **QUALITATIVE RESEARCH** 3e

Juliet Corbin
Anselm Strauss

www.sagepub.co.uk

 **SAGE**

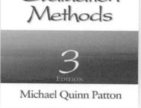
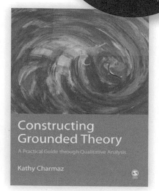
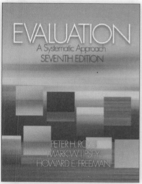
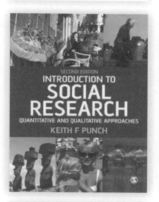
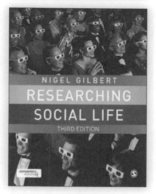
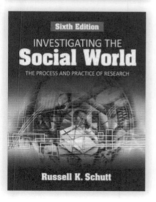